Ḧistory of the Tow

Vernon, New Hampshire

Charles James Smith

Alpha Editions

This edition published in 2020

ISBN : 9789354013744

Design and Setting By
Alpha Editions
email - alphaedis@gmail.com

PREFACE.

The preparation of the History of the Town of Mont Vernon has involved the outlay of considerable time and patience, and like other publications of the same character can not be perfect.

The author of the History of Amherst, the late Mr. D. F. Secombe, in acknowledging the incompleteness of that publication very justly remarks that the proper preparation of a town history is the work of a lifetime, and not of three or four years.

The History of Mont Vernon is necessarily brief. Its history was merged in that of Amherst, the parent town, until the year 1803, from which it was then severed.

The town is small in population; its largest number of inhabitants, being 763—in 1830—small in industries and business, but the enterprise of its people is not to be measured by these things. The writer has been unable to gather much material in the shape of records, personal intercourse with old settlers, etc., upon which to work as a basis. Had he anticipated some fifty years since, that it was to be his task to prepare at some future time a history of the Town of Mont Vernon, he might then have collected much valuable material from interviews with aged people, who have passed away since, which would have proved entertaining and interesting. As it is, there is scarcely a person living, who could furnish facts concerning the early history of the town.

The writer has collected and put into shape all available material.

Taking all these facts into consideration the reader must see that the History of Mont Vernon would be short, that it would be impossible to make it a book of much size.

After all we know but comparatively nothing of the perils and privations of the pioneer's life. They toiled amid dangers and difficulties of which we have no adequate conception.

Rough, hardy, worthy people were they, having a constant struggle for existence, with little pleasure in their lives. Such as these were the founders of this great republic, which they left behind them as an imperishable monument.

Let us who come after them strive to cherish and perpetuate these institutions, which they founded, for our children, as they cherished and perpetuated them for us.

The writer hopes that this work will prove readable, and also be a valuable book of reference, perhaps not so much to the present generation as it will to the future generation.

The map of the old church was drawn and presented by Mrs. S. J. Bunton.

GENERAL INDEX.

LIST OF ILLUSTRATIONS.

CHAPTER I.

CHAPTER II.

CHAPTER III.

CHAPTER IV.

CHAPTER V.

CHAPTER VI.

CHAPTER VII.

CHAPTER VIII.

CHAPTER IX.

CHAPTER X.

CHAPTER XI.

CHAPTER XII.

CHAPTER XIII.

CHAPTER XIV.

CHAPTER XV.

HISTORY OF MT. VERNON.

CHAPTER I.

EARLY HISTORY AND EARLY SETTLERS.

Narragansett Townships—Meeting of Proprietors of Souhegan West—Towns to which Proprietors Belonged—First Settlement in Township—Lieut. Joseph Prince—Pioneers' Difficulties—Sawmill—Establishment of Boundaries Between New Hampshire and Massachusetts—Grist-Mill Built—Incorporation of Amherst—Pioneer Settlers of Mont Vernon—Desire of the Northwest* Part of Town to be Set Off Into a Second Parish—Exertions of Northwest to be Set off—Second Church of Amherst—Building of Church—Petition of Northwest Part of Town—Act of Incorporation of Second Parish—Warrant for Parish Meeting—Actions of Parish Meeting—Hiring of Mr. Bruce Establishment of Parish Boundaries—Completion of Church Edifice—Miscellaneous Proceedings.

IN 1733 the Province of Massachusetts assigned certain unsettled tracts of territory, afterwards formed into townships, as a reward of valor, to seven companies composed of those who were officers and soldiers in King Philip's War (which occurred in 1675-76), and particularly those who were in the Narragansett expedition, and took part in the Swamp Fight on December 19th, 1675, under Captain Benjamin Church. They were known as the Narragansett townships, from the name of the leading tribe with which King Philip's War was waged.

The grantees were surviving officers and soldiers, or their legal representatives. Each company was composed of one hundred and twenty grantees. The seven Narragansett townships were located as follows: Massachusetts, three; New Hampshire, two; Maine, two. Grant Number Three, located in New Hampshire, was called Souhegan West, and comprised all of Amherst and Milford, and the larger parts of Merrimack and Mont Vernon. Grant Number Five, known as Souhegan East, embraced the present town of Bedford and parts of Merrimack, and of what is now the city of Manchester.

The first meeting of the proprietors of Souhegan West was held at Salem, July 17, 1734. A committee of three was appointed to take a "particular view of the circumference of said township and make report to the Grantees on the second Tuesday in September next." They were authorized to employ a surveyor and such guides as might be necessary, at the expense of the proprietors. Another committee of eight was appointed to sub-divide the township. In September, 1734, the proprietors met to hear the report of their viewing committee, who stated that they had been disappointed in the surveyor they had engaged, but "they had been on the land and found it well timbered." The sub-dividing committee was directed to lay out sixty acres to each proprietor for his, or her, first home lot; what was wanting in quality to be made up in quantity.

At a meeting January 8, 1735, it was voted that three lots be reserved: one for the first settled minister; one for the ministry; and one for the school. The lots laid out by the committee appear to have been drawn by the proprietors at this meeting. The towns to which the proprietors belonged, and the number in each town, were as follows: Andover, 9; Beverly, 14; Boxford, 4; Bradford, 1; Chatham, 1; Falmouth, 2; Gloucester, 5; Lynn, 27; Marblehead, 7; Reading, 2; Salem, 29; Scarborough, 1; Topsfield, 13; Wenham, 4; York, 1. Of these, two were females, and one hundred and eighteen were males; twenty-nine were survivors of the fight at Narragansett fort, December, 1675, and ninety-one were children or legal heirs of those to whom territory was assigned.

At a meeting May 1, 1735, a committee of three was appointed to visit the township and find and lay out the most commodious places whereon to erect a public meeting-house, a convenient public burying ground, another for a training field, moreover one for the ministry, one for the minister, and one for the school, and make a return to the clerk, that he may record the same.

The first settlement in this township was probably made in 1735, by Samuel Lamson and Samuel Walton, both from Reading, Massachusetts, a mile south of Amherst Plain, where they built a log-house. Lamson, about 1740, removed to Mont Vernon. In 1765 he removed to Billerica, Massachusetts, and died there in 1779. His sons, Jonathan and John, passed their lives and died in Mont Vernon. Sarah, daughter of Jonathan, married Deacon Jacob Kendall, of Mont Vernon, in 1782. Four daughters and one son of John spent most of their lives in this town. Lieut. Joseph Prince, of Salem Village, now Danvers, was the only one of the original proprietors who settled in the township. He was a proprietor in the right of his uncle, Richard Prince. According to a family tradition, he once owned a belt of land extending from Bedford line westward to near where Mont Vernon village now stands. He first located about 1740, and lived some years on the farm about one mile southeast from Mont Vernon village known as the Jones farm, for many years owned by Samuel Campbell, now by William Gurdy. The cellar of the log house Prince occupied has been discovered by Mr. Gurdy in the southern part of his farm, near where it adjoins George C. Hadley's farm. He [Prince] removed thence to the easterly part of Amherst, lived, and died there in November, 1789, on the farm now the homestead of his great grand-son, Solomon Prince. Other settlers followed Prince, mostly from the vicinity of Salem, but the progress of the settlement was slow, notwithstanding that the proprietors voted sums of money and made great efforts to induce settlers to locate in the township.

The lives of the first settlers in the New Hampshire townships were a constant struggle for existence. A settler in one of them thus describes his town in its infancy: "A howling wilderness it was, where no man dwelt. The hideous yells of wolves, the shrieks of owls, the gobbling of turkeys, and the barking of foxes were all the music we heard. All a dreary waste and exposed to a thousand difficulties." In 1736 a bridge was built over the Souhegan River, for which the proprietors paid £95.

The building of a sawmill was now in order, and in April, 1737, the proprietors appointed a committee "to secure the building of the same upon Beaver Brook where it may be most convenient, provided that said mill be fit to saw the first of November next, and that it shall be kept in good repair for ten years, and to saw for the proprietors by the halves during that time," and £120 was levied upon the proprietors to pay for the same.

March 5, 1740, the King in council established boundaries between the provinces of Massachusetts and New Hampshire, which had been in dispute, which have remained unchanged until the present time. By this decision Souhegan West, with twenty-seven other townships, which had been granted by Massachusetts, with large quantities of ungranted land intermixed among them, became parts of New Hampshire.

April, 1741, it was voted that the proprietors give to John Shepard, of Concord, Massachusetts, one hundred and twenty acres on the Souhegan River, to begin at William Peabody's line and run down to the bottom of the falls, he to build a good grist-mill and a good sawmill on said river against the aforesaid land, and to keep them in good repair for the use of said proprietors, having the liberty to cut such white oak timber for the mill as he wants." The same year he built the mill, and became a useful and honored citizen of the town.

At the same meeting they voted to build a bridge over the Souhegan River, and appointed a committee of three to say where it should be built and to get it done. This committee was composed of Capt. Samuel Bancroft, Capt. Thomas Tarbox, and Joshua Hicks. They also voted that they "will give no encouragement to a blacksmith to settle among them," but they soon thought better of it, for on the 22d of May, 1745, they voted that they "will give encouragement for a blacksmith to settle with them, and that Capt. Parker, Lieut. Prince, and Mr. Lamson be desired to agree with a good smith to settle with them." Capt. Parker and Mr. Lamson resided in the district now included in Mont Vernon.

As the sixty families required by the grant had not settled in the township, the proprietors voted, March, 1747, to choose a committee to treat with and get an obligation to secure at least sixty families with those that are already there to settle immediately, agreeably to the grant.

In January, 1753, a petition was presented to the Governor and Council of New Hampshire by thirty-two citizens of Souhegan West, for incorporation as a town. Seven of these citizens lived in that part of the town which is now Mont Vernon. They were Ebenezer Ellinwood, Ebenezer Ellinwood, jr., Samuel Lamson, Samuel Lamson, jr., Ebenezer Lyon, Joseph Steel, and Caleb Stiles. This petition failed. Seven years later, January, 1760, in answer to another larger petition by the inhabitants, Governor Benning Wentworth, with the advice and consent of the Council, granted a charter incorporating Souhegan West into a town by the name of Amherst, "reserving to us, our heirs and successors, the power and the right of dividing said town when it shall appear necessary and convenient to the inhabitants thereof." Lieut.-Col. John Goffe was appointed "to call the first meeting of inhabitants of said town within forty days," at which meeting Col. Goffe read the charter. He was chosen moderator, and the town voted to accept the charter. Col. Goffe was then the leading citizen of the town.

The resident tax-payers in Amherst in 1760 were one hundred and ten. Of these certainly twenty-two lived in what is now Mont Vernon. These original settlers bore the names of Averill, Bradford, Carlton, Cole, Curtis, Ellinwood, Gould, Harwood, Holt, Lovejoy, Lamson, Odell, Smith, Steel, Stiles, Weston, Wilkins.

From this date the growth of the northwest part of the town, afterwards known as the Northwest Parish, now as Mont Vernon, was rapid.

The pioneer settlers of Mont Vernon were a rough, hardy, worthy people. In many of them the religious element was strong. Their attendance at church was regular, though the route was long and tedious. They early looked forward to the time when this section should become a separate parish. In 1777 Rev. Daniel Wilkins, the first minister of Amherst, had become so enfeebled by age as to be incapable of performing his duties acceptably; the town sought to obtain a colleague pastor. The people of the northwest part of the town made this an occasion for a strong and persistent effort for organization into a separate parish.

In the winter of 1777-78, the church and town extended a call to Mr. John Blydenburg to become associated with Mr. Wilkins as a colleague pastor. Against this action seventeen citizens of what is now Mont Vernon made a written protest, demanding that it be placed on the town records. Mr. Blydenburg declined the call.

In the spring of 1779 petitions were presented to the General Court by sundry persons belonging to the northwesterly part of the town to be set off as a parish. The town chose a committee to treat with these petitions, in March, 1779, and at a subsequent meeting on the 31st of said month, after hearing the report of the committee, voted not to set them off.

In August, 1779, the town appointed an agent to prepare and present reasons why this petition should not be granted before the General Court.

December 6, 1779, sundry inhabitants of the northwest part of the town asked to be voted off as a parish, on condition that the inhabitants of that part of the town should pay their full proportion towards the support of Rev. Mr. Wilkins and every charge of the town, except the settlement of a minister, until they could supply

themselves with preaching in the parish, but the town refused to
grant their request.

In December, 1779, the church and town united in inviting Mr.
Jeremiah Barnard to become their minister, whereupon thirty-two
residents of the northwest part of the town filed a protest setting forth
"That having repeatedly petitioned to be set off as a distinct parish,
and their petitions having been rejected, they enter their protest
against Mr. Barnard's being settled, or any other minister, while they
remained in conjunction with the town and their request not granted."
It would seem that their opposition to their ministerial candidates
was almost wholly based on their desire to be made a distinct parish.
Mr. Barnard, having accepted his call, was ordained March 3, 1780,
prior to which a lengthy and earnest remonstrance was addressed to
the ordaining council, by thirty-seven residents of what is now Mont
Vernon, and a few others.

Another committee was appointed by the town September 11,
1780, to show cause before the General Court why the prayer of a
number of the inhabitants of the town residing in the northwesterly
part of the same, asking to be set off as a separate parish, should not
be granted. But the people of this part of the town insisted upon
having a ministry of their own selection, and in September, 1780,
called a council, which organized here, what was called the Second
Church of Amherst. No records of these transactions, or of the
church for the first thirteen years exist, but it is known that the first
deacons were Oliver Carlton, Nathaniel Heywood, and Richard Ward,
all men of sound orthodoxy and fervid piety.

Immediately after the organization of the church, the Rev. Mr.
Coggin, of Chelmsford, Massachusetts, preached to a large congregation in Major Cole's barn on the Capt. Kittredge place, in the south
part of what is now Mont Vernon, upon the importance of immediately
erecting a house of worship. This, in the poverty of those Revolutionary times, was no slight undertaking; but in the month of April,
following, each farm in the community had contributed its free-will
offering of timber for the frame and covering of the edifice, which still
stands on the summit of the hill, a monument to those brave christian
men. It is related that the heaviest timber was drawn upon the
snow-crust the last of April, without obstruction from walls or
fences.

Lieut. James Woodbury gave the land where the church, now

converted into a town house, stands, and also another lot one-fourth of a mile above, for the burial ground.

So urgent was the demand for the house, that as soon as the frame was covered, and before the floor timber was laid, it was occupied without any formal dedication. They finished the house gradually, as they were able. The first worshipers here sat upon rough benches, with a single open floor, with nothing to warm them but the glad tidings of salvation. The old-fashioned square pews were constructed as the families felt able, "the pew-ground" merely being deeded by the parish.

The organization of a church and providing a place of worship were but preliminary to the renewal of their effort to be legally set off into a second parish. They, in March, 1781, presented to the General Court convened at Exeter, an extensive petition, setting forth their reasons in asking for a separation.

"To the Hon'ble the Council & Gents of the Hon'ble House of Representative in General Assembly Convened at Exeter in the State of New Hampshire, March 14, 1781:

"The humble petitions of the several persons whose names are hereto set and subscribed. Inhabitants of Amherst in the County of Hillsborough, living chiefly in the northwest part of said town. Sheweth that the Rev. Daniel Wilkins, the former minister of Amherst, Being by Age and Infirmities Rendered incapable of Duty, the Town chose a committee to hire preaching until another minister should be ordained. By which means the Reverend Mr. Jeremiah Barnard was introduced into the church there only by Way of Supply, the town not being in a proper situation for settling a minister. However, the s'd Mr. Barnard officiated there some time. That your petitioners for Reasons hereafter mentioned, Could by no Means Rest Satisfied under his Ministry and openly disapproved of him. Notwithstanding which a party was form'd in favor of s'd Barnard, which party taking advantage of Calling Church and Town Meetings, when the severity of the season was such, and times when such an abundance of snow had fallen that it was extremely Difficult if not morally impossible to have a general attendance of the town's inhabitants, it was carried by a very small majority, to give the s'd Mr. Barnard a call. An Ecclesiastical Council was convened at Amherst on the first day of March, 1780, for the purpose of ordaining him. That although your petitioners were convinced to their great Grief and Sorrow (by being out voted) that they were not the greatest part of the inhabitants of said Town, yet being Conscious of their weight and Importance (as paying a greater part of the Taxes than those that voted in favor of Mr. Barnard's settling) they did think themselves aggrieved in having the s'd Mr. Barnard *imposed* upon them in that *unfair manner*; and they did, previous to the s'd ordination, sign and address a Memorial and Remonstrance, Conched in the strongest but most modest Terms, to the s'd Council, setting forth among other things that with Regard to Mr. Barnard, they must say that he was not a man of their choice, that he was not the man they should choose for their Spiritual Guide, for their Instructor in the Great and Deep Mysteries of the Gospel of Jesus Christ, and that his, the s'd Mr. Barnard's, discourses—however Doctrinally sound they might be—did not appear to be delivered in the demonstration of the spirit, and with that *life*, *power*, and *energy* which they could wish for, nor yet with that clearness and perspicuity which they thought they had a right to expect from a man thoroughly furnished to every good work, and from one who might come to them in the fulness of the blessings of the Gospel of Peace.

"And in conclusion, hoping that the bare sight of such a number of names as would be annexed to s'd memorial might be sufficient to convince Mr. Barnard that he ought not to think of settling where there was so little prospect of his being Beneficial to the people and comfortable to himself. And praying the Venerable Council that the said Mr. Barnard might not be ordained,—to which Memorial your Petitioners pray leave to refer themselves, and that it may be taken as part of this petition. That notwithstanding there are some few of your petitioners who did not sign said memorial, yet did they oppose Mr. Barnard's being settled as their minister, and did in the strongest (though) modest terms manifest to the said Council their disapprobation of the said Mr. Barnard's being ordained as a minister of the Church and People of this town.

"That notwithstanding the said Memorial and Remonstrance, the Council thought fit to ordain, and did accordingly ordain the said Mr. Barnard. In consequence whereof for the reasons aforesaid, and also because the said Mr. Barnard and his party carry the Advantage they have gained in manner as before set forth, with a high hand, your Petitioners cannot in conscience resort to the now place of Public Worship in Amherst, nor can they join in prayer, nor in communication with the said Mr. Barnard, nor reap any benefit from his discourses, so that they wholly absent themselves and may be said to be without any settled minister. Moreover, under all these difficulties and hardships which they labor under, your Petitioners are liable to be rated with their equal proportion of rates toward the support of the said Mr. Barnard, and as under the foregoing circumstances your Petitioners think hard of paying them; it seems to open a door of Contention and Lawsuit, which they would avoid.

"That your humble petitioners in Expectation; of Being sett off as a separate parish, did some time ago at their own proper charge, build a commodious Meeting-House at the said northwest part of said Amherst, and have hired preaching for some time past, hoping at the same time to have enjoyed the privilege of a minister of their own choosing, our local situation being such as required the same. But that not being granted by the then Hon'ble Assembly, your Petitioners now have recourse to your Honors, praying that you should take their most unhappy cases into your Serious Consideration, and that they may be at liberty to bring in a bill whereby they may be severed from the said New Meeting-House and Minister, and from any future minister there, and from paying any rates for the repairs of the said meeting-house, or support of the new minister of the same, and that your Petitioners may be invested with the power of assessing, levying, and raising money for keeping their said meeting-house in Repair, when the same shall be in want thereof, and for settling and constantly maintaining a Gospel Ministry in said Northwest Meeting-House, and that it may and shall be lawful for any now minor children or servants of your Pet'rs, as soon as they shall come of age, to poll off, if they see fit, and join such future Minister or Ministers of the Gospel at the said Northwest Meeting-House, and may be in like manner declared Independent of said Mr. Barnard's Meeting-House, and separate therefrom, & from all rates whatsoever incident to the support of that meeting-house or minister, provided that such child or children, servant or servants, so coming of age do signify to the Town Cl'k of Amherst in writing his, her, or their desire of joining and becoming members of the said Society of the Northwest Parish, or that your Hon's will grant your Pet'rs Relief in such other manner as you in your great wisdom shall deem most meet. And your Petitioners, as in duty bound, will ever pray."

This was signed by John Averill and fifty-one others. With the foregoing petition we have the following record:

"STATE OF NEW HAMPSHIRE.

"In the House of Representatives, June 20,1781. Upon reading and considering the foregoing petition: Voted that the prayer thereof be granted, and that the Petitioners have leave to bring in a bill accordingly.

"Sent up for Concurrence.

"JOHN LANGDON, Speaker.

"In Council June 21, 1781. Read and Concurred.

"E. THOMPSON, Sec'y."

The act for the incorporation of the Second or Northwest Parish is as follows:

"STATE OF NEW HAMPSHIRE.

"In the year of our Lord one thousand seven hundred and eighty-one.

"An act to enable sundry inhabitants of the Town of Amherst to

erect a new parish in the northwest part of said town for transacting ministerial affairs only.

"Whereas sundry inhabitants of Amherst in the county of
Hillsborough have petitioned the General Assembly, setting forth
(among other things) that in humble expectation of being sett off
from the Society and Meeting-House whereof the Rev. Jeremiah
Barnard is now minister in said town, they had at their own proper
charge built a commodious meeting-house in the northwest part of
said town, and hired preaching for some time past and praying that
they might be severed from said Mr. Barnard's church in future by an
especial act, and be exempt in future from paying any rates towards
the repairs of the said Mr. Barnard's meeting-house, or the support
of him or any future minister of the same, upon which petition, the
Agents of said town having been heard and the prayer appearing
reasonable. Therefore be it enacted and it is hereby in Council and
House of Representatives in general assembly convened and by the
authority of the same petition above referred to, viz.: Nathaniel
Heywood, Oliver Carlton, Amos Stickney, John Cole, John Mills, Jo-
seph Farnum, Daniel Wilkins, Joseph Langdell, Josiah Dodge, William
Lamson, Abijah Wilkins, James Smith, Jacob Smith, John Averill,
Joseph Lovejoy, Nathan Jones, Joshua and Eli Elkins, Joseph Tuck,
Timothy Smith, jr., Nathan and Nathan Flint, jr., Daniel Simonds,
Peter Woodbury, William Bradford, jr., Daniel Smith, Isaac Smith,
Samuel Winchester, Andrew Leavitt, Knight Nichols, James Wood-
bury, Thomas Carlton, Joseph Perkins, Joseph Duncklee, John
Duncklee, Allen Goodrich, Richard Gould, Thomas Town, jr., Nathan
Cole, Richard Ward, Jeremiah Burnham, Samuel Sterns, John Har-
wood, Enos Upton, Ezekiel Upton, Hannah Peabody, Wm. Wilkins,
James Hopkins, Daniel Gould, Robert Parker, Joseph Steel, and
Timothy Smith be and they hereby are separated, exonerated, and
discharged from paying any taxes towards the support of the Gospel
Ministry and Public worship, in said town of Amherst, from and
hereafter the day of the date hereof excepting in the Parish hereby
erected, together with all the polls belonging to their respective families, and all the estates which they do now or shall hereafter own,
being in said town, and the said persons, polls and estates be and
they hereby are erected and incorporated into a new parish, and invested with the privileges and authorities of a parish, separate and
distinct from the other parts of said town, and the parishioners of
the said new parish are hereby enabled to raise money as there shall
be occasion, on the polls and estates thereto belonging for the maintenance of the Minister of the Gospel, and the repairs of their
meeting-house when necessary, and the support of Public Worship
amongst themselves, and assess any necessary taxes on the said polls
and estates for that end, and to levy and collect the same in the same
manner that town taxes are levied and collected, and for that purpose
to choose any number of suitable persons belonging to said parish in
the month of March annually, for assessors or a collector or collectors

thereof, who shall have the same power to levy and collect such taxes, and in default of the due discharge of said office to be subject to the same pains and penalties as the constables of Towns in this state are liable by law, and also choose any other persons to such offices and trusts as the said parishioners shall judge proper, and they are hereby authorized to act accordingly.

"And be it further enacted that any minor children of said parishioners, any persons who may hereafter come and settle in said town and inhabit the town, and their minor children, who shall in time to come be desirous of belonging to the new perish, who shall within six months after such new settler coming into said town, and after such minor children attaining the age of 21 years giving their names and signifying their desire and design in writing to the clerk of said town, for the time being, which being done, such future settlers and minors shall be entitled to every privilege in this act with said parishioners, otherwise to be precluded therefrom, and the parishioners of the said new parish are hereby authorized to meet and to choose all necessary officers for the service of said parish for the current year, and until their next meeting in March next, and at any time in the month of July next, and Nathaniel Heywood is authorized to call the same. Provided nevertheless that nothing in this act shall be construed to exempt any of said parishioners, their polls or estates, from paying their just proportion of all ministerial charges arising in said town of Amherst, nor from the future support of Rev. Daniel Wilkins, the late minister of said town, and now living according to contract."

"STATE OF NEW HAMPSHIRE.

"In the House of Representatives, June 28th, 1781.

"The foregoing bill having been read a third time. Voted that it pass to be enacted.

"Sent up for Concurrence.

"JOHN LANGDON, Speaker."

"In Council, June 30th, 1781. This bill was read a third time and voted it should be enacted. M. Weare, president. Copy examined by E. Thompson, Sec'y."

Of the names found in the act of incorporation, some are interesting as being the progenitors of present active residents of at least the fourth generation.

"STATE OF NEW HAMPSHIRE.

"HILLSBOROUGH, ss.   July 11, 1781.

"To the Inhabitants of the Second Parish in Amherst, Greeting:

"Whereas the Honorable Council and House of Representatives

of this state have ordered,—That the inhabitants of this parish should meet some time in this month to choose parish officers, and have authorized me to call said meeting; therefore I, the subscriber, by virtue of said authority, hereby warn all the freeholders and other inhabitants belonging to the said second parish of Amherst who are qualified to act in such parish meetings to meet at the meeting-house in said parish on Tuesday, the 24th day of July, at three o'clock in the afternoon, for the following purposes, viz.:

"1st. To choose a Moderator for said meeting.

"2d. To choose a parish clerk and other parish officers.

"3d. To choose a committee to hire preaching in said parish.

"4th. To transact such other business as may appear needful."

The first parish meeting was held 24th July, 1781. Nathaniel Heywood was chosen moderator; Eli Wilkins, clerk; Peter Woodbury, Nathaniel Heywood, and Abijah Wilkins, assessors; James Woodbury, treasurer; Nathan Flint, collector; Oliver Carlton, Richard Gould, and Wm. Bradford a committee to hire preaching. Lieut. James Woodbury, Ensign Thomas Stickney, and Abijah Wilkins were chosen a committee to lay the lower floor and sell the pew-ground in the meeting-house at public vendue. July 1, 1782. It was voted to hire preachers on probation "and that the committee apply to such gentlemen to preach as they think proper." August 29, 1782. Voted to hire Mr. Powers to preach in said parish. At the same meeting a proposition to unite with the Southwest Parish in hiring preaching at Mr. Abner Hutchinson's was rejected.

January 13, 1783. John Mills, moderator. Voted to hire Mr. Allen to preach four Sundays if his services can be procured.

March 1, 1783. At the annual meeting chose Peter Woodbury, Nathaniel Heywood, Abijah Wilkins assessors, Richard Gould, Timothy Smith, Richard Ward a committee to hire preaching. Voted £50 to defray parish expenses.

September 9, 1783. Capt. J. Mills, moderator. Voted not to hire Mr. Allen any longer. Voted not to send to Dartmouth College for a preacher.

December 9, 1783. Voted to concur with the church in giving Mr. Samuel Sargent a call to settle in the gospel ministry in said parish. The effort to settle Mr. Sargent failed, for on the 29th of December, 1784, they voted to concur with the church in giving Mr. John Bruce a call to settle in the gospel ministry of this parish. Voted to give Mr. Bruce £120 lawful money as a settlement and £60 lawful money and twenty cords of wood yearly as long as he supplies the pulpit, and £30 and 20 cords of wood during life, after he had ceased to supply the pulpit. Voted Nath'l Heywood, Dea. Oliver Carlton, and Lieut. Wm. Bradford a committee to treat with him relative to his settlement. Voted Capt. John Mills, Joseph Langdell, Daniel Smith to be a committee to take a deed from Lieut. Woodbury of the ground on which the meeting-house stands. Mr. Bruce accepted the call after some delay, and was ordained the 3d of November, 1785. He continued pastor of the parish and town until his death, which took place the 12th of March, 1809.

An act defining the boundaries of the Second Parish in Amherst was passed by the legislature the 24th of January, 1789.

January 7, 1790. The First Parish having petitioned for the repeal of the act establishing the boundaries of the Second Parish, William Lamson, Henry Campbell, Capt. William Bradford were appointed a committee to appear before the General Court and show cause why the prayer of this petition should not be granted.

June 4, 1790. Capt. William Bradford and Henry Campbell were appointed a committee to go to Concord to hear the report of a committee appointed by the General Court respecting the alteration of the boundary lines between Mr. Bruce's and Mr. Barnard's parishes.

April 26, 1790. The meeting-house still remaining unfinished, the parish chose a committee to finish the same, as was voted, the committee to return any overplus that might arise from the sale of the pews to the treasurer.

October 15, 1790. Voted that the committee for the time being furnish the ministerial pew on the spot reserved for that purpose.

January 25, 1791. Another act establishing the boundaries of the Second parish was passed by the legislature, changing them somewhat from those fixed by the former act.

March 21, 1791. Voted to accept a strip of land lying in the easterly part of Lyndeborough, with the inhabitants living thereon, as a part of the parish, provided the consent of Lyndeborough is obtained.

1792. Voted J. Mills 9 shillings for sweeping the meeting-house.

March, 1792. Dea. Oliver Carlton and others chosen a committee to complete the meeting-house were instructed to finish the whole of the joiner work inside, not already let out.

May 24, 1792. Eli Wilkins being the only Justice of the Peace in the Northwest parish, at a town meeting on that date it was voted that "John Conant, of Beverly, Massachusetts Bay, is a person most suitable to be recommended" for a commission of Justice of the Peace.

May 25, 1792. Voted to build a wall by the highway against the burying-ground. Voted that the bass-viol be not carried into the meeting-house in time of exercise. Voted that £6 be paid to the minister, instead of 20 cords of wood, annually, "if he agrees to accept the change." Andrew Leavitt built the graveyard gate, and John Mills made the hinges and bolts.

October 25, 1792. It was voted to allow the bill of the committee for building the gate in front of the burying-ground amounting to £4. 19s. 5d.

Voted to build another piece of wall by the side of the burying-ground.

March 18, 1793. Voted a pew in the gallery of the meeting-house to the use of the singers.

March 12, 1794. Voted Capt. Mills 12 shillings for sweeping the meeting-house 4 times, and caring for the same 1 year.

March 21, 1796. An article having been inserted in the warrant calling the meeting holden this day, asking for the consent of the parish that the bass-viol be used in the meeting-house on Sunday to assist the singers in time of public worship, failed of approval. Eben Fisk was sexton, and Dea. J. Carlton, parish clerk, 1799-1804.

CHAPTER II.

CONDITIONS PRELIMINARY TO THE SEPARATION FROM THE PARENT TOWN.

PUBLIC EVENTS—LOYALISTS—SKETCH OF JOSHUA ATHERTON—SKETCH OF CHARLES H. ATHERTON—SKETCH OF CHARLES G. ATHERTON—SKETCH OF SAMUEL DANA—REV. JEREMIAH BARNARD—LOYALISTS' INFLUENCE IN POLITICS—TROUBLOUS TIMES IN THE COUNTRY—ESTABLISHMENT OF CONSTITUTION—MR. ATHERTON'S OBJECTION TO CONSTITUTION—ORGANIZATION OF THIRD OR SOUTHWEST PARISH INCORPORATION OF MILFORD—DISSENSION BETWEEN PARISHES—PETITION OF FIRST PARISH—POLITICAL PARTIES—EXTRACT FROM A TOWN MEETING—OR A TOUCH AT THE TIMES AT A   —MEETING BETWEEN BRADFORD AND AUTHOR OF POEM—FEELING BETWEEN FIRST AND SECOND PARISHES—SKETCH OF MAJOR WILLIAM BRADFORD—SKETCH OF DR. ROGERS SMITH.

A GLANCE at public events of this period, and their effect in influencing local conditions, so as to require for the peace and order of both communities a complete severance of all corporate interests, will give to those interested a clear idea of the influence of the various causes which converted the northwest parish of Amherst into the town of Mont Vernon.

For several years prior to the War for Independence, and even after the breaking out of hostilities, while the majority of the colonists were bitterly hostile to King George and his ministry, and regarded his policy as so unjust and tyrannical as to justify revolt, and yet hoped for a reconciliation with the mother country, there was yet a considerable minority loyal to the royal government. They believed the attempt at independence would not succeed, that it was madness; that the trained troops sent over by the King would overpower the raw militia, and the result would be the ruin of the colonies. They were generally rich and prosperous, of aristocratic tendencies, but mostly men of moral worth. These loyalists were vulgarly called

tories, and were in excessive odium among the patriots. Many of
them who did not flee, acquiesced in the order of things, but it was
conformity without change of opinion. Those who were most uncompromising were exiles and their property was seized and confiscated
during the war. The provinces of New Brunswick and Nova Scotia
were their refuge, and among the valuable citizens of those provinces
today are many descendants from the tory refugees of the United
States. John Holland, a rank tory, nephew of Joshua Atherton, of
Amherst, was seized and banished to New Brunswick, where he died.

When Gen. Gage evacuated Boston, in March, 1776, twelve
hundred American loyalists went with him to Halifax, but few of
whom returned. Prophetic were the words of the brave Dr. Warren
who fell at Bunker Hill: ''The contest may be severe, but the end
will be glorious.''

Joshua Atherton was at this time easily, in reputation, ability,
and influence, the first man in Amherst. Born in Lancaster, Massachusetts, in 1737, after graduating at Harvard, he studied law and
practised six years in Merrimack. In the summer of 1773 he moved
from Merrimack to Amherst, and being an able lawyer, was soon
busily employed in the practice of his profession. As the dispute
between the mother country and her American colonies increased in
bitterness, he, being an open and avowed loyalist, became exceedingly
unpopular.

September 20, 1774, some three hundred men from Bedford,
Amherst, and vicinity, assembled at Amherst and chose a committee
to wait upon Mr. Atherton and request him to come to the court-
house, which he did, and sign a declaration and read it to the people,
who accepted it. Notwithstanding this declaration, the persecution
continued, but he was not cured of his loyalty.

In 1776 he refused to sign the Association Test Paper when it
was presented to him. Finally he was arrested and placed in Exeter
jail ''as a person at large whose presence would be dangerous to the
liberties of the country.'' He was afterwards transferred from Exeter
to Amherst jail. He was ultimately liberated in June, 1778. At the
January term of court, 1779, he took the oath of allegiance and
attorney's oath, and was again admitted to practice. The good will
of his fellow citizens began to return to him, and his business became
lucrative. He was a warm friend of Mr. Barnard, and took an active
part in his ordination in 1780. During the rest of his life he was
Senator in the state legislature, and attorney-general of the state,

Many young men, afterwards distinguished, resorted to his office for instruction in their chosen profession. He died in 1809.

The name of Atherton among his descendants is now extinct. But among the Atherton female branch, those bearing the name of Spaulding, Gordon, Means, Bigelow, and others have achieved honorable distinction.

His son, Charles Humphrey Atherton, born August, 1773, died January, 1853, was for many years one of the most prominent lawyer, of Hillsborough county, and as a probate lawyer had no superior in the state.

He was a high-toned Federalist, and in religious belief a Unitarian of the Channing type. He was Register of Probate three years, also representative three years, and many years on the superintending school committee. He had a great interest in historical and genealogical researches, and was a Master Mason. By close attention to money matters, he accumulated one of the largest estates ever left in Amherst.

His son, Hon. Charles Gordon Atherton, graduated at Harvard in 1822, and in 1825 entered upon the practice of law at Nashua, New Hampshire. He early engaged in politics, and being ambitious, identified himself with the Democratic, then the ruling party in the state, and likely to remain so for many years. He was five years representative in the state legislature, and four years speaker of the House. In 1837 he took his seat as a Representative in Congress, which he held four years December 10, 1838, he introduced into Congress what was famous as the "Gag," a rule which provided that all petitions for the abolition of slavery should be laid upon the table without further action. This was in force until 1845, but this, like all other measures to stay the anti-slavery agitation, increased it. In 1843 he was elected United States Senator, and served a full term of six years. In 1853, through the influence of the President-elect, Franklin Pierce, he was again returned to the Senate, to be the organ in that body for the incoming administration, but died suddenly while attending court at Manchester, November 14, 1853, aged 49. He was a man of acute and scholarly intellect, a fluent and polished speaker, and ranked high as a counsellor and advocate. In temperament he was cold, distant, and aristocratic in bearing, and won no followers by personal magnetism. He married the grand-daughter of the life-long personal and political friend of his immediate ancestor, Rev. Jeremiah Barnard, by whom he had no children.

Another of these loyalists active in this community was Hon. Sam'l Dana. He was graduated early at Harvard College, fitted for the ministry, and was settled at Groton, Massachusetts, in 1761, and remained in office until May, 1775, when he resigned. Being a rank tory, the affections of a larger part of his people had been diverted from him by the course he pursued during the Revolution. In 1780 he became a law student at the office of his friend, Joshua Atherton. In the spring of 1781 he purchased a small tenement of Mr. Atherton and moved his family from Groton to Amherst. In the autumn following he was admitted to practice as an attorney, and soon acquired a large business. In 1782 he purchased a farm and buildings at the west end of the plain, and built the mansion that was afterwards for many years the homestead of Dr. Matthias Spalding, where he died April, 1798.

During his residence in Amherst, he was successively Register and Judge of Probate, and a member of the state Senate. He was the father of Benevolent Lodge of Amherst, and was its first Grand Master. In 1826 this institution was removed to Milford, where it now flourishes. His religion was liberal (Unitarian), and he was a close friend and supporter of Rev. Mr. Barnard. He exhibited talents as a lawyer above mediocrity. His daughter Mehitable married Sam'l Bell in 1807, and became the mother of Chief Justice Samuel Dana Bell of New Hampshire, and James Bell, United States Senator. A son of Samuel Dana Bell was Samuel N. Bell, a representative in Congress, who in 1874 declined the offer of appointment as Chief Justice tendered him by Gov. James A. Weston.

Rev. Jeremiah Barnard settled in 1780 in Amherst, and died January 15, 1835, on his farm on Christian Hill, Amherst, aged 85. He was a man of more than ordinary abilities. His lot was cast in a stormy time, as religious and political divisions prevailed in the parish for the first thirty-five years of his ministry. But his will and energy enabled him to breast the storm, when a man of more peaceable and quiet disposition would have been overcome by the contending factions. Of religious differences he was very tolerant, but not so of political. He was warmly attached to the Federal school of politics, and denounced the opposition in and out of the pulpit with great zeal. He was most emphatically a fighting political parson, but his marked social qualities, his general good sense, warm attachment to friends, and kindness of heart enabled him to prosper through his long ministry. These men of aristocratic predilections and others of like tendencies largely controlled public sentiment in Amherst, and their influence at the time of intense political excitement gave complexion to the politics of the citizens of what is now the town of Amherst.

The sketches of the lives of these men do not bear directly upon the history of Mont Vernon, but they had important and indirect influence in shaping opinions and events, which led to a final separation.

The War for Independence had closed. But the whole country was in a most unsatisfactory condition. The colonies were very poor. A period of distress and depression prevailed, sharper than at any crisis of the Revolutionary struggle. Their money had so declined in value that it took one hundred paper dollars to buy a pair of shoes.

The government of the League of Confederation was weak and inefficient. The people were so jealous of it that they had hardly given Congress means of action. It could not raise money by taxes or establish rates of duties on foreign goods imported, nor compel obedience to any law. It was so loose and feeble that treaties with foreign countries were impossible. Washington said: "We are one nation today and thirteen tomorrow." The people were heavily in debt. Public and private credit was destroyed. A rebellion broke out in Massachusetts, called "Shay's Rebellion," composed of men who thought that all taxes and debts should be suspended at such a time. Complaints were rife that attorneys and officers of the law sought to advance their selfish interests to the ruin of their fellow-citizens. In the midst of these troubles, a petition from fifty citizens of Amherst, and mostly of the Northwest Parish, was presented to the General Court in February, 1783, asking for some legislation to relieve the situation. These financial troubles continued for some years, but the establishment of the Federal Constitution, taking effect in 1788, in a large measure operated to close them. In 1787 a convention met in Philadelphia, to form a new constitution, which, if adopted, would insure a stronger government. After many weeks' discussion, September 17, 1787, the convention finally adopted what is substantially the present United States Constitution, and sent it to the thirteen colonies for acceptance.

In the New Hampshire State Convention, Col. Ebenezer Webster (father of Daniel Webster), who was a delegate from Salisbury, did not vote at all on the question of acceptance or rejection. January 1, 1788, ten citizens of Amherst were chosen a committee to examine this form of government and report their judgment upon it. They reported that they could not recommend it to the acceptance of the town in its present form. The only member of the committee from the Northwest parish was Rev. John Bruce. Three others of the ten, Messrs. Atherton, Dana, and Barnard, were men of liberal education. January 15, 1788, the town chose Joshua Atherton to represent it in the state convention to decide upon the adoption of the present constitution. In that body Mr. Atherton made a very sensible and feeling speech against Section IX Article I. of that instrument, which tolerated the African slave trade for a term of years. His objections were not heeded, as the constitution in its entirety was ratified at an adjourned session held in Concord the following June, though sixteen out of the twenty-five delegates from the old county of Hillsborough voted against its acceptance.

What is now Mont Vernon having become the Second Parish in Amherst, forty-seven residents of the southwest part of the town petitioned the General Court at its session March 1, 1782, to be set off into a third parish.

September 9, 1782, the first parish appointed Messrs. Blanchard, Dana, and Wilkins to show cause before the legislature why the prayer of this petition should not be granted. Their efforts were unsuccessful, for November 23, 1782, the General Court constituted the petitioners as the Third or Southwest Parish of Amherst, "for transacting ministerial affairs only." Being thus severed from the First Parish, they organized, January 9, 1783, and voted "to build a meeting-house of the same size and bigness as the Northwest Parish has built except the porches." The frame of this meeting-house was erected in the summer of 1784, but not completed until eight years afterward. This building for nearly half a century was the place of worship for the Congregational church in Milford, and also its town-house. It was in the center of what is now Union Square, now located on the east side of the Square, and known as Eagle Hall, which has been refitted and is used for business purposes.

In October, 1793, at a parish meeting, it was voted to petition the General Court to set them off as a separate town in connection with the Mile Slip and Duxbury School Farm, and a part of Hollis. Therefore January, 1794, the town of Milford was incorporated, consisting of one hundred and forty-two tax-payers, and preceding the organization of the Northwest Parish into Mont Vernon just ten years.

The dissensions between the different sections of Amherst, which commenced with the building of the second meeting-house in 1771-74, and aggravated by the settlement of Mr. Barnard, were in no wise healed by the division of the town into parishes.

A lengthy application, signed by one hundred and twenty inhabitants of the old parish, was sent to the General Court in February, 1783, setting forth an unhappy state of affairs. This document recites that in May, 1781, sundry persons, whose names are given, obtained an act erecting them into a distinct parish, still leaving them to act with the town of Amherst in all matters, save religious, proper to such a corporate body. That whereas disuniting in some things disunites them in other things. This unfortunate act had operated to create variance and discord, that their town meetings were scenes of confusion, irregularity, and vexation, therefore they invoked the General Court to relieve their unhappy situation and extricate them from the bondage of continual discord and party factions. They specified the remedy they wished applied as follows: "Permit us to part with one of them, and to ask your Honors that the persons above named, who have chosen to be separated in part, may be separated from us wholly. Your Honors have ample powers to complete the separation in all matters whatsoever, as we do not wish to retain them to our mutual vexation."

This was aimed at the Northwest Parish only. Though respectful in form, it indirectly censured the action of a previous legislature, in setting off a fractious minority against the remonstrance of a majority of the voters in Amherst. The legislature took no action upon this doleful petition, but twenty years later the desired relief came, to the satisfaction of both communities.

The establishment of the Federal Constitution divided the people into political parties, a division which became more acute after the breaking out of the French Revolution, hailed, with all its terrible excesses, by one party as a triumph of the people, and regarded by the other side as the precedent of destruction of all government among men. Jay's treaty with Great Britain during Washington's administration was very much opposed by the Republicans, but more odious to them was the "Alien and Sedition Law," and the "Land Tax Law," both passed during the administration of John Adams, which greatly intensified the divisions among the people.

At the annual meeting in March, 1799, the selectmen were appointed a committee to petition Congress to repeal the "Alien and Sedition Law," and to change the mode of assessing and collecting

the land tax. The selectmen declined the appointment, whereupon
Major William Bradford, Eli Wilkins, Esq., of the Second Parish,
and William Low, of the First Parish, all Republicans, were chosen
as the committee. At an adjourned meeting the next Tuesday, they
presented a report, which the town by a majority vote accepted, which
greatly exasperated the Federalists. The Northwest Parish, being
almost entirely Republican, voted almost unanimously for the report,
and this will explain the following description of the meeting, which
made its appearance in the "*Village Messenger*" of March, 1799, and
which is introduced here to show the bitterness prevalent in this
community at that period:

"Extract From a Town-Meeting. Or a Touch of the Times at
    Am......t:

> "March comes, the first born child of Spring:
> The bells for annual meeting ring:
> Joy smiles in every patriot's face,
> And Am......t dreams not of disgrace.
> Forth from the North in crowds came down
> Old age, on crutch, and youth, half-grown:
> Old age, whose one foot in the grave is,
> Whose other to the gout a slave is:
> And youth, not yet arrived at freedom,
> Who need their nurses still to lead 'em:
> All, all came down, a motley nation,
> As tho' 'in hell there were vacation.'
> Burning with Jacobinic zeal,
> To overturn the public weal,
> Before them stalked a man of stature,
> Designed a Jacobin by nature,
> Whose mind and mien strong traces bore
> Of that great Jacobin of yore,
> Who, for Sedition, forth was driven,
> Eternal from the gates of heaven.
> Despising peace and lawful labors,
> He sows sedition 'mong his neighbors:
> Tells them that governments are knaves,
> That they, poor souls, will soon be slaves,
> And those that rule them soon will stand
> The lords and sovereigns of the land.
> To church he goes, but not for preaching:
> He gives his precious time to teaching
> That those that dare not tell a lie
> Have surely lost their liberty.
> He at his heels the rabble brought.

Who long beneath his eye were taught
To banish order, stir up evil,
And serve their lord and master, Devil.
    *   *   *   *   *   *
At length the cause of all their ills,
The Alien and Sedition Bills,
The tax direct on land and houses,
Which every foe to peace arouses,
Comes publickly to be discussed
By friend and foe, by blest and cursed.
A solemn pause—debates proceeded,
As though the Jacos some man needed
Some natural son of base sedition,
To rise and speak for their petition.
Their chief arose. 'Tis strange,' he cries,
'Since freedom is our blood-earned prize,
That we, like slaves, should be debarred
The use of speech,—indeed, that's hard.
No more shall scandal charm our souls,
Since government our tongues controls
Aliens no more with monied reason
Shall stir up faction, death and treason;
But under harrows, saws and axes,
We be compelled to pay our taxes,
Support our Congressmen in style,
By cruel, unrewarded toil.
Till we, at last, O, dreadful thought!
Beneath those tyrants shall be brought,
And see in tears the fatal day
When we to tyrant laws gave way.
Beware, my friends, 'tis our condition!
O, curse the law against sedition!
O, curse the Pres——no, no, I fear
Some friend to government may hear,
And I like friend and brother Lyon,*
Be tried and feel the power of iron.
O, Liberty, 'tis but a name,
When we no longer can defame!"
Reasons were offered when he ended,
And government and laws defended;
But sense and reason all are vain,
When faction rules the heated brain;
For ignorance, deceived by lies,
All human argument defies.
The question put, the chief uprose.

---

*Matthew Lyon was at that time a Republican member of the National House of Representatives. A motion to expel him from the House had just failed.

Surveyed his friends, surveyed his foes:
His minion friends united stand,
Instructed by his factious hand.
Their chief they watch, his actions view,
And when he votes, why they vote too.
Such are Columbia's servile foes.
Led on, like asses, by the nose;
Seduced from order by a villian,
Whose honor is not worth a shilling.
Who, worse than Judas and such gents.
Would sell our State for thirty cents.
O, would he ape that child of hell
In all his actions 't would be well;
His neck, too, then, a rope would grace,
And he depart to his own place.

                                                AMPHION.

The Jacobin who was so offensively caricatured and so insolently abused was Major William Bradford, an active and influential citizen of the Northwest Parish, and for the next three years representative from Amherst. A few days afterward he repaired to Amherst, intending to inflict personal chastisement upon the writer of this abuse. He demanded of the editor the name of the author and where he might be found, and was pointed to a certain law office and was told that he would there find a student who would respond to his call. Major Bradford had been through the Revolution, was a man of stately proportions and in the full vigor of manhood, and would be a formidable antagonist in a personal encounter. He went as directed, and was presented to a young man, in whom he beheld his match, a six-footer of stalwart proportions, a very Hercules in muscle, and he deemed it discreet to retire without stating his errand "Amphion" was a young Wilton Federalist, who studied law and taught school in Amherst, and in later life was known as the Hon. William Abbott, of Bangor, Maine.

The Northwest Parish folks bore the dwellers on the plain and the lowlands in the neighborhood no good-will. They called it Sodom, and spoke of seeing "the smoke of its torment ascending to the heavens on frosty mornings." This was somewhat akin to the spirit of one of their number who, in the days when Parson Barnard was prophesying against the Democracy, gave as a Fourth of July toast: "Amherst:—It has a big meeting-house with a tall steeple, an Arminian preacher, and a cursed people."

The time was now approaching for an entire separation from the parent town. Twenty-three years before, this had been partially accomplished by the formation of the Second Parish as religiously independent of the First, but this, we have seen, did not tend to unity of thought or action.

In the party divisions, which distinguished the close of the last and the beginning of the present century, the ruling influences in the Second Parish were as decidedly Republican or "Jeffersonian" as were those of the First in an opposite direction.

For three years, 1800-1802 inclusive, the offensive "Jacobin," Major Bradford, represented Amherst in the General Court, with the aid of the Second Parish vote, and the Federal elements anticipated a restoration of their local ascendency by freedom from this connection. Here it may be proper to remark that in the First Parish itself there was a minority of active Republicans, conspicuous among whom were Hon. William Fiske, Cols. Daniel Warner and Paul D. Sargent, and Capt. Eli Brown.

Major William Bradford, so stigmatized by Mr. Abbott in his "Extract from a Town Meeting," a leading Republican of Mont Vernon, was a man of note. His father was William Bradford, from Middleton, Massachusetts, who settled in Souhegan West previous to its incorporation as a town. The son was born here in 1753. He was a sergeant at the age of 22, in Capt. Josiah Crosby's company at Bunker Hill, and an ensign in Capt. Wilkins's company at the Cedars, where he was taken prisoner and abused by the Indians. He afterwards served as a lieutenant in the Continental Army. In 1800, 1801, 1802 he represented Amherst, and in 1804, 1805, 1806 he represented Mont Vernon in the New Hampshire Legislature. He was the active promoter of the incorporation of Mont Vernon as a separate town. In 1812 he received a major's commission in the 1st Regiment New Hampshire Volunteers. He married for his second wife Mrs. Lois, widow of Rev. John Bruce. He had two brothers, Samuel and Joseph, who were in the Revolution, and his first cousin, Capt. John Bradford, of Hancock, commanded a company in the battle of Bennington, and was the first man to scale the enemy's breastworks. Major Bradford removed in 1815 to Barre, Vermont, where he died October 25, 1816, aged 63. For record of his children, see Family Register.

Another citizen prominent in political and town affairs during this period was Dr. Rogers Smith. He was the eldest son of James and Moriah (Rolfe) Smith, and was born in Middleton, Massachusetts, June 12, 1776. His parents a few months later moved to Mont Vernon. He studied medicine with Dr. William Jones, of Lyndeborough, commenced practice in Amherst in 1802, removed to Mont Vernon in 1805, to Greenbush, New York, as surgeon in the army, in 1813, and in 1816 to Weston, Vermont, where he died March 25, 1845. During his seven years' residence in Mont Vernon, he was three years moderator of the town meeting, once selectman, three years town clerk, and three years on the School Board. He was a man of fine literary taste, a cultivated writer, and a well informed and ardent politician. He was the father of Asa Dodge Smith, president of Dartmouth College from 1863 to 1877.

CHAPTER III.

SEPARATION FROM AMHERST.

VOTING ACTIONS OF NORTHWEST PARISH— ACT OF INCORPORATION OF
NEW TOWN—NAME BOUNDARY LINES OF NEW TOWN—BOUNDARY
OF NEW TOWN—NAME OF TAX PAYERS—FIRST TOWN MEETING.

ON the third day of May, 1802, the Northwest Parish voted to
take measures to effect a separation from the town of Amherst, and a
committee consisting of Major William Bradford, John Carlton, Capt.
John Batchelder, Capt. Joseph Perkins, Capt. Thomas Cloutman,
Dea. Jacob Kendall, Lieut. Benjamin Parker, Lieut. Joseph Farnum,
Eli Wilkins, Parker Richardson, Nathan Jones, and Lieut. Timothy
Hill were appointed a committee to petition the town relative thereto.

On the last Thursday of May, 1802, the Parish voted to petition
the General Court to incorporate them into a new town, with the same
boundaries as those established between the First and Second Parishes.

On the first Monday of June, 1802, chose Nathan Jones, Capt.
Joseph Perkins, and Capt. Benjamin Parker to present the petition to
the General Court.

May 2, 1803, at a town meeting held that day, Col. Robert
Means, Samuel Wilkins, Daniel Warner, Samuel Whiting, and William
Fisk, of the First Parish, and William Bradford, Josiah Perkins, Eli
Wilkins, Ebenezer Odell, and Joseph Langdell, of the Second Parish,
were chosen to confer together upon a division of the town, and were
instructed to report at this meeting. After an hour's session the
committee reported verbally, "not agreed." Whereupon the town of
Amherst chose Col. Daniel Warner agent to attend the General Court
in the matter of the Second Parish petition. Daniel Campbell, Samuel
Wilkins, and Chas. H. Atherton were appointed a committee to con-
sult with said agent and give him such advice and instruction as they
think proper, before he shall attend the General Court.

However, an act incorporating the town of Mont Vernon was

completed by the signature of Gov. John Taylor Gilman, Dec. 15, 1803.

The verdure of the farms, which cluster about the eminence upon which the village is located, it is said by some, suggested the name of Mont Vernon for the town. A statement like this may be found in the sketch of the town by the Rev. C. D. Herbert (once settled over the church at Mont Vernon) in Lawrence's History of the New Hampshire Churches, published in Claremont, in 1856. But this explanation seems to be open to doubt. The English name " Vernon," is not at all the same as the French word from which are derived such words as "verdure," "verdant," etc., signifying greenness. And, referring to the probabilities, the Rev. C. C. Carpenter of Andover, Mass., who also occupied the position of pastor of the church for several years, and who is a past master in historical research, says : " I do not think the hard-headed farmers of our hill were so imaginative, in the month of November, 1803, as to consider their pastures green enough to suggest the name for the town." And he adds : " Per contra, it seems to me the preponderating likelihood is that the name was intended to be in memory of Washington's home, the beloved Father of his Country having then so recently died." The name " Mont," which seems to have been used in the act of incorporation, was probably due to a blunder in transcription. The original act cannot be found, but a certified copy gives it " Mont." The postoffice name is, however, " Mount" Vernon, and the name is sometimes given as " Mont," and sometimes as " Mount," in official or semi-official volumes. Washington's home, Mount Vernon, was named for Admiral Vernon of the Royal Navy.

Its boundaries, as given in the act of incorporation, were as follows : "Beginning at the northwest corner of Amherst, on New Boston, south line, thence running sutherly on the west line of Amherst about four miles and a half to the northwest corner of the town of Milford, thence easterly on the north line of Milford to the southeast corner of a lot of land now in possession of David Dodge and John Cochran, thence northerly to the northwest corner thereof, thence easterly to the southwest corner of a lot now in possession of Nathan Fuller and John Fuller, thence northerly to the northwest corner thereof, thence easterly on the north line of said Fuller's lot and the north line of Elisha Felton's house lot, and the same course on the line of Enos Bradford's and Lambert Bradford's land to the southwest corner of land now or lately owned by Enos Bradford, thence northerly on the

east line of said land and the east line of a lot now owned by John
Clap to the northeast corner of said Clap's land, thence a few rods to
the southwest corner of a lot now in possession of Andrew Leavitt,
thence northerly on the west line of said lot in possession of said
Leavitt and on the west line of a lot now owned by Col. Robert Means
and others to the southeast corner of land now owned by Joseph
Nichols, thence northerly on the west line of said Nichols's land to the
northwest corner thereof, thence easterly on the north line of said
Nichols's land to a line running south from the east side of Henry
Spaulding's land and on the easterly line thereof until it intersects
New Boston line, thence westerly to the place of beginning."

　The following one hundred and thirty-five tax-payers were resi-
dent in Mont Vernon, April 1, 1804 : Timothy Austin, Jesse Averill,
John Averill, jr., Eben Batchelder, Israel Batchelder, John Batchelder,
James Bennett, Ebenezer Bills, Jonathan Bixby, Enos Bradford,
Lambert Bradford, Widow Bradford, William Bradford, William
Bradford, jr , Mark Burnam, Charles Cambridge, John Carlton, Mrs.
Emma Carlton, Nathan Cleaves, Josiah Coburn, Thomas Cloutman,
Henry Codman, Joseph Coggin, William Coggin, Jonathan Conant,
Jonathan Conant, jr. Lot Conant, Nathan Cross, Jacob Curtis, Jacob
Curtis, jr., Allen Dodge, Joseph Dodge, Josiah Dodge, Malachi
Dodge, Jonathan Duncklee, Benjamin Durant, Israel Farnum, Joseph
Farnum, Thomas Farnum, John Fisk, John B. Flanigan, Nathan
Flint, Samuel Flint, Lieut. Allen Goodridge, Allen Goodridge, Nathan
Green, John Harwood, John Harwood, jr., William Hastings, Lieut.
Josiah Herrick, Peter Herrick, Mrs. Judith Hill, Timothy Hill,
Ebenezer Holt Ezekiel Holt James Hopkins, James Hopkins, jr.,
Robert Hosea, Nathan Jones, Peter Jones, Daniel Kendall, Jacob
Kendall, John Kendall, Lieut. Thaddeus Kendall, William L. Kidder,
Josiah Kittredge, Solomon Kittredge, Dr. Zephaniah Kittredge, Jesse
Lamson, Jonathan Lamson, jr., Mrs. Mary Lamson, Joseph Langdell,
Jonathan Low, Isaac Manning, John Manning, David Marshall,
Ebenezer Mills, Samuel Mitchell, Lieut. Ebenezer Odell, Ebenezer
Odell, jr., Capt. Benjamin Parker, Robert Parker, jr., Aaron Peabody,
John Peabody, Moses Peabody. Samuel Peabody, Capt. Joseph
Perkins, Joseph Perkins jr., Samuel Phelps, Ensign Benjamin Pike,
Ephraim Pike, James Ray, James Ray, jr., Levi Ray, Mrs. Phœbe
Raymond, John Roby, John Roby, jr., John Rollins, Daniel Secombe,
Dea. Daniel Smith, Daniel Smith, jr., David Smith, Eben Smith,
Isaac Smith, Isaac Smith, jr., Jacob Smith, James Smith, Jeremiah

Smith, Nathan Smith, Timothy Smith, Abijah Spofford, Benjamin Stearns, Cyrus Styles, Josiah Swinington, Robert Taggart, Henry Treavitt, Allen Towne, John Trow, Joseph Trow. Joseph Trow, jr., Enos Upton, Dea. Ezekiel Upton, Lieut. Ezekiel Upton, Nehemiah Upton, Isaac Weston, John Weston. Thomas Weston. Abial Wilkins, Abijah Wilkins, Eli Wilkins, Jonathan Wilkins, Peter Wilkins, James Woodbury.

The first town meeting was held January 23, 1804, at the Center school-house. Joseph Langdell was chosen moderator, John Carlton, town clerk, and John Carlton, Jos. Langdell, and Jacob Kendall, selectmen.

At the first annual town meeting, March 13, 1804, the same town officers were re-elected, and Major William Bradford was chosen as representative.

CHAPTER IV.

DESCRIPTION AND BOUNDARIES.

THE town of Mont Vernon is situated in the county of Hills-borough in the State of New Hampshire. It lies a little southward from the territorial center of Hillsborough County, being third in the tier of towns northward from the Massachusetts line. It is situated in latitude 42 degrees 51 minutes north. Mont Vernon is irregular in shape, averaging four and one-half miles in length, and three and one-half in width. It covers an area of about 10,000 acres, of which a very small part is covered with water.

The towns which bound it are : New Boston on the north, Am-herst on the east, Amherst and Milford on the south, and Lyndeborough on the west.

It is twenty-eight miles south by southwest from Concord, fifteen miles southwest from Manchester, fourteen miles northwest from Nashua, and four and one-half miles north from the line of the Nashua and Wilton railroad at Milford village. Its distance from Boston is about fifty-five miles.

The surface is hilly, the larger part of the town being a lofty ridge lying between the valley of the south branch of the Piscataquog River on the north, and that of the Souhegan on the south. It is emphatically an upland town. The soil is rocky, but generally deep and fertile, well repaying careful cultivation. It seems especially adapted to the apple, several thousand barrels of this fruit being the annual product of its orchards ; and the winter apples grown here have long been known as not excelled by any for their keeping quali-ties. The annual crop of blueberries gathered from its pastures is many hundred bushels.

Its water courses are limited to five brooks, of any considerable size, four of which flow southerly to the Souhegan, and one northerly to the Piscataquog. The largest of these streams has its rise in the northeasterly part of the town, flows southerly some four miles, (furnishing in the easterly part of the town two mill sites,) to Holt's Meadow, in Amherst, where it unites with Cæsar Brook, which rises in Mont Vernon village, two miles above, and unitedly they form Beaver Brook, which courses southward, and, after furnishing the water power to Amherst village, makes its confluence with the Souhegan River, three miles below. The Indian name of this stream as given on some maps is the "Quohquinnepassakessananagnog." This name excites much interest among those who come to Mont Vernon as strangers. A third brook, known as Harwood's, rises in the meadow northwest from Mont Vernon village, and after a journey southward from three to four miles, empties into the Souhegan, one and one-half miles above Milford village.

Black, or Purgatory, Brook issues from Smith's Pond, one mile northerly from the village, has a course of some five miles, and after receiving a large tributary from Lyndeborough, known as Curtis Brook, empties into the Souhegan River about three miles above Milford village.

A fifth stream rises in the northwest part of the town, and after a course of two miles northward, discharges itself into the Piscataquog at the hamlet known as Paper Mill Village, in New Boston. It is generally known as Baldwin brook, or sometimes called Colby.

Smith's Pond a body of water located one mile north from the village, covers an area of twenty-five acres. This name, Smith's Pond, is not usually applied to it, "The Old Pond," being its common designation.

Joe English Pond is divided between Mont Vernon, New Boston, and Amherst, the larger part being in Amherst.

Roby's Hill, rising in the northeast part of the town near Joe English Pond, forms the highest elevation.

Other conspicuous prominences are McCollom Hill, on the northerly line of the town; Beech Hill, in the northwesterly section; Carleton Hill, in the southwesterly part of the town; and near the village easterly and southeasterly are Campbell Hill and Prospect Hill. From the summit of the latter, which is a broad plateau elevated some one hundred feet above the village, is obtained a prospect most varied and extensive.   An expanse of country forty miles in every direction is seen with the naked eye.

Mont Vernon is on an eminence nearly 1000 feet above mean tide water.

Nearly all the different kinds of forest trees and shrubs, usual in southern New Hampshire, abound in Mont Vernon.   Hard wood is found chiefly here, largely beech, birch, maple, and chestnut, also soft wood including pine, hemlock, and spruce.

A little granite is to be found, principally in the southern part of the town, being of a fair quality.   What granite has been quarried here, has been mainly used for door-stones and underpinning.

The smaller wild and cultivated fruits, blackberries, blueberries, raspberries, and strawberries, are plentifully produced, and hundreds of bushels of the different kinds, more especially blueberries, are sold at the boarding houses, while more are sent to Boston and other cities.   Forty years ago the wild fruits were available to any who might desire to gather them.   But of late years they have become so valuable that in most blueberry pastures the public are warned not to gather them.   In the north and east parts of the town certain persons make a business, in the season, of picking, or hiring others to pick, blueberries, and each day carry crates of them, in quart boxes, to Milford, whence they are shipped by rail to Lowell and Boston.

As not any of the ponds of Mont Vernon are of any considerable size, no fish of much consequence are to be found in them.   The brooks above named, however, still abound in small trout, except Purgatory brook.   The brooks are, however, so persistently fished, and dry summers are so frequent, that the fishing is not at all what it used to be, although every year several hundred trout are taken within the limits of the town.   Large game was abundant in the early days of the town, and small game is now.   Within late years Mont Vernon has had many famous hunters for a town of its size.   The smaller animals, as the mink, coon, musk-rat, otter, fox, rabbit, or hare, etc., are frequently met with.   Squirrels are very common. Even now a deer is seen occasionally.   In fact, within ten years these animals have become quite common.   At present no shooting of deer is allowed, and they bid fair to become detrimentally plenty to the farmers.   Formerly the birds that were to be found in the country were more common than at the present day.   Robins, bluebirds, sparrows, bobolinks, swallows, orioles, or golden robins, partridges, quail, and a host of others appear every summer.   The voice of the whip-poor-will is a pleasant feature of the summer evenings. Often in their semi-annual migration wild geese are seen or heard coursing through the air. Rattlesnakes are very rare. Only one has been seen here within the memory of the present generation, a large one being killed in 1840 by Mr. Chester B. Southworth, in the garden attached to his house, on the west side of the cemetery. Adders, water and spotted, also black, green, and striped snakes are common.

Sudden and extreme changes in temperature occasionally occur, as great and sudden as fifty degrees in eighteen hours have been noticed The average snow fall for each of the forty last winters has been a little less than seven feet. The greatest rain fall within that time is believed to have been in October, 1869, when, after a drought of three months, nearly eight inches of water fell, damaging hillside highways and dams. The damage amounted to $3,000 in this town, and the sawmill of Arthur A. Trow and Daniel W. Trow on the Harwood Brook was swept away. The old turnpike, near the old Town Farm, was so washed out at this time that it was discontinued as a highway.

PURGATORY.

"Purgatory" is the name given to a rocky gorge two miles west of Mont Vernon, forming part of the boundary lines between the towns of Mont Vernon and Lyndeborough. It is a deep ravine, more than half a mile in length, through which Black Brook makes its way. At the "Upper Falls" the brook plunges perpendicularly about fifty feet into a deep chasm or pit, from which the view upward of a solid wall of rock on either side and dense overhanging forest is one of singular wildness and grandeur. One hundred rods down this steep gorge, the stream makes several further leaps known as "Lower Falls." Close by the channel at the "Upper Falls" is the "Devil's Beanpot," a circular excavation or "pot-hole" several feet deep in the ledge, and hard by is a perfect imprint as of a human foot, seven feet long, embedded in the rock, and known as the "Devil's Footprint." In the gulf below are the "Pulpit," the "Overhanging Rock," the "Devil's Den," the "Old Boy's Face," (sometimes called the "Giant's Head") "Hog Rock," and many other points in this museum of Nature's wonder works.

There is a fine grove near the "Upper Falls" which is fitted up for picnic parties. The approach to the glen is down a steep hill one-half mile long from the Mont Vernon side, on the old highway from Amherst to Lyndeborough, and a domestic once remarked, after emerging from its gloom, that this Purgatory was as hard to get out of as the other.

Doubtless this gorge had a human history long ere the Anglo-Saxon set foot here. The dusky tribes of the forest no doubt frequented it to gaze in awe and wonder. The students at the village academy were accustomed to make weekly picnic excursions to Purgatory; but the name has no particular significance.

For some years, one day in the latter part of August of each year, hundreds of dwellers in Mont Vernon and adjacent towns had been accustomed to resort to Purgatory on a picnic excursion. In July, 1889, Mr. H. A. Hutchinson, the owner of the Falls and lands in the vicinity, associating himself with Messrs. Henry F. Dodge and Joseph G. Carleton, formed the plan of improving the grounds and providing the requisite accommodation for the entertainment of any number of excursionists who might be attracted thither. A band stand, dancing platform, bowling alley, and other facilities were erected. In short, they designed to enlarge the gathering and make Purgatory Picnic a permanent institution. So, in August, 1889, over two thousand persons assembled to inaugurate the scheme. J. H. A. Bruce, Esq., then the proprietor of the Hotel Bellevue, presided. The survivors of the world-renowned family of Hutchinson singers, John W. Hutchinson, of Lynn, and his sister, Mrs. Abby H. Patton, of New York, who led a choir composed of such other members of the "Tribe of Jesse" as had inherited something of that rare gift, thrilled and charmed the vast audience by the sweetest music.

Hon. Charles J. Smith delivered a very acceptable historical address on "Purgatory and Surroundings," which was published. Since then, on the Thursday next the 20th of August, not less than 1500 to 2500 persons from near and far have annually gathered here to honor the occasion and make it permanent; and these throngs coming each returning August, establish the fact that the festivity is popular.

CHAPTER V.

POLITICS, ROADS AND BRIDGES, NOTABLE EVENTS.

POLITICAL FEELING BETWEEN AMHERST AND MONT VERNON—THE
FREE SOIL PARTY GROWTH—VOTES AT SEVERAL ELECTIONS—
BOY SPELLBINDERS—CAREERS OF MARDEN AND BRUCE—HIGH-
WAYS AND BRIDGES—THE OLD TURNPIKE CHARTERS—SECOND
TURNPIKE ROAD OF NEW HAMPSHIRE—THE AMHERST TURNPIKE
CORPORATION—TURNPIKE TAVERNS—OTHER ROADS—NOTABLE
EVENTS—SPOTTED FEVER—TEMPESTS—FROSTS—RAIN STORMS—
FLOODS—GRASSHOPPERS—"DARK" AND "YELLOW" DAYS—LONG
WINTERS.

AT the time of the incorporation of the Northwest Parish of Amherst into the town of Mont Vernon, Thomas Jefferson was President
and Aaron Burr was Vice President of the United States. Both were
Republicans.

The country was divided into two large political parties, intensely
antagonistic to each other, and this party rancor affected the social
relations of every community in this country. The aversion of the
Amherst Federalists to the leading influences of Mont Vernon continued until the incoming of President Munroe's administration, when
the "era of good feeling" began to pervade the country. The following well-authenticated anecdote furnishes an instance of the feeling.
A prominent citizen of Concord, who was born in Amherst in 1801,
left in 1822, and died in 1883, was noted for his quaint and original
sayings. Whenever the town of Mont Vernon was mentioned he
would scowl and express himself thus: "Mont Vernon! Mont Vernon!
it was nothing but a community of savages before the advent of Dr.
Adams, whose coming brought civilization into the town."

Politically, Mont Vernon, in its early days was overwhelmingly
Republican, as what afterward became the Democratic party was then

called. The opposing party was the Federalist party, which later was known as the Whig party. The anti-slavery sentiment grew very strong in the early forties, and when the "Liberty," afterwards the "Free Soil," and, later still, the modern "Republican" parties were organized, there was a strong minority of anti-slavery men to join those organizations. The town, however, was almost uniformly Democratic.

In 1804 the national vote was: Federalist 3, Republican 74.

State vote—Gilman, Federalist 13, Langdon, Republican 129.

1812—National vote: Federalists 35, Republicans 120,

1836—National vote: Whigs 26, Democrats 61.

1840—National vote: Whigs 67, Democrats 92, Liberty 4.

1844—National vote: Whigs, 18, Democrats 77, Liberty 40.

1846—State election: Governor, Colby, Whig 18; Berry, Liberty 56; Williams, Democrat 80.

1851—Governor vote: Atwood, Liberty 98; Sawyer, Whig 11; Dinsmore, Democrat 48.

1852—Governor vote: Martin, Democrat 80; Atwood, Liberty 61; Sawyer, Whig 18.

National vote: Democrats 77, Liberty 57, Whigs 12.

1856—National vote: Democrats 110, Republicans 86.

1860—National vote: Breckenridge and Lane 6, Douglas 83, Lincoln 80.

1868—National vote: Democrats 95, Republicans 83.

1876—National vote: Democrats 96, Republicans 74.

1880—National vote: Democrats 104, Republicans 63.

1884—National vote: Democrats 76, Republicans 64.

1892—National vote: Democrats 79, Republicans 60.

1896—National vote: Palmer, Gold Democrat 15, Bryan, Silver Democrat 27, McKinley, Republican 86.

1898—Governor vote: Rollins, Republican 65, Stone, Democrat 63.

A good many of these anti-slavery men lived in the village, and at the Lyceums, which used to convene in the old red school house, many of the debates were on anti-slavery "questions." It was at these meetings that young Geo. A. Bruce and Geo. A. Marden, both little lads and chums in the primary classes, being duly coached by their respective fathers, who were rank abolitionists, began their careers as public speakers.

The town threatened to become anti-democratic under this con-

stant hammering of the anti-slavery element. but it was saved to the
democratic party by a timely annexation of a democratic strip of
Lyndeboro' along the west line. in 1852.   This annexation had been
petitioned for the year before by Abraham French and others. but
was not enacted by the Legislature.   In the town warrant for the
March meeting in 1852. Article 6 was as follows: "In consequence
of a petition signed by Hiram Perkins and others. to see if the town
will vote in favor of disannexing a part of Lyndeboro', and annexing
the same to Mont Vernon. it being the same as that petitioned for by
Abraham French and others at the last session of the Legislature."
The vote was 76 yeas. to 22 nays.   At the March meeting in 1853 it
was voted to raise $105.00 to defray the expenses of said annexation.

In 1860. when Lincoln was elected President. the anti-democratic
voters, having joined hands as modern Republicans. were exceedingly
jubilant. and. a few evenings after the election. celebrated the victory
in most enthusiastic style.   A company of "Wide Awakes." as the
campaign organizations of the party were known. paraded the streets
in uniform hats and capes. and carrying lighted torches.   Every Republican house in the village was illuminated, in the way then in
vogue. with a lighted candle in each window pane.   A brass band escorted the procession with martial music. and a mass meeting crowded
the "New Academy Hall." where speeches were made by several
local orators, including young Bruce and Marden. who were now class-
mates and room-mates in Dartmouth College. where they graduated
the next summer.   Marden was just old enough to cast his first vote
for Abraham Lincoln. but Bruce. whose birthday did not come until
November 19. was a bit too young to share in that glory.

It may not be out of place here to record certain facts in the
careers of these two young men. which were. at that time. considered
somewhat remarkable.   Both were born on the main village street,
within a few rods of each other — Marden. August 9. and Bruce
November 19. 1839.   They attended the same district school. drove
the family cows to the same pasture. were always together in their
studies and their sports. entered Appleton Academy together. graduated in the same class. entered Dartmouth College together. roomed
in the same rooms and ate at the same tables, through the entire four
years, belonged to the same society, and graduated together in the
class of 1861.   They did not serve together during the war, but were
both in the service about three years.   Both studied law after the
war, but Marden drifted into journalism. and Bruce was admitted to

the bar; and in 1867 they were both in Boston, again sleeping in the same room and sitting at the same table. In 1884, Bruce was elected President of the Massachusetts Senate, and Marden was elected, for the second time, to the Speakership of the Massachusetts House of Representatives.

HIGHWAYS AND BRIDGES.

The town of Mont Vernon as constituted at this writing (1904) has about 60 miles of public highways within its limits. It has no bridges of any great importance to maintain. Its roads are fairly well kept, and the annual expense of maintenance, including road-breaking in winter, is now about $1400. The modern "road-machine" has done much to improve those roads which are not too much used, but the main travelled roads often are made worse by the scraping from the gutters into the middle of the highways, of the worn out material which has so long been subjected to the wear of travel.

It is difficult to learn the details of the laying out of the earliest roads, but among them it is certain that the old Turnpike is one of early enterprises in this direction.

THE TURNPIKE.

The "Second Turnpike Road in New Hampshire" was incorporated in 1779. We are indebted to the Hon. E. N. Pearson, Secretary of State, for a copy of its charter, which was as follows:

STATE OF NEW HAMPSHIRE.

[L. S.]

IN THE YEAR OF OUR LORD ONE THOUSAND SEVEN HUNDRED AND NINETY NINE.

AN ACT TO INCORPORATE A COMPANY BY THE NAME OF THE PROPRIETORS OF THE SECOND TURNPIKE ROAD IN NEW HAMPSHIRE.

Be it enacted by the Senate and House of Representatives in General Court convened, that Josiah Stevens, Isaac Green, and Nathan Coolidge, and their associates and successors be, and they are hereby incorporated and made a body corporate and politic under the name of the Proprietors of the Second Turnpike Road in New Hampshire, and in that name may sue and prosecute & be sued and prosecuted to final judgment and execution, and shall be, and hereby are vested with all the powers and privileges, which by law are incident to corporations of a similar nature.

And be it further enacted that the said Josiah Stevens shall call a meeting of said proprietors by advertisement in the newspapers printed at Walpole and Amherst to be holden at any suitable time and place, at least fourteen days from the first publication of said advertisement & the proprietors by a vote of a majority of those present or represented at said meeting, accounting and allowing one vote to each share in all cases, shall choose a clerk, who shall be sworn to the faithful discharge of said office, and shall also agree on the method of calling future meetings, and at the same time, or at any subsequent meetings, may elect such officers and make and establish such rules and by-laws, as to them shall seem necessary and convenient for the regulation and government of said corporation for carrying into effect the purpose aforesaid, and for collecting the tolls herein after established, and the same by-laws may cause to be executed and annex penalties to the breach thereof, provided the said rules and by-laws are not repugnant to the constitution and laws of this state; and all representations shall be proved by writing signed by the person to be represented, which shall be filed with the clerk, and this act, and all rules, by-laws, regulations and proceedings of said corporation shall be fairly and truly recorded by the clerk in a book or books provided and kept for that purpose.

And be it further enacted that the said corporation are empowered to survey, lay out, make and keep in repair a turnpike road of four rods wide, in such rout or tracts, as in the best of their judgment and skill, shall combine shortness of distance, with the most practicable ground, from the lottery bridge in Claremont, to the plain in Amherst in this state, near the court house.

And be it further enacted, that if the said proprietors, and the owners of land, over which the road may run, shall disagree on the compensation to be made for said land, and the building or buildings thereon standing, and shall not agree in appointing persons to ascertain such compensation, the judges of the court of common pleas in the county in which said land lies, if not interested, and if interested, the judges of the superior court, upon application of the said proprietors, or the owners of the land, reasonable notice of such application having been given, by the applicants, to the adverse party, shall appoint a committee, who shall ascertain the same, in the same way as compensation is made to owners of land for highways as usually laid out, and execution on nonpayment, against said proprietors shall issue of course.

And be it further enacted, that the corporation may erect and fix, such, and so many gates or turnpikes upon and across said road, as will be necessary and sufficient to collect the tolls and duties hereinafter granted to the said company, from all persons travelling in the same, with horses, cattle, carts and carriages.

And be it further enacted, that it shall and may be lawful for said company to appoint such and so many toll gatherers, as they shall think proper, to collect and receive of and from all and every person or persons using said road, the tolls and rates herein after mentioned, and to stop any person riding, leading, or driving any horses, cattle, hogs, sheep, sulkey, chair, chaise, phaeton, coach, chariot, cart, wagon, sleigh, sled, or other carriage of burden or pleasure from passing through the said gates or turnpikes, until they shall have respectively paid the same; that is to say, for every mile of said road, and so in proportion, for a greater or less distance, or greater or smaller number of sheep, hogs or cattle (viz) for every ten sheep or hogs one cent, for every ten cattle or horses two cents; for every horse & his rider, or led horse one cent; for every sulkey, chair, or chaise, with one horse and two wheels, two cents; for every chariot, coach, stage-wagon, phaeton or chaise with two horses and four wheels, three cents, for either of the carriages last mentioned with four horses, four cents; for every other carriage of pleasure the like sums, according to the number of wheels and horses; drawing the same; for each cart, or other carriage of burden, drawn by one beast, one cent; for each wagon, cart, or other carriage of burden, drawn by two beasts, one cent and an half; if by more than two beasts, one cent for each additional yoke of oxen or horse; for each sleigh drawn by one horse, one cent; if drawn by two horses, two cents; and if by more than two horses one cent for every additional horse; for each sled drawn by one horse one cent; for each sled drawn by two horses or a yoke of oxen, one and a quarter cent, and if by more than two horses, or one yoke of oxen, one cent for each additional pair of horses, or yoke of oxen; and at all times when the toll-gatherer shall not attend his duty the gates shall be left open; and if any person shall with his carriage, team, cattle or horses turn out of the said road to pass the said turnpike gate, or ground adjacent thereto, with intent to avoid the payment of the toll due, by virtue of this act, such person shall forfeit and pay three times so much as the legal toll would have been, to be recovered by the treasurer of the said corporation to the use thereof in an action of debt or on the case; provided that nothing in this act shall extend to entitle the said corporation to demand toll of any person who shall be passing with his horse or carriage to or from public worship, or with his horse, team or cattle, or on foot, to or from any mill, or on the common and ordinary business of family concerns within the same town.

And be it further enacted, that the said proprietors are hereby empowered to purchase and hold in fee simple, so much land as will be necessary for said turnpike road; and the share or shares of any of said proprietors may be transferred by deed duly executed and acknowledged and recorded by the clerk of said proprietors on their records, and the share or shares of any proprietors may be sold by said corporation on nonpayment of assessments duly made agreeable to the by-laws that may be agreed upon by said corporation.

And be it further enacted, that no toll shall be taken by said corporation for any mile of said road until eight hundred dollars shall have been expended thereon, or a proportionate sum upon the whole number of miles, reckoning from the Lottery Bridge in Claremont to the place where said road may terminate.

And be it further enacted, that said corporation may be indicted for defect of repairs of said road after the toll gates are erected, and fined in the same way and manner as towns are by law fineable for suffering roads to be out of repair, and said fine may be levied on the profits and tolls arising or accruing to said proprietors.

Provided nevertheless, and be it further enacted, that if the said turnpike road shall in any part be the same with any highway now used, it shall not be lawful for said corporation to erect a gate or turnpike on or across said part of the road that now is used and occupied as a public highway anything in this act to the contrary notwithstanding.

And be it further enacted, that when said proprietors shall make it appear to the judges of the superior court of judicature that they have expended said sum of eight hundred dollars on each mile, or a proportionable sum as before mentioned the proprietors shall have the liberty to erect the gates as aforesaid.

And be it further enacted, that at the end of every ten years after the setting up any toll gate an account of the expenditures upon said

road, and the profits arising therefrom shall be laid before the judges
of the superior court for the time being, under forfeiture of the privileges of this act in future, and if the neat profits of the said ten years
shall exceed twelve per cent. per annum, the said court may reduce the
future toll so far as that it may not exceed twelve per cent.; and if the
profits shall not amount to six per cent., the said court may raise the
toll so that it shall not be less than six, nor exceed twelve per cent.

And be it further enacted, that if in ten years the said road shall
not be completed according to the provision in this act, every part and
clause thereof shall be null and void; Provided also that the State of
New Hampshire may at any time after the expiration of forty years
from the passing of this act, repay the proprietors of said road, the
amount of the sum expended by them thereon, with twelve per cent. per
annum in addition thereto, deducting the toll actually received by the
proprietors, in that case the said road shall to all intents and purposes
be the property of the State of New Hampshire, anything in this act
to the contrary notwithstanding.

State of New Hampshire.

In the House of Representatives, Decr. 20th, 1799.

The foregoing bill having had three several readings passed to be
enacted.

Sent up for concurrence,

JOHN PRENTICE, Speaker.

In Senate Decr. 23d. 1799. This Bill having been read a third time,
was enacted.

AMOS SHEPARD, President.

Approved Decr. 26th, 1799.

J. T. GILMAN, Governor.

A true copy,

Attest, PHILIP CARRIGAIN.

In 1812 "The Amherst Turnpike Corporation" was chartered,
and as it was a continuation of the Second Turnpike Road, above referred to, it is of interest in connection therewith, and its charter
was as follows:

STATE OF NEW HAMPSHIRE.

[L. S.]

IN THE YEAR OF OUR LORD ONE THOUSAND EIGHT HUNDRED AND
TWELVE.

AN ACT TO INCORPORATE A COMPANY BY THE NAME OF
THE AMHERST TURNPIKE CORPORATION.

Section 1. Be it enacted by the Senate and House of Representatives in General Court convened, that David Dexter, Josiah Stevens and
Samuel Fiske and their associates and successors be and they hereby
are incorporated and made a body corporate & politic forever, under
the name of the Amherst Turnpike corporation and in that name may
sue and prosecute, and be sued and prosecuted until final judgment and

execution; and shall be and hereby are vested with all the privileges and powers which by law are incident to corporations of a similar nature.

Sec. 2. And be it further enacted, that the said David Dexter and Josiah Stevens or either of them, shall call a meeting of said proprietors, to be holden at any suitable time and place, by posting notifications, one at least in some public place in each town through which said road is contemplated to pass, at least fourteen days before the time of holding said meeting expressing the time, place and design of said meeting; and the proprietors by a majority present or represented at said meeting, accounting and allowing one vote to each share in all cases, shall choose a clerk who shall be sworn to the faithful discharge of the duties of his Office; and shall agree on a method of calling future meetings; and at the same or at any subsequent meeting, may elect such officers and make and establish such rules and by-laws as to them shall seem necessary and convenient, for the regulation and government of said corporation for carrying into effect the purposes aforesaid, and for collecting the tolls hereinafter established; and the same by-laws may cause to be executed and annex penalties to the breach thereof; provided said rules and by-laws are not repugnant to the laws of this State. And all representations at any meeting shall be proved by writing signed by the person to be represented, which shall be filed by the clerk in a book or books provided and kept for that purpose.

Sec. 3. And be it further enacted, that the said corporation are hereby empowered, to lay out, make and keep in repair a turnpike road of four rods wide, beginning at the end of the second New Hampshire turnpike on Amherst plain thence running to the line between the State of New Hampshire and Commonwealth of Massachusetts in a direction to meet the Turnpike road in Tyngsborough in the Commonwealth of Massachusetts, conforming to the survey lately made by Daniel Warner Esquire as near as the nature of the ground will permit.

Sec. 4. And be it further enacted, that if the said proprietors, and the owners of land over which said road may run, shall not agree on the compensation to be made for such land, and shall not agree in appointing persons to ascertain such compensation, the Justices of the Court of Common pleas in the County where such land lies, if not interested, and if interested the Justices of the Superior Court, upon the application of the proprietors or owners of the land, reasonable notice having been given to the adverse party, of such application shall appoint a committee who shall ascertain the same in the same way as compensation is made to the owners of land for highways as usually laid out. Provided nevertheless that it shall not be lawful for said proprietors to make such road until the damages done the owner or owners of the land through which the same is laid out, is ascertained and paid, or tender thereof made, or security given for the payment of the same to the said owner thereof to his or their satisfaction.

Sec. 5. And be it further enacted, that the said corporation may erect and fix such and so many gates or turnpikes upon and across said road as will be necessary and sufficient to collect the tolls and duties herein after granted to said company, from all persons travelling the same with horses, cattle, carts or carriages.

Sec. 6. And be it further enacted, that it shall and may be lawful for said company, to appoint such and so many toll-gatherers as they shall think proper, to collect of and from all and every person or persons using said road, the rates and tolls herein after mentioned, and to stop any person riding, leading or driving any horses, cattle, carts or carriages from passing through said gates or turnpikes, until they shall respectively have paid the same; that is to say for every mile of said road, and so in proportion for a greater or less distance, or greater or smaller number of horses, cattle or carriages Viz. for every ten sheep or swine one half cent; for every ten neat cattle, horses or mules one cent; for every horse and his rider or led horse one cent; for every sulkey, chair or chaise, with one horse and two wheels two cents; for every coach, chariot, stage, phaeton or chaise with two horses and four wheels, three cents; for either of the carriages last mentioned with four horses, four cents; for every other carriage of pleasure, the like sums according to the number of wheels and horses drawing the same; for each cart, waggon or other carriage of burthen drawn by one beast, one cent; for the like carriages drawn by two beasts, one and a half cents; if by more than two beasts, one cent for each additional yoke of oxen or pair of horses; for each pleasure sleigh drawn by one horse, one cent and a half; if drawn by two horses, two cents; if drawn by more than two horses, one cent for each additional horse; for each sled or sleigh of burthen drawn by one horse, three quarters of a cent; if by two horses or one yoke of oxen, one cent; if by more than two horses or one yoke of oxen, one cent for each additional yoke of oxen or pair of horses; and at all times when the toll gatherer does not attend his duty the gates shall be left open; and if any person shall with his carriage, team, cattle or horses turn off the said road to pass the said turnpike gate on ground adjacent thereto, not being a public highway, with an intent to avoid the payment of the toll due by virtue of this act, such person shall forfeit and pay three times as much as the legal toll would have been; provided that nothing in this act shall extend to entitle said corporation to demand or receive toll of any person who is an inhabitant of any town where any gate may be erected, nor any officer or soldier of the militia under arms, going to or from the place of military duty nor to any funeral that may have occasion to pass said gate.

Sec. 7.   And be it further enacted, that the said corporation are hereby empowered to purchase and hold in fee simple, so much land as will be necessary for said turnpike road, and the share or shares of any proprietor may be transferred by deed, duly executed, acknowledged and recorded by the clerk of said corporation on their records; and said shares may be sold by said corporation on non-payment of assessments duly made, agreeable to the by-laws of said corporation.

Sec. 8.   And be it further enacted, that the said corporation shall take no toll for any mile of said road until six hundred dollars shall have been expended thereon, reckoning a proportionate sum upon the whole number of miles from the second New Hampshire turnpike road on Amherst plain, to the line between the State of New Hampshire and the Commonwealth of Massachusetts; nor shall any toll be taken for any mile of said road until the Justices of the superior court shall adjudge that said road is sufficiently made to entitle the said corporation to receive toll, at which time said incorporation may erect gates thereon according to the provisions of this act.

Sec. 9.   And be it further enacted, that said corporation may be indicted for want of repairs on said road after the toll gates are erected, and fined in the same way and manner as towns are by law fineable for suffering highways and bridges to be out of repair; and said fines may be levied on the profits and tolls accruing to said corporation provided that if said Turnpike road shall in any part be the same with any highway now used, it shall not be lawful for said corporation to erect any gate or turnpike upon or across that part of said road which is now used as a public highway, anything herein to the contrary notwithstanding.

Sec. 10. And be it further enacted, that at the end of every six years after the setting up of any Toll-gate upon the road aforesaid an account of the expenditures upon said road and the profits arising therefrom, shall be laid before the Justices of the superior court for the time being under the forfeiture of the privileges of this grant in future; and if the net profits for the said six years shall exceed nine per centum per annum, the said court may reduce the future rates of toll so far as that it may not exceed nine per centum per annum; and if the said profits shall not amount to six per centum per annum, the said court may raise the future rates of toll, so that it shall not be less than six per centum per annum nor more than nine per cent. per annum.

Sec. 11. And be it further enacted, that if in four years from the passing of this act, the said road and every part thereof shall not be completed, agreeable to the provisions of this act, every part and clause thereof shall be null and void — provided also that the State of New Hampshire may at any time after the passing hereof repay the proprietors of the said road the amount of the sums expended by them thereon, with nine per cent. per annum in addition thereto, deducting the toll actually received by said corporation; in that case the road shall, to all intents and purposes, be the property of the State of New Hampshire, provided further that the Legislature of this State shall have a right to adopt such measures in future, as shall by them be considered necessary or expedient, to compel said proprietors to keep said road in good repair.

State of New Hampshire.

In the House of Representatives, June 17, 1812.

The foregoing Bill having had three several readings passed to be enacted.

Sent up for concurrence.

CLEMENT STORER, Speaker.

In the Senate, June 18, 1812. This Bill having been read a third time was enacted.

JOSHUA DARLING, President.

By the Governor, the same day, approved.

WILLIAM PLUMER.

Recorded agreeably to the original.
Attest:

SAML. SPARHAWK, Secretary.

The Second Turnpike Road of New Hampshire was built in 1802. It ran from the southern line of Mont Vernon, through the center of the town and its entire length, making its distance in the town about five miles. The first toll-house above Amherst was in the north-westerly part of Mont Vernon, and was kept by James McCauley forty years. The stage ran daily on this road from Amherst to Windsor, Vermont, for more than fifty years.

The turnpike built by the two corporations ran southerly through Amherst and South Merrimack to Nashua, and so on to Boston,

though it was not a turnpike for the entire distance. To the north it
passed directly to Francestown, and thence down the long hill to
Cork Plain to Hillsborough, and through Hillsborough Lower and
Upper Villages, Washington, Lempster, Goshen, and Unity, to Claremont, and thence to Windsor, Vermont, crossing the Connecticut
river by a bridge. In the days before railroads were established,
this thoroughfare was, at certain seasons, filled with teams of the
farmers, of one, two, four or six horses, carrying their produce to
Boston, and returning, to the country stores and homes, groceries,
liquors, dry goods, etc., demanded for home use. A most interesting description of things in this regard will be found in the admirable
historical address given by Col. Bruce at the centennial celebration
of the town in 1903, which is printed elsewhere in this volume.

"On the 15th of April, 1837, agreeably to a vote of the Proprietors, all the gates on the Second New Hampshire Turnpike were
thrown open, and the road was made free from that day." The
foregoing is found in Secombe's History of Amherst, p. 453. No
mention is made of the discontinuance of the road built by the "Amherst Turnpike Corporation," but as the latter was only an extension
of the former, and the proprietors were the same, probably the whole
turnpike was discontinued at the same time. Mr. Secombe's History
adds that the act of incorporation was repealed by the General Court
July 4, 1837, and the care of the road thenceforth devolved upon the
towns through which it passed.

On the 3d and 4th of October, 1869, occurred the very heavy
rain, above noted, which so washed out the turnpike near the foot of
the hill close by what had been the "Town Farm," that it was discontinued, as not worth repairing for the small amount of travel
passing over it.

To accommodate the travel on the turnpike in its palmy days,
there were numerous taverns, at intervals of two or three miles, some
of which are still standing, though their use as places of refreshment
for man and beast has been rendered obsolete. In those days, however, they must have sheltered many a weary teamster, and their
open fire-places must have brewed many a mug of flip, and the bars
must have dispensed many a glass of rum and "black-strap." Then
everybody imbibed, and rum was no small item in the freights of the
returning teams.

Among these is a tavern about a mile from the village, which
used to be kept by Zephaniah Kittredge. It is now owned by Mr.

Lucius B. Hutchinson, who bought the place for its lumber. The house is occupied at intervals by more or less transient people, and the buildings are fast going to ruin.

A large house standing, at the junction of the Turnpike and the road to Paper-Mill Village in New Boston, was once a tavern, which went out of commission when the teaming business lapsed. It was occupied afterwards by the late Stephen G. Dunbar, and later still by the late David McCollom.

Not far east of this is a house in which Nelson E. Shedd kept tavern, but it is now in poor condition. All these landmarks will soon disappear.

The old turnpike is a notably hard road as far as it runs in Mont Vernon. It is rocky and in places sandy, and just at the New Boston line, beyond the McCollom, or as it used to known, the Parker place, is a long and very sandy hill, known as Warner Hill, which was always the bane of the stage-driver and the teamster.

Sept. 30, 1823. "Voted to lay out a road from the meeting-house down the hill to the old road between William Richardson's and Joshua Cleaves's place."

This is the road to the "Maple Tree." probably, striking the road which led easterly to Amherst, and westerly to Lyndeboro'.

A new road from Amherst to Weare was built in 1828. It passes through the entire length of the easterly part of Mont Vernon, and its construction and maintenance have been a heavy burden to this town. The road is direct from Amherst village to New Boston village, and follows the stream known as the Quohquinnepassakessananagnog to its source.

March 10, 1840. Hiram Perkins having presented a petition that about 25 rods of the road south of his house (the Woodbury place, later owned and occupied by Hiram Perkins, and at this writing known as "the Hearthstone) be discontinued, and a new road be laid out, it was voted to discontinue said piece of road and lay out one on the north of his house, provided said Perkins will give the land and wall the same — and the selectmen were authorized to lay out the same, which was very soon done.

In 1853 was built the new road from "the Maple tree" to Milford, a direct line through the woods and passing what is now Hartshorn's Mill. Formerly to get to Milford, Mont Vernon people had to go round by the south school-house, and the Raymond and Hutchinson places. The new road is much shorter and easier.

In 1878 the town built from the corner near John A. Carleton's, in the southerly part of the town, a road to connect with the road which formerly ended at Josiah Swinington's. A new road was also built from the East main road to John Elliot's.

In 1890, the road known as the "Boulevard" was built from Main Street to the top of Prospect Hill.

In 1893 two short pieces of road were built. The first one began at the north road to Amherst, near the house of Edward Hildreth, having its terminus on the south road to Amherst, near the house of Jesse S. Trow.

The second one beginning on the Lyndeborough road, near the house of Joseph G. Carleton, formerly the John A. Carleton place, extends to the Purgatory road, near the foot of Harwood's Hill, forming with its connections a convenient route from Mont Vernon to West Milford and Wilton.

From the foot of the Harwood hill to the turnpike or Francestown road, near Coggin's blacksmith shop, is a delightful piece of road through the woods, and it is known as "Lovers' Lane." It was built in 1860.

In 1903 a piece of road was built from the place owned by Charles Blood, just off the road to New Boston, at the north-east part of the town, across to the road from the east part of the town to Joe English Hill, near the farm now owned by J. F. Best.

NOTABLE FACTS AND EVENTS

In the winter and spring of 1812 a new and most virulent epidemic, known as the spotted fever, appeared. Very few physicians could treat it skilfully. Its attack was as sudden and violent as the cholera or plague. Its progress was rapid, and it terminated fatally in most cases. This scourge brought death into many families in Mont Vernon. The services of Dr. Matthias Spalding, of Amherst, who was credited with more than average success in coping with this fearful disease, were in requisition day and night for several months.

One of the most severe tempests ever experienced here occurred on the 22d of September, 1815. It began at 11:30 A. M., and continued with great violence for two hours. Trees were uprooted, fences blown down, buildings unroofed, and their fragments scattered in all directions. No lives were lost here.

The year 1816 was remarkable for its unusual severity of weather. Snow fell every month, causing light crops.

July 15, 1818. This day was of unusual darkness in New England, probably caused by the uncommon smoke produced by the burning of woodlands on the mountains, and of brush fires in all directions.

1826 is remembered as the grasshopper year. So plenty were these insects that they devoured every green thing. In some places they were caught in nets and fed to the hogs. The last week in August a great rain storm occurred which largely destroyed them. More water fell than had fallen in the same length of time for many years. It was during this storm that the White Mountain slide took place, by which the Willey family were destroyed. It was a year of disease and death. Whooping cough, measles, and an epidemic form of dysentery of a malignant type prevailed through this county, and swept away old and young.

November 13, 1833, there occurred the grandest meteoric display ever witnessed in America, at half-past five in the morning. Thousands of meteors might be seen flying in every direction through a clear, unclouded sky. As daylight approached they appeared less frequent, but they were seen as long as the stars were visible.

Three severe thunder storms occurred June 30, 1841. The second of these was accompanied by furious wind and hail, which did an immense amount of damage. Some hailstones were as large as good sized hen's eggs. Nearly ten thousand lights of glass were broken in this town alone. A terribly cold storm of wind and snow occurred June 11, 1842, and at its close, snow to the depth of four inches covered the ground, and the next day a very high wind prevailed, which would have done credit to November.

The latter part of the winter of 1842-43 was remarkably long and severe. Sleighs were used until late in April, and on the 17th of that month snow was three feet deep on a level. There was very little fruit that season.

In April, 1860, the tannery, owned by Starrett and Kittredge, was entirely destroyed by fire.

In August, 1864, the spacious fancy box shop of H. H. Bragg was destroyed by fire and not rebuilt.

October 3, 1869. There had been no rain of any consequence for nearly three months. Seven or eight inches of water fell October 3d and 4th, doing a great amount of damage, entirely destroying the mill

of Arthur A. Trow and Daniel W. Trow in the southerly part of the
town, also rendering the old turnpike road and several hillside roads
impassable. Neighboring towns suffered more than Mont Vernon.
The damage done in this town was between two and three thousand
dollars.

In July, 1879, the steam mill of Track W. Averill, on the old
tannery site, was burned.

Sept. 5, 1881, occurred what has generally been known as the
"Yellow Day." It grew very dark after the morning had passed,
and the atmosphere had a brazen appearance. The Rev. C. C. Carpenter was then pastor of the church, and on that day attended a
meeting of the Hollis Association of Ministers at New Ipswich. In
writing about it to the Farmer's Cabinet, he says: "The wonder of the
day was the brazen sky above, the tinted world beneath, and the mid-
day darkness, which compelled the lighting of lamps. The Association
actually dined with two full-burning "student" lamps on the table, at
half-past one o'clock p. m., and it was not a *light* dinner even then."
Whether the darkness was due to prevalent fires in the woods, or
some other cause, is not known. The darkness was reported over a
considerable area. On the ponds and streams of New Hampshire
and Massachusetts was found a yellow deposit, which some took for
sulphur, and others said it was a substance like pollen, and came from
certain trees, but it does not appear what trees would be in blossom
and in a stage to supply pollen so late in the season.

In the winter of 1880-1881 the stage went "on runners" to Milford 105 days, and on roads north of the village there was continuous
sleighing for 120 days.

November 27, 1881. The horse-sheds were partially destroyed
by fire, the old meeting-house and the parsonage narrowly escaping
destruction. The horse-sheds were rebuilt the next year.

July 8, 1882. Telephonic communication established. There
never was a telegraphic service, all messages having to be brought
up from or sent to Milford. The telephone enabled the sending of
messages to Milford, and thence by telegraph elsewhere.

[October, 1905. Local telephones put in, there being about a
dozen subscribers, affording facilities for communicating with other
parts of the town, or with other towns, without rendering it necessary
for those having telephones to go to the store which was the central
"pay station." Before this the only telephones in the village were
in the store and the Grand Hotel.]

March 23, 1883. W. H. Conant's box-shop (standing where store now stands) and Peter F. Pike's house adjoining, burned. The box-shop was formerly Hollis's boot and shoe shop.

October 27, 1883. William G. Bruce, aged 64, accidentally shot himself in taking his gun from his wagon, while on a hunting expedition in New Boston.

October, 1883. T. H. Richardson's store, the only one then in the village, which stood at the junction of the old turnpike and the main street, in front of the Hotel Bellevue, and ta the corner of the village Park, was moved to the site of W. H. Conant's box-shop, where it now (1905) stands.

October, 1883. The Park was graded by the Village Improvement Association.

January 10, 1884. The Capt. Timothy Kittredge house, the old Kittredge homestead, (owned by Dr. Charles M. Kittredge), destroyed by fire.

June 17, 1884. New school-house in the South District dedicated, with historical address by the Hon. Charles J. Smith, and a poem written by Mrs. Emily Dodge Simpson of New York, daughter of Henry C. Dodge, and in girlhood a pupil of the school.

June, 1884. Granite watering trough set up at the old well near the site of the store at northwest corner of the Park, the gift of C. Amory Stevens, of New York, son of Calvin Stevens, and grandson of Asa Stevens.

April 27, 1885. Woods Brothers, (John A. and Willard P), sons of Walter Woods, both of whom were born in Paper Mill Village in New Boston, succeeded Thomas Haskell Richardson, in the village store. Mr. Richardson, who always was called by his second name, "Haskell" Richardson or by his initials, "T. H." Richardson, began trade in a very small way in the old box-shop of Deacon William Conant, which was situated on the other side of the street nearly opposite. He bought out J. E. Bruce, who traded at the store situated then near what is now the Park, about 1847, and remained in trade till this date after the store was moved to where it now stands.

June 14, 1886. The Park was laid out with walks, trees were set out, and the Village Improvement Society determined to raise money to build a summer house on the Park, which was put up the next May.

April 25, 1887. John M. Fox & Co. (the "Co." being the son

William P.) bought out Woods Brothers (John and Willard P.)

June 15, 1888. The Dr. Daniel Adams House struck by lightning and burned.

March 7, 1888. Dwelling house in south part of town, owned by Elmer E. Carlton destroyed by fire.

April 16. Residence, barn and shed of Milton W. Wallace and Asa Carson, being the old Upton place on Beech Hill, destroyed by fire.

April 7. Store of John M. Fox entered, and $100 worth of goods and $15 worth of postage stamps stolen.

May. Village drain running from the bog hole in rear of the Tabitha Stevens residence across to Campbell hill, down through the Bragg field, and under the old Baker store, (then the old Hillsborough house) under the park, completed. This drain was made as a sanitary measure, but it was never adequate, and the assessments levied as for betterments on account of it caused much dissatisfaction, and were never fully collected.

June 29, 1889. Dr. Frederick Chandler assumed office of postmaster.

September, 1889. The three cottages on the hill where the Grand hotel was erected later on, then belonging respectively to Frank Marden, Mrs. Lauretta E. Phillips, and John A. Spalding of Nashua, in process of erection.

October 1, 1889. Hotel Bellevue leased to Willard P. Woods, by George E. Boutell, the owner.

Stage and mail route from Milford to Mont Vernon and North Lyndeboro purchased by Elmer E. Smith of Hillsboro. Mr. Smith also bought out Mr. Walter Woods, who had been proprietor of the stage line for 17 years.

The Dr. J. K. Smith house, next to the old Baker store, purchased by Elbridge F. Trow, and occupied by John M. Fox.

August, 1890. Dr. F. Chandler resigned as postmaster, and sold his real estate to John M. Fox. It was the house next south of the Bellevue, and is now occupied by Mr. Fox, although from 1900 to 1904 Mr. Fox resided and conducted a grocery business in Rochester, N. H. He returned to Mont Vernon in 1904.

December, 1890. Elmer E. Smith sold out his mail route contract and stage line to Willard P. Woods.

June 17, 1892. Barn on the William G. Bruce place struck by lightning and entirely consumed.

April 13. O. W. Battles sold his farm and removed to Sequachee, Tenn.

Alonzo Winn sold his farm and removed to Wilton.

September, 1892. William E. Robinson harvested 1000 baskets of peaches from his orchard of 300 trees.

Alonzo Travis' cottage and barn sold to Dea. William H. Conant. This cottage stood on the main village street, next above the McCollom Institute. It was moved back, facing the road across from the main street to the old turnpike, and a fine new house was erected on its former site, which up to this time (1905) has been occupied by W. H. Conant and his family.

December 31. W. F. Pinkham presented a piano to Prospect Grange (Patrons of Husbandry) and to the Congregational Society for their joint use.

January 20, 1903. Mont Vernon post-office made a money-order office.

September 15, 1893. W. P. Woods sold stage route to Herbert C. Dickey, of Manchester.

May 13, 1896. A supplemental grading-bee for new church ground.

May 15, 1896. Conant Hall destroyed by fire—cause unknown. It burned about 9 o'clock p. m.

CHAPTER VI.

ECCLESIASTICAL HISTORY.

THE troubles and dissensions which the people of the Northwest
Parish, now the town of Mont Vernon, had with the Amherst church,
which led to the formation of a new religious society, and subsequently to the erection of a new town, have been described in the chapters
on "Early History and Early Settlers" and "Conditions Preliminary
to Separation From the Parent Town," as has also the early ecclesiastical history of the only church in Mont Vernon.

LIST OF MINISTERS.

The following is a list of ministers who have preached for any length of time in Mont Vernon since the organization of the church in 1780. There having been but the one church organization, it is a simple matter to make a record of its pastors, and it is clear, all the way through this history, that whenever the church is referred to, the First (and only) Congregational church of Mont Vernon is meant.

From the organization of the church in 1780, to 1782, there apparently was not a "stated supply" for the pulpit. August 29, 1782, a "Mr. Powers" was invited to supply for a year.

In 1783 a "Mr. Allen" is said to have been called to supply for a year. Then a Mr. Samuel Sargent was invited to settle, but declined.

After this came the following succession of ministers, all of them supposedly having been duly "settled" over the parish by ordination or installation, down to Rev. Dr. Keeler's time. Since then Rev. Mr. Carpenter and Rev. Mr. McGown are the only ones who were installed.

Rev. John Bruce began preaching in 1784, was ordained Nov. 3, 1785, and died while in service, March 12, 1809, aged 54.

Rev. Stephen Chapin, D.D., installed Nov. 15, 1809; dismissed, at his own request, Nov. 18, 1818.

Rev. Ebenezer Cheever, ordained Dec. 8, 1819; dismissed April 8, 1823.

Rev. Nathaniel Kingsbury, ordained Nov. 8, 1823; dismissed April 6, 1836; died July 12, 1843, aged 49.

Rev. Edwin Jennison, installed April 6, 1836; dismissed Aug. 19, 1841 (on account of ill health); died at Conway, Mass., Dec. 25, 1887.

Rev. Bezaleel Smith, installed Aug. 19, 1841; dismissed April 30, 1850; died at Randolph, Vt., May 15, 1879.

Rev. Charles D. Herbert began preaching July 5, 1850; installed Nov. 6, 1850; dismissed July 21, 1856; died at Hebron, N. Y., Oct. 13, 1893, aged 75.

Rev. Chas. E. Lord began preaching Oct. 1, 1856; installed Feb. 4, 1857; dismissed April 2, 1861; died at Newburyport, Mass., Feb. 19, 1902, aged 90.

Rev. George E. Sanborne, installed April 2, 1862; dismissed May 29, 1865; died at Hartford, Conn., Jan. 7, 1900.

Rev. Benson M. Frink, installed Nov. 1, 1865; dismissed Nov. 1, 1867. Living (June, 1905) at West Brookfield, Mass., but not settled in any pastorate.

Rev. Seth H. Keeler, D.D., began preaching Jan. 9, 1868; dismissed Sept. 24, 1875; died at Somerville, Mass., Dec. 26, 1896, aged 86.

Rev. Wm. H. Woodwell, began preaching Nov. 1, 1875; closed his service March 28, 1880. Now (June, 1905) living at Seabrook, N. H.

Rev. Charles C. Carpenter, began preaching Nov. 1, 1880; installed July 12, 1881; dismissed Sept. 19, 1885. Now (June, 1905) living at Andover, Mass.

Rev. Richard H. McGown, began preaching Jan. 10, 1886; installed June 23, 1886; dismissed Feb. 28, 1888. Died at Everett, Mass., April 1, 1900.

Rev. John Thorpe preached for the first time April 15, 1888; May 18, same year, accepted engagement to preach as supply; and served till Sept. 1, 1894. Now (June, 1905) pastor of Congregational church at Center Harbor, N. H.

Rev. Thomas J. Lewis began preaching as supply Nov. 11, 1894; and closed his labors at Mont Vernon Dec. 5, 1897. Now (June, 1905) pastor of the Congregational church at Conway, N. H.

Rev. Donald Browne began preaching in November, 1898, and ceased service in November, 1900. Now (June 1905) he is serving as rector of an Episcopal church at South Groveland, Mass.

Rev. Henry Porter Peck assumed the duties of pastor Jan. 1, 1901, and still continues (June, 1905).

DEACONS.

It seems to be impossible to secure the full details as to the dates of appointment and terms of service of all those who have been deacons of the church at Mont Vernon. It is probable that the following list comprises all who have been deacons, however, and the dates of appointment are nearly all given, but only a part of the dates of resignation or death. Doubtless most of the deacons served as long as they lived, the office having a life tenure. The following names are taken from a list published in the Mont Vernon Annual Church and Town Record for 1891:

Between 1780 and 1795, Oliver Carlton, Nathaniel Heywood,

and Richard Ward are supposed to have been the deacons. From that time on, the appointments are on record:

Appointed March 28, 1794, John Carlton, Ezekiel Upton, Daniel Smith.

Appointed October, 1800, John Carlton, Jacob Kendall.

Appointed May 27, 1817, Jonathan S. Adams.

Appointed April 27, 1820, John Bruce; died Jan. 19, 1872, aged 83.

Appointed April, 1829, Josiah Kittredge 2d.

Appointed Aug. 31, 1832, William Conant; resigned Aug. 15, 1875; died at Somerville, Mass., Feb. 20, 1890.

Appointed Nov. 10, 1836, Joseph A. Starrett; resigned March, 1858; died May 22, 1895, aged 89 years, 9 months.

Appointed April 4, 1858, Geo. E. Dean. Died Feb. 26, 1891.

Appointed Aug. 22, 1875, William H. Conant; died May 19, 1903.

Appointed May 2, 1889, Geo. G. Batchelder; died Jan. 8, 1896.

Appointed October 29, 1891, Maj. Charles F. Stinson and William H. Kendall. Major Stinson died March 10, 1893, aged 52 years, 5 months. Deacon Kendall is still serving (1905).

Appointed April, 1899, Jay M. Gleason; still serving (1905).

SKETCHES OF THE MINISTERS.

Concerning the temporary ministers, who preceded, or were asked to precede, Rev. Mr. Bruce, the following facts are furnished by the Rev. C. C. Carpenter:

"Mr. Powers, who was called to supply for the year 1782, was doubtless Rev. Peter Powers, son of Capt. Peter Powers, first settler of Hollis; was born in old Dunstable, Nov. 29, 1729, and came to the Hollis part of Dunstable in 1730; graduated at Harvard in 1754, the first college graduate from Hollis. In 1764 was settled in Haverhill, N. H., and Newbury, Vt., on opposite sides of the Connecticut. The towns were opposite in sentiment, as in location, and didn't agree in politics. Powers was a "high whig," and was persona non grata to the Newbury folk; removed to Haverhill in 1781, in spring. Continued to preach a year or two, and dismissed sometime in 1782. He soon after settled in Deer Isle, Maine. I find no hint of his going to Mont Vernon, but it is very probable that he would have been the likely man to be called at just that time, because he was just getting through at Newbury and Haverhill, and because as a Hollis man he would be well known in Amherst. I do not understand that he actually preached in Mont Vernon, only was asked to do so."

"The Mr. Allen of the 1783 call, was presumably Ebenezer Allen, born in Martha's Vineyard in 1746, graduated from Harvard in 1771. He was settled in Wolfeboro in 1792. When he came there he had recommendations from ministers in Andover, Haverhill, Plaistow, Stratham, etc., showing that he was known all about, and was perhaps seeking a parish in New Hampshire about those days."

"I find no Samuel Sargent to answer the demand of the '83 man at all, which is singular, as it is a familiar New Hampshire name, although not perhaps in the ministerial line."

THE FIRST PASTOR was the Rev. John Bruce, who ministered to Mont Vernon church from 1784 until his sudden death of apoplexy March 12, 1809. He was born in Marlborough, Massachusetts, August 31, 1757, and graduated at Dartmouth College in 1781.

The following is an interesting extract from the records of the Second Parish of Amherst:

Second Parish of Amherst, N. H., Dec. 29, 1784.

At a legal meeting, duly warned, voted to concur with the Church in giving Mr. John Bruce a call to settle in the gospel ministry in this Parish.

Voted to give him one hundred and twenty pounds Incouragement as settlement.

Voted to give Mr. Bruce sixty Pounds sallery and twenty cord of wood annually, as long as he carry's on the gospel ministry in this place, and if in case he should be disinabled to carry on the work of ministry by Infirmness of Body or old age, to give him thirty pounds, and twenty cords of wood annually as long as he remains our Minister.

Of the first ten and last eight years of his pastorate there are no church records. A list of the members of the church, in Mr. Bruce's hand-writing, about 1798, makes its membership one hundred and ten. The next fifty were added by profession. This revival was the first known in this section, and it awakened much interest far and near.

In 1809 there were printed by Richard Boylston (Farmers' Cabinet Press), Amherst, in a small pamphlet, a copy of which is extant, two sermons preached at Mont Vernon by the Rev. Stephen Chapin, Mr. Bruce's successor, the second Sabbath after his installation, Nov.

26, 1809, from the text, "Now then we are ambassadors for Christ, as though God did beseech you by us, we pray you in Christ's stead be ye reconciled to God." The title page bears the subject, "On the duties of an ambassador of Christ," and "Published by desire." Doubtless one sermon was preached in the forenoon and the other in the afternoon.

In the same pamphlet appears a considerable sketch "On the Life and Character of the Rev. John Bruce, by A Parishioner," from which the following is condensed:

The Rev. John Bruce was born in Marlborough, Massachusetts, August 31, 1757, of respectable and pious parents. He lost his mother at the age of seven. His father was a farmer. He fitted for college in some school not named in the sketch, and entered Dartmouth College in 1777, and graduated in 1781, and "by his teachable disposition, gentleness of manners, mild, serious and dutiful behavior in all respects, he obtained, it is said from the highest authority of the college, the distinguishing appellation of 'the good Mr. Bruce.'" He afterwards received from his alma mater the degree of M. A. Soon after leaving college he began the study of divinity, and in due time was licensed to preach. After preaching on probation for several years in various places, and a sufficient time in the Second Parish of Amherst, New Hampshire, now Mont Vernon, he received and accepted a call to the pastoral care of the church and congregation in that place, and was ordained Nov. 3, 1785. On the 15th of December following he married Lois Wilkins of Marlborough, whom he left a widowed mother of six children. He continued with faithfulness to fulfil the various duties of his sacred office, from the time of his ordination till his death, a period of twenty-three years and four months.

"His constitution was not firm and robust, being probably enervated by study and a sedentary life, although his stature was considerably above the middle size, well proportioned, and of an athletic appearance. For several years before his death, his health sensibly decayed, and for more than one year he was afflicted with almost a total blindness of one eye, which necessitated him to extemporize in his public discourses, instead of using notes, which had been his custom. On Saturday morning, March 11, 1809, he arose early, as was his usual practice, and complained of a slight headache, which however, he mentioned but once, and appeared as usual till he sat down to breakfast. He had taken but little food; when he was suddenly attacked with a Hemiplegia, or palsy of the right side, accompanied with an entire loss of reason and alarming symptoms of apoplexy. Medical aid was immediately called in, but in vain. The lethargic and apoplectic symptoms, in defiance to every exertion to procure relief, continued to grow more profound, and to assume a more threatening aspect, till nearly three o'clock on Sunday morning, when he slept the sleep of death.   Thus ended the life of this excellent man ; thus sudden and unexpected, though insensible to the pangs of dissolving nature, was his transit to eternity.

"He was meek, pious and humble ; kind, gentle, and easy to be entreated   He 'became all things to all men, that if possible he might gain some ;' while at the same time he steadfastly adhered to 'the faith once delivered to the saints.'   He possessed in an eminent degree that charity which 'suffereth long and is kind,' which 'beareth all things, believeth all things, hopeth all things, endureth all things.' But the most distinguishing traits in his character, next to his love of piety and religion, were prudence and a peaceable disposition.   He was prudent and discreet in all things, and eminently entitled to the appellation of a peace-maker.   These virtues were so conspicuously displayed by him, that he had not a personal enemy in the world, but all who knew esteemed and revered him.   As a husband he was faithful, affectionate, tender, and sincere.   As a parent he was kind, indulgent, and anxiously solicitous for the temporal, but chiefly for the eternal, well-being of his children.   As a neighbor he was friendly and hospitable ; as a citizen patriotic, and friendly ; as a man, in all respects, a true and sincere christian."

The sons, John, James, William and Nathaniel, were heads of families, all worthy citizens, and lifelong residents of Mont Vernon. Their united ages at their decease were three hundred and twenty-two years.

The Second Pastor was the Rev. Stephen Chapin, who on the decease of Mr. Bruce, immediately received a call from this church, but was not installed until November 15, 1809.   Born at Milford, Massachusetts, in 1788, a graduate of Harvard in 1804, a pupil in divinity with the famous Dr. Nathaniel Emmons, of Franklin, Massachusetts, his first settlement was in the neighboring town of Hillsborough, four years, from 1805 to 1809. Mr. Chapin was a man of positive conviction, and bold, unadorned, and uncompromising in his style of preaching.   His earnest, able preaching, and stringent discipline made a deep impression upon his people.   During a pastorate of nine years one hundred and fifteen were added to the church.   On one Sabbath in 1817, fifty-one converts were received into fellowship.   While all hearts were completely united in him, the day of separation came from a quarter least expected.   In October, 1818, the pastor suddenly announced a change in his views respecting the mode and subjects of baptism.   He was a man sincere and true, and conscientiously embraced Calvinistic Baptist views.   He at once resigned his pastorate here, and was dismissed in November, 1818. After a three years' pastorate as a Baptist clergyman at North Yarmouth, Maine, he was, in 1822, called to a professorship at Waterville College, Maine, and thence to the presidency of Columbia College at Washington, D. C., which he occupied for many years. The salary of Mr. Chapin was stipulated at four hundred dollars per annum, and if, from any cause, he was unable to preach, no abatement, unless such absence exceeded six weeks.

Relative to the great revival of 1817, the Farmers' Cabinet of Oct. 25, 1817, had an editorial commenting on a meeting held on the previous Thursday, at which fifty-one persons came forward for admission to the church, the fruits of the revival which had been going on the past summer. "We have," said the editor, "seldom witnessed a scene more solemn and interesting."

About 1821 a Baptist meeting was appointed at the red schoolhouse in the Center District. This would have a divisive tendency. One morning Dea. John Carlton, a staunch Congregationalist, whose self-appointed function was to protect the fold from intrusion, was heard, before the regular church meeting commenced, haranguing a company of his brethren in front of the old yellow church in this wise : "If so be that our minister preaches the gospel, we have the gospel. If so be he preaches not the gospel, we want not the gospel."

THE THIRD PASTOR, called after an interval of a little more than a year from Mr. Chapin's dismissal, was the Rev. Ebenezer Cheever, a native of Reading, Vermont, a graduate of Bowdoin College. He was ordained December 8, 1819. He continued pastor till April 8, 1823, with an addition to the church in the meantime of twenty-two members. He baptized thirty-nine children in less than three years. In the spring of 1820 the first Sabbath School was organized here, being held in the school-house and composed exclusively of children.

THE FOURTH PASTOR was the Rev. Nathaniel Kingsbury, from Connecticut, and a graduate of Amherst College, who commenced his labors two weeks after Mr. Cheever's dismissal. He was ordained November 8, 1823, and dismissed April 6, 1836. The following were the exercises at his ordination : Ordaining Prayer, Rev. E. P. Bradford, New Boston; Sermon, Rev. Chancy Booth, of Coventry, Connecticut; Consecrating Prayer, Rev. Moses Bradford, Francestown; Charge, Rev. Humphrey Moore, Milford; Fellowship of

Churches, Rev. N. Merrill, Lyndeborough; Address to Congregation, Rev. E. P. Bradford, New Boston; Concluding Prayer, Rev. Nathan Lord, Amherst. Hon. C. Claggett, of Amherst, and Sol K. Livermore, of Milford, were members of the ordaining council.

Mr. Kingsbury removed West and died some years since in Wisconsin. He was not a man of marked ability, but his ministry here was prosperous, and during it one hundred and fifty-four were received into the church. Two periods of peculiar interest occurred, the former in 1828, when thirty-four were added, the latter in 1831, when nearly sixty united by profession.

These were revival days when the ministers aided each other in what were called "protracted meetings," which were often seasons of thrilling interest and great power. Never before nor since, has this church been the scene of such religious activity, scenes still living vividly in the remembrance of some among us.

It was in 1830, during Mr. Kingsbury's pastorate, that the temperance reform began in the church, and was vigorously and steadily prosecuted outside until it expelled liquors from the town. The youth of the present day can hardly imagine the condition of this small community, with eight tavern licenses signed in a single year. In some places they sold a hogshead of liquor a month; and though but a small portion of this quantity was dispensed to residents, it was enough to alarm the thoughtful and virtuous. At that period two public roads led northward, through different sections of the town. They were thoroughfares thronged with light and heavy travel. At all hours of the day lines of canvas-covered six-horse merchandise wagons might be seen bearing their heavy freight from and to the seaboard. To modify and control public opinion was no easy matter, work which required strong heads and true hands. Dr. Daniel Adams may be named as one early prominent in this movement of philanthropy. He delivered convincing and effective addresses on this subject in this and other towns.

THE FIFTH PASTOR, Rev. Edwin Jennison, was born in Walpole, N. H., August 26, 1805, being the son of Maj. William and Phebe (Field) Jennison. He fitted for college at Alstead, N. H., and Windsor, Vt., and graduated at Dartmouth College in 1827; and at Andover, (Mass.), Theological Seminary in 1830. August 16, 1831, he was ordained pastor of the Congregational church in his native town, and was dismissed therefrom March 18, 1835. He was called to the church at Mont Vernon to succeed the Rev. Nathaniel Kingsbury, and was installed April 6, 1836. The installing prayer was by the Rev. A. Burgess, Hancock; the sermon by Rev. Nathaniel Kingsbury, the retiring pastor, who also delivered the address to the church and society. The charge and concluding prayer were by the Rev. E. P. Bradford of New Boston; and the fellowship of the churches, by the Rev. William Richardson of Lyndeboro. He was dismissed on account of ill health, August 19, 1841. After recruiting his health, and visiting England and Scotland, he was called to the church in Ashburnham, Mass., where he was installed May 12, 1842, from which pastorate he was dismissed in 1846. He then accepted a call to Hopkinton, N. H., where he was installed June 6, 1847, and dismissed June 6, 1849. He preached in Alstead in 1850-2, and in Langdon, 1852-4. His health became so much impaired that he was compelled to abandon the active ministry, and in 1860 retired to a small farm in Winchester, N. H., whence, in 1880, he removed to Conway, Mass., to be, with his wife, under the more immediate care of their children.

Mr. Jennison was married in Ipswich, Mass., January 25, 1832, to Miss Mary Barker Shannon, daughter of Dr. Richard Cutts and Mary (Tebbetts) Shannon, of Saco, Me. They had four children—Edwin Shannon, born at Walpole, December 13, 1832; William Cutts, born at Mont Vernon, May 29, 1837; Mary Theresa, born at Mont Vernon, April 4, 1840; and Helen Maria, born at Ashburnham, November 23, 1844. The second and third of these children died and were buried while Mr. Jennison was in England. Mrs. Jennison died November 22, 1885; and Mr. Jennison, December 25, 1887, at the ripe old age of 82 years and 4 months.

It was during his pastorate that the following Church Covenant was adopted, at a church meeting held September 21, 1837:

CONFESSION OF FAITH.

You believe, 1st, That there is one God and but one, who is the Creator, Preserver, and Governor of the Universe, and who possesses every natural and moral perfection.

2nd, That the Bible was written by holy men, as they were moved by the Holy Spirit, and is a perfect rule of faith and practice.

3d, That God exists in three persons—the Father, the Son and the Holy Spirit, and these three are one God, the same in essence and equal in every divine perfection.

4th, That God has made all things for himself, and that known unto him are all his works from the beginning; that he governs and controls all things, creatures and events, according to the council of his own will; and that the administration of his government is perfectly holy, just and good.

5th. That God created Adam perfectly holy, and constituted him the representative of all his posterity, suspending their moral character upon his probationary conduct.

6th, That in consequence of the fall of Adam all mankind are by nature entirely sinful and deserve to be punished with eternal death.

7th. That the Lord Jesus Christ, who is God and man, has by His death on the cross, made an atonement for the sins of the whole world.

8th. That through the atonement, salvation is freely offered to sinners, in the Gospel: Yet they all naturally reject this gracious offer, and refuse to come to Christ that they may have eternal life.

9th. That God in the covenant of redemption chose all who ever obtain salvation by Christ in him from before the foundation of the world, and from eternity predestined them to be holy heirs of eternal glory.

10th. That the Holy Spirit, by an act of special grace, renews the heart of all the elect, and causes them in the present life to accept the salvation of the Gospel.

11th. That the foundation of the forgiveness of believers is the atonement of Christ; in this atonement they become interested by true faith alone. Yet God will reward them for all their holy services.

12th, That God promises to preserve all who have been renewed in the spirit and temper of their minds from final apostacy, and conduct them through the sanctification of the spirit and belief of the truth into the Kingdom of Glory.

13th. That none but those who really and truly love the Lord Jesus Christ ought to partake of the Lord's Supper; every church ought to require a profession of love to the Redeemer, of all whom they admit to their communion.

14th, That adult believers who have not been baptized are subjects of baptism, and the children of professing believers.

15th. That God has appointed a day in which he will judge the world in righteousness by Jesus Christ, who will then receive the righteous to endless happiness, and the wicked to everlasting punishment.

A true record: 　　　　　　　　　　J. BRUCE, Secretary.

It was also during Mr. Jennison's pastorate in 1837, that the meeting-house was removed from the easterly to the westerly side of the street, and remodeled and furnished with a belfry, bell and organ, an account of which is given elsewhere. Mr. Jennison occupied, during his residence in Mont Vernon, the house opposite the entrance to the cemetery, now known as " Elm Cottage." His salary was $500. Dr. Daniel Adams led the choir in those days. The deacons were John Bruce, William Conant and Joseph A. Starrett. During his pastorate twenty-three persons were admitted to the church. It is said of him that as a sermonizer he excelled, but as pastor he did very little visiting. During his pastorate the slavery question somewhat agitated the church and disturbed its peace. A very good portrait appears of him elsewhere, made from a daguerreotype, furnished by a daughter, Mrs. Chelsea Cook of Conway, Mass.

THE SIXTH PASTOR was the Rev. Bezaleel Smith, a native of Randolph, Vt., a farmer's boy, whose parents were John and Sarah (Lawrence) Smith, who were married in Lexington, Mass., Nov. 15, 1781, and removed to Randolph, Vt., about 1790. They had nine children—four sons and five daughters. The father was in the battle of Lexington. Bezaleel was born April 2, 1797, and was named for his maternal grand-father, Bezaleel Lawrence.

He was born and grew up as most New England farmers' boys do, fitting for college at Randolph, and graduating at Dartmouth with the class of 1825.

He became a Christian when nineteen years of age. His conversion was of the rugged sort of those days, and the struggle through which he passed stamped his character with earnestness and fervor, that permeated his subsequent religious life. Writing of this in later years, he says, " Returning from a meeting on a certain Sabbath, I took up my Bible to read, when I felt a rising opposition in my mind to what I read. My heart was filled with hate and blasphemy. It went out in opposition to Christ, and to whatever was in His praise." This hostility continued for several weeks, but terminated by the complete surrender of himself to Christ, whom he ever after delighted to love and honor, as his rightful Master.

Mr. Smith soon decided to prepare for the ministry, anticipating with great delight, that his business would be to meditate upon the truths of the Bible and lead others to this enjoyment. His college life was marked by a high standard of religious thought and life. On graduating, he taught in the Academy at Hampton, N. H. One of his pupils was Eliza Esther Morrison, daughter of John B. Morrison, a merchant of that place. Shortly after Mr. Smith's first settlement in the ministry, that pupil became his wife. She died at Mont Vernon, where she was laid to rest in the village cemetery, mourned by a large circle of devoted friends. Eight children were born to them. He married for a second wife Mrs. Laura S. Brown, daughter of Belcher Salisbury of Randolph, who died in 1896.

After teaching for a time at Hampton, Mr. Smith returned to Hanover to study theology under President Tyler. A written sermon, forenoon and afternoon was then required. The writer of this sketch remembers his father telling him, that when he handed President

Tyler his second sermon, after it had been duly criticised, the president said, " Now you can preach all day."

Mr. Smith received his license from the Harmony Association at Plymouth, N. H., November 14, 1827. He preached at different places, until the spring of 1829, when he was ordained and installed over the church at Rye, N. H., as associate pastor, with Rev. Huntington Porter. From Rye he went to Mont Vernon in 1841, where he was installed August 19 of that year.

The exercises were as follows : — Invocation and Reading, Rev. John Haven, Stoneham, Mass.; Introductory Prayer and Right Hand of Fellowship, Rev. Austin Richards, Nashua ; Sermon and Installing Prayer, Rev. Jonathan French, North Hampton, N. H.; Charge to the Pastor, Rev. E. P. Bradford, New Boston ; Addresses to the People and Concluding Prayer, Rev. H. Moore, Milford.

He remained in this pastorate nine years, being dismissed April 30, 1850.

He was a sound but not brilliant preacher ; cautious and discreet, a pastor who made no enemies. Slaveholders were by vote excluded from church fellowship and from the Lord's table, and thirty-two persons were added to the church during his pastorate. He removed from here to Roxbury, N. H., and laboring there two years was called to the pastorate of the church in New Alstead, N. H., and thence to the church in Hanover Centre, N. H., in 1861, where he remained for ten years. His final ministry was at West Hartford, Vt., from which church he retired as an active minister, December, 1877.

The last days were passed in his native town. During his half-century in the ministry, there were only five Sundays when he did not preach ; twice only, when he was detained from the pulpit by illness. A brother minister said, at the time of his death, " The elements of character which combined to make him a success in the ministry were, energy of purpose, a ready acquiescence in the call of duty, self-devotion to all the interests of the church, generosity in his religious sympathies, and the retention of a youthful spirit." He died in Randolph, Vt., May 15, 1894.

The following interesting paragraph concerning Mr. Smith is from the *Congregationalist* in December, 1877, from the pen of the late Rev. Lewis Grout, of Brattleboro, Vt. :

A LIVE MAN.

"Here is a young man for you; not that he is wanting a call or waiting for a parish. He could not be spared from the parish he now occupies and serves—West Hartford, Vt. He has been here a a little more than five years, and in that time has seen the resident membership of his church more than doubled by the addition of more than forty to their number. He will be only eighty years old next April, and has been in the ministry as yet only fifty years. Yesterday (Dec. 10) was one of the coldest of wintry days. On the day previous a foot of snow fell, and the wind blew furiously all day Saturday and all night, putting the snow in piles, putting the railroad trains from three to six hours behind time even with engines doubled. And yet, with the mercury below zero, our octogenarian, the Rev. Bezaleel Smith, for such is his name, started out Sabbath morning with his own team, to drive to a neighboring parish, six miles away, to honor an appointment for an exchange of pulpits, and reached there just in time to astonish his stalwart brother of thirty-five and inspire him with courage to start out and meet his part of the engagement. Let the men of years take heart and work on, and let the young men see to it that they are not outdone by the fathers."

THE SEVENTH PASTOR, the Rev. Charles D. Herbert, youngest son of Hon. George Herbert, of Ellsworth, Me., was born at that place, September 18, 1818; graduated at Bowdoin College in 1841; and three years later at Bangor Theological Seminary. He was immediately ordained, and went as a home missionary to the West. After several years on the frontier in this service, he returned to New England. He commenced preaching in Mont Vernon, July 5, 1850, and was installed pastor, November 6, 1850, the exercises being as follows: Invocation and Reading of Scriptures, Rev. W. G. Tuttle, Littleton, Mass.; Reading First Hymn, Rev. D. Goodwin, Brookline; First Prayer, Rev. L. Swain, Nashua; Second Hymn and Sermon, Rev. J. Maltby, Bangor; Installing Prayer, Rev. J. Willey, Goffstown; Charge to Pastor, Rev. J. G. Davis, Amherst; Fellowship, Rev. E. B. Claggett, Lyndeborough; Address to the People, Rev. E. N. Hidden, Milford; Concluding Prayer, Rev. Mr. Kellogg, New Boston.

Coming here young and enthusiastic Mr. Herbert devoted himself with singleness of aim and Christian zeal to his work. His labors here exhibited him as a kind, sympathetic and sincere friend, and an earnest and consecrated man. Under his ministry in 1851 and 1852, quite a number of young people in the academy and outside attained the Christian hope. The whole number added to the

church during his ministry was fifty-five. He closed his labors here
early in 1856, and was soon after settled over a church in West
Newbury, Mass. After a ministry there of many years, he qualified
himself for the practice of medicine, and labored in Rutland, Mass.,
some years, both preaching and practising. Some years since he
was recalled to his former parish at West Newbury, both preaching
and practising medicine there. In 1887 he became pastor of the
Presbyterian Church in Hebron, N. Y., which he resigned on account
of ill health. He was then much prostrated by an attack of la grippe,
and continued to decline slowly but steadily, to a peaceful and pain-
less end, October 13, 1893. The burial was at Mt. Auburn, Mass.,
October 17, 1893.

THE EIGHTH PASTOR was the Rev. Charles E. Lord, who having
commenced preaching October 1, 1856, was installed February 4,
1857, the exercises being as follows: Scribe, Rev. J. G. Davis,
Amherst; Reading Scripture and Opening Prayer, Rev. Lothrop
Taylor, Francestown; Sermon, Rev. Dr. J. P. Cleveland, Appleton
Street Church, Lowell, Mass.; Installing Prayer, Rev. E. B. Clag-
gett, Lyndeborough; Fellowship, Rev. E. N. Hidden, Milford;
Address to the People, Rev. E. C. Cogswell, New Boston.

Mr. Lord was dismissed April 2, 1861. He was born in Portsmouth, N. H., February 11, 1817, the son of John Perkins Lord, a
brother of the famous historical writer, Rev. John Lord, and a
nephew of the still more famous educator and theologian, Rev.
Nathan Lord, D. D., for thirty years President of Dartmouth
College. The subject of this sketch fitted for college in South
Berwick, Me., to which town his parents removed in his early childhood. He also studied at Phillips Academy at Andover, Mass., and
graduated at Dartmouth College with the class of 1838. He taught
in the South Berwick, Me., Academy for a year, and for two years
had charge of an academy at Kingston, N. C. He studied theology
at Union Theological Seminary, New York, and was at the Theological school at New Haven for two years, and studied one year at
Auburn, N. H. He was ordained to the ministry at Jonesville, Ind.,
May 8, 1844. In 1845 he preached at Marshall, Mich. November
17, 1846, he was installed as pastor of a Presbyterian church at
Niles, Mich., being dismissed therefrom in 1849. He was one year
with the Presbyterian church at Evansville, Ind., and subsequently
preached at Mont Vernon, Chester, Vt., 1865-1869, Beverly, New

Jersey, 1869, 1870, North Easton Mass., Pelham, N. Y., and from 1888 till his death conducted a mission under the name of Hope Chapel at Salisbury Beach, near Newburyport, where he resided. He received his degree of D. D., from East Tennessee Wesleyan University in 1873.

Dr. Lord was a voluminous writer on theological and ethical topics. He was an ardent abolitionist and a warm patriot. At the breaking out of the Civil War he preached two war sermons at Mont Vernon (April 28, 1861) which were published. The text of his morning sermon was " Speak unto the children of Israel that they go forward." Exodus, XIV : 12. The afternoon text was, " And he that hath no sword, let him sell his garment and buy one." Luke XXII : 36. The two discourses well fitted the strenuous texts.

The Congregational Year-Book for 1903, in a sketch of his career makes the following mention of his teaching and other service, and published works :

"Made a member of the Society of Science, Letters, and Art, London, 1888; professor of Christianity and Church History in Talmage's Lay College, Brooklyn, N. Y., 1873; professor in Lay College, Revere, Mass.; secretary of Peace Society, New York, 1874. Publications: Natural and Revealed Theology, J. B. Lippincott & Co., Philadelphia, 1870, pp. 550. Possibilities of the African Race, a lecture before the National House of Representatives, Washington, D. C., 1869. Pamphlet on Slavery, Secession, and the Constitution, and Our Country's Crisis, 1861. An Appeal to Our Country's Loyalty, 1864. History of Congregational Church, Chester, Vt., 1868."

Dr. Lord was married, January 15, 1857, soon after he came to Mont Vernon, to Miss Eunice Elizabeth Smith Pike, daughter of Joseph Smith and Sarah (Pettengill) Pike, of Newburyport, who still (May, 1905,) survives him, having reached the age of ninety in August, 1903.

Hope Chapel was burned in the autumn of 1902, and Dr. Lord was actively engaged in securing its rebuilding at the time of his death, which occurred very suddenly, February 19, 1904, from heart failure.

THE NINTH PASTOR, the Rev. George E. Sanborne, was the son of Rev. Peter and Martha (Wakefield) Sanborne, and was born at Reading, Mass., April 16, 1827. He fitted for college at Williston Seminary and Monson Academy, and graduated at Amherst College in 1853. He took the full course at Andover Theological Seminary, 1853 to 1856, and February 12, 1856, was licensed to preach by the Andover Association in Lowell. January 1, 1857, he was ordained pastor of the church in Georgia, Vt., and served that church until 1861, and having served as acting pastor of a church in Portsmouth, N. H. for a year, he was installed over the church at Mont Vernon, April 2, 1862.

The exercises were as follows, Rev. William Clark, of Amherst, being moderator, and Rev. Charles Cutter, of Francestown, scribe :— Reading Scriptures, Rev. Darwin E. Adams, Wilton ; Prayer, Rev. E. B. Claggett, Lyndeborough ; Sermon, Rev. C. W. Wallace, D.D., Manchester ; Charge, Rev. C. E. Lord, retiring pastor ; Fellowship, Rev. J. T. Hill, Nashua ; Charge to the People, Rev. Augustus Berry, Pelham ; Concluding Prayer, Rev. C. Cutter, Rochester, N. H.

He was dismissed May 29, 1865, and went to a church in Northboro, Mass., where he remained until 1870. From 1870 to 1875 he was Superintendent of the Hartford, (Conn.,) Orphan Asylum, also preaching in 1870-1872 at Tolland, Conn., at Wethersfield Avenue church in Hartford (which he organized), and in 1875 at Enfield, Conn. He then became steward of the Retreat for the Insane at Hartford, in which capacity he served till 1895, when owing to feeble health he was obliged to retire, although he continued to live in Hartford until he died of sclerosis of the spinal cord, January 7, 1900.

Mr. Sanborne was married June 10, 1858, to Annie E. Knowlton, daughter of Dea. John Knowlton of Portsmouth, and she survived him. He was much beloved by his parishoners of Mont Vernon for his genial manners and kindly courtesy, and he was a preacher of many rare qualities.

The ministry of both Messrs. Lord and Sanborne was barren of noteworthy incidents and the numerical increase to the church slight. The Civil War was waging, and public attention was concentrated upon it, to the exclusion of other interests. The clergymen of Mont Vernon, like most of their brethren, during that eventful period, omitted no effort to set and keep the public opinion around them in what they deemed the right channel —the prosecution of the war for the destruction of slavery, and the conquest of rebellion as the only basis for a re-united country. They sought in and out of the pulpit to stimulate the zeal and sustain the courage of the people. And the event has justified their patriotism as of the true quality. A peace based on righteousness conquered.

THE TENTH PASTOR was the Rev. Benson M. Frink, who in response to a request for the salient points in his life sent the following personal sketch:—

I was born in Bartlett, Carroll County, N. H., June 20th, 1838; the youngest of four sons of the Rev. Silas and Sarah P. Frink. When I was two years of age, my family moved to Conway Center in the same County, where my father died when I was fifteen years old. I received my early educational training in my native town, and in the Academy in Fryeburg, Maine, and in Beloit, Wisconsin.

In October, 1859, I entered Bangor Theological Seminary with my brother, from which we were graduated in a class of 23 in 1862.

After engaging in missionary work in Quebec and the Townships, for one year, I was called to the pastorate of the Congregational Church in Derby, Vermont. Here I was pastor for two years, during which time, I opened the long closed Academy, serving as principal for one term; but the added responsibility of sixty-six pupils and three assistants was more than my strength would permit, with my other work, and I declined to continue my connection with the school.

During the month of August, 1865, I supplied the church in Mont Vernon. While there, I received a very urgent call to the pastorate, which I accepted, beginning my work September 24th, and was installed November 1st. In October, 1867, I received a unanimous call from the Central Congregational Church, Portland, Maine, and November 1st. I was dismissed from the Mont Vernon Church, that I might accept the call extended me from Maine. Since then I have been pastor in Saco, Maine; Beverly, Hamilton, Whitman, Shelburne and West Brookfield, all in Massachusetts, and in this last place I now (May, 1905) reside without a permanent pastorate.

August 28th, 1859, I was married to Miss Mary E. Webb, in Bridgton, Maine, to whom I am largely indebted for any success which I may have had in the Christian ministry.

Of the two years service in Mont Vernon, much was accomplished by our united effort. During the first winter, every activity was turned toward the special work of the church. Mr. Charles A. Towle was then the principal of the Academy, (succeeding Rev. C. P. Bancroft,) who gave to us his earnest and faithful service, and for five evenings each week for seventeen weeks, meetings were held in the various school districts of the town, and in the spring 57 persons united with the church.

When I went to Mont Vernon, its beautiful scenery, location and the intellectual character of the people, having made it a center of attraction, it was impossible to procure a house in which to reside, and

we found a home in the family of Dea. George E. Dean; and in the
following spring, the little room off the chapel was fitted up for a study.
At that time it became evident that a special effort should be made to
secure a parsonage if possible; but the usual hinderances were freely
presented, and to these was added the forceful argument that, "Every
minister has tried and failed, for we cannot raise the amount necessary for such a house as we need and ought to have." Nothing daunted,
and seeing that something heroic must be done, I drew up a simple
subscription paper, and wrote down 18 names of leading people whose
ability I learned from the town taxes and report, and attached the
amount I thought each ought to contribute to make the enterprise a success. The list of names was headed by Dea. William Conant, and
Mrs. Asa Stevens, each for $200, it being my belief that the beginning
would decide the result, and they must set the example of doing great
things; and after a little delightful diplomacy each wrote "Approved"
against their names. Then followed Messrs. F. O. Kittredge, H. H.
Bragg, Capt. Timothy Kittredge, Dea. Joseph A. Starrett, Dea. John
Bruce, and others of like willingness to help on the good cause, after
which it was plain sailing, and in eight days I had secured the pledge
of $2,400, a small part of which was to be paid in labor, and I am hap-
py to record that every dollar subscribed was paid, and much more was
freely given in drawing timber, grading, and other work in and about
the building of the house by the generous and enthusiastic friends.

I immediately drew plans for the house to be submitted to a carpenter to determine if it were a workable plan; and it was approved by the
building committee and the builder. The contract was made, and work
immediately begun in the early summer, and on October 25th, 1866, we
moved into the new home, and it would be difficult to decide which were
the happier, the people or ourselves; certainly the people manifested a
full measure of appreciation, and generous hearts added much to the
pleasure of the "House Warming" which followed. Every one seemed
to take pride in the movement, and the guests were kind and generous
to the young pastor and his family.

As I look over my old records I find these entries that tell a story
of commendable liberality for that people, none of whom could be rated
as rich, but they were heartily in earnest and gave to the limit in every
demand made upon them. Here are a few figures that may interest
those who were young people then:

For Parsonage,		$2,500
"	New Pulpit furniture and carpet,	100
"	Communion Service,	75
"	Changes and repairs in chapel,	25
		$2,700

This did not lessen the benevolences of the church, or the prompt
payment of my salary. The many summer guests who came to this
town were of a very high order, and very many of them were constant

in their attendance on the Sabbath services. They were considerate and generous, and I recall that the first year I was handed an envelope containing $130 from the boarders at the hotel (the old Mount Vernon House, kept by Mr. F. O. Kittredge) and Mr. Dean's. The following year another purse was presented to us from the guests of $80. I cannot refrain from making mention of like kindnesses from our people in ways not measured by dollars. I recall that one Monday morning I entered the "Box Shop" as was my custom, when I was met by some young ladies working there, who handed me a package, requesting me not to open until I reached home. To our very great delight it contained the works of Dr. Horace Bushnell, V Vols.—each volume inscribed thus:

"Rev. Benson M. Frink,

From his friends,

MARTHA E. CONANT,
CORDELIA M. J. BRAGG,
ELLEN M. BRAGG,
MARY E. CLOUTMAN,
MRS. JOHN F. COLBY."

December 25, 1865.

Few communities could then, or can today, boast of more delightful homes or educated sons and daughters who have exerted a wide and lasting influence in educational, religious and business circles. I have believed, and shall continue to believe, that the long and faithful ministry of Rev. Mr. Bruce and his successors, and the inspiration of the honored and distinguished principal of the Academy, the late Rev. C. F. P. Bancroft, D.D., Ph.D., had much to do in guiding to high purposes the young men and women who have honored their native town in church and state.

The fathers and mothers sleep; sowers and reapers pass on, but their work abides in the Old Granite State, and the Christian democracy of this nation.

The clock that was presented to us Christmas Evening, 1865, at the home gathering of Dea. W. H. Conant, has ticked away the years from then until now; changes have come to all, and many we then knew as our people rest in silence; but memory brings back their sacred names, and their deeds of kindness and love troop in to make glad the years we now live; and no years of my public life are more cherished than those spent among the good people of Mont Vernon, N. H.

Our only child, a daughter, Florence Leonola, was born September 6, 1863, at Magog, Province of Quebec.

THE ELEVENTH PASTOR was the Rev. Seth Harrison Keeler, D.D., who was born in Brandon, Vt., Sept. 24, 1800. In 1823 he entered the Sophomore class at Middlebury College, graduating in 1826, and entering Andover Theological Seminary the same year. Soon after his graduation from there he was called to the church in South Berwick, Me., and was ordained as its pastor in October, 1829. The following winter he was married to Mary Felt, of New Ipswich, N. H., of whom he said: "Not a little of my success as a pastor I gratefully ascribe to her example and influence." In the autumn of 1836 he accepted a call to the church in Amesbury Mills, Mass., and after a successful ministry of three years, (April 18, 1836 to December 7, 1839), by the advice of a council of clergymen, answered the call to a church in Calais, Me. There he remained for twenty-seven years, (November 30, 1839, to October 22, 1874), extending his usefulness so much beyond his own church that he was called the "Bishop of Washington County." In 1865 the trustees of Middlebury College conferred upon him the degree of D.D. Full of patriotism, and longing for some share in the Country's sacrifice, he asked permission from his people to serve in the Christian Commission at Washington, and was there for some weeks, comforting the sick, and sustaining many a soldier in his last hours. In 1866 he resigned his pastorate at Calais, and came to Reading, Mass., purposing to rest, and preach occasionally as he might have opportunity; but at the close of 1867, through his friend Dr. Clark, of Amherst, he went to preach at Mont Vernon, New Hampshire, and, receiving a unanimous call from the church, entered once more upon the labors he loved as pastor, continuing at Mont Vernon from 1867 to 1875. He often spoke of the eight years he spent there as most happy. He delighted in the beautiful scenery, and said the fine air gave him a new lease of life. He took a lively interest in Appleton Academy. This was his last pastorate. In 1875 he removed to Somerville, Mass., to be near a son and daughter, and lived there until 1886. On Christmas day of that year he died in church, just as he had risen to join in singing—a most fitting ending to an exceptionally beautiful and useful life. He was 86 years, 3 months and 2 days old at the time of his death. Though advanced in years when his service to this people commenced, he proved himself as an able, scholarly and faithful religious teacher. In 1873 and 1874 some forty people united with the church as the result of special religious interest in the community.

On the 5th of September, 1880, Dr. Keeler came and preached a centennial sermon, the church having been organized in 1780.

THE TWELFTH PASTOR was the Rev. William H. Woodwell, who was born at Newbury (now Newburyport), Mass., September 9,

1844. He attended the public schools of Newburyport, graduating from the High school in 1862. Between that date and the time he entered Bowdoin College in 1865, he was employed a part of the time as a special reporter on the Boston Transcript. He graduated at Bowdoin in 1869, and at once entered the Andover Theological Seminary, where he graduated in 1872. He was ordained as a minister at Wells, Me., June 12, 1873, and was pastor of the Congregational church at that place until May, 1875. In November of that year he became pastor of the church at Mont Vernon, serving until about April, 1880. In January, 1881, he went to Hawaii, Sandwich Islands, and was pastor and teacher there until May, 1882. He was called to the pastorate of the Congregational church at Orient, N. Y., and served that church from 1883 to 1887. After a short pastorate at New Marlborough, Mass., he was called to the Congregational church at Sandwich, Mass., and was there from near the close of 1888 to October, 1898. He soon after removed with his family to Washington, D. C., and supplied pulpits of churches of his denomination in Washington and elsewhere until April, 1901, when he preached at Hampton, Conn., where he remained till April, 1904, when he assumed the pastoral care of the Congregational churches at Hampton Falls and Seabrook, N. H., where he now is (May, 1905).

On the 18th of April, 1873, Mr. Woodwell was married to Miss Martha Haskell, of Newburyport. The following children have been born to them : —

Julian Ernest, born at Wells, Me., Jan. 7, 1874, who graduated from the Massachusetts Institute of Technology.

Eva Cecilia, born at Mont Vernon, N. H., and graduated at Mount Holyoke in 1900.

William Herbert, born at Pohala, Hawaii, May 5, 1881, and was a member of the Law School of George Washington University, at Washington, D. C.

Archer Roscoe, born at Newburyport, May 23, 1883, now (1905) residing at Fredericksburg, Va.

Carolus Sylvester, born at New Marlborough, Mass., February 9, 1889, and now a member of Phillips Academy at Exeter, N. H.

THE THIRTEENTH PASTOR was Rev. C. C. Carpenter, who began his pastorate simultaneously with the second century of the church, occupying the pulpit of the church first on September 19, 1880, and removing his family here from Peabody, Mass., in November following.

Charles Carroll Carpenter was born in Bernardston, Mass., July 9, 1836, the son of Dr. Elijah W. Carpenter, for forty years a physician in that town, and Vallonia Slate. He was of the eighth generation from William Carpenter, an English emigrant of 1638, who had been influenced to join the Plymouth Colony by Governor Bradford, husband of Alice Carpenter, a cousin. He settled first at Weymouth, Mass., soon after at Rehoboth, where the successive generations dwelt until Dr Carpenter's father, after his service in the Revolutionary army, removed to Vermont.

Mr. Carpenter fitted for college at Goodale Academy in his native town, at Williston Seminary, and at Kimball Union Academy in Meriden, N. H., but the complete break-down of his health prevented him from pursuing his studies further. A health excursion to the coast of Labrador led him, after two years spent in business, to visit that coast again in 1858, under the auspices of the Canada Foreign Missionary Society to see what could be done for the unprivileged inhabitants. He took lumber down the St. Lawrence, built a mission-house on Caribou Island, in the Straits of Belle Isle, and at that station, and at a winter station on the banks of Eskimo River, served as missionary among the sailors and shoremen until the fall of 1865, when the severity of the climate compelled him to retire. In the meantime he had visited "the States" repeatedly, attending lectures at Harvard Medical College, receiving ordination at Montreal in 1860, marrying in 1862, and spending the last winter of the Civil War in the service of the U S. Christian Commission in the Army of the Potomac.

From 1866 to 1872 he was superintendent of the Lookout Mountain (Tenn.) Educational Institutions for white youth, having for associates, for a part of the time, Principal Cecil F. P. Bancroft and his Mont Vernon wife, Frances Kittredge. He was a student at Andover Theological Seminary from 1872 to 1875, then minister at South and West Peabody, Mass. (two parishes), until 1880. He was formally installed pastor at Mont Vernon, July 1, 1881, and closed his pastorate, Sept. 20, 1885. He has since resided in Andover, Mass., without pastoral charge, occasionally preaching, but mostly engaged in literary work; was editor of the *Andover Townsman* for two years, and has been a contributing editor of the *Congregationalist* from 1886 ; he published a Biographical Catalogue of

Phillips Academy, Andover (1778-1830), and is now preparing a general catalogue of Andover Seminary. He received the honorary degree of A. M. from Hamilton College in 1869, and from Dartmouth College in 1887.

Mr. Carpenter married, May 1, 1862, Miss Feronia N. Rice, of Auburn, Mass. They have had five children: George R., Harvard College, 1886, professor in Columbia University; Charles L., Dartmouth College, 1887, civil engineer on the Panama Canal; William Bancroft, Harvard College, 1890, teacher in Boston public schools; Jane B., Mt. Holyoke College, 1897, teacher; Miriam F. (born in Mont Vernon), Colorado College, 1905.

The Fourteenth Pastor was the Rev. Richard Hastings McGown, who commenced preaching here January 10, 1886, and was installed June 23, 1886. He was born at North Ellsworth, Me., May 13, 1850, was educated principally at the Eastern State Normal School at Castine, and graduated in 1878 from the Bangor Theological Seminary. Became a preacher of the Methodist Conference, and as such was stationed at Dover, Tremont, and Pembroke, Me. March 7, 1882, he was ordained as a Congregational minister at Harrington, Me., was acting pastor at Turner, Me., from December, 1883, to November, 1885, and at Mont Vernon from December, 1885, until February 26, 1888. He was afterwards two years each at Cornish, Me., and at Northwood, N. H. His last pastorate was at the Courtland street Congregational church in Everett, Mass., where he died in the service, April 1, 1900, after a brief illness. His wife and two sons and two daughters survived him; also two brothers, Dr. Wilkes McGown, of Lynn, Mass., and the Rev. A. J. McGown, now (1905) pastor of the Congregational church at Amherst, N. H.

Sept. 25, 1875, he married Abby Frances Rowe, of Ellsworth, Me. Five children were born to them: Ruth May, Ralph Sumner, Anna Estella, Roy Edmund, and Ernest Alfred, the last named child dying in infancy.

A newspaper account of his death says: " Wherever he has been he has left the impress of his faithfulness, and people were everywhere impressed by the integrity and faithfulness of his Christian life and ministry; and everywhere he was called 'a good man.' While his life was comparatively short it would be hard to estimate the good he has done."

THE FIFTEENTH REGULAR PASTOR was the Rev. John Thorpe, who was born May 4th, 1845, in the village of Newton Heath, three miles from the city of Manchester, England, which, at this writing (1904), is a ward of said city. His father, Joel Thorpe, was born in Moston, a suburb of Manchester, and died in October, 1880, at the age of 75. His mother's maiden name was Sarah Brown, and she was born at Compstall Bridge, Derbyshire, England, Jan. 5, 1814, and is still (1904) living with grandchildren. Both father and mother were silk weavers on the hand loom. There were eleven children, of whom John was the sixth. He went to school at three years of age, and at eight worked in the print works at what was known as a "half-timer." At thirteen he began to work as a "full-timer," and attended a night school until he was twenty. He began work as a local preacher at the age of sixteen for the "Methodist New Connexion," still working as a calico printer, at the Clayton Vale Print Works, Manchester. At twenty-one he went to work in a Manchester ware-house, first as a porter and messenger, then as travelling salesman. At the age of twenty-four he married Miss Emily A. C. Bennett, eldest daughter of Alfred and Sarah Ann Bennett, of Newton Heath. Mr. Bennett was superintendent of a cotton mill at the time of his death in 1870. Her mother is still (1904) living in Failsworth, Manchester, at the age of 76.

At the age of twenty-five John Thorpe sailed for New York, and after a rough passage of 52 days in a clipper ship, landed at Castle Garden, New York, May 8, 1871. He worked three months in a woolen mill at Raritan, N. J., and then went to Lawrence, Mass., and at first worked as a cloth-folder in the Washington Mills, and later as a cloth-inspector. On Sundays he was engaged in mission services, supplying pulpits in various places, and following his occupation in the mill during the week.

In May, 1874, he returned with his wife to England. Leaving her with her mother, he went to London, and in June, 1874, sailed for Quebec, Canada, removing to Upper Canada, and then to Detroit, and Chicago, at which last named place he was employed by a surveyor for a brief time. Then he went to Elgin, Ill., as an attendant in a hospital. On the first of March, 1875, he went to Washington, D. C., and thence to Baltimore, and later to Philadelphia, from which place he shipped in a Guion steamer for London, and later rejoined his wife in Manchester. They soon went to house-keeping in the Lancashire seaport town of Southport, where he did odd jobs for a

hardware dealer, and finally acted as a salesman. He afterward was
employed as lodge-keeper and messenger at the Lancashire Independent College at Whalley Range, Manchester; and later as librarian at
the Longsight (Manchester) Mechanics Institute.

In January, 1880, he returned to Lawrence, Mass., as a cloth-
inspector, and also resumed religious work under his local preacher's
license. In 1884 he served the Tower Hill Congregational church of
Lawrence as pulpit supply. In 1885 he removed to South Weare,
N. H., as preacher and missionary, and Dec 30, 1885, was ordained
and installed as a Congregational minister in the Congregational
church at South Weare. On Sunday afternoons he also supplied the
pulpit at North Weare, also preaching often for the Free Baptists.

June 17, 1888, he began his pastorate of the Congregational
church at Mont Vernon, where he preached until Sept. 1, 1894. On
this date he began service as pastor of the Congregational churches
at Andover and East Andover, N. H., laboring there until March 1,
1899, when he removed to Brookline, N. H., where he served as pastor of the Congregational church until June 1, 1902, when he began
his labors with the Congregational church at Center Harbor (on Lake
Winnepesaukee), N. H., under an engagement on a mutual basis for
what is called "An Indefinite Time"—which connection he still holds
(June, 1905).

In the Old Scholars' Union Magazine, a Sunday-school publication, issued in 1891, Mr. Thorpe gives a good many facts in his
career. His call to be a preacher, he says, came when he was a
child, when his ambition was to enter the ministry. At 16 he joined
the church, at 18 he preached his first sermon in the old Culcheth
school, at 19 he was put on the "plan," and at 21 went to work in
the city of Manchester. At 24, he says, he "married the prettiest
Lancashire lass in the whole county." At 25 he set sail for New
York, where he landed, May 8, 1871. At 26 he joined the Free Congregational church at Lawrence, Mass., and the next year preached
for the Methodists at various places in Massachusetts and New
Hampshire.

One who knows him well says :

"The free, frank, independent, happy-go-lucky, roaming, rhym-
ing, contented, rollicking spirit of John Thorpe was learned by him
from reading and assimilating over and over again the life of John
Wesley, who said : 'I look upon the World as my parish. I have

no time to be in a hurry. God buries his workmen, but continues
his work. The best of all is, God is with us '"

> "No foot of land do I possess,
> No cottage in this wilderness
> A poor way-faring man:
> I lodge awhile in tents below,
> And gladly wander to and fro,
> Till I may Canaan gain."

Mr. Thorpe's ministry at Mont Vernon was busy and successful.
He might well be called a "hearty" minister, both in his preaching
and in his parish work. His varied experiences made him a fit ex-
emplar of St. Paul's note of his own course in "becoming all things
to all men," and he had a whole-souled manner which made him welcome in every household.

THE SIXTEENTH PASTOR was the Rev. Thomas Jones Lewis, son
of Thomas and Susan (Jones) Lewis, and he was born in Swansea,
Wales, July 2, 1857. He attended the public schools in his native
place, and began to preach when only eighteen years of age in a Congregational church in Swansea. He came to the United States in
August, 1883, and was a student at Marietta, Ohio, in that and the
succeeding year. From 1884 to 1887 he was a student at the Theological Seminary at Bangor, Me., graduating with his class.

After graduation he preached two years at Deer Isle, Me., but
was not ordained to the gospel ministry until Dec. 5, 1889. This
occurred at Southwest Harbor, Me., where he began preaching in
September of that year, and continued until April, 1891. In May,
1891, he became pastor of the church at East Andover, N. H., and
served there until July, 1894, when he succeeded the Rev. John
Thorpe as pastor of the Congregational church at Mont Vernon, who
in turn succeeded him at East Andover. Mr. Lewis remained at
Mont Vernon until December, 1897, when he went to Wales, supplying a pulpit at Porthcawl for about a year. In 1899, having returned
to this country, he was recalled to the pulpit at East Andover, N.
H., which he served until January, 1901. At this time he was
called to the pastorate of the Congregational church at Conway, N.
H., where he is still serving successfully and happily (June, 1905).

On the 19th of February, 1878, Mr. Lewis was united in marriage to Miss Annie Daniels, by whom he has had four children, of
whom three are living.

Mr. Lewis's pastorate at Mont Vernon was successful in every respect. It was during this pastorate that the new meeting-house was dedicated. Mr. Lewis was an honest, faithful, and devoted Christian minister, and a preacher of no mean abilities. He possessed the entire respect and esteem of all his people.

THE SEVENTEENTH PASTOR, the Rev. Donald Browne, commenced preaching here November, 1898. He was born at London, England, November 3d, 1851, son of Donald and Sarah (Humphrey) Browne. Educated in Devonshire, then became teacher. He took charge of an Episcopal Mission School in Newfoundland four years. He was Judge of District Court six years at St. Barbes, Newfoundland. He studied in the theological department of Boston University, was ordained over a Congregational church at Tiverton, R. I., in 1889, remaining there three years. In 1892 he went to the Broadway Congregational church, Fall River, preaching there several years. He closed his two years' pastorate here November, 1900. Mr. Browne while here assisted in the work of Grace Episcopal Church of Manchester, N. H., of which the Rev. W. Jones was rector. Mr. and Mrs. Browne were very highly esteemed here, and the universal sentiment of the parish was of much regret at their departure. He went from Mont Vernon to pastoral work in Manchester, N. H., and later to Derry, N. H., and at this writing (June, 1905,) he is at South Groveland, Mass. These last two charges were in the Episcopal denomination.

THE EIGHTEENTH PASTOR of the church (who is serving at this date, June, 1905,) is the Rev. Henry Porter Peck. He was born in Kalamazoo, Michigan, Oct. 25, 1853, and spent his boyhood and early manhood in Norfolk, Conn. He fitted for college at Williston Seminary, at Easthampton, Mass., and graduated at Amherst College in the class of 1878. He spent two years in the study of theology at Auburn, N. Y., and two years at Andover Theological Seminary, where he graduated in 1882. May 1, 1882, he was called to the pastorate of the Congregational church at Plymouth, N. H., where he served from 1882 to 1889. October 1, 1889, he was called to the Second Congregational church at Winsted, Conn., where he remained until Oct. 1, 1891, and May 1, 1892, was settled over the Congregational church at Milford, N. H., until Oct. 1, 1899. He began his ministry at Mont Vernon in the winter of 1900-1901, where he still

continues (June, 1905.)   Mr. Peck is a preacher of unusual ability,
always discoursing without notes, and his sermons are plain, practical
Christian utterances, illustrated by a fund of ready reference to current events and up-to-date thought.

For the last twenty-five years the strength of the church and society has waned, by the death, or departure from Mont Vernon, of a
considerable number on which both relied for strength and support.
A considerable summer clientage, however, helps to maintain public
worship in the decidedly handsome and commodious little meeting-
house, which is among the most attractive in the country.

CHAPTER VII.

THE OLD MEETING-HOUSE.

Pew-Grounds—Pew-Spots—Alterations and Repairs—Transfer
of Parish Matters to Town—Horse-Sheds—Buildings on the
Common—Call to Rev. Stephen Chapin—His Dismissal—The
Ministerial Fund—Extensive Repairs—Parsonage—Fire in
Meeting House—New Modelling the House—Its Removal
Across the Road—Hearse and Hearse House—Last Service
in Old House—As a Town Hall—Town and Society Quit-
claim to Each Other—Co-partnership Ended—Certain
Rights Reserved—Appropriation to Change Meeting-House
to Town Hall—The Changes—Old Baptismal Bowl Found
—Town Hall Dedicated.

The story of the building of the first meeting-house in 1781, is
given at some length in the first chapter of this history, as well as
sundry notes relative to changes therein, and to the "burying-
ground," which is about a quarter of a mile from the meeting-house,
towards Francestown. The accounts of what has been done, from
time to time, to the building are meagre.

1784, Dec. 29, the Parish voted a deed of "pew ground," No.
33, ' to the Widow Hannah Peabody, of Amherst, 6 ft. 1 in. long
by 4 ft. 11 in. wide, according to a scheme of ground plot or plan of
land now lodged with the public record of said Parish:" which is of
interest as fixing the size of the "pew-grounds."

When the new meeting-house was built in 1896, some of these
"pew-ground" deeds, which had descended by inheritance or otherwise to persons then living, were offered in exchange for pews in the
new edifice, but of course that could not be allowed, as the old pew-
grounds were then valueless; nor was such an exchange necessary,

as no pews were sold, or even rented in the new meeting-house, sittings in which were made free to all.

1790, April 26, the Parish voted "to allow 4 pews more in front of those now built on the lower floor, in said house."

Also voted "6 'pew-spots' more in the gallery," and chose a committee to sell the "spots" to the highest bidder.

Voted "to impower the committee to pay up the arrearages and finish the meeting-house."

1791, July 9. Voted "to find stuff and to build the seats in said meeting-house, except the front of the brestworks in said seats."

1792, Oct. 25. Voted "not to have the Small Pox any longer in said Parish after the House now infected can be cleaned."

1801, March 13. The new Town of Mont Vernon had an article in the warrant "to see if they will acknowledge all former contracts of the Second Parish of Amherst not legally discharged, as their own, and order the selectmen for the time being to call for a transfer of all monies, grants and obligations in favor of said Parish." Under this article it was

Voted "to take a transfer of all parish matters to the Town of Mont Vernon, and acknowledge them as their own."

Here ended the Parish, and the Town succeeded to its privileges and obligations.

1808, April 13. An article was put in the warrant "to see if the town will agree to 1 t old buildings that is halled on to the Common in said Town and left there by John Averill, jr., and Jesse Averill, still continue there; if not, to see if said Town will allow said building to have a place anywhere on the common near said meeting-house."

"To see what method said Town will take in future in regard to the building of horse-sheds, and the methods the inhabitants shall take to obtain leave for that purpose."

At the meeting held May 16, 1808, Voted "there should not any buildings stand in front or in rear of said meeting-house."

Voted "that all the horse-sheds and other buildings should not stand where they now stand."

Voted "to choose a committee of seven persons to say where the said sheds should stand."

The committee was at once named, and reported to the meeting, and it was voted "that persons having buildings should be notified to move them within 30 days."

The agency of the Town as a successor of the Parish in manag-

THE OLD MEETING HOUSE
(Erected in 1781)
Before Remodelled as Town Hall.

ing the affairs of the church is shown in a vote, April 11, 1809, "to choose a committee to hire a candidate to supply the pulpit; also to raise $127 for hiring preaching, and to appropriate the school land money in place of the $127."

1809, Sept. 25. There was an article in the warrant "to see if the Town will concur with the Church in said town, in giving a call to the Rev. Stephen Chapin to settle with said church." The vote was in the affirmative, and a committee appointed to report "what encouragement ought to be given to said Chapin." After a recess of three-quarters of an hour, the committee reported that he should be paid an annual salary of $400 "including the annual interest on the ministerial money." Later, a day was voted by the town for Mr. Chapin's installation, and a committee was appointed to manage it, so far as the town was concerned.

1813, March 9. Voted "to remove the seats (except the front ones) on the lower floor of the meeting-house, and sell the ground at vendue on the day appointed for selling the Town's poor."

1818, Nov. 9. In consequence of a petition signed by Asa Stevens and others, an article was put in the warrant "to see what measures the Town will take relative to the situation of the Rev. Stephen Chapin and the People of his charge concerning some scriptural points."

Voted "to choose a committee to wait on Mr. Chapin and request him to come forward and make a publick statement, relative to his disposition."

Also voted "that Mr. Chapin be dismissed agreeable to his request."

For many years the town voted to appropriate the income of what was commonly known as the "funded money" towards the "support of the Gospel." The term for the same money was, sometimes, "ministerial fund." The Rev. C. C. Carpenter says :

"The 'ministerial fund' was created by the sale of the 'ministerial land,' an hundred acres or so, originally set aside in the settlement of a town, for the use of the minister as long as he remained such. In process of time, because they were remote from the center of the town, or for other reasons, this was sold — in whole or part — and the proceeds made a fund, the income of which was to be used for the support of preaching — not so much as an addition to his salary, as for helping the people to make up the amount they had pledged. Some times this fund, through mismanagement, was lost, and in other cases — perhaps the most — used in some emergency for paying debt to the pastor. In some other cases, when other denominations than the 'standing order' sprang up, they claimed a share of it, and it was turned over to them. The sum was not large in any case, as the lands did not usually bring much."

1821, in June, there was an article in the warrant "to see if the town will vote to repair the outside of the meeting-house, agreeably to an act of the Legislature passed in 1819, and raise money for that purpose."

On this it was voted (June 15, 1821) "to repair the outside of the meeting-house. To choose a committee to report the repairs necessary to be made, and the best manner of effecting them."

The committee were evidently prepared beforehand, for after a recess of half an hour, they reported: "To right the underpinning, and point it with lime, supply the water-tables and clapboards that are wanting, and secure all the clapboards by sufficient nailing, shingle the two porches, and the roof on the backside with good 15-inch shingles, laying 4½ inches to the weather, supply glass and putty and mend the window sashes, make a new front door, and door-stools to all the doors; and paint the house with two coats of good paint and oil, the trimmings with white lead, and the body of the house a bright yellow, composed of 2-5 of white and 3-5 a French yellow, the doors of a mogany [mahogany] color."

The committee added that the repairs were recommended "to be let out to the lowest bidder in two separate jobs or lots, viz.: The painting, glass and putty in one lot, and all the other repairs specified in another, reserving the privilege of letting the whole job together, if it can be done cheaper."

The Town voted to accept the report, and that the repairs must be done by the last day of September; and chose a committee of three to oversee and accept them. Mr. Porter Kimball offered to do the entire job for $239, and it was "struck off" to him, and the Treasurer was authorized to borrow the money and pay him.

About all that is in the Town records for several years after this relative to the church, is a vote each year that the income of the "funded money" be paid to the religious society for the support of the ministry; but in 1825 there was an article in the warrant "to see if the Town would vote to purchase a parsonage" with the funded money, or a part of it. Instead of voting this, however, it was voted "that the interest be appropriated (as last year) to the support of the Gospel; that the selectmen collect the funded money as soon as consistent, and loan it to the Rev. N. Kingsbury, by his giving good security — providing he may want it."

At the same meeting a committee was appointed to make arrangements for letting individuals "build horse-sheds on the common." It does not appear that anything was done under this vote, as in 1831 it was voted "to grant individuals the privilege to erect horse-sheds near the meeting-house."

1832, March 13, it was again voted "to let Rev. N. Kingsbury have the use of the funded money, by his giving satisfactory security."

At the same meeting it was voted that "the Rev. N. Kingsbury's society keep the meeting-house in repair the present year."

It was also voted "that the selectmen see that the meeting-house is properly swept after this meeting has adjourned."

It seems that the meeting-house caught fire in the winter of 1833-34, for at an adjourned Town meeting held April 7, 1834, it was voted "to repair the meeeting-house"; and further it was voted "to pay those who watched the meeting-house on the night of the fire 5 shillings each "

1836, March 22, at an adjourned meeting, there being no article in the warrant on that subject, it was

Voted, "to take the money called the Ministerial Money to defray the expenses of the Town, to be paid into the town treasury "

1837, March 14 There was an article in the warrant "to see if the town will hear any proposition that may be made by the Congregational Society in this place for new-modelling the meeting-house "

On this it was voted to choose a committee to confer with a committee of the Congregational Society respecting this article, and Allen Goodridge, George Raymond, and Jonathan Herrick were appointed

This committee reported at an adjourned meeting and the report was accepted The following votes were then passed:

1. "That the Town unite with the Congregational Society in this place in new-modelling the meeting-house.

2. "That one-half the ground floor of said meeting-house be appropriated for a Town Hall.

3. "That the Town furnish the Town Hall appropriated for their use, and that they sustain the roof of said house, making all repairs which may be required from time to time.

4. "That the Congregational Society be at the expense of all alter-

ations, excepting what pertains to the Town Hall, that they sustain the body of said house, making all repairs which may be required from time to time, and that the said Congregational Society have sole control of said house, excepting the Town Hall for the transaction of town business.

5.   "That the town chose an agent to convey their right or interest in the Meeting-House to the Congregational Society, reserving the right to the Town, agreeably to the above votes."

Chose Jonathan Herrick to make the above conveyance.

This contract was scrupulously adhered to fifty-nine years, and the church and town occupied the edifice harmoniously, within clearly defined limits, until the building of the new church in 1896

Until this time (1837) the meeting-house had stood on the common, on the easterly side of the main road to Milford and Amherst; but when this new modelling took place, it was moved to its present site on the westerly side of the road.   There seems to be no record of just what was done by the way of change in the building, but it was undoubtedly finished in two stories, and was furnished with a bell and an organ   It is also probable that the "two porches" spoken of in earlier records were removed, and an addition was made of the present front, on which was erected the steeple and belfry   Two front doors were put in, and a "vestry" was put in the lower story, while the rear half of the ground floor was finished as a town hall, and here the meetings of the Town were held until the entire building was taken for a Town Hall in 1897.

Rev. Mr. Jennison, who was pastor at the time, has said there was no formal dedication sermon at the occupation of the new modelled building.

1838, March 13   It was voted "to finish the Town Hall the present year;" also

"That the selectmen cause the Town Hall to be finished the present year, with as many new windows as they shall deem needful;" also

"That the town pay for ringing the bell for funerals, and on all occasions except for Society meetings, at $7.50 per year."

1840, March 10   Voted "that Nathaniel Bruce be a committee to ascertain if the town have a right to sell the land on the common east of the road passing by the Meeting-House."

1841, March 9   Voted "that the bell be rung at 12 of the clock, noon, and at nine of the clock at night, and the town pay Mr. Shattuck a reasonable compensation."

1842, March 8. Voted "that the Town buy or procure a Hearse, Hearse-house and harness for the use of the town :

"That N. Bruce be a committee to procure the same :

"That the selectmen cause the necessary repairs to be made on the outside of the Meeting-House as soon as practicable.

"That the Town pay for ringing the bell once in a day. That it be rung at noon

"That if the person who rings the bell fails to ring it at the true time, as a general thing, he shall have nothing for the same."

1843, March 14. Voted, "That the Town rebuild the wall in front of the burying-ground

"To buy a stove for the Town-house."

The last service in the old meeting-house occurred on Sunday, July 5, 1896, the sermon being preached by the Rev. C. F. P. Bancroft, D D , Principal of Phillips Academy, Andover, Mass. The then Pastor, Rev. T. J. Lewis, conducted the devotional exercises. It was an occasion of surpassing interest. For something over 116 years the venerable building had been used as a place of worship on this hill-top. It had been hallowed by many prayers and sermons, christenings and baptisms, marriages and funerals. It was dear to all the people of the town, and however much more comely and comfortable the new meeting-house might be, the old house of worship held a place in their hearts which no more modern structure could fill.

AS A TOWN HALL.

The frame of the old meeting-house was of the durable character of buildings constructed in those days. It is of hewn oak, and as the building has always stood upon the solid rock, which, in many points near the site crops out in a ledgy surface, it has mainly kept sound until this day

When the new meeting-house was completed, in 1896, a movement was started to dispose of the Congregational Society's right and interest in the old meeting-house. The first suggestion was that the town should buy out the society's interest in the land and building, and pay $1500 therefor. At the March meeting of 1895 such an article was put into the warrant, but it was voted "to pass by the article." Similar action was taken in 1896. In 1897 at the March meeting, it was voted "to appoint a committee of five to report a bill

covering the whole matter." The committee consisted of Willard
P. Woods, Daniel Richardson, Geo. W. Averill, Wm. G. Burnham,
and Henry F. Dodge, and they reported the following resolution,
which was adopted:

"Resolved, That the selectmen be instructed to quitclaim to the
Mont Vernon Congregational church Society all right and title to land
and buildings on east side of road, known as the Woodbury land,
upon condition that said Society quitclaim all right and title to land
on west side of said road including buildings thereon."

The deed of conveyance was as follows:

KNOW ALL MEN BY THESE PRESENTS.

THAT the Town of Mont Vernon, County of Hillsborough
and State of New Hampshire, for and in consideration of
the sum of One Dollar and valuable considerations before the
delivery hereof, well and truly paid by the First Congregational Society of Mont Vernon, New Hampshire aforesaid,
the receipt whereof it doth hereby acknowledge, have remised, released, and forever QUITCLAIMED, and do by
these presents remise, release, and forever QUITCLAIM
unto the said First Congregational Society of Mont Vernon
and its assigns forever:

All that certain piece, tract or parcel of land situated,
lying and being in said Mont Vernon in the County of Hillsborough and said State of New Hampshire, and described
as follows: so much of the "Meeting House lot" so called,
as is situated east of the main road leading from Mont Vernon
village to Milford, and the buildings "New Church and Parsonage" thereon.

TO HAVE AND TO HOLD the afore-described premises,
with all the privileges and appurtenances thereunto belonging
to the said First Congregational Church and Society and
assigns, to its and their use and behoof forever.

IN WITNESS WHEREOF, the Town of Mont Vernon
by its selectmen have hereunto set their hand and seals this
eighth day of April, in the Year of Our Lord, One Thousand
Eight Hundred and Ninety-seven.

Signed, sealed and delivered in presence of us:

   HARRY G. BLOOD,) Selectmen
   W. L. ROBINSON, of
   W. H. KENDALL,) Mont Vernon.

It may be as well to give, here, the corresponding deed given by
the Society to the Town, which was as follows:

First Congregational Society of Mont Vernon to Town of Mont Vernon.

KNOW ALL MEN BY THESE PRESENTS

THAT the First Congregational Society of Mont Vernon, New Hampshire, a corporation duly established under the laws of the State of New Hampshire, for and in consideration of the sum of One Dollar and other good and valuable considerations to it before the delivery hereof, well and truly paid by the Town of Mont Vernon, the receipt whereof it doth hereby acknowledge, hath remised, released and forever QUITCLAIMED and by these presents doth remise, release and forever QUITCLAIM unto the said Town of Mont Vernon, and its assigns forever:

All that certain piece, tract or parcel of land situate, lying and being in said Mont Vernon, in the County of Hillsborough and said State of New Hampshire, and described as follows: So much of the "Meeting House lot" so called, as is situated west of the main road, including the premises acquired by said Society from Israel Burnham and from George W. Averill, excepting so much thereof as has been heretofore released to the said Averill, together with the Meeting House thereon, subject, however, to the following conditions: First, that this release shall not in any wise affect the rights and privileges of the owners of the horsesheds on said premises. Second, that said Town shall maintain a bell on the building, on said premises, which bell said Society and the Church connected therewith shall have the right to ring for all meetings of said Church or Society.

Third, that said Church or Society shall have the right to use the hall in said building for business meetings or entertainments without charge, except for the cost of heating and lighting. TO HAVE AND TO HOLD the said granted premises with all the privileges and appurtenances to the same belonging to the said Town of Mont Vernon and its assigns, to its and their own proper use and benefit forever.

In witness whereof the said First Congregational Society has caused a seal to be hereto affixed and these presents to be signed, acknowledged and delivered in its name and behalf by Frances A. Holt as Treasurer, hereunto duly authorized this eighth day of April in the year one thousand eight hundred and ninety-seven. Signed, sealed and delivered in presence of:

W. H. CONANT, } Witnesses.
W. H. KENDALL, }

First Congregational
Society
of Mont Vernon.
FRANCES A. HOLT, Treasurer.

At a special meeting of the First Congregational Society of Mont Vernon, New Hampshire, duly called for the purpose and held in said Mont Vernon on the twenty-second day of March, A. D. 1897, and adjourned to the twenty-fourth day of March, the foregoing deed having been read and considered, the following vote was passed:

Voted, that Frances A. Holt, the Treasurer, is hereby authorized and instructed to execute, acknowledge and deliver in the name and behalf of the Society, the deed from said Society to the Town of Mont Vernon which has just been read.

A true copy: Attest.   CLARK CAMPBELL, Clerk.

Here ended, finally, the co-partnership between the Town and the Church and Congregational Society, which formally began in 1837, but which was really initiated when the town was incorporated in 1803, and which grew out of that union of "church and state," which existed from the beginning of New England history. But even at this writing, as will be seen from the deeds which passed between the Town and the Society, there are still vestiges of the old partnership left, as in the provisions of the deed of the Society to the Town, the right was reserved to use the bell, which was allowed to remain in its old place in the belfry of the old meeting house, for summoning its worshipers to all meetings, and also the right to use the Town Hall for business meetings and entertainments, free of charge, except for the cost of heating and lighting. Furthermore the rights of the individual owners of the horse-sheds were reserved to them, under the transfer. It was said that the bell was allowed to remain in the old belfry to head off the mischievous youth of the town, who were accustomed to break into the building on the night before the Fourth of July, and begin the celebration of Independence at midnight in the way which Daniel Webster said John Adams would have recommended. It might be considered an open question whether the Town needed specifically to convey the new meeting-house and parsonage, for if any buildings ever belonged to the Society, which built them, with no aid from the Town, these two did. However, it was only a swapping of any and all possible rights, giving the Town a clear and indisputable right to the property on the west side of the road, subject only to the reservations named above, and the Society an equally clear title to the property on the east side of the road.

It is supposed, however, that another vestige of the Town and Society partnership remains, in a joint ownership of the building originally erected for an Academy, and a school room for the Centre district, long known as the Chapel, and used for many years as such

by the church. It is believed, without any conclusive documentary
evidence, that the upper part of this building was given to the Society by the proprietors, who built it by issuing shares at $5 each,
as will be seen later in the chapter relating to schools. Since the
new meeting-house was built, the church has had no use for it, and
at this writing it is rented by the Grange, or "Patrons of Husbandry." It is understood that this piece of land was not a part
of the "meeting-house lot" quitclaimed in above deed.

The tendency to such partnerships seems to have been strong in
Mont Vernon, and about this time, the Congregational Society and
the Trustees of McCollom Institute established a new and better line
between their adjoining premises by a similar device of quitclaiming
to each other.

The vote of the Town above recorded was supplemented by
votes appropriating the sum of fifteen hundred dollars "to reconstruct
the old church into a town hall;" and Wm. G. Burnham, Geo. W.
Averill, Clark Campbell, Wm. H. Kendall, and Joseph W. Averill
were appointed a committee to carry out the vote.

At a special town meeting held Aug. 16, 1897, it was voted to
appropriate not exceeding five hundred dollars "to complete the Town
House;" and also "to purchase the seats for the town hall."

In making the changes the floor of the old church, running on an
incline from the entrance to the back of the auditorium, was taken
out, and replaced in such a way as to make the rooms below a little
higher posted and more usable than before. A dining room, selectmen's room, and kitchen were arranged on the ground floor, in the place
of the old basement, used partly as a town hall, and partly as a furnace
room. The two entrances on the east end were closed, and a large
one made in the centre. The two short flights of stairs on either side
of the lower entry, leading to one of corresponding size above, were
torn out, and a wider stairway made on right of entrance. The same
arrangement regarding changes of entrances into the church auditorium were made in the upper hallway. The main hall is exactly
the same in size and form as was the old church auditorium, the only
changes being in making the floor level and in the frescoing of walls
and ceiling. The stone steps were not changed The furnace was
in use in the old church. The windows were changed from small
panes of glass to larger ones, but not as to the size of the frames.
The space formerly occupied by the choir loft has been made into a

commodious stage, with curtains and foot-lights, and an ante-room on either side.

When the building was remodelled into a town hall there were found sundry interesting relics of former times, which had gotten out of sight in the unfinished roof or in the belfry tower. The most interesting was a baptismal bowl made of white metal, pewter or Britannia, about nine and one-half inches in diameter and two a half inches in depth. It is of "repousse" or hammered work on the side, with a rim apparently turned on a lathe, and in the centre of the bottom inside, it has, in relief, as a crest, a stag's head, and underneath a monogram, the lower part of which is worn smooth, but the upper part shows half of two letters in script which may be "P. R." or "B. R." or B. B." or some combination similar. None who have seen the bowl can recall that it was ever in use in their day. It apparently must have disappeared in 1837, when the meeting-house was moved and remodelled, and some who have examined it are of the opinion that it is a piece of Paul Revere's handiwork, and that it is his monogram which is on the bottom of the bowl. The crest, however, is not identified as his, even if he had one, and the letters of the monogram are too indistinct as to their lower half to be legible.

The other things found at the same time were an old-fashioned tin lantern, with holes all around to let the light shine through, two very old-fashioned oil lamps of metal, made to hang on the wall, and an old-fashioned whale-oil hand lamp of the style known as the "petticoat" lamp.

The new town hall was dedicated on the evening of September 8, 1897. Speeches were made by chairman of the committee, W. G. Burnham, who introduced Hon. Geo. A. Marden, of Lowell, Mass., as president of the evening, who introduced the following speakers: Gov. Geo. A. Ramsdell, a former student at the Academy here, who made a reminiscent and very interesting speech; Hon. Chas. H. Burns, of Wilton; John H. Colby, Esq., of Boston; Hon. Arthur H. Wellman, of Malden; Hon. George A. Bruce, of Somerville; Col. W. H. Stinson, of Dunbarton; Mr. Chas. E. Osgood, of Boston.

CHAPTER VIII.

THE NEW MEETING-HOUSE.

How the Project Started—Building Committee—The Dedication
—Dedicatory Service—Full Programme of Exercises—Report of Building Committee—The New Meeting-House
Turned Over to the Society—Accepted by the Society—
Dedication Sermon—Full Description of the Edifice—Memorial Windows.

Just when the project for a new meeting-house took definite shape is not known. As early as 1890 a movement was begun to raise money for remodelling the old meeting-house, which had become an apparent necessity. The pulpit was located at the easterly end of the audience room, between the doors of entrance, and everybody who entered the room had to "face the congregation;" while the floor had a determined slope, rising several inches from front to rear, to enable all readily to see the occupant of the pulpit. It was very awkward for the late comer, no matter how great his or her assurance or lack of self-consciousness. The whole building needed renovation and repair.

After considerable agitation in this direction, without making much progress, the project of building a new meeting-house was suggested, but it was considered almost preposterous to expect to secure the necessary funds. A timely and most generous offer, however, from two ladies, descendants of a native of the town, opened the way, and in a short time the necessary amount was secured.

A building committee was chosen by the Society, consisting of Hon. Geo. A. Marden, of Lowell, John H. Colby, Esq., of Boston, Clark Campbell, John T. McCollom and Wm. H. Kendall of Mont Vernon, who were empowered to report on a site, and, later, were authorized to erect a new church building. As the report of this committee made at the dedication gives, in detail, the story of the enterprise, it will be necessary only to refer to it as given quite fully below. It was a strenuous enterprise for the little community, even to raise the $6000, required to secure the liberal donations of Mrs. Richardson and Miss Stevens, but there was a generous rivalry among former citizens, natives, summer visitors, and local organizations, in contributing money, and on the 7th of July, 1896, the fine little church edifice was complete, both in finishing and furnishing, and ready for dedication. The *Manchester Daily Union*, which published an extended report of the dedication, said:

"The dedication of the church had been carefully planned, and it was not the committee's fault that the weather kept away many who might otherwise have attended. Meteorological conditions were anything but favorable. There had been a steady drizzle for three days, and this morning found no change. A heavy black cloud hung ominously over the hill, and the rain drizzled and dripped in the most approved fashion until noon. Then the cloud settled down over the hill and enveloped the entire town.

"Then it poured. Great basketfuls of rain fell out of that cloud and anybody who happened to be out got wet. But there was quite a crowd out to the dedication with all the disadvantages. The morning train brought along a few visitors and many others interested in the church drove into town.

Among the visitors were the Rev. D. W. Waldron, Boston city missionary, and Miss Waldron; I. E. Noyes, president of the Metropolitan National bank, Boston; Sydney F. Squires, Boston; the Rev. F. H. Page, Lawrence, Mass.; the Rev. H. P. Peck, Milford; the Rev. Dr. R. A. Beard, Nashua; Miss Catherine A. Stevens, New York city; the Rev. C. A. Towle, Iowa; Prof. C. S. Campbell, Pinkerton academy, Derry; the Rev. C. F. P. Bancroft, principal of Phillips academy, Andover, Mass.; Dr. C. M. Kittredge, Fishkill-on-the-Hudson; ex-Sheriff John M. Clark, Boston; Col. James F. Hill, Boston; H. Porter Smith, Cambridge, Mass.; Mrs. Asa Stevens, New York city; Mrs. J. A. Parker, Summit, N. J.; the Rev. William H. Hopkins, Poughkeepsie, N. Y.; the Rev. R. H. McGown, a former pastor of the church, Everett, Mass.; the Rev. T. M. Davies and wife, Manchester, and the Rev. Dr. W. R. Cochrane, Antrim.

THE DEDICATORY SERVICES.

The dedicatory exercises began promptly at 1:30 o'clock, and the church was comfortably filled, although a few chairs were arranged in the aisles for the slight overflow.

THE NEW MEETING HOUSE.
Dedicated July 7, 1896.

There were on the platform, the Rev. R. H. McGown of Everett, Mass.; Rev. Dr. Warren R. Cochrane of Antrim; the Rev. Nehemiah Boynton D.D., of Detroit, Mich., and Deacon William H. Kendall, George A. Marden, Clark Campbell, John T. McCollom, and John H. Colby of the building committee.

The following was the order of exercises:

EXERCISES.

1. ORGAN PRELUDE.
   SOLON W. STEVENS, Esq.,
   Organist First Congregational Church, Lowell, Mass.

2. INVOCATION.
   REV. JOHN THORPE, Andover, N. H.,
   A Former Pastor.

3. ANTHEM—"Except the Lord Build the House,"   *Gilchrist*
   BY THE CHOIR.

4. SCRIPTURE LESSON.
   REV. AUGUSTUS BERRY, Pelham, N. H.,
   Former principal of Appleton Academy.

5. ARIA—"With Verdure Clad,"   *From The Creation*
   MRS. O. F. DAVIS, Plymouth, Mass.,
   A former preceptress of the Academy.

6. REPORT OF BUILDING COMMITTEE AND TRANSFER TO FIRST CON-
   GREGATIONAL SOCIETY.
   HON. GEO. A. MARDEN, Lowell, Mass., Chairman.

7. ACCEPTANCE BY FIRST CONGREGATIONAL SOCIETY.
   DEACON WM. H. CONANT, President.

8. OFFERTORY.

9. HYMN—Written by Mr. H. Porter Smith, Cambridge, Mass.
   Tune "Anvern."

Choir and Congregation.

God of our fathers' here we raise
A grateful song, a hymn of praise,—
Thou safely didst the fathers lead,
And hast supplied their children's need.

With a new song to-day we come
Within these walls, our Sabbath home;
Firm on this mount our temple stands,
Accept the labor of our hands.

In what our hands, dear Lord, have done,
Our hearts have been with love led on;
The gifts a joy, the labors sweet—
Behold this house of Thine, complete!

This house shall be a beacon light,
Far reaching from its beauteous height;
Triumphant Faith its walls inspire,
Its altar burn with heavenly fire.

Now may Thy grace our souls renew,
Give us of Thee a clearer view,
May all our lives be sanctified,
And, like this temple, beautified.

Then shall the prophecy of old,
Be here fulfilled to bless this fold,
And ours the word of promise be—
The Lord will build a house for thee.

10.   DEDICATION SERMON.
          REV. NEHEMIAH BOYNTON, D.D., Detroit, Mich.

11.   HYMN Written by Dea. W. H. Conant,   *Tune, "Italian Hymn."*
                    Choir and Congregation.

Oh, Thou whose presence fills
These temples of the hills
    With light and power,
Enter this sacred place
With consecrating grace,
While now we seek Thy face,
    This holy hour.

Here, where our fathers prayed,
And sure foundations laid,
    In early days,
Memorial stones we place,
That future years may trace
Thy wondrous love and grace,
    And speak Thy praise.

Here may a fruitful soil
Reward the lab'rer's toil
    An hundrol fold,
Endue Thy Church with power,
Send Pentecostal shower,
Bring Zion's favored hour
    To young and old.

Stand on this hill-top, then,
Thou witness unto men,
    In His dear name.
Sound out o'er hill and plain—
God's Love and Truth remain,
Christ and His Cross are gain—
    Ever the same.

12.   DEDICATORY PRAYER.
          REV. WARREN R. COCHRANE, D.D., Antrim.

13.   BENEDICTION.
          BY THE PASTOR. REV. T. J. LEWIS.

After the introductory exercises, in accordance with the above
program, George A. Marden of Lowell, Mass., chairman of the building committee, then transferred the keys of the church to the society.
His words were :

CHAIRMAN MARDEN'S REPORT.

I do not know just when this movement for building a new meeting
house was started. The original proposition was to remodel the old
meeting house, and the first money raised by that indefatigable and
most successful organization, the Ladies' Home Circle, for improved
church accommodations, was for remodeling.

Later a most generous proposition was made by Mrs. M. Grace
Richardson and Miss Catherine A. Stevens of New York, daughters of
the late Calvin Stevens, a native of this town, that if the sum of $6000
should be pledged towards the building of a new church edifice, they
would each add the sum of $2500 to the fund. This proposition gave
new impetus to the enterprise, and subscriptions began to come in so
freely that active steps were taken to put the society in shape to utilize
them. It was found on investigation that the society had virtually
lapsed, from failure to hold its annual meetings legally, and the first
step taken was to resuscitate the organization by petitioning a justice of
the peace to call a meeting, as provided in the Public Statutes, when
the society could be re-organized.

This meeting was held May 11, 1895. Officers were duly chosen,
a code of by-laws was adopted, and it was voted that names of a building committee of five members, "to erect a new church building", should
be reported at the next meeting of the society.

A subsequent meeting was called on the 25th of May, and a full discussion of the enterprise was had, and announcements were made as to funds pledged, from which it appeared that the amount required by Mrs. Richardson and Miss Stevens, to wit: $6000, had been pledged. The society then unanimously voted that a new church should be built, and a committee of five should be appointed to carry this vote into effect. It is in behalf of that committee that I now beg leave to report.

Your committee was first instructed to inquire as to the cost of several lots which had been suggested as a site for the new meeting house, and at an adjourned meeting held June 8, 1895, it was voted that the building committee "be given full powers as to the location and erection of the church." The committee at once organized and investigated the several sites proposed, and at a special meeting of the society, held August 17, 1895, it was further voted that "the building committee have full power to locate, build and equip a church edifice for the first Congregational society." The money subscribed was at once called for, and a large proportion of it was soon in the hands of the treasurer of the committee.

The site selected for the new building was this spot, on the land originally given by James Woodbury, and conveyed by him January 5, 1786, to the Second parish of Amherst "for the use of a meeting house spot, and likewise for a common." Mont Vernon did not at that time exist as a town, and Mr. Woodbury was a citizen of Amherst, occupying the house across the way, now owned by Dr. C. M. Kittredge. The Second parish had been incorporated in 1781 "for transacting ministerial affairs," and the petition for the act of incorporation alleges that the petitioners had for some time maintained public worship in a commodious meeting house erected for the purpose, and on this same land, which in 1786 was conveyed by Mr. Woodbury to the parish. For in 1784 the parish voted to "to choose a committee to take a deed from Lieutenant Woodbury in behalf of said parish for the ground that the meeting-house stands on," a copy of which deed is now in our possession.

In 1802 the parish voted to petition the Legislature to set it off from Amherst, and incorporate it as "a distinct town," and also to ask that a strip half a mile wide from Lyndeborough be joined with it. In 1803, December 15, the new town was incorporated under the name of Mont Vernon.

In 1804 the town voted to "take a transfer of all parish matters" including all moneys, grants and obligations in favor of said parish, and thus the town succeeded the parish as trustee under the Woodbury deed, of the property conveyed by him to the parish. The town records show that the town exercised all parish functions in transacting ministerial affairs (to use the exact language of the act incorporating the parish), including the repairs and alterations in the meeting house, the care of and jurisdiction over the Woodbury property, the calling, settling and dismissing of the minister in connection with the church, and levying taxes to pay the minister's salary voted by the town.

No mention of a "society" appears in the records until 1821, when the town voted "the interest of the funded money" (whatever that might have been), to "the Congregational society for the support of of the Gospel," and this was passed annually for several years, and it seems that this was the town's only contribution to the minister's salary, there being no mention of any tax levied for this purpose.

In 1832 it was voted by the town that "the Rev. N. Kingsbury's society keep the meeting house in repair the present year."

In 1836 it was voted "to take the money called the ministerial money to defray the expenses of the town, to be paid into the town treasury." This indicated a growing divorce between the town and its original parish functions, and in 1837 the town voted to choose a committee to confer with a committee of the Congregational society concerning "any proposition which might be made by said society for new modelling of the meeting house."

The two committees were chosen and met and reported, and the town accepted the report and passed the following votes:

1. That the town unite with the Congregational society in this place in remodeling the meeting house.

2. That one-half the ground floor of said meeting house be appropriated for a Town Hall.

3. That the town finish the Town Hall appropriated for their use, and that they sustain the roof of said house, making all repairs which may be required from time to time.

4. That the Congregational society be at the expense of all alterations excepting what pertain to the Town Hall; that they sustain the body of the house, making all repairs which may be required from time to time, and that the said Congregational society have sole control of said house, excepting the Town Hall for the transaction of town business.

5. That the town choose an agent to convey their right or interest in the meeting house to the Congregational society, reserving the right to the town agreeably to the above votes.

Jonathan Herrick was chosen the agent to make the conveyance, and he probably made it in due form, although there is no record of the same, any more than there is a record of the original conveyance by the parish to the town.

It is not probable that any action has been taken on this subject by the town since 1837, until January 18, 1890, when it was voted that "the town relinquish all claims to the Town Hall, provided that another place is provided for town meetings."

I have recapitulated these facts to show that this Congregational society had an existence many years ago, which was recognized by the town, and that it had and still has certain clear and indisputable rights in the property, jointly with the town; further, that it undoubtedly succeeded to the functions for which the parish was established originally, and which the town for several years exercised, but finally transferred to, or allowed to be assumed by, the Congregational society.

These facts had not become definitely and fully established by the record when your committee began its work, but they were assumed to exist because they coincided with the known practice of both the town and the society, and hence it was decided, on the whole, to be best to locate the new meeting house on the Woodbury lot, as retaining all rights of the society, which might be lost by removing its place of worship to another locality, and on the whole, as being as convenient a location as could be found.

To utilize this location it seemed wise to move the parsonage down the hill and erect the meeting house substantially on the vacated site. This job was let to Mr. Haviland Thompson of Milford, who began work in August, and had completed the same about the first of September. This change has been a great improvement to the parsonage, which now has a large, high-posted cellar, in place of a little hole in the ledge, and by the kindness of Dr. Kittredge has an ample supply of excellent water, whereas before it had next to none. The change also enabled other improvements to be made in the parsonage, and a considerable portion of the amount expended upon it out of the church building fund would properly be chargeable to some other account.

The total amount of money, including that represented by savings bank books at their face value received up to date, has been $11,702.01.

Of this amount, including interest reckoned to July 1, 1894, there is $832.73 on three books in the Milford Savings bank, on which only 10 per cent has been paid, leaving to be collected in the uncertain future, if ever, $749.47. There have been sundry subscriptions in work, the exact amount of which can only be estimated. The cost of the church, including the moving and improvements of the parsonage, the carpet, the chairs for the vestry, the furnaces and the pulpit, architect's services and insurance is, in round numbers, $12,000. The original proposition was to build the church, without furnishings, for $11,000. This has actually been bettered, and if our Milford Saving bank money had been good for its face, we should have come out without any considerable shortage. As it is, we shall need a round $1000 to clear up our obligations, leaving the money at Milford as, perhaps, a "permanent investment."

It is impossible to estimate accurately the number of individual contributors, as the money deposited in the savings banks represent many whose names are not known, as well as sums accumulated by the Home Circle and the King's Daughters. But of the total amount received, $8233 in spot cash was given by persons non-resident in the town, and aside from the amounts coming from the savings banks, the individual contributions of residents of the town is less than $1150, and of this amount $825 was contributed by five persons.

And now, Mr. President, in behalf of the committee, I turn over to you the keys of this beautiful house of worship, so well appointed for its purposes, and in which every citizen of this little town may, if he will, have an equal proprietary interest, and in which all should feel a common pride. Beyond and beside the sacred use to which it is about to be dedicated, it will prove that "thing of beauty" which "is a joy forever," and a material minister to the needs and wants of a community which depends so largely on the outside world for its subsistence.

The society which you represent, as I have shown, is an ancient organization, with an honorable and self-denying record. It has maintained the faith of the fathers these many years in the old meeting house, it will do no less in this more modern temple as the years go by.

DEACON CONANT ACCEPTS.

The acceptance of the building was by the president of the society, Deacon William H. Conant. The deacon spoke as follows:

"It becomes my pleasant duty as president of the Congregational society to extend our heartfelt gratitude to the building committee for its self-denying faithfulness and devotion in the months past, until they present today this completed and beautiful church edifice, admirably adapted to the purpose for which it was designed. A good Providence has raised up and qualified these men to call forth gifts, quicken enthusiasm, inspire confidence, harmonize conflicting views and manage, with wisdom and discretion, this work so as to get the best results for the amount expended. And they have spared no time or effort to make the enterprise a success.

"We also wish to express our obligation to those kind and benevolent ladies whose ancestors lived here for many generations, who suggested the building of a new church instead of repairing the old one, and who contributed so large a proportion of the amount necessary to its accomplishment. Also to the numerous friends and donors, many of whom are with us today; to the Home Circle, the King's Daughters and other organizations who have for years worked patiently and saved for this object; and to all who have by the smallest word of encouragement or in the humblest way contributed to the result.

"I accept in behalf of the society the keys to the building with a sense of the obligation which they imply and the labor and sacrifice which this finished temple represents. The Lord has indeed done great things for us, whereof we are glad. We promise that it shall be held for the high and sacred purposes for which it was intended and to which today it is dedicated. We hope it will enable us to hold the Christian Sabbath and Christian worship to us and our children in the coming years.

"And while some have thought that this church is too good for this little town on the hilltop, we regard it as none too good for the Master we love and the God we serve. It must be our effort to avail ourselves of our new and increased facilities for worship, to enlarge our faith, our zeal, our Christian hope, to the full measure of our enlarged privileges and opportunities, and to make this church a witness to the truth in the present and in coming years."

When Deacon Conant had finished and a collection had been taken, the choir and congregation sang a hymn written for the occasion by H. Porter Smith of Cambridge, Mass.

The dedicatory sermon was preached by the Rev. Dr. Nehemiah Boynton of Detroit, Mich., formerly pastor of the Union Congregational Church, Boston. His address was a masterly effort and thrilled his congregation with its eloquence. His text was found in Ephesians v : 27. "That he might present it to himself a glorious church, not having spot or wrinkle, or any such thing : but that it should be holy and without blemish."

Dr. Boynton's address was a strong dissertation on the church. He began by defining the church as the "social state permeated by the spirit of Jesus Christ." He enlarged upon his theme and painted beautifully the majestic life of love and sanctity passed by the Saviour.

Speaking of the motive of the church, Dr Boynton said it was the worship of God. "Go where you may," he argued, "and you will find that the instinct to worship will show itself in some form, even though the manifestation be a feeble one."

The preacher advocated beautiful church buildings, arguing that the beautiful is sometimes more useful than the useful itself. "No church is too beautiful for God," he said.

Rev. William H. Hopkins of Poughkeepsie read a hymn, written for the occasion by Deacon W. H Conant.

The dedicatory prayer was offered by the Rev. Warren R.

Cochrane, D.D., of Antrim, and the benediction was given by the pastor, the Rev. T. J. Lewis.

In the evening a somewhat informal meeting was held in the church, at which Hon. Geo. A. Marden presided. Addresses were made by several gentlemen, and there was music. The chief feature, however, was the raising about a thousand dollars to provide for that amount of indebtedness, due to the fact that money subscribed was locked up in several suspended New Hampshire savings banks. It is but fair to say that nearly all this amount was afterwards paid by the banks. The proceedings in raising the money were exceeding merry, and the result was that every dollar required was pledged before the meeting adjourned.

THE CHURCH EDIFICE.

The architect to whose skill and taste the little church owes its beauty, elegance and adaptedness to its purpose, was Mr. G. Wilton Lewis, of Boston. It is a model structure, and is one of the chief attractions of the village.

The general design of the new edifice is of the picturesque colonial, with details of the renaissance, and is charmingly adapted to its situation, overlooking from its lofty eminence a wide prospect over the plains below, with the neighboring villages of Milford, Amherst, and Merrimack, and the cities of Nashua, Manchester and Lowell.

The walls, to the height of the window sills, are of field stones; thence to the ridge-pole is frame, clothed with shingles. The roof is olive-stained, to complement the rustic, moss-covered field stone, separated by walls of yellow brown and trimmings of cream white. Many of the stones used in the wall were brought by persons interested in the building, picking up here and there in their drives about the country any that were distinguished for their beauty.

In plan it forms a cross, with the apse at the north, lighted by five small windows, and flanked on the east by the organ loft and choir gallery, and on the west by the pastor's room.

The auditory is 53x36 feet in area, and has a seating capacity of 300. It is well lighted at the east and west by large triple windows under the gables. Under the roof of the cloister and in the opposite wall these windows are filled with bevel plate glass, providing a fresco of nature, far exceeding that of art, in the wide and distant expanse of mountain and valley.

The remainder of the windows above are memorials in artistic stained glass, set in lead, giving richness of effect. At the south three large flexifold doors screen the Sunday school and prayer meeting room, which is of a semi-circular shape, with a seating capacity of 150; also a ladies' parlor and primary department, with 50 sittings. These last rooms open into each other, as well as the auditory, making a comfortable capacity for 500 sittings, all within good view of the pulpit.

There is an ample supper room for special occasions, provided with kitchen conveniences complete.

A ladies' room is provided, with a large brick fir place, securing comfort and ventilation.

The Sunday school library is in a niche provided for that purpose, enclosed in diamond sash doors.

The finish of the building is quartered oak, finished light, making the interior of the Puritan order, while the walls are tinted with colors complementing the woodwork, and ornamented in graceful designs. The building is heated by a wood furnace of great capacity.

There is a porte cochere at the tower entrance. The tower is large, surmounted by a belfry and lookout.

The building is practically a memorial church. The two chief donors to the building fund, Mrs. Richardson and Miss Stevens, made their contributions in memory of their father, Calvin Stevens, a native of this town, the son of Asa Stevens, and the grandson of Calvin Stevens, a Revolutionary soldier, who fought at Bunker Hill, and who spent his last years in Mont Vernon, where he lies buried; also in memory of their mother, who in earlier years was a frequent visitor in the town. There are fourteen memorial windows in the edifice, several of them large and of artistic beauty. One of these is for Deacon William Conant and his wife, given by their grandchildren. It is a figure of the Madonna and Child. Mrs. Charles F. Frasse of New York, provided a beautiful window in memory of her father, Asa Stevens, a brother of Calvin. The figure is that of St. John, and it is perhaps the finest window in the church. The friends of the late John F. Colby, Esq., of Boston, gave an elegant window bearing a representation of Hoffman's Christ, standing with outstretched arms and open hands. Mr. Colby graduated at Appleton Academy, married Miss Ruth E. Cloutman, a native of Mont Vernon, had a summer home in town for many years, and was one of its most ardent admirers. He was the father of John H. Colby of the building committee. Another of the large windows is in memory of Capt. Timothy Kittredge and his wife, the former a native, and both life-long residents of the town, and very prominent in the town and church. The window was given by their children.

Other windows are in memory of Esther Cloutman Gray, who for many years was organist of the church, one in memory of Thomas Henry Stinson, another in memory of Deacon George E. Dean, given by his daughter, Miss Harriet A. Dean of Dorchester, (Boston) Mass.; and one for John Smith.

A handsome communion table is a memorial of the late Major Charles F. Stinson, a veteran of the Civil War and a deacon of the church; this table being a gift of his widow.

The pulpit was the gift of the pastor, Rev. Thomas J. Lewis.

The old organ in the old meeting-house was considered past usefulness. The resources of the people were not sufficient to warrant a new up-to-date pipe organ. But a very acceptable substitute was found in a Mason & Risch Vocalion, built in Worcester, Mass., which is described as "a reed organ with pipe effects." It cost $855, and was paid for, $300 down, and balance in instalments, chiefly through the efforts of the Home Circle. It is substantially the equivalent of a pipe organ that would have cost $2500, and was pronounced, by prominent organists who have tried it, a very satisfactory substitute for a pipe organ. It was set up and in order for the dedicatory services.

The deed of the land by James Woodbury to the Second Parish of Amherst, for a meeting-house site, provided that if it were not used for this purpose, it should revert to the heirs of James Woodbury.

The deed was drawn by James Woodbury himself, in 1787. He was an ancestor of Judge Charles Levi Woodbury of Boston. He was a surveyor, and was granted a square mile of land on top of this hill "in consideration for services rendered as surveyor."

CHAPTER IX.

EDUCATIONAL.

The Public Schools—Before the Town Was Incorporated—
Names of Early Pupils—Aurean Academy at Amherst—A
Latin Grammar School—Money Appropriated to North-
west Parish—Appropriations Since Incorporation of Town
—The Literary Fund—Decline in Population—Increase of
Appropriations—Superintending Committees—Appleton
Academy—Its Real Beginning—First Academy Hall—Built
by Shareholders—Incorporation of Academy—Meagre Records—Organization of Trustees—Names of Pupils First
Term—Mr. Clough as Principal—Mr. George Stevens's
Success—First Printed Catalogue—His Assistants—When
and Why He Left—The New Academy Building—Purchase
of Kittredge Place by Mr. Stevens—Sale of Lot for Academy Site—Name of Academy—Library Given by Mr. Appleton—Building Fund Subscriptions—Erection of Building—
A Permanent Fund—Sketches of King, Berry, Bancroft
and Other Principals.

Mont Vernon, prior to the close of 1803, was an integral part of
Amherst. Whatever of schooling its adult inhabitants had received
they had obtained from the school privileges provided by the mother
town, and used by them as a part of its population.

By the records we find that in 1762 it was voted, "To keep a
school in five divisions, the selectmen to divide;" but as no appropriation was made, this was only a prophecy of what they would do
years later. The first appropriation was made in 1771, when the
town of Amherst voted twenty pounds lawful money for schooling,
and that "the school be kept some part of the time in several parts
of the town." Also voted that the people of the town "keep as many
schools as they see fit, and each family that does keep a school
shall be entitled to draw their proportion of the money above granted."

The next year twenty-six pounds and two-thirds of a pound were voted.

But little attention was paid to other than private instruction through the Revolutionary War. In 1778 it was "Voted to keep a grammar school," and in that and the year following the names of two teachers appear as thus employed. March 8, 1779, the town was divided into "squadrons" for schools, each to draw its proportion of the money appropriated. They made an appropriation this year, and gradually increased it each subsequent year.

In 1781 it was voted "the schools be kept by each neighborhood classing together." In 1787 a grammar school in the Centre District of Amherst was provided for, conditioned "that the district shall make up to the master in a private way what their proportion of the school money falls short of an adequate salary."

This year at same meeting, a committee of whom Rev. John Bruce was one, was appointed "to examine the ability of schoolmasters and mistresses," and none should be employed in any district, but those recommended by them. From 1787 to 1793 the annual appropriation for schools was one hundred and fifty pounds. In 1789 the town voted to "excuse such as had united for the support of an academy from the payment of any school tax, so long as they should sustain the proposed academy." The use of the townhouse for school purposes was also granted them.

Isaac Brooks of Woburn, Mass., afterwards for many years Register of Deeds at Amherst, N. H., kept a private school in the North-West Parish as follows: —

"Tuesday 8 December, 1789, began a school at the North West Parish, by an agreement with Dr. Zeph. Kittredge. The names of pupils are as follows:

Dorcas Cleaves,	Jno. Fuller,
Betsey Cleaves,	Wm. Fuller,
Sally Cleaves,	Hannah Hazelton,
Nath'l Cleaves,	Zeph. Kittredge,
Polly Cleaves,	Asa Kittredge,
Huldah Cleaves,	Ingalls Kittredge,
Amos Dodge,	Sally Kittredge,
Sam'l Duncklee,	Peter Kittredge,
Sally Duncklee,	Nabby Kittredge,
Polly Duncklee,	Rob't Parker,
Anna Duncklee,	Hannah Perkins.

Jno. Felton,   Mark Perkins,

Elisha Felton.   Sally Stearns.

Rachel Felton,

"Wednesday March 10th, 1790, finished keeping three yearly months' school."

February 10, 1791, an act of incorporation was granted for the "Aurean Academy" at Amherst. Twenty-six of the thirty-one grantees were of Amherst, and five from other towns. Nathan Cleaves was the only grantee in the Second Parish. This school soon after went into operation. It had an existence of ten years, and ten preceptors, among whom were J. Heywood and Daniel Weston from the North West Parish. In 1810 this academy was finally closed for lack of funds.

At that time a law was in effect requiring that "in shire and half-shire towns, a portion of the school money shall be applied for the support of a Latin Grammar School" or a school in which that language might be taught, if desired. This will explain the following votes:

April 13, 1801, Voted, "that the grammar school be kept eight months in the First Parish and four months in the Second Parish, this year."

March 3, 1803, seven hundred dollars was appropriated for schools, three hundred dollars of which was to be used for the support of grammar schools, the Centre District of the First Parish to have two hundred dollars, and that of the Second Parish to have one hundred dollars; and it was provided that every person in town have liberty to send to the grammar school.

These votes will explain the fact that for several years immediately preceding the incorporation of Mont Vernon, a school of high character had been kept in the Center District—a select school, open to any in the parish. David Dodge and Ephraim P. Bradford were two of its teachers.

At the first annual meeting of the new town, March 13, 1804, it was voted to raise two hundred dollars for schooling, and to choose a committee of twelve persons to class the town for the convenience of schooling. March 27th this committee presented their report, dividing the town into five school districts [classes] and defining their respective limits.

May 1, 1804, accepted the report of committee, and voted to

raise money to build new school-houses in three of the districts; voted to raise one thousand dollars for this purpose.

March 12, 1805, appropriated three hundred dollars for schooling during the current year. This sum was raised each successive year until 1822, when it was increased to three hundred and fifty dollars. In 1830, there having been a small source of revenue (about thirty dollars) derived from the "literary fund," applied to schools, the town voted but three hundred dollars which was the amount of appropriation, until, in the year 1851, it was increased to four hundred dollars, in 1853 advanced to four hundred and fifty dollars, and in 1854 fixed at five hundred dollars; which being augmented by the "literary fund" amounted to five hundred and sixty dollars, the average amount devoted to schools between 1854 and 1870. In the latter year two hundred dollars additional school money was voted, and it was continued annually for fifteen years, making an average of seven hundred and sixty dollars expended upon the district schools annually.

From 1889 until 1893, the town voted seven hundred dollars annually for schools; in 1893, eight hundred dollars; 1894, nine hundred dollars; 1895, nine hundred dollars; 1896, seven hundred dollars; 1897, nine hundred dollars; 1898, one thousand dollars; and each year thereafter to this writing (1905) one thousand dollars.

Additional to this, since 1871, the town has given McCollom Institute a total of over $7000, in payment of tuition of town pupils in this institution, in annual grants of from $200 to $300 to pay the tuition of town scholars who attended it.

The "Literary Fund" is fully explained in the following extracts from the compilation of the "Laws of New Hampshire Relating to Public Schools," by the Department of Public Instruction, from the Public Statutes, and the Session Laws, 189-1905 inclusive;

"All taxes collected by the state upon the deposits, stock and attending accumulations of depositors and stock-holders of savings banks, trust companies, loan and trust companies, loan and banking companies, building and loan associations, and other similar corporations, who do not reside in this state, or whose residence is unknown, shall be known as the 'literary fund.'

"The state treasurer shall assign and distribute, in November of each year, the literary fund among the towns and places in proportion to the number of scholars not less than five years of age who shall, by the last reports of the school boards returned to the superintendent of public instruction, appear to have attended the public schools in such towns and places not less than two weeks within that year.

"No unincorporated place shall receive its portion until a treasurer or school agent shall have been chosen to receive and appropriate the same as required by law.

"The portion of the literary fund so received by any town or place shall be assigned to the districts as other school money, and shall be applied to the maintenance of the public schools during the current year; one fifth part thereof may be applied by the school board to the purchase of blackboards, dictionaries, maps, charts, and school apparatus.

"If any town or incorporated place or the agent of any unincorporated place shall apply any money so received to any other purpose, the town, place, or agent so offending shall refund to the state treasury double the sum so misapplied."

With the decline of population has come a diminution of the number of pupils in our district schools. In 1850, the whole number was one hundred and forty-nine; and in 1860, was one hundred and sixty-seven. For the years 1884-1885 it was less than one hundred of total attendance, and now (1905) is barely fifty. The school money has increased about in the ratio that the number of those receiving its benefits have been diminished.

From 1803 to 1818, there is no record of any special superintendence of schools by an examining committee. For ten years, inclusive, from 1818, a superintending committee, consisting of three persons, were chosen by the voters at the annual town meeting. Below are the names of these, with the number of years they served:

Dr. Daniel Adams, ten years; Jonathan S. Adams, nine years; John Prentiss, one year; Artemas Wood, four years; Rev. Ebenezer Cheever, three years; Aaron F. Sawyer, three years. From 1827 to 1840-41, there is no trace of a superintending committee. The Board of Selectmen made the appointment from 1841 to 1877, since which the voters have done it at the March meeting for the choice of town officers. The persons who held the office from 1841 to 1853 were Dr. Daniel Adams, Rev. Bezaleel Smith, Samuel Campbell, Dr. Samuel G. Dearborn and Rev. C. D. Herbert. From 1852 until 1887 the committee consisted of one person only: 1853-56, Rev. Charles D. Herbert; 1857-59, Rev. Augustus Berry; 1860-64, Charles J. Smith; 1865-66, Charles A. Towle; 1867, Joshua V. Smith; 1868-72, Charles J. Smith; 1873-77, George W. Todd; 1878, J. W. Carson; 1879, Charles J. Smith; 1880, William H. Ray; 1881-86, inclusive, Charles J. Smith.

A new educational law took effect in 1886 providing for a school board of three persons after the first election, one to be elected every year, each board consisting of three persons; the first election being one for one year, one for two years, one for three years, after which every newly elected member of the board served for three years.

Charles J. Smith served in 1886, '88, '89, '90; John W. Carson, 1886, '87; William H. Kendall, 1886 to 1892, six years; Mrs. Clark Campbell, nine years, 1887-'93, '95-'98; Col. W. H. Stinson, three years, 1892-'95; F. O. Lamson, ten years, 1891-1900; W. F. Pinkham, one year, 1893; Joseph G. Carleton, two years, 1894-'96; Mrs. Annie E. Perham, 1896-1900, four years; Henry F. Dodge, three years, 1898-1901; Marietta A. Lamson, 1901-'03; Mrs. C. H. Trow, 1902-'04; Mrs. W. H. Kendall, 1903, '04. At this time the incumbents all resigned, and Messrs. Jay M. Gleason, George C. Hadley, and Willard P. Woods were elected, and are serving at this writing (1905).

The schools of late years have suffered as in all sparsely settled New England towns, from the paucity of children, the lack of money, and the scattered school districts. So few pupils were in attendance that there was a lack of the stimulus which in larger schools encourages competition in study, and excites an interest which is so healthful to the minds and efforts of children. Attempts have been made at several times to induce the town to abolish the district system, as may be done under existing laws, and to assemble all the children of school age at the Center district, where a single properly graded school might be conducted, with competent teachers, and by a concentration of money expended, longer terms might be had, as well as schools much better in character and efficiency. The wages paid are so small that it is impossible to secure trained and experienced teachers, and the entire condition conduces to inefficient and inadequate school privileges.

APPLETON ACADEMY.

The chief factor and feature in the educational history of Mont Vernon has been its Academy. This institution was incorporated in 1850, and bore the name "Appleton Academy" until 1871, when it was renamed The "McCollom Institute", which name it still bears, though it has ceased to perform the functions of an Academy, owing to changed conditions, and does duty, without change of name, as the Mont Vernon High school, having not, at this writing, a single pupil from beyond the limits of th town, and only eleven all told.

The history of this institution of learning is most interesting, and is a monument to the aspirations and achievements of the men who lived in this town about the middle of the first century of its existence, as well as to their sacrifices that their children might have better educational advantages.

The real genesis of the Academy antedates its incorporation some three years, and is to be found in a fall term of a "high school", as it was called, in the vestry in the first story of the old Meeting-House, and taught by George Stevens, in the autumn of 1847. Mr. Stevens was the son of the widow Tabitha Stevens, who had lately removed from Hancock to Mont Vernon. He was at the time a junior in Dartmouth college, where he graduated in the class of 1849.

This sort of a school had been of nearly, if not quite, annual occurrence since 1835, usually being taught by college undergraduates, and naturally many of them came from Dartmouth. Mr Stevens was a teacher of rare capacity. He not only knew, but he had an unusual faculty for making others know and remember. In this special term he so aroused the interest of the people that they were more than ever eager to establish a permanent school. And they at once set about getting ready for one.

The Centre District school-house was then a typical New England "little red school-house," standing where its successor was so soon to be erected. It was too small to accommodate the children in the district.

In 1848 the district voted to build a new school house. This seemed a favorable opportunity to secure some sort of quarters for the proposed higher school, and in November of that year the following subscription paper was started, to raise money with which to house the Academy which it was proposed to establish, by putting on a second story over the room to be devoted to the district school. The response, as will be seen below, was quick and generous.

November, 1848.

Whereas the Centre School District in the town of Mont Vernon is about to build a school house, and at a legal Meeting of said District, they voted that individuals might have the privilege of putting on a second story on said schoolhouse for a public school, etc., by paying the expense thereof,

Therefore, it is thought best to raise the sum necessary to carry into effect the aforesaid object, that it be made into shares of five dollars each, and we severally agree to take the number of shares set to our names, and pay the same when wanted to any person authorized by said shareholders to receive the same, providing enough be raised to defray the whole expense.

APPLETON ACADEMY—McCOLLOM INSTITUTE.
First occupied in fall of 1853.
(Piazza and Porte Cochere added later.)

NAMES.	NO. SHARES.	NAMES.	NO. SHARES.
Wm. Conant,	6	Asa Kendall,	1
Luther Wisewell,	2	S. N. Stevens,	1
Newell D. Foster,	1	William H. Conant,	1
H. H. Bragg,	3	I. C. Richardson,	1
J. A. Starrett,	5	David Boardman,	2
Wm. A. Starrett,	1	David Dutton,	1
John Elliott,	1	Nathaniel Bruce,	2
John Bruce,	5	D. W. Baker,	3
J. K. Smith,	5	Wm. A. Stinson,	2
Thos. H. Richardson,	3	Mrs. Hanah Whittemore,	1
Chas. A. Gray,	1	Jesse Averill,	3
Thomas Cloutman,	3	Z. Kittredge, 3d,	1
Wm. Bruce,	1	John Carleton,	1
Isaac Foster,	1	James Bruce,	2
Asa Wetherbee,	1	Mrs. Elizabeth Bruce,	1
F. O. Kittredge,	5	Timothy Kittredge,	2
Hiram Perkins,	2	Joseph Harwood,	2
Charles Marble,	1	Luther Odell,	2
C. B. Southworth,	1	Milton McCollom,	2
H. C. Dodge,	1	Joseph P. Trow,	1
Ira Kendall,	1	Daniel Adams,	3
Zephaniah Kittredge,	2	J. E. Bruce,	1
S. Bancroft,	1	Clinton Roby,	1
Joseph Trow, Jr.,	1	Bezaleel Smith,	1
Porter Kendall,	1	Mr. Joseph Perkins,	1
Matthew G. Rotch,	2	Dr. Dearborn,	1
Mark D. Perkins,	1	Albert G. Starrett,	1
Wm. G. Bruce,	1	Rev. Mr. Herbert,	2

Total. 102 shares.

The names comprise an undoubted majority of all the legal voters in the district, and also some women who had no male representatives in their families. As was to have been expected, Dea. Wm. Conant, Mr F O. Kittredge, Dea John Bruce, Dr. J K Smith, and Dea J A Starrett were the largest subscribers. The amounts were not large, but for the immediate purpose they were sufficient. The number of shares at first subscribed was 102, and the capital stock amounted to $510. Later when the Academy had been incorporated, and a commodious new Academy building was called for, these same men and women subscribed what were, for them, large sums for the object they had so much at heart.

The school-house was a very well constructed building, with a district school-room and entry on the first floor, and a room for "higher education," reached by a stairway in the corner opposite the district school entry, and an ante-room over the same. To the admiring youth and their ambitious parents it seemed a very spacious and commodious educational home. Just when it was opened for use does not appear. But at the June session of the Legislature, 1850, the following act of incorporation was passed, it being Chapter 105, of the Laws of 1850:

STATE OF NEW HAMPSHIRE.

In the year of our Lord one thousand eight hundred and fifty. An act to incorporate the Appleton Academy.

SECTION 1. Be it enacted by the Senate and House of Representatives in General Court convened that Nathaniel Bruce, D. W. Baker, Wm. Conant, S. G. Dearborn, J. A. Starrett, F. O. Kittredge, their associates and successors, be and hereby are incorporated by the name of the Appleton Academy, and by that name may sue and be sued, prosecute and defend to final judgment and execution, and shall be and hereby are vested with all the powers and privileges, and subject to all the liabilities which by law are incident to corporations of a similar character.

SECTION 2. That said corporation is hereby authorized and empowered to acquire by purchase or otherwise, suitable buildings for academical purposes, and may hold real estate to the amount of three thousand dollars, and the same may sell, convey and dispose of, at pleasure, and may receive by donation or otherwise personal estate to the amount of twenty thousand dollars, the interest of which shall be expended to defray the expenses of said Academy.

SECTION 3. That said Academy shall be located in the town of Mont Vernon, in the county of Hillsborough, and Nathaniel Bruce, D. W. Baker, and William Conant or any two of the aforesaid grantees, may call the first meeting of said corporation by giving ten days' personal notice or by posting up three notices of the time and place of meeting in the most public places in said town of Mont Vernon, at least fifteen days prior to said meeting, at which meeting, or some subsequent one, they shall choose all necessary officers and adopt such rules and regulations as may be necessary or useful, not being contrary to the laws of the State.

SECTION 4. The legislature may alter, amend or repeal this act at any time when the public good may require it.

N. B. BAKER,
Speaker of the House of Representatives.

RICHARD JENNESS, President of the Senate.

Approved July 13, 1850.

SAM'L DINSMOOR, Governor.

The "Grantees and Associates" were summoned to meet at "Academy Hall," on Monday, August 5, 1850, at five o'clock p. m., "to see if they would accept the act of incorporation," and, if they did, "to choose all necessary officers, and adopt such rules and regulations as may be necessary to carry into effect the objects of the grantees." The notice was signed by Nathaniel Bruce and William Conant, two of the grantees, authorized to call the first meeting.

It appears from this that the "Academy Hall" must have been
finished. The grantees met and were called to order by Nathaniel
Bruce who was chosen moderator, and Dr. S. G. Dearborn, clerk, pro
tem. It was voted to accept the act of incorporation, and that shareholders might become "associate grantees," and Newell D. Foster,
Dea. John Bruce, Thos. H. Richardson, Thomas Cloutman, Isaac C.
Richardson and James Bruce were added to the list of grantees.
Messrs. N. Bruce and Dr. Dearborn were appointed to draft "rules
and regulations for the corporation," and the meeting adjourned to
meet "on Monday next."

At the adjourned meeting by-laws were reported and adopted,
and a committee was chosen to invite the rest of the share-holders to
become "associates," which seem to have been the same as "grantees."

August 17, an adjourned meeting of the corporation was held,
and S. G. Dearborn was elected clerk, and Matthew G. Rotch, treasurer. William Conant, Nathaniel Bruce, Samuel G. Dearborn,
Franklin O. Kittredge, Joseph A. Starrett, James Bruce, and Hiram
Perkins were elected as the first Board of Trustees. A large number
of shareholders were voted in as associates or grantees.

August 23, a set of By-Laws of Appleton Academy were adopted,
and as they show the animus of the founders of the institution the
salient points are given herewith.

The annual meeting was fixed for the first Monday in August.
The officers of the corporation were a Clerk, a Treasurer and seven
Trustees, to be elected by major vote of the shareholders, each share
being entitled to one vote. Section 3 was as follows :

"All persons who have paid five dollars or more towards the
building which is contemplated for a public school, shall be Associates
unless they shall object thereto; and any person who has not already
paid anything toward the aforesaid building may become associated
with us, on recommendation of the Trustees, and the payment of five
dollars to the Treasurer of said corporation, taking his receipt therefor."

The Board were to choose one of their own number as President,
who was to appoint "a visiting committee, whose duty it shall be to
visit the school from time to time, and make such examination as
may be necessary to see that the school is conducted in the best possible manner; and if anything is ascertained by them which they
think is wrong, or anything is suggested to their minds which would
be beneficial to said school, they shall report the same to the Board of
Trustees, who shall forthwith take such action as is necessary in the

premises. The trustees shall also transact any business to the sustaining of the aforesaid Academy.

"They may agree with some suitable person to open a school so many terms as may be thought best, during the year, providing he will take the use of the room and open the school upon his own responsibility. But in no case shall they have power to hir teachers without being directed by a special vote of said corporation."

After providing for filling vacancies, etc., the following article, showing the expectations for future prosperity was adopted:

"ART. 9. All moneys received by donation or otherwise, after paying for the Academy building and fixtures, shall be appropriated for the purchase of such apparatus as is most needed, until said Academy is well supplied, and the residue to be retained as a fund of said corporation to be placed at interest with good security.

"ART. 10. As this corporation was not intended for a moneymaking business, but simply for educational purposes, therefore no officer in this corporation shall receive any compensation for his services, except the honor which he may win fulfilling them satisfactorily to himself and others."

The Board then organized by the choice of Nathaniel Bruce as President, and Rev. Charles D. Herbert, Dr. S. G. Dearborn, Samuel Campbell, Capt. Timothy Kittredge, George E. Dean, George W. Stinson, John Averill, Ira Kendall, Jesse Robinson, T. H. Richardson, Rev. Bezaleel Smith, Dea. John Bruce, J. H. Goodale, esq., Rev. J. G. Davis and Edward D. Boylston of Amherst, Rev. E. B. Claggett of Lyndeboro, Dr. Kittredge of Nashua, Dr. Daniel Adams of Keene, Oliver Bixby and Rev. E. N. Hidden of Milford, as a visiting commitee. The Rev. Mr. Herbert had just been called to succeed the Rev. Bezaleel Smith as pastor, and the latter had not left town, which accounts for both being on the list.

Strangely enough the record book of the Trustees of Appleton Academy does not contain any account of the first term of school which was conducted after the passage of, if not under, the act of incorporation. It was held in the new Academy Hall, however, in the autumn of 1850. Lucien B. Clough was its first principal, assisted by John Ordronaux, a graduate of Dartmouth, and since a distinguished professor of Medical Jurisprudence in Columbia College for many years. The first was afterward a most respectable lawyer in Manchester, and the last has long enjoyed wide celebrity for his ability as a public teacher of law and medicine in the city of New York.

The announcement of the opening of the school appeared in the *Farmers' Cabinet* of Aug. 15, 1850, and was as follows:

APPLETON ACADEMY
AT
MONT VERNON, N. H.

The Trustees of Appleton Academy take pleasure in announcing to the friends of education, that they have recently completed their building, and are now prepared to open it to the public.

They feel assured that the pleasant location of this Institution, and the universal interest of the people of ont Vernon will insure success. And they also flatter themselves that they have secured such Teachers as will entitle them to a patronage and give satisfaction to those who may avail themselves of the opportunity offered them.

The First Session will commence Aug. 21, and continue 12 weeks, under the instruction of L. B. Clough, A.B., aided by competent assistants. Tuition: Common English Branches, $3.50. Latin and Higher Branches, $4.00.

Board can be had in good families, including rooms and lights, for $1.50 per week. Rooms can be obtained by students wishing to board themselves.

Per order of the Trustees.

For more particular information address

NATHANIEL BRUCE, Esq.,
DEA. WM. CONANT,
D. W. BAKER, Esq.,
THOMAS CLOUTMAN, Esq.,
F. O. KITTREDGE, Esq.

The following is a list of the pupils during the term. There was no printed catalogue, but the list was preserved by Principal Clough and furnished by him, in response to a request made by the Rev. C. C. Carpenter, under date of August 16, 1884:

Averill, Almira J.	Clough, M. C.
Averill, Carrie	Clough, Abbie C.
Baldwin, Sabrina F.	Clough, F. V. B.
Baldwin, Susan A.	Conant, Walter S.
Baldwin, Maria S.	Dunbar, Annette E.
Bancroft, Wm. H. C.	Dunklee, G. W.
Batchelder, Charles	Foster, Samuel K.
Batchelder, John A.	French, Almira
Batchelder, Nancy R.	French, Clinton
Brown, ———?	Hartshorn, John A.
Bruce, Clarinda F.	Hutchinson, ———?
Bruce, George A.	Jones, Jane M. W.
Bruce, James P.	Kendall, Emeline
Campbell, Wm. H.	Kendall, Cyrene E.
Campbell, Elizabeth M.	Kittredge, Charles
Cloutman, Sarah Emeline	Kittredge, Harriet E.

Kittredge, Nancy M.
Langdell, Frances
Perkins, Ann M.
Putnam, Helen M.
Robinson, Mary E.
Roby, Kilburn
Rotch, Albert M.
Rotch, Maria Adelaide
Smith, Augusta

Smith, Elizabeth J.
Smith, H. Porter
Starrett, Henrietta M.
Stewart, Edmund P.
Stinson, Sarah Ann
Towne, Emily
Wheeler, E. M.
Wilkins, Nancy H.

The total number of names above given is 49, which was a very good number to begin with, before the school had fairly been organized. With half a dozen exceptions the pupils were residents in Mont Vernon. Mr. Clough taught but a single term.

Nothing was done towards permanently starting the school until January 26, 1851, when at a special meeting it was voted to make immediate arrangement for a Spring session of school, and Dea. Wm. Conant was authorized to procure a teacher.

A week later the Deacon reported that it was thought that the encouragement was not sufficient for a Spring term of school, and it was voted to arrange for a Fall session.

On the 3d of May, 1851, at a special meeting it was voted that individual members of the Board should "gather the necessary information relative to the school;" and on the 17th of May, Deacons Starrett and Conant were made a committee "to confer with George Stevens in regard to engaging his services as an instructor," and Nathaniel Bruce and F. O. Kittredge, were requested to draw up a paper certifying Mr. Stevens' terms, and to present the same to citizens soliciting their names to become responsible for the specified sum.

June 16, at another special meeting, Hiram Perkins and Deacon Conant were a committee to secure board and rooms for students, and Esquire N. Bruce, S. G. Dearborn and F. O. Kittredge were appointed to prepare a notice or announcement of the commencement of the school; and at an adjourned meeting June 23d, the notice was reported and adopted. The committee on board and rooms reported that they "had made ample provision."

August 8, 1851, the stockholders of the corporation elected N. Bruce, moderator; S. G. Dearborn, clerk; Wm. A. Stinson, treasurer; and N. Bruce, J. A. Starrett, Wm. Conant, John Bruce, James Bruce, Thomas Cloutman, and F. O. Kittredge, trustees for the ensuing year.

There is no further record of anything more done by the Board of Trustees this year, except to appoint, at a special meeting held Sept. 12, 1851, a large committee "to visit and report the appearance of the school at its close." No record appears of the agreement made with Mr. Stevens, or of the fact that he was engaged to teach the school at all. But there is extant a copy of the first catalogue that was printed, and its title page shows that it was "A Catalogue of the Trustees, Instructors and Students of Appleton Academy at Mont Vernon, N. H., for the Academical year ending August, 1852." "Concord: Steam Power Press of McFarland & Jenks." The year began in August, 1851.

The second page contains the names of the Trustees, Nathaniel Bruce, Esq., Chairman, Dea. Wm. Conant, F. O. Kittredge, Dea. J. A. Starrett, Jno. Bruce, Esq., Thomas Cloutman, James Bruce, S. G. Dearborn, M. D., Secretary. "Board of Teachers: Mr. Geo. Stevens, A. B., Principal; Mrs. Elizabeth R. Stevens, Preceptress, and Teacher in French, Drawing and Painting; Mr. James M. Emerson, Assistant Pupil, and Mr. Josiah M. Blood, Teacher of Penmanship."

It is perhaps a matter of sufficient interest to reproduce the names of these charter members, so to speak, of the Academy, and to give also the other pages of this first catalogue, as showing how the school started out.

STUDENTS—FALL TERM, 1851.

GENTLEMEN.

NAME.	RESIDENCE.	NAME.	RESIDENCE.
Batchelder, John A.	Mont Vernon	Hutchinson, Jesse L.	Milford
Blood, Josiah M.	Hollis	Kittredge, Charles M.	Mont Vernon
Brown, Joshua	Mont Vernon	Marden, George A.	Mont Vernon
Brown, Leonard J.	Amherst	Norton, John	Hudson, N. Y.
Bruce, George A.	Mont Vernon	Paige, Benjamin F.	Pittsfield
Buzell, George B.	Northwood	Parker, Charles I.	Bedford
Campbell, William H.	Mont Vernon	Rotch, Albert A.	Mont Vernon
Cleaves, William L.	Mont Vernon	Smith, Daniel H.	Mont Vernon
Conant, Albert	Mont Vernon	Smith, David A.	Antrim
Conant, Charles E.	Mont Vernon	Stearns, Charles H.	Lowell, Mass
Conant, Harlan P.	Mont Vernon	Stuart, Edmund	Amherst
Dudley, Lorenzo E.	Mt. Holly, Vt	Thorndike, Thomas H.	Pittsfield
Emerson, James M.	Barnstead	Trow, Henry H.	Mont Vernon
Goffe, Nathan	Bedford	Upham, Phineas E.	Amherst
Hanson, Caleb W.	Barnstead	Vent, Charles F.	Pittsfield
Hartshorn, John L.	Amherst	Wheeler, John E.	Amherst
Hutchinson, Elias S.	Milford		

LADIES.

NAME.	RESIDENCE.	NAME.	RESIDENCE.
Adams, Lucy M. K.	Littleton, Mass	Perkins, Ann A.	Mont Vernon
Averill, Caroline S.	Mont Vernon	Perkins, Emily L.	Mont Vernon
Averill, Sarah F.	Mont Vernon	Perkins, Mary F.	Mont Vernon
Baldwin, Maria S.	Mont Vernon	Phelps, Sophia E.	Amherst
Baldwin, Mary	Mont Vernon	Rand, Nancy E.	Lyndeborough
Baldwin, Susan A.	Mont Vernon	Robinson, Harriet A.	Mont Vernon
Batchelder, Mary J.	Mont Vernon	Robinson, Mary E.	Mont Vernon
Batchelder, Nancy R.	Mont Vernon	Rotch, Maria A.	Mont Vernon
Beard, Sarah W.	Mont Vernon	Sawyer, Miranda L.	Mt. Holly, Vt
Brown, Rebecca D.	Mont Vernon	Smith, Augusta S.	Mont Vernon
Campbell, Elizabeth M.		Smith, Elizabeth J.	Mont Vernon
	Mont Vernon	Smith, Maria S.	Mont Vernon
Cressy, Martha F.	Beverly, Mass	Smith, Theresa M.	Deering
Hartshorn, Elizabeth S.	Amherst	Stevens, Caroline A.	Mont Vernon
Hutchinson, Georgiana	Milford	Starrett, Henrietta M.	
Kendall, Elizabeth C.	Mont Vernon		Mont Vernon
Kittredge, Harriet E.	Mont Vernon	Underwood, Ellen J.	Amherst
Parker, Philinda P.	Piscataquog	Weston, Mary J.	Mont Vernon

WINTER TERM. 1851-2.

GENTLEMEN.

NAME.	RESIDENCE.	NAME.	RESIDENCE.
Blood, Josiah M.	Hollis	Hutchinson, Andrew B.	
Brown, Joshua	Mont Vernon		Mont Vernon
Bruce, George A.	Mont Vernon	Hutchinson, Elias S.	Milford
Campbell, William H.	Mont Vernon	Hutchinson, Hayward	Milford
Coburn, George E.	Mont Vernon	Marden, George A.	Mont Vernon
Conant, Walter H.	Mont Vernon	Morrill, Ashley C.	Canterbury
Dunbar, Stephen H.	New Boston	Paige, Benjamin F.	Pittsfield
Emerson, James M.	Barnstead	Parker, Francis W.	Piscataquog
Hanson, Caleb W.	Barnstead	Rotch, Albert A.	Mont Vernon
Hanson, John	Barnstead	Thorndike, Thomas H.	Pittsfield
		Upham, Phinehas C.	Amherst

LADIES.

NAME.	RESIDENCE.	NAME.	RESIDENCE.
Baldwin, Almira J.	Mont Vernon	Marden, Sarah L.	Mont Vernon
Baldwin, Maria S.	Mont Vernon	Parker, Philinda P.	Piscataquog
Baldwin, Susan A.	Mont Vernon	Perkins, Ann A.	Mont Vernon
Brown, Rebecca D.	Mont Vernon	Perkins, Emily L.	Mont Vernon
Campbell, Elizabeth M.		Perkins, Mary F.	Mont Vernon
	Mont Vernon	Rotch, Maria A.	Mont Vernon
Cloutman, Sarah E.	Mont Vernon	Smith, Maria S.	Mont Vernon
Hartshorn, Elizabeth S.	Amherst	Stevens, Caroline A.	Mont Vernon
Hutchinson, Georgianna,	Milford	Sawyer, Miranda L.	Mt. Holly, Vt
Jones, Jane M. W.	Amherst		

SPRING TERM, 1852.

GENTLEMEN.

NAME.	RESIDENCE.	NAME.	RESIDENCE.
Adams, Leonard B.	Littleton, Mass	Kittredge, Charles F.	Mont Vernon
Adams, John W.	Littleton, Mass	Kittredge, Charles M.	Mont Vernon
Blood, Josiah M.	Hollis	Marden, George A.	Mont Vernon
Bruce, George A.	Mont Vernon	Moore, Gilman D.	Bedford
Buzell, George B.	Northwood	Morrill, Ashley C.	Fisherville
Campbell, William H.	Mont Vernon	Parker, Charles J.	Bedford
Conant, Walter H.	Mont Vernon	Parker, Francis W.	Piscataquog
Emerson, James M.	Barnstead	Perkins, John T.	Mont Vernon
Fletcher, Edward	Littleton, Mass	Roby, Kilburn H.	Mont Vernon
Hanson, Caleb W.	Barnstead	Smith, H. Porter	New Alstead
Hanson, John	Barnstead	Starrett, William S. A.	
Hutchins, Charles L.	Concord		Mont Vernon
Hutchinson, Andrew B.		Thorndike, Thomas H.	Pittsfield
	Mont Vernon	Trow, Arthur A.	Mont Vernon
Hutchinson, Hayward	Milford	Upham, Phinehas C.	Amherst
Hutchinson, Justin E.	Milford	Vent, Charles F.	Pittsfield
Hutchinson, Jesse L.	Milford	Wheeler, John E.	Amherst

LADIES.

NAME.	RESIDENCE.	NAME.	RESIDENCE.
Adams, Lucy M. K.	Littleton, Mass	Kittredge, Lauretta E.	*
Baldwin, Susan A.	Mont Vernon		Mont Vernon
Beard, Sarah W.	Mont Vernon	Manning, Mary E.	
Bragg, Cordelia M. J.	*		Littleton, Mass
	Mont Vernon	Moore, Hannah St.	Stephens, N. B
Bruce, Frances C.	Mont Vernon	Morrill, Mary A.	Fisherville
Bruce, L. Augusta	Mont Vernon	Otis, Elizabeth E.	New Boston
Butterfield, Ann W.	New Boston	Parker, Emily J.	Piscataquog
Campbell, Elizabeth M.		Parker, Philinda P.	Piscataquog
	Mont Vernon	Perkins, Ann A.	Mont Vernon
Cloutman, Ellen R.	* Mont Vernon	Perkins, Mary F.	Mont Vernon
Cloutman, Sarah E.	Mont Vernon	Rotch, Maria A.	Mont Vernon
Davis, Harriet W.	Brownsville, Me	Starrett, Henrietta M.	
Hutchinson, Georgianna.	Milford		Mont Vernon
Hutchinson, Laura A.	Milford	Stevens, Caroline A.	Mont Vernon
Hutchinson, Mary Josephine		Stinson, Mary A.	Mont Vernon
	Milford	Stinson, Sarah A.	Mont Vernon
Jones, Jane M. W.	Amherst	Underwood, Ellen J.	Amherst
Kimball, Sarah E.	Littleton, Mass	Wallace, Marion	Manchester
Kittredge, Harriet E.	Mont Vernon	Wilson, Georgianna E.	
			Mont Vernon

* Students in Drawing.

SUMMER TERM, 1852.

GENTLEMEN.

NAME.	RESIDENCE.	NAME.	RESIDENCE.
Adams, John W.	Littleton, Mass	Ramsdell, George A.	Milford
Bruce, George A.	Mont Vernon	Ramsdell, George T.	Milford
Conant, Harlan P.	Mont Vernon	Rotch, Albert A.	Mont Vernon
Emerson, James M.	Barnstead	Smith, H. Porter	New Alstead
Hartshorn, John L.	Amherst	Thorndike, Thomas H.	Pittsfield
Kittredge, Charles F.	Mont Vernon	Tuten, Edward T.	Mont Vernon
Morrill, Ashley C.	Fisherville	Vent, Charles F.	Pittsfield
Perkins, James W.	Mont Vernon		

LADIES.

NAME.	RESIDENCE.	NAME.	RESIDENCE.
Bragg, Cordelia M. J. *		Kittredge, Ellen J.	Mont Vernon
	Mont Vernon	Kittredge, Lauretta E.	
Cleaves, Augusta, L.	Mont Vernon		Mont Vernon
Cloutman, Ellen R. *	Mont Vernon	Perkins, Mary F.	Mont Vernon
Cloutman, Mary E.	Mont Vernon	Rotch, Maria A.	Mont Vernon
Conant, Martha E.	Mont Vernon	Stinson, Mary A.	Mont Vernon
Elliott, Sarah E.	Amherst	Upton, Jane *	Mont Vernon
Harwood, Mary J. *	Mont Vernon		

* Students in Drawing.

SUMMARY.

Fall Term, ...	66
Winter Term, ...	38
Spring Term, ...	66
Summer Term, ...	28

Total.   198

TEXT BOOKS.

ENGLISH.

American School Reader; Smith's Quarto Geography; Weld's New Grammar; Parker's Aids to English Composition; Weld's Parsing Book; Paradise Lost; Goodrich's Pictoral History; Worcester's Elements of Universal History; Comstock's Natural Philosophy; Comstock's Chemistry, Revised; Wood's Botany; Hitchcock's Geology; Abercrombie's Intellectual Philosophy; Wayland's Moral Science; Cutter's Physiology; Colburn's Decimal Arithmetic; Adams' Arithmetic, Revised; Robinson's Algebra; Robinson's Astronomy; Davies' Surveying; Davies' Legendre's Geometry; Preston's Book-keeping; Wilson's Punctuation; Greene's Analysis.

LATIN.

Weld's Latin Lessons and Reader; Andrews and Stoddard's Latin Grammar; Cæsar's Commentaries; Cicero's Select Orations; Sallust; Virgil; Cicero de Senectute; Horace; Livy; Ovid; Arnold's Latin Prose Composition; Andrews' or Leverett's Latin Lexicon; Butler's Atlas Classica; Ramshorn's Latin Synonyms; Anthon's Classical Dictionary; Smith's Greek and Roman Antiquities.

GREEK.

Crosby's Greek Lessons; Crosby's Grammar; Crosby's Xenohpon's Anabasis; Greek Testament; Homer's Iliad; Liddell and Scott's or Pickering's Greek Lexicon; Sophocles Greek Verbs; Arnold's Greek Prose Composition.

FRENCH.

Bugard's French Translator; Telemaque; Charles XII; Racine; Madame DeStael's L'Allemagne; Surrenne's Dictionary; Ollendorff's Exercises.

GENERAL REMARKS.

This Institution has now been in operation one year. The success which has attended it encourages the Trustees in the prosecution of their original plan, to make it a permanent school. The uncommon fitness of the locality requires no comment to recommend it to all who have visited the place. Fanned by the purest of New England's breezes, it also enjoys the healthiest moral tone. Transgression is difficult where there are no possible means by which to transgress.

All scholars are required to attend church upon the Sabbath, also a Biblical exercise.

Especial attention will be given to such as may wish to fit for College. It is intended to make the instruction in the Classical Department of the most thorough character, and to present advantages surpassed by none, to those who may enter upon such a course of study. While no branches shall suffer neglect, Classical and Mathematical studies shall receive their place as the foundation of a thorough education.

A Teachers' Class will be formed in the Fall and Spring Terms, if desired.

APPARATUS.

A new Philosophical Apparatus will be procured before the commencement of the Fall Term. The school-room is already adorned with Geographical Maps, and both Lambert's and Cutter's Physiological Charts.

LECTURES, ETC.

The Teachers will, in the course of each Term, give lectures upon Philosophy, Chemistry, Physiology, Geography, Teaching and Morals. Physiology will be made a general exercise. There is also a general exercise daily in Mental Arithmetic.

WEEKLY EXERCISES.

There will be weekly exercises in Declamation, Composition, Spelling, Analysis of words, and Punctuation. The prominence which will be given to any one of these branches will depend upon the deficiencies of scholars.

FRENCH, DRAWING AND PAINTING.

To those who may wish to pursue these branches, unusual facilities are afforded here. Skillful instruction will be given in Pencil Drawing, Black and Colored Crayoning, Painting in water colors and oils.

EXAMINATIONS.

Public examinations are had at the close of each Term, under the charge of a committee selected by the Trustees.

CALENDAR.

There are Four Terms annually of Eleven Weeks each, commencing for the ensuing year as follows:

Fall Term,	.	.	.	Aug. 30
Winter Term,	.	.	.	Nov. 29
Spring Term,	.	.	.	Feb. 28
Summer Term,	.	.	.	May 29

EXPENSES.

Common English Branches, per term,	$3.50
Higher English and Languages,	4.00
Drawing (extra),	2.00
Painting in Water Colors,	2 00
Painting in Oils,	10.00
Music,	8.00
Writing,	1.00

Bills are made out for one half of a term, or for the whole, only.

Board in good families at reasonable rates. Conveniences are good for those who may wish to board themselves.

TEACHERS FOR THE ENSUING YEAR.

Mr. George Stevens, A. B., Principal.

Mr. John Colby, A. B., Assistant.

Mrs. Elizabeth R. Stevens, Preceptress, and Teacher in French, Drawing and Painting.

Miss Caroline M. Burnham, Teacher in Music.

Catalogues will be sent, or any information in respect to the school given on application to the Principal or either of the Trusees.

Mrs. Stevens came to Mont Vernon a bride. She was a native of Littleton, Mass., and a most worthy helpmeet as a member of the board of instruction with her husband. Mr. Emerson came over from Pittsfield, N. H., where Mr. Stevens had been teaching the Pittsfield Aeademy since his graduation from Dartmouth in the class of 1849. The residences of the pupils show that many of his students followed him to Mont Vernon. Mrs. Stevens, then Miss Kimball, was his assistant at Pittsfield.

The second catalogue contains the added names of Miss Abby W. Jaquith as Preceptress, with Mrs. Stevens as teacher of drawing and painting, Mr. W. S. B. Mathews as instructor on the piano forte, and George Bowers as teacher of penmanship and book-keeping. Inadvertantly the name of Mr. John Colby, A. B., was omitted from the list as Assistant Principal. He had just graduated at Dartmouth (class 1852), and had intended to go directly to Andover Theological Seminary, but in order to earn some money he engaged to teach for Mr. Stevens during the fall term of 1852. Mr. Colby again assisted Mr. Stevens during the fall term of 1853. In a letter written from Fitzwilliam, N. H., under date of January 18, 1905, (where Mr. Colby was then living as a retired clergyman, he having been settled over the Congregational church there for several years) he says: "I think the fall term of 1853 was the largest in numbers known to Appleton Academy. My impression is strong that it was the last term of Mr. Stevens as Principal of the institution. I cannot speak definitely of the time Mr. Stevens closed his connection with 'Appleton.' But I was there with him in the same relation to the Academy in the Fall term of '53 as in the Fall term of '52. I boarded in his family in '53. It would be difficult to estimate the number of times I took little George about the house in a baby carriage, with the announcement—'Music and Drawing taught here'—little George furnishing the Music and I the Drawing. The exact date when Mr. Stevens gave up his position of Principal I cannot give. But in a little time after my return to Andover, at the close of the Fall term, Mr. F. O. Kittredge, as Chairman of the Board of Trustees, came to Andover, and in an interview with him he expressed the desire of the Board that I would take the position which Mr. Stevens had given up. But I could not think of postponing my Seminary studies."

The above reference to "little George" may explain why Mrs. Stevens did not act as full Preceptress during the second year. In the second catalogue the classification of students is not by terms, but by classes, and into "Classical" and "English" Departments. But in the summary it is shown that during the fall term there were 101 students; winter term, 37; spring term, 80; summer term, 47. Total, 265. Whole number of different students, 160. It was, as Mr. Colby says, the largest number known at Appleton Academy.

It is probable that Mr. Colby is not quite right in assuming that Mr. Stevens left the school at the end of the Fall term, 1853, for Chapman's History of Dartmouth College has this statement concerning Mr. Stevens, which probably he furnished himself: "He taught at Gilmanton Academy from 1849 to 1850; Pittsfield Academy, 1850 to 1851; Mont Vernon Academy, August 1851 to March 1854." This book was published as early as 1867, and is probably correct.

Mr. Colby delivered the address at the first meeting of the Alumni, which occurred August 31, 1854. In this address he alluded to the completed new building, so that it must have been finished sometime during the fall term of 1853; for the closing exhibition that term was in the new building, which was so crowded with a standing audience—the settees having been removed—that the "exhibition" could not take place, and was adjourned indefinitely. But early in the morning, long before daybreak, after a big contingent of rude visitors from outer places had departed, the boys aroused the sleeping students and villagers, and the exhibition was gone through with successfully, concluding about the time it had come to be broad daylight.

The New Academy hall was the pride of the Trustees, the teachers, the students, and the people of the town. It is unfortunate that the Academy records are so meagre. It is impossible now to trace its progress to completion, its cost, or the sources of all the money which was secured for building and equipping it.

The records of the Trustees are very meagre and unsatisfactory, after the organization had been effected. Just why it was named "Appleton Academy" is not told in the records. Neither does it appear what were the conditions on which Mr. Stevens undertook to carry on the school. January 1, 1853, there was a meeting to consider a request of Mr. Stevens to be released from his contract, although there is no record of his having preferred such a request. The school had started out splendidly under his management, and the people were much disappointed at the prospect of losing him. The trustees voted, however, at this first of January meeting to comply with his request, "providing we can procure a good teacher to take his place."

January 8, 1853. Voted "to release Mr. Stevens agreeable to his request," and Nathaniel Bruce and J. A. Starrett were chosen a committee "to notify Mr. Stevens that after the close of the present term he is released from his agreement unconditionally." Two days later the trustees were informed that Mr. Stevens had been notified, and the members of the Board were "severally requested to exert themselves to find a good teacher."

The project for erecting a new Academy building must have been well underway before this, and the people were incited to effort to achieve this by the success which the school had met, and by the personal push and spirit of the Principal. His release did not seem to dampen their ardor. This enthusiasm was general, and in no wise contined to the Trustees. It seems that the corporation had already run behind.

On the 13th of May there was a meeting of the "Trustees and others" and a committee was appointed "to collect what money they could" for the Academy, and on the 20th, the committee was authorized "to see if they could procure $250 towards paying the debts of the corporation."

May 14, 1853, the Trustees voted "to build a new Academy building, and that it be placed on land of George Stevens, if the land can be bought." F. O. Kittredge, William Conant and Nathaniel Bruce were appointed a building committee, and it was voted that "the building be 38 by 58;" also voted "that the building committee trade with Mr. Stevens for land, if they can."

On the 24th William H. Conant was chosen Clerk both of the corporation and the Trustees, and Dea. Starrett was appointed a committee to procure a teacher for the Fall term of 1853.

It is exasperating to the historian, who is trying to make out a clear and connected story, to find breaks in the very official records which should make it plain sailing for him; and to be obliged to search here and there contemporary records, and miscellaneous sources of information. In this case the records of the trustees fail to tell us when Mr. Stevens was allowed to leave the school. Nor is there any story in detail as to how the new Academy was built, or just when it was finished. This much, however, is certain : A deed found in Hillsborough county records shows that on the 27th day of May, 1853, George Stevens conveyed to the Trustees of Appleton Academy the land on which the Academy was subsequently erected, the consideration being $215. In further consideration the Trustees were "to build a good picket, or tight board or other fence against the Stevens land," and it was provided that "no building or other incumbrance should be placed on the piece of land reserved for a street on the north side of the above lot, providing it is not used for a street."

This land so conveyed, was a part of the old Dr. Zephaniah Kittredge place, which was afterwards "Conant Hall," burned in 1896, and now (1905) the site of a fine summer cottage owned by Mr. C. E. Osgood of Boston. Zephaniah Kittredge, (son of Dr. Zephaniah) and Charles Wilkins are named in the deed as the grantors to Mr. Stevens. There were about seven acres in the lot, and it extended on the turnpike from the old tavern line of Thomas Cloutman to the place of S. O. La Forest (now owned by A. W. Bragg), and on the Milford road from the old blacksmith shop of Capt. William Bruce, just below the southwest corner of the Park, to the meeting-house lot, north of the new meeting-house. The deed to Mr. Stevens was dated February 6, 1852, and the consideration named was $1500. The roadway reserved was evidently the present street, running from the Milford road, just south of the William H. Conant house, since built, to the turnpike, just below George W. Averill's house, which was built by John Kidder, after this transaction.

Of course when Mr. Stevens purchased this place, he must have intended to remain more or less permanently at Mont Vernon. And the committee having been "able to trade with Mr. Stevens for the land," they must now push for the new building, that was to furnish a permanent home for their Academy, which had made so auspicious a beginning.

The institution had no doubt been named Appleton Academy in honor of William Appleton of Boston, one of her wealthy business men, and afterwards the representative of one of the Boston districts in Congress.

In the book of the treasurer, Mr. William A. Stinson, under date of November, 1853, is the following entry:

"Received of the Hon. William Appleton, by donation, a library containing about seven hundred volumes, for the use of the Institution"

It is not of record whether there had been any promise or intimation of this gift, before the school was named, but its founders evidently had "expectations" from the namesake of their academy. Mr. Appleton had often visited the town, where his mother and three sisters had resided for some years. It is said that he was not consulted as to the name, and it was felt by some that he did not very warmly appreciate the honor done him. The library was, however, a very welcome adjunct to the equipment of of the school, and was a well-selected and valuable collection of books, which have been freely used by teachers and pupils, and which were accessible to the towns-people, and to this day, are in constant use. Mr. Appleton also added one hundred dollars in cash, to his donation, in the spring of 1855.

The propriety of the name "Appleton" was enhanced by a donation of $500 in money by Samuel Appleton, a cousin of William, as is shown by an entry on a page of the Record book of the Trustees, next following a record of a meeting held August 16, 1852, but which is itself without date, to the effect that the Trustees requested that a record be made upon the book of records, "of a donation of the Hon. Samuel Appleton towards the New Academy of Five hundred Dollars, also a donation of Two hundred and fifty dollars from Dr. Ingalls Kittredge of Beverly, Mass., for the same building."

In the Treasurer's book for 1853 (William A. Stinson, Treasurer) is the following entry of donations and loans to build the new Academy, which were received in cash:

Samuel Appleton,	$500.00
Dr. Daniel Adams,	25.00

Dea. William Conant,	300.00
F. O. Kittredge,	250.00
M. G. Rotch,	50.00
Thos. Cloutman,	100.00
Timothy Kittredge.	125.00
Albert Conant,	25.00
Ladies Levee,	64.11
W. H. & A. Conant,	50.00
Rev. C. D. Herbert,	15.00
Nathaniel Bruce,	50.00
Zephaniah Kittredge,	25.00
Wm. A. Stinson,	50.00
John Trevitt,	25.00
H. H. Bragg,	100.00
John Bruce,	50.00
James Bruce,	50.00
Dea. Geo. E. Dean,	50.00
George Stevens,	50.00
Joshua Cleaves,	10.55
Ira Kendall.	5.00
Wm. L. Cleaves,	10.00
Ezra Batchelder,	3.00
Henry Batchelder,	3.00
Clinton Roby,	5.00
Daniel P. Kendall.	5.00
Ira Wilkins,	5.00
Warren Williams,	1.00
Thos. H. Richardson,	100.00
Dr. Ingalls Kittredge,	250.00
Dea. Alvah Kittredge,	100.00
Ezra Holt,	3.00
Fines of Burnham & Langdell,	8.75
Interest and Lumber,	1.95
Building Committee, (Money Borrowed,)	1625.00
N. Bruce, Auction bills,	4.76
Levee Feb. 22nd, 1854,	59.50
Asa Stevens,	50.00
Building Committee, (Note given John Elliott,)	175.00
Wm. T. Haskell,	25.00
Lumber sold at Auction,	6.75

Geo. E. Dean,	(Money Borrowed,)	60.00
Hannah Lamson,	'' ''	25.00
Greenough Marden,	'' ''	300.00
Widow Blanchard,	'' ''	400.00
Donation of T. H. Richardson,		25.00
'' '' D. R. Baker,		25.00
'' '' A. A. Gerrish,		10.00
'' '' J. A. Starrett,		25.00
'' '' Chas. G. Perkins,		5.00
'' '' C. D. Herbert,		5.00
'' '' Jos. W. Perkins,		3.00
'' '' Mrs. Whittemore,		3.00
'' '' John Bruce,		5.00
'' '' Joseph Underwood,		3.00
'' '' Samuel Baldwin,		1.50
'' '' Ira Kendall,		2.00
'' '' Sardis Johnson,		3.00
'' '' Perley Batchelder,		2.00
'' '' Henry Batchelder,		1.00
'' '' B. F. Marden,		5.00

$5319.85

This was the beginning of the enterprise of building the Academy. It is a pity that the story cannot be told more in detail. It was no small undertaking for these men, none of them of more than moderate means, to raise upwards of five thousand dollars for such a purpose. It was secured only by the co-operation of some men who could but little more than support their families, and by the widows' mites.

The Trustees' records are silent as to when work on the Academy was begun, or as to what its entire cost was. In his "Annals," read at the Quarter-Centennial celebration in 1875, Mr. H. Porter Smith says: "We remember the day that Capt. Kittredge and others came with their oxen and broke ground for its foundation." He does not give the date when this happened, but as the above list of donations is dated March, 1853, the breaking of ground most likely occurred as early that spring as the ground could be worked.

The Treasurer's book shows in detail to whom the money which had been raised was paid, but it does not furnish much information as to the details of what was done. There is no mention of any contract entered into by the building committee, and perhaps there was none. The construction was superintended by Mr. Samuel Marden, of Newton, Mass., a contractor and builder of large experience, and whose wife (born Eliza Ann Young) was formerly a resident of Mont Vernon. Mr. Marden did a remarkably good job. The Academy, which still stands apparently as sound as ever, is a handsome structure, 40 feet by 60 in size, the upper story mainly devoted to a fine hall, nearly 40 x 50, with 12 foot posts, and well adapted to the purpose for which it was erected. Work on it was rapidly pushed all summer, and the disbursements shown on the Treasurer's book indicate that about every mechanic and farmer in town was more or less employed on the building. There were frequent loans of not large amounts, from time to time, as exigences arose, and all the time there were accessions to the funds by contribution.

Not only were these contributions for the erection and equipment of the building, but there were long lists of contributions "towards defraying the deficiency for teachers' services, after deducting tuition for the year ending in 1856." Thirteen citizens are recorded as having paid an assessment of $20.43 each towards this deficiency.

There was still another subscription towards "paying the Academy debt." It is dated 1855 and 1856, and is worth reproducing, as showing the devotion and persistence of the men who were pushing the enterprise.

Dea. William Conant,	$750.00
F. O. Kittredge,	400.00
J. A Starrett,	150.00
Timothy Kittredge,	150.00
Geo. E. Dean,	100.00
James Bruce,	171.90
John Bruce,	100.00
Thomas Cloutman,	50.00
C. B. Southworth,	10.00
Wm. A. Stinson,	25 00
Samuel Campbell,	35.00
Dr. A. A. Gerrish,	25.00
Hiram Perkins,	20.00
Newell D. Foster,	5.00
Chas. R. Beard,	25.00
Daniel R. Baker,	25.00
Wm. H. Conant,	25.00

William Lamson,	20 00
John Weston,	10.00
Trask W. Averill,	10.00
Nathaniel Bruce,	25.00
Wm. O. Lamson,	10.00
Mrs. E. W. Bruce,	25.00
Matthew G. Rotch.	25.00
Joshua Cleaves,	10.00

The donation of $750 by Dea. Wm. Conant was the valuation of a house bought by him probably for a boarding house for pupils. It is now known as the "Sunset House" for summer boarders owned by W. H. Marvel.

Besides these there were several small contributions, including sundry amounts of interest due on money loaned—and very likely some of the subscriptions represented the principal of loans to the Academy. In fact in addition to the above is an entry of "Cash received of Dea. John Bruce, balance of note given up, $27.00."

The records of the Trustees, until the endowment by Mr. McCollom in 1871, and the change of name, abound in entries showing frequent "taxes" as they were sometimes called, or "assessments," or "subscriptions" to make up deficiencies of teachers' salaries, or to pay debts. But these records almost every time fail to give the details which would be most interesting.

In the catalogue issued at the close of the school year (August, 1853,) it is remarked that "the Institution has now been in operation two years. The unexpected success which has attended it encourages the Trustees to prosecute their plan of making it a permanent school. A new, elegant and spacious building, now in process of erection, will be opened for the school at the commencement of the Fall Term, 1853."

It is also remarked that "the school is furnished with a good Philosophical Apparatus." Several pieces of this apparatus are still in use.

It is also noted that "the Philorrhetorian Society, a Literary Association connected with the school is already in possession of a valuable library, which is to be enlarged the present season by books to the value of five hundred dollars presented for that purpose by the Hon. William Appleton, of Boston." This last came duly to hand in November, and was housed in a room set apart for a library in the new building.

Without finding any record showing that the Fall Term of 1853 began in the new building, it seems to be established that Mr. Stevens began the year as principal, and that the new building was moved into late in the term, and it is certain, as previously narrated, that the "closing exhibition" was given there.

Geo. Stevens was a remarkable teacher. He was not only a scholar of high attainments, but he had the rare gift of arousing the interest and enthusiasm of his pupils, and an unusual ability in imparting instruction, and in making the student work for himself. He was the prime cause of the establishment of the Academy, in securing the new building, and in starting the school on a prosperous career. Rev. Dr. Bancroft of Phillips Academy at Andover, one of Mr. Stevens's successors, in a paper read at the alumni meeting in 1890, said: "There were many who might properly be mentioned as founders of this school. It is doing none of them injustice to say Mr. Stevens was at the head of the column, and that but for him the thing would not have happened as it did, or when it did."

Mr. Stevens not only planned and pushed the erection of the new building, but he gave, from first to last, most liberally in a pecuniary way to its success, even in years after he had left it. When he came to Mont Vernon from Pittsfield Academy, he brought with him a considerable number of young men who had attended his school there, and whose character and attainments did much to give the school a reputation. They had tested Mr. Stevens's abilities as a teacher and followed him in order to further profit by them. They not only included the Pittsfield names which appear in the first catalogue (1851-52) given above, but those of Buzzell of Northwood, Emerson and the Hansons of Barnstead, Wheeler of Amherst and Morrill of Canterbury.

Mr. Stevens was born in Stoddard, N. H., October 23, 1824. His father was Daniel Stevens, a farmer, and his mother was Tabitha (Sawyer) Stevens. Later the family removed to Hancock, and later still to Mont Vernon. He worked his way through a preparation for college, and entered Dartmouth in 1845, paying his way chiefly by teaching. He graduated with his class in 1849, and at once began teaching at Gilmanton Academy, and the study of law in the office of Ira Allen Eastman, who was a Dartmouth man of 1829. The next year (1850-51) he taught the Pittsfield Academy, continuing his law studies with the Hon. Moses Norris of that town. In the fall of 1851 he came to Mont Vernon, where it is to be presumed that he contin-

ued his law studies as he found opportunity. When he had gotten
the school well started, he asked to be released from his contract with
the Trustees, and they released him. He removed to Lowell in
March, 1854, and finished his law studies in the office of the Hon.
William A. Richardson, afterwards Secretary of the Treasury under
President Grant. Three of the young men who had begun to fit for
college with him at Mont Vernon, followed him to Lowell and finished their preparation under his tuition there. They were Ainsworth E. Blunt and John F. Colby, who subsequently graduated at
Dartmouth, and William E. Barrett, who graduated at Harvard.

Mrs. Stevens was Elizabeth R. Kimball, daughter of Mr. James
Kimball of Littleton, Mass. She graduated at Mount Holyoke Female Seminary in the class of 1847, and for a time occupied the
position of secretary to Mary Lyon. She assisted Mr. Stevens at
Pittsfield Academy. They were married at Littleton, September 19,
1850.

On his admission to the bar at Lowell in 1854, Mr. Stevens at
once began to achieve success in his profession. On January 1,
1856, he was appointed Clerk of the Police Court in Lowell and
served in that capacity until August 1, 1857. The Justice of the
court at that time was the Hon. Nathan Crosby, a prominent graduate of Dartmouth. From 1858 to 1874 Mr. Stevens was an Associate Justice of the same court, and frequently presided at its sessions.
In 1858 he served in the Massachusetts House of Representatives,
but declined a re-election, saying he could not afford to spare the
time from his practice. In 1867 and 1868 he held the office of City
Solicitor of Lowell, and for five years (1874-1879) he served in the
position of District Attorney of the North Middlesex District.

There seems to have been no catalogue published of the last
(partial) year of Mr. Stevens's administration. But there is in possession of the Rev. John Colby, his assistant, a list of names of
those in attendance during the fall term (1853) who presented Mr.
Colby with "a very valuable book in 2 volumes" as "a token of their
respect and regard." The names of 41 ladies and 37 gentlemen appear on this list, and it is not improbable that there were some who
could not afford to enroll themselves; so that there must have been
over 78 pupils in attendance that term.

It is a remarkable fact that neither the records of the Trustees
nor the Treasurer's book make the slightest reference to the school
year 1854-55, during which Mr. Fenner E. King was the third prin-

cipal of the Academy. There was no catalogue published of Mr.
King's year. There is extant, however, the circular issued by the
Trustees under date of August 1, 1854, from which we learn that—

The Board of Instruction consisted of Fenner E. King, A. B.,
Principal; Miss Elizabeth A. Neilson, Preceptress; Miss Sophia M.
Neilson, Associate Preceptress. The following paragraphs, among
others, appeared in the circular:

"The new and splendid Academy Building erected the past year,
is completely finished."

"MEETING OF THE ALUMNI.—In accordance with the wish of
many of those who have enjoyed the privileges of Appleton Academy,
the Trustees hereby extend an invitation to all its former students, as
well as those who propose attending the ensuing Fall Term, to meet at
Academy Hall, Mont Vernon, on Thursday, Aug. 31, 1854, at 10 o'clock
A. M., to review the pleasant social feelings of the past; and at 2 o'clock
P. M., listen to an address from the Rev. John Colby, a former Instructor,
and remarks from those who have been connected with the school.

Per order of the Trustees,
WM. H. CONANT, Clerk."

This was to be the first of a long list of alumni meetings, a
somewhat detailed account of which will appear later on.

Mr. King had a fairly prosperous year. He was a most courteous and dignified gentleman. He was married either before the
school opened, or during the first term, as Miss Elizabeth A. Neilson
became Mrs. King before the school closed.

Mr. Augustus Berry was the fourth principal. Under date of
October 12, 1855, the Trustees are recorded to have chosen Mr. F.
O. Kittredge a committee "to wait on Mr. Berry and invite him to
meet them." Also "instructed Mr. Berry to ascertain what Miss
Bradbury's terms would be for assisting in instruction one year."
The next evening Mr. Berry reported that Miss Bradbury would not
want to stay less than $250 per year. It would seem to have been
even more important to have recorded under what conditions Mr.
Berry and Miss Bradbury began their work. No catalogue of 1855-
56 (Mr. Berry's first year) seems to have been published. But one
was published under date of January 1, 1857, which must have covered a portion at least of the year 1856, and perhaps it was intended
to cover the whole of Mr. Berry's first year. It gives the names of
the students in the "Male," and "Female" departments—the males
numbering 66 and the females 52—being, no doubt, the number of
different pupils for the year.

The catalogue, under the head of "Expenses" says that "board can be obtained at various prices, according to the quality and distance from the Academy. The usual terms per week are $2.25 for males and $2.00 for females." It was at this time that Mr. F. O. Kittredge's Mont Vernon House, (the old Cloutman tavern,) which had been purchased by himself and Captain Timothy Kittredge on purpose to furnish boarding accommodations for teachers and students, was used for that purpose, and was announced in this catalogue as available. Mr. and Mrs. Berry boarded there.

This catalogue gives the name of Augustus Berry, A. B., as Principal, and Miss Martha W. Bradbury as Preceptress and Teacher of French and Music.

The next catalogue is dated April 1, 1858, and was "published by the students," as the title page informs us. Miss Bradbury is succeeded by Miss Emily A. Snow (a sister of Mrs. Berry) as Preceptress. The number of students in the Male department foots up 89, and in the Female department, 75. But this is not very intelligible, and it is not certain just what time is covered. The names of George A. Bruce and George A. Marden are among those in this catalogue, though both left at the end of the summer term of 1856-57 and entered Dartmouth College in the autumn of 1857.

The next catalogue is dated April 1, 1859, and as before, is "published by the students." There were 96 students in the Male department and 86 in the Female department.

April 10, 1856, the Trustees chose a committee "to raise funds to pay the debt on the Academy."

June 18, 1857, a committee was named "to make the tax on the arrearages of the past year of the school, and to collect the same, and to obtain names to be responsible for Mr. Berry's salary another year."

June 28, 1858, the Trustees met to take measures to settle the Academy expenses in relation to hiring Mr. Berry another year.

July 2, it was voted by the Trustees to "continue the school another year, and that a committee be raised to make a bargain with Mr. Berry for his services as teacher." A committee was also chosen "to draw up a paper for the support of the school another year, and spend one day soliciting names or signers to bear their proportion of the deficiency if any should occur."

None of these committees seem to have reported anything, but the debts were paid, and the deficiencies were made up.

July 1, 1858, the Trustees voted "to write to Dr. Ingalls Kittredge, of Beverly, in relation to the farm willed to the Academy by his father." But there is no solution of the mysterious vote on the subsequent records.

There seems to have been a permanent fund established during Mr. Berry's term of service, though just how much it amounted to, or how it was raised is not clear. Under date of May 15, 1857, the Treasurer's book contains the following entry: "Received of the Ladies' Circle in Mont Vernon, one hundred and sixty-seven dollars for a permanent fund for Appleton Academy, the interest only to be used yearly for the support of said institution. The above loaned to the Town of Mont Vernon."

In the Trustees' records for March 30, 1859, it was voted "That the treasurer obtain what donations he can for the Academy, and that he collect the interest on the fund, on or before the 1st of July next; also that he obtain a note of Capt. Timothy Kittredge for the amount of the fund in his hands ($500), said note to be lodged with the Treasurer."

There are two more references to a "fund," but we look in vain for any clear information in the records. It is evident that there was some difficulty about insurance on the Academy, and under the last named date, the following queer vote was taken:

"Voted, that any persons applying to the Treasurer shall receive from him a receipt or certificate that they are proprietors in the House to the amount they have paid in towards the New Academy Building, and if they choose to get their property insured they can do so."

March 31, 1860, there is another reference to the "fund" in the choice of a committee "to wait on Capt Kittredge and ascertain if he intends to pay the interest on his fund annually which he promised the Academy when the debts were paid." April 13, the committee reported, and the report was accepted, but there is no clew as to what the report was.

This is the financial story of the school during Mr. Berry's stay. It was a constant task to keep the school going and the bills paid— but it was done.

As is seen by the figures given above, in numbers the Academy was growingly prosperous under Mr. Berry's charge. He was a man of rather stern demeanor, and called boys and girls alike by their first names, and was disciplinary in a familiar way. He was thoroughly conscientious, and did his best by all. Everybody gave him sincere respect and admiration as a teacher and as a man. He closed his connection with the school at the end of the summer term of 1860. In a letter written at the time of the quarter-centennial of the school, Mr. Berry said: "There was not a term while I was there, that there were not individuals who have since made their mark." "The period in which I had charge, I think was distinguished by nothing more than by the union of effort on the part of the citizens in sustaining the school, and its increasing prosperity was the result of that effort."

Miss Bradbury, his first assistant, was a most vivacious, charming and delightful woman, and a brilliant teacher. Her pupils all doted on her. Miss Emily C. Snow, who succeeded her, and remained as long as Mr. Berry did, was also a most faithful and competent teacher.

Augustus Berry was born in Concord, N. H., October 27, 1824, the son of Washington and Maria (Dale) Berry. He fitted for college at Francestown Academy, and graduated at Amherst College in 1851. He was principal of an academy at Limerick, Me., 1851-53, at Lyndon, Vt., 1853-55. Appleton Academy, Mont Vernon, 1855-60. While at Mont Vernon he was licensed to preach by the Hollis Association, and often supplied the pulpit at Mont Vernon, and in the neighboring towns. After leaving Mont Vernon, he studied at Andover Theological Seminary as a resident licentiate, and was ordained as pastor of the Congregational church at Pelham, N. H., October 30, 1861. It was his only pastorate. He died suddenly in the harness, of heart failure, after a service to one church of nearly 38 years, October 4, 1899, aged 74 years, 11 months and 27 days. He was married November 24, 1853, to Dora Richardson Snow of Dublin, N. H., who died March 15, 1875. January 30, 1877, he was married a second time, to Mary Currier Richardson, of Pelham, who was then a teacher in Bradford Academy, and who survives him, and is still (1906) a resident of Pelham.

Cecil Franklin Patch Bancroft was the fifth principal, who came fresh from Dartmouth College, where he graduated in July, 1860, the fourth in rank in a class of sixty-five. He was not only a brilliant scholar, but he became one of the most eminent of American educators, being at his death in the twenty-eighth year of consecutive service as Principal of that famous fitting school Phillips Academy, at Andover, Mass. He came to Mont Vernon with only the degree of A. B. to ornament his name. He died entitled to write A. M.,

Litt. D., Ph. D., and LL. D., after the A. B., and with a record fully entitling him to the honors.

In a letter to H. Porter Smith, which is published in the "Annals" of Appleton Academy prepared by Mr. Smith for the Quarter-Centennial of the Academy, Dr. Bancroft said: "I went to Mont Vernon in August, 1860, and remained four years. My sister (now Mrs. A. Conant) was my assistant, and George A. Marden, Miss Sarah A. Stinson, and Miss Martha E. Conant, also had classes for a short time. At that time the Academy had a fund of seven hundred dollars, and no boarding-house. One fall I had eighty scholars, and it was regarded as a great success. One year, when all my 'big' boys had gone to war, my salary amounted to four hundred and twenty dollars, and some of the time I taught ten hours a day."

After naming some of the most prominent of his pupils, he adds: "The war interest was the great one in my time, and our schools all suffered for want of men and means. I remember W. H. Conant's coming in, pale with excitement one evening, in my first spring term, April, 1861, with the news of Massachusetts men slain in Baltimore. When I resigned in 1864, our armies were lying about Petersburg apparently idle; prices went up, and receipts went down, and the wonder to my mind now is, that we accomplished as much as we did. But the people of Mont Vernon were always kind and appreciative, and my residence there, though not without many drawbacks to usefulness and happiness and personal improvement, was one for which I have every reason to be grateful. I was invited to the place without seeking it, and left it without pressure, to pursue my further studies. My interest in the school will never die. May the school flourish forever, and its friends rise up to make it a blessing to the ends of the earth, and to the end of time."

As usual the records are silent as to the coming of Mr. Bancroft or his assistant, and as to the arrangements under which he was to conduct the school. But at the annual meeting, March 30, 1861, a committee was appointed "to engage the services of Mr. Bancroft another year;" and, if possible, "on the same terms as last year." These terms are now stated, viz: "he is to take the school on his own responsibility, and if his receipts during the year do not amount to $900, he is to have the interest of the fund." In the language quotted above, Mr. Bancroft put the fund at $700, which must chiefly have been made up of the $167 received from the Ladies' Circle, and the $500 in the hands of Captain Kittredge.

On this same 30th of March it was voted "that a committee be raised to prepare a communication to be presented to Hon. William Appleton of Boston, soliciting from him an addition to the fund of the Academy." The committee made a report, but "in consequence of the exciting war news" action was postponed. Mr. Bancroft said he would stay another year if the Trustees "would find him in wood," and they at once set about raising money to buy the wood.

Mr. Bancroft continued in charge of the school through to the close of the summer term of 1864, with a hundred dollars increase of salary, and with a release from the requirement to have an assistant during the winter and summer terms. As usual a subscription was started to raise the hundred dollars increase in salary, and for money enough to pay the Hillsborough Fire Insurance Company what was due it for insurance.

Cecil Franklin Patch Bancroft was born in New Ipswich, N. H., November 25, 1839, and died at Andover, Mass., October 4, 1901. He was of plain, sturdy, honest patriotic New England ancestry. In childhood he was practically though not legally adopted by a Mr. and Mrs. Patch, of Ashby, Mass. He fitted for college at Appleton Academy, New Ipswich, graduated at Dartmouth in 1860, taught at Mont Vernon 1860-1864, graduated at Andover Theological Seminary in 1867. At his death, his close friend, the Rev. C. C. Carpenter, wrote as follows of him in the *Congregationalist* of October 12, 1901:

"Although ordained to the Congregational ministry (at Mont Vernon, May 1, 1867) he was never a settled pastor, choosing teaching as his life work, a service long and grandly fulfilled. From 1867 to 1872 he was principal of C. R. Robert's institution for white youth on the summit of Lookout Mountain, Tenn., gaining the lasting affection of many men and women of the Southern States. After a year of European travel and study (in the University of Halle) he was elected in 1873 to the principalship of Phillips Academy—the position filled for thirty-four years by Dr. Samuel H. Taylor.

"He was a worthy successor of that great teacher, though with a rule less stern as befitted the changing times. With marvellous tact, with most kindly heart and most genial temperament, with a phenomenal remembrance of names and faces, seeming to know every 'Phillips boy,' from the oldest alumnus to the youngest under-graduate, he impressed himself strongly alike on the student body and the hosts of alumni, about five thousand of whom had been in the school in his twenty-eight years of service. *   *   *   *

"As a citizen of Andover he was greatly honored and beloved.

Like his intimate friend, the late Professor Churchill, his heart and hand were in every good work, public and private. The University of the State of New York gave him the degree of Ph. D. in 1874, Williams College that of Litt. D. in 1891, and Yale University that of LL. D. in 1892. Since 1897 he has been a trustee of Dartmouth College. He was also a trustee of the state institutions at Tewksbury and Bridgewater, and had been President of the Dartmouth Alumni Association, the Merrimack Valley Congregational Club, and of the Head Masters' Association of the United States. He found time to prepare many addresses on educational topics, and to write valuable articles.

"Dr. Bancroft was also, during the whole period of his principalship, a member of the board of trustees having charge of the Theological Seminary as well as of Phillips Academy. As resident member of the board and its clerk he had a large additional responsibility, which only his ceaseless activity and his genius for hard work and for minute details enabled him to meet.

"Dr. Bancroft married, May 6, 1867, Miss Frances A. Kittredge of Mont Vernon, N. H. She died in 1898. Four children survive, Mrs. William J. Long of Stamford, Conn., Cecil K. Bancroft, instructor in Yale University, Phillips Bancroft, a student at Yale and Miss Mary E. Bancroft, a student at Smith College."

Mrs. Bancroft was the daughter of Capt. Timothy Kittredge, and was a pupil of Mr. Bancroft while he was Principal of Appleton Academy.

Again do the records of the Trustees fail in neglecting to record the engagement of Mr. Bancroft's successor, but during the summer, a committee were at work on the problem, and by the records of July 17, 1865, we find a resolution "expressing appreciation of the services of our worthy Preceptor, Mr. Towle," and a desire to retain him another year, and he was pledged cordial co-operation, and $250 in addition to the tuitions for the year ensuing—1865-66. This was Charles Augustus Towle, a native of Epsom, N. H., born June 20, 1837, fitted for college at Pembroke Academy, and at Pinkerton Academy, graduated at Dartmouth in 1864, was principal of Appleton Academy at Mont Vernon two years, 1864-65 and 1865-66, studied at Andover Theological Seminary, 1866-68, and graduated at Chicago Theological Seminary in 1869, ordained pastor of the Congregational church at Sandwich, Ill., June 9, 1869, and remained there until 1873; pastor of the church at South Chicago, 1874-76; pastor of Bethany church, Chicago, 1877-82; at Monticello, Ia., 1882-86; state superintendent for Iowa of the Congregational Sunday school and Publishing society, 1886-89, residing at Cedar Rapids 1886-89, and at Grinnell, Ia., until his death, February 22, 1899,

aged 61 years. 8 months and 2 days. While in college he enlisted for
nine months in the 15th N. H. Volunteers. He was married December
14, 1869, to Mary Jane Lay, of Chicago, who died May 8, 1881.
Was married again August 30, 1894, to Ella Reinking of Des Moines,
Ia., who survived him, with three sons and one daughter,—a married
daughter having died in 1896.

Mr. Towle was a man of stalwart physique, and a conscientious,
hard-working teacher of sterling character. There are no catalogues
of his day, so far as can be learned, and the school was diminishing
in numbers. He had two lady assistants, one being Miss Martha E.
Conant, and the name of the other is not recalled.

Joshua V. Smith, a graduate of Bowdoin College, succeeded Mr.
Towle as principal, and is said to have remained two years, presumably 1866-67 and 1867-68. The only entry on the records (and this
is on the Treasurer's book) which names Mr. Smith, is under date of
June 25, 1868, crediting the treasurer with a payment of "$20.64 to
J. V. Smith." There is no record of any meeting of the Trustees
between July 17, 1865 and March 23, 1867.

On the last named date there was a meeting of the corporation
"to take into consideration the expediency of offering the use of the
Academy property to the State for a Normal School;" and it was
unanimously voted "to make over to the use of the State for a Normal School the Academy building and grounds, with library, philosophical apparatus, piano, cabinet, etc., so long as the Normal School
shall be continued here."

A committee of three was appointed to communicate the action
of the corporation to the State commissioner, and they were requested
to communicate "what action the Town had taken relative to the
establishment of a Normal School here."

The town had begun to agitate the matter, and December 25,
1866, at a special town meeting, it was voted "to instruct the Selectmen to cause application to be made at the next session of the New
Hampshire legislature for an enabling act giving to the town of Mont
Vernon power to raise and appropriate money to aid the establishment
of a State Normal School in said town."

It was further voted that the sum which might be raised should
be $5000.

Evidently the work of keeping the Academy in operation was
becoming burdensome. Conditions which have since almost abolished
the country academy in New England had begun to come.

Nothing, however, was done under the vote above recorded, and on the 18th of August, 1868, at a meeting of the Trustees, it was voted, as a means of broadening the interest in the school, "to make some addition to the board of trustees of gentlemen interested in the cause of education, resident among us," and Rev. Dr. Keeler, Mr. Albert Conant, Mr. William Stevens, Mr. H. H. Bragg and Charles J. Smith were unanimously chosen. These must have been considered honorary elections, as the number of trustees was fixed.

August 24, 1868, a committee was appointed to make to the coming alumni meeting, to be holden August 26, some statement of the present conditions of the institution; and at an adjourned meeting August 31, a committee was appointed to consider a proposition of William H. and Albert Conant, in regard to a boarding-house, which proposition is stated further on.

Meantime Mr. Smith had continued at the head of the school, which could hardly have been counted prosperous. There seem to have been no catalogues issued, and nothing further put on record concerning the Academy.

Sometime in the summer of 1868 there was a determined effort to secure a fund of $5000 for the support of the Academy. A subscription of a considerable amount was made, which resulted, in the end, in action at the meeting of the alumni as thus described in the *Farmers' Cabinet* containing a report of the meeting:

" It appeared that it had been in contemplation for some time to endeavor to do something toward raising a fund for the school, and put it on a firm foundation. As a step in that direction, William H. Conant of Mont Vernon and Albert Conant of Boston, had purchased the Campbell place (the old Dr. Kittredge place) which they proposed to fit up for a boarding-house for the school, provided a fund of $5000 could be raised. In a brief speech, George Stevens, Esq., the founder of the school, urged energetic action, and as evidence that his heart was in the work, booked his name for $500. Mr. Asa Stevens of New York, came down with a round $1000; and Messrs. William Stevens and F. O. Kittredge, of Mont Vernon followed with subscriptions of $500 each. Other sums varying from $25 to $200 were subscribed, and at the close of the dinner the sum of $1100.00 was pledged. A committee of ten (five ladies and five gentlemen) was appointed to solicit further donations, and it is hoped that the sum will be raised to $10,000."

The original subscription paper is in the hand writing of George Stevens, and is as follows :

We the undersigned, agree to give our several notes to the corporation known as "Appleton Academy," for the sums set against our
respective names, of which we will annually pay to the Trustees of
said corporation the interest for the use of said Academy located in
Mont Vernon. N. H., and for the support of a school therein, and the
principal thereof we agree to pay in ten years from date.   These
subscriptions however are upon the express condition that a permanent fund of Five Thousand Dollars at least, including these subscriptions, shall be raised for the support and maintenance of said school
in said Academy, of which fund no more than the income or interest
shall ever be used for said purpose.

NAME.	RESIDENCE.	AMOUNT.
Geo. Stevens,	Lowell.	$ 500
Geo. A. Marden,	Lowell,	100
Geo. A. Bruce,	Boston.	100
T. L. Livermore.		25
Asa Stevens.	New York,	1000
W. Stevens.		500
T. H. Richardson,		100
C. F. Kittredge,		100
F. O. Kittredge.		500
H. H. Bragg.		100
John Bruce,		50
Walter S. Conant,		100
H. P. Conant.		200
Augustus Berry,		25
Chas. F. Stinson,		25
Henry E. Spalding,		25
J. V. Smith.		100
J. E. Bruce,	Milford.	50
John F. Colby,		100
W. H. Curtis,		50
H. C. Shaw,		25
Mrs. J. J. Phillips,		100
Geo. E. Dean.		25
A. W. Bragg.		25
Geo. W. Ordway,	Chicago.	25
Geo. W. McCollom.		100
Chas. E. Conant,		200
Henry A. Kendall,		100

Andrew Dutton,	100
H. Porter Smith,	100
Benj. J. Boutwell,	50
Mrs. Loveredge,	50
D. E. Kittredge,	25
Timothy Kittredge,	500
C. F. P. Bancroft,	50

Dated, Sept. 1, 1868.

The subscriptions were not in cash, but notes, which were printed as follows :

APPLETON ACADEMY.

WHEREAS, divers persons, of whom I am one, have agreed with each other and with the APPLETON ACADEMY, an incorporated educational institution, located in Mont Vernon, in the State of New Hampshire, to give and to pay to said APPLETON ACADEMY, each a certain sum of money, which he has set against his name upon a paper of subscriptions signed by him, and which is named in the note hereon written, in ten years from date, with interest to be paid annually, for the purpose of making in the aggregate a fund of not less than five thousand dollars, for the purposes of education in the Academical School of said body corporate ; which fund is to be managed and invested by the trustees of said APPLETON ACADEMY, and the income thereof and no more ever to be used for the purpose of giving education to the youth of both sexes, in the Latin, Greek, and Modern languages, and also in the various branches of a thorough literary, mathematical and scientific education in the English language :

Now, in consideration of the above agreements and subscriptions, and of the acceptance hereof by said APPLETON ACADEMY, and that the said fund shall not be less than five thousand dollars, I hereby make the promissory note written hereon, the proceeds of which are to be used in the manner and for the purposes set forth above, and no other.

$100.   Mont Vernon, Sept. 1st, 1868.

Ten years after date, for value received, I promise the APPLETON ACADEMY, a body corporate, located in Mont Vernon, in the State of New Hampshire, to pay it one hundred dollars, with interest at the rate of six per cent. per annum, payable annually.

. . . .

Of these notes there still remain "alive" but those of W. H. and A. Conant ($1500), and John F. Colby ($100) on which the interest has been regularly collected to date. Of the others many were paid in full, or "settled" on some basis, though why for less than their face does not appear. There still remain in the hands of the Treasurer notes amounting to $1200 on which interest was collected only a few years, and which are now of course "outlawed," and are without value, even where the makers are still living.

It is of record that at a meeting of the Trustees August 31, 1868, it was voted that the Secretary be instructed to write to Asa Stevens of New York and George Stevens of Lowell, and others, expressing the thanks of the Trustees for their generous donations to the institution.

The Academy was now "in fund," if not "in funds." The notes above referred to were mostly dated September 1, 1868, and at once began to draw interest. It might have been expected that the names of William H. and A. Conant would have appeared in the list of note contributors; but they two had purchased the old Kittredge or Campbell place (the same place which Mr. George Stevens had bought when he first took the Academy) and had agreed to give it to the institution for a boarding house. January 9, 1869, at a meeting of the Trustees, it was voted:

"That if W. H. and Albert Conant shall give to the Appleton Academy corporation their note for fifteen hundred dollars, with interest annually, the same as other members of the alumni, that they shall be released from all obligation in regard to the Campbell Place, so-called, as a boarding-house for the Academy, and they shall have full control of the same, this sum being the original cost of the place."

Under date of June 25, 1869, the Treasurer's book records the fund account as consisting of the Town Note (money raised by the Ladies' Circle, and loaned to the Town) $167.00. Notes on hand, as per subscription list, $5225.00. W. H. and A. Conant's note taken in lieu of the Campbell place, $1500.00. There was a small note besides, of Deacon J. A. Starrett, of $23.12, and the total fund figured up $6915.12. The Treasurer added all the accrued income, during the year, making a total of $7369.22, but of course this was a mixing of fund account and cash account not quite intelligible. The income at 6 per cent, which was the legal rate, amounted, however, to over four hundred dollars a year, and that was a great relief to the over-burdened promoters of the school.

Still the Academy was languishing, and we have to go outside the scrappy records of the board to gather that Mr. Smith left at the close of the school year 1867-68. Nor do we learn, except by implication, that there was no school at all during the year 1868-69, or what was doing, if anything, during that year. There is no record of the engagement of Prof. Lucien Hunt to teach for the year begin-

ning in August, 1869, but in the Treasurer's book, under date of May
25, 1869, it is stated that there was paid to Prof. L. Hunt, to date,
$500.00; and tradition says that he was principal until the close of
the school year 1869-70. His assistants were Mr. S. A. Holton (afterwards Principal of Lawrence Academy, Falmouth, Mass.,) Mr.
A. M. Goodspeed of Falmouth, and Mrs. Hunt.

And now reappeared the scheme to get the state to locate its
proposed Normal School at Mont Vernon, and September 20, 1870,
the Trustees held a meeting to consider the proposition of the state
for a Normal School location, and on motion of Deacon William
Conant, it was unanimously voted—

"That the Trustees of the Appleton Academy offer to the state
the use of all the property belonging to the corporation, provided the
State Normal school shall be located in this place, during its contin-
uance here, provided the state shall keep the buildings and other
property in good repair;" also voted—

"That the Secretary and Rev. Dr. Keeler be a committee to
write to the different donors to the fund of the Academy to obtain
their consent to allow the funds to be used in aid of the Normal
school;" also voted that the same committee —

"Make out a statement of the property belonging to the Academy, and offer the same to the State. Voted, further, that the same
committee take measures to have the selectmen of the Town call a
town meeting to see if the Town will make any appropriation for the
support of said Normal School."

Again we learn, from sources outside the records of the Trustees,
that Mr. D. A. Anderson, a Dartmouth graduate, was the principal
of the school, beginning with the Fall term of 1870, and that he
remained two years, with very moderate success. A catalogue was
issued in November, 1871, which shows that the Trustees were Dea.
George E. Dean, President; Rev. Seth Keeler, D. D., Sylvanus
Bunton, M. D., William A. Stinson, William Conant, William
Stevens, Dea. John Bruce, Thomas H. Richardson, George Stevens
(honorary member) Lowell, Mass.; George W. McCollom (honorary
member) New York; William H. Conant, secretary, and F. O.
Kittredge, treasurer.

The instructors were D. A. Anderson, A. M., Principal; Miss
Martha E. Conant, Preceptress; Miss Mary C. McIntire, assistant
pupil; Miss Laurania Smith, teacher of music; A. F. Newton,
teacher of penmanship.

There was one in the graduating class, Frank Richardson of Milford. There were seven gentlemen and nine ladies in the classical department, forty gentlemen and twenty-five ladies in the English department, and there were in all twenty-eight pupils during the winter term, twenty-eight in the spring, and fifty-four in the fall.

The catalogue gives the information that "the discipline of the school is entrusted to the Principal," and that "it is intended to be mild but efficient." A capacious boarding-house is kept by William H. Conant, and expenses are: tuition, English branches, $5.00 a term; languages, $7.00; music, $10.00; use of piano, $2.00; board per week, including room-rent and washing for bed, $3.50.

Presumably, this catalogue was for the school year 1870-71—but this is only a guess. It may have been for a part of the two years covered by Mr. Anderson.

CHAPTER X.

EDUCATIONAL CONTINUED.

McCollom Institute Succeeds Appleton Academy—Endowment by George W. McCollom of New York—Charter Amended—Mr. Anderson's Principalship—He Served both Appleton Academy and McCollom Institute—A Liberal Fund Well Invested—George W. Todd as Principal—Great Prosperity—Large Classes—Dissatisfaction among Donors at Change of Name—Affects the "Gratuity Notes"—Why Prof. Todd Left—Principalship of W. H. Ray—Prof. Lucien Hunt (who takes the school a second time)—Hiram Q. Ward—Cassius S. Campbell—Improvements to Building and Apparatus—Oscar S. Davis as Principal—Prof. J. B. Welch Succeeds Davis—The Dean Place Bought for Principal to Live In—Trustees Authorized to Hold More Property—Trustees Incorporated and Why—By-Laws of New Corporation—G. W. Cox as Principal—G. S. Chapin Succeeds Him—School Suspended for Year 1900-1901—Building Repaired—Rev. H. P. Peck Conducts the School for the Year 1901-1902—The Institute as a Town High School—Rev. Mr. Peck and Miss A. L. Williams Teachers—Mr. and Mrs. Leslie A. Bailey Succeed Them—Then Prof. Henry W. Delano—Triennial Alumni Reunions.

Early in the year, 1871, George W. McCollom, then of New York City, offered to the Trustees, as a permanent endowment, the sum of ten thousand dollars, provided that they would cause the name to be changed from Appleton Academy to that of McCollom Academy, and provided further that the town of Mont Vernon should for five successive years, raise and pay to the institution the sum of three hundred dollars, being an aggregate amount of fifteen hundred dollars. The conditions were complied with, and now for thirty-four years the school has enjoyed the income from this valuable endowment. Mr.

McCollom was a native of New Boston, but came with his parents to Mont Vernon to reside in early life. He married the eldest daughter of Asa and Mary A. (Appleton) Stevens of this town. She died in New York in 1865, and her husband's donation was intended as a grateful memorial of her. A marble tablet p'aced by him in the hall of the Institute bears this inscription: "Endowed by George W. McCollom in memory of his wife Mary Ann S. McCollom."

Mr. McCollom died in New York, September 4th, 1878.

Just how the proposition came to be made for a change of name of Appleton Academy to McCollom Institute does not appear; but it was probably owing to a suggestion made by the Treasurer, William H. Conant, who was fertile in plans for securing advantages for the school.

At a meeting of the board of trustees June 5, 1871, it was voted:

"That in consideration of the offer of George W. McCollom of New York to give an endowment of ten thousand dollars if the name of the institution shall be changed from Appleton Academy to McCollom Academy, that the trustees comply with that condition;" and also voted:

"That Dea. Bruce and Rev. Dr. Keeler be a committee to carry out the above vote by petitioning the Legislature for such a change of name."

The Trustees met on the 8th of June to hear the report, and recommitted it for the petition to be revised and amended, and forwarded to the Legislature at an early day.

On the 12th of June the Trustees voted that when the name is changed it be called McCollom Institute, provided Mr. McCollom did not object. Whose idea this was does not appear, but it was a most unfortunate change, and the name "Institute" has been a constant burden to the school ever since.

The name of the institution was changed to McCollom Institute by the following act, which was approved, July 7, 1871:

STATE OF NEW HAMPSHIRE.

In the year of our Lord, one thousand eight hundred and seventy-one. An act in amendment of an act to incorporate the Appleton Academy, Mont Vernon, N. H.

Be it enacted by the Senate and House of Representatives in General Court convened.

SECTION 1. That section one of the act entitled an "Act to incorporate the Appleton Academy" be amended by striking out the words

"Appleton Academy" and inserting instead thereof the words "McCollom Institute."

Section 2. All acts or parts of acts inconsistent with this act are hereby repealed, and this act shall take effect from and after its passage.

WILLIAM H. GOVE,

Speaker of the House of Representatives.

G. W. M. PITMAN, President of the Senate.

Approved July 7th A. D., 1871.

JAMES A. WESTON, Governor.

Messrs. F. O. Kittredge, W. H. Conant and William Stevens were a committee to thank Mr. McCollom for his generous endowment, and to receive and invest the amount as a fund for the benefit of the Institute.

Mr. Anderson's second year was as principal of the " McCollom Institute," and the Trustees, being now well-to-do financially, voted him four hundred and seventy-five dollars in addition to the tuitions. The Treasurer's book for October, 1871, shows a fund amounting to $17,206.87. The subscription notes contributed in 1868 were all paying six per cent., and one of the halves of Mr. McCollom's endowment was in a western railroad bond which paid seven per cent. The other half was in a good 7 per cent. mortgage.

In the spring of 1872 a proposition was made to enclose the Academy grounds with a fence, and in the autumn of the succeeding year it was done. It was not many years, however, before the community were as anxious to get rid of the fence as they had been to have it built.

In 1872 George W. Todd, of Rindge, N. H., became the tenth principal, a man of untiring zeal, great executive ability and experience. He at once associated with himself, as classical teacher, Rev. Charles P. Mills, an accomplished scholar, a graduate of Amherst College, and later in the ministry at Newburyport, Mass., and serving afterward with distinction in the Legislature of Massachusetts. Mr. Todd held the office of principal six years, retiring in 1878. His later assistants were Messsrs. F. A. Eldredge and G. W. Putnam, graduates respectively of Harvard and Dartmouth.

The first year, Mr. Todd was to receive from the fund income six hundred dollars, in addition to the tuitions, and the Trustees were to pay the salary of Miss Martha E. Conant as assistant, but Mr. Todd was to pay all the other expenses of the school.

The change of name of the institution gave great offence to some of the previous benefactors of the school, and the interest on some of

the subscription notes was defaulted, and later the principal. In one
or two instances the givers of the notes compromised by paying a
reduced sum.

Of the notes given, the following were at different times paid in
full to the institution:

George Stevens,	Lowell,	$500.00
George A. Marden,	"	100.00
George A. Bruce,	Boston,	100.00
Thomas L. Livermore,	"	25.00
William Stevens,	Mont Vernon,	500 00
T. H. Richardson,	"	100.00
H H. Bragg,	"	100.00
John Bruce,	"	50.00
H. P. Conant	Boston,	200.00
Augustus Berry,	Pelham,	25 00
Henry E Spalding, M. D.,	Boston,	25.00
J V. Smith,		100.00
J. E. Bruce,	Milford,	50.00
George E. Dean,	Mont Vernon,	25.00
Alonzo W. Bragg,	Boston,	25.00
George W. Ordway,	Chicago,	25.00
George W. McCollom,	New York,	100.00
Charles E. Conant,	Boston,	200.00
Andrew Dutton,	"	100.00
Benjamin J. Boutwell,		50.00
Mrs Loveredge,	New York,	50.00
Darwin E. Kittredge,		25.00
Timothy Kittredge,	Mont Vernon,	500.00
C. F. P. Bancroft,	Andover, Mass..	50.00
Asa Stevens's note for $1000 (compromised),		350 00

With the exception of the note of W. H. & A. Conant of $1500,
and John F. Colby's note for $100 (which has been assumed by his
son, John H. Colby) and which are still alive, the interest having
been paid up to date, all the notes given in 1868, not paid, as shown
above, have become void under the statute of limitations This
shows $3375 collected, and $1600 still collectible—a total of $4975.
About $1100 seems to have defaulted.

There was a catalogue issued for 1873-74, which was probably
the first one of Mr. Todd's administration. The Trustees of McCollom Institute at this time were Rev. Seth H. K eler, D. D., President,

Dea. George E. Dean, Sylvanus Bunton, M. D., William A. Stinson, Dea. William Conant. William Stevens, and Thomas H. Richardson. George W. McCollom of New York, George Stevens of Lowell, and Albert Conant of Boston were recorded as "Honorary Trustees;" William H. Conant was Secretary, and Daniel R. Baker, Treasurer.

The board of teachers consisted of George W. Todd, LL. B., Principal, Miss Martha E. Conant, First Assistant, Mrs. George W. Todd, Second Assistant, Miss Martha Aldrich, Assistant. Spring term, Miss Emma D. Putnam, Assistant Pupil. Winter term, Miss Laurania Smith and Miss Ellen B. Richardson, teachers of music.

The summary gives twenty-four gentlemen and twenty-two ladies in the Classical Department, forty gentlemen and twenty-nine ladies in the Higher English, and fifteen gentlemen and six ladies in the Common English. In the Fall term (1873) the total number of pupils was eighty-one, in the Winter (1873-74) eighty-eight, and in the Spring (1874) ninety-one.

For the first time the catalogue is adorned with a lithographic cut of the Academy building, which shows the new fence which had been built around the grounds.

The students were furnished board at various homes in the village, and Conant Hall, which had been first purchased and fitted up and presented to the Trustees for a boarding-house, was now advertised as a place where pupils could engage board of William H. Conant, who had become its proprietor, and who also conducted it most successfully as a summer boarding-house.

The catalogue gives other information as to the Institute, under its new career: "The average age of students here is 18 years and 4 months—a significant fact," says the catalogue. "The prosperity of this school for the past two years," it goes on. "has been almost unparalleled, having risen in average attendance from 36 in 1871-72 to 86 in '73-'74."

"The Principal has taught twenty-four years, and is engaged for the third year," Mr. Todd having begun his work with the Fall term of 1872.

August 25, 1873, the Trustees voted Mr. Todd the sum of one hundred dollars to purchase apparatus.

October 30, the same year, the Trustees met "to consider the matter of building a Hotel in accordance with a vote of the town to appropriate five thousand dollars for the purpose." A committee of five—Rev. Dr. Keeler, W. H. Conant, Daniel R. Baker, William

Stevens, and Prof. G. W. Todd—was appointed "to prepare a subscription paper and solicit funds for the purpose."

July 27, 1874, the Trustees voted to offer the position of assistant
the coming year, to Mr. Charles P. Mills, a recent graduate of
Amherst College, and to offer him two hundred and fifty dollars per
term, it being a proposition of Mr. Todd "to pay fifty dollars of this
amount per term, provided the Trustees would in some way raise the
balance."

As usual there is no record that the committee appointed to carry
out this vote ever reported, but Mr. Mills came, and in April, 1875,
they voted to endeavor to engage Mr. Mills for another year on the
same terms. This was done, and a lack of boarding places was made
good by special effort. The price for board had increased like everything else, but "including room and washing for bed" it was still but
three dollars and fifty cents per week.

In April, 1876, Mr. Todd was engaged for the school year
beginning in September, he to furnish all the assistance, and pay all
the running expenses, and to receive, in addition to the tuitions, the
sum of eight hundred dollars from the Trustees.

This agreement was renewed for the next school year, (1877-78),
at the close of which, Mr. Todd's connection with the school ceased.

Mr. Todd was a most energetic and pushing man, and the school
was quite prosperous under his administration. Mr. Mills proved a
most valuable assistant. It does not appear who succeeded him, but
in the catalogue for 1876-77 under the head of First Assistant, no
name appears, but the words "Best man and ripest scholar that can
be obtained." In this catalogue also appears the name of Mrs. S. J.
(Trevitt) Bunton as "teacher of all kinds of painting." G. L. Adams
was teacher of penmanship.

As was the custom, the principal of the Institute was usually
elected (when he would accept it) as Superintending committee of
the Town schools. Mr. Todd filled this position several of the years
while in Mont Vernon, and he carried the same energy and push into
his administration of this office as he did in managing McCollom
Institute.

In his last report to the town as Superintending committee, made
in the spring of 1878, he gives a brief history of his connection with
the Institute, which was thoroughly characteristic, and which contains
the reasons why he left, as follows:

"Nearly six years ago we became principal of this school. Before we came into town we were strongly advised not to come, for we could not succeed without much expense and much opposition in various forms. But not afraid of soiled clothes, bare hands or hard work, we went to work with high hope and good resolution. We were self-conceited enough to think we knew how to manage a school of this kind successfully. With these feelings we made our preparations. The first year the school was small, but larger than for some years previous. It required the first year to decide the people whether we were capacious enough to fill the place. During the next four years (12 terms) most of the terms numbered eighty,—ranging from that to one hundred and two,—the average being above eighty for the whole four years. To keep the school up to a high standard we have paid out (including next term) $1650 for assistance, upwards of $1000 for stationery, postage and printers' bills, above $700 for fuel, and $200 for repairs to building and furniture, improvement of grounds and apparatus. This last sum we have mostly raised by Exhibitions. During these four years we claim that our labors have resulted in bringing more dollars into town than those of any other man. By far the largest portion of the money paid us here has been spent and in this town, too, when we could obtain what we needed, paying above $1000 over the counter of one store for supplies, and above another $1000 for fuel and farm products. We claim also to have contributed our full share to benevolent objects abroad, to public enterprises at home, and to the support of preaching and other religious matters in town. In these respects conscience does not reprove us in the least.

"Two years ago at this time the school reached its highest point. For a good while about that time we heard, and heard of, a good deal of talk about the enormous sum of money we were making and how fast we were getting rich. We were often told and knew as well, that we had reached the zenith of our glory here. One year we paid Mr. Mills $150, the next year $175. The retention of Mr. Mills left the trustees nearly $300 in debt.—Now every dollar of that debt is liquidated by reduction of our income during these last two years. It is admitted, we have made some money; but have we not worked hard for it? We took the school in a very reduced condition and furnished the needful to raise it to a good standing. Surely we have a right to reap where we sow. Honestly, we believe the net income from one of our largest boarding-houses is better for six months than is ours for six years. We mean to give full credit for what the town, the Board of Trustees, and friends have done for the school and for us. We feel that we have worked faithfully for the interests of the town, the Institute and the public schools, and the varied enterprises of home interest since we have been a citizen of the town. At the close of the Spring term we are to dissolve our connection with the school, trusting as the rising sun eclipses the setting sun, and the welcome new takes the place of the departing old, the school will witness a return of patronage, a new revival of interest, a new and long lease of prosperity. It has had a season of remarkable prosperity and usefulness. Twenty-four have graduated the last three years. Representatives of that number are in five different New England colleges now. A fair sized class is expected to graduate next term. We do not take this step because we feel entirely devoid of friends. Kinder-hearted, more obliging, or more accommodating neighbors we never had and never desire to have while we live. Our reasons for this step are various. The school is much reduced in numbers.— *We do not feel it* to be our fault. The causes are various.—Some out of town, and in town, say the people are not in harmony with us,— some, that the Trustees desire this step,—some, that our politics are in the way—but most say it is the 'hard times,' little business and less money.

"1st.—No man can run the school, as a scientific and classical school, without an able male assistant. No one female teacher in a thousand could fill the place of Messrs. Mills, Chapman, Putnam or Eldridge, and that one would want, and could command as good pay as either of them had. The income, with present patronage, will not meet expenses. We can not lay up a dollar this year beyond moderate day wages for a common farm laborer.

"2nd.—Compared with two years ago the town has withdrawn above 40 per cent. of its patronage this year.

"3rd.—We are well acquainted with the schools of this town and see but very few in them who will be fitted to enter the Institute for three or four years to come.

"4th.—A good many of our patrons are slow in the payment of bills, so slow that we have twice had to discount notes at the bank to pay our assistants. At the time of writing we hold fifty unpaid tuition bills, mostly against our friends in town. These bills vary in time from a few weeks to three years.

"5th.—Not to attend church regularly would be a scandal. To attend is to suffer for the next day or two, and the prospect of a better state of things very soon is dim. Smoke is bad to breathe.

"Last and not least.— We need release and rest from the long and constant anxiety, severe labor, continued care and nervous wear peculiarly incident upon a school of this kind."

Mr. Todd was elected to the New Hampshire State Senate from this district in 1879-80. His death occurred from typhoid pneumonia at Norridgewock, Maine, where he had just gone to assume the position of Master of the High School, on the 15th of April, 1884.

William H. Ray, a Dartmouth graduate, succeeded Mr. Todd, at the beginning of the Fall term, 1878. He was to have seven hundred dollars from the fund income, and all the tuitions, was to furnish a competent female assistant, and pay all the running expenses of the school, and the Trustees' records add:

"It is also expected that he will remain at least five years."

PROF. LUCIEN HUNT.

In April, 1879, the length of the Fall and Winter terms was made thirteen weeks each, and the Spring term twelve weeks, thus lengthening the school year by two weeks. Capt. John Trevitt and the Rev. W. H. Woodwell, the latter having succeeded the Rev. Dr. Keeler as pastor of the church, now appear on the list of Trustees, though no record of their being elected is found. Daniel R. Baker, Treasurer, having died, Capt. John Trevitt was chosen in his place.

Mr. Ray resigned in February, 1881, to take effect at the end of the school year, and the school was kept through by Mr. William Whiting of Dartmouth College. Mr. Ray going to a position in the public schools in Yonkers, N. Y.

The catalogue for 1878-80 shows that Mr. Ray was assisted by Miss Mary A. Loveland, Miss Ellen F. Conant, Mr. George W. Putnam, A. B., and Miss W. Farwell. It was the most elaborate catalogue ever published of the school, and contained an earnest appeal for an addition to the funds and equipment. Mr. Ray was an accomplished teacher, and held several important positions after he left Yonkers, being finally at Hyde Park, Ill., a suburb of Chicago, where he died.

Mr. Lucien Hunt, who was the eighth principal in 1869-70, was invited to return and take charge of the school as the eleventh principal after Mr. Ray's last year. He was to have eight hundred dollars a year from the income of the fund for two years, and after that seven hundred dollars. He was to have all the tuition, all income from any use of the hall, and was to pay all the expenses of the school, the Trustees to keep the building repaired. The Trustees put this declaration on record: "We hope this arrangement will be so satisfactory to both parties that it will be a permanent one, and for the lasting benefit of the institution."

January 22, 1882, the board chose the Rev. C. C. Carpenter, president, and Prof. Hunt, a member of the board.

Mr. Hunt was a most excellent teacher, and a very valuable man for the social as well as material interests of the town and school. He bore an active part in everything, and was much esteemed. His assistant was Mr. Arthur V. Goss, of Chelsea, Vt., a Dartmouth graduate.

The hope of permanence, however, failed again, and Prof. Hunt declined to serve longer than two years.

The next principal was Mr. Hiram Q. Ward of St. Johnsbury, Vt., a Dartmouth graduate. He remained but a single year. His assistant was a Miss Doane. The school seems to have fallen to an average of about thirty pupils each term, though no catalogues were published.

Mr. Ward was to have seven hundred dollars from the income of the fund, the three hundred dollars appropriated by the town to pay tuition of town pupils, all tuitions received from out of town pupils, and all income from use of hall, and he was to pay all expenses.

Prof. Hunt remained in town for some time after his connection with the school had ceased, and was active on the board of Trustees. Mr. Ward was succeeded as principal by Prof. Cassius S. Campbell, Prof. Hunt having presented a strong endorsement of him from a friend in Hastings, Minn., where Mr. Campbell had served as superintendent of schools for some time. He was born in Windham, N. H., Nov. 19, 1845, which town was originally a part of Londonderry, and his first paternal ancestor in America emigrated from Londonderry, Ireland, in 1733, settling in the New Hampshire town of the same name.

Cassius fitted for college at Pinkerton Academy, and graduated at Dartmouth in the class of 1868, and at once became superintendent of schools at Hastings, Minn., where he remained for ten years. He then became Principal of the High school at St. Paul, which place he held for five years, and then came to McCollom Institute, where he did as good work as the school had ever known; and where he remained until 1888, when he became one of the faculty at Pinkerton Academy, where he remains at this writing (1906.)

Mr. Campbell's forte was in Physics, Mathematics and the natural sciences. The school flourished with new vigor under Prof. Campbell's all-round ability, and his pervasive energy and enthusiasm. Everybody liked him, and his rare acquirements and ability made a lasting impression. Especially did he set about putting the school-building and its equipment in order. The following resumé of what was accomplished during his term of service was furnished by him at the special request of the editor of this history :

"The condition of the building was not attractive when I took possession of it. The basement was nearly full of all kinds of rubbish apparently dating from its erection, and was used by the school instead of outbuildings without any provision being made therefor. One of the rooms was filled to the ceiling with disabled settees and other rubbish, etc., etc. Fortunately the wind and snow had the freedom of the basement so that the health of the school did not suffer except from occasional colds through the winter. A cam-

paign of repairs and improvements was at once begun, and at the end
of my four years the building was clean and wholesome throughout;
every foot of plastering in it, if I remember rightly, had been newly
papered by Mr. Mixer; the building fully equipped with new stoves,
lamps and automatic electric bells for the school programme; an
up-to-date chemical laboratory and other apparatus fully equal to the
demands of the school; the library newly arranged and a new catalogue
made and printed; the piazza and porte-cochere built.

"All this was paid for primarily out of my pocket, with the distinct
understanding that the Trustees should never be under the least
obligation to make up to me any deficiency that might exist.

"The following is an abstract from my personal account of the
whole matter:—

Chemical laboratory and apparatus,	$871
Programme clock, Electric bells, Stoves and pipe, Plumbing materials,	85
Paint, Paper, Shades, Desks, Cases, Carpet, Glass, Hardware and Piazza,	629
	$1585

Trustees of McCollom Institute,	$100
24 Lectures and School Entertainments,	297
Materials sold and unsolicited donations,	77
	$474

"When I left Mont Vernon I took with me the three principal
pieces of apparatus I had bought and the Trustees gave me a check
for $435, which came within about $125 of balancing the account.
This was abundantly satisfactory to me, and if it was not satisfactory
to the Trustees it was their own fault."

The amount which Mr. Campbell was to receive from the income
of the fund was only six hundred and seventy-five dollars. The other
conditions were substantially as with his predecessors.

It was he who proposed the piazza in front of the building, and
the porte-cochere, which was a great convenience, and the Trustees
voted that he might build it "at his pleasure," adding: "the understanding is that he will not hold the Trustees, as such, responsible for
any expense that may be incurred."

At this same time the following significant vote was passed by
the board: "That Prof. Campbell may allow the Academy bell to be
rung only for one hour at sunrise and sunset on July Fourth, and
that the Trustees will prosecute any person who shall break into or
enter the building at night, for any purpose."

May 9, 1886, the Trustees authorized the Treasurer to expend one hundred dollars for tables, chemical apparatus, etc.

Dr. Frederick H. Chandler having come into town as a practising physician, he was at this time elected a Trustee.

Prof. Campbell carried on many enterprises to raise money for improvements and apparatus during his stay. The Trustees seem to have thought he was not giving quite as much attention to the "classics" and some "practical" branches, as they should receive, and suggested certain changes in this regard. But Prof. Campbell's administration was considered almost a new era of prosperity, and when he resigned to accept a place in the Pinkerton faculty, his leaving was very much regretted.

August 3, 1888, the Trustees accepted Mr. Campbell's resignation as Principal, and that of Prof. Lucien Hunt as a Trustee. The matter of selecting a new Principal was delegated to a committee, and Col. William H. Stinson was elected a Trustee.

August 11, it was voted to engage Mr. Oscar F. Davis of Bellows Falls, Vt., as Principal, on same conditions as previous principals, except that the amount allowed from the income of the fund was reduced to seven hundred dollars. Mr. Davis was a graduate of the University of Vermont. His wife was his assistant. The school was fairly prosperous. He remained until 1891, when he resigned to accept the position of the head of an important educational institution in Salt Lake City.

Mr. Davis afterward entered the ministry, and was for some time settled at Plymouth, Mass., and later removed to Vermont. He was later located in New Richmond, Wis.

John B. Welch, A. M., a veteran teacher, succeeded Prof. Davis in 1891. He was a native of Onondagua County, N. Y., a graduate of Wesleyan University, Middletown, Conn., and had been teacher for a period covering twenty years at Willimantic, Conn., and Westfield and Pittsfield, Mass. Mrs. Welch was his assistant the first three years, and the last year George S. Chapin. Prof. Welch was a thorough scholar and rigid disciplinarian. He left here in 1895 to take charge of Marmaduke Military Institute, Sweet Springs, Missouri. He was later principal of a preparatory school at Columbia, Missouri, for Missouri State University.

The terms under which Prof. Welch was engaged were like those of former principals, except that the amount granted him from the fund income was increased to eight hundred dollars, "for the first year only."

In November, 1891, Charles H. Raymond and Henry F. Dodge were elected Trustees, and Hon. George A. Marden of Lowell, Charles M. Kittredge, M. D., of Fishkill, N. Y., and William F. Pinkham of Mont Vernon were chosen honorary members of the board

On the first of August, 1892, Messrs. Albert Conant and W. F. Pinkham were chosen active members of the board, and the latter was chosen President, but declined to serve.

August 13, 1892, the Trustees voted "that the Trustees hereby express to Prof. Welch their confidence in him as a competent teacher, and desire that he will remain with us as Principal of McCollom Institute at least five years; and if, to that end, he will purchase or build a permanent home among us, they will loan him for that purpose a reasonable amount on mortgage of the same at five per cent. per annum; and that the Clerk forward a copy of this vote to Prof. Welch."

No response to this communication is on record, but a proposition was received from Mr. W. F. Pinkham who had some time before purchased the Dean p'ace, so-called, to sell the buildings and about one acre of the land of said place to the Trustees "for the use of the Institution." This proposition was accepted, and the property was bought for two thousand dollars, and was occupied by Prof. Welch and his family as long as he remained Principal. This no doubt accomplished the purpose of the above-named "proposition." Prof. Welch inaugurated, in his new home, the practice of taking a few boys into his family to be specially instructed, and made more of an income than any previous Principal. Of course he paid a rental for the Dean place, which was at the rate of one hundred and twenty-five dollars per year.

The changes made in the personnel of the Trustees are not all accounted for in the records. At the beginning of the school year, August, 1894, the list appears as follows: F. O. Kittredge, Clark Campbell, Charles H. Raymond, William H. Conant, Albert Conant, George A. Marden and John H. Colby. It was voted that John H. Colby and George A. Marden be a committee to secure a new charter for the corporation, if necessary, and take measures to legalize past acts of the corporation. This was to enable the corporation to acquire more real estate than the charter already allowed, and to cover any possible illegality in the methods of electing Trustees.

The committee referred to at the next session of the Legislature (1895) secured the passage of the following act:

CHAPTER 201.

An act to authorize McCollom Institute to acquire, hold and convey real estate, and receive donations.

Be it enacted by the Senate and House of Representatives in General Court convened.

SECTION 1. That McCollom Institute, which was incorporated by the laws of 1850, chapter 1051, under the name of Appleton Academy, is hereby authorized and empowered to acquire by purchase or otherwise suitable buildings for academical purposes, and may hold real estate to the amount of ten thousand dollars, and the same may sell, convey and dispose of at pleasure, and may receive by donation or otherwise personal estate to the amount of fifty thousand dollars, the interest of which shall be expended to defray the expenses of said academy.

SECTION 2. The trustees of said institute shall be elected annually and shall hold their office until their successors are elected.

SECTION 3. The acts of the acting trustees heretofore within the scope of the powers of actual trustees are hereby ratified and confirmed.

SECTION 4. This act shall take effect upon its passage. (Approved March 5, 1895.)

The original corporators were shareholders in the original building, and others were afterwards voted in on payment of a certain sum.

Of late years it had been found difficult to secure the attendance of any considerable number of the members of the corporation at the annual meeting, and accordingly the names of nearly every one of them, who survived, was obtained to a petition to the Legislature to have the Trustees incorporated, with the power to fill vacancies, in order that there might be a certain perpetual, definite and accessible body to hold the property belonging to the institution, and to execute its purposes.

The result was the passage of the following act:

STATE OF NEW HAMPSHIRE.

In the year of our Lord one thousand eight hundred and ninety-seven.

An act to incorporate the Trustees of McCollom Institute.

Be it enacted by the Senate and House of Representatives in General Court convened.

SECTION 1. William H. Conant, Franklin O. Kittredge, Clark Campbell, Charles H. Raymond, George A. Marden, Albert Conant and John H. Colby, and their successors, are hereby made a corporation by the name of the "Trustees of McCollom Institute," for the purpose of maintaining a school in the town of Mont Vernon, with all the powers and privileges, and subject to all the duties, restrictions and liabilities set forth in all general laws, which now are, or may hereafter be in force and applicable to such corporations.

SECTION 2. Said corporation shall have authority to receive, hold and manage the funds and property now held by McCollom Institute, and any other donations or bequests which may be made for its benefit, and may hold, for the purposes aforesaid, real and personal estate to an amount not exceeding One Hundred Thousand Dollars.

SECTION 3. The said Trustees shall have the power to adopt such by-laws as may be useful or necessary, with authority to elect one of their own number as President, also a Treasurer and a Secretary who may or may not be members of the corporation. Whenever a vacancy shall occur in the Trustees by the death, resignation or disability of any member, a successor shall be elected by the remaining Trustees, who shall thereby become a member of the corporation.

SECTION 4. All the acts and transactions of the Trustees acting under supposed authority as said Trustees, up to the present time, are hereby legalized and made valid.

SECTION 5. The purpose of this act is to continue the work contemplated in the establishment of the McCollom Institute under Chap. 1051 of the Laws of the year 1850 and acts amendatory thereof and additional thereto.

SECTION 6. This act shall take effect on its passage.

The first meeting of the corporation under the act above quoted, was called by George A. Marden, the President of the old Board, and assembled at Institute Hall on Wednesday, September 8, 1897, at four o'clock, all the corporators named in the act being present.

Mr. Marden called the meeting to order, and read the act of incorporation.

Mr. Colby thereupon presented for consideration the following by-laws, which were unanimously adopted:

TRUSTEES OF THE McCOLLOM INSTITUTE.

BY-LAWS.

ART. 1. The officers of this Corporation shall be a President, a Treasurer and a Secretary, all of whom shall be members thereof.

ART. 2. The officers of this Corporation shall be elected by ballot each year at the annual meeting, to hold office until their successors are duly elected.

ART. 3. The annual meeting, after 1897, shall be held in Mont Vernon on such day in August as may be designated by the President of the Corporation. Special meetings may be called by the President whenever he deems it necessary, and he shall call a special meeting whenever three members of the Corporation shall so request in writing. Special meetings may be held elsewhere than in Mont Vernon.

ART. 4. Notice of meetings shall be given either by personal service on each member by the Secretary or President, or by mailing notice a sufficient time before the meeting is to be held.

ART. 5. The Treasurer shall have the custody of all the funds and securities of the Corporation, shall collect all money due the Corporation and disburse all moneys to be paid out, under direction of the President and Secretary, but he shall make no permanent change of investment of any money in the funds without the authority of the board. He may be required to give such bond with such securities as the board may determine.

ART. 6. Four members of the board of trustees may be a quorum to do business.

ART. 7. Any of these by-laws may be suspended or amended by a three-fourths vote.

George A. Marden was then elected President of the Corporation by ballot, having six votes which was the total number cast. Albert Conant was in like manner elected Secretary and Treasurer, Deacon William H. Conant, who had for many years served the old corporation in those capacities, declining further service.

On the 6th of February, 1895, at a special meeting of the Trustees held in Boston, it was voted inexpedient to retain Prof. Welch another year, and G. Wilbert Cox, a graduate of Harvard, 1895, who had been graduated from Acadia College, Wolfeville, N. S., was hired as teacher, remaining here three years; his wife, Mrs. E. D. Cox, furnishing such assistance as he required. The last year of his residence here, he supplied the pulpit to the acceptance of the church. He was a patient, faithful and laborious teacher much beloved by the students. He took an active interest in town affairs and was much respected by all. He left here in 1898 to accept a more lucrative position of Superintendent of Schools at Bellows Falls, Vt.

He was succeeded in September, 1898, by George S. Chapin, who was an assistant under Prof. J. B. Welch, a graduate of Bowdoin (1893), an accomplished scholar, who designed to pursue teaching as his life vocation.

At the first meeting of the new corporation, September 8, 1897, it was voted to sell the Dean place so called to Mrs. Ellen F. Stinson for two thousand dollars, and to take a mortgage for that amount on the place at five per cent, the taxes to be paid by the mortgagor. Mrs. Stinson either managed the place or rented it season by season as a summer boarding-house, until 1905, when the Trustees again came into possession through a deed from Mrs. Stinson.

Mr. Chapin remained in charge of the school, which was small in numbers, and consisted only of pupils resident in the town, until the end of the school year of 1898-99.

At the annual meeting August 25, 1900, it was voted to put the building in charge of a janitor "until a school is opened," and though various plans for opening the school were considered with some arrangement between the town and the Trustees, nothing came of them, and there was no school during the year 1900-'01.

Extensive repairs were made on the building during the interregnum, a new furnace was put in, and the premises were put in most excellent condition, which used up a good portion of the income of the fund during the school suspension.

The regular triennial alumni meeting was due to have occurred in 1899, but as the next year would be the semi-centennial of the founding of the school, it was voted to postpone the alumni meeting till 1900.

During the year while the Institute was closed, the board of education of the town undertook to provide suitable school privileges for the town pupils who would have attended the Institute, and the Trustees voted one hundred dollars toward paying for the same.

For the school year beginning September 3, 1901, an arrangement was made with the Rev. H. P. Peck, pastor of the Congregational church, to conduct the school in connection with his pastoral work, he to act as Principal, and to receive five hundred dollars from the Trustees, together with any sum appropriated by the town for the Institute.

And Mr. Peck was also authorized to make such arrangements with the town board of education with reference to the joint use of the Institute building by such of the town schools as they may mutually agree upon.

June 28, 1902, an informal conference was held by the Trustees and the town board of education as to what should be done with the school the coming year. The arrangement of the previous year had not proved satisfactory, because it did not furnish full High school privileges, without which, approved by the State Superintendent of Public Instruction, any parent might send a child competent to enter a High school, to any High school in the state, and the town would have to pay the tuition therefor. There was an animated discussion, but no action.

At the annual meeting held August 16, 1902, it was voted that owing to the complete and long-continued disability of W. H. Conant, which rendered him incapable of performing the duties as a member of the board, this position was hereby declared vacant; and a highly complimentary resolution to the retiring member was passed.

A resolution expressive of the valued services of F. O. Kittredge, one of the charter members of the Trustees, who had recently died, was passed. Dea. William H. Kendall and Mr. Willard P. Woods, both residents of Mont Vernon, were elected to fill the vacancies, and on the organization of the board, Mr. Marden was re-elected President, and Mr. Woods Secretary.

The report of the conference between the town school board, and the Trustees was then taken up, and a proposition to be made to Rev.

Mr. Peck to take the school another year was read and discussed, but no final action was taken.

September 1, 1902, a plan was adopted to provide such a curriculum and such instruction as should meet the approval of the State Superintendent of Public Instruction, and required by law for a High school. This plan was jointly signed by the Trustees and the town board. The Trustees were to pay towards the expenses five hundred dollars from the income of the fund, and to allow the use of the Institute building and its appurtenances. The town was to pay the two hundred dollars appropriated already, and to use its best endeavors to secure a further town appropriation of three hundred dollars for the balance of the year. The Trustees were to hire a Principal and an Assistant, satisfactory to the town board, and the Assistant was to be satisfactory to the Principal. The balance of the money, after reserving a sufficient amount to pay for heating, lighting, care and school supplies, was to be divided between the Principal and Assistant, as the Trustees might deem best. If the town should fail to appropriate the three hundred dollars, then the school was to be closed after as many weeks as the money provided would pay for; and the arrangement was to last but one school year, unless renewed.

A course of study was made up from suggestions of the State Superintendent, which was approved by him, and McCollom Institute was designated as an institution acceptable as a High school.

Rev. Mr. Peck was engaged as Principal, and Miss Annie Louise Williams of Brattleboro, Vt., a graduate of Brown University, as Assistant. The nine hundred dollars remaining after the expense of care, heating, etc. (which was fixed at one hundred dollars) was divided equally between the Principal and Assistant.

Miss Williams proved a teacher of rare ability, and it was with regret that the Trustees received her declination to serve another year, which she offered in order to accept a better position in the High school of Whitefield.

The High school for the year was fairly successful, but was under the disadvantage of so large a number of classes as the law required, with so few pupils—the maximum number being not more than twenty.

The triennial meeting of the alumni for 1903 was voted by the Trustees to be held on the 5th of September, in connection with the annual celebration of the Old Home Week, and the Centennial anniversary of the town, for which arrangements were making.

Prof. Leslie A. Bailey and his wife, of Dresden, Maine, were engaged as Principal and Assistant for the year beginning in September, 1903, the High school arrangement being continued as before.

Mr. and Mrs. Bailey remained but a single year, he resigning to accept a school in Maine, very much to the regret of the Trustees.

For the next year, 1904-05, Mr. Henry W. Delano, a Dartmouth graduate, and a resident of Marion, Mass., was secured as Principal, and Clarence H. Hallowell, M. D., was induced to act as Assistant.

It was a most satisfactory combination, and was renewed for the succeeding year. Dr. Hallowell, however, removed from town, in January, 1906, and Prof. Delano, with the assistance of Miss Annie Hazen, an advanced pupil, continued the school.

Mr. Delano was one of the best principals the school has ever known. But the number of pupils of High school age and capacity had now become reduced to eleven, and there was small encouragement to continue the school as a High school.

For some years the permanent population of the town had been diminishing, and the surrounding towns, also growing smaller, were sending their children to High schools in towns which were large enough to support them. The regular fitting schools had, by their superior advantages, drawn many of the class that formerly came to Mont Vernon, and McCollom Institute could no longer compete in the work.

REUNIONS OF ALUMNI.

It was early determined that it would be pleasant and valuable for those who had been pupils at Appleton Academy to have frequent reunion meetings. As there was no complete and formal curriculum ending with graduation by classes, every pupil who attended the school was accounted as an alumnus. It is a great pity that complete records of these reunions were not kept and deposited in the Academy library. But from the files of the *Farmers' Cabinet*, and other sources have been gleaned a considerable number of facts concerning all the meetings held.

Beginning in 1854, reunions were as follows, generally with a regular period of three years intervening, but not always:

No. 1, 1854, August 31.

No. 2, 1857, August 19.

No. 3, 1859, August 24.
No. 4, 1862, August 28.
No. 5, 1865, August 30.
No. 6, 1868, August 26.
No. 7, 1872, August 28.
No. 8, 1875, July 20, (25th Anniversary).
No. 9, 1878, August 28.
No. 10, 1881, August 24.
No. 11, 1884, August 27.
No. 12, 1887, August 24.
No. 13, 1890, August 21.
Fo. 14. 1893, August 23.
No. 15, 1896, August 19.
No. 16, 1900, August 15, (50th Anniversary).
No. 17, 1903, September 5, (Town Centennial).

No. 1. The first meeting was held in Academy hall, Aug. 31, 1854, beginning at 10 a. m. George A. Ramsdell was chosen president; Ainsworth E. Blunt, vice president; George Bowers, of Hancock, secretary; John D. Nutter, John F. Colby and H. Perham were marshals. The Amherst Brass Band furnished the music. As the *Cabinet* put it, "the procession proceeded to the dinner tables collocated under a covert of verdant bowers, and spread with the luxuries of a prolific season. The pastor of the church, Rev. C. D. Herbert, asked a blessing. Toasts offered by the alumni called out a cheerful and pathetic response from Rev. Mr. Colby, Rev. Mr. Herbert, Mr. King and others." The location of the tables is not mentioned, but it probably was just above the Dr. Kittredge place, afterwards Conant Hall. The Rev. Mr. Colby was John Colby, one of the early assistant principals of the school; and the Mr. King was Prof. Fenner E. King, the third regular principal after the school was incorporated.

When the dinner was over, the procession was reformed, and returned to the hall, where the Rev. John Colby delivered an address, his subject being "Our Influence on Others, a Stimulus to Right Action."

There was a committee appointed for the purpose, consisting of Prof. King, Mr. Blunt and George A. Spalding, who reported a series of resolutions, which were adopted, pledging hearty co-operation with the trustees, teachers and parents in promoting the interests of the Academy, declaring their gratitude to and friendship for the former

OLD MOUNT VERNON HOUSE.
F. O. Kittredge, Prop. Burned.

teachers, Mr. Clough, Mr. and Mrs. Stevens, Mr. Colby and Miss
Jaquith, and their appreciation of the work of the trustees, and of the
citizens of Mont Vernon. The second resolution was as follows:

Resolved—That we tender to Hon. William Appleton, of Boston, our grateful acknowledgments for the liberality manifested in
the donation of our Library, and the generous aid afforded in the
erection and establishment of the Appleton Academy

After some responses to toasts, the meeting adjourned till evening, when a pleasant social hour, with miscellaneous entertainment
of speeches and singing, was enjoyed.

No. 2. The second alumni meeting was held August 26, 1857,
at half-past ten in the forenoon in Academy hall. The names of the
officers are not given. "Hundreds" were in attendance, and the
exercises were prayer by the then pastor, Rev. Charles E. Lord, music
by the Glee Club, and an oration by John E. Wheeler, A. B., of
Amherst, on "Literature;" a poem by Dr. George E. Bowers, of
Nashua, on "Progress." We have the word of the reporter that Mr.
Wheeler's address was one of "rare excellence," and that Dentist
Bowers's poem evinced that "its author possessed much taste and
cultivation."

A procession was formed at the close of the exercises and
marched to F. O. Kittredge's Mount Vernon House, where dinner was
served to the merry crowd. The procession then returned to the hall,
where the Matrimonial Statistics were read by A. E. Blunt of Dartmouth College, and the Obituary Record by J. F. Colby also of
Dartmouth College. A toastmaster was chosen and the "most prominent members" of the alumni were called out. After singing "Old
Hundred," the meeting was "adjourned for two years."

It is a pity the reports were not fuller. It would be interesting
to know who were the officers, what band furnished music (if they
had a band) and why they adjourned for "two" years, instead of
three. Perhaps the triennial custom had not then been adopted.

No. 3. The third meeting was held August 24, 1859, probably
in Academy hall. William Barrett presided, the oration on "Amusements," was by George A. Ramsdell, then hailing from Peterboro;
and the poem by Ainsworth E. Blunt. In the evening there was a
social reunion in the hall, the only formality recorded being the reading of an ode written by Eliza Boutelle of Wilton.

No. 4. The fourth alumni meeting was held on Thursday, August
28, 1862, in the midst of the time of the Civil war. It was largely

attended. The president of the day was John F. Colby, Esq., of
Boston. Rev. Augustus Berry, of Pelham, officiated as chaplain, and
William Barrett, then practising law in Nashua, delivered the
address, his subject being "Books: their Uses, etc." The Poem was
by J. M. Blood, M. D., then of Temple, and it was described as
"amusing and sprightly," and in the metre of Hiawatha. The Annals
had been written in the field, in Virginia, and in the hospital after
the "Seven Days Fight," by George A. Marden, who had not expected
to be present at the meeting, but it so happened that he got a fur-
lough just in time to appear and read the paper himself. The toast-
master was George A. Bruce, then engaged in recruiting a company
for the Thirteenth New Hampshire Volunteers. The Matrimonial
Record was read by Frank G. Clark, of Lyndeborough, and the
Obituary notices by Charles M. Kittredge, who soon after was commissioned a Second Lieutenant in the Thirteenth. The Ode was
written by Charles F. Kittredge, who also, with Clark Campbell,
officiated as Marshal, and they formed a procession of the alumni at
the Academy hall where the exercises were held, and, with the New
Boston Brass band, marched to Baker & Campbell's hall, where
dinner was served. Toasts were given, and responses made by Dea.
William Conant, Jonas Hutchinson and Lieut. George A. Marden,
who, after serving about eight months as a private and non-commis-
sioned officer in the Berdan U. S. Sharp-Shooters, had just received a
commission as first lieutenant.

In the evening there was a social reunion at the Academy hall,
where addresses were made by Rev. Augustus Berry and others.

No. 5. The fifth meeting of the alumni was held on Wednesday,
August 30, 1865, the number attending being described as "unprec-
edented." The weather was delightful. At eleven o'clock, under the
marshal-ship of Clark Campbell, a procession was formed at the Mount
Vernon House, with the Wilton Cornet Band furnishing the music,
and proceeded to Academy Hall, which had been elaborately deco-
rated for the occasion, and which was filled to overflowing. William
Barrett, Esq., of Nashua, presided, and prayer was offered by Rev.
John E. Wheeler. John F. Colby, Esq., of Boston, delivered the
oration, his subject being "America and Her Institutions." George
A. Marden read the poem. A Military record was read by Prof.
C. F. P. Bancroft. There was no Matrimonial or Obituary
record, owing to some oversight. An ode was sung, written by Miss
Mary Frances Perkins. After the exercises at the hall, a procession

of four hundred was formed and marched to the Hiram Perkins grove, where a dinner prepared by the ladies of the town was served. Harlan P. Conant, of Boston, was toastmaster, and responses were made by George Stevens, Esq., of Lowell, Mass., Rev. Augustus Berry, of Pelham, and Dr C. F. P. Bancroft, all former principals, Prof. Charles A. Towle, the present principal, Capt. George A. Bruce, Lieut. George A. Marden, Rev. John E. Wheeler, George A. Ramsdell, Jonas Hutchinson and Dr. J. M. Blood.

At the conclusion of the exercises, the procession marched back to the village. In the evening the hall was again filled for a promenade concert and a social reunion. The Wilton band was then a crack organization, led by Carl Krebs, and its music was a great attraction. Miss Agnes Giles, (since Mrs. Agnes (Giles) Spring, of Boston,) was just coming into notice as a fine contralto singer, and she was a member of the school. Her singing added much to the evening's pleasure.

Arrangements were made for the next Triennial to be held on the last Wednesday in August, 1868.

No. 6. The sixth triennial occurred at the Academy Hall, Wednesday, August 26, 1868. The Hall was beautifully decorated with bunting. The services were opened with prayer by the Rev. Augustus Berry, of Pelham, a former principal. William H. Towne, Esq., of Boston, presided, and gave an address of welcome, Col. George A. Bruce, of Boston, delivered an address on "American Culture," and as Mr. George B. Buzell, of Portland, Maine, one of the earliest alumni, who had been appointed poet, failed to appear, George A. Marden, editor of the *Lowell* (Mass.) *Daily Courier*, read a poem written for another occasion, in his stead. The Matrimonial Record was read by Maj. Charles F. Stinson, of Charlestown, and the Obituary Record by Henry E. Spalding, M. D., of Hingham, Mass. The closing ode was written by Miss Ellen C. Sawtelle, of Brookline.

A committee of five was chosen to make arrangements and select officers for the next triennial.

A photograph of the alumni, assembled in front of the Academy, was taken, after which the multitude marched to the Mount Vernon House to dinner. After "the cloth was removed," John F. Colby, Esq., was introduced as toast-master, and responses were made by George Stevens, Rev Augustus Berry and Charles A. Towle, former principals, and Rev. John Colby, former assistant. J. V. Smith the present principal, W. H. Conant. George A. Bruce, George A. Marden, Dr. Henry E. Spalding, Col. Thomas L. Livermore, and Maj. Charles F. Stinson.

The music for this gathering was by the Nashua Cornet band, E. T. Baldwin, director, which gave a delightful promenade concert in the evening. The marshals were Col. Thomas L. Livermore, Clark Campbell, and Darwin E. Kittredge.

No. 7. The next meeting of the alumni was held in the meeting-house, Wednesday, August 28, 1872. The weather was fine and there was a large gathering. The morning meeting at 11 o'clock saw a church filled with people. Prayer was offered by the Rev. William H. Cutler, of Westminster, Mass., who was once a pupil of the school from Lowell, Mass. George Stevens presided, and made an address of welcome. Rev. Augustus Berry, of Pelham, a former Principal, delivered an address on "What education do the masses need, and how better to secure it?" Rev. C. F. P. Bancroft, a former Principal, and lately from Look-out Mountain, Tenn., where he had been Principal of a successful educational institution, read a poem. The Annals were read by Chestina A. Hutchinson, the Matrimonial Record by Harlan P. Conant of Somerville, Mass., and the Obituary Record by Mrs. Ellen J. (Kittredge) Drury, of Lowell, Mass. The Milford Cornet Band furnished music. The exercises at the church closed with an Ode to the tune of "Auld Lang Syne"—the name of the author not being given in the report.

The alumni then marched to Academy (now Institute) Hall where dinner was served. After dinner George A. Marden, of Lowell, was introduced as toast-master, opening with a brief poem of his own composition, and offering the successive toasts in rhyme. These were responded to by Rev. Dr. Seth H. Keeler, then pastor, George A. Ramsdell, Esq., of Nashua, Clerk of the Supreme Court of New Hampshire, Rev. Augustus Berry, Dea. William H. Conant (who also read letters from Rev. John E. Wheeler and Rev. Vaola J. Hartshorn,) George A. Bruce, H. P. Conant, Prof. George W. Todd present Principal, just beginning his first term, Rev. W. H. Cutler, Prof. Andrews of Boston, A. A. Rotch, junior editor of the *Cabinet*, and Dr. Bunton. Prof. J. H. Morey of Concord, being present, favored the alumni with some most delightful music on the piano. The church and hall were profusely decorated with the national colors.

In the evening the usual promenade concert was given by the band, with additional piano music by Prof. Morey, and the singing of the Star Spangled Banner by Miss Mary Miller, of Salem, an alumnus of the school noted for her fine vocalism. W. H. Conant, George O. Whiting, Henry T. Stinson, George A. Ramsdell and George A. Marden were appointed a committee of arrangements for the next triennial and twenty-fifth anniversary, to be held in 1875.

No. 8. This triennial was held July 20, 1875, in celebration of the twenty-fifth anniversary of the founding of Appleton Academy in 1850. In 1871, Mr. George W. McCollom of New York City, who was once a resident of the town, and whose wife, Mary Ann (Stevens) McCollom, was a native, gave the school an endowment of $10,000, in consideration of which its name was changed to "McCollom Institute." Mrs. McCollom was a daughter of Asa Stevens, and her mother was Mary (Appleton) Stevens, who was a sister of the William Appleton, for whom Appleton Academy was named. The day of celebration was, for some reason, changed from Wednesday to Tuesday, and the month from August to July. The increased importance of the quarter-centennial anniversary was recognized in the decorations on the village street and the "Institute" (as the building has been called since the change of name.) On the outside, in large letters and figures in evergreen, was the inscription "1850—WELCOME—1875," and the hall was also decorated within, as was also the Meeting-House, where the literary exercises were held, beginning at 11 o'clock, A. M. The excellent Wilton Cornet Band furnished the instrumental music, during the day, and in the evening, Curtis's orchestra. The exercises were opened with prayer by Rev. Frank G. Clark, of Rindge, a native of Lyndeboro, and a graduate of the school, and of Amherst College. George A. Ramsdell was President of the day, and made an appropriate welcome address. The oration was by Col. Frank W. Parker, of Quincy, Mass., on "New England Culture and its Influences." The poem was by Edward E. Parker, Esq., of Nashua. Mr. H. Porter Smith, a merchant of Boston, read the Annals, giving a brief historical sketch of the school and its teachers. The Marriage Record was read by Henry T. Stinson, and the Obituary Record by Wendell P. Marden. The closing ode was written by Miss Emily (Dodge) Simpson, of Lawrence, Mass.

Maj. Nathan B. Boutwell, an officer in the Boston Custom House, was marshal, and under his direction a procession was formed at the close of the exercises in the meeting-house and marched to Institute Hall, where dinner was served by J. H. A. Bruce, the then landlord of Hotel Bellevue. Over the platform was the inscription

"'50—ALL HAIL—'75", while the walls were hung with flags, pictures, mottoes, etc.   Col. George A. Bruce officiated as toast-master, and responses were made by Rev. Dr. S. H. Keeler, then pastor at Mont Vernon, George W. McCollom, of New York, for whom the Institute was named, Hon. Lucien B. Clough, the first principal after the school was incorporated, William Barrett, Esq., of Nashua, Rev. F. G. Clark, Rev. Henry Marden, a native of New Boston, a graduate of the school and of Dartmouth College, and a Missionary in Turkey, who was home on a leave of absence, John F. Colby, Dr. C. M. Kittredge, of Fishkill-on-the-Hudson, N. Y., Rev. Augustus Berry, of Pelham, Rev. C. F. P. Bancroft, Principal of Phillips Academy of Andover, Mass., Prof. Lucien Hunt of Falmouth, Mass., a former Principal, Rev. Vaola J. Hartshorn of Hyannis, Mass., Prof. George W. Todd the present Principal, Rev. Darwin E. Adams of Wilton, a grandson of Dr. Daniel Adams, for many years a prominent physician of the town, Hon. George A. Marden of Lowell, Mass., Clerk of the Massachusetts House of Representatives and editor of the *Lowell Daily Courier*, George W. Putnam of Amherst, Rev. Bezaleel Smith of West Hartford, Vt., pastor of the church at Mont Vernon from 1841 to 1850, and Charles H. Hopkins, an undergraduate.

This long list of speakers did not allow an adjournment until six o'clock P. M.   Mr. McCollom was honored with demonstrations of great appreciation of his generous endowment of the Institute, and he gave to the school portraits of himself and his departed wife, which were hung in the hall.   Of the ten Principals of the school, six were present: Judge Clough, Rev. A. Berry, Dr. Bancroft, Prof. Hunt, D. A. Anderson of Newton, N. J., and George W. Todd.

In the evening there was the usual promenade concert and social reunion.   Resolutions of gratitude to Mr. McCollom were passed, and thanks to those who had so successfully managed the celebration. There was singing by Maj. N. B. Boutwell and Dr. C. M. Kittredge. The teachers at this time were Prof. Todd, Charles P. Mills and Mrs. Todd, and there were ninety pupils.

No. 9.   This reunion was held on Wednesday, August 28, 1878, and was largely attended.   Institute Hall was handsomely decorated, and the exercises began there at 11 o'clock.   Music was furnished by Curtis & White's orchestra.   Hon. George A. Bruce presided, prayer was offered by Rev. Augustus Berry, Charles P. Mills of Andover, Mass., a former assistant teacher, delivered the address, and Newton H. Wilson, Goffstown, the poem. Mrs. Elizabeth (Boutwell) Parkhurst, of Boston read some happy "Reminiscences of School Life," the Marriage Record was by William H. Stinson, of Dunbarton, and the Obituary Record by George W. Putnam, of Amherst. The ode sung was written by Emma F. Wyman, of Mont Vernon.

At the close of the exercises, Clark Campbell, as chief marshal, conducted the alumni procession to Hotel Bellevue, where, in the orchard in rear of the house, tables had been spread for the dinner by Landlord J. H. A. Bruce, at which 250 sat down. No toast-master had been appointed, but the President of the day officiated in the double capacity, and drew speeches from Hon. George A. Ramsdell. Rev. Dr. Keeler, of Somerville, Mass., who spoke in behalf of Dea. William Conant (who was unable to be at the dinner,) Samuel Hodgkins, Henry Robinson, George A. Marden, A. A. Rotch, Rev. A. Berry, Rev. W. H. Woodwell (present pastor,) Dr. George Bowers, Col. F. W. Parker, Prof. C. P. Mills, Prof. George W. Todd, and Prof. William H. Ray, who had just assumed the Principalship. There was singing by a male quartette, led by Maj. Boutwell. The sad news was received that Mr. George W. McCollom of New York, had been stricken with paralysis.

In the evening a promenade concert was held at Institute Hall, and appropriate resolutions relative to the report as to Mr. McCollom were adopted. The social reunion was enjoyed with singing and other music, and the reunion wound up with dancing. This is the first record of any dancing at one of these reunions.

No. 10. The tenth reunion was held Wednesday, August 24, 1881, with "an unexpectedly large attendance." Col. Thomas L. Livermore, of Manchester, was President of the day. The alumni met in the Meeting-house at 10.30 in the forenoon, and prayer was offered by Rev. Dr. Bancroft, of Andover, Mass. John H. Hardy, Esq., of Boston, delivered an address on "Freedom of Thought," and John W. Adams, of Littleton, Mass., read a poem. Henry F. Robinson, of Hancock, read the Matrimonial Record, and Mrs. Ann A. (Perkins) Campbell, of Mont Vernon, the Obituary Record. The ode sung was written by Miss Lucia E. Trevitt. Music both day and evening was furnished by Nickles' Orchestra of Milford. It is not stated in the report, but probably these exercises were held in the Meeting-house, and that the dinner, which was served to 300 persons by George E. Boutell, landlord of Hotel Bellevue, was in Institute

Hall. The after-dinner speaking (no mention being made of a toast-master) was participated in by George Stevens, Esq., of Lowell, Mass., John F. Colby, Esq., of Boston, Rev. C. C. Carpenter (then pastor), George A. Marden, of Lowell, Prof. Lucien Hunt, Dr. Bancroft of Andover, and Dr. John P. Brown, Supt. Taunton (Mass.) Insane Hospital, (who married Caroline A. Stevens, sister of George Stevens.) There was the customary social reunion in the evening.

No 11. This reunion was held Wednesday, August 27, 1884, with the morning exercises in the church. Hon. George A. Marden, of the *Lowell Courier*, and Speaker of the Massachusetts House of Representatives, was President of the Day. Rev. Charles P. Mills, of Newburyport, offered prayer, the oration was by Hon. Augustus E. Sanderson, of New Jersey, one of the early graduates, and the poem by Mrs. Emily Dodge Simpson, of New York, the Marriage Record by George W. Putnam, of Lowell, Mass., and the Obituary Record by Mrs. Carrie (Averill) Trow, of Amherst. This record was notable, in that it recorded the deaths of George Stevens, the founder of the school, Hon. George W. Todd, a recent principal, and Miss Martha Ellen Conant, daughter of Dea. William Conant, who had been for several terms an assistant teacher. The exercises closed with the singing of an Ode written by Alice Hammond Peaslee, of Bradford. Appropriate memorial addresses on the several teachers above mentioned were read, that on George Stevens by H. Porter Smith, that on Prof. Todd by G W. Putnam, and that on Miss Conant by Rev. Mr Berry.

Dinner was served to as many as Institute Hall would hold, and the after-dinner speakers were Hon. George W. Sanderson, of Littleton, Mass., who, as a member of the Massachusetts Senate, was asked to report for Hon. George A. Bruce, President of that body, who was unable to be present, Hon. A. E. Sanderson, the orator of the day, and brother of the preceding speaker, Rev. C. C. Carpenter, Rev. R. R. Meredith, D. D., pastor of the Union Congregational church, Boston, and a summer resident of Mont Vernon, Rev. A. Berry, Prof. Hunt, Rev. C. P. Mills and Prof. C. S. Campbell, who was just assuming the position of Principal.

In the evening the social reunion was furnished with instrumental music by Nickles' Orchestra of Milford, and the assembled alumni and friends were delighted with singing by Mr. Ludlow Patton of New York, and his wife Abby (Hutchinson) Patton, the soprano of the famous Hutchinson Family, who gave a number of the old-time Hutchinson songs.

No. 12. The twelfth reunion was held Wednesday, August 24, 1887. It rained when the alumni gathered in the church at 11 o'clock, but the house was filled. Clark Campbell was marshal. Nickles' Orchestra furnished the music, Rev. Dr. Bancroft officiated as Chaplain, Dr. C. M. Kittredge was president, and Hon. E. Moody Boynton, of Newbury, Mass., a friend of several prominent members of the alumni, delivered the address, his subject being "Our Western Christian Civilization, the product of three forces—the Teacher, the Preacher, and the Inventor." The poem was written by Henry A. Kendall, of Somerville, Mass., and read by H. Porter Smith, and the Ode by Henrietta N. Hanford, of Danville, Ill. The Matrimonial Record was read by Henry T. Stinson, of Winchester, Mass., and the Obituary Record by J. B. Twiss, of Jaffrey. This latter recorded the death of Dr. J. V. Smith, a former Principal, at Melrose, Mass., also the death of a Trustee, William Stevens.

Dinner was served in Institute Hall. Dr. Kittredge presided, and the speakers were Hon. George A. Marden, Prof. Hunt, Prof. Campbell, John F. Colby, Lucius B. Hutchinson of New York City, Dr. W. H. Weston of New York, and H. P. Smith. Among those present was F. O. Kittredge of West Medford, one of the charter trustees. The reunion closed as usual with a social gathering in the hall.

No. 13. The fortieth anniversary and the regular triennial reunion were held on Thursday, August 21, 1890, meeting at the church at 10.30. Eastman's orchestra of Manchester was in attendance. Hon. George A. Ramsdell of Nashua presided, and Hon. George A. Marden of Lowell, Mass., Treasurer and Receiver General of Massachusetts, delivered an address on "The Relation between the Country Academy and the People among whom it is Located." The poem was "Reminiscences of School Life," by Rev. J. P. Mills of Michigan. The Matrimonial Record was by Alice P. Campbell, and the Obituary Record by Charles C. Stinson, of Portland, Me. The record noted the following deaths, among others, since the last report: John F. Colby, Boston; Jesse Hutchinson, Baltimore; William Barrett, St. Paul; Rev. Henry Marden, Turkey; John W. Adams, Littleton, Mass.; Dr. J. M. Emerson, Barnstead; Thomas H. Thorndike, Pittsfield—all early graduates.

Memorial sketches were then presented—on Dea. William

Conant, by Dr. Bancroft; on John F. Colby, Esq., by H. P. Smith; on Rev. Henry Marden, by Rev. F. G. Clark; on Prof. W. H. Ray, by Miss L. E. Trevitt. An ode was then sung which was written by Dr. H. E. Spalding of Boston.

Dinner was then served in Institute Hall, and speeches were made by Dea. W. H. Conant, Rev. John Thorpe, (then pastor), E. B. Gould, Esq., Nashua, Hon. J. P. Bartlett, Manchester, Rev. Frank G. Clark, Plymouth, Dr. William H. Weston, New York, Rev. A. Berry, Mrs. Berry, Prof. C. S. Campbell of Pinkerton Academy, Derry, Prof. Oscar F. Davis (present principal), Col. W. H. Stinson, Hon. Charles H. Burns, Wilton, Hon. George A. Marden, John H. Colby, Esq., Boston, H. P. Smith, Lucius B. Hutchinson, Rev. George E. Sanborne of Hartford, Conn., a former pastor, and Maj. D. E. Proctor of Wilton.

In the evening there was the usual promenade concert and social gathering in the Hall.

No. 14. This reunion was held August 23, 1893. The morning exercises were in the Meeting-house at 10.30. H. Porter Smith presided, Rev. John Thorpe was chaplain. Hon. John P. Bartlett, of Manchester, delivered the oration on "The Educational System of our Country—its Moulding Influence on Character;" the poem was by Hon. Edward E. Parker, Judge of Probate, Nashua; the Matrimonial Record was by Mrs. Fannie (Dodge) Clark, of Amherst; the Obituary Record by Clarence Trow, of Amherst; and the ode was written by Mrs. Emma F. Abbott, Wilton. Music was by Custer's Grand Hotel Orchestra.

Memorial sketches were read by Dr. Bancroft, on Dea. George E. Dean, Thomas H. Richardson, and Capt. John Trevitt, three members of the Board of Trustees.

Dinner was served by the Ladies' Home Circle in Institute Hall, and the after-dinner speakers were Dea. W. H. Conant, Rev. John Thorpe, Dr. W. H. Weston, Judge Bartlett, Judge Parker, George A. Marden, F. C. McLaughlin of Somerville, Mass., a summer boarder, John H. Colby, and Prof. John B. Welch, the new Principal.

In the evening Custer's Orchestra (from the Grand Hotel just opened) gave a concert in the Hall, and a social hour was enjoyed.

No. 15. The date of this reunion was August 19, 1896, the exercises being in the church. Dr. W. H. Weston, of New York City, presided; Rev. C. P. Mills, of Newburyport, was chaplain; Rev. Frank G. Clark, of Plymouth, was the orator; Miss Lucia E. Trevitt read

the poem; the Matrimonial Record was by Emily C. A. Starrett, of
Mont Vernon; the Obituary Record was by Hon. A. M. Wilkins, of
Amherst; and the ode by Jennie B. Carpenter, of Andover, Mass.

Dinner was served in Institute Hall by the Home Circle. The
after-dinner exercises had begun most merrily. Mr. F. O. Kittredge,
the venerable and only surviving original Trustee, had been honored
with great applause. Dea. Albert Conant had made an interesting
speech on some of the Institution's financial trials; Mr. Willard P.
Woods had spoken with his accustomed energy on "The relation of
the Academy to the Town;" Rev. Thomas J. Lewis, then pastor, had
made a happy speech on "The Church and the School;" and the next
speaker was Dr. C. M. Kittredge (or, as his boyhood familiars knew
him, "Charlie M.") And there are few efforts on such occasions so
happy, bright, cheerful and witty as his. He had especial delight in
recalling boyish pranks and incidents with his old chums, and told,
with great glee, and with evident looking forward to what would be
said in reply, by his especially close chum, George A. Marden, a
story of the time when they played pick-a-back and frightened an ox
in a yoke belonging to Hiram Perkins as he stood chained to a stake
at Capt. William Bruce's blacksmith shop, waiting while his mate was
in "the swing" being shod, and so disturbed the animal that he flew
around and broke the yoke. As the Doctor sat down amid cheers
and laughter, at the close of his speech, he was noticed to fall back
in his chair, and with a gurgle in his throat he became unconscious.
Drs. Dearborn and Weston were at once by his side, and he was
removed to the lower rooms, where he died almost at once. The lately
merry gathering was awe-stricken at the sudden calamity. At the
suggestion of Rev. Mr. Mills, two verses of "Nearer, My God, to
Thee" were sung, and, when this had been done, Dr. Weston returned
to the presiding officer's chair, and said, in tremulous voice, to the
hushed audience, "the Doctor has gone from us."

Of course this ended the alumni reunion, but at a business meeting held later L. B. Hutchinson moved that Mr. Marden, Rev. Mr.
Mills and Prof. George W. Cox, the incoming new principal, be a
committee to frame appropriate resolutions for the occasion, which
was done, and they were adopted.

No. 16. This triennial reunion was due to have been held in
regular course in 1899. But as the year 1900 would be the fiftieth
anniversary it was postponed a year, in order that the two events
might come together. The semi-centennial celebration was held

Wednesday, August 15, 1900.   This was also the first day of the town's celebration of "Old Home Week," and the reunion and semi-centennial were, therefore, made a part of the town celebration. The exercises were held in the new meeting-house for the first time, and began at half past ten o'clock.   After an organ prelude, prayer was offered by the Rev. Dr. Bancroft, Principal of Phillips Academy, Andover, an address followed by Hon. Geo. A. Marden of Lowell, Assistant United States Treasurer at Boston, and President of the Board of Trustees.   This was followed by a duet, "O Salutaris," sung by Mrs. Browne, wife of the Rev. Donald Browne, then pastor of the church, and Mrs. John A. Woods of Manchester.   An able historical address was then delivered by Col. Wm. H. Stinson of Dunbarton. The Matrimonial Record was by Mrs. Henry F. Robinson, Hancock, and was followed by a vocal solo by Harry M. Kittredge, of Fishkill, N. Y., son of the late Dr. C. M. Kittredge.   The Obituary Record was by Edgar J. Kendall, Esq., of Milford, and the Ode was written by Geo. A. Marden.

At the close of the exercises dinner was served in Institute Hall, but without the usual after-dinner formalities and speaking.

In the evening there was a social reunion in the Town Hall, followed by a fine concert by the Tabasco Banjo, Mandolin and Guitar Club of Lowell, with singing and dancing.

The seventeenth triennial reunion was held on Saturday, September 15, 1903, in connection with the celebration of Old Home Week, and also in connection with the centennial celebration of the incorporation of the town.   As a full chapter further on gives a report of this joint celebration, it is unnecessary to give the details in this place.

CHAPTER XI.

OLD HOME WEEK.

Establishment in 1899 by Gov. Frank W. Rollins—Mont Vernon First Town to Respond—Elaborate Preparations—The Governor Attends—Three Days' Festivities—Illuminations, Fire Works, Sports, Sunday Services, Etc.—Celebrations Every Year from 1899 to Date of this History.

It was a happy thought of His Excellency Frank W. Rollins, Governor of New Hampshire in 1899, to issue the following proclamation, which explains itself:

Old Home Week
in
New Hampshire
Aug. 26 to Sept. 1, 1899.

STATE OF NEW HAMPSHIRE
EXECUTIVE DEPARTMENT.

The residents of New Hampshire have conceived the idea of celebrating the week of August 26 to September 1 of the present year as "Old Home Week," and of inviting every person who ever resided in New Hampshire, and the descendants of former residents, to return and visit the scenes of their youth and renew acquaintance with our people.

It affords me pleasure as governor of New Hampshire to extend this invitation in behalf of our people, and to assure those who may be able to accept that they will receive a cordial greeting in any section of the Old Granite State.

During this week our people intend to keep open house, and the doors of our hospitality will be swung wide open. A large number of towns and cities in the state will have local celebrations during the week, to which all are cordially invited.

Old Home appeals to every person of mature years, father, mother, and childhood, and when you think of the old home, you bring back the tenderest memories possessed by man; true love, perfect faith, holy reverence, high ambitions—"the long, long thoughts of youth." Few states have furnished more men and women who have achieved distinction and renown than New Hampshire, and our people hold these sons and daughters in high regard. In behalf of the people of New Hampshire, I heartily invite all to whom New Hampshire is a former home or place of nativity, to visit the State during Old Home Week.

(Signed) F. W. ROLLINS,
Governor.

Mont Vernon was the very first town to respond to the Governor's summons, and as an initial step an Old Home Week Association was formed, with the Hon. Geo. A. Marden as President, and Miss Ruth S. Conant as Secretary. The necessary committees were appointed, and every arrangement was made for a first celebration of the new anniversary. An elaborate invitation was prepared, published in the newspapers, and sent to every native and former resident of the town, whose address could be learned, giving the details of the proposed celebration, which was to begin on the 26th of August, 1899, and to continue three days. This invitation was as follows:

TO ANY AND ALL WHO HAVE EVER LIVED AT MONT VERNON, N. H.

You are hereby cordially invited to come back to the old place to celebrate "Old Home Week" as recommended by Governor Rollins.

The local celebration will begin on Saturday Evening, August 26, 1899, and the following programme will be carried out as far as possible:

Saturday Evening, August 26. Town Social at the Town Hall. To this everybody in town at the time is cordially invited. There will be an informal social meeting for interchange of greetings, to be followed by dancing. Good music will be in attendance. If the Town Hall should prove inadequate, Institute Hall will also be thrown open.

A Grand Illumination of the streets and houses will be made during the evening, and a huge Bonfire will be lighted on one of the hills of the town nearby.

Sunday Morning, August 27. There will be, in the new Meeting-House, a service appropriate to the occasion, to be conducted by Clergymen who have either been settled in the town over the Congregational Church, or who have at some time resided in the town.

Sunday Evening, August 27. The Evening Service will be conducted by distinguished laymen who have been residents of the town.

A special double quartette of good singers will furnish music for both the above services.

Monday, August 28. The morning will be devoted to rides and walks, golf, bicycling, tennis, and social calls; and in the afternoon a Basket Town Picnic may be held in the Splendid Pine Grove near the Grand Hotel, with such sports and entertainment as may be devised.

There will be ample accommodation at the various summer boarding-houses, and at private houses, for all who desire, and at very reasonable rates. Those desiring to secure rooms and meals will be provided by addressing Mr. Will P. Woods, Chairman of Entertainment Committee.

Come back to the old hearthstone, and see what a nice, tidy, attractive village old Mont Vernon has become, and renew old associations, and meet old friends.

GEO. A. MARDEN,
President Old Home Week Association of Mont Vernon.

Of the way in which these promises were carried out, the following dispatch to the *Boston Daily Globe*, from its special reporter, will give information:

MT. VERNON, N. H., Aug. 26, 1899.—The "home week" celebration began here today, under the happiest auspices, the weather being all that could be wished for, and the projectors of the affair showing notable enthusiasm in the enterprise.

Already it is evident that the inhabitants of this enterprising and hustling little town are determined to make their celebration the most notable one ever held in this part of the state.

To Mt. Vernon belongs the credit of having the first "Home Week" celebration in the state. The hotels, boarding-houses, and private residences are jammed full of visiting natives.

Today a large number came from Boston and other points to join in the week's festivities. The fame and beauty of the town also brought many strangers, who have entered into the spirit of the occasion as if they had been born and bred in the granite State.

Early this forenoon the people began to decorate their establishments, and by noon almost every residence and other building was swathed in bunting and flags.

Soon after sunset hundreds of Japanese lanterns, which adorned the more pretentious residences along the main streets, were lighted. With the green foliage for a background they made a pretty picture.

Gov. Rollins's portrait, garlanded with flags and bunting, was to be seen as a part of the decorations on several public buildings.

By 8 o'clock bonfires and fireworks illuminated the town and made merry the crowds that perambulated the streets until midnight. Everyone, practically, kept open house. At 9 the town hall was opened to the public, and then the "home week" committee held an informal reception, enlivened by music furnished by the Second Regiment Band. Dancing was indulged in until midnight.

The most elaborate decorations of a public character are on the town hall, school-house, academy, and the Grand, Bellevue, and Campbell hotels.

Private displays worthy of special note, many of them made by people who are summer residents only, are given by Alderman J. H. Colby, Capt. E. G. Martin, F. O. Kittredge, A. W. Bragg, Paul Stucklen, all of Boston; Hon. Geo. A. Marden of Lowell, Dr. J. P.

Brown of Taunton, Hon. H. P. Moulton of Salem, Hon. A. H. Wellman of Malden, J. T. Bridge of Medford, J. F. Wellington and A. D. Clark of Somerville, Dr. C. F. P. Bancroft of Andover, and the following local residents: Deacon A. Conant, Mrs. Blood, John T. McCollom, Col. Clark Campbell, G. W. Averill, Rev. Donald Browne, Benjamin F. Davis, W. H. Conant, Mrs. J. A. Holt, Lincoln Hall, W. P. Fox, Dr. W. I. Blanchard, W. H Kendall & Co., Mrs. P. F. Pike, George D. Pike, the Cutter cottage, Mrs. Fred W. Davis, Mrs. Maria Bruce, Walter Woods, Mrs. O. C. White, Mrs. William Stevens, W. S. A. Starrett, William H. Marvell, J. M. Gleason, Joseph W. Averill, W. F. Jenkins, Frank Smith.

It is worth while to go a little more into detail in narrating the story of these celebrations of Old Home Week, because the town has not been much given to celebrations generally, and because in those which have been held in connection with the Academy, and Old Home Week, there has always been a somewhat remarkable exuberance and enthusiasm.

On Sunday, Aug. 27, the second day, there was a special religious service in the morning at 10.45 o'clock, in the charming little new meeting-house, every seat in which was occupied, and many chairs in addition were brought in, and some persons even had to stand.

The service began with an organ prelude by Mrs. J. F. Choate of Malden, a summer guest in the town, followed by the singing by a double quartette of "The King of Love My Shepherd Is," a hymn by the congregation, responsive Scripture readings, Scripture lessons, prayer, and a selection by a male quartette, "I Cannot Always Trace the Way." An offertory followed, and then came an able Old Home Week discourse by the Rev. Donald Browne, pastor of the church, dwelling chiefly on the duty of the sons and daughters of New Hampshire who have left the old state towards the home from which they had departed.

Addresses were also made by the Rev. Chas. E. Lord, D.D., of Newburyport, Mass., who was pastor of the church from 1856 to 1861, and by Rev. C. F. P. Bancroft, Ph. D., Principal of Phillips Academy, Andover, Mass., who was Principal of Appleton Academy in this town from 1860 to 1864. The double quartette then sang a selection entitled "The Homeland," the congregation sang "America," and the morning exercises closed with the benediction by Rev. Dr. Bancroft.

Governor Rollins did not arrive in town until 4 o'clock in the

SUMMER HOUSE OF J. FRANK WELLINGTON
Erected on site of old Dr. Daniel Adams House.

afternoon, when he became the guest of an old schoolmate and townsman of his, Walter I. Blanchard, M. D., the medical practitioner in the village.

The evening exercises were denominated "A Laymen's Service," over which the Hon. Geo. A. Marden presided, and made an opening address of welcome to those who had returned to the old hearthstones, and congratulated everybody on the entire success of the celebration, due to the hearty interest which everybody had manifested in carrying it on.

Mr. Marden then introduced Governor Rollins, who was greeted with great enthusiasm. The handsome little church had been appropriately decorated and it was crowded to the doors.

The governor proceeded to make a plain statement of facts, as he said. He said that New Hampshire had been a farming state until fifty years ago, when the great west began to compete with the farmers of New England and rendered farming unprofitable. Then came the manufacturing. To his mind no country can be prosperous without a happy and contented yeomanry. It is the foundation of civilization and good government, he asserted. He spoke of the centralization of people in large cities, told of the evils springing from the crowding of people into cities, and pictured how much better off they would be if they would make their homes in the country instead of living in city tenements.

He dwelt upon the large number of New Hampshire men who had taken up their abode in other states of the union, and pointed out what they had accomplished in building up the American nation. He expressed the hope of getting some of them back to their native soil, if only for a week in the summer time.

Governor Rollins then went on to tell the people what was needed. The first thing that should be done, he said, was to build some good roads. He intended to see that a start was made in this direction before he went out of office. The next thing was to protect the forests of the state, he said. And the next was to improve the district schools. He favored state supervision. He paid a warm tribute to the state grange, and told how much it was doing to improve the condition of New Hampshire farmers.

He said that he was very much pleased with the way the people had taken hold of home week, and that it was sure to be a permanent feature every year in New Hampshire. He especially complimented

Mont Vernon on its celebration, saying that outside of Concord's celebration Mont Vernon's was by far the best held.

Gov. Rollins was followed by Hon. George A. Bruce of Somerville, Mass., a native of the town, and former President of the Massachusetts Senate. He made an eloquent and stirring speech, as did Lucius B. Hutchinson of New York city, another native, and Mr. H. Porter Smith of Cambridge, Mass.

The exercises closed by appropriate singing, and benediction by the pastor, and the formal home week celebration so far as Mont Vernon was concerned was over.

The exercises on Monday were mainly informal, the visitors enjoying themselves in any way which seemed good to them, finding every latchstring out; and in the evening an impromptu reception was given the Rev. Benson M. Frink, a former pastor of the church, and to Mrs. Frink, they having arrived in town during the day, having been unable to be present sooner.

In 1900 the second Old Home Week celebration took place, in connection with the semi-centennial anniversary of the incorporation of Appleton Academy. As before, circular invitations were sent to everybody whose address was known. The Academy anniversary was celebrated on Wednesday, Aug. 15, and on the next day there was a golf tournament, and the day was given up to various informal social events. On Friday, Aug. 17, there was no formal exercise, but a good many people had arrived in town and were enjoying themselves.

On Saturday, Aug. 18, the Old Home Week celebration proper was begun with a Clam Bake in the beautiful pine grove on the old Woodbury (later the Hiram Perkins) farm, owned at this writing by the estate of Dr. Chas. M. Kittredge. It was a delicious summer day, and the First Regiment Band of Boston, a crack musical organization, furnished most delightful music at the grove. About 5 o'clock in the afternoon Governor Rollins and his staff arrived in a tally-ho coach with four horses, driven by Hon. John A. Spaulding of Nashua, who owned and occupied one of the cottages on Prospect Hill, and an experienced whip. The gubernatorial party were received at the Town Hall by a battalion consisting of a company of 44 young ladies in white, and a company of golf-players and caddies armed with golf clubs, commanded by Maj. W. I. Blanchard, M. D., and headed by the First Regiment Band. The party thus escorted marched to the

Golf Links, and a charming dress-parade was held, the Governor and his party reviewing the parade. A pretty episode occurred, when the parade was dismissed, in a grand rush of the young ladies in white surrounding Governor Rollins and his staff and showering them with bouquets of flowers.

The Governor and staff then took supper at the Grand Hotel, and in the evening a complete illumination of the village occurred, and there was a parade, led by the caddies and the young ladies in a four-horse barge, with other vehicles, and with the band, and numerous banners, which made the tour of the village, preceded by a band concert on the Park. Fireworks closed the day, outside, and a fine ball was given at the Grand in honor of the distinguished guests.

Sunday morning a special Old Home Week service was held in the new meeting-house with a sermon by the pastor, Rev. Donald Browne, and with special music fitted to the occasion. The evening, as last year, was devoted to a Laymen's service presided over by Hon. Geo. A. Marden. There was singing by Col. Coit of the Governor's staff, Mrs. John A. Woods, Miss Kitty Osgood, and Miss Gertrude M. Sewall. Governor Rollins delivered an earnest and eloquent address in which he enlarged on the practical as well as sentimental value of Old Home Week, and Michael J. Murray, Esq., one of Boston's finest orators, followed in an address of rare power.

The celebration in 1901 occurred on Saturday and Sunday, August 24 and 25. The Saturday evening illumination and out-door concert were interfered with by a heavy rain, but the First Regiment Band of Nashua, a very fine organization, gave a concert in the Town Hall, where the crowd assembled, and passed a delightful evening in social festivities.

The Sunday morning service was conducted by the Rev. Henry Porter Peck, who had succeeded to the pastorate of the church, and who preached from a text taken from the 103d Psalm: "How shall we sing the Lord's song in a strange land?" An orchestra from the band played at the service, and a charming violin solo was given by Miss Grace Whitmore of Boston, a summer guest. The band gave a sacred concert on the Park toward evening; and at 8 o'clock the now customary Laymen's service was held in the meeting-house, with Mr. Marden presiding, the orchestra helping out the music, and eloquent addresses were made by the Hon. Chas. J. Noyes, former Speaker of the Massachusetts House of Representatives, Hon. Harrison Hume, formerly a member of the Maine Senate, and Col. J. P. Bradley, and the Hon. Thomas M. Babson, all of Boston, and the last two summer residents in town.

The celebration in 1902 occurred on Saturday and Sunday, August 23 and 24. The afternoon of Saturday was devoted to a grand coaching parade, which was organized by a committee headed by Mrs. H. P. Peck. Mr. J. F. Wellington served as Marshal, with ten aids. There were nearly thirty entries in all classes, and prize banners were awarded by a committee to the following :

First prize for Tally-ho coaches to the Hotel Bellevue ; second, to a coach entered by Col. W. B. Rotch, proprietor of the *Milford Cabinet.*

Double Teams—First prize to Mr. J. F. Wellington ; second to Mr. C. E. Osgood.

Single Teams—First prize to Mrs. R. F. Marden and Miss Bessie B. Hadley, both of Lowell, Mass., and summer guests.

There was a fine illumination in the evening, and very profuse decoration of the residences, public buildings and grounds. The First Regiment Band of Nashua, was again in attendance, and gave a concert on the Park.

The Sunday morning service was conducted by Rev. H. P. Peck, and a chorus choir of sixteen voices furnished the music. A most able and impressive sermon was preached by the Rev. A. A. Berle, D.D., of Boston, from Exodus iii :6 : "I am the God of thy fathers, the God of Abraham ; the God of Isaac ; the God of Jacob." At the laymen's service in the evening, presided over by Mr. Marden, as usual, a masterly address was delivered by the Hon. Chas. H. Burns of Wilton.

The celebration of 1903 was held in connection with the centennial celebration of the incorporation of the town, and an account of what was done will appear in a later chapter devoted to the centennial.

The celebration in 1904 occurred on Saturday and Sunday, August 20 and 21, but a heavy rain prevented the customary illumination and decorations and the band concert. On Friday evening there had been a fine musical entertainment at the Town Hall for the benefit of the Golf Club by a number of the First Corps of Cadets of Boston, and a quartette of their number had been engaged to remain over and furnish music in the church at the Old Home Week Sunday services.

As the storm prevented the carrying out of the out-door plans on Saturday, the Colonial Quartette (which was the name of the Cadet quartette) volunteered, with several of the members outside the quartette, who had remained in town, to give an impromptu entertainment on Saturday afternoon, and the hall was well filled, and those present were royally entertained.

Sunday morning was perfect as to weather. Rev. Henry Porter Peck preached a sermon exactly appropriate to the anniversary, and the singing by the Cadets made as complete a celebration service as could have been asked for. In the evening at the Laymen's service Guy A. Ham, Esq., assistant U. S. district attorney at Boston, delivered an eloquent address, and there were other brief addresses, which with the music, concluded the exercises of the sixth Old Home Week celebration.

The seventh annual celebration in 1905, was limited to Sunday, August 20, so far as the official exercises were concerned : but some of the villagers felt that there ought to be something doing on Saturday evening, and they hired the Laurel Band of Milford to come up, and there was quite a fine illumination of many of the residences and grounds, and though the affair was virtually impromptu the streets were quite full of pedestrians, carriages and automobiles. The Golf Club house was decorated and illuminated, and quite an elaborate display of fireworks was given on the golf links in front of the house.

The Sunday services were conducted by the Rev. H. P. Peck, and the sermon was preached by the Rev. Geo. L. Perin of Brookline, who was spending the summer at the neighboring town of Brookline, N. H. The music was by a double quartette. The church was beautifully decorated with clematis and golden rod by the young lady guests of the Mount Vernon house. The evening Laymen's service was in charge of John H. Colby, Esq., of Boston, and a most eloquent address was delivered by Solon W. Stevens, Esq., of Lowell, Mass., a member of the Middlesex County bar, supplemented by a brief and inspiring talk by the Rev. Francis H. Rowley, D.D., of the First Baptist church of Boston.

The town made quite a reputation by these observances of Gov. Rollins's popular celebration, and they contributed to the material advancement of the town, which at this time had become to depend so much on what is known as the "summer business," as well as to the enjoyment of both its permanent residents and summer guests. The "sprucing up" of the village, in getting ready for the Old Home Week holiday, led to permanent village improvement, and while the village had always been noted for its tidy and well-kept condition, its attractiveness was enhanced by these special efforts, and the reports of its vivacious observance of the new idea were spread abroad over the country, and secured for it a valuable interest.

OTHER CELEBRATIONS.

It does not appear that the people of the town were much given to celebrations before the days of the Academy. At any rate the records of such events are most meagre.

There was a Fourth of July celebration in 1808, but there is no full account of it to be found. There is, however, a printed copy of the Oration delivered on that occasion by Dr. Rogers Smith. It was printed at Amherst by Joseph Cushing, and on the title page appears this quotation, credited to Washington's Legacy: "Why quit our own, to stand on foreign ground?" William Bradford, John Carlton and Zephaniah Kittredge were appointed to wait on the Doctor and "present the thanks of the Committee of Arrangements for his ingenious and patriotic oration," and "to request the favor of a copy for the Press."

To this the orator replied:

"GENTLEMEN: I herewith submit the copy requested, with all its imperfections, to your disposal, and to the candor of the public. Permit me to express the high sense I feel of the honor done me by the Committee of Arrangements, and of the flattering terms in which you have been pleased to communicate their request.
"I am, Gentlemen,
most respectfully,
your sincere friend,
and obliged humble servant,
"R. SMITH."

The address was quaint, as from its date would be expected. It was but the thirty-second anniversary of the Declaration, and the orator started with an apology that he was "unused to public declamation," and "too young to recollect the important events we this day celebrate." But he was old enough and bold enough to discuss "the nature, design and end of civil government."

The writer recalls but one other Fourth of July celebration, and

that was in the late forties or early fifties, and took the shape of a
Sunday School picnic in the Hiram Perkins grove.

An account of the celebration by the republicans of the election
of Abraham Lincoln, in November, 1860, has already been given.

The democrats took their turn at celebrating a national victory
when Grover Cleveland was elected President a second time.   On the
21st of November, 1892, the democrats had a grand jubilee at Institute Hall.   They brought the old Revolutionary cannon, "Molly
Stark," from New Boston, and fired a hundred guns from Campbell's
hill.   The village was more or less illuminated.

October 21, 1892, Columbus Day was celebrated by the schools,
it being the 400th anniversary of the discovery of America.

CHAPTER XII.

THE CENTENNIAL CELEBRATION.

THREE CELEBRATIONS IN ONE—THE TRIENNIAL ALUMNI REUNION—
OLD HOME WEEK—THE HUNDREDTH ANNIVERSARY OF THE IN-
CORPORATION OF THE TOWN—AN OUTLINE REPORT OF ALL THREE
—COL. GEO. A. BRUCE'S ORATION—H. PORTER SMITH'S CHURCH
STORY—REMINISCENCES BY REV. C. C. CARPENTER.

So important an event as the celebration of the one hundredth
anniversary of the incorporation of the town certainly deserves an
important place in the town history. It can hardly be accomplished
better than by reproducing most of the contents of a pamphlet printed
at the time by the *Milford Cabinet*, which Col. W. B. Rotch, proprietor of that journal, himself the son of a Mont Vernon ancestry,
kindly allowed the use of in the preparation of this history.

It preserves in full the admirable oration of Mont Vernon's
gifted and distinguished son, the Hon. Geo. A. Bruce, the most
interesting story of the old church, and the personnel of its congre-
gations of fifty years ago, by Mr. H. Porter Smith, the son of one of
its pastors of that time, and appropriate reminiscences by the Rev.
C. C. Carpenter, who once occupied its pulpit.

It also gives a brief account of what was done, as well as said,
at the celebration, and the names of many who took part therein.

STORY OF THE CELEBRATION.

The exact date of the hundredth anniversary of the incorporation
of the Town of Mont Vernon would have been December 15th, 1903.
But in a hill town, away from the railroad, such a celebration could
not be conveniently held in the winter. Besides, it was deemed best
to combine with the centennial celebration, the seventeenth triennial

reunion of the Alumni of the McCollom Institute, which was due to be held this year, and the fifth annual observance of "Old Home Week," which had been postponed from August.

At the annual March meeting the town voted an appropriation of $200.00 towards the centennial celebration, and appointed the following named gentlemen to act as a committee, with full powers to expend this money: Dea. W. H. Kendall, Chas. H. Raymond, Lucius B. Hutchinson, Frank O. Lamson, and Hon. Geo. A. Marden of Lowell, having a summer residence in the village. All the committee, except Mr. Marden, were citizens of the town.

Messrs. Kendall, Raymond and Marden being members of the Board of Trustees of McCollom Institute, and Mr. Marden being President of the Mont Vernon Old Home Week Association, it was easy to secure the co-operation of both these organizations in a triple celebration.

The necessary sub-committes were appointed, and the date of the celebration was fixed on September 5th and 6th.

Saturday, September 5th, opened auspiciously, and the celebration began at sunrise, with the ringing of the bells upon the Institute and Town Hall, and the firing of a national salute on the grounds of the Mont Vernon Golf Club, under the direction of Colonel J. Payson Bradley of Boston, a summer resident of the village, a former commander of the Ancient and Honorable Artillery Company of Boston, and a veteran of the Artillery service of the Civil War. Col. Bradley had brought from Boston two light guns from his yacht, and paid all the expense of the salute, which was also repeated at sunset.

Meanwhile, the Town Hall (the old Meeting House), the new Meeting House, the Institute building, and the district school house, together with practically every private residence in the village, had been profusely decorated with the national colors, wild flowers and other adornments, and preparations were made on a large scale for the evening illumination, which has always been a prominent feature in the Old Home Week celebrations.

At 10:30 many members of the Alumni of McCollom Institute (and Appleton Academy as it used to be named) and others assembled in the new Meeting House for the Triennial Reunion. The meeting was called to order by Mr. W. P. Woods, of the committee of arrangements appointed three years ago, and H. E. Spaulding, M. D., of Boston, was introduced as President of the Day. Dr. Spaulding made a brief and feeling address of welcome, after which the Triennial Matrimonial Record was read by Miss Emily Starrett of Mont Vernon, and the Mortuary Record by Mrs. Fannie Dodge Clarke of Amherst. Instead of the usual formal address, brief remarks were made by Gen. A. E. Blunt of Wellesley, Mass.; Hon. Geo. A. Bruce, Hon. A. M. Wilkins of Amherst; Levi A. Bruce, M. D., of Utica, N. Y., and Hon. Geo. A. Marden, all former pupils of the institution, Messrs. G. A. Bruce, Blunt and Marden having been members of the earliest class in Appleton Academy. The speakers were all fluent in happy reminiscence, and a very lively meeting was enjoyed.

During the exercises the Schubert Quartette of Boston, and the First Infantry Band of Nashua, arrived, and the Quartette sang several selections, and the Band played under the trees in front of the meeting house.

At 12 : 30 an abundant dinner was served in the dining-room under the Town Hall, by the Ladies' Home Circle, to such as desired, at the price of fifty cents. The band entertained the crowd with numerous selections.

At 1 o'clock P. M., a heavy shower came up, with sharp lightning and heavy thunder, and with a dash of hailstones as large as marbles. The lightning struck twice in the upper part of the village, but did no material damage. The storm did little harm to the decorations, as the Chinese lanterns, which had been hung out for the illumination, were all taken in. The shower cleared off about two o'clock.

At 2 : 30 the Centennial celebration occurred in the Meeting-House. Prayer was offered by the Rev. H. P. Peck, pastor of the Congregational church. Hon. Geo. A. Marden presided, and delivered a brief address of welcome to the returning sons and daughters of the old town and other visitors. The church was filled with an interested audience, including many who were natives, or had at some time been residents of the town. Inspiring music was furnished by the Schubert Quartette of Boston and the First Infantry Band of Nashua.

The chief address was delivered by the Hon. Geo. A. Bruce of Boston, a native of the town, and a grandson of the first pastor, the Rev. John Bruce. Colonel Bruce's oration is given in full elsewhere.

After the Centennial exercises, a social hour was enjoyed, with many greetings between those who had not met for many years. Meantime, the villagers and the committee on decorations and illuminations were busily engaged in preparing for the evening. The weather had become pleasant, there was no wind, and a profusion of Chinese and Japanese lanterns, fancy lights, red, white and blue and colonial buff bunting, and flags and streamers were displayed, and the illumination was one of the finest ever known.

The band gave a concert from a temporary band stand erected on the Park, and later played on the pavilion at the Golf Club House, while a grand display of fireworks was made by a committee consisting of Mr. J. F. Wellington of Somerville, and John H. Colby, Esq., of Boston. The village street was filled with carriages and the sidewalks with pedestrian visitors, viewing the continuous illuminations of the streets and buildings, and the crowd centered at the Golf Club for the final display.

The celebration was continued on Sunday, which dawned clear and beautiful, and with a most comfortable temperature. The people filled the new Meeting-House at half-past ten. Preliminary devotional exercises were conducted by the pastor, with special and most charming music by the Quartette, with a prelude by Mr. Charles Clemens of Cleveland, Ohio, who was a guest at the Grand Hotel, and kindly consented to preside at the organ; and with Congregational hymns. Then followed "An Historical Sketch of the Church," by Mr. H. Porter Smith of Cambridge, a Boston merchant, son of the Rev. B. Smith, who was pastor of the church in the forties. It is given in full elsewhere, and was hugely enjoyed for its interesting reminiscences and historical facts, and especially for the merry humor which pervaded the entire address.

Mr. Smith was followed by the Rev. C. C. Carpenter of Andover, Mass., a former pastor, with reminiscences of his pastorate, which were exceedingly interesting.

In the evening the customary Old Home Week laymen's service was presided over by Hon. Geo. A. Marden, the Rev. Mr. Peck conducting the preliminary devotional service. Mr. Marden delivered a brief informal address, "taking his text" from the History of Amherst, of which Mont Vernon was formerly the Northwest Parish, and dwelling somewhat on the historical genesis of the town as the result of a theological schism in the Amherst church. The Quartette furnished delightful music, and the congregation sang familiar hymns.

A most fitting address was also made by Mrs. Elizabeth Frances Bennett of Lowell, Mass., president of the Middlesex Woman's Club, who was a temporary guest at Hotel Bellevue.   Col. J. P. Bradley also gave a stirring talk, and Mr. C. E. Osgood spoke briefly.

Collections to help defray the expenses were taken up at both morning and evening services, resulting in $109.00.   In addition to this and the town's appropriation of $200.00, the expenses were provided for by a guaranty fund pledged in sums of $25.00 each, by Messrs. G. A. Marden, A. Conant, Colby, Best, Baker, Wellington, Kendall, Osgood, Bragg and L. B. Hutchinson, and by contributions of $10.00 by Mr. Henry F. Dodge and $15.00 by Mr. W. P. Woods. Only 50 per cent. of the guaranty subscription was finally needed to pay all the bills.

Messrs. C E. Osgood and A. Conant were a committee on decorations and illumination; J. F. Wellington and J. H. Colby were a committee on fireworks; Frank Smith, Will P. Fox, Will Jenkins and Miles Wallace furnished the bandstand; Daniel Richardson and wife were in general charge of the dinner provided by the Ladies' Home Circle, from which about $50.00 profit was realized for the treasury of that organization; W. P. Woods and Deacon W. H. Kendall were the committee on invited guests and entertainment; Geo. A. Marden on music and publicity.

No effort was made to have a very formal celebration, but, on the whole, it was a most satisfactory affair

ADDRESS BY COL. GEORGE A. BRUCE.

Mr. President, Ladies and Gentlemen :

The town of Mont Vernon has invited all her children wherever scattered over the earth's broad surface to return to their old home to assist in commemorating the hundredth anniversary of her birth.   If any there be who are not able to be present on this occasion we know that it is not from lack of interest or desire.   To all here present she extends a hearty welcome, and to the absent, like a good mother, she sends her warm good wishes and kindly benediction.   This gathering is little more than a family reunion on a large scale.   Time has made this occasion for us, and we are here to enjoy it all by ourselves.   We do not challenge the world's attention to what we do or say here, but none the less it is for us an event filled with satisfaction and joy as great as if it were to be seen and heard of all men.

In many ways the observance of those years which mark the close of periods in our civic life are of value not only to us but to those who are to come after us.   They tend to turn inquiry backward, and are the cause of gathering and preserving in enduring form the record of events in our history which otherwise might be forever lost; they tend to excite and cultivate a strong local attachment which cannot fail to be of service and value to this town; they tend to lead us to reflect upon what a town's good name and prosperity rests, and help to make more sure the future which now begins to unfold before us.

Very fortunately some years ago, in anticipation of this celebration, it was decided to have prepared a complete and full history of Mont Vernon from the earliest date, and this important work was confided to the most competent person that could have been found, and very soon, I doubt not, the finished labors of the Hon. Charles J. Smith will be in the possession of every citizen.

In the opinion of most men the settlement of Plymouth in 1620 is the most conspicuous and important event in the history of New England. It is, perhaps, the most important act of colonization in the annals of mankind. History has gathered up and preserved in her treasury every event in the lives of the Pilgrims, while art, poetry and eloquence have exhausted their powers in presenting to our imagination the story of their hardships, their sufferings, their heroism, their virtues and their unchangeable devotion to religious and political freedom. We do not complain of this. They caught and hold that added glory which comes to those who stand first in a long series of events which culminate in great and fortunate results. This it is which gives renown to Lexington, and to the first shot at Fort Sumter in the Civil War.

There is, however, but little difference in the character and motives of the men and women who came to Plymouth and those who soon followed them to the settlement of Charlestown, Boston, Salem, and the other towns of New England. They left alike the most beautiful country the sun in all his course is permitted to look down upon to seek a new home in the wilderness; they encountered the same hardships; they came face to face with the same difficulties and dangers; and they bore in their bosoms hearts as brave, wills as strong, faith as pure, convictions as unchangeable and a reverent trust in God which never knew shade of doubt. While the world will continue to hold in its especial care the name and fame of the Pilgrims of Plymouth, here at least we are bound to give to the first pilgrims to Mont Vernon the same measure of praise and admiration which in a wider field has been so abundantly accorded to them.

We are living now in an age of great events and great things. We have a great nation, great cities, great towns, great railroads and great everything else. Small things and small events are passed by as unworthy of attention in a great age. Any number less than a million has been lost from our common speech.

It is well for us once in a while to remember that a million is made up of units, and that there is value in small things as well as in large things. To be a small good man is better than to be a large bad one, and a small town with a virtuous population is better than a large city filled with a vicious population.

Mont Vernon is one of many small towns in New Hampshire, and though its story resembles very closely that of many others, yet to us, her children, it is full of interest and tender memories. It has a local flavor all its own and readily distinguished from that of all others. Though but little of the heroic and tragic has been enacted here, yet the simple annals of the years that bound her history are full of lessons of private and public devotion that appeal to the heart of civilized man. No great battles for civil and religious liberty have been fought here to attract the world's attention to this spot: no martyr has enriched our fields with his blood or sanctified them by his sufferings: but the simple living of plain New England people has furnished many examples of how a man should live to gain most of that which God intended he should gain through his gift of human existence.

For forty-three years Mont Vernon formed a part of the town of Amherst, which was incorporated in 1760. It owed its settlement to a grant made by the Massachusetts Bay Colony to soldiers who had taken part in King Philip's war in 1675, or to their descendants and representatives. It was 120 years from the landing of the Pilgrims when the first house was built in the eastern part of this town on land included in what for half a century has been known as the Samuel Campbell farm. At that time what may be termed the heroic age in New England colonization had passed. The Indian wars were then a matter of history. The eastern part of Massachusetts and the whole surface of Rhode Island and Connecticut were dotted with cultivated farms and growing villages. Boston contained a population of about ten thousand, and Charlestown, Marblehead, Salem and Newburyport were busy ports crowded with ships engaged in the fisheries and colonial trade. In the whole of New England there were at least 300,000 white men and women. There was a large population born upon the soil who were beginning to think of themselves as Americans and not as Englishmen. There were five newspapers published weekly in Boston alone. Benjamin Franklin had begun his great career and was even then the most conspicuous person in America. Jonathan Edwards, who ranks among the brightest ornaments of the Christian Church in any age and any country, had been settled for 15 years in Northampton. A new nation was in process of formation and the instinct of nationality was asserting itself in every one of the older colonies. Only five years later, Massachusetts, just to try her wings for independent flight, with slight aid from Connecticut and Rhode Island, captured the fortress of Louisburg, which was considered the Gibraltar of America.

At the time Mont Vernon was first being settled, the American Colonies contained a larger population than had ever before gone out from any nation for such a purpose. All this had been accomplished, not by aid of the English government, but in spite of it. Religious persecution had in part started it, and subsequently helped it. A political revolution had given it a new impulse; but the real explanation of its great success is to be found in causes that reach back as far as the Norman Conquest. For nearly a thousand years the title to the greater part of the soil of England has been vested in the hands of less than a hundred men. In the estimation of mankind nothing gives to the individual so much importance and dignity, so much of all that which makes life attractive as the possession of great landed estates. The passion to own land is inborn in every Englishman. He looks upon it as the crown and glory of life. What one sees to be so advantageous to others he desires to possess for himself. It was this passion for the ownership of lands, of estates great or small according to the means possessed for acquiring them, that led most of the English colonists to found their homes in America. They did not come here in quest of gold, or glory or adventure or novel excitements, but to build up homes for themselves and their children. Unfortunately the information which we possess in regard to the earliest settlers upon this hill is very meagre. We know the names of some of them, but no memorial of their existence remains save that which they have left on the surface of the earth which we daily tread.

How we should treasure and with what delight we should now read a well-kept diary by one of our earliest settlers covering the first fifty years of our history! Not Pepy's or Evelyn's or Fannie Burney's would be to us half as interesting and instructive. It would be what Bradford's history is to a wider circle of readers. By its aid we should almost be able to see passing before our eyes the transformation of a wilderness into a prosperous and civilized town. Perhaps, too, we might learn what were his emotions and what was his wonder as he gazed for the first time from the brow of this hill upon the most extended view obtainable in New England from any spot habitable by man and saw no trace of man's existence; how he received and with what delight he welcomed the incoming of other settlers to become his neighbors and friends, each in turn making a new opening in the forest where for centuries the giant trees had wrestled with wind and storm and tossed them off from their branches in the glory of their strength; when and who brought under cultivation Prospect Hill, our highest elevation, where now the summer visitor from the piazza of the "Grand" can enjoy a view of surpassing loveliness by day or watch the coast-wise lights send out their friendly rays to the wandering ship by night; when and who wrought into lawn-like smoothness the waving lines of Campbell's hill where the golfer of today at the ninth tee looks up to catch a smile or receive a frown from Crotchet Mountain at the success or failure of his stroke; by what way and when the first horse and cow and pig and sheep and hen were brought here to equip the shaping farm; when the footpaths leading from house to house were transformed into roadways for more convenient travel; how long it was before the blueberry, raspberry and blackberry bushes sprang up and bore fruit from the burnt-over soil; when, too, was the house ready for the incoming of the wife to cheer and encourage all with her genial presence, and when and where did the first-born see the light on Mont Vernon soil; who first discovered and with venturesome step descended into the gloomy depths of Purgatory — facilis descensus Averno, sed revocare gradum superasque, evadere ad auras, hoc opus, hic labor est — these and a thousand other facts of greater or less interest we should know, if only Lamson, Wilkins, Carleton, Averill or Smith could have foreseen that a century and a half later this church, which has taken the place of the one they helped to build, would be crowded with their descendants and successors to bless their memories for such a gift.

As early as 1760 there were fourteen taxpayers in the town, and after that date its settlement must have been very rapid, for during the Revolutionary War our territory furnished about fifty soldiers and two commissioned officers, Stephen Peabody attaining the rank of Lieutenant Colonel, with the command of a battalion of infantry before its close.

It is almost certain that before the end of the century every acre of land which we now see cleared and many more now grown up into woodland had been brought into cultivation, and the houses now standing, with a few exceptions, had been built. I am amazed as I attempt to compute the amount of labor which this achievement represents. What workers these early Mont Vernon men must have been! The only thought then could have been how short could the hours of sleep and how long could the hours of labor each day be made. The "walking delegate" was the creation of a later day

We hear much at the present time of what is called the strenuous life — of urgent and persistent labor in one way or another that taxes strength to its utmost limit of endurance, of a determination to do things that never ceases until the spring is broken or the sands of life have run out. It is spoken of as if it were an incident of our day only, and is held up as a racial menace. But there were heroes before Agamemnon and hard workers before the age of Roosevelt. The man, who, with a warrant for 120 acres in his pocket, a rifle on his shoulder, and an axe in his hand, first came upon this hill, and during a lifetime, by the labor of his own hands, transformed his wilderness tract into fields of timothy and clover, of wheat and rye, barley and oats, corn and potatoes; who erected a commodious house for a large family, and a barn ample for fifty sheep, twenty head of cattle and the necessary winter supplies; who in the off-days of the year constructed ten miles of fencing from the loose and half-buried boulders that some prehistoric glacier had scattered about his fields, apparently for the very purpose of keeping him from idleness; who had reared a family of eight or ten children and given them a good education; who had fulfilled all the duties of a good citizen in helping to keep the town up to a high standard of excellence in all things; the wife of this man who did a full share in this great accomplishment, who rose

before the lark in summer and before the weasel in winter just to put
the house in order for a good day's work; who with her own hand
made the butter and cheese from the milk of twenty cows, washed
and spun the wool from forty sheep, became the mother of ten children
and did all the work for such a household without the aid of any
servant; who tried out the lard from the fat of half a dozen hogs; and
who made the candles to light the house through the long nights of winter
when she knit the stockings and from the waste pieces of woolen
braided the mats that were scattered over the floor of every room in
the house, including the front entry; who cultivated her own little
flower-bed, set out and watered the hollyhocks that bloomed on either
side of the front door and made it look like an entrance into paradise;
who dispelled the wintry gloom by filling the sunward windows with
flowers almost as bright and cheerful as her own warm and sunny
heart; who held herself in readiness every day of the year to sit by
the bed of sickness at the summons of any neighbor in distress; who
found her only recreation in going to church on Sunday three miles
away to listen to a sermon three hours long, keeping off the chilblains
by a little portable stove filled with coals from the parish fire,—this
man and this woman knew something of a strenuous life that the men
and women of our day little dream of.

From the beginning of time did the Infinite Eye ever look down
upon brighter examples of absolute consecration to duty than the
fathers and mothers who made this beautiful New England in order
that they might leave to their children and those who were to come
after them something which they may have dreamt of but never
realized?

Can it be a matter of wonder to us that in the early ages of our
kind, among children of such parents as these, if such there were,
who had heard from the lips of father and mother and in part seen
with their own eyes the long story of their toil and struggle to build
up a home in order that they might bequeath to them that which they
did not inherit, there should have sprung up the thought and feeling
for ancestral worship that still survives as one of the religions of the
world? In life they had been their earthly parents seen, and in death
they became their heavenly parents unseen.

Though we know but little of the first generation of Mont Vernon
men and women individually, we know much of them collectively.
They were a strong, vigorous, God-fearing race, who never turned
from the path of duty as they saw it until the race of life was run.
Religion was to them something more than a formality; it was a
stern, living, ever present reality.

The inconvenience of going from two to six miles to church, at
a time when no roads existed, was very great, yet it is doubtful if
there was a family here that failed in going to Amherst every Sunday
of the year to hear the preaching of the Gospel until a house of worship of their own had been provided. As early as 1779 many residents

petitioned the General Court of New Hampshire to be set off as the second parish of Amherst, but the petition was not granted until two years later. Before this, however, a church had been organized and the building across the way from this in which we are now assembled had been constructed, every farmer in the town having contributed of the materials entering into it, the heavy timbers having been hauled to this spot by oxen over the snow then piled so high and crusted so hard that stone walls were invisible and a straight, smooth road was open from one place to another in any direction.

The Rev. John Bruce from Marlborough, Mass., a graduate of Dartmouth College, was the first ordained minister, of whose qualifications I am unable to speak for two reasons: First, that I never heard him; and second, that I am one of his direct descendants.

Separated as the people here then were from Amherst ecclesiastically, the ties that bound them to the old town became very slight, and from ecclesiastic to political independence was a natural and easy step. In 1783, 121 residents petitioned that the second parish of Amherst might be set off as an independent town, but then as now such applications were not readily granted, and it was not until 1803 that an act of incorporation was obtained and Mont Vernon then became and has ever since remained one of the brightest of all the jewels that adorn the crown of New Hampshire. It is this event and that which flowed from it that we have met here today to commemorate.

It was right and proper that the people living upon this hill should form a little commonwealth by themselves, and govern it as they deemed best. They were in numbers sufficient, their wealth was equal to it, and in intelligence and capacity they were in no way lacking. They felt for this land so lifted up towards the heavens all the passionate love which the Swiss feel for their snow-clad mountains or the highlander of Scotland for Ben Nevis or Ben Lomond. They took a pride in their lofty isolation and desired to give to it a local habitation and a name, and the mention of that name has never yet brought a blush of shame to the check of one of its citizens.

It was, is, and always has been a little town. In population it never reached much beyond seven hundred, but it has succeeded in always making itself known and felt, sometimes in one way and sometimes in another. It is always throwing out its banners, and when one grows dim, it lifts up another. Into obscurity and neglect it will never consent to drop. When the cultivation of the soil began to fail, its enterprising citizens turned their attention to manufacturing, and there was not a town or city in the country that did not hear of it through its fancy boxes and portable writing desks. And even before new fashions threw these into innocuous desuetude the same men erected a temple of learning on this hill which for half a century has shed its light over the surrounding country and spread the fame of Mont Vernon far and wide. Finally, she invited the world to come and see her as she is when she puts on her summer robes of beauty, to breathe her air as pure as that which mantled Eden ere sin polluted it in spots, to drink of the waters that gush from her granite breast, to look up into her heavenly dome of a blue not less lovely than that o'erarching the Ionian land, to open their eyes upon a landscape of surpassing loveliness and of endless extent, to gaze upon her western skies when in autumn the sun drops behind the Lyndeborough mountains and paints the piled-up clouds in colors more brilliant and variegated than Turner saw when looking over Venice from the Lido; and the world came and still comes and will continue to come as long as men seek heal h, beauty and rest, where health, beauty and rest are found.

Mont Vernon followed the order which is observed in the evolution of nearly all of our New England towns. The farms came first and then the village. When the population was sufficient they first erected a church. For convenience it was located near the territorial center and around it the village grew. First came the doctor, then followed in natural succession the blacksmith, the shoemaker, the storekeeper, the carpenter, and these, with the few owners of nearby lands which they cultivated, make up with their homes the typical New England village. Such was the little village of Mont Vernon a few years after the erection of the church already spoken of, and it has continued in the form in which it was originally constructed to the present day, with only few changes and some additions. For a generation after its incorporation the citizens of Mont Vernon were almost entirely engaged in agriculture and prosperously so until 1840 or a few years later. The decline in this industry was due to causes beyond their control. They affected every agricultural community in New England to a greater or less degree. Events are every day happening in this busy world that bring a blessing to one place and a blight to another. We can neither foretell them, nor guard against their effects. A Portuguese navigator passing around the Cape of Good Hope to India destroyed the commerce of the Mediterranean and built up that of the English Channel and the North Sea. Eli Whitney invented the cotton gin and indirectly brought on the Civil War. England repealing her corn laws reduced the value of her farming lands one-half and made herself the greatest manufacturing nation in the world. When our railway system was extended into the valley of the Mississippi our New England farmers found that they could no longer raise corn and wheat and oats and barley in competition with the owners of more fertile lands and easier of cultivation, and from that date and for this cause began the abandonment of our Mont Vernon farms, and I fear the end has not yet been reached. Not only man and his belongings, but the birds of the air even are subject to the decrees that evolution is issuing from her irresistible throne.

Where now are those flocks of wild pigeons that in the gloom and glory of an autumnal morning fifty years ago darkened the sun in their flight like the arrows of Xerxes at Thermopylæ? When the wheat and rye fields disappeared they took their flight and not one from their untold millions remained to remind us of their existence.

After the Revolutionary War the process of settling of New Hampshire continued with an accelerated pace, and before the close of the century our eager home builders had pushed northward to the very borders of Canada and filled up the lands between. Though a farming population is the most independent and self-sustaining of all, yet there is no such thing as real independence. We are always leaning one upon another. The city is dependent upon the town and the town upon the city. One nation draws from another and gives of her own what is wanted in exchange. As New Hampshire did not possess navigable rivers, and was unable to construct canals as did New York, Pennsylvania and Maryland, they were obliged to build roadways to meet the demands of trade. In 1802 the Second New Hampshire turnpike was completed from Amherst through this town to Claremont, and later by extension to Windsor in Vermont. They imitated the Romans and laid it out in a straight line, neither turning to the right nor left, whatever might be the difficulties in the way. Our sturdy ancestors seemed to delight in overcoming obstacles and never turned aside to avoid them. The opening up of this road was an event of great importance to Mont Vernon. It was the avenue through which passed the travel of northern New Hampshire and Vermont to the metropolis of New England. It continued to hold it until the Concord and Nashua Railroad was opened in 1857, when the toll-gates were pulled down and its glory was a thing of the past

I have heard my father say that he has seen 125 two horse teams, loaded with the products of the farm, passing one after the other through this village on their way to Boston. Scarcely a day would pass in the appropriate season of each year when droves of cattle and sheep and swine were not seen passing in the same direction. To accommodate this immense traffic taverns were built every two or three miles along the pike, and there were some capable of providing for the care of forty horses at one time. The town then could boast of four stores, and it has been said that the village tavern, located on what is now the public square, was in the habit one time of dispensing to its customers a barrel of rum a week This period marked the culmination of the prosperity of Mont Vernon as an agricultural community, and can be looked back to as its most picturesque and busy age. Fortunately for its future there were then growing up here a group of men of high intelligence and ambitious views who gave a new impulse to the town and for a generation kept it in prosperous ways

The manufacture of desks and fancy boxes was carried on by William Conant and Harry H. Bragg, which at times gave employment to fifty people; a large tannery was established by Joseph A. Starrett; the husk business was the conception of F. O. Kittredge,

and besides these, clocks and organs were sent out from here that
kept good time and made fine music, and as they bore the name of the
place of their manufacture upon them, they sold readily without a
warranty.

In 1850 the men whose names have just been given, joining
hands with several other of the prominent citizens, learning from their
own experience the value of a good education, and desiring that the
rising generation should have within their reach opportunities beyond
that which they had enjoyed, resolved that an academy of the first
order should be erected, and the result of their labors and contributions was soon seen in the institution which for a long time flourished
here under the names of Appleton Academy and McCollom Institute.
Since then I have mingled somewhat widely with men and affairs, but
there has never come under my observation or within my knowledge
an instance of such liberality or such great personal sacrifices as were
made by these men in the establishment of this school. It is certain
that one of them gave to it at least one-fifth of all his wealth, which
was limited to a few thousand dollars.

There was a time when 125 scholars were being educated in
yonder building, and the flourishing years of the academy gave to
the village a life and vivacity to which before it had been a stranger,
and to hundreds of boys and girls the opportunity of gaining an education, which, but for the labor and sacrifice of these men, they never
could have gained.

The next stage in the history of Mont Vernon is due to the
sagacity, good judgment and business enterprise of F. O. Kittredge.
His love for his native town was intense and beyond that of most
other men. What he thought to be so attractive and beautiful, he
believed other people would also enjoy, and in the fifties he erected
in the village a hotel for summer boarders that in outward appearance and interior equipment was the equal of any house of the same
character in New England. From the date of its construction until
its destruction by fire in 1872 it was annually filled with guests of
high standing and refinement, whose presence was welcomed with the
same pleasure and cordiality by the people of the town as they extend to their successors of the present year.

It is not possible to close the history of Mont Vernon, that seems
to be so far removed from the rush and roar and turmoil of the great
world as to be hardly in touch with it, without reminding you that it
is one of the little units that forms a part of a mighty nation. Though
far removed the nerves of human allegiance reach here and thrill here,
and nowhere have human hearts moved more deeply and responded
more quickly to the demands of patriotism.

To the men and women of Mont Vernon, to the men and women
of every city and town and hamlet of the North, the year of 1861
stands out in the background of their lives as the one most memorable and eventful. It presents itself to us still in a dual aspect—

filled with light the brightest, and with shadow the darkest. It is a canvas from which stands out the majestic figure of America, full of strong and lusty life, in the act of putting on her armor and taking up the sword, set in a frame of mourning.

I need not tell you how the currents of our lives began to widen and to flow into the broad stream of the Nation's life, helping it and strengthening it with heart and hand, with thought and deed.

No longer then were the thoughts uppermost in the minds of men when would the warm and mellow earth be ready for the seed, no fear of summer drought to wither or early frosts to kill the growing corn. All the hopes and fears of everyday life were overshadowed by the impending national calamity and the resolution and work to avert it. It was a conflict on our part not of aggression, but of preservation. We were a people unused to arms. The story of our wars had been told to us, if told at all, by the descendants of those who had participated in them. The actors had passed away.

But when the nation rose from its sleep of security to put forth its strength in defense of life and honor, we recall with what quickness of decision and alacrity of step our young men left field and workshop, school and college, home and friends to meet the unknown but certain perils of war. They were caught up and carried along almost joyously to the strife by that spirit which kindleth a flame in the hearts of a people when great dangers threaten and heroic work is laid upon them to perform. They made no excuses; they asked not for delay, but to the call gave the quick response, "We are ready."

The Union soldier was gifted with that intelligence which enabled him to see the importance of the conflict in which he was engaged, and its relation and bearing upon the nation's history and that of the civilized world. He knew and felt that though his own name might soon be forgotten, yet his valor, aiding and stimulating that of his fellows, was being wrought and spent in deeds which were to live through all human story, and, with this foretaste of immortality charged home against the foe. Thus and thus only have the great battles of freedom been won. From the beginning to the close of the war Mont Vernon furnished four commissioned officers and about fifty enlisted men.

The names of your soldiers were upon the muster-roll of every army; they followed the fortunes of the Army of the Potomac from the beginning to the end: they were present at the taking of New Orleans; they joined in the assault at Port Hudson, and helped to open up the Mississippi to the peaceful commerce of the world; they endured the hardships and experienced the pangs of hunger without complaint under Burnside in the siege of Knoxville, and marched with happy hearts under Sherman from Atlanta to the sea.

And now the hour has struck and the story is ended. We stand face to face with the new century. We will not attempt to penetrate into the future, but await its unfolding as surely it will unfold with its duties and responsibilities, with its joys and sorrows, its smiles and tears. The good God has set your lives in pleasant places and scattered around you with prodigal hand the beauties of wood and field, of hill and mountain, the wavy lines of the smiling plains that stretch and prolong themselves till they meet the sea at its margin.

In my day I have traveled far and wide and seen many of the places famed for their beauty and loveliness. I have stood on Castle Hill in Edinborough and looked down upon the contrasted picture of water and cultivated earth and far-off hills that spread out before and around you there; I have seen the fields and meadows that roll away from the foot of Windsor Castle in all their wealth of rural loveliness; I have gazed upon the wonders of an Italian landscape, crowded with the fig, the pomegranate, the orange and the lemon when they burst forth into what seems a springtide of eternal bloom; I have crossed and recrossed our great continental uplift, seamed with marvelous canyons, whose granite, iron and marble walls, painted by storms, gleam with wonders of color as brilliant and variegated as sunset clouds, broken by lofty mountain ranges, whose peaks are covered with eternal snow, where from the mists of ocean are brewed the storm-cloud, which moving from their mountain home and spreading their wings in flight until they cover a continent, fertilize it with a wealth of generous waters, and at times terrify it with the wrath of tempests, but nowhere have I looked upon that which has left a more enduring and pleasing recollection upon the mind than that which for a hundred times I have looked out upon from the top of Prospect Hill.

When a century hence some one shall fill the place which I now hold, and to the generation of Mont Vernon men and women then living shall unfold the annals of the hundred years then passed, may the record be as white and free from blot or stain as that which I have been able, all inadequately, to record to you.

SOME HISTORICAL SKETCHES OF THE CONGREGATIONAL CHURCH.

By Huntington Porter Smith, Cambridge, Mass.

The fathers and mothers of this church were of Puritan stock. They had the Puritan spirit, the Puritan religious principle, the Puritan faith in God which overcomes the world. They were resolute, intelligent, worthy pioneers, who began the settlement of the place about 1765. They were accustomed to walk from the extreme borders five or six miles to the village below for public worship. This they did cheerfully until their hearts were moved to prepare a church home nearer their dwellings. In the winter it was common for whole families to ride down to church on their ox-sleds. In the summer, during the week, they occasionally had preaching in the barns of these remote districts, but they early looked forward to the time when this section should become a separate parish. For this they planned. When a majority of the church in Amherst extended a call to Rev. Jeremiah Barnard, they said they should object to any other settlement until their request to form another parish was granted. "They insisted," says a writer at a later period, "upon having a more pious and more orthodox ministry and proceeded to supply themselves." In September, 1780, a council was convened which organized here what was called the Second Church in Amherst.

No records of this church for the first thirteen years are to be found; but aged men who were living here fifty years ago said the first deacons were Nathaniel Hayward, Richard Ward and Oliver Carlton. These aged men also gave other information concerning the early days which happily has been preserved. For example, that Rev. Mr. Coggin from Chelmsford, Mass., preached to a large audience in Major Cole's barn which was said to have been just south of the spot where the old meeting-house stands. His sermon was upon the importance of immediately erecting a house of worship. This was in revolutionary times and a large thing for these farmers to undertake, but on the following April, each farm in the community sent in its free will offering of timber for the frame and covering for their house of worship.

The first settler on the hill, Lieut. James Woodbury, presented land for the church. Those venerable men to whom we have alluded as living here fifty years ago said that the heaviest timber was drawn upon the snow across the fields and over the walls and fences without obstruction. This was in the month of April, 1781. David said, looking forward to the time when there should be a suitable resting place for the ark of God, "I will not give sleep to mine eyes, or slumber to my eyelids until I find out a place for the Lord, a tabernacle for the mighty one of Jacob." Of like spirit were these progenitors. In June, 1781, fifty-four individuals were constituted by the General Court the Second Parish of Amherst. So urgent was the demand for the house that before the floor timbers were laid, it was occupied without any formal dedication. We may well imagine the unfinished walls and roof resounded with fervent prayer and praise. As they were able, they slowly but steadily completed what their longing hearts had prompted them to begin.

During the first winter they worshiped there, sitting upon rough benches, with a single floor, and most of the windows loosely boarded up. "To this place came men and women walking even from the Chestnut Hills, five miles distant, with nothing to warm them but the glad tidings of salvation, which they could scarcely hear for the raging of the wind without." So says one who wrote at a later day of this beginning. The old fashioned square pews were constructed as families felt able, the "pew-ground," as it was called, being deeded

by the parish. There was for a time much space left for the benches.
The ground for four or five of the square pews was elevated in front
of the pulpit and reserved for free seats.

We say of such men, we say of these men, "they builded better
than they knew"; but we also say of them they knew they were building well. They knew that the timber that they drew from their farms
was the soundest and the best. They knew the foundation upon
which they placed those timbers was not shifting sand, but a rock.
They knew that they were not building for themselves alone but for
future generations, and they knew they were building a church for
God.

There is an old couplet that runs:

> "He who builds a church for God and not for fame
> Will never mark the marble with his name."

Name and fame were not their ambition.

"Though dead they speak in reason's ear and in example live,
Their faith, and hope, and mighty zeal still fresh instruction give."

Looking up to the old meeting-house, recalling its history, and
the lives of these faithful men and women, one has an impulse to
stand with uncovered head. Men and women of the present day,
you have done well to preserve this ever sacred edifice, which from
afar as well as near "many an eye has danced to see." You have
perpetuated that which shall be an inspiration for braver, nobler living to yourselves and children, a cause for gratitude to every home-
comer. To a remarkable degree the church here and the town have
ever been interwoven. Though you now have a more beautiful house
of worship, the old meeting-house as the fathers planned, and for
which they toiled, is still a link that unites the town and the church.

In 1780 and 1781, there was no regular minister. In 1782, a
Mr. Powers supplied. In 1783, Mr. Samuel Sargent was called to
settle, but declined the call. Rev. John Bruce was the first pastor,
and this was his first and only pastorate. He was born in Marlboro,
Mass., in 1757, and entered Dartmouth College at the age of twenty,
graduated in 1781, with honor and greatly beloved by his instructors.
In 1781, he came here from his theological studies, having declined
an invitation to be the pastor at Mason. He remained twenty-five
years, this being nearly twice as long as any other minister, and died
suddenly, March 12, 1809. The people had gathered as usual on
that Sabbath morning for the service when the announcement of his
death was made.

Mr. Bruce was eminently a successful minister, greatly endeared
to his people, and deeply mourned. The lapse of time has not been
permitted to efface his memory, for children's children have sacredly
kept it as a rich legacy. Though but fifty-two years of age at the
time of his death, such was his dignity of character and gracious-

bearing that he was known as "Father Bruce." For the first ten years and the last eight when he was here, there are no church records, but in the handwriting of Mr. Bruce there has been brought to light what is undoubtedly a list of members of the church when he became pastor, numbering 110. During the seven years, from 1794 to 1801, it appears that 83 members were added by letter or profession: 50 were added by profession in the year 1799. This revival was the first one known in this section, and awakened much interest far and wide.

As will be noticed, it was in his day that the town was incorporated. Who first so happily suggested the name of this town? I waited in vain for the town historian to tell us yesterday. Though the right name is as we now see it, others must have been suggested :— West Amherst, Montville, perhaps. But who naturally would be the one to give a name in which all would unite, but the man in whom all hearts were united — the intelligent, sweet-spirited pastor? One afternoon he rides in a chaise from Chestnut hill where he has been making calls. Looking off from a hill-top to this one he has new views or new impressions of the beauty and the verdure of the fields and farms clustering here, and he says "Mont Vernon." So the town votes Mont Vernon. Thus the imagination pictures it.

Rev. John Bruce had four sons, all of whom lived beyond the alloted age of man and passed their entire lives in this town. Deacon John, "Squire Nat," James, and Captain William. How familiar their names! In our boyhood days how familiar their forms and features. Intelligent men, men of worth, they faithfully served the church and the town.

Just eighty years after the first pastor graduated at Dartmouth College his grandson, George Anson Bruce, son of Nathaniel, received his diploma from his grandfather's college, and at the same time and place his townsman and boon companion, George Augustus Marden. The historian of 2003 will have ample occasion to speak of these men.

I will not tarry here to enlarge upon their distinguished record, but simply say that side by side they prepared for college, and passed their four years together there; both served our country in the Civil War, and since then in legislative halls as well as in the arena of life they have greatly honored their native town and state. The future historian will doubtless refer to this period as the "time of the Georges."

The second pastor was the Rev. Stephen Chapin. He had been dismissed from a neighboring church, so I find it written, on account of his "deep and discriminating orthodoxy, and his bold, unadorned, uncompromising style of preaching." He immediately received a call to this church. He remained here nine years, during which time large numbers were added to the church. He was a graduate of Harvard College, and died while President of The Columbian College, Washington, D. C. The cause of his separation from this church was from a quarter least expected. A child being presented for baptism. Mr. Chapin refused to administer the rite, announcing a change in his views respecting the mode and subject of baptism. So completely were the hearts of the people united in him, that it was supposed that the flock would follow the shepherd, but led by the Rev. Humphrey Moore of Milford, they stood their ground in argument, and not a single individual swerved from the faith. "Yet," says the record, "they treated Mr. Chapin with great affection and tenderness."

After an interval of more than a year, Rev. Ebenezer Cheever, a graduate of Bowdoin College, became pastor. He continued until 1823. In 1820, the first Sabbath School was organized. It was held in the old red school-house which stood where the village school-house now stands. The Sabbath School was composed only of children.

Rev. Nathaniel Kingsbury followed Mr. Cheever in a prosperous ministry of thirteen years. The temperance movement began early in Mr. Kingsbury's time. It is on record that there were eight tavern licenses given in one year here. In some of the places a barrel of liquor was sold per week. It was no easy matter to control public opinion. The church seemed on the point of being rent asunder and the minister driven from his post. There is an anecdote which illustrates the times: The new road was being built south of the church. Mr. Kingsbury, passing that way, overtook one of his deacons with "two pails full of grog." The deacon advised the pastor to go on the old road as the workmen were so drunk that he would be insulted. It is mentioned that church members would angrily leave the sanctuary if the subject of temperance was alluded to. But the pastor was faithful; devout men and women stood by him, and the truth was finally triumphant. "Intemperance was excommunicated from the community, as well as from the church."

In this ministry, I notice that on September 4th, 1831, the following persons were received into the church: William Conant and wife, Thomas Cloutman and wife, John Carlton, Timothy Kittredge, Susan Marden, Dr. Daniel Adams. Dr. Adams was a man of considerable fame, being the author of Adams's Arithmetic which, in after years some of us boys and girls knew to a very limited extent and not by heart. In the days of his medical practice, the doctor was a great favorite. To quote from one of the Hutchinsons' well known songs, he was one of those doctors who came "like post with mail but ne'er forgot his calomel." If the baby died, it was a great consolation to feel that it had been under Dr. Adams's care. There was a time when the good doctor led the choir, and with a tuning fork pitched the tune. Here I may as well pause, and speak of some of the traditions and recollections of the choir in the thirties and forties.

Thomas Cloutman was chorister after Dr. Adams. Capt. Cloutman was a sturdy man, erect in figure and with upright hair; prompt, a good timist and drill master. It was "Down, left, right, up, Sing!" with him. Are there any members of Dr. Adams's choir here?

I hardly dare assume it, but I am confident there are enough of Thomas Cloutman's choir who could, if they would, give us an Old Folks' Concert that would be interesting and inspiring. How we should like to hear them sing:—

"Fly like a youthful hart or roe
Over the hills where spices grow"

to the accompaniment of violins and bass viol. Most of that choir are members of the Choir Invisible, but some of them are spared to us.

More of you remember the choirs in the forties rather than in the thirties. Some are born singers. Such were some of these. The pastor enjoyed the singing beyond expression. "How beautifully Emeline sang today," I heard him exclaim more than once as he came home from a Sabbath service. Emeline Cloutman was only twelve years old when she became a member of the choir. They had an organ then and Esther Cloutman played it. When she was called to join that choir above, her father could no longer remain in this one. If she has her earthly form and face there, it is in harmony with all we imagine of that home. Laurana Smith, the village music teacher and, after Esther Cloutman, church organist, ever faithful at her post of duty; Levi Averill, the organ blower, shall I not speak of him? An illness in childhood left him not entirely what he would otherwise have been; but he was all there, body and soul, when he "played the organ," as he called it.

As you see, I have anticipated the years. Let me again refer to Mr. Kingsbury's time. It was in the latter part of his ministry that a stove was procured for the church. Some few regarded it "too oppressive an innovation to be borne." They claimed it reflected upon the habits of those earlier days. It may also be recorded that in 1837 the church was removed to the other side of the street, remodeled, and furnished with bell and organ. In 1855, I may add, "with all needed repairs it was supplied with furnaces."

Rev. Edwin Jennison, introduced by Mr. Kingsbury, was installed on the day the latter was dismissed, April 6, 1836. The people regarded Mr. Jennison as unsurpassed by any minister in the county as a sermonizer. On account of failing health he asked for dismissal, and took a voyage to Europe.

Rev. Bezaleel Smith was installed August 19th, 1841, and continued for about nine years. The pastor's son, though but a small boy, may be supposed to have considerable to say of this period, but ministers' children should be careful what they say. You have probably noticed that they are. That was a basic principle in this family. Still the size of the family and that of the salary is public property, therefore this minister's son does not make any break in saying that the family consisted of the parents, six children, and a grandmother. The annual salary was $500, with an annual donation party, if memory serves. The donation parties were memorable occasions. On the pages of the church book there are no itemized accounts or statements of gross receipts, but this child can testify that anything nourishing was acceptable in the family, from a string of onions or a string of dried apples up to a barrel of flour. The children's warmest thanks were bestowed upon those who sent in pumpkin pies and doughnuts. Alas! for those country minister's children who never know the joys of the old fashioned donation party. Oh that some genius like the one who wrote of the moss-covered bucket would sing of those joys!

Not only at those parties, but usually, this minister's son was a pretty happy boy. But for a time he felt that he did not have a fair and square deal with the world because he was a minister's son. To him the air upon this hilltop seemed to be blue with that old Satanic falsehood about "ministers' sons and deacons' daughters." The atmosphere was cleared one day as by a bolt from heaven when Dr. Davis of Amherst preached upon that subject. He vividly and eloquently illustrated his sermon with anecdotes of successful and distinguished men and women who were children of Christian parents, ministers and deacons especially included. The boy does not remember one of the sermons of Humphrey Moore who often supplied his father's pulpit, and not all of his father's, but he does remember that one of Dr. Davis's, and that he went out of church that day, his head erect and as he believes a stronger, better boy. These were the days of tin foot stoves which we boys had to fill from the red hot stove in the vestibule and deposit at our mothers' and grandmothers' feet.

A majority of the church at this time took ultra ground against African slavery and voted, as did other New England churches, to exclude all slave-holders from the pulpit and the Lord's table. Mr. Smith, while abhorring slavery as much as any one, did not believe in that method of expressing his abhorrence. There were those in the South, sincere Christians, who had come into possession of slaves which they thought it their duty to retain and care for. He had a college classmate who was that kind of a slave-holder. The pastor felt that such men should not be excluded from the communion table. We cannot hide that the saints had their little differences then as now. You know the old hymn says:

> "They wrestled hard as we do now
> With sins and doubts and fears,"

and probably with one another, as we do now. It is remembered that the pastor said in his farewell sermon:

"When I am willing to have my wife and children placed upon the auction block and sold one by one to the highest bidder, then you may accuse me of being pro-slavery." But these conflicting opinions left no scars which time did not soon obliterate. Nothing has ever been wanting on the part of this people to show their affectionate regard for this pastor his wife, and their children. While here, the wife of his youth was taken from him and her tranquil grave is in yonder cemetery. Later, three of their children were brought here, and are resting by their mother's side.

The name of Conant has been identified with the history of this church for more than eighty years. As we have noticed, William Conant and wife united here on profession of faith September 1st, 1831. The church was not long in finding out that it had in this young man good material for a deacon. May I not say — many deacons, since it was well grounded in the doctrines of foreordination and predestination. Mr. Conant was unanimously chosen for high office just a year after he united with the church. "Once a deacon always a deacon" by Divine right, when such as he are elected. Not a tall man in stature — measured by his soul, he was a large man. He had five sons and three daughters—two pews full, counting the father and mother. They were round, smiling faces. Smiles are usually responsive with children, often leading up to an explosion. I remember, one of this deacon's sons got one of the minister's sons into trouble just by a smile, and the latter came very near being invited into the pulpit. I once heard a talented young minister say at a Council in reply to the question, "What led him to choose the ministry," that he thought it must have been because he always saw the humorous side of things. Was it for this reason that William Conant's five mirthful boys all became the best of deacons? Yes, and because the father's veins were full of deacon blood, I should say, and the daughters were of the same type and mould as the sons. From this country church they went, one remaining to fill the father's place. This family fully demonstrates what is undeniably true, that country churches furnish in a large measure the life and strength of the city churches. I wonder if those children heard that sermon alluded to, preached by Dr. Davis more than fifty years ago. They are an illustrious example of the truth that was proclaimed that day.

William H. succeeded his father in office here, and faithfully served the church until laid aside by illness. Only a few months ago some of us came to this fair village and stood beside the open grave of this good friend of the church and our good friend.

The eighth minister of this church was the Rev. Charles D. Herbert, who remained nearly six years. Mr. Herbert was a man of ardent religious spirit. The Academy was incorporated about the commencement of his ministry. Several of the students took an active part in the work of the church. John F. Colby, of enduring memory, was among these, uniting with the church at that time. With the pastor he was holding neighborhood meetings that fall, 1852, beginning then the work of an earnest Christian from which he never ceased.

The next pastor was the Rev. Charles E. Lord, who served the church a little more than four years, leaving here on account of Mrs. Lord's health. The letter of the church to them on their departure is one of special affection and appreciation.

The Rev. George E. Sanborne followed, and although he continued only three years, his ministry was one of great usefulness in uniting more closely the hearts of the people in Christian fellowship. Mr. Sanborne was a man of tender, persuasive spirit, and the light of it pervaded the whole community.

Rev. Benson M. Frink was the next pastor for two years. He was a young man of exceptional ability, fully consecrated to his high calling. He went from this church to the Central Church, Portland, Maine. The Council in granting the letter of dismission expressed their warm sympathy in the frequent trials of the church in its changes of ministers, and said: "The ministry of our young brother has been largely blessed in this place."

The parsonage was built at this time. One other special event which occurred during Mr. Frink's stay was the ordination here of C. F. P. Bancroft, Ph. D., who went as teacher and pastor to Lookout Mountain. Dr. Bancroft's wider fame is that of Andover, but he was the successful principal of our Academy for four years. He closely identified himself with the work of the church, often supplying the pulpit in the absence of the pastor. While I am not expected to speak here of the Academy, I cannot forbear quoting from the annals published on the 25th anniversary in 1875: "He" [Mr. Bancroft] "came immediately after graduating at Dartmouth, and when he was but twenty years of age. We are told that his rule was one of love, and not of terror, — a rule that worked very satisfactorily for him since one of his pupils was so effectually subdued that she has been willing to be governed by it to this day." To this quotation let me add, that from this favored spot no choicer spirits have ever gone forth than Cecil and Fannie Kittredge Bancroft. Lovely and pleasant in their lives, in their death they were not long divided.

The next pastor, Dr. S. H. Keeler, was here eight years. That this was a ministry of strength and uplifting power is abundantly testified by living witnesses, although the records are very meagre. John Bruce, after a continued service of fifty years as deacon, resigned the office about this time. At his death he left a legacy to the church of $400.

Deacon J. A. Starrett and Deacon William Conant also, after their long years of service, resigned. Tender and appreciative letters were given to each of these faithful servants of God, which are placed in your records. Deacons Bruce, Starrett, and Conant! — a cluster of names that will ever add bright lustre to the pages of the history of Mont Vernon church!

Rev. W. H. Woodwell, of Hampton, Connecticut, followed, and remained nearly four years and a half, having endeared himself to the church by his wisdom and sympathy.

Rev. C. C. Carpenter commenced his labors here Nov. 1st, 1880. After nearly five years of generous toil he laid aside the work on account of impaired health and by advice of his physician. I find on his leaving, a tribute of great respect and affectionate esteem, voted by the church and signed by a committee consisting of these beloved brothers who have now all passed on — Wm. H. Conant, George E. Dean, Thomas H. Richardson.

Mr. Carpenter is the man above all others to prepare the annals of this church, and would have done so now, had he felt that health permitted. By good fortune he is with us today, bringing his greeting and his own account of the church and people in his time.

After him came Richard A. McGown, John Thorpe, T. J. Lewis, Donald Brown, and H. P. Peck, the present pastor.

On some future occasion, others will speak more fittingly of these later pastorates, of the new church building, of the large gifts for it, from distant friends, as well as smaller gifts from equally devoted and loving hearts. Especially will they tell how the last thousand dollars of the debt was raised on a Sunday evening by George A Marden, when by mirthful personal appeals, witty anecdotes, and characteristic persuasion he gathered the needed sum, an entertainment never excelled on this hilltop, besides being the most profitable one. But is mine to speak of earlier days.

Let me give you one or two more pictures of the long ago. When I was a boy, I saw as a boy, I thought as a boy. The old meeting-house was the centre of all things here, and from its belfry you could see everywhere. Go up into the belfry and I will show you the cyclorama on a Sunday morning of that time. Everybody is on his way to meeting. Looking east, you see winding along the side of Preble Hill (they give it a grander name new, because the city folks require it) a long row of wagons loaded down almost to the axles with Batchelders, Kendalls, Wilkinses, Robies, Robinsons, McColloms. Coming across Cloutman's blueberry pasture is Mr. Eliot, the village carpenter who lives outside the village. Samuel, John and Jane are with him. Look north, and you see wagon loads of Battleses, Averills, Lamsons, Westons, Richardsons, Smiths, Perkinses, Trows, and many others on foot. Look east by south,—those are the Campbells, Baldwins, Browns, Trevitts. That is Sarah Jane Trevitt with a beautiful bouquet of flowers for the pulpit. Toiling slowly up the hill, from the south, with his horse stopping to puff at every other "thank-you-marm," is Joshua Cleaves with his wife and two daughters, Lydia and Augusta. The latter teaches the village school held in the old red school-house. The former has also taught there. Mr. Cleaves's brother John and his son William are walking. Uncle Joshua will have a comfortable nap before he returns. Another wagon is that of William Richardson. He is driving his son Justin's white mare, "pushing on the reins" continuously. Justin is walking. Then Capt. Kittredge's family (where the minister was never allowed to be criticized), two loads of them, one wagon and a rockaway, the latter the toniest vehicle in town. They have with them old lady Coburn and the widow Kittredge. Sabrina Coburn is also on the way. Charles and George Kittredge are walking up the old road with their two cousins, Nancy and Harriet. There is James Bruce with his three daughters. Behind them is Deacon John Carlton, son of the first deacon Carlton, and wife, with Harriet and Abbie. Joseph and John are walking cross-lots. The Trows of the south part of the town are on their way: also a stray Hutchinson (most of them go to Milford). Turn in a westerly direction, and you see the Uptons coming over the old, uneven Purgatory road, and Henry Dodge's family, who live at the Old Homestead. The Dodges are in a double-seated "democrat" wagon, good, honest Democrat that he is. He is fair to middling in size and weight (rather more so), but there is room for his wife and four little girls besides little Henry Francis, who adds his mite to help bring down the wagon springs. From different points of the compass, as you see, they all come "with one accord to one place." They bring their luncheons and stay all day. You cannot see how they and the village folks can crowd in, but I remind you that it is a very large meeting-house, and they are all there, except those whom the minister mentions in his "long" prayer as "not present on account of severe illness or the infirmities of age."

Come down from the belfry and look in with me over the audience. You see Bruces enough and those connected with them by the "ties of nature and affection" to fill a fair-sized meeting-house. The Conants are there all right, about two-thirds up the right aisle. The Stevens pews are full, and a portion in the singers' seats. There is a full pew of Cloutmans, and the balance in the choir. How it would delight President Roosevelt's heart to see that row of chubby Marden children. They are all young, but George is old enough to repeat to his Sabbath School teacher.

"Though I am young, a little one.
Yet I can speak and go alone."

Zephaniah Kittredge, his sons and daughters and grandchildren, Starretts, Stinsons, Marbles, Dunbars, Odells, Smiths, Bakers, Braggs. If I have omitted anyone, he need not speak, for him I have not offended!

Ah! these "scenes that once were mine and are no longer mine!" It does not harm us to have smiles as well as tears in God's House as we recall them, especially at such a time as this. We will turn from these things but cannot forget them, certainly not the hallowed names. We will "look up and not down, look forward and not backward," and we will "lend a hand," and "all abide in the deepening conviction that there is no institution like the Christian church, nothing that is worthy of one's utmost devotion save the kingdom of our Master."

ADDRESS BY REV. C. C. CARPENTER.

The speaker selected for this commemoration of the first hundred years of the Mont Vernon church, to whose interesting address we have just listened, is certainly far better fitted for that service than I, for he belonged to that century and I did not! He came to the town to reside, with his reverend father—at an early age, to be sure—nearly forty years before I set foot within its borders. My pastorate began indeed on the very boundary line of the church's second century. When I first visited Mont Vernon in September, 1880, I was told that the venerable Dr. Keeler had preached, two Sabbaths before, a centennial sermon in recognition of the original organization of the church in September, 1780. That first century had been blessed with twelve pastors—the full apostolic number—and when after the true Congregational fashion the people gave forth their lots, the lot fell upon me to be numbered with them and to take part in their ministry. And I always felt that I entered into their labors, and to a good extent reaped what they had sown. All praise to the memory of those early pastors; their faithful ministrations moulded a whole generation of strong-hearted, true-hearted men and women who believed in God, in the Bible, in the Church, in the Sabbath, in the seriousness of the life that now is, because connected with the life which is to come!

I have been asked for some remembrances of my pastorate. Memories I surely have, vivid and tender, of those five happy years of humble service here, although they ended nearly a score of years ago. I remember that first Sunday on the hilltop in the autumn of 1880, and the dear old meeting-house in which I preached—learning afterwards that my coming had been kindly arranged by my good friend, Dr. Bancroft, in the capacity of a candidate! And when the days of candidacy were over and the family had come to the parsonage—then of course standing on this site, and so ensuring still more of the brisk and beautiful breezes of winter than in its present humbler location—I remember that characteristic hospitality of Mont Vernon homes, which though not always entertaining angels always seemed to provide "angels' food"—and this hospitality continued unto the end.

The elder Bruces and Kittredges had passed on, but good old Deacon Conant remained—though only in the summer time—as also Mr. Cloutman, who lived till he was able to say with Joshua, "Lo, I am this day fourscore and five years old." Hiram Perkins died on the morning of the first Sunday of my pastorate. How well I remember all the rest: Deacon Starrett, Deacon Dean, Deacon Wm. H. Conant, Haskell Richardson—and his brother Nathan "in the singers' seats"—Capt. Trevitt from his fertile farm in the valley, and Porter Kendall from his rocky farm in the East,—a farm which seemed to bring forth "honey out of the rock" according to the

Scripture!—Dr. Bunton in his last days, Charles J. Smith, with his encyclopediac memory of all the past, B. F. Marden with his originality and mental independence, Major Stinson, the Batchelders, the Battleses, the Averills, the McColloms, the Lamsons, the Smiths, the dwellers in the North District, in the South District, in the East District, in the West District and on Beech Hill, and godly women not a few, such as Mrs. Trask Averill, Mrs. Nancy Stinson, Mrs. Mary Starrett, Jane Elliott, yes, and Laurania Smith with her passion for music, and many others, both men and women, whom time, not memory, fails me to tell of.

I remember the Academy and its work—education and religion co-operating after the plan of the fathers (the handmaids standing side by side now, instead of on opposite sides of the road)—the shorter principalships of Ray and Ward and Hunt, the longer one of Cassius Campbell, who was a tower of strength to church and pastor. I remember the Center school and the children who successively attended it—I still preserve tenderly a big bunch of their letters written when I came away; they are children no longer, and although I remember all their names, I wonder whether I shall recognize all their faces if I see them today! I remember the Sunday School, with Deacon Dean as superintendent and George Starrett and afterward Lucia Trevitt as librarians, and the quarterly concerts where were exhibited the rolls of honor for faithful attendance. I sent up to Mr. Marden the other day some of the lists executed in red crayon. I remember the Home Circle, with its pleasant entertainments, its beneficent and comprehensive work—repairing the chapel, painting the parsonage, building a parsonage barn, blowing the organ, plowing out the sidewalks in winter; I remember the training of the Buds of Promise—promise well fulfilled!—the levees and the lyceums and the Village Improvement Society, and, perhaps, best of all, the formation at the parsonage one stormy winter evening of the Christian Endeavor Society, the influence of which proved the glad beginning of open Christian life for many of our youth. I have brought back that precious roll of beginners to the church.

I remember seasons of joy and sorrow almost too sacred to mention—bride and bridegroom taking the glad vows of marriage, and the times of mourning, as one after another of our townsfolk departed hence, or sons and daughters of the town were brought back to be laid among their kindred in "God's acre." One specially tender incident I remember at the funeral of a dear old mother in Israel, whose name I need not speak, brought back from Somerville for burial here, when her seven sons and daughters, in a few minutes of waiting at the close of the service in the old meeting-house, as by common impulse sang together "In the sweet by and by, we shall meet on the beautiful shore."

You must pardon me, friends, if as I recall the pastors who preceded me and the parishioners of my time, one sad thought is for the moment uppermost in my mind. Of that roll of twelve pastors of the first century closing in 1880, five have died since that date — Jennison, Herbert, Lord, Sanborn, and Keeler — only Frink and Woodwell remain.   Mingled with the joy of meeting old friends is the sadness of not meeting others.   Of those whom I used to see before me in the old meeting-house, how many I miss!   I found most of their names this early morning in the quiet city of the dead : Dea. William Conant, Dea. Starrett, Dea. and Mrs. Dean, Mrs. Mary Starrett, Mrs. Nancy Stinson, Mrs. Bunton, Mr. and Mrs. Richardson, Mr. and Mrs. Porter Kendall, Capt. Trevitt, Mr. and Mrs. Batchelder, Mr. and Mrs. Trask Averill, Mr. and Mrs. Travis, Mr. and Mrs. Marden, Mr. and Mrs. Marble, Mr. and Mrs. Stinson, Mr. Stevens, Alonzo Bruce, Mr. and Mrs. Joseph Perkins, Justin Richardson, and I presume this does not include all.   Besides these I think of friends closely identified in our minds with Mont Vernon : John F. Colby, Augustus Berry, Dr. Bancroft and Mrs. Bancroft, Dr. Kittredge, Prof. Ray, Chas. P. Mills and others.   Last of all, and in respect of church associations nearest of all, I think of Dea. William H. Conant, gone so lately to realize what he often used to quote in our prayer meetings — we can almost hear his familiar voice even now — "Though our outward man perish, yet the inward man is renewed day by day : for our light affliction, which is but for a moment, worketh for us a far more exceeding and eternal weight of glory : while we look not at the things which are seen, but at the things which are not seen, for the things which are seen are temporal, but the things which are not seen are eternal."

But in place of this sad note — which is not really sad — let me add words of greeting, of cheer, of promise.   Instead of the past, we have the present, and future.   In an old exhibition program of your academy, twenty years ago, I noticed the other day the title of an essay written by one of your girls — "Mt. Vernon a Hundred Years Hence."   What is the outlook for the town's new century?   There are many elements of encouragement : a new sanctuary of "strength and beauty" ; instead of the fathers are the children ; new friends are added to the old who remain ; the never failing freshness of this air, the never fading beauty of these hills.   But let religion and education have the first place.   Mt. Vernon's second century will be largely what the church and the school shall make it, shall mould it!   The children of my time are the citizens of today : the children of today will be the citizens of your second century.   For the best and truest prosperity of Mt. Vernon's future, make sure that these institutions are constantly, heartily, strongly sustained!

Nor let us be disturbed because the thoughts and ways, the sermons and experiences of those ministers and people in the past differ so much in appearance from those of the present day.   Were they all wrong in the past?   Are we all wrong now?   Neither!   I have just read over the sermon of Stephen Chapin in commemoration of John Bruce, whose pastorate was not only the first, but by far the longest of all — how fitting that his honored grandson can be the historical orator at this time!—and I read such stern doctrine and gloomy exhortation as no preacher of today would think of using, and no congregation would listen to. I used to read when in Mt. Vernon an old set of written experiences of candidates for membership which some pastor had preserved, describing in stereotyped doctrinal phraseology their feelings, or what they thought their feelings ought to be. We could not possibly feel so or speak so. But they were right in their time—noble, sturdy men and women, true to their light and their consciences. We are right in thinking and speaking differently; the differences, however great they may seem, are really small—they represent the unimportant and the transient. Under these differences, these changing creeds and forms of statement, is the same truth—that is vital and enduring: "The things which cannot be shaken remain." Like the rock under your ancient church, like the hills which surround you as the mountains about Jerusalem, so the Rock of Ages is beneath all, the great facts of reason and revelation stand firm as the everlasting hills. Dear Dr. Bancroft, a few days before his death, said to me, "There are a few great, simple verities to be thought of now!" Let us keep them uppermost; God's existence, God's love for his children on the earth. His immortality and ours, Jesus Christ the same, yesterday and today and forever; these make what John Fiske called "the everlasting value of religion"—these are the simple, blessed verities which abide—we can trust them!

For all the past ministers of the dear old church on the hill-top, I will now say, "peace be within thee!" God grant that it may still be as a city set on a hill, as a light on a candle-stick, attracting and guiding children and youth, men and women, into an earnest faith in great and blessed things, training them for pure and honest and useful lives, so that they may enjoy whatever is true and right and good here, and thus be best fitted to inherit and enjoy that grander life, veiled now from our eyes, but not far away from us in elder years—not very far from any of us—when we shall come to Mount Zion and dwell at home, not for one "home week," but forevermore, all God's children united in the Father's House.

Mr. Carpenter closed with an exhortation to the maintenance of the precious heritage of the past—not to be content with praising the fathers but to imitate them—and recited Dr. Bacon's old hymn of the Pilgrim Fathers, "O God, beneath Thy guiding hand," the last stanza of which was especially appropriate:

> "And here thy name, O God of love,
> Their children's children shall adore,
> Till these eternal hills remove,
> And spring adorns the earth no more."

CHAPTER XIII.

MILITARY HISTORY.

French and Indian War Soldiers—The Revolutionary War—The War of 1812—Militia Musters—The Mexican War—The Civil War—Action of Town as to Bounties—Men Furnished Under Different Calls—Men in the Second, Third, Fifth, Eighth, Tenth, Eleventh, Thirteenth and Sixteenth New Hampshire Regiments, and the United States Sharp-Shooters—Town Agent For Raising Quotas—Action as to Drafted Men or Substitutes.

Mont Vernon, as small as she is, has had a part in all the wars which have taken place in this country, except the Spanish War. That part has not been large, but it has in every case been creditable. The story is a brief one, but it is honorable. Men went from this town to nearly all the New Hampshire organizations in the several wars, but the greater number served in the Civil War, and in the Thirteenth New Hampshire Volunteers, enlisting in Company B, with George A. Bruce, who was early chosen First Lieutenant, and with Charles M. Kittredge, who was later First Sergeant and then Second Lieutenant of the same Company. This company and regiment saw much active service.

Six soldiers who at that time lived in what is now Mont Vernon served in the French and Indian War, closing in 1763. They were Samuel Lamson, Jonathan Lamson, John Mills, Samuel Bradford and Daniel Weston. Stephen Peabody was a sub-officer.

Mont Vernon acted in conjunction with Amherst, it being a part of that town, in military affairs, until its entire separation in 1803.

About fifty soldiers served from what is now Mont Vernon, in the War for Independence. The following are their names: John

Averill, Daniel Averill, Sr., Enos Bradford, Joseph Bradford, John Cole, Nathan Cole, Isaac Palmer Curtice, John Carleton, Enoch Carleton, Jacob Curtice, Benjamin Dike, corporal, Stephen Dike, Amos Flint, Asa Farnum, John Farnum, Joseph Farnum, Stephen Farnum, John Farnham, Stephen Gould, Allen Goodrich, Silas Gould, Joshua Haywood, William Haywood, Zephaniah Kittredge, Soloman Kittredge, Joseph Lovejoy, Samuel Lamson, Andrew Leavitt, Joseph Leavitt, Jeremiah Lamson, John Mills, John Odell, Ebenezer Odell, Joseph Perkins, William Parker, Robert Parker, James Ray, Peter Robertson, Moses Sawyer, Daniel Smith, Asa Swinnerton (Swinington?), Samuel Sterns, Henry Trivet (Trevitt?), Eli Wilkins, Lemuel Winchester, Levi Woodbury, Jesse Woodbury.

Stephen Peabody was Adjutant of Col. Reed's regiment.

Levi Woodbury, uncle of Judge Levi Woodbury, who died in 1850, served on the privateer Essex, which was taken by the British. He was carried to England, a prisoner of war, where he died.

The following Mont Vernon soldiers died in the Revolutionary War: Lieut. Joseph Bradford, John Cole, Benjamin Dike, Jeremiah Lamson, Sylvester Wilkins.

The people of Mont Vernon, believing that the War of 1812 was just and necessary, ardently favored its prosecution, and quite a number enlisted for permanent service.

Captain James T. Trevitt, commanding a company in Colonel Steel's regiment, was for sixty days at Portsmouth, where was expected an attack from a British fleet cruising near by. This company was made up of men drafted for special service. Dr. John Trevitt was a surgeon, who continued permanently in the service after the conclusion of peace, and died in 1821 at Augusta, Ga., at his post of duty.

Dr. Rogers Smith was an assistant surgeon on the frontier.

In the days of "militia musters" Mont Vernon was always represented. For thirty years a first-class company of infantry was sustained here under the militia law. It would be exceedingly interesting to have a roster of the company or companies, or detachments, of the militia organizations in which there were Mont Vernon representatives, but the names are not known to be on record. Within the last half-century there were officers living in the town who probably gained their titles in the military service—such as Capt. Thomas Cloutman, Capt. N. R. Marden, (who later lived in Francestown). Capt. William Lamson. Capt. Joseph A. Starrett. Capt. William Bruce, and others.

In the war with Mexico. Chandler Averill was a volunteer. Capt. John Trevitt, a graduate of West Point in 1840, being in the regular army, served in this war.

THE CIVIL WAR.

The Civil War affected the little town of Mont Vernon much as it affected all rural New Hampshire. A spirit of intense patriotism was aroused, and the town was stirred to its depths by a determination to do anything within its power to aid in preserving the Union. The official action in town meeting is perhaps the best story of what was done in this direction :

1861. In a warrant for a special town-meeting, called for May 15, was the following article :

"2. To see if the Town will make the wages of those that volunteer to serve their country up to $18 per month, and furnish them with a suitable outfit, or make them a donation equal thereto, and make suitable provision for their families, or make as much provision for them as those that volunteer are accustomed to do for the families with which they are connected."

The vote on this article seems to have been somewhat extraordinary, in view of the proposition made therein. It was :

"Voted, that the Selectmen of Mont Vernon be directed to order paid from the treasury of said town to the following persons, who have enlisted in the volunteer service of the United States, the sum of seven dollars per month each, for a period not exceeding three months from the date of their enlistment in such service, viz : George Farnam, A. E. Bennett, John H. Smith, James Marvell, James Beard, Albert York, and also George W. Kittredge, if he has not been guaranteed extra wages by any association of persons, or by any town. Also that said Selectmen be instructed to pay an expense of board incurred for said individuals while drilling at Milford, and their wages at said Milford at eleven dollars per month, and also to pay for any material used in garments made and furnished to them as an outfit prior to their leaving for the point of rendezvous of their regiment in this state ; Conditioned, however, that if the Legislature of this state shall, at its next ensuing session make any appropriations covering any of the above expenses, only such money shall be paid under this vote for those of the above specified objects as are not provided for by such legislative acts."

It was also voted "to give to each of the above named persons who have volunteered a revolver, or twelve dollars in money."

At a special meeting held Oct. 18, 1861, there was an article in the warrant

"To see if the Town would raise money, or authorize the Selectmen to borrow money, to carry out the votes above recorded."

"Also to see if the town would pay for the soldiers' rubber blankets or overcoats, which were furnished by Milford people to those who first volunteered for three months from said Mont Vernon."

Art. 3. Also to see if the Town will pay the amount to each soldier for the support of his family, as provided by the law passed at the last session of the Legislature in this state."

At the meeting it was voted "That the Selectmen be instructed to borrow money to pay the bills which have been contracted for those who have volunteered for three months' service in the present war from the town of Mont Vernon."

Voted "That the town adopt the law in regard to paying each soldier for the support of his family, as provided by the law passed by the last session of the Legislature in this state."

August 12, 1862, at a special meeting, there was an article in the warrant

"To see if the Town will pay any amount of money as an inducement to persons to enlist into the military service of the United States, that drafting may be dispensed with."

On this the following vote was passed:

"That the town of Mont Vernon shall pay to any citizen of this Town who shall volunteer into the U. S. service for the term of three years, unless they shall sooner be discharged, the sum of one hundred dollars, which shall be paid to each volunteer upon his being mustered into the U. S. service."

Sept. 19, 1862. At a special town meeting, there was an article in the warrant

"To see what action the Town will take to encourage enlistments under the last call of the President of the United States."

On this article it was voted—

"To pay each person who will enlist into the United States service for the term of nine months, one hundred dollars, on his being mustered into the United States service."

1863, Sept. 4. At a special town meeting called for this date, an article in the warrant was—

"To see if the town will pay those that may be drafted and go into the service, or their substitutes who may perform the service.

three hundred dollars each, or any other sum, as part compensation for their service."

"On this it was voted—

"That the Selectmen of Mont Vernon be instructed to pay to each of the drafted men from this Town, under the present call, or their substitutes, three hundred dollars, after their being mustered into the United States service ten days."

Dec. 2, 1863, at a special town meeting called to see what action would be taken in regard to furnishing men for the United States service under the recent call of the President, it was voted—

"That the chairman of the board of Selectmen be authorized to furnish the substitutes for this Town on the best terms he can, under the last call of the President."

Also, "That James Upton be authorized, in behalf of said town, to borrow money sufficient to pay the substitutes for the quota required of Mont Vernon, and receive from the Government and the State the amount to be paid, and pay the same into the treasury, to be appropriated in liquidating the debt thus incurred by the Town."

James Upton was the chairman of the board of Selectmen.

March 8, 1864, there was an article in the warrant "To see if the town will make an appropriation in favor of all or any of the soldiers who enlisted from the town in 1861."

Voted—To pass by the article.

June 2, 1864, a special meeting was called "To see if the town will pay the soldiers about to be drafted, the sum of three hundred dollars each, or any other sum the town may see fit to give."

Voted—That the Selectmen be instructed to pay to volunteers, drafted men, or their substitutes, three hundred dollars on their being mustered into the United States service, and this vote to hold good till the next annual March meeting in 1865.

Voted—That the Selectmen be authorized to fill our quotas with volunteers or substitutes, and the Town will pay any sum over three hundred dollars which the same requires.

June 27, 1864, a special meeting was held "To see if the town will vote to raise a sum of three hundred dollars in gold, or its equivalent, for each drafted man or their substitutes, for the present call, and volunteers or drafted men or their substitutes for all calls that may take place before the annual meeting in March next."

The following resolutions were passed:

"Resolved, That the sum of three hundred dollars in gold be raised and paid to every man who has been drafted and held to service from Mont Vernon under the last call of the President for 200,-000 men; or to his substitute on his being mustered into the United

States service, if the Selectmen and Town Agent (to fill quotas) shall deem it expedient to do so.

"Resolved, That Charles J. Smith, who was chosen, on the second day of June, agent for the Town of Mont Vernon, to look out for the interests of the Town and fill our quotas with volunteers or substitutes, to hold said office until our annual meeting in March, 1865, be authorized, empowered and invested with the amplest general discretion to expend such sums of money as may be raised, in such a manner as he may deem best calculated to promote the pecuniary interests of the Town, and to fill any quotas of Mont Vernon under present or future calls of the President for troops, promptly, according to his best judgment.

"Resolved, That a sum not exceeding $10,000 be raised to carry into effect the votes passed at the Town meeting held on June 2nd and the vote passed this day."

March 14, 1865, an article in the warrant was—"To see what action the town will take in furnishing men that may be called for by the President for the Army for the coming year."

Voted, "To take no further action on the subject, the number of men to answer all calls not yet having been contracted for by the Town's agent for this purpose."

Article 6 was "To see what action the town will take with regard to paying those men that furnished substitutes under the call for two hundred thousand men."

Voted, "To dismiss the article."

When President Lincoln made a call for 75,000 volunteers for three months' service in 1861, no one went from this town, though three who have since resided here enlisted at that time in other parts of the state. They were Samuel J. Beard, New Boston, John M. Fox, Amherst, and Daniel H. Green, Milford, all enlisting in the 2nd N. H. Regiment. They enlisted in April for three months, and re-enlisted in May for three years as privates. Mr. Beard was wounded at Oak Green, Va., and was discharged on account of his wounds. Mr. Green was wounded at Gettysburg, Pa., and appointed a corporal. He lived on the old Nathaniel Bruce place in the village, which he had purchased, for some years, and died there in 1896. Mr. Beard lived in town, mainly at Mr. Henry F. Dodge's, but afterwards entered the Soldiers' Home at Tilton, where he died May 29, 1902, aged 66. Mr. John M. Fox lived in Mont Vernon, when he enlisted, on the farm formerly owned by William H. Ireland. He at first carried on the tailor's trade, having a shop in the D. W. Baker store. Later he bought out the store so long kept by T. H. Richardson, and for some years was postmaster. In May, 1898, having sold his store to Dea. W. H. Kendall, he removed to Rochester, N. H., where he kept a grocery store until May, 1903, when he returned to Mont Vernon, where at this writing (1906) he still lives, not being engaged in any regular business.

In the latter part of 1861 several went into service from this town, also one from Danbury—Warren D. Johnson—who enlisted in the 5th New Hampshire Regiment, and subsequently moved here, and died in 1893. He was a native of Danbury, and enlisted in Company I, of the Fifth Regiment, Oct. 5, 1861. He re-enlisted Jan. 1, 1864, and was promoted to Sergeant, being mustered out Jan. 12, 1865. He is said to have been several times wounded, and about a year before he died he received a pension. He came to Mont Vernon from New Boston, May 8, 1876, and died here Sept. 6, 1903, aged 50. He was in the battles of Chancellorsville, Vicksburg, Lookout Mountain, Wilderness, Cold Harbor, Petersburg, Five Forks and others.

Augustus Johnson enlisted from Nashua in 1861, in the Third New Hampshire Regiment, and was discharged for disability the same year. He enlisted again in the Tenth New Hampshire, July 30, 1862, and was discharged Nov. 10, 1865. He was a pensioner and came to Mont Vernon, where he married the widow of James Smith. After her death he entered the Soldiers' Home at Tilton, where he still is (July 5, 1906).

Matthew F. Burnham enlisted in the Third N. H. Regiment in 1861; was discharged, disabled, in 1863. He died at Mont Vernon in 1896.

George H. Farnum enlisted in 1861 in the Fifth N. H. Regiment as musician, was wounded at Fredericksburg, Va., Dec. 13, 1862, transferred to Veteran Reserve Corps, and was discharged May 4, 1867.

Henry N. McQuestion enlisted in the Fifth N. H. Regiment in 1861, as private, and died of disease June 6, 1862, at Newport News, Va.

The following men enlisted in the Eighth N. H. Regiment in 1861: Charles W. Brooks, as private. He died in Roxbury, Mass., in May, 1890.

George W. Brown, as private, died May 25, 1863, at New Orleans, La.

John Follansbee, as corporal, was wounded twice, was discharged disabled, Nov. 18, 1864. He died at Nashua, May 2, 1881.

William E. Ireland, as private. He was drowned July 26, 1864, in the Mississippi River at Morganzia, La.

Howard B. Ames enlisted from Lyndeborough in 1862, in the Eleventh New Hampshire Regiment. He moved to Mont Vernon and died here Nov. 12, 1876.

The following men enlisted in the Thirteenth N. H. Regiment in 1862:

George G. Averill, as private; afterwards detailed as musician.

George A. Bruce, as private; appointed 1st Lieut. 1862, appointed Capt. Co. A, May 30th, 1864; wounded, 1864, at Fort Harrison, Va., appointed Brevet Lt.-Col., Maj. and Capt. U. S. V. to March 13th, 1865, for gallant and meritorious services during the war. He now resides in Boston, Mass.

Albert Burnham, as private—was wounded June 1, 1864, at Cold Harbor, Va.

Israel Burnham, as private; discharged disabled, May 20th, 1864. He now lives in Nashua.

Charles W. Dodge, as private; appointed Corporal 1863, discharged to accept promotion to U. S. Colored Troops, Dec. 22, 1863, appointed 2nd Lieutenant Veteran Reserve Corps, 1865.

Charles M. Kittredge, 1st Sergeant; commissioned 2nd Lieut., resigned 1863. He moved to Fishkill-on-the-Hudson. He died in Mont Vernon, August 19th, 1896.

John T. Perkins enlisted as a private; appointed Corporal, 1864, wounded slightly May 16, 1864 at Drewry's Bluff, Va. He lives at Westboro', having a position there in the Massachusetts Insane Hospital.

Peter F. Pike enlisted as private. He died in September, 1898.

Charles H. Robinson, as private. He died May 23, 1864, at Milford.

Henry K. Shattuck, as private. Died of disease Nov. 23, 1863.

John H. Smith, as private. Discharged disabled, at Newport News, Va., March 12, 1863.

William S. A. Starrett, as private; discharged disabled, March 21, 1863.

Charles F. Stinson enlisted as a private; was discharged 1863, to accept promotion as Captain and Brevet Major. U. S. Colored Troops. He died March 10th, 1893.

Elbridge F. Trow enlisted as private; was discharged disabled, Oct. 23, 1862. He died March 19th, 1892, at New Boston.

Solomon Jones, private; mustered in Sept. 18, 1862, mustered out, June 21, 1865.

George N. Copp, private; discharged Jan. 19, 1864, to accept an appointment as First Lieut. in Thirtieth Regiment U. S. Colored Troops.

Cyrus P. Douglass, private; mustered out with regiment, June 21, 1865.

Albert Yorke enlisted as a private, in the Third N. H. Regiment in 1861; was appointed Sergeant, wounded in 1865, at Fort Fisher, N. C.

Alfred Yorke enlisted in the State Service as a private.

John P. Alexander enlisted in the Sixteenth Regiment N. H. Volunteer Infantry in 1862 as private; discharged August, 1863; died at Mattoon, Ill., Sept. 20th, 1863.

Nathan F. Kendall enlisted as private in the Sixteenth N. H. Regiment in 1862; died of disease Aug. 13, 1863, at Concord.

Oramus W. Burnham enlisted from Hillsborough in 1862 as private in the Sixteenth N. H. Regiment; was appointed 1st Lieut. in 1862, and resigned in 1863. He moved to Mont Vernon in 1888.

George H. Blood enlisted as private from Bedford, in 1864, in the Second Regiment Berdan's U. S. Sharpshooters. He died in Mont Vernon in 1898.

George A. Marden enlisted in Company G, Second Regiment Berdan's U. S. Sharpshooters, Dec. 10, 1861, as private; appointed 3rd Sergeant on organization of Company; appointed Quartermaster of 1st Regiment Berdan's U. S. Sharpshooters, July, 1862; discharged, 1864. He died in Lowell, Mass., Dec. 19, 1906.

James D. Towne enlisted as private in 1861, in the Second Regiment Berdan's U. S. Sharpshooters. He died of disease, Dec. 20, 1861, at Washington, D. C., Camp of Instruction, U. S. S.

William H. Upton enlisted in the Sixteenth N. H. Regiment, in 1862, as private. He died Feb. 18th, 1863, at New Orleans, La.

The editor hereof wrote to the Adjutant General of New Hampshire asking for a list of all soldiers from Mont Vernon who served in the several wars, and the names of all who were credited to the

Town during the Civil War. To this the following reply was received:

Concord, Feb. 19, 1906.

Hon. George A. Marden,
    Assistant Treasurer, U. S.
        Boston, Mass.

Dear Sir:

I have the honor to acknowledge receipt of your letter of Feb. 17, in relation to the soldiers of Mont Vernon in the several wars, and regret to say there is nothing in any of our state offices giving just the information you desire.

The Revolutionary records give the towns from which men went in but very few cases. There are no records whatever of the War of 1812 and Mexican War in this office save as published in Nat Head's reports for 1868, which are not official and which do not give the residence of the men. In the Civil War I can give you all the men credited to Mont Vernon under the call of July 1. 1862 and subsequent calls, but for some reason when the credits to towns were made up they did not go back of the above date. I enclose the list. I think you will find some men whose names are given as of the quota of Mont Vernon were not from the Town, and were picked up either as substitutes or to fill the quota.

The Revolutionary-rolls in possession of the state have all been published in Vols. 14, 15, 16 & 17 of State Papers, also called Vols. 1, 2, 3 & 4 of Revolutionary-rolls, with index to each volume. These books are in the Public Library at Mont Vernon and also in the rooms of the Massachusetts Historical Society.

Very Respectfully,
A. D. AYLING,
Adjutant General.

List of men mustered into the U. S. Service from New Hampshire, under the call of July 2, 1862, and subsequent calls, and assigned to the quota of the Town of Mont Vernon.

Lewis Green (Gerrie),	3rd Regiment.
John Burns,	" "
Daniel Bradbury,	5th "
Edwin Austin,	" "
Peter Adams,	6th "
George Werner,	" "
Joseph Farley,	7th "
William J. Harding,	" "
Henry Stewart,	8th "
John Petty,	" "
John Riley,	9th "

Melchoir Warsch,	9th Regiment.
William G. Holt.	10th "
Marius Blanc.	11th "
James Davis.	" "
Thomas Martin.	" "
Charles Lynch.	" "
George White.	" "
James Calligan.	" "
Henry K. Shattuck.	13th "
Solomon Jones.	" "
George G. Averill.	" "
Albert Burnham.	" "
Israel Burnham.	" "
George N. Copp.	" "
Charles W. Dodge.	" "
Cyrus P. Douglass.	" "
Peter F. Pike.	" "
John T. Perkins.	" "
Charles H. Robinson.	" "
John H. Smith.	" "
William S. A. Starrett.	" "
Charles F. Stinson.	" "
Charles M. Kittredge.	" "
Elbridge T. Trow,	" "
George A. Bruce.	" "
Nathan F. Randall.	16th "
John P. Alexander.	" "
William H. Upton.	" "
John Brown.	18th "
Edward Lockwood.	1st Cavalry.
Robert Murry.	" "
John Gilbert.	" "
John Mackey,	" "
Robert Cowell.	" "
Morris Costoloo.	" "
John McIntyre.	" "
John Leary,	Heavy Artillery.
James E. Follansbee.	U. S. Sharpshooters.
George Turner.	U. S. Colored Troops.

James Wallace,　　　　　　U. S. Colored Troops.
Patrick Sullivan,　　　　　　　U. S. Navy.
Edward Williams,　　　　　　　"　　"　　"
Aaron B. Hutchinson,　　　　Lafayette Artillery.

It is probable that from all the foregoing, every man who served from or for Mont Vernon in the Civil War is accounted for.

CHAPTER XIV.

STATISTICAL.

For sixty years after its incorporation Mont Vernon varied but little, from decade to decade, in population. Just how many people it had at the very beginning of its corporate existence does not appear to have been a matter of record. As stated in chapter three, there were one hundred and thirty-five tax-payers on the list in 1804, which should represent somewhere about six hundred to seven hundred population. The successive census periods show the following number:

1810,	762.	1860,	725.
1820,	729.	1870,	604.
1830,	763.	1880,	516.
1840,	720.	1890,	475.
1850,	722.	1900,	453.

Up to 1860 the conditions upon which the population depended were not much changed. There was, in the period preceding, quite a variety of manufactures carried on in a small way, which tended to keep a considerable number of families here. But the whole trend of things about this time was to carry manufacturing where railroads existed, and where power could be obtained at reasonable cost. The old families, which had been fairly large, began to lose their maturing members, who must find a wider field for their enterprise, and the farming interests were interfered with, as the manufactures were, by changed conditions, and chiefly by western competition, in the growing of staple products. Changed conditions in education tended to keep away children from abroad, who formerly depended on the Academy, and this was another factor in the reduction of the population.

THE TOWN DEBT.

The indebtedness of the town prior to the Civil War was not large. In 1848 it was only $2097.28. The Town reports were rather meagre, and often gave no statement as to the condition of the Town treasury. In 1851, the debt is reported as $837.72. In 1852, it was $511.40. In 1857, it had risen to $3601.27. In 1858, it was $3221.99. In 1859, it was $3308.60. In 1860, it was $3459.06. In 1861, it was $3619.87. In 1864, the debt had risen to $10,911.71. In 1865, it was $15,779.29. In 1866, it had fallen to $14,036.15. In 1867, to $13,715.07. In 1868, to $12,099.18.

Of course the rapid increase during the years of the war is readily accounted for by all sorts of war expenses—the chief of which was the filling of quotas, the payment of bounties, the aid given to soldiers' families, etc. But it is also to be remarked that the Town reports varied more or less in their methods of accounting, so that it is not possible to say exactly what the real indebtedness at any given time was. It was paid off in part soon after 1872, by the sale of certain "town bonds," as the treasurer's report calls them. In answer to an inquiry made by the editor of this history of the Hon. Solon A. Carter, State Treasurer of New Hampshire, as to what these "bonds" were, and how many the town had, the following communication was received.

Concord, Feb. 23, 1906.

Hon. George A. Marden,
    Asst. Treasurer, U. S.
        Boston, Mass.
My dear Marden:
    Your note of 21st inst. duly received.
    The New Hampshire legislature of 1871 authorized an issue of State bonds, styled municipal war loan bonds, to be dated Jan. 1, 1872, maturing in 20 to 33 years. These bonds were given outright to the towns on the basis of $100 for each three years' man credited

on the quota of the town under the President's call of July 2, 1862, and subsequent calls, and a proportional amount for longer and shorter terms of enlistment.

The total issued was $2,206,100. The amount apportioned to each town was determined by a Commission.

This Commission found Mont Vernon entitled to the following credits:

Term.	No. men.	Amt. awarded.
Four years enlistment.	1	$ 133.33
Three " "	49	4900.00
One " "	1	33.33
Nine months "	3	75.00
Three " "	1	8.34
	55	$5150.00

On the 20th of April, 1872, the record shows that D. R. Baker, Agent for the town, received

Cash.		$ 50.00
$100 Bonds (Nos 471 to 476) (6 pieces)		600.00
$500 " (Nos. 328 to 332) (5 pieces)		2500.00
$1000 " (Nos. 198 & 199) (2 pieces)		2000.00
		$5150.00

Gen. Ayling informs me that he has furnished you the names of the men credited to Mont Vernon by the Commission.

The list does not include the names of those who enlisted prior to July 2, 1862.

If I can serve you further command me.

Yours truly.

SOLON A. CARTER.

Treasurer.

LONGEVITY.

The Town has always been noted for the "length of days" of many of its inhabitants. No attempt has been made to make a full record of those who have reached an advanced age as residents of the Town; but in 1882 there were eight persons in town eighty years old and upward. In 1883 there were four more who came into the list. In 1899 there were six.

MODERATORS OF TOWN MEETINGS.

The following is believed to be a complete list of those who have served as moderators at Town meetings since the incorporation of the Town, giving also the years in which they served:

Joseph Langdell, 1804, 1805, 1806.

Dr Rogers Smith, 1807, 1809.

A. F. Sawyer, 1808, 1810, 1811, 1812.

Ephraim Pike, 1813, 1815.

Thomas Needham, 1814; Andrew Wallace, 1816.

Elijah Beard, 1817; Nathan Jones, 1818.

Levi Jones, 1819, 1820, 1821, 1822, 1823, 1824, 1825.

Aaron F. Sawyer, 1826, 1827, 1828, 1830, 1831.

Dr. Daniel Adams, 1832, 1833.

Porter Kimball, 1834, 1835.

Z. Kittredge Jr., 1835, 1839, 1840, 1841.

William Bruce, 1837, 1850; C. R. Beard, 1838.

Leander Smith, 1842, 1843, 1844, 1845, 1846, 1847, 1848, 1849, 1851, 1854, 1855, 1856.

Charles J. Smith, 1852, 1853, 1857, 1858, 1859, 1860, 1861, 1862, 1863, 1864, 1868, 1881, 1883.

Alonzo Travis, 1865, 1866, 1869, 1870, 1871, 1872, 1873, 1874, 1875, 1876, 1877, 1878, 1879, 1880.

C. F. Kittredge, 1867.

J. W. Carson, 1882.

Clark Campbell, 1884, 1885, 1886, 1887, 1888, 1889, 1890, 1891, 1892, 1893, 1894, 1895, 1896, 1897, 1900 (Fall meeting.)

William H. Kendall, 1898, 1900 (March meeting), 1902, 1903, 1904, 1905, 1906.

TOWN CLERKS.

John Carleton, 1803, 1804, 1805.

Benjamin Durant, 1806, 1807, 1811, 1812, 1813, 1814.

Dr. Rogers Smith, 1808, 1809, 1810.

John Bruce, 1815, 1816, 1817, 1819, 1820, 1822, 1823, 1824, 1825.

Elijah Beard, 1818.   Dr. Daniel Adams, 1821, 1833.

Timothy Kittredge, 1826, 1827, 1828, 1830.

C. R. Beard, 1831, 1832, 1834, 1835, 1836.

Nathaniel Bruce, 1837, 1838, 1839, 1840, 1841, 1842, 1844, 1845.

F. O. Kittredge, 1843.   J. E. Bruce, 1846, 1847.

Alonzo Travis, 1848, 1849, 1850, 1852, 1853, 1854, 1855, 1856, 1857, 1858.

J. D. Nutter, 1851.

W. H. Conant, 1859.

Clark Campbell, 1860, 1861, 1862, 1863, 1864, 1871, 1872.

Charles J. Smith, 1865, 1866, 1873.

John Kidder, 1867.

George W. Averill, 1868, 1869, 1870, 1880, 1881, 1882, 1883.

John M. Fox, 1874, 1875, 1876, 1877, 1878, 1879, 1886, 1887, 1888, 1889, 1890, 1891, 1892, 1893, 1894, 1895, 1896, 1897, 1898.

Dr. Frederic Chandler, 1884, 1885.

William H. Marvell, 1899.

Arthur P. Temple, 1900, 1901, 1902, 1904, 1905, 1906.

Joseph H. Blood, 1903.

SELECTMEN.

John Carleton, 1803, 1804, 1805, 1806.

John Langdell, 1803, 1804, 1805, 1806, 1807, 1808.

Jacob Kendall, 1803, 1804, 1805, 1806, 1807, 1808, 1809, 1810.

Benjamin Durant, 1807, 1808, 1811, 1812, 1813, 1814.

Dr. Rogers Smith, 1809, 1810.

Eben Odell, 1809, 1810, 1811, 1812, 1813.

Jonathan Herrick, 1811, 1812, 1815, 1816, 1817, 1818, 1820, 1822.

Edmund Batchelder, 1813, 1814, 1815, 1816, 1817.

Dr. Zephaniah Kittredge Sr., 1824.

Ezekiel Upton, 1815, 1816, 1817, 1818, 1819, 1820, 1822, 1823, 1824, 1825, 1826, 1827, 1828.

Zephaniah Kittredge Jr., 1824, 1826, 1836, 1843, 1856.

John Bruce, 1818, 1819, 1820.

John S. Adams, 1819, 1821, 1823, 1824.

George Raymond, 1821, 1822, 1823, 1832, 1833, 1837, 1838.

Asa Webber, 1821.

Allen Goodrich, 1825, 1826, 1827, 1828, 1830, 1831.

Nathaniel Bruce, 1826, 1827, 1829, 1830, 1831, 1832, 1833, 1834, 1835, 1837, 1838, 1839, 1842, 1848, 1849.

Ezra Langdell, 1830, 1832, 1833, 1834.

Timothy Kittredge, 1831, 1847, 1848.

Capt. Leander Smith, 1834, 1835.

Josiah Russell, Jr., 1835, 1836.

William Coggin, 1836.

Ira Kendall, 1837, 1838, 1839, 1840, 1843, 1844, 1845, 1850, 1852, 1853, 1854, 1857, 1858, 1859.

John Averill Jr., 1839, 1840, 1841, 1844, 1845, 1851, 1852.

Henry C. Dodge, 1840, 1841, 1842, 1846, 1847, 1850, 1853, 1855.

Clinton Roby, 1841, 1842, 1843, 1851.

John Carleton, 1844, 1845, 1846, 1849.

Trask W. Averill, 1846, 1847, 1857, 1860.

Andrew W. Raymond, 1848, 1853, 1854, 1857, 1858.

James Weston, 1849.   F. O. Kittredge, 1850.

George E. Dean, 1851, 1860, 1867.

C. R. Beard, 1852, 1864.

William Bruce, 1854, 1855, 1859, 1861, 1862, 1865.

J. P. Trow, 1855, 1856.

J. D. Towne, 1856.

Alonzo Travis, 1857, 1858, 1879, 1880.

Nelson E. Shedd, 1860, 1861.

James Upton, 1861, 1862, 1863, 1876, 1877, 1883, 1894, 1895.

George W. Averill, 1862, 1863, 1864, 1865, 1866, 1874, 1875, 1887.

Samuel F. Livingston, 1863, 1864, 1865.

Henry H. Trow, 1866, 1868, 1869, 1870, 1879, 1900.

Captain John Trevitt, 1866, 1868, 1871, 1872, 1873.

J. H. Tarbell, 1867.

Thomas Wason, 1867.

Charles J. Smith, 1868, 1869, 1870, 1871.

Daniel R. Baker, 1869, 1870.   David Marden, 1871.

John T. McCollom, 1871, 1872, 1873.

Cornelius Green, 1874.

Henry F. Dodge, 1873, 1874, 1876, 1877, 1878, 1892, 1893.

David Stiles, 1875.   Jesse Wilkins, 1875.

Thomas H. McQuestion, 1876, 1877, 1878.

Charles H. Raymond, 1878, 1879, 1880, 1881, 1885, 1886, 1890, 1891, 1896, 1899, 1900, 1902, 1905, 1906.

Benjamin F. Davis, 1881, 1882.

George G. Batchelder, 1880, 1882.

Josiah Swinnington, 1881, 1883.

John W. Carson, 1882, 1883, 1884.

Frank O. Lamson. 1884, 1888, 1906.

Joseph W. Averill, 1884, 1885, 1886, 1888, 1900.

George A. McQuestion, 1885, 1886, 1887.

William F. Hadley, 1887, 1889, 1890.

Joseph G. Carleton. 1888, 1889, 1901, 1902.

Willard P. Woods, 1889, 1890.

William G. Burnham, 1891, 1892, 1893.

George C. Hadley, 1891, 1892, 1893, 1894, 1895.

Daniel Richardson, 1894.

Harry G. Blood, 1895, 1896, 1897, 1901, 1903, 1904.

William L. Robinson, 1896, 1897, 1898.

William H. Kendall, 1897, 1898, 1899.

Charles H. Trow, 1898.

Charles O. Ingalls, 1899.

Louis A. Trow, 1901, 1902, 1903.

Joel F. Perham, 1903.

Leander F. Humphrey, 1904.

Nathaniel F. Hooper, 1904.

John M. Fox, 1905.

Edward W. Trow, 1905.

John M. Fox, 1906.

There has been no fixed compensation for town officers, and no records have been kept of this, except in the annual town reports which commenced about 1868.

For the year ending Feb. 28th, 1871, the selectmen's bills amounted to $174.00.

For the year ending February 28th, 1882, $123.50.

"   "   "   "   March 1st, 1891, 133.00.

"   "   "   "   February 15th, 1896, $140.25.

"   "   "   "   "   "   1897, $121.00.

"   "   "   "   "   "   1898, $141.25.

"   "   "   "   "   "   1899, $140.00.

REPRESENTATIVES.

In giving a list of the names of those who have served the town as representatives in the legislature, it is interesting to recall a petition to the General Court, dated Mont Vernon, December 20, 1803, which was just after the town had been incorporated. The petition is given as recorded, both in spelling and punctuation:

To the Honorable Sennate and House of Representatives in General Court conviened sheweth, that our present Situation, is sutch, that we cannot be conveniantly Anexed to Any other Corporation for the benefit of representation, in said General Court, As our present Numbers Amount to no more than one hundred and twenty seven — votable polls—Therefore your petitioners pray that we may have liberty to send a representative to represent us in your Honorable House the Next Session and so in futer.

Mont Vernon December 1803.

Eli Wilkins	Joseph Trow, Jn'r
David Smith	Ezekiel Upton, Jr
Ebenezer Mills	Enos Bradford
William Hastings	Joseph Farnum
John Harwood	Isack Weston
Josiah Kittredge	Isac Smith
Joseph Cogin	Sollomon Kettredge
Benj'n Durant	Cyrus Stiles
Thos. Kendall	Ebenezer Holt
Jonathan Lord	Mun Dodge
James Ray	Benjamin Pike
Parker Richardson	Jacob Smith
Joseph Dodge	Wiliam Cogen
Joseph Perkins, jr	John Batchelor
John Colburn Kendall	Lant Kidder
Benjamin Stearns	John Lamson
Nathan Jones	John Weston
Abijah Spofford	Allen Goodridge
Jake Peabody	Eben'r Batchelder
William Bradford	Lamb't Bradford
Samuel Phelps	Aaron Peabody
Wm. Bradford, jun	John Peabody
Jonathan Wilkins	Timothy Hill
James Woodbury	Samuel Mitchell
Peter Herrick	Moses Peabody
James Bennett	John Rollings
John Fisk	Daniel Smith
John Trow	Nathan Flint
Nehemiah Upton	Jacob Curtice
Joseph Langdell	William Lamore
Jesse Avrell	Nathan Smith
James Smith	Dan'l Kendall
Joseph Perkins	Jacob Kendall
John Averel	Josiah Dodge
John Averill, Jun	Abial Wilkins
Mark Burnham	William Wilkins
John Carleton	Joseph Trow

This petition was referred to a joint committee of the two branches, who after investigation reported that the prayer of the petitioners be granted, and this report seems to have been accepted. Whether any formal enabling act was passed is doubtful. At any rate, Major William Bradford represented the town in 1804. The following is a list of the several representatives and the years in which they served:

Major William Bradford, 1804, 1805, 1806.

1807, no representative.

Capt. John Batchelder, 1808, 1809, 1810.

Benjamin Durant, 1811, 1812, 1813, 1814, 1815.

Andrew Wallace, 1816.

Ezekiel Upton, 1817, 1818, 1819, 1820, 1821.

Dea. John Bruce, 1822, 1823, 1824, 1825, 1826.

Aaron F. Sawyer, 1827, 1828, 1829.

Nathaniel Bruce, 1830, 1831, 1832, 1833, 1840, 1841.

Daniel W. Baker, 1834, 1835.

Porter Kimball, 1836.

George Raymond, 1837, 1838, 1839, 1842.

Zephaniah Kittredge, jr., 1843.

William Conant, 1844.

Leander Smith, 1845, 1846, 1847, 1851, 1852.

John Averill, 1848.

J. A. Starrett, 1849.

William Bruce, 1850.

Alonzo Travis, 1853, 1854, 1855.

Charles R. Beard, 1856, 1857.

Ira Kendall, 1858, 1859.

Charles J. Smith, 1860, 1861.

Ira Roby, 1862.

Wm. G. Bruce, 1863, 1864.

Henry C. Dodge, 1865.

Geo. A. Bruce, 1866.

Charles F. Kittredge, 1867.

Andrew W. Raymond, 1868, 1869.

Joseph H. A. Bruce, 1870, 1871.

James Upton, 1872, 1873.

John Trevitt, 1874, 1875.

Dan'l P. Kendall, 1876, 1877.

Elbridge F. Trow, 1880, 1882.
1884, voted not to send.
1886, not entitled.
Henry F. Dodge, 1888.
John M. Fox, 1890.
Wm. G. Burnham, 1892, 1894.
Not entitled, 1896.
Franklin Marden, 1898.
Charles H. Raymond, 1900, 1902.
William H. Kendall, 1903, 1904.
Joseph G. Carlton, 1905, 1906.

JUSTICES OF THE PEACE.

The following citizens of Mont Vernon have been commissioned as Justices of the Peace: Eli Wilkins, Jonathan Conant, Dea. John Carleton, Aaron F. Sawyer, Dr. Dan'l Adams, Elijah Beard, John Bruce, Nathaniel Bruce, George Raymond, Alonzo Travis, John Trevitt, Franklin O. Kittredge, Charles J. Smith, Wm. H. Conant, Clark Campbell, Alonzo S. Bruce, Wm. F. Hadley, John M. Fox, Wm. H. Stinson, Oramus W. Burnham, Wm. H. Kendall, Arthur P. Temple.

CHAPTER XV.

CONCLUSION.

In writing this, the closing chapter, it is left only to record the testimonial of our citizens to the splendid work done by those who have with great painstaking labor compiled the interesting data of these pages.

In 1890 the town voted to publish a history and appointed a committee of three, William H. Conant, Charles H. Raymond, and Charles F. Stinson, to have charge of the arrangements for the compilation of it. In the same meeting the sum of five hundred dollars was appropriated for the use of the committee.

Hon. Charles J. Smith at once commenced work, and the assembling of facts for a true history of the generations past and present has been carried on until now. As usual where much time is required to sift and sort the facts from the fiction, to verify tradition and hearsay, it has seemed to those waiting that the history would have to repeat itself.

Only one, Mr. Raymond, of the original committee remains, the others having passed from amongst us; his associates now being Henry F. Dodge and Willard P. Woods.

It is a pleasure as well as a measure of justice to say that out of a mind stored with accumulated facts acquired through a long life of vital, active interest in the affairs of Mont Vernon we secured results which money could not buy in the work of Mr. Smith. Having been endowed with a wonderful memory, he has given to us a genealogical record simply beyond comparison, and we are deeply grateful for his life and work.

In the original resolution it was written that a final revision of the work should be made by Hon. George A. Marden. During the past four years, through failing health and great physical discomfort, he has worked on this with a thoroughness and fidelity which can never be overestimated.

He died December 19, 1906, before entirely completing the work, and it is unusually fitting that this book should close with a tribute of love and praise for the absolutely unselfish interest, for the self sacrifice and the limitless generosity which has characterized his whole life. Living as he has through the epoch making period of our country's existence and taking no small part in shaping its truer life, he ever and always stood staunchly for justice and the right. It is with honest pride of justification that we treasure the honor of his complete life as our heritage.

.

PART II

GENEALOGY

GENEALOGY

LIST OF ABBREVIATIONS

---

b.—born.

ch.—child or children.

d.—died.

dau.—daughter.

dys.—days.

grad.—graduated.

m.—married.

mos.—months.

Mt. V.—Mont Vernon.

res.—resides or resided.

unm.—unmarried.

wid.—widow.

yrs.—years.

&—and.

rem.—removed.

Regt.—Regiment.

Dist.—District.

There are the usual abbreviations for months of the year, and states of the Union.

EXPLANATORY NOTES.

The sign * before a given name denotes that that person is mentioned at length afterward, or mentioned elsewhere.

The numeral placed after a given name denotes the number of the generation of such person reckoning from his earliest ancestor, mentioned in the genealogy. Where cities and towns in New Hampshire are referred to, the name of the state is not given, nor is it given, if the city mentioned is a well-known city.

DANIEL ADAMS, M. D.

ABBOTT.

1. Deacon Ephraim Abbott, b. December 16, 1742, m. Dorothy, dau. of Caleb Stiles. She was b. September 2, 1740. Deacon Abbott lived on the place now occupied by Miss Lizzie R. Parker. He was a Baptist deacon, and d. in Goffstown, 1827.

2. His son, Rev. Samuel Abbott, b. in Mont Vernon in 1777, m. in 1798, Sarah, dau. of Rev. John Rand of Lyndeborough. He was pastor of Baptist churches at Middleboro, Bridgewater and Chester, Mass., and Londonderry, N. H. He was the inventor of "Abbott's Window Shades," 1825, went to Antrim in 1838 and bought an estate in Clinton Village, where he remained until his death in 1853. Mr. Abbott was wholly uneducated in the schools, but had strong native abilities, was a good sermonizer, and an impressive preacher. In style, he was bold, incisive and logical. As a minister he was honest and fearless. He never wrote a sermon. He had nine children, one of whom, Rev. Stephen G. Abbott, was b. in Bridgewater, Mass., November 9, 1819.

3. Sarah, dau. of Deacon Ephraim and Dorothy Stiles Abbott, m. Rev. Jonathan Rand, one of the seven children of Rev. John Rand, first minister of the Congregational Church, Lyndeboro. They moved to Antrim in 1844. She d. in 1848. They had seven children.

4. Rev. Stephen G. Abbott, son of Rev. Samuel Abbott, b. Bridgewater, Mass., November 9, 1819. He studied theology at New Hampton, settled in Needham, Mass., and other places. He m. in 1846 Sarah B. Cheney of Holderness. He received the degree of A. M. from Bates College in 1870. Has one child who is:

5. Hon. John T. Abbott, b. Antrim, 1850, graduated from Bates College, 1871, is now a lawyer in Keene.

ADAMS.

Dr. Daniel Adams was b. in Townsend, Mass., September 9, 1773, graduated at Dartmouth College in 1797, and at its medical school in 1799. After residing several years at Leominster he removed to Boston. For a period was engaged in publishing an agricultural journal in Boston; came to reside in Mont Vernon in 1813, and was employed in preparing his various publications and in his profession here until his removal to Keene, in 1846. His "Scholar's Arithmetic," Adams' "New" and "Revised" all were in very extensive use for many years. He wrote and published several pamphlets. Dr. Adams was very highly esteemed in Mont Vernon, and during his thirty-three years' residence here, he wielded a controlling influence in behalf of temperance, education and morality. In 1839 and 1840 he was a member of the New Hampshire Senate from the district where he resided. He m. August 17, 1800, Nancy, dau. of Dr. Mulliken of Townsend, Mass. She d. at Keene in 1851. He d. at Keene, June 8, 1854, aged 90 years, 9 months. Their ch. were:

1. *Rev. Darwin Adams, b. Leominster, Mass., October 10, 1801.
2. Arabella, b. Leominster, September 9, 1803, d. in infancy.
3. Nancy, b. Leominster, July 7, 1810, d. June 1, 1820.
4. *Dr. Daniel Lucius, b. Mont Vernon, November 1, 1814.
5. *Nancy Ann, b. Mont Vernon, December 3, 1821.

Rev. Darwin Adams, eldest son Dr. Adams, b. Leominster, October 10, 1801, graduated at Dartmouth College 1824, at Andover Theological Seminary 1827, m. October 9, 1828, Catherine H. Smith of Hollis, N. H., who d. at Wellesley Hills, Mass., July 1897, aged 95 years. He d. in Groton, Mass., August 16, 1889. Their children were:

1. George Darwin, b. Camden, Me., April 18, 1830, m. Eliza Ann Brown of Ohio, resides at Tanesfield, Ohio.
2. *Rev. Daniel Emerson Adams, b. Camden, Me., June 22, 1832.
3. Mary Emelia, b. Alstead, N. H., April 1, 1835, d. Dunstable, Mass., July 5, 1855.
4. Catharine Lucretia, b. Alstead, November 12, 1836, d. Alstead, December 31, 1845.
5. John Smith, b. Alstead, October 7, 1839, enlisted in Company F., Sixth N. H. Regiment in 1862 as 2nd Lieutenant, was with Gen. Burnside at Hatteras Inlet, and Roanoke Island, was wounded in the second Bull Run battle, and reported as killed, laid on the field from Thursday until Monday afternoon, and lived to return to his father's home in Alstead. He was afterwards Commissary of Stores in Hospitals at Brattleboro, Montpelier and Bennington, Vt. Was promoted to Captain. He was at the time of his death, March 11, 1869, engaged in the wholesale linen business in New York City. He was in his youth a student at Appleton Academy (McCollom Institute.).

Dr. Daniel Lucius Adams, second son of Dr. Adams, was b. at Mont Vernon, November 1, 1814, graduated at Yale College, 1835, m. Cornelia A. Cook of New York City, March 7, 1861. He d. at New Haven, Conn., January 3, 1899. Their ch. were:

1. Charles C., b. Ridgefield, Conn., August 24, 1864, d. September 21, 1864.
2. Catharine, b. Ridgefield, Conn., May 3, 1866, m. April 23, 1896, Dr. William L. Elkin, Professor in Yale University.
3. Mary W., b. Ridgefield, Conn., October 15, 1869, resides New Haven, Conn.
4. Frank M., b. Ridgefield, Conn., June 7, 1871, Professor in Yale University.

5. Roger C., b. Ridgefield, Conn., May 1, 1874, electrician in Buffalo, N. Y.

Nancy Ann Adams, youngest dau. of Dr. Adams, b. Mont Vernon, December 3, 1821, m. May 18, 1841, William S. Briggs of Keene. She d. February 14, 1868. Ch:

1. Daniel A. Briggs, d. in infancy.

2. William A Briggs, b. July 31, 1848, m. November 27, 1872, Emelia F. Whiting of Montpelier, Vt.

Rev. Daniel Emerson Adams, second son of Dr. Darwin Adams, b. Camden, Me., June 22, 1832, graduated Bangor Theological Seminary, was settled over a parish in Wilton, N. H., where he was the beloved pastor of the Congregational Church many years. He was then called to the pastorate of a church at Wellesley Hills, Mass. He is now (1902) preaching in Mason, N. H. He was at one time Supt. of Public Schools for Hillsboro' County, m. (1) September 16, 1854, Ellen F. Kingsbury of Keene, who d. at Ashburnham, May 21, 1882. He m. (2) Marion E. Center of Wilton, February 28, 1884. Ch., all by first wife, were:

1. Charles Darwin, b. Keene, October 21, 1856, m. August 24, 1881, Julia A. Stevens of Wilton, graduated Dartmouth College, 1877; is Professor of Greek in Dartmouth College, has three children.

2. Mary Catherine, b. Wilton, April 7, 1863, m. December 4, 1899, Rev. Martin F. Nevis, Pastor Pilgrim Congregational Church, Southboro', Mass., 1 child.

3. George Wilton, b. Wilton, April 27, 1873, m. June 8, 1899, Grace A. Turner of Natick, Mass., has one ch., residence Mattapan, Mass.

Dea. Jonathan S. Adams, brother Dr. Daniel Adams, trader here several yrs. He d. 1867, age 81. His wife Betsey W. Adams d. 1866, age 79.

ALEXANDER.

1. James Alexander, b. in Londonderry, April 19, 1802, m. (1) Eliza M. Dickey, June 14, 1835. She was b. May 31, 1813, d. June 25, 1854; m. (2) Elizabeth L. Reed, December 1, 1854, settled in the easterly part of Mont Vernon, adjoining Amherst, about 1836. He died July 24, 1885. Their ch. were:

1. William E., b. July 13, 1837, m. Emma F. Keith, July 5, 1871. He is a soap manufacturer, resides on what was formerly the Daniel Campbell farm in Amherst, and has five children.

2. James A., b. November 17, 1838, m. (1) Mary L. Sargent, December 3, 1860, resides in Boston, Mass. He m (2) Evaline Gusting, March 7, 1879.

3. John P., b. April 20, 1840, d. September 20, 1863, Mattoon, Ill., was a member of the Sixteenth N. H. Volunteer Infantry.

4. Harriet M., b. April 2, 1842, m. Ira Chase, October 5, 1862; resides in Milford.

5. Mary E., b. May 6, 1844, m. William D. Robbins of Brookline, N. H., April 23, 1884, one daughter.

6. Sarah J., b. January 6, 1846, m. January 1, 1867, John T. Grafton of Milford. They have two sons.

7. Ellen F., b. March 6, 1850, m. Edward Cloutman of Lynn, Mass., December 17, 1879. She d. at Milford, a widow, March 6, 1893.

8. Daniel C. Alexander came to Mont Vernon from Nashua in 1896, and has since resided in the East District. He was b. in Vermont, January 25, 1865, m. May 30, 1891, Mary Alice Grant of Craftsbury, Vt. She was b. February 16, 1866.

ALCOTT.

Gilman Alcott, son of Benj. Alcott, a native of Bedford (now West Manchester), moved here from Lowell in 1843, and bought the Goodrich farm (now belonging to Mrs. Joseph H. Tarbell). He was a tin pedler. He removed to Lowell in 1848 and d. there September 11, 1858, aged 47 years. He m. (1) June 24, 1837, Lucy Ann, dau. of Ezra and Rebecca Langdell of this town. She was b. August 6, 1814, d. March 12, 1838. He m. (2) Mary F. Langdell, sister of his first wife. She was b. April 6, 1829. By his second wife he had children.

ANDERSON.

Edwin L. Anderson, b. Limington, Me., October 20, 1853, m. Abbie C. Leavitt, August, 1880. She was b. in Tuftonboro', N. H., December 28, 1862. Mr. Anderson and family came from Parsonsfield, Me., to Mont Vernon in August, 1897. He works on the Edward H. Best farm in the East District, and resides in East District. Their children were:

1. Jessie May, b. Parsonsfield, November 18, 1882.

2. Annie Ruth, b. Parsonsfield, October 20, 1886.

3. Marion Mabel, b. Parsonsfield, November 30, 1895.

4. Grace Verna, b. Mont Vernon, September 3, 1898, d. January 26, 1900.

Mr. D. A. Anderson, a native of Goffstown, N. H., a graduate of Dartmouth, was the ninth principal of McCollom Institute, remaining two years, from 1870 to 1872.

AVERILL.

John Averill, the ancestor of all the name in Mont Vernon, was b. in Middleton, Mass., June 2, 1740, m. Mary Bradford, dau. of William and Mary Lambert Bradford (Bradford was the ancestor of the Mont Vernon

Bradfords). She was b. in 1741. They came to what is now Mont Vernon in 1763. He d. May 21, 1815, aged 75. His wife d. August 21, 1814,
aged 73. Their children were:

1. Naomi.
2. *Daniel.
3. Mary m. Benjamin Simonds of Mont Vernon, whither he removed to Antrim in 1793. They had eight children, of whom four were
born in Mont Vernon, and four in Antrim.
4. Anna, m. —— McAllister.
5. *John, Jr., b. October 13, 1767.
6. *Jesse, b. 1772, d. March 2, 1840, aged 67.
7. *Levi.

Daniel Averill, son of John and Mary (Bradford) Averill, m. (1)
April 24, 1783, Mary, dau. of Daniel and Mary (Hartshorn) Weston.
She was b. Mont Vernon, February 20, 1766. He m. (2) April 26, 1827,
Mrs. Manning. He was a Revolutionary soldier, and d. in Barre,
Vt., April 21, 1848, aged 86 yrs. He lived on the Odell farm in West
District (now J. Hazens). He had several ch. all by first wife, of them:
1. Mary, b. Oct. 26, 1783, m. May 16, 1805, *David Smith of Mont
Vernon, d. Aug. 25, 1864.

Of his sons:
David W., m. Aug. 27, 1809, Submit French (sister of Abraham and
Dolly French).
Daniel, m. July 17, 1809, Dolly French (sister Abraham and Submit
French). Both sons settled in Barre, Vt., and among their descendants
are prominent merchants of that city.
Sylvia, a dau., m. Nov. 11, 1824, *Timothy Baldwin. She d. March
28, 1867, age 62 years, 6 months.

John Averill, Jr., son of John and Mary Averill, b. Oct. 13, 1767,
d. Oct. 26, 1844, m. Anna, dau. of James and Hannah (Trask) Woodbury.
She was b. Aug. 4, 1774, d. May 9, 1858. They lived in the west part of
the town, near Beech Hill. Their children were:
1. Nancy, b. Feb. 19, 1792, m. Asa Wallace of Milford, Aug. 16,
1814, who d. in Tennessee, Feb. 5, 1815. Mrs. W., afterwards m. William
Bradford of Goshen, and d. Aug. 13, 1837, aged 45, leaving one child,
Asa Wallace.
2. Betsey, b. Feb. 7, 1794, m. Levi Trow of Mont Vernon, May 5,
1812. They moved to Goshen.
3. *John, b. March 10, 1796.
4. Bernard, b. April 26, 1798, m. Harriet Richardson, Nov. 4, 1829,
settled and d. in Farmington, N. H., leaving five daughters and two sons.
5. Hannah, b. May 13, 1800, d. July 23, 1803.
6. Mary, b. July 13, 1802, m. Nathaniel Cutter of Jaffrey, N. H.,
Oct. 11, 1827.

7. Hannah, b. Jan. 7, 1805, m. William Butterfield of New Boston, Dec. 26, 1835. She d. Oct. 13, 1890, leaving four children.

8. Fanny, b. June 5, 1807, d. June 6, 1814.

9. Lucretia, b. March 5, 1809, m. Joel W. Duncklee of Milford, March 8, 1832. She d. Aug. 25, 1844, leaving seven children.

10. *Trask Woodbury b. March 20, 1841.

Jesse Averill, son of John and Mary (Bradford) Averill, b. 1772, d. March 2, 1840, age 67 years. He d. at small house near Henry F. Dodge's old farm. He m. (1) *Sarah, dau. Andrew Leavitt. He m. (2) Dec. 4, 1825, Abigail Swinnington (sister Elisha and Job Swinnington).

Children by first wife:

1. Joseph, settled in Lowell.

2. *Jesse, b. 1799.

3. Franklin, m. —— Flanders, 4 children: three daughters and one son.

4. Chili, b. 1805, d. Coburg, Ontario, Oct. 11, 1884, aged 78 yrs.

5. William, d. Merrill, Wis., 1885, age 78.

6. Chandler, d. Mont Vernon, July 6, 1853, aged 43. He was a soldier in the Mexican War. He left one son.

7. Jonathan, d. Mont Vernon, May 28, 1831, age 19 years, 4 months.

8. A dau. Sarah of Jesse and Sarah (Leavitt) Averill, m. Dr. Abram McMillen of New Boston.

Children by second wife:

9. Miles, d. July 4, 1847, aged 26.

10. Rensalaer, left home when about 18, and was never heard from.

Levi Averill, youngest son of John and Mary (Bradford) Averill, m. Mary Jones of Wilton. He lived in the West District, on the place now occupied by George Stearns. He d. Aug. 31, 1868, age 85. She d. November 28, 1864, age 80. Their children were:

1. Mary Bishop, b. Feb. 19, 1804, m. Thomas Dunlap of Antrim. He d. Aug. 17, 1865, aged 62. She d. June 18, 1874, age 70. They had thirteen children.

2. Hiram, b. Oct. 21, 1805, d. Warren, R. I., Feb. 1, 1886, aged 80. He was a brush manufacturer in Charlestown, Mass., of the firm of Averill and Hunting.

3. Lucinda, b. Sept. 8, 1809, m. Nov. 16, 1829, Alexander Jameson of Antrim. She d. Nov. 26, 1843, aged 34, leaving three daughters, viz:

1. Mary R., m. D. F. French of Washington, N. H., d. three weeks after marriage.

2. Anne W., m. Harris E. Cutter, lives in Chicago.

3. Emily S., d. 1869, aged 27.

4. Lucy, m. Sumner French, lived in Milford.

5. Mark, settled in Tewksbury, Mass.

6 and 7. Nancy and Hannah, twins. Nancy m. —— Carter, lived in

Somerville, Mass. Hannah m. (1) —— Clough, (2) —— Seaver of Enfield, N. H.

8. John P., graduated Dartmouth College, was for many years principal of the Chapman School, East Boston, Mass., is now living in Concord, N. H. Has two children.

9. Thomas, lived in New Boston and Francestown, d. in Francestown.

10. Levi, b. April, 1821, d. May 26, 1892.

John Averill, son of John and Anna (Woodbury) Averill, b. March 10, 1796, m. (1) Dec. 15, 1825, Hannah, dau. of Abraham and Naomi French. She was b. Mont Vernon, Jan. 9, 1804, d. July 10, 1855. He m. (2) Dec., 1856, Dorcas Smiley. She d. March 21, 1885, age 71. He d. May 3, 1883, age 87 years. He lived on the farm, now of Henry H. Trow, but moved to the village, where he died. His children, all by his first wife were born at Mont Vernon:

1. Charles Frank, b. Nov. 4, 1826, now living unm. in California, where he emigrated in 1850.

2. *George Woodbury, b. March 10, 1829.

3. Harriet Frances, b. Dec. 31, 1830, d. April 16, 1850, unm.

4. Caroline S., b. Nov. 15, 1832, m. Sept. 22, 1859, *Benjamin F. Davis, resides Mont Vernon.

Trask W. Averill, youngest child of John and Anna (Woodbury) Averill, b. March 20, 1811, m. (1) Hannah W., dau. of Joseph and Sally (Smith) Perkins, April 9, 1835. She was b. April 24, 1816, d. May 2, 1849. He m. (2) Oct. 11, 1849, Hannah, dau. of Silas and Martha (Farnum) Wilkins. She was b. May 11, 1816, d. Feb. 28, 1900. He d. May 26, 1899. He resided in the North District for many years. His children by first wife were b. Mont Vernon:

1. Sarah Frances, b. March 24, 1836, m. Oct. 19, 1858, Capt. Brown Flanders of Boston. She d. Sept. 15, 1881. She left one dau. Lilla.

2. Nancy Maria, b. May 21, 1838, m. (1) *Plumer Jones, by whom she had one son. She m. (2) his brother *Solomon Jones, by whom she had one dau. and two sons. She d. Nov. 16, 1876.

3. Emily Caroline, b. Jan. 3, 1840, m. (1) Mr. Hutchinson, m. (2) Frank H. Hopkins. She d. Feb. 15, 1900, leaving no children.

4. *Woodbury T., b. Sept. 6, 1841.

5. Josephine Eliza, b. Sept. 23, 1843, m. (1) 1867, *Stephen G. Clement, m. (2) Frank Brooks of Greenfield, Sept. 23, 1892. She d., Greenfield, May 20, 1901, leaving one daughter. Gertrude E. Clement.

6. Mary Henrietta, b. May 27, 1846, m. Samuel Leadbetter of East Boston, Mass. They had one son, William. She d. Aug. 27, 1882.

7. Franklin Perkins, b. April 6, 1849, now (1902) resides in Mont Vernon, has spent many years in California.

By his second wife:

8. *Charles Eugene, b. August 6, 1855.

Jesse Averill, Jr., son of Jesse and Sarah (Leavitt) Averill, b. 1799, m. 1820, Eliza, dau. of Lot Conant. He d. May 24, 1850, age 51 years. She d. May 21, 1872, age 67. Their children were:

1. Joanna G., b. Jan. 12, 1821, m. 1843, Jeremiah O. Pulsifer of Manchester. She d. July 22, 1855, no children.

2. Eliza M., b. 1824, m. *Newell D. Foster, June 10, 1846, d. June 5, 1852, age 28, three children.

3. Charlotte W., b. Sept. 6, 1827, m. George H. Chandler of Manchester. She d. January 3, 1854.

4. *Joseph Woodbury, b. Dec. 1, 1829.

5. George G., b. Feb. 8, 1831, m. March 9, 1868, Sarah L., dau. of Benjamin F. and Betsey (Buss) Marden. She was b. May 9, 1835, no ch. He was in the 13th N. H. Reg't in Civil War. Farmer, residence Mont Vernon Village.

6. Almira J., m. James Gilmore of Manchester, not living.

7. Mary M., b. July, 1840, m. Orville B. Stevens, d. May 1, 1870, age 29 years, 9 months. He d. Jan. 30, 1869, age 29 years, 5 months.

8. Angelia M., b. 1835, m. Jonathan F. Williams of Lowell. She d. April 15, 1898, age 53 years, 11 months; one son, George.

George Woodbury Averill, son of John and Hannah (French) Averill, b. March 10, 1839, m. Nov. 10, 1857, Nancy E., dau. of William and Serviah Lamson. She was b. Oct. 7, 1827. He has been repeatedly elected selectman of this town and is an industrious and skillful farmer. Their children are:

1. Ella Augusta, b. Nov. 2, 1858, attended Wellesley College two years, was for three years a teacher in South Africa, m. Dec. 25, 1889, Henry F. Robinson of Hancock, has four children, resides in Hancock.

2. Carrie Frances, b. Aug. 24, 1861, m. *Charles H. Trow of Mont Vernon, Dec. 19, 1882, one son.

3. George Franklin, b. April 18, 1866, m. Oct. 26, 1893, Fanny L., dau. of John A. and Amanda (Wilson) Carleton of Mont Vernon. He is an enterprising and successful merchant of Milford, N. H.

Woodbury T., son of Trask W. and Hannah (Perkins) Averill, b. Sept. 6, 1841, m. Rebecca, dau. of George Jones of New Boston. She d. West Medford, Mass., March 23, 1885, age 35. He lived in Hancock from 1873 to 1877, went to Manchester, thence to Boston, where he d. Feb. 23, 1895, age 53. He was a massage physician, also a great hunter and fisher. Their children were:

1. Belle, b. Mont Vernon, July 31, 1867, m. Albert Shepard of Ipswich, Mass.

2. Alonzo W., b. Hancock, Nov. 14, 1868, resides in Boston.

3. Willie, b. April 4, 1877, d. Dec. 26, 1895.

Charles E. Averill, son of Trask W. and Hannah (Wilkins) Averill, b. Aug. 6, 1855, m. Sept. 1, 1875, Ruth A., only child of Almus and Lydia A. Fairfield of Antrim. She was b. Nov. 12, 1853. He d. Nashua, Sept. 20, 1883, leaving one son, Ernest.

Joseph W. Averill, son of Jesse and Eliza (Conant) Averill, b. Dec. 1, 1829, m. Sabrina F., dau. of Timothy and Sylvia (Averill) Baldwin, Dec. 3. 1857. She was b. March 15, 1836, d. June 16, 1896. He has been five years selectman, and is respected by all. They had one son.

1. Chester B., b. Jan. 17, 1867, m. Oct. 19, 1892, to Edith Leonard of Warren, N. H. They reside in Warren, N. H., and have one daughter.

James J. Averill, son of Ebenezer and Anna (Johnson) Averill, b. Milford, Aug. 6, 1778, m. March 3, 1807, Lucy Wallace Burnham of Milford, b. March 20, 1785, d. Jan. 16, 1855. He lived for many years in the South District on the farm known as "Chas. H. Raymond's old farm." He d. here July 11, 1867. Children:

1. Mary Ann, b. Milford, June 1, 1809, d. unm. in Mont Vernon, May 24, 1883.

2. Lucy B., b. Oct. 4, 1816, in Mont Vernon, m. 1844, Stephen C. Langdell. She d. Feb. 9, 1903. Four children.

3. Helen M., b. Mont Vernon, March 15, 1827, m. March 28, 1847, *Joseph Fitch Crosby. She d. Milford, Nov. 14, 1879.

Granville C. Averill, b. Mont Vernon, Dec. 21, 1832, was reared in the family of his grandfather, James Hopkins, m. 1867, Nancy Jane, only ch. of George and Hannah P. (Stearns) Green. She was b. Feb. 8, 1843, d. Dec. 4, 1900. He d. June 24, 1901. They lived in the West District. Their children were:

1. *Edward G., b. April 6, 1868, New Boston.

2. Rufus G., b. Jan. 6, 1876, resides Mont Vernon.

3. Hannah J., b. June 29, 1878, m. (1) Dec. 15, 1895, Walter J. Blanchard, by whom she had one son, m. (2) George Page, 1901, d. July 18, 1901.

Edward G. Averill, son of G. C. and N. J. (Green) Averill, b. April 6, 1868, at New Boston, m. March 9, 1892, Mrs. Abbie M. (Pollard) Pease. She was b. Jan. 27, 1871. They reside in Mont Vernon. Ch:

1. Eva Belle Pease (Mrs. Averill's ch. by first husband), b. Epping. Feb. 2, 1890.

2. Ina May, b. Mont Vernon, Oct. 1893.

Moses Averill, Jr., was a son of Moses, who was a son of Ebenezer, who was the first Averill to settle in Milford. He was b. in Mont Vernon, Jan. 26, 1785. Came from New Boston to Milford in 1824, d. Milford, July 14, 1861, m. Sally Odell, June 6, 1811. She was b. Mont Vernon, Feb. 21, 1787, d. Milford, Nov. 30, 1873. Ch:

1. Sophronia, b. Mont Vernon, Nov. 4, 1811, m. Oct. 11, 1832, John B. Wilson of Canaan, d. Oct. 18, 1897.

2. Sarah L., b. Sept. 16, 1813, m. 1834, Joseph P. Myrick, resided Cleveland, O., d. March, 1891.

3. Clementine, b. Aug. 9, 1815, resided Valrico, Fla.

4. Abby L. O., b. New Boston, May 5, 1820, m. 1850, resided Cleveland, Ohio.

5. Calvin H., b. New Boston, Dec. 29, 1822. Came to Milford in 1824 with his father, was a matchmaker, m. Sept. 1848, Mary B., dau. of Amos and Mary (Burns) Gutterson, b. Milford, March 27, 1831, d. April 30, 1865, one dau.

6. Clementine Elexene, b. Milford, March 9, 1850, m. Herbert O. Lilly, resided Cleveland, Ohio.

BAKER.

Daniel W. Baker, b. Stoddard, N. H., June 13, 1795, m. (1) Desire Rose, dau. of Abraham Rose of Lyndeborough, Nov., 1823. She was b. Nov. 5, 1802, d. June 30, 1828, m. (2) Mrs. Delinda Dutton, Jan. 6, 1851. She d. March 29, 1862, m. (3) Mrs. Helena C. Atherton of Nashua, Sept. 8, 1863. He d. at Nashua, Jan. 11, 1865. He was appointed postmaster in 1829, serving as such until 1832. He was Representative to the Legislature in 1834-1835. By his first wife he had one child.

1. Daniel Rose Baker, b. June 17, 1828, m. Dec. 20, 1860, Mary E., dau. of Milton and Sophronia (Trow) McCollom. She was b. May 5, 1860. He was postmaster from 1835 to 1842 and from 1853 to 1861. He d. July 25, 1879, aged 51 years. They had no children.

BALDWIN.

Timothy Baldwin, b. Billerica, Mass., Oct. 11, 1791, m. (1) Sally Marshall, June, 1815. She d. May 21, 1824, age 32 years. He m. (2) Sylvia, dau. of Daniel and Mary (Weston) Averill, Nov. 11, 1824. She d. March 28, 1867, age 62 years, 6 months. He d. May 25, 1869. His ch., five by his first wife, were:

1. Lydia J., b. June 30, 1816, Mt. Vernon, m. *Wm. Harrison Smith. She d. April 26, 1868, leaving three daughters.

2. Ruth A., b. Sept. 19, 1818, Mt. Vernon, d. Dec. 22, 1853, unm.

3. Hannah, b. April 14, 1820, Mt. Vernon, d. April 7, 1861, unm.

4. Samuel B., b. Jan. 1, 1822, Mt. Vernon, d. Sept. 18, 1822.

5. John B., b. Aug. 8, 1823, Mt Vernon, d. Nov. 20, 1823.

By his second wife he had:

6. Sarah C., b. Sept. 27, 1830, Mt. Vernon, d. March 3, 1832.

7. Mary A., b. Aug. 2, 1832, Mt. Vernon, d. Aug. 21, 1834.

8. Sabrina Frances, b. March 15, 1836, Mont Vernon, m. *Joseph G. Averill, Dec. 3, 1857. She d. June 16, 1896, leaving one son.

Samuel Baldwin owned and occupied the farm now of E. C. Flanders. He was b. Wilmington, Mass., Sept. 7, 1789, d. Mont Vernon, July 8, 1856, m. Mary Dane, Feb. 1, 1816. She was b. Chelmsford, Mass., April 18, 1794, d. Bedford, Nov. 23, 1874. Children:

1.   Samuel Dane, b. Oct. 4, 1817, m. (1) June 3, 1840, Clarissa Hildreth. She d. July 24, 1852, m. (2) Sarah S. Sanders, Sept. 28, 1853, resided Nashua. He d. Feb. 18, 1885.

2.   Silas H., b. June 20, 1819, d. Dec. 13, 1844.

3.   William O., minister, b. Aug. 25, 1821, m. (1) Oct. 4, 1854, Mary Proctor. She d. Jan. 24, 1872. He m. (2) Letty A. Gilman. He graduated Amherst College, settled in Central New York as a Presbyterian clergyman, and d. there.

4.   Jonathan N., b. Jan. 19, 1824, d. Oct. 12, 1825.

5.   Mary, b. June 26, 1826, m. Daniel K. Mack of Manchester, Oct. 8, 1856.

6.   Susan A., b. Francestown, Nov. 2, 1828, m. Leonard C. Farwell, Dec. 10, 1856, resided Temple. d. Sept. 4, 1895. 3 children.

7.   Sophia J., b. Dec. 23, 1830, d. March 17, 1832.

8.   Sophia M., b. July 18, 1832, unm.

9.   Charles H., b. March 7, 1835, d. May 20, 1836.

10.   Almira J., b. March 25, 1838, m. Isaac G. Wheeler, Jan. 12, 1864, d. Allston, Mass., March 26, 1895.

BANCROFT.

Stowell Bancroft, b. Groton, Mass., April 11, 1799, m. Martha D., dau. of Joseph and Betsey (Perkins) Trow, July 3, 1825. She was b. Mont Vernon, Feb. 7, 1796, d. Dec. 15, 1876. He was a brick-mason, and lived in the North District. He d. at Lancaster, Mass., Feb. 14, 1883, age 83. Their children were:

1.   Emily, b. Lowell, Mass., July 29, 1826, m. John P. Batchelder of Lowell, d. at Worcester, Mass., Dec. 29, 1826, leaving four children.

2.   Andrew J., b. Dunstable, Mass., April 28, 1829, m. Mary A. Clough of Lowell. He is a prominent and wealthy citizen of Lancaster, Mass. They have five children, viz.: Edward E. M. Bancroft, M. D.; William L., lumber dealer; George A. Bancroft, M. D.; Charles G., a lawyer; Martha S., a teacher.

3.   Sabrina F., b. Amherst, Aug. 28, 1831, lives unm. in Lancaster, Mass.

4.   William H., b. Mont Vernon, Aug. 10, 1833, m. Martha Varney of Lowell, lives in Lancaster, Mass., has three children, two sons and one daughter.

5.   Charles B., b. Mont Vernon, Sept. 4, 1838, m. Eunice Billings of Newton, Mass., has ch., resides in Lunenburg, Mass., d. June 3, 1903.

Dr. Cecil Franklin Patch Bancroft, son of Dea. James and Sarah W. (Kendall) Bancroft of New Ipswich, N. H., was b. in that town, Nov. 25, 1839. He fitted for college at Appleton Academy, New Ipswich, graduated at Dartmouth College in 1860. He came here in Aug., 1860, as Principal of Appleton Academy (now McCollom Institute), remaining four years. He was young, genial and enthusiastic, with conceded ability and soundness in judgment. He graduated at Andover Theological Seminary, 1867, was ordained at Mont Vernon, 1867. He then went to take charge of Robert College on Lookout Mountain, Tenn. He remained there five years. In 1873 he was chosen Principal of Phillips Andover Academy, which position he filled with eminent success until his death, Oct. 4, 1901. He received the degree of Doctor of Philosophy from New York State University, 1874, the degree of Doctor of Laws from Yale University in 1892. He was appointed a trustee of Dartmouth College in 1897. He was one of the most accomplished educators in America, and prepared for college a larger number of boys than any other American teacher, by whom he was universally beloved and honored. He was a man of rare insight and wonderful business ability. One of his townsmen said of him, "Had Dr. Bancroft been a business man, he would have become a millionaire." He had a gracious kindly manner, and was ever courteous to all.

In Andover, he won his way up to being "the first citizen of the town." He was a man of tireless energy, and wrought so intensely as to probably shorten his life. He d. Oct. 4, 1901, loved and esteemed by all who knew him. For several summers preceding his death, he made his summer home at "The Hearthstone," and ever manifested a cordial interest in the welfare of Mont Vernon. May 6, 1867, he m. Frances Adelia, dau. of Capt. Timothy and Frances (Marsh) Kittredge, an accomplished and lovely lady. She was b. Feb. 15, 1844, d. at Andover, Mass., March 29, 1898. Their children are:

1.   Cecil Kittredge, b. Dec. 15, 1868; is a Professor in Yale University.
2.   Frances Marsh, b. Sept. 12, 1872, m. Sept. 5, 1900, Rev. William J. Long of Stamford, Conn., has one daughter.
3.   Arthur Kendall, b. March 10, 1874, d. Aug. 9, 1880.
4.   Phillips, b. April 21, 1878.
5.   Mary Ethel, b. May 22, 1882.

BATCHELDER.

Ebenezer Batchelder, b. Nov. 24, 1710, m. Jerusha Kimball in 1740, settled in Wenham, Mass. Their children were:

1.   Anna, b. 1741.
2.   Mary, b. 1743.
3.   Lydia, b. 1745.
4.   Jerusha, b. 1747.

5. *Ebenezer, b. Nov. 5, 1750, settled in Amherst (now Mont Vernon).

6. Elizabeth, b. Jan. 25, 1753.

7. *John, b. Aug. 16, 1755, settled in Amherst (now Mont Vernon).

8. Mehitable, b. March 9, 1761.

9. Samuel, b. June 15, 1763.

*Ebenezer Batchelder, son of Ebenezer and Jerusha (Kimball) Batchelder, b. Wenham, Mass., Nov. 5, 1750, m. Elizabeth (Thompson) Sherwin. He settled in the East District, Mont Vernon about 1778, where he d. April 24, 1849, aged 98 years. She d. March 10, 1841, aged 85 years. Their children were:

Children probably b. Mt. Vernon.

1. Betsey, b. July 18, 1779, m. David Wiley, d. in Landgrove, Vt.

2. Joseph, b. Nov. 21, 1781, m. Anna Cochran, lived in Landgrove, Vt., and afterward in Illinois.

3. *Ebenezer, b. March 16, 1783.

4. Fanny, b. July 8, 1785, m. *Robert Parker, May 29, 1806, d. in Landgrove, Vt.

5. Lydia, b. Nov. 21, 1786, m. Benjamin Wilkins, Nov. 27, 1806, d. in Hillsborough.

6. Mehitable, b. Aug. 25, 1788, m. *Isaac Weston.

7. *Reuben Kimball, b. Feb. 7, 1790.

8. *Ezra, b. March 2, 1792.

9. Atness, b. April 5, 1794, m. *William Coggin, 2nd, Dec, 1814, settled in Mt. Vernon, d. Oct. 4, 1835.

10. Levi, b. March 10, 1797, m. Mary Peabody, d. Landgrove, Vt., Aug. 10, 1856, father of E. C. Batchelder, who was a well known merchant of Milford.

Capt. John Batchelder, son of Ebenezer and Jerusha (Kimball) Batchelder, b. Wenham, Mass., Aug. 16, 1755, m. his second cousin Betsey or Elizabeth Batchelder, dau. of Amos Batchelder of Woburn, Mass. She was b. Nov. 20, 1758, d. April 15, 1815. Capt. Batchelder settled in Mont Vernon in the East Ditsrict, on the farm now (1902) owned by Edward H. Best. He represented the town 1808, 1809, 1810. He d. Dec. 8, 1848. Their children were b. in Mt. Vernon.

1. *John, b. July 6, 1780.

2. Israel, b. Oct. 18, 1782, m. July 28, 1805, Abigail Wiley. He d. Peru, Vt., Aug. 31, 1858. She d. April 20, 1842. Had two daughters, Mary Jane and Abigail.

3. Betsey, b. Jan. 19, 1785, m. John Haseltine of Amherst, Dec. 25, 1805. She d. April 20, 1842, had eight children.

4. *Edmund, b. Aug. 5, 1787.

5. Nancy, b. Oct. 19, 1789, m. Dec. 26, 1808, Robert Wason, settled in

New Boston, d. July 28, 1863, had nine children, viz.: Elbridge, Louisa, Hiram, Nancy, Mary, Robert B., Adeline, Caroline, George Austin.

6. *Lydia, b. Feb. 11, 1792, m. her cousin *Ezra Batchelder, d. Sept. 29, 1882.

7. *Perley, b. July 26, 1794.

8. *Relief, b. Dec. 16, 1796, m. Sept. 2, 1830, *Dea. Josiah Kittredge, of Mont Vernon. She d. July 19, 1868.

9. *Amos, b. June 4, 1799.

10. Cyrene, b. Oct. 17, 1803, m. May 10, 1832, *Ira Kendall. She d. Goffstown, Dec. 16, 1872.

Ebenezer Batchelder, son of Ebenezer and Elizabeth Batchelder, b. March 16, 1783, m. June 30, 1811, Rachel, dau. of Timothy and Elizabeth (Kendrick) Jones of Amherst. She was b. 1786, d. Jan. 9, 1863, in Amherst, aged 76. He d. Feb. 26, 1815. Had several children. A daughter, Mrs. Fanny (Batchelder) Blaisdell, d. San Francisco, Cal., Dec. 28, 1890, aged 76 years. His son, William Batchelder, d. Feb. 20, 1860, aged 48. There were other daughters.

Reuben K. Batchelder, son of Ebenezer and Elizabeth T. S. Batchelder, b. Feb. 7, 1790. He m. (1) Alice, dau. of Daniel and Sarah (Lovejoy) Kendall. She was b. August 1, 1800, d. June 26, 1846. He m. (2) Mary, dau. of John and Abigail (Haseltine) Weston. She d. July 22, 1877, age 66 years, 28 days. He d. Dec. 13, 1867, age 77 years, 10 months. Two children by first wife, b. Mt. Vernon:

1. Reuben K., b. Feb. 17, 1836, left Mt. Vernon, 1861, lived in Milford. Has resided in Nashua for several years, is unm.

2. Sarah Eliza, b. March 30, 1838, m. Dr. David P. Stowell, resides at Waterville, Maine, no children.

18. Ezra Batchelder, son of Ebenezer and Elizabeth Batchelder, b. March 2, 1792, m. his cousin, Lydia Batchelder, dau. of Capt. John Batchelder, d. May 19, 1875. She was b. February 11, 1792, d. Sept. 29, 1882. He lived on his father's farm in the East District. Their children were b. in Mont Vernon.

1. *Hiram, b. April 20, 1820.

2. *George Gage, b. Nov. 16, 1824.

3. Susan Frances, b. Aug. 4, 1827, m. Sanford Trow, Aug. 3, 1847, son of Richard Trow of Hopkinton. They lived in Milford, moved from there to Haverhill, Mass., had several children.

4. Charles, b. Jan. 29, 1830, m. Dec. 15, 1853, Sarah J. Dinsmore of Londonderry, N. H., she d. Feb. 5, 1858, aged 28 years, 1 month. He d. Jan. 18, 1856, Nashua, N. H.

5. John A., b. Dec. 29, 1831, d. March 24, 1850.

6. Nancy Richards, b. Feb. 4, 1834, d. at Wareham, Mass., unm., Jan. 26, 1892.

Deacon John Batchelder, son of Capt. John and Betsey B. Batchelder, b. Mont Vernon, Nov. 14, 1780, m. (1) Sept. 13, 1802, Polly Hildreth, m. (2) Nancy Barnard of Peru, Vt. He d. Peru, Vt., June 9, 1851. By his first wife he had eight children:

1. Mark.
2. Fanny.
3. Eliza.
4. John.
5. Lucy Ann.
6. Edmund.
7. Mary Ann.
8. Mahala.

By his second wife he had:

9. Josiah.

Edmund Batchelder, son of Capt. John and Betsey B. Batchelder, b. Aug. 5, 1787, m. Betsey, dau. of Timothy and Elizabeth (Kendrick) Jones of Amherst. She d. in Peru, Vt., July 9, 1869, aged 83 years, 3 months. He d. at Peru, Vt., July 23, 1869. Children probably b. in Vermont. Their children were:

1. Ira K.
2. Frances.
3. Porter.
4. Roxana.
5. Amos.
6. Hannah.
7. Daniel.
8. Charles.
9. James.

Perley Batchelder, son of Capt. John and Betsey B. Batchelder, b. July 26, 1794, m. (1) 1823, Rebecca, dau. of Benjamin and Mary (Hosea) Damon of Amherst. She was b. Feb. 12, 1800, d. July 4, 1840. He m. (2) Alsinda Wason of New Boston, who d. Nov. 18, 1870, age 66. He d. Oct. 22, 1878. He lived on the farm and buildings in the East District, now owned by Edward H. Best. His children, all by first wife, were:

1. Clarissa D., b. June 12, 1825, d. Nov. 12, 1850, unm.

2. Rebecca Jane, b. Aug. 4, 1827, d. July 28, 1828.

3. Henry, b. July 28, 1829, m. Mary Anna, dau. of Samuel Brown of New Boston, Dec. 18, 1861. He d. of consumption, Jan. 19, 1863, aged 33 years. His widow m. for second husband, Prescott Farrar of Hillsboro', April 11, 1866.

4. Mary Jane, b. July 26, 1831, d. Lowell, 1903, m. Dec. 10, 1862, William A. Mack of Lowell, Mass., formerly of Amherst, where all their children were born. Maria A., b. Feb. 1, 1864; Emma, b. April 18, 1866; William L., b. July 13, 1868; Julia, b. July 27, 1870, d. Aug. 15, 1870.

29. Amos·Batchelder, son of Capt. John and Betsey B. Batchelder, b. June 4, 1799, m. Sept. 1, 1831, Nancy, dau. of William L. and Nabby (Jenkins) Kidder. He lived in the smaller house on the farm in the East District now owned by E. H. Best. He d. Feb. 10, 1847. Their ch. were:

1. Eliza E., b. Aug. 15, 1833.

2. Abby Maria. b. Oct. 9, 1838, m. (1) Henry Winchester, Feb. 14, 1855. He d. 1856. She m. (2) William Ryerson of Roxbury, Mass, children: William H., b. Wisconsin, March 31, 1859; Abby Francis, b. Dec. 8, 1862; Edith L., b. Wisconsin, April 9, 1865; Tillar, b. Aug. 2, 1870.

33. Hiram Batchelder, son of Ezra and Lydia Batchelder, b. April 20, 1820, m. (1) Jane Howard of Amherst, dau. of Henry and Polly O. Howard, Nov. 10, 1842. She was b. April 10, 1818, d. May 25, 1857. He m. (2) Mrs. Sarah A. Decatur of Mont Vernon, b. July 27, 1826. She was the dau. of James and Jane (Bixby) Upton, d. June 22, 1897. He settled in Reading, Mass., was a foundryman, children b. Reading. He d. Feb. 1, 1883. His children all by first wife were:

1. Nelson, b. Nov. 6, 1844, d. Feb. 19, 1857.

2. Eleanor, b. Sept. 16, 1846, m. April 16, 1868, Edward Eaton.

3. George, b. May 11, 1849, m. Jennie Wylie, July 31, 1870.

4. Harlon, b. Jan. 6, 1852.

5. Willie, b. April 27, 1854.

Deacon George Gage Batchelder, son of Ezra and Lydia Batchelder, b. Nov. 16, 1824, m. Nov. 25, 1849, Mary Elizabeth Horne of Dover, N. H. She was b. Aug. 10, 1826, d. June 23, 1899. He d. Jan. 8, 1896. Lived on his father's farm in East District, now owned by Vict. D. Gustine. Their children were b. Mont Vernon:

1. Charles Albert, b. Oct. 20, 1850, d. unm., Nov. 11, 1885.

2. George Herbert, b. July 18, 1852.

3. Marcia Ellen, b. March 3, 1864, m. Jan. 9, 1890, Frank O. Lamson of Mt. Vernon, has three children.

Susan Frances Batchelder, dau. of Ezra and Lydia Batchelder, b. Aug. 4, 1827, m. Aug. 3, 1847, Sanford Trow, resided Milford, children were:

1. Willie A., b. Sept. 26, 1860.

2. Charles Albert, b. Sept. 3, 1863.

3. Gracie Eaton, b. Dec. 10, 1869.

4. George Eaton, b. April 14, 1876.

BATTLES.

Samuel Battles, Sr., came to Mont Vernon from Plymouth, Mass., in 1813. He m. Deborah Atwood. He settled on the farm now of C. W.

Blood, in the East District. Three children, viz.: 1. William, 2. William, 3. Louis, d. in infancy at Plymouth. He had six children when he came here, Deborah, Samuel, Jr., John, Edward, Louis and Sarah. Of these Edward and Louis grew up, but were not m. He d. 1864, age 93. Ch:

  1. Deborah, m. *Daniel Kendall, Dec. 31, 1818. She d. April 24, 1871.

  2. Samuel Battles, Jr., m. Lydia Holmes, about 1820, moved from Mont Vernon to North Randolph, Vt., d. there April 16, 1880, had three sons, Charles, Lysander, and Edward (killed in the army) and several daughters.

  3. John, b. Aug. 14, 1797, m. Sarah Kendall, dau. Daniel and Sarah (Lovejoy) Kendall in year about 1827. She was b. July 26, 1794, d. March 6, 1858. He d. Dec. 11, 1877, had adopted son, Samuel F. Livingstone.

  4. Edward.

  5. Louis.

  6. Sarah, m. *George Jones, about 1831. She had three sons and three daughters. She d. Jan. 2, 1894.

  7. *Thomas W., b. Mont Vernon, Feb. 17, 1817.

Thomas W. Battles, son of Samuel, Sr., and Deborah (Atwood) Battles, b. Mont Vernon, Feb. 17, 1817, m. Lucy M. Stevens, June 1, 1837. She was b. in Mont Vernon, Oct. 23, 1818, d. Decatur, Ill., Aug. 8, 1900. He lived for many years on the farm owned and occupied by Charles W. Blood. He moved to Decatur, Ill., several years since, where he now resides. Children b. Mont Vernon:

  1. Orintha M., b. March 5, 1838, m. March 14, 1861, John C. Roby, resides Decatur, Ill.

  2. Charles W., b. August 18, 1843, m. Emma L. Spring, Aug. 18, 1869, has two daughters, Flora E., and Ella L., both b. in Decatur, Ill., where he resides. Carpenter.

  3. George W., b. March 23, 1851, m. Lizzie A. Parker of Goffstown, March 25, 1880, is in shoe business, resides Decatur, Ill.

  4. Orrin W., b. Sept. 30, 1852, m. Ella E. Whittemore of Goffstown, June 15, 1886. Resides Decatur, Ill.

  Children b. Mont Vernon:

  1. Alice E., b. Nov. 5, 1887.

  2. Maude, b. Aug. 29, 1889.

BEARD.

Charles Rodney Beard, b. New Ipswich, N. H., 1799, moved to Mont Vernon about 1825, formed a partnership in the tannery with Dea. Joseph A. Starrett, sold out and removed to Newport, N. H., came back here after his first wife's death, and bought out D. W. Baker's half of store. He was representative in 1856-1857. He d. in New Ipswich, Dec. 16,

1880, age 81 years. He m. (1) 1829, his cousin, Betsey J., dau. of Mark and Mahala Perkins, she d. Jan. 26, 1850, age 40. He m. (2) Fanny, dau. of Capt. William Bruce of Mont Vernon. She was the widow of David Boardman. She d. Nov. 13, 1873, age 62. Three children by first wife:

    1. Charles E., b. May 31, 1832, lived in New Ipswich.

    2. Sarah W., b. May 24, 1835, m. Jesse Hutchinson of Milford, lived in Baltimore.

    3. Frank.

Samuel J. Beard, son of Samuel Beard, b. in Hollis, N. H., March 23, 1836, came to Mont Vernon in 1860, enlisted in 22d N. H. Regiment; discharged for wound in knee, Dec., 1862. He was a helper in the families of John Follansbee and Henry F. Dodge many years. He entered the Soldiers' Home at Tilton in 1897, where he d. May 29, 1902. He was unm.

Elijah Beard, came here from Hillsboro'. Children Elijah and Lucy Beard.

    1. Cyrene Adeline, b. Feb. 17, 1816.

    2. Stillman A., b. Dec. 17, 1817.

BENNETT

John H. Bennett of Canterbury, N. H., m. Polly Johnonnot of Goffstown, N. H. He d. in Mont Vernon, Aug. 28, 1871, aged 58. She d. Aug. 5, 1895, aged 89 years, 4 months. Children all b. in Mont Vernon were:

    1. Marden J., b. Dec. 3, 1836, d. Feb. 2, 1893, was a carpenter, unm.

    2. Elizabeth, b. March, 1839, d. Nov. 29, 1888. She m. *Clinton May, who d. May 18, 1877, age 46. They had three children.

    3. Alvan E., b. July 23, 1841, m. April, 1861, Ellen, dau. of Mark and Mary (Twiss) Putnam of Amherst, has three children, George, Mark P., Florence.

    4. Harvey, d. May 28, 1868, age 16 years (adopted son).

BISHOP.

Henry Bishop came from Marblehead, Mass., lived on the Joseph Conant farm in the East District 15 years, moved to the village and d. there Nov. 8, 1860, age 66. His wife, Sally D. (Barker) Bishop, d. Marblehead, Oct. 16, 1890, age 89. A child d. in infancy, March 13, 1841.

BLANCHARD.

George Walter, son of Timothy and Dorcas (Hood) Blanchard, b. Milford, Nov. 19, 1824, moved in the West District, Mont Vernon in 1876. He d. Nov. 2, 1896. He m. Delia Finnerty, b. Aug. 5, 1835, children:

    1. George D., b. 1862, farmer, lives Mont Vernon.

    2. James, b. March 4, 1865, d. at San Bernardino, Cal., Dec. 13, 1891.

    3. Walter J., b. July 6, 1870, m. 1895, Hannah J. Averill, one child. She d., 1901.

BERRY.

Rev. Augustus Berry, b. Concord, N. H., Oct. 17, 1824, was principal of McCollom Institute from 1856 to 1860, thence went to Andover, Mass., to study theology, was settled as minister of the Congregational Church, Pelham, until his death, Oct. 10, 1899. He m. (1) Nov. 24, 1853, Miss Dora Richardson Snow of Peterborough, who d. March 15, 1873. He m. (2) in 1877, Miss Mary Currier Richardson of Pelham. No children.

BLOOD.

George A. Blood, b. Merrimack, N. H., 1804, was a soldier in the 10th New Hampshire Regiment, d. in hospital, Nov., 1863, m. 1839, Alice Seavey Butterfield, b. Feb. 19, 1821, in Bedford. Children:

1. *George Henry, b. Bedford, Aug. 5, 1845.

2. Alonzo, b. Merrimack, 1846, m. Clara Pearson, has three sons, lives in New Boston.

3. Mary Ann, b. Bedford, June 19, 1848, m. Henry J. West, of Amherst, d. 1866.

4. Eliza J., b. Merrimack, Sept. 27, 1854, m. Jan., 1874, J. Minot Harvell, resides in Milford. Children: Sarah Alice, b. at Mont Vernon, Sept. 5, 1875, m. Chandler of New Boston. Herbert Minot, b. Dec. 1, 1880, at Mont Vernon, resides Milford.

5. Elizabeth E., b. Merrimack, Sept. 27, 1858, m. Dec. 28, 1880, James Kennett of Beverly, Mass., has two sons.

6. Ida E., b. Bedford, July 16, 1860, dressmaker, unm., resides Mont Vernon.

7. *Charles W., b. March 26, 1862.

George Henry Blood, b. Aug. 5, 1845, m. Nov. 27, 1897, Mary J. West of Amherst, b. Sept. 9, 1850. He d. Sept. 21, 1898. Farmer. Resided in North and South District (Justin Richardson farm). Children except Bessie b. Amherst.

1. Harry G., b. May 2, 1869, m. April 27, 1892, Harriet M. Kittredge, dau. of Henry J. and Jane (Murray) Kittredge. Farmer. Resides North District.

2. *Joseph H., b. June 24, 1872.

3. Alice R., b. March 3, 1876, clerk, resides Mont Vernon.

4. Charles E., b. March 25, 1879, m. Feb. 12, 1900, Ida Millay, resides Stoddard. One son.

5. Bessie May, b. Mont Vernon, April 21, 1895.

*Charles W. Blood, b. March 26, 1862, m. June 21, 1890, Ida J. Codman, dau. of Nathan and Hannah (Cree) Codman. She was b. W. Deering, Sept. 27, 1869. Children b. Mont Vernon.

1. Helen M., b. March 18, 1891.

2. Olive E., b. Feb. 28, 1893.

Joseph H. Blood, b. June 24, 1872, m. Jan. 10, 1900, Myrtie A., dau. of Frank Brooks of Greenfield. He is senior partner of firm of Blood & Temple, village grocers. Children b. Mont Vernon:

1. George B., b. Dec. 8, 1900.
2. Jennie A., b. June 1, 1902.

BOARDMAN.

David Boardman from Halifax, Vt., settled in Mont Vernon in 1840, m. Oct. 6, 1842, Frances E., dau. of Capt. William Bruce. He d. July 25, 1850, age 42. She d. Nov. 13, 1873, age 52. They had three children:

1. Irving went to western New York, studied medicine, and is a practising physician there.
2. Frances Estelle, d. Sept. 2, 1852, age 6½ years.
3. Emily, d. March 14, 1849, age 18 months.

BOHONAN.

Walter Bohonan, son of Jonathan and Elizabeth (Whitcomb) Bohonan, b. Temple, N. H., Dec. 22, 1856, came to Mont Vernon in 1895, and settled on the Simeon F. Kendall farm in the East District. He m. Estella F., dau. of Henry and Frances (Marshall) Heald of Milford. She was b. April 22, 1868. Children:

1. Elsie Marion, b. Milford, April 28, 1893.
2. Frances Elizabeth, b. Mont Vernon, Jan. 3, 1896.
3. Hattie Florence, b. Mont Vernon, Nov. 17, 1897.
4. Bertha May, b. Mont Vernon, Nov. 3, 1899.
5. George W., b. Mont Vernon, Sept., 1901.

BOUTELLE.

Lilly E. Boutelle, son of Joseph and Sarah (Eaton) Boutell, b. Amherst, 1796, m. Feb., 1820, Phebe Holt of Temple. She was b. Jan. 8, 1793, d. Oct. 27, 1847. He d. July 24, 1839, age 33, children were:

1. George E., b. Amherst, June 29, 1825, m. (1) Mrs. Nancy S. Bohonan of Nashua, she d. March, 1867, m. (2) Ella A., dau. Albert B. and Harriet E. (Cummings) McCrillis of Francestown, b. Nov. 19, 1848. Children: Georgia Ella, d. young; George Curtis, b. Feb. 12, 1871, insurance solicitor, m. and res. Buffalo, N. Y.; Edwin Tracy, b. Sept. 10, 1873, d. Feb. 14, 1878; Carl Vernon, b. Mont Vernon, Dec. 26, 1884.
2. Phebe A., b. Amherst, Dec. 26, 1826, d. Nashua, June 17, 1899, unm.

BOUTELL.

Horace S. Boutell, son of Calvin Boutell, b. Amherst, N. H., Jan. 24, 1822, m. Martha A., dau. Jesse and Nancy (Cochran) Trow of Mont Vernon, June 6, 1848. She was b. Mont Vernon, March 10, 1825, d. Amherst, N. H., Aug. 18, 1893. Mr. Boutell was a railroad engineer in Hillsborough, removed to Mont Vernon, lived on the farm now occupied by Maurice Herlihy in the South District, and on the Harwood place west of the village, thence removed to the Moses Hill's Place in Amherst, where he d. Oct. 14, 1896. Children:

    1. Martha E., b. Hillsboro', May 6, 1850, m. Henry A. Hill of Stoneham, Mass., April 23, 1871, d. Amherst, N. H., April 18, 1876.

    2. Frank T., b. Hillsboro', March 22, 1854, m. Delia Foster of Marlboro', Mass., Jan. 11, 1879, res. Amherst, N. H.

    3. George P., b. Mont Vernon, July 29, 1861, m. Hattie B. Tobin of Amherst, N. H., Oct. 14, 1896, d. Amherst, Oct. 25, 1897.

    4. Fred, b. Mont Vernon, Jan. 21, 1865, m. Martha E. Boutelle of Corinth, Me., June 10, 1897, lives at Amherst.

    5. Harry, b. Stoneham, Mass., Dec. 27, 1869, m. Anna C. Whiting, dau. Benj. B. Whiting of Amherst, Dec. 27, 1893, lives at Amherst.

Reuben Boutell, b. Reading, Mass., 1760, m. Olive Bradford, moved from here to Antrim. A son, Chandler B., b. March.

BRADFORD.

William Bradford came here early in life from Middleton, Mass., m. (1) Mary Lambert, Jan. 18, 1737. She was b. March 11, 1718, d. Feb. 18, 1770. He m. (2) Rachel Small. She was b. May 7, 1738, d. Jan. 26, 1802. He d. 1791.

Children by first wife:

    1. Samuel, b. about 1738, was a Revolutionary soldier, m. Anna Washer, d. in Antrim at Elijah Gold's, Feb. 5, 1813.

    2. Patience, m. Joseph Lovejoy of Amherst, July 9, 1761, had eight children, d. in Amherst, March 3, 1826, aged 85.

    3. Mary, m. *John Averill, d. Mont Vernon, August 21, 1814, aged 73. She was baptized in Middleton, Mass., 1742.

    4. *Enos, b. Nov. 3, 1744, m. Sarah Chandler of Bedford, Jan. 24, 1769, d. of starvation, from a disease of the throat which prevented him from swallowing food.

    5. *Joseph.

    6. *William.

    7. Huldah, unm.

    8. Olive, m. Reuben Boutell, Jr., Nov. 11, 1789, removed to Antrim, 1783.

    9. Eunice, m. Moses Pettengill, Feb. 4, 1779.

By second wife:

    10. Hannah, b. May 20, 1773, m. James Tuttle, July 5, 1798.

    11. *Lambert, b. March 18, 1775.

Enos Bradford, son of (1) William and Mary (Lambert) Bradford, b. Nov. 3, 1744, m. Sarah Chandler of Bedford, Jan. 24, 1769. He settled near his father in Mont Vernon. Their children were:
1. Chandler, b. Nov. 20, 1772, d. Jan. 29, 1775.
2. Enos, b. Dec. 26, 1774, d. Sept., 1797.
3. Lambert.
4. Sarah, b. 1780.
5. Chandler, b. Aug. 13, 1783, d. Feb. 22, 1784.
6. Nancy, b. 1792, m. Sept. 10, 1809, *John L. Lamson of Mont Vernon, d. Jan. 23, 1812.

Joseph Bradford, son of William and Mary (Lambert) Bradford, was a Revolutionary soldier, d. Medford, Mass., July, 1775, left two children:
1. Molly, m. Robert Taggard, Sept. 20, 1793.
2. Lavina.
They were placed under guardianship, April 28, 1779. They had been previously cared for by Nathan Jones.

William Bradford, Jr., son of William and Mary (Lambert) Bradford, m. (1) Hannah ———, and settled in Mont Vernon. She d. Sept. 1, 1812, age 56; m. (2) Mrs. Lois Bruce, widow of Rev. John Bruce. She d. 1828, age 67. He was a Revolutionary soldier, and a prominent character in the early history of the town. He removed in his old age to Barre, Vt., where he d. Oct. 25, 1816, aged 63 years. Maj. William Bradford, though and old man, commanded under Gen. Miller at "Lundy's Lane." He lived on the John Averill farm in North District. His ch. were:
1. William, b. 1780, m. Mary Green, d. Barre, Vt., March 3, 1866.
2. Joseph, d. Winchester, Tenn., Jan. 19, 1859, age 72 years.
3. Mary, m. Daniel L. Stearns, d. Goshen, Aug. 1849.
4. Leonard, m. Betsey, dau. Phinehas and Sarah (Hildreth) Jones, May 4, 1815, settled in Washington, N. H.
5. Anne, d. unm. in Goshen.
6. Lucy, m. Eber Curtis of Antrim, had seven children.
7. Fanny, an adopted dau., m. Eben Averill of Milford, d. Feb. 12, 1850, age 66.

Lambert Bradford, son of William and Mary (Lambert) Bradford, m. Phebe Farnum. He d. Merrimack, Feb. 12, 1850, aged 75. Their children were:
1. Polly, b. March 9, 1795, m. George Wiley, Jan. 1, 1818.
2. William, b. March 16, 1797, m. Ruth Whiting of Merrimack, March 16, 1826.
3. Minerva, b. Aug. 11, 1799.
4. Nabby, b. Dec. 1, 1801.
5. Susannah, b. April 6, 1802.

HARRY H. BRAGG.

BRAGG.

Harry H. Bragg, b. Springfield, Vt., Jan. 4, 1813, m. (1) Malvina M. Wilkins, dau. Frederick Wilkins, Dec. 24, 1839. She was b. Feb. 25, 1819, d. Oct. 19, 1873. He m. (2) Mrs. Mary S. Bruce of Milford, N. H., Feb. 11, 1875. He d. Nov. 11, 1883. He was an honest, straightforward man of business, kind and friendly disposition, and during the 30 years he was a citizen of Mont Vernon, his enterprise contributed largely to the prosperity of the town and his removal after the burning of his factory in 1864, was a serious loss. His children were all b. in Mont Vernon.

1. Cordelia M. J., b. Feb. 3, 1841, m. Henry J. Allen of Boston, Dec. 3, 1874. She d. Feb. 19, 1882; no children.

2. Alonzo W., b. Oct. 29, 1842, m. (1) Sept. 26, 1865, Sarah N. Holland of Boston, who d. He m. (2) Mrs. Mary E. Lamb of Revere, who d. He m. (3) March 20, 1884, Miss Mary Edgerly of Boston. He was engaged in active business, as a manufacturer and merchant in Boston for 25 years, is now successfully retired with an ample estate which has been increased by fortunate investments. He is sharp and shrewd in financial matters.

3. Ellen M., b. April 27, 1845, m. Nov. 1, 1868, Arthur J. Haseltine of Manchester, N. H., by whom she had one daughter. She m. (2) Feb. 8, 1893, William G. Burnham of Mt. Vernon. She d. at Sharon, Mass., March 18, 1896.

4. Henrietta E., b. June 29, 1849, m. Charles B. Dodge of Milford, Dec. 24, 1870, d. Aug. 2, 1873.

5. Harry A., b. Nov. 29, 1854, d. Dec. 28, 1860.

BROWN.

Amasa, son of Joshua and Sally Potter Brown, b. Concord, Mass., April 16, 1808, d. March 10, 1883, settled in Mont Vernon in 1833, m. Sept. 3, 1833, Maria, dau. of James Wilkins and Hannah Brown Wilkins of Carlisle, b. July 17, 1808. She d. Oct. 29, 1900. Children all b. in Mont Vernon.

1. Joshua, b. June 29, 1834, d. Aug. 11, 1853.

2. Rebecca D., b. March 6, 1836, m. October, 1859, Lorenzo A. Lane of Ashburnham; one son, Elmer C., b. Oct. 15, 1867, m. Nov. 27, 1889, Mary Allen of Alfred, Me., have two children, res. Dorchester, Mass., Mrs. Rebecca (Brown) Lane d. Feb. 12, 1881.

3. *James A., b. Nov. 7, 1837.

4. Sarah P., b. May 25, 1840, lives on homestead, unm.

5. Susan B., b. May 25, 1840, d. May 26, 1840.

6. George W., b. Feb. 11, 1842, d. while a member of Company B., Eighth N. H. Regiment at New Orleans, May 25, 1863.

7. Hiram W., b. July 7, 1844, lives Mont Vernon.

8. Charles D., b. Dec. 6, 1850, lives Mont Vernon.

James A. Brown, son of Amasa and Maria Wilkins Brown, b. Nov. 7, 1837, m. (1) May, 1856, Adeline L. Small. She d. Dec., 1863. He m. (2) Adeline A. Davis of Ashby, March 24, 1865. She was b. Dec. 21, 1850. Children by first wife were:

1. James, b. March, 1857, d. April , 1857.
2. Clara M., b. May, 1860, d. Feb. 25, 1879.
3. Sarah J., b. May, 1863, d. Dec., 1863.

Children by second wife were:

4. Susan E., b. July 17, 1866, m. Chas. Johnnott, resides in Nashua; one child.
5. James W., b. Dec. 19, 1868, engineer.
6. Albert Irving, b. June 23, 1870, m. resides in New Boston; has two children.
7. Joseph Derby, b. July 8, 1873.
8. Charles Reuben, b. Jan. 22, 1876.
9. George Amasa, b. Nov. 8, 1878.
10. Sarah Ellen, b. Oct. 16, 1881.
11. Warren F., d. Feb. 24, 1887, age two years.
12. Marion Blanche, b. July 9, 1889.

John Dalton Brown, son of William and Tabitha (Boutelle) Brown, b. Amherst, Sept. 28, 1818, m. Dec. 25, 1849, Mary dau. Eli and Polly (Hidden) Buttrick. She was b. Pelham, N. H., April 11, 1828, d. Feb. 22, 1903, at Milford. He came here from Amherst about 1864, lived on the farm by the big maple tree, now owned by C. O. Ingalls, then on the old poor-farm (now Edw. Hildreth's), thence to the Rollins' farm in East District. While driving his team, one of the stakes struck him in the neck inflicting a wound from which he died the next day, May 29, 1879.

Children were:

1. Alvah, b. Amherst, Feb. 12, 1850, d. April 14, 1850.
2. Elwin, b. Amherst, July 11, 1852, d. Aug. 30, 1854.
3. Martha J., b. Amherst, May 27, 1855, m. (1) Chas. O. Brooks of Greenfield, Sept. 23, 1874, by whom she had two children; m. (2) Elbridge K. Jewett, Dec. 25, 1844, four children, res. in Milford.
4. Lewis W., b. Amherst, Sept. 3, 1857, m. Martha Granicher, Dec. 22, 1887; eight children; reside in California.
5. Ellen M., b. Amherst, Dec. 5, 1859, m. Hubbard H. Sanderson, Nov. 23, 1881; two children; res. Milford.
6. Otis G., b. Amherst, Jan. 21, 1862, res. in Milford, unm.
7. Martin L., b. Mont Vernon, Jan. 16, 1866, m. Sept. 30, 1897, Bertha M. Lund, one child, res. in Milford.
8. Hattie Eva, b. Mont Vernon, Sept. 4, 1868, d. Milford, Dec. 25, 1888.
9. Clara M., b. Mont Vernon, March 8, 1871, d. Milford, Dec. 7, 1883.

Mrs. Charlotte Brown, lived where Jay M. Gleason now does, in the forties and fifties. One dau. Charlotte, d. Sept. 9, 1844, aged 28. A dau. Julia Ann, m. *Elisha R. Manning, d. Sept. 9, 1877, aged 56 years.

BROWNE.

Rev. Donald Browne, b. London, England, Nov. 3, 1851, son of Donald and Sarah (Humphrey) Browne, educated in Devonshire, was a teacher, had charge of an Episcopal Mission School four years. Judge of District of St. Barbe's, Bombay, Newfoundland six years, studied theology at Boston University, ordained 1889, preached at Tiverton, R. I., 1889 to 1892, was pastor of Broadway Congregational Church at Fall River, Mass., 1892 to 1895, at Mont Vernon N. H. Congregational Church from Nov. 1898 to Nov. 1900. He is now Rector of the Episcopal Church at Derry, N. H. He m. (1) 1874, in Birmingham, Eng., Miss Agnes Anderson, who d. 1890, two children by first wife. He m. (2) Mrs. Caroline (Crapo) Swain of Fall River, Mass., one child.

   3. Donald, b. Nov. 26, 1897.

BRUCE.

Rev. John Bruce, b. Marlborough, Mass., Aug. 31, 1757, d. in Mont Vernon, March 12, 1809, m. Lois Wilkins of Marlborough, Dec. 15, 1785, who after his death m. Major William Bradford. She d. in Mont Vernon, Feb. 12, 1828, aged 67. He settled in Mont Vernon in 1785, was the pastor of the Congregational Church from 1785 until his death in 1809. He was called the "good Mr. Bruce." He lived on the farm, now occupied by Miles E. Wallace, west of village. Their ch. were b. Mont Vernon.

   1. John, d. Dec. 14, 1786, age 6 weeks, 6 days.

   2. *John, b. Feb. 11, 1788.

   3. *James, b. Nov. 15, 1789.

   4. *William, b. Aug. 7, 1791.

   5. Lois, b. 1793, m. William S. Stinson, Sept. 12, 1816, d. Oct. 5, 1823, had three sons.

   6. *Nathaniel, b. 1794, d. March 2, 1874.

   7. Fanny, m. Stephen Peabody, by whom she had children, lived in Montpelier, Vt.

Deacon John Bruce, son of Rev. John and Lois (Wilkins) Bruce, b. Feb. 11, 1788, was representative, moderator, and deacon in the church here. He m. Dolly Durant. She was b. May 3, 1792, d. Aug. 28, 1871. He d. Jan. 19, 1872. He lived on his father's farm. He was also County Treasurer several years. Their children were b. Mont Vernon.

   1. Maria Jane, b. Aug. 21, 1814, m. Dec. 10, 1833, Dea. Joseph A. Starrett, d. Oct. 20, 1869, had four children.

   2. *John Erastus, b. Nov. 4, 1817.
   3. *Levi W., b. July 21, 1821.
   4. *Alonzo Swan, b. July 3, 1826.
   5. Emily Frances, m. Nov. 15, 1849, William A. Starrett of Francestown, d. Mont Vernon, Aug. 19, 1853, age 23.

James Bruce, son of Rev. John and Lois (Wilkins) Bruce, b. Nov.
5, 1789, m. (1) Sarah, dau. of Thomas Parker of New Boston. She was
b. March 11, 1794, d. at Mont Vernon, Nov. 28, 1844, age 50 years. He m.
(2) Mrs. Elizabeth Wheelwright. She d. May 1, 1883, age 82. He d.
July 19, 1869, age 79 years, 8 months. He moved in Mont Vernon, moved
to Lyndeboro', thence removed to Mont Vernon, where he d. Children all
by first wife.
   1. John W., b. July 30, 1816, resides Medford, Mass.
   2. Sarah, b. April 14, 1820, m. May 6, 1846, Nathan Richardson of
Lyndeborough, where she d. Aug. 3, 1888. She had four children, viz.:
1. Edward B.; 2. Sarah E., m. Stephen H. Dunbar of Wilton; 3. Ella F.,
m. Eli Curtis of Wilton; 4. Harry J., lives in Lyndeborough.
   3. *Elizabeth, b. April 24, 1825.
   4. Clarinda F., b. Jan. 10, 1831, m. James H. Carr of Lyndeborough,
has one son, Frederic B. Carr.
   5. James P., b. May 3, 1834, d. at Mont Vernon, April 11, 1854.

Capt. William Bruce, son of Rev. John and Lois (Wilkins) Bruce, b.
Aug. 7, 1791, in Mont Vernon. Lived in the village, was a blacksmith, m.
Dec. 1, 1814, Hannah, dau. Peter and Betsey Woodbury Jones. She was
b. Mont Vernon, Nov. 20, 1793, d July 18, 1871. He d. July 21, 1871. Ch.
b. Mont Vernon.
   1. Jane T., b. Jan. 1, 1816, m. March 26, 1833, Stephen Dunbar of
Milford, son Rev. Elijah Dunbar, d. Manchester, Feb. 8, 1890.
   2. William G., b. Feb. 1, 1819, mechanic, lived in village, m. Augusta,
dau. James and Hannah (Stevens) Whittemore. She was b. May 12,
1825, d. Sept. 6, 1891. He, while hunting in New Boston, shot himself, and
d. as a result, Oct. 27, 1883. He was representative in 1862 and 1863,
two years.
   3. Frances E., b. 1821, m. (1) Oct. 6, 1852, *David Boardman, m. (2)
Chas. R. Beard. She d. Nov. 13, 1873.
   4. Nancy B., b. Oct. 1, 1825, m. Sept. 23, 1843, *Thos. Haskell
Richardson. She d. June 6, 1892.
   5. Artemas F., d. July 18, 1831, aged 10 months, 15 days.

Nathaniel Bruce, son of Rev. John and Lois (Wilkins) Bruce, b.
1795, m. (1) Frances Tay of Bedford, m. (2) Lucy Butterfield of Lyndeboro'. She was b. Dec. 12, 1803, d. Jan. 11, 1880. He lived first in South
District, then in village where Walter Woods now lives. He d. March 2,

NATHANIAL BRUCE, ESQ.

JOSEPH H. A. BRUCE.

1874. Was a justice of the peace. He was County Treasurer from 1843 to 1846. He was appointed postmaster in 1861 to 1873, and representative in 1830, 1831, 1832, 1833, 1840, 1841. Children by first wife.

    1. Maria, b. Feb. 10, 1817, d. young.

    2. Nathaniel F., b. May 25, 1819, m. (1) Harriet N. Oliver of Stoneham, Mass., kept store in Wakefield and Billerica, Mass., 28 years (14 years in each place). His ch. are: 1. Clarence M., a merchant of Billerica; 2. Jasper, res. Billerica; 3. Romanzo L., Methodist preacher of Vermont Conference, lives California; 4. Eva Caroline, m. Orlando Hoyt, res. Stoneham, Mass.; 5. Louis F., resides Stoneham; 6. Nathaniel E., m. Emily J. Hatch, resides Stoneham.

    3. Frances Maria, d. at 12 years of age.

    4. Caroline, d. at 10 years of age.

    5. Mary, m. John Oliver, d. Portsmouth, N. H., where she resided.

    6. Sarah Ann, m. Henry Oliver of Stoneham, Mass., d. there Jan. 31, 1884.

    7. Joseph Harvey Appleton, b. Oct. 30, 1833, m. (1) Emily, dau. Mark D. and Mahala (Jones) Perkins of Mont Vernon. She d. June 19, 1860, age 26 years, 9 months. He m. (2) Elvira, dau. George Hoyt of Francestown. They had one dau. Emilie (now Mrs. Chas. Abbe of Pittsburg, Pa.), m. (3) Mrs. Emma (Burton) Hoyt of Wilton. He was representative in 1870 and 1871. He is the proprietor of a summer hotel at Bethlehem, N. H., and a winter hotel at Lakeland, Fla.

    8. Frances M., m. Henry Mosman, by whom she had three dau. Gertrude, Jennie, Frances. He d. April 23, 1880. She m. (2) June, 1887, Daniel Holley, res. San Jose, Cal.

By second wife, Lucy Butterfield Bruce:

    9. *George Anson, b. Nov. 19, 1839.

    10. Lucy Augusta, b. May 28, 1841, m. July 10, 1861, Alfred Kirke, b. Harrison Co., Ohio, Feb. 16, 1832. Children: Allen B., b. June 2, 1868; Harold B., b. Sept. 20, 1876. They reside in Chicago.

John Erastus Bruce, b. Nov. 4, 1817, went to Milford, 1849, was a merchant there many years, m. June 16, 1846, Sarah J., dau. of James and Hannah (Stevens) Whittemore, b. Weymouth, Mass., May 22, 1827. Ch:

    1. Charles E., b. Mont Vernon, Dec. 18, 1846, manufacturer, res. Elmira, N. Y., m. 1873, Fanny McMurray, Troy, N. Y.

    2. Josiephine F., b. Mont Vernon, Aug. 26, 1848, teacher, res. Medford, Mass.

    3. Ella A., b. Milford, Nov. 24, 1850, m. Nov. 16, 1870, W. N. Robinson, has three children, res. Milford.

    4. Emily F., b. July 2, 1853, m. Nov. 1874, Judge Walter H. Sanborn, res. St. Paul, Minn.

    5. Sarah W., b. Sept. 6, 1859, m. April 29, 1891, Edwin A. McCrillis, res. Milford.

Levi W. Bruce, b. July 21, 1821, d. July 2, 1855, m. Dec. 18, 1851, Alma, dau. Daniel and Olive (Proctor) Holt of Milford. She was b. Milford, May 24, 1834. She m. (2) 1857, *Dea. George E. Dean of Mont Vernon. She d. Mont Vernon, Dec. 31, 1891. Mr. Bruce was a merchant tailor and lived in Milford. Children:

1. Augustus Levi, b. Milford, Nov. 24, 1854, grew up in Mont Vernon, graduated McCollom Institute, graduated at a homeopathic school in Chicago, Ill., is a successful physician of the osteopathy method at Utica, N. Y., has been an instructor in the Atlantic School of Osteopathy, Wilkesbarre, Pa. He m. Nov. 29, 1888, Miss Elizabeth Harris of Victory, N. Y.

Alonzo Swan Bruce, son of Deacon John and Dolly (Durant) Bruce, b. July 3, 1826, d. April 27, 1892, m. May 31, 1865, Maria N., dau. Robert and Nancy (Smith) Tuten. She was b. Cambridge, Mass., Sept. 20, 1843. He was postmaster for several years. Children:

1. John Alonzo, b. May 1, 1868, m. Nov. 22, 1894, Lizzie Blanche, dau. John F. and Mary E. (Hatch) Amsden, one ch., is a clerk and res. in Milford.

2. Alice Frances, b. Nov. 22, 1874, d. Nov. 12, 1895.

3. Robert Tuten, b. Dec. 26, 1876, res. at Mont Vernon.

Elizabeth Bruce, dau. of James and Sarah (Parker) Bruce, b. April 24, 1825, m. Dea. Nathaniel F. McIntire of Lyndeborough, April 12, 1848, d. Feb. 2, 1903, in Lyndeborough. Children:

1. Mary C., b. Feb. 28, 1851, m. June 9, 1874, *Jay M. Gleason, two children.

2. Lois E., b. Oct. 11, 1854, lives in Lyndeboro'.

3. Herbert B., b. July 3, 1857, m. Ida Woodward of Marlboro', N. H., is a doctor in Cambridge, Mass.

George Anson Bruce, son of Nathaniel and Lucy (Butterfield) Bruce, b. Nov. 19, 1839, fitted for college at Mont Vernon, graduated at Dartmouth in 1861, studied law one year with Hon. D. S. Richardson at Lowell. In August, 1862, he enlisted in the Thirteenth N. H. Regiment, and went to the front as first lieutenant of Company B. He served with distinguished bravery until the close of the war, holding at its close the position of brevet lieutenant-colonel. In 1865 he resumed his legal studies at Lowell. In 1866 he represented Mont Vernon in the N. H. Legislature. In 1866 he was admitted to the bar and opened an office in Boston, where he pursued his profession with an assured reputation as an able counsellor and advocate until recently. He is now retired. Establishing his residence in the city of Somerville, he was in 1877 elected its Mayor, holding the office three consecutive years. In 1883 and again in 1884 he was in the State Senate from his district, and the latter year its presiding officer.

HON. GEORGE A. BRUCE.

SYLVANUS BUNTON, M.D.

He now lives in Boston. He m. Clara M. Hall of Groton, Mass., by
whom he has one child, who survives.

1. Clara Augusta, b. Nov. 19, 1882.

BULLARD.

Edmund E. Bullard, son of Nahum and Keziah (Peabody) Bullard,
b. Amherst, March 25, 1835, m. June 22, 1863, Rachel E. Roberts of Hub-
bardton, Vt. He lived in the Proctor house (now burnt), near George
C. Hadley, several years, moving to Amherst in the eighties. He d. Aug.
6, 1901, at Amherst. Their children were:

1. Lovicey J., b. March 23, 1864, d. Nov. 22, 1864.

2. Charles D., b. Nov. 7, 1868, m. Abby A. White, June 26, 1890,
lives in Amherst.

3. Anna E., b. Oct. 29, 1871, m. Sept. 2, 1891, Willis M. Chandler,
one daughter.

John A. Bullard, son of Nahum and Keziah (Peabody) Bullard, b.
Amherst, June 26, 1851, m. Nov. 23, 1875, Ida B., dau. Josiah and Sally
(Farnum) Swinnington, b. May 25, 1860, Mont Vernon. He resides in
Lyndeborough. Their children are:

1. Harry Orville, b. Mont Vernon, July 17, 1877.

2. Winfield Stetson, b. Amherst, Sept. 5, 1880.

3. Arthur Brooks, b. Mont Vernon, June 26, 1886.

BUXTON.

Dr. Sylvanus Buxton, b. Allenstown, N. H., March 8, 1812, graduated
Dartmouth College, 1840, studied medicine in Baltimore. First settled
in his profession in Manchester, N. H., where he continued until June,
1864, when he was appointed assistant surgeon of Seventh N. H. Regiment,
promoted to surgeon, mustered out July 20, 1865. Then he settled in his
profession at Hollis, and in 1868 removed to Mont Vernon, N. H., where
he d. Aug. 13, 1884. He m. (1) Dec. 17, 1846, Clarissa Conant. She was
b. Hollis, May 1, 1814, d. at Mont Vernon, July 3, 1873. He m. (2) Dec.
1874, Sarah J., dau. Capt. James T. and Sally (Gillis) Trevitt. She was
b. Mont Vernon, Sept. 22, 1818, d. Mont Vernon, Dec. 26, 1899. Children
by first wife:

1. Henry S., b. Manchester, N. H., April 6, 1848, m. in Winthrop,
Mass., May 9, 1880, Mary G. Giles. He is treasurer Hyde Park Savings
Bank, Hyde Park, Mass.

2. Leonard J., b. Dec. 29, 1858, d. 1859.

BURNHAM.

Azel W. Burnham, son of Col. Joshua Burnham of Milford, b. Milford, May 15, 1787, was a farmer in Mont Vernon, where he d. April 24,

1865, m. Sept. 20, 1816, Lydia H. Peabody of Mont Vernon, had eight ch
who reached adult age.

1. David, d. Wilton.
2. Azel, d. in Concord.
3. Sabrina, d. Nov. 9, 1846, age 24, unm.
4. Moses.
5. *William P.
6. Hiram, lives in Prescott, Minn.
7. Matthew F., b. 1832, m. Fanny Follansbee, three children d. Tilton, N. H. He d. April 28, 1895, aged 62 years.
8. Walter, d. in Milford, leaving children.

William P. Burnham, son of Azel W. and Lydia (Peabody) Burn-
ham, b. Mont Vernon, Feb. 22, 1827, resided on farm of John Bartlett in
Milford, d. there May 3, 1885, m. Nov. 12, 1850, Frances C., dau. John
Bartlett. She was b. June 15, 1831. Children b. in Milford.

1. Ella S., b. Nov. 30, 1851, m. Dec. 23, 1885, George C. Evans, resides Jefferson, N. H.
2. Annie J., b. Aug. 5, 1853, m. Oct. 16, 1890, Walter Warren.
3. Mary F., b. June 12, 1856, m. Sept. 23, 1880, George C. Hadley of
Mont Vernon. She d. Mont Vernon, Dec. 15, 1881.
4. Myra E., b. July 4, 1859, m. Oct. 5, 1882, Frank L. Macomber of
Boston, resides Nashua.
5. William W., b. May 17, 1862, res. Milford.
6. Carrie I., b. July 24, 1869, m. Jan. 1, 1891, Cyrus W. Foss of East
Raymond, Me., resides Nashua.

Oramus Walter Burnham, youngest son of Thomas and Rachel
(Conant) Burnham, and grandson of Col. Joshua Burnham of Milford,
b. Antrim, May 25, 1827, m. (1) July 30, 1857, Ellen, youngest dau. of
Capt. Daniel Hartshorn of Amherst, m. (2) Mrs. Ellen J. (Kittredge)
Drury, dau. of Zephaniah and Elizabeth (McIntire) Kittredge, Nov. 27,
1884. She was b. Jan. 24, 1841. They lived in Mont Vernon, on the farm
occupied by Stephen M. Carpenter, from 1888 to 1902, when they moved
to Waltham, Mass.

John Burnham, b. Dunbarton, d. 1826, aged 46, m. Sarah Hook
Appleton, dau. of Rev. Joseph Appleton, D. D., of North Brookfield, Mass.
She d. Boston, Nov. 11, 1884, aged 90 years. Their children were:

1. John A., b. Hillsboro', N. H., June 16, 1813, m. Miss Dennison of
Stonington, Conn., had several children, graduate of Amherst College,
1833, was first agent of the Stark Mills, Manchester, from 1839 to 1847,
was then a cotton broker in Boston and travelled through the South buy-
ing cotton for New England manufacturers; accumulated a large fortune,
estimated at $100,000, d. Aug. 23, 1883, aged 70.
2. William, engaged in the cotton business in the South, d. unm.

3. Sarah, m. Capt. Augustus Whittemore, lived in Boston, had two daughters.

4. Maria Theresa. m. George Dodge of Attleboro', Mass., resided Boston.

William Gage Burnham, son of Norman and Nancy (Gage) Burnham, b. Lowell, Mass., Sept. 15, 1850, m. (1) Oct. 20, 1875, Ellen, dau. of Thomas H. and Nancy (Bruce) Richardson. She was b. Dec. 1, 1847, d. July 22, 1887. He m. (2) Feb. 8, 1893, Mrs. Ellen (Bragg) Haseltine, dau. Harry H. and Malvina (Wilkins) Bragg, and widow of Arthur Haseltine. She was b. April 27, 1845, d. Sharon, Mass., March 18, 1896. He d. at Holliston, Mass., April 18, 1901.

1. Nellie Blanche, b. Mont Vernon, Aug. 19, 1877, d. Aug. 24, 1877.

Andrew Burnham, b. Wilton, Sept. 3, 1800, d. May 1880, m. Martha Hutchinson, June, 1823. She was b. Milford, Feb. 27, 1801, d. Oct. 17, 1887. Came to Mont Vernon from Lyndeboro'. Lived in West District.

1. William S., b. Feb., 1823, m. —— Gibbons, has children, res. Hartford, Conn.

2. George W., b. Lyndeboro', May, 1824, m., lived in Nashua, is not living.

3. Mary Jane, m. Charles Eaton, lives Long Island, has ch.
Twins.

4. Louisa, b. Lyndeboro', March 4, 1827, m. William Southworth, lived in Ashburnham.

5. Lavinia, b. Lyndeboro', March 4, 1827, m. Daniel Kendall of Brookline, left children, is not living.

6. James A., b. Lyndeboro', drowned in Trow's Pond, June 22, 1851, aged 18.

7. Israel, was a butcher, had a slaughter house in Mont Vernon several years, res. Nashua.

8. Albert. b. Lyndeboro', Jan. 7, 1839.

CAMBRIDGE.

Charles Cambridge, an Englishman, lived in the South District, in a house, now torn down, on the Carleton farm. He had several children, one of whom, Edward, was an apprentice in the Cabinet office at Amherst, d. of consumption, Aug. 1, 1807.

Charles, m. Anna, dau. of Joseph Langdell, July 2, 1810, had five sons and two daughters:

1. *Joseph L.

2. William G., was a Universalist minister.

3. Arthur.

4. Eleanor, was m. and lived in Lowell.
5. Mary Ann, was m. and lived in Lowell.
6. Henry.
7. Charles.

Joseph L. Cambridge, b. Mont Vernon, moved to Lowell, then to Amherst, practised as a Botanic physician. He returned to Lowell.

CAMPBELL.

Henry Campbell came to Mont Vernon from Windham, between 1780 and 1790. He was an active citizen here. He went to Antrim in 1793, and opened a store in the east part of Antrim, where he traded 8 years. In 1801 he was drowned while bathing in the Charles River near Boston, whither he had gone to purchase goods. He m. Amy, youngest dau. of Dea. Oliver Carleton. She was b. May 24, 1769. She m. after her husband's death, William Grout of Acworth, had several children by him. She moved to Ohio and d. there. Henry and Amy Campbell had two ch. who were buried on "Meeting House Hill," in Antrim, in 1793 and 1796. He is supposed to have been the Henry Campbell who signed the Association Test in Windham in 1776.

Samuel Campbell, b. New Boston, long a single man, and long a teacher in Massachusetts, d. Sept. 27, 1867, aged 86. He came to Mont Vernon about 1830 and bought the Gurdy farm in the Southeast part of the town. He moved to the village about two years before his death. He was a quiet, sensible man, much respected, and served as school committee for several years. He m. Rebecca Kingsbury of Dedham, Mass. She d. July 24, 1878, aged 77 years, 5 months. Children:

1. Elizabeth, d. Oct. 15, 1855, aged 22 years.
2. *William Henry, b. July 30, 1835.

William Henry Campbell, b. July 30, 1835, at Mont Vernon. He was of the firm of Conant (Walter S. Conant) & Campbell, in New York City 12 years. He commenced the manufacture of paper boxes in Nashua, Nov. 1, 1886, as successor to S. S. Davis. He m. (1) March 14, 1864, Helen A. George of Newport, N. H. She d. July 14, 1865. He m. (2) Helen A. Wing, dau. of Phillip Wing of Grafton, Mass., Nov. 24, 1870. She d. Aug. 26, 1891. Children:

1. George Wing, b. Oct. 30, 1871, m. Frances Freeman of Boston, res. Nashua.
2. Bessie Rebecca, b. Aug. 14, 1874, m. Seth S. Staples of Rondout, N. Y., res. there.

Clark Campbell, son of Captain Daniel and Sabrina (Moor) Campbell, b. New Boston, March 17, 1836, m. (1) Ann A., dau. of Hiram and Serviah (Lamson) Perkins, Nov. 27, 1862. She was b. Jan. 15, 1838, d. August 16, 1900. He m. (2) July 2, 1902, Lillian J., dau. of William P.

CLARK CAMPBELL.

CASSIUS S. CAMPBELL,

Cooke of Revere, Mass. In 1857 he became associated in the store here with Daniel R. Baker, having purchased the interest of C. R. Beard. He was town treasurer from 1876 to 1899; representative, 1878 and 1879, and served as moderator many years. He was Democratic candidate for State Senator and High Sheriff at one time. He served from 1894 to 1899 as United States Marshall for the State of New Hampshire. Was appointed Rural Mail Inspector in 1900. Children:

    1. Alice Perkins, b. Sept. 22, 1870, graduated Wellesley College, 1895, assistant teacher in Milford High School, 1895-1898, m. June 6, 1899, Fred A. Wilson of Nahant, one child, Constance P. Campbell, b. April 13, 1900, lives in Nahant.

    2. Mary Grace, b. Oct. 14, 1873, d. Aug. 20, 1882.

CARKIN.

Charles Carkin of Lyndeborough, lived with his sister, Mrs. John Hartshorn several years on the Beech Hill Road. He d. unm., April 9, 1888, aged 72 years.

CARLETON.

Edward Carleton, a freeman and man of importance in Rowley, Mass., in 1642, lived in Rowley some years, returned to England, b. in England about 1630.

John settled in Haverhill, m. Hannah Jewett, had several children, d. Nov. 16, 1668. His son, Thomas, lived in Bradford, had five children, of whom George, the third child, was b. Sept. 26, 1702, in Bradford, m. Nov. 9, 1725, Mary, dau. of Samuel Hale of Boxford, to which place they removed in 1727 where she d. Nov. 28, 1780, age 73. He d. Feb. 13, 1783, age 80. They had five sons and two daughters, of whom the third, Thomas, b. Nov. 10, 1730, m. Jane Stickney, Nov. 28, 1754. She d. between 1760 and 1770. He moved to Mont Vernon, m. (2) Mrs. Mary (Hartshorn) Weston, widow Daniel Weston, dau. of David and Sarah (Phelps) Hartshorn. Children:

    1. Thomas.
    2. Sally.
    3. David Hartshorn, left Antrim, 1820.
    4. Joseph Stickney, moved to Antrim, 1790, lived there in 1816.

    1. Edward Carleton.
    2. John Carleton.
    3. Thomas Carleton.
    4. George Carleton.

Deacon Oliver Carleton, son of George and Mary (Hale) Carleton of Boxford, Mass., b. Boxford, Sept. 11, 1732, came to Mont Vernon about 1760. He was a prominent man in the Northwest parish, now Mont Vernon. He was on the Committee that provided for soldiers' families in the War for Independence. It was related that he was so zealous to accomplish the completion of the first church building here (being on the Building Committee), that he neglected his own work so, that he was obliged to sell a pair of steers to cancel his indebtedness. He m. Amy dau. of John and Hannah (Wilkins) Washer, 1761. She was b. in Middleton, Mass., d. 1812. He d. 1801. He lived on farm in South District occupied by his great-great-grandson, Joseph G. Carleton. Children:

    1. *John, b. Oct. 16, 1762.

    2. Rebecca, b. Jan. 21, 1764, m. Sept. 11, 1783, *Robert Parker, Jr.

    3. *Enoch, b. Sept. 15, 1765.

    4. Oliver, b. Aug. 23, 1767, m. Mary, dau. of Lieut. Joseph Farnum, removed to Vermont before 1800, had a large family mostly sons, and d. in Claremont about 1860, aged 92. He was a carpenter by trade.

    5. Amy, b. May 24, 1769, m. (1) *Henry Campbell, m. (2) Wm. Grout.

    6. Stephen, b. Oct. 23, 1771, studied medicine with Dr. B. Jones of Lyndeboro', settled in Acworth as a physician in 1803, and d. there in 1857, aged 86 years, never married. He was a man of few words, a gentleman, very much esteemed as a physician, and valued as a citizen, was noted for his kind and generous assistance to deserving young men. He represented Acworth in the Legislature several years.

Deacon John Carleton, son of Deacon Oliver and Amy (Washer) Carleton, b. Mont Vernon, Oct. 16, 1762, d. Dec. 20, 1838, m. (1) Judith Weston, dau. of Daniel and Mary (Hartshorn) Weston. She was b. March 29, 1763, d. Nov. 25, 1824. He m. (2) Mrs. Tabitha (Wilkins) Gilmore, March 30, 1825. She was b. Oct. 28, 1774, d. in South Marlow, Sept. 16, 1848. He was a prominent, public spirited and respected citizen for many years, a Justice of the Peace, selectman and town clerk. In 1800 he was elected a deacon of the church in place of his father who d. that year. Lived on the Carleton farm in South District. Children b. Mont Vernon.

    1. Clarissa, b. Sept. 9, 1781, m. William Davis of Acworth, who settled in Denmark, Me. She d. in 1869, had five sons and three daughters. 1. William; 2. John, settled in Naples, Me., was a state senator two years; 3. Josiah; 4. Oliver; 5. Ezra, settled in Nashua, was first lieutenant in Company B., 7th N. H. Regiment, d. on board transport, New York harbor, July 30, 1863; 6. Clarissa, d. unm.; 7. Emma, m. a Mr. Pingree of Denmark, Me., had three sons; 8. Elizabeth, m. (1) Oliver Smith of Denmark, Me., by whom she had one son, Peleg Smith, m. (2) George E. Dean of Rockford, Ill.

    2. Judith, b. July 8, 1783, m. April 21, 1804, *Josiah Coburn, d. Oct. 5, 1864.

    3. Emma, b. Aug. 21, 1785, d. of spotted fever, Feb., 1812.

4. *John, b. July 26, 1787, d. Jan. 14, 1868.

5. Mary, b. Jan. 19, 1790, m. *Dr. Luther Smith, July 22, 1817, d. March 20, 1872.

6. Daniel Weston, b. Dec. 5, 1791, d. in infancy.

7. Daniel Weston, b. Nov. 26, 1793, d. in infancy.

8. Achsah, b. July 21, 1795, d. Jan. 2, 1842.

9. George, b. May 16, 1797, d. young.

10. Lucy, b. May 2, 1799 d. young.

11. *Oliver, b. July 20, 1801.

12. *Daniel, b. Oct. 27, 1805, m. Hannah Goodrich of Biddeford, Me., had four sons and a daughter.

John Carleton, son of Dea. John and Judith (Weston) Carleton, b. July 26, 1787, d. Jan. 14, 1868, m. Fanny Lewis of Milford, b. April 9, 1791, d. Sept. 10, 1863. He was an industrious, worthy farmer, living on the Carleton farm in the South District. Ch. all b. in Mont Vernon.

1. *William Davis, b. June 15, 1815.

2. Emma Frances, b. July 19, 1818, d. April 20, 1826.

3. Harriet Elizabeth, b. Sept. 19, 1823, m. Sept. 19, 1846, Luther Wiswell. She d. Sept. 25, 1859, one child, Emma F. Wiswell, b. July 9, 1854, m. Gilbert A. Heald.

4. *John Adams, b. Aug. 8, 1826.

5. Abby Temple, b. Jan. 29, 1829, m. Spencer Guild of Milford, Oct. 16, 1850. He was b. in June, 1820, d. Nov. 17, 1885. Children: 1. Fanny Carleton, b. Sept. 17, 1856, head Miss Gilman School, Boston; 2. William Albert, b. March 7, 1862, insurance business, Boston; 3. Frank Spencer, b. April 12, 1866, Art Editor, Ladies' Home Journal, Philadelphia.

Enoch Carleton, son of Deacon Oliver and Amy (Washer) Carleton, b. Mont Vernon, Sept. 1, 1765, m. (1) Hannah, eldest dau. of Col. Stephen Peabody. She was b. July 2, 1768. He moved to Cambridge, Vt., prior to 1800, had four children by this wife, viz.:

1. Enoch, Jr., m. Rosamond Chadwick, had nine children.

2. George, accidentally killed.

3. Stephen Peabody, twice married, d. Dixon, N. Y., about 1842, left four children.

4. Hannah, m. Luke Nichols. They d. about 1850, leaving four sons, 1. Jonathan, lives Westford, Vt.; 2. Franklin, d. at 25; 3. Chandler, lives northwest part of Illinois; 4. Levi, lives Westford, Vt. They are all sterling and energetic men.

Enoch Carleton, Sr., m. (2) Eliza Thurston, two children. He d. Richford, Vt., Sept., 1845, age 80.

5. Levi Atwood, m. a Warner, both d. leaving a son Charles, who d. and left a widow and daughter in New York City.

6. Caroline, m. Alden Sears, had six children, most of whom grew up and settled in California, and ultimately went to Oregon.

7. *Andrew J., b. July 23, 1828, m. Esther Brown, had three ch., lives Springfield, Mass.

E. Carleton, m. (3) Clarissa (Goffe) descendant of Wm. Goffe.

Oliver Carleton, Esq., son of Deacon John and Judith (Weston) Carleton, b. July 29, 1801, at Mont Vernon, prepared for college at Phillips' Academy, Andover, graduated Dartmouth College, 1824, tutor in Dartmouth College, Aug. 1824 to Aug., 1826, principal of Academies in various places in Mass. and N. H. From 1832 to 1856 was principal of the Salem Latin School, Salem, where he distinguished himself as an able educator. He was afterwards head of private schools in Portsmouth. N. H. and Salem, Mass. He d. Salem, Mass., June 21, 1882. He m. (1) Margaretta, dau. Hon. Clifton and Margaret (McQuestion) Clagget of Amherst. She d. March 13, 1829, age 26. He m. (2) Louisa A., dau. Hon. Bailey Bartlett of Haverhill, Mass. She was b. Oct. 17, 1809, d. June 20, 1840. He m. (3) Aug. 18, 1841, Mary Smith of Salem, Mass. She was b. Bath, N. H., July 23, 1803, d. Salem, 1874.

Children by first wife:

1. Clifton C., d. in infancy.

Children by second wife:

2. Edwin Bartlett, b. Nov. 2, 1832, drowned at sea in 1851.

3. William Jarvis, b. May 12, 1835, d. 1861, m. Eliza Ham of Danvers.

4. Joseph George Sprague, b. Aug. 10, 1837, resides Lynn, Mass.

5. Mary Louisa, b. Oct. 16, 1838, res. Salem, Mass., unm.

Children by third wife:

6. Harriet E., b. July 21, 1842, res. Salem, Mass., unm.

Daniel Carleton, youngest son of Dea. John and Judith (Weston) Carleton, b. Oct. 27, 1805, m. Hannah Goodrich of Biddeford, Me., had five children. He d. in Biddeford, Me., in 1852. Children were:

1. Caroline.

2. Chas. Henry, d. at about 18 years of age.

3. Daniel Freeman, lives in Springfield, Mass.

4. Thomas Lord.

5. Benjamin, d. young.

William Davis Carleton, son of John and Fanny (Lewis) Carleton, b. Mont Vernon, June 15, 1815, m. Dec. 27, 1840, Clarissa J. Wells of Goffstown, b. June 25, 1818. He was for a time Master of the Yard of the Stark Corporation, Manchester, went West in 1847, settled respectively in Trenton, Beaver Dam, and Sun Prairie, Wis. He lived for many years and d. at Sun Prairie, Oct. 5, 1900. He was an active business man. Mrs. Carleton d. 1898. Children:

Yours cordially,
C. C. Carpenter.

REV. CHARLES C. CARPENTER.
Thirteenth Pastor, 1880-1885.

1. Frances Jane, b. Manchester, Feb. 23, 1842.

2. William Munroe, b. Manchester, Nov. 27, 1844, m. Margaret Graham, lives in Minneapolis, has two daughters.

Twins.

3. Emma Ellen, b. Sept. 14, 1847, in Wis., m. Oct., 1865, David Samuels, has two children.

4. Anna Viola, b. Sept. 14, 1847, in Wis., m.

5. Charles Edwin, b. Sept. 26, 1850.

6. Mary Alletta, b. Feb. 20, 1852.

7. John, b. July 10, 1858.

8. Ernest, b. May, 1862.

John Adams Carleton, son of John and Fanny (Lewis) Carleton, b. Aug. 8, 1826, m. June 14, 1848, Amanda Wilson, b. Norwich, Vt., Jan. 21, 1827, d. April 28, 1896. He d. Milford, May 29, 1898. He lived on his father's farm in South District. His children were all b. in Mont Vernon.

1. Ella Amanda, b. July 16, 1850, d. Sept. 2, 1852.

2. John William, b. Dec. 17, 1852, m. June 12, 1883, Ida M. Adams, resides Manchester.

3. Charles Frederic, b. Jan. 1, 1857, d. Jan. 4, 1857.

4. Lilla, b. Aug. 4, 1858, m. William F. Easton, Dec. 25, 1880, lives in Wilton.

5. Elmer E., b. June 29, 1861, m. 1894, Dora J. Pillsbury, d. Oct. 4, 1894.

6. *Joseph George, b. May 20, 1863.

7. Will Stearns, b. Oct. 31, 1864, lives in Manchester.

8. Fannie Lewis, b. Nov. 7, 1866, m. Oct. 26, 1893, George F. Averill, lives in Milford.

9. Charles Gage, b. June 1, 1868, m. Oct. 11, 1894, Lillie M. Butler of Lyndeborough, has one son, and resides in Nashua, is a clerk.

Joseph G. Carleton, son of John A. and Amanda (Wilson) Carleton, b. May 20, 1863, m. Nov. 25, 1891, Minnie B., dau. of Otis and Hannah (Swinnington) Spaulding, of Mont Vernon. She was b. Milford, Sept. 1, 1869. He resides on the ancestral farm in the South District. Children b. Mont Vernon.

1. George Otis, b. April 29, 1894.

2. Elmer Ellsworth, b. April 25, 1896.

3. Alwin, b. April 7, 1897.

4. Oliver Wilson, b. April 10, 1901.

5. Abby, b. Dec. 7, 1902.

CARPENTER.

Rev. Charles C. Carpenter, was b. at Bernardston, Mass., July 9, 1836. His father was Dr. Elijah W. Carpenter, a physician of that town.

Mr. Carpenter fitted for college at Williston Seminary, Mass., and at Kimball Union Academy, New Hampshire. He studied theology at Andover, and was ordained to the ministry at Montreal in 1860. He was in the service of the Canada Foreign Missionary Society, principally at Caribou Island, Labrador, from 1858 to 1867. In 1866 he was appointed financial superintendent of Robert College, Lookout Mt., Tenn., where he remained until 1872. In 1875 he became pastor of a church at South Peabody, Mass., resigning in 1880, to accept a call to a less arduous charge at Mont Vernon. The honorary degree of A. M. was conferred on Mr. Carpenter by Hamilton College, New York. In 1885 he removed to Andover, Mass. Mr. Carpenter performed his work here with energy and fidelity, so diligently and thoroughly that the impress long abided. He was a beloved pastor. He now (1902) preaches occasionally, and is editor of a department in the *Congregationalist.* He is a man of antiquarian tastes, and is extensively and accurately informed in many lines. He m. May 1, 1862, Feronia Rice of Auburn, Mass. Children:

1. George Rice, b. Labrador, Oct. 25, 1863, graduated Harvard University, 1886, now Prof. Rhetoric, Columbia University, m. Mary Seymour, has one daughter.

2. Charles Lincoln, b. June 17, 1867, a graduate and post-graduate of Scientific School, Dartmouth College, 1888, m. Catherine F. Sullivan of Charlestown, Mass., one child.

3. William, b. Feb. 9, 1869, studied at Amherst, three years, graduated Harvard University, 1890, m. Catherine Hoyt of Newfane, Vt. Sub-Master High School, Woonsocket, R. I. One son.

4. Jennie Bradie, b. Nov. 14, 1871, graduate Mt. Holyoke Seminary, 1896.

5. Miriam Feronia, b. Mont Vernon, Sept. 21, 1881.

CARSON.

John J. Carson, son of John Carson and Hannah (Austin) Carson, of Lyndeborough, b. Lyndeborough, March 3, 1816, lived on the Carleton farm in the South District, and on the farm now owned by his son in the West District, m. Sarah Hopkins, dau. of James and Azabah (Curtis) Hopkins. She was b. in Mont Vernon in 1816, and d. Mont Vernon, Nov. 18, 1887, age 71 years. He d. Sept. 15, 1896, age 80 years. Children all b. in Mont Vernon except Emily.

1. Emily J., b. Jan. 16, 1843, Milford, m. *David E. Upton of New Boston, resides New Boston, had four children.

2. *George J., b. Oct. 18, 1848.

3. Harriet L., b. Oct. 19, 1852, m. June 24, 1879, Ira A. Parker of Mont Vernon, d. June 26, 1881, Deering.

4. *Frank, b. March 26, 1855.

George J. Carson, son of John J. and Sarah (Hopkins) Carson, b.

Mont Vernon, Oct. 18, 1848, m. Laura A., dau. David D. and Sophronia (Dickinson) Clark, of Lyndeboro'. She was b. Lyndeboro', March 7, 1852. Farmer, lives in Lyndeboro'. Children b. Mont Vernon.

1. Roy Clark, b. Dec. 8, 1879.
2. Cora Alice, b. Sept. 20, 1881, d. March 5, 1889.
3. Hattie Marion, b. Aug. 13, 1883.

Frank Carson, son of John J. and Sarah (Hopkins) Carson, b. Mont Vernon, March 26, 1855, m. Aug. 24, 1880, Eda M., dau. of Frank and Mary G. (Hooper) Carson. She was b. New Boston, July 21, 1862, farmer, res. West District. Ch.:

1. Fred, b. Mont Vernon, April 14, 1881.

Alexander Carson, brother of John J. Carson, b. Lyndeborough, Dec., 1822, settled in the South District, m. Dec. 23, 1843, Margaretta, d. u. James and Azubah (Curtis) Hopkins. She was b. Dec. 14, 1823. Ch: Twins.

1. Sarah Helen, b. Sept. 30, 1844, d. Oct. 14, 1867.
2. Mary Ellen, b. Sept. 30, 1844, d. May 4, 1860.
3. Martha Ann, b. Feb. 28, 1846, m. *Wallace D. Hooper.
4. John Washington, b. Nov. 16, 1848, m. Julia Dodge of Francestown, Dec., 1884. She was b. June, 1850, dau. Adoniram and Maria (Bixby) Dodge of Francestown, lives in Francestown. Have ch., Ralph D., b. Mont Vernon, Feb. 23, 1886; Forrest G., b. Francestown, Jan. 18, 1890.
5. Abbie L., b. June 9, 1854, d. Oct. 14, 1867.
6. Alwilda, b. July, 1855, d. Oct. 16, 1867.
7. Nettie M., b. Feb. 20, 1860, m. March 25, 1898, Nathaniel F. Hooper of Mont Vernon, one child.
8. Theresa D., b. May 6, 1861, d. May 16, 1867.

Asa Carson, b. Francestown, March 10, 1810, m. (1) Edah Cooper. She d. Sept. 3, 1858, m. (2) Miss Annette Lee. She d. Sept. 6, 1886, age 47. He d.

Children by first wife:

1. Jacob W., b. May 27, 1840, d. unm.
2. Frank S., b. Sept. 26, 1842.
3. Alonzo S., b. May 15, 1845.
4. Eugene S., b. August 10, 1849.
5. Edwin H., b. Dec. 26, 1855, lives Nashua, m. Miss Hall, dau. Samuel Hall.

Frank S. Carson, b. Sept. 26, 1842, son of Asa and Edah (Cooper) Carson, m. Mary G., dau. of Nathaniel and Lucy (Carson) Hooper. Ch:

1. Eda M., b. New Boston, July 21, 1862, m. Aug. 24, 1880, Frank Carson.
2. Jessie Estella, b. Brooklyn, N. Y., March 9, 1864, m. John Har-

vell of Amherst, May 2, 1884, two children. She d. April 26, 1900 in Somerville, Mass.

CHAPIN.

Rev. Stephen Chapin, b. Milford, Mass., in 1778, a graduate of Harvard in 1804, a pupil in divinity with the famous Dr. Nathaniel Emmons of Franklin, Mass., his first settlement was in Hillsborough from 1805 to 1809. He was Pastor of the Mont Vernon church from 1809 to Oct. 1818. Having embraced Calvinistic Baptist views he resigned his pastorate. After a three years' pastorate as a Baptist clergyman at North Yarmouth, Me., he was in 1822, called to a professorship in Waterville College, Me., and thence to the presidency of Columbia College at Washington, D. C., which he occupied many years

Mr. Chapin was a man of positive convictions and bold, unadorned and uncompromising in his style of preaching. His earnest, able preaching and stringent discipline made a deep impression upon his people.

He m. Sally Mosher, adopted dau. of Rev. Daniel Emerson of Hollis, Dec. 21, 1809. They had children.

George S. Chapin of Auburndale, Mass., graduate of Bowdoin College in 1893, was the principal of McCollom Institute from 1898 to 1900.

CHEEVER.

Rev. Ebenezer Cheever was ordained minister of the Congregational Church here, Dec. 8, 1819. He continued pastor until April 8, 1823, with an addition to the church in the meantime, of twenty-two members. He baptized thirty-nine children in less than three years. In the spring of 1820, the first Sabbath School was organized here, being held in the schoolhouse and composed exclusively of children. After leaving here, Mr. Cheever was pastor of a church in Waterford, N. Y., and at other places and d. in 1866, age 75 years, in New Jersey. He was married twice, his first wife dying in Mont Vernon.

CLEAVES.

Nathan Cleaves, b. July 11, 1748, came to Mont Vernon, and settled before the Revolution. He was a tailor by trade, and owned and occupied the farm now Jesse S. Trow's. He d. Aug. 25, 1812, age 64. His wife, Sarah, d. July 1, 1817, age 67. His children were:

1. *Dr. Nathan Cleaves, b. Mont Vernon.

2. Betsey, b. Mont Vernon, m. Oct. 2, 1796, Samuel Clark of Hopkinton, had several daughters.

3. *Nathaniel, b. Mont Vernon, 1778.

4. Dorcas, b. Mont Vernon, m. John Kelso of New Boston, had several children.

5. *Joshua, b. Mont Vernon.
6. John, b. Mont Vernon, lived with his brother Joshua, was never m.

Dr. Nathan W. Cleaves, son of Nathan and Sarah Cleaves, b. Mt. Vernon, 1773, studied his profession with Dr. Benj. Jones of Lyndeboro', settled in Antrim in 1795, and d. there in 1807, age 33. His fever was caused by a ten-mile walk on snow shoes to visit a sick woman. He m. Jennie Hopkins of Antrim. Ch.: Dorcas W.; m. James Jameson, June, 1812, d. in 1848. She was the mother of Nathan W. C. Jameson, who is the father of Nathan C. Jameson of Antrim, a Democratic politician of much note. 2nd ch. Robert Hopkins, m. Anne Jameson, Sept. 24, 1818, lived where his father died, was killed by a fall, Dec., 1843, left five ch.: Dr. C. left four other ch.: Solomon, John, Luther and Calvin.

Nathaniel, son of Nathan and Sarah Cleaves, b. Mont Vernon, m. (1) Hannah Bradford, April 10, 1794, m. (2) Relief, dau. of Dea. Ephraim Barker, Jan., 1806. He lived in Amherst many years. He d. in Mont Vernon, Dec. 16, 1850, age 72. Children:
    1. Miranda, d. April, 1803, age 5 years.
    2. James Barker, b. Constable, N. Y., Sept. 7, 1820, d. Amherst, Nov. 18, 1850, m. Joanna, dau. of Capt. Daniel and Dolly (Hastings) Hartshorn of Amherst. She was b. 1824, m. (2) —— Torrey, he d. Waltham, Mass., April 9, 1867, one ch., Lucy. Nathaniel Cleaves had other children.

Joshua, son of Nathan and Sarah Cleaves, b. Mt. Vernon, 1787, was a farmer, lived on his father's farm, m. Elizabeth Lincoln of Leominster, Mass. He d. Jan. 13, 1868, age 80. She d. Nov. 4, 1856, aged 72. Ch. b. Mt. Vernon:
    1. Elizabeth, b. 1808, d. Jan. 17, 1840, age 32 years, 6 mos.
    2. Nathan, graduate Dartmouth College, studied medicine, located in Mexico, and at Rio Grande, Mexico, was shot by two negroes, Feb., 1849. His age was 30.
    3. *Wm. Lincoln, b. April 11, 1821.
    4. Lydia Ann, b. June 8, 1823, m. June 8, 1843, Charles B. Tuttle of Amherst, had seven ch. She d. Milford, July 26, 1866.
    5. Augusta, b. April, 1826, a teacher, m. Benj. C. Jones of Chicago, had one daughter, d. Chicago, June 5, 1894, age 68 years, 2 months.

William Lincoln Cleaves, son of Joshua and Elizabeth (Lincoln) Cleaves, b. Mt. Vernon, April 11, 1821, farmer, lived on his father's farm, also dealer in lumber, m. Dec. 8, 1856, Harriet, dau. Rufus and Ann (Blanchard) Crosby of Milford. She was b. March 3, 1832, in Milford. He d. Sept. 26, 1860. One child:
    1. William C., b. Milford, Jan. 12, 1861, farmer, res. with mother, is unm.

CLEMENT.

Jesse Clement, son of Jesse and Mary (Cram) Clement, b. Weare, Sept. 1, 1796. His grandmother Clement was the youngest daughter of Hannah Dustin, of Indian fame. He moved with his parents to Unity, N. H., in 1805; m. June 30, 1829, Eliza Glidden, who d. Sept. 10, 1891, age 86 years. She was the dau. of Stephen and Elizabeth (Jones) Glidden of Unity, and was b. July 20, 1805. In 1832, Jesse Clement removed to Lowell, represented Lowell in the Massachusetts legislature in 1837, thence to Mont Vernon in 1844, then Lyndeboro'. In 1850 he sat in the New Hampshire Constitutional Convention as delegate from Lyndeboro'. In 1852 he was an efficient promoter of annexing the part of Lyndeboro' to Mt. Vernon, in which his farm was located. The place is now owned by Edward G. Averill. He d. July 28, 1858, age 62. Children:

1. Harriet Celinda, b. Lowell, Dec. 8, 1830, m. *Henry Hiram Trow, Oct. 8, 1856, d. March 31, 1897.

2. *Stephen Glidden. b. Lowell, June 15, 1833.

3. Henry J., b. Lowell, June 16, 1837, d. Sept. 15, 1840.

4. Mary E., b. Lowell, Dec. 26, 1838, d. Sept. 16, 1840.

5. Ellen J., b. Lowell, July 13, 1841, d. at Antrim, Sept. 30, 1870.

Stephen Glidden Clement, son of Jesse and Eliza (Glidden) Clement, b. Lowell, June 15, 1833, m. (1) 1865, Susan M. Butler of Antrim, who d. Sept. 18, 1867, age 33, m. (2) Josiephine E., dau. of Trask W. and Hannah (Perkins) Averill, b. Sept. 23, 1843, in Mont Vernon. He moved here from Antrim in 1877. He lived on the farm in North District, now occupied by Harry G. Blood. He d. here, Oct. 21, 1888. She m. (2) Sept. 23, 1892, Frank Brooks of Greenfield. He d. May 20, 1903, one ch.:

1. Gertrude E., b. Antrim, Nov. 30, 1872, res. Melrose Highlands, Mass.

Dr. Thomas R. Clement, b. Landaff, N. H., was taxed here from 1852 to 1860, in East District, served in 8th N. H. Regt., 10th N. H. Regt., and 18th Regt., in Civil War, m. May 2, 1855, Juliette, dau. Timothy and Betsey P. (Gay) Hartshorn of Amherst, now resides Osterville, Mass.

CLOUTMAN.

Capt. Thomas Cloutman, b. Marblehead, Mass., Oct. 1, 1761, moved to Mont Vernon, about 1800, d. Nov. 18, 1825. He lived where C. J. Smith does, farmer. He m. Sept., 1788, Susannah Haskell, b. Sept. 23, 1759, d. Jan. 31, 1838. Their children were:

1. Susannah, b. Dec. 26, 1789, d. Nov. 27, 1794.

2. Ruthy, b. Oct. 23, 1791, m. *Jotham Richardson, Dec. 1, 1814

3. Sukey, b. June 5, 1795, d. June 13, 1812.

4 *Thomas, b. May 13, 1799.

Thomas Cloutman, Jr., son of Capt. Thomas and Susannah (Haskell) Cloutman, b. Marblehead, Mass., May 13, 1799, d. Mont Vernon, Nov. 8, 1884, m. Jan. 23, 1822, Nancy, dau. of Calvin and Esther (Wilkins) Stevens. She was b. Feb. 11, 1800, d. Feb. 15, 1877. He lived on Cloutman farm (C. J. Smith's) farmer, moved into village, was a tavern keeper. Children were b. in Mont Vernon.

1. Susan, b. March 13, 1823, m. May 30, 1850, *Daniel Porter Kendall. She d. Jan. 8, 1897.

2. Nancy A., b. Oct. 26, 1824, m. Sept. 24, 1846, *William A. Stinson. She d. Oct. 18, 1898.

3. Esther Stevens, b. Sept. 28, 1826, d. July 30, 1828.

4. Esther Stevens, b. June 21, 1828, m. Charles Gray, Nov. 16, 1848. She d. Feb. 2, 1851, age 22 years, 8 months, leaving one daughter, Mary A., who m. *Thomas Winters and res. Milford.

5. Ruthey Ellen, b. Feb. 20, 1830, m. *John F. Colby.

6. Thomas Haskell, b. March 7, 1832, d. Dec. 8, 1833.

7. Sarah Emeline, b. May 6, 1834, m. *William H. Conant.

8. Mary, b. 1836, d. March 15, 1841, age 4 years, 10 months.

9. Elizabeth H. D., d. Sept. 4, 1840, age 2 years, 6 days.

10. Mary Elizabeth, b. Oct. 24, 1840, m. Nov. 24, 1870, Frederick Davis of Falmouth, Mass. Ch.: 1. Adolphus, b. Dec. 23, 1871, d. young; 2. Marian Elizabeth, b. June 9, 1873, m. June 3, 1896, Alden R. Palmer of Wellington, O., one ch., Lawrence, b. 1899. She d. at Mont Vernon, Sept. 1, 1901; 3. Edith Frances, b. Oct. 11, 1880.

COBURN.

Josiah Coburn, b. Dracut, Mass., March 31, 1775, lived there until 10 years of age, d. Mont Vernon, April, 1826, m. April 26, 1804, Judith, dau. of Dea. John and Judith (Weston) Carleton. She was b. Mont Vernon, July 8, 1783, d. Oct. 5, 1864. Lived on Beech Hill Road. Children were all b. Mont Vernon.

1. Daniel Weston, b. March 11, 1805, d. Oct. 18, 1835.

2. *George Clinton, b. July 14, 1806, d. Nov. 24, 1835.
Twins.

3. Sabrina, b. Sept. 29, 1807, d. Feb. 9, 1808.

4. Servilla, b. Sept. 29, 1807, d. Dec. 29, 1807.

5. Sabrina, b. Aug. 31, 1809, d. Feb. 9, 1867, unm.

6. *John Carleton, b. July 21, 1811, d. Dec. 17, 1856.

7. Emma Carleton, b. Dec. 10, 1812, d. Dec. 27, 1854.

8. Hannah, b. July 21, 1815, d. Dec. 31, 1842, m. Charles C. Durgin of Gilmanton. No children.

9. Clarissa Davis, b. April 29, 1818. She m. Geo. W. Burns of Milford, had one dau., d. Nov. 3, 1843.

10. Samuel, b. Dec. 31, 1820, d. March 20, 1844. He m. Laura Lunkin of Jay, Me.

11.   Henry, b. Dec. 3, 1823, d. Jan. 30, 1895, at Strafford, N. H., became a spiritualistic doctor, had an adopted dau.

12.   *Stephen Chapin, b. Nov. 19, 1825.

George Clinton Coburn, son of Josiah and Judith (Carleton) Coburn, b. Mont Vernon, July 14, 1806, m. March 30, 1831, Mahala, dau. of Daniel and Betsey (Durant) Secombe.   She was b. in Mont Vernon, July 27, 1806.   He was a worthy mechanic and a devout Christian.   He d. Nov. 24, 1835, ch. b. Amherst.

1.   George E., b. March 11, 1832, m. Ellen Davenport of Canton, Mass., May 21, 1863, d. Fitchburg, Mass., Feb. 22, 1881, two children.

2.   Sabrina Frances, b. Aug. 2, 1833, d. May 14, 1848.

John Carleton Coburn, son of Josiah and Judith (Carleton) Coburn, b. Mont Vernon, July 21, 1811, d. Mont Vernon, Dec. 17, 1856, m. July 6, 1835, at Lowell, Julia Holbrook.   She was b. Frankfort, Me., Sept. 27, 1809, d. July 20, 1892, at Salina, Kan.   Children all b. in Lowell.   He lived in Auburn, N. Y. several years.

1.   Charlotte Emma, b. Nov. 22, 1839, d. Auburn, N. Y., April 21, 1869.

2.   Julia Amanda, b. March 2, 1843, m. July 28, 1860, Rev. William Simpkins of Auburn, N. Y.   They now (1902) reside in Salina, Kansas, ch: 1. Albert Gallatin, b. Auburn, N. Y., Nov. 28, 1870, d. Dec. 23, 1872; 2. Emma Coburn, b. Salina, Kas., Nov. 15, 1873; 3. Louise Holbrook, b, Salina, Kas., Oct. 30, 1876; 4. Florence Lee, b. Salina, Kas., May 28, 1881.

3.   Elizabeth Alden, b. June 10, 1850, d. June 17, 1870.

Stephen Chapin Coburn, son of Josiah and Judith (Carleton) Coburn, b. Mont Vernon, Nov. 14, 1825, moved to Milford in the fifties.   He carried on a shoe store there many years.   He was Representative from Milford from 1879 to 1883, five years; Selectman, being Chairman of the Board four years.   He now (1902) lives on a farm in the south part of Milford. He m. Sept. 11, 1856, Ann, dau. of Aaron K. Putnam and Polly (Shattuck) Putnam of Wilton.   She was b. Wilton, July 26, 1826, children b. Milford.

1.   Mary E., b. July 9, 1857, m. April 8, 1880, Albert A. Gilson of Milford, two children, res. Walpole, N. H.

2.   Florence S., b. April 13, 1859, m. July 13, 1887, Wm. H. Whitmore, res. Cleveland, O.

3.   Grace P., b. Sept. 9, 1862, m. April 30, 1865, Geo. A. McIntire, one child, res. Milford.

4.   S. Carroll, b. June 26, 1866, m. 1896, Belle Goodwin of Milford, one child, grocer in Milford.

5.   Charles H., b. April 4, 1871, druggist in Barton, Vt.

CODMAN.

Dr. Henry Codman, b. Middleton, Mass., Jan. 25, 1744, d. in Amherst,

March 14, 1812. His wife, Agnes, d. Jan. 19, 1808, age 69. He practised medicine in Amherst. Children:

1. Henry Codman, Jr., studied medicine, practised in Mont Vernon, where he d. July 31, 1806, age 29 years. He m. Feb. 19, 1796, Rebecca, dau. of Joseph Langdell. She m. (2) Thos. Hamlin, May 3, 1837, and d. May 5, 1855, aged 76. Her remains rest by the side of her first husband in Mont Vernon Cemetery.

2. Catherine, d. June 10, 1781, age 2 years, 3 months.

Nathan Codman, b. Hillsboro' Bridge, m. Hannah Cree of New Boston. He d. Dec. 17, 1874. She d. Aug. 29, 1881. Children b. West Deering, N. H.

1. George N., b. July 11, 1867, res. Mont Vernon, laborer.

2. Ida Jennie, b. Sept. 27, 1869, m. June 21, 1890, *Charles W. Blood.

3. Harry W., b. March 9, 1873.

COGGIN.

Joseph Coggin, son of Joseph and Mary Coggin, b. Reading, Mass., March 26, 1740, m. Ruth Hopkins, moved from Wilmington to Mont Vernon about 1778 and settled on Potato Street, in the East District. Their children were:

1. *William, b. Wilmington, Mass., March, 1767.

2. *Joseph, Jr., b. Wilmington, 1771.

3. Hannah, m. (1) —— Fairfield, m. (2) —— Fairfield, d. in New Boston.

4. Ruth, m. —— Fairfield, settled and d. in New Boston.

5. Sally, b. August 28, 1782, m. —— McMillen, d. in New Boston.

William Coggin, son of Joseph and Ruth (Hopkins) Coggin, b. Wilmington, in March, 1767, lived on the Stiles' farm, on Potato Street in the East District, was a blacksmith and farmer, d. Mont Vernon, Sept. 18, 1856, age 89 years, 6 months, m. (1) Susannah Haseltine. She d. Sept. 20, 1835, age 65; m. (2) Mrs. Mary Reed. She d. Sept. 20, 1871, aged 85 years and 3 months. His children were b. Mont Vernon.

1. Susan, b. Mont Vernon.

2. *Nathaniel, b. Mont Vernon, 1802.

3. John, m. Lucinda Lund, was a furniture dealer in Nashua.

4. Nancy, m. William Kelso of New Boston.

Joseph Coggin, Jr., son of Joseph and Ruth (Hopkins) Coggin, b. Wilmington, 1771, m. Sept. 5, 1795, Betsey, dau. of Josiah and Mary (Low) Herrick of Amherst. She was b. in Wenham, Mass., May 7, 1769, d. in Mont Vernon, April 6, 1846. He d. in Milford, Jan. 10, 1849. They settled on the Coggin homestead on Potato Street in the East District, where they resided more than fifty years. Children all b. in Mont Vernon.

1. William, b. July 22, 1790, m. (1) Atness Batchelder, Dec. 1, 1814, m. (2) Mrs. Sarah (Duncklee) Peacock. He d. in Nashua, May 17, 1864.

2. *Daniel, b. June 23, 1792, m. (1) Rebecca Brigham of Goshen, m. (2) Elizabeth Briar. He d. in Milford, Aug. 24, 1872.

3. Betsey, b. May 22, 1796, d. in Amherst, Sept. 28, 1881, unm.

4. Fanny, b. April 27, 1799, m. Moses Foster of Milford, d. May 9, 1842.

5.   *Luther, b. Aug. 16, 1801.
6.   Mary, b. May 23, 1805, m. Levi Duncklee, d. Milford, Dec. 4, 1871.

Nathaniel Coggin, son of William, Sr., and Susannah Haseltine Coggin, b. Mont Vernon, 1802, moved to Milford in 1835, resided in the South part of the town, was a blacksmith and operated a sawmill, removed to Wilton in 1855, d. 1870, m. (1) 1832, Hannah, dau. of Isaac and Mary (Dodge) Peabody, b. New Boston, 1805, d. Milford, Dec. 14, 1853. He m. (2) Eliza H., widow of Shubael Shattuck. She was the dau. of John and Sarah (Holden) Knowlton, and was b. in New Ipswich, July 12, 1799. She d. Jan. 23, 1863. Children:
     1.   Chas. Henry, b. Mont Vernon, July, 1835, is a mechanic, resides San Francisco, m. (1) Oct., 1857, Julia A., dau. Eldad and Mary (Peterson) Sawtelle of Brookline, N. H., m. (2) Emily C., dau. of George W. and Clarissa D. (Coburn) Burns of Milford, Nov., 1866, m. (3) Hannah Wright, a widow, dau. of Daniel and Elizabeth (Davis) McAdam, Jan. 1877.
     2.   Isaac Clinton, b. Milford, 1837, is a musician in San Francisco, m. July, 1860, Clara, dau. of Lemuel and Rebecca (Shattuck) Hall of Brookline, N. H.

Daniel Coggin, son of Joseph, Jr., and Betsey (Herrick) Coggin, b. June 23, 1792, at Mont Vernon, was a farmer in Milford, resided on place near road to Amherst, where he d. Aug. 31, 1872, m. (1) Rebecca Brigham of Goshen, m. (2) Elizabeth, dau. of Joseph and Jane (Kelly) Bryer (or Briar), Feb. 1, 1845. She was b. Boothbay, Me., June 13, 1808. Children by first wife:
     1.   Eunice B., m. Joseph Sanderson of Nashua, d. there, 1892.
     2.   Eliza, m. a Mr. Black of Roxbury, Mass., d. there.
     3.   Rebecca, m. a Mr. Coolidge of Somerville.
     4.   Emily, m. a Mr. Bemis of Waltham.
     5.   Joseph, m. Roselle Bundy.
     6.   Henry.
By second wife:
     7.   Frank F., b. Milford, March 9, 1847, resides Lynn Centre, Mass., m. Ellen M. Holmes, has three children.

Luther Coggin, son of Joseph, Jr., and Betsey (Herrick) Coggin, b. Mont Vernon, Aug. 16, 1801, d. Amherst, Jan. 18, 1877, m. (1) Mary Harwood, Sept. 13, 1827. She was the dau. of John and Mary (Carlton) Harwood, and was b. in Mont Vernon, April 13, 1807, d. Nov. 4, 1859. He m. (2) Mrs. M. W. Warriner of Bedford, March 15, 1860. He settled in New Boston, where he resided several years, thence he removed to the Fletcher tavern stand in Amherst, where he d. Children were:
     1.   Mary Augusta, b. March 16, 1830, m. Sept. 23, 1854.
     2.   Luther, Jr., b. Jan. 2, 1835, m. Mary L. Carleton, May 9, 1861 lives in Amherst, one son.
     3.   *John H., b. March 10, 1838.

John H. Coggin, son of Luther and Mary (Harwood) Coggin, b. New Boston, March 10, 1838, m. (1) Harriet N., dau. of Daniel and Elizabeth (Austin) Secombe, April 9, 1866. She was b. Nov. 9, 1838, d. Jan. 8, 1882, m. (2) Mrs. Dell Seavey of Nashua, Oct. 23, 1882, resides on the Fletcher place in Amherst, formerly owned by his father. Children:
     1.   Frederick Lampson, b. June 11, 1870.
     2.   *George Whitfield, b. Nov. 28, 1871.

JOHN H. COLBY.

George Whitfield Coggin, b. Nov. 28, 1871, moved to Mont Vernon, 1897, is a blacksmith, m. Sept. 30, 1895, Nellie A., dau. of John and Frances (Little) Murphy of Milford. She was b. Milford, March 31, 1874, one child:

    1. Guy, b. Mont Vernon, Aug. 23, 1897.

Francis Coggin, son of William and Atness (Batchelder) Coggin, was b. in Mont Vernon, March 17, 1820. He moved to Nashua early in life. He spent much of his time before and since the Civil War in the South. He was a pioneer in the cotton business, and a heavy owner in a large number of mills. He also owned a controlling interest in the Augusta, Ga., *Chronicle*, one of the largest newspapers in the South, of which he was formerly editor. Prior to the Civil War he was a slave owner. He d. in Nashua, Jan. 19, 1903. He was m. but left no children.

COLBY.

John Colby, son of John and Prudence (Dane) Colby, b. Weare, April, 1801, m. April 29, 1831, Mary H. Holt of Lyndeboro'. He d. Nov. 5, 1849. She d. at her daughter's, Mrs. John M. Haggett in Wilton in 1880. Children b. in Bennington.

    1. Samantha A., b. March 7, 1832, m. Nov. 11, 1851, John M. Haggett, son of James and Charlotte (Merrill) Haggett of Lyndeboro'. She d. Boston, May 16, 1884, one child, Carrie A., b. April 30, 1858.

    2. *John Freeman, b. March 3, 1834.

    3. Augustus Grovesnor, b. May 23, 1838, m. Dec. 31, 1859, Sarah M. Ames of Milford. She d. Aug. 26, 1867. One child, Charles F., b. Jan. 31, 1861, d. July 17, 1861. Mr. A. G. Colby attended the academy here, and lived some years in Mont Vernon. He enlisted in the army from Milford in May, 1861, discharged for disability in Aug., 1861. He enlisted at Lowell in 1862 in Second Mass. Cavalry under General Butler. Was wounded in engagement at Port Hudson in summer of 1863, carried to hospital at Baton Rouge, La., where he d. Sept. 2, 1863.

John Freeman Colby, son of John and Mary H. (Holt) Colby, b. Bennington, March 3, 1834, d. while visiting in Hillsboro', June 7, 1890. He m. Jan. 24, 1861, Ruthey E., dau. of Thomas and Nancy (Stevens) Cloutman. She was b. Mont Vernon, Feb. 20, 1830. For extended account of John F. Colby, see Chapter on "Prominent Men," in History Manuscript. Their children were:

    1. John Henry, b. Randolph, Mass., June 13, 1862, m. 1891, Annie E. Corneilus of Boston, is a Boston lawyer, spends his summers at Mont Vernon, one child, John.

    2. Charles Dane, b. Mont Vernon, June 30, 1865, d. Sept. 2, 1865.

    3. Arthur Stevens, b. Boston, March 23, 1869, d. Mont Vernon, Aug. 25, 1889.

COLE.

John and Tyler Cole lived in South District. John Cole was killed at the Battle of Bunker Hill, June 17, 1775.

CONANT.

Roger Conant, son of Richard and Agnes Clarke Conant, b. East Budleigh, Devonshire Co., England, baptized April 9, 1592, m. in London, Nov.

1618 to Sarah Norton, emigrated with his brother, Christopher, arriving at Plymouth in July, 1623, he being a Puritan and Separatist did not like and after a year went to Nantasket Hull in 1624. The next winter, 1624-1625, he was employed by the Dorchester Co., to manage all their affairs in fishing and planting as agent, and Governor in the fall of 1625, and there may still be seen the remains of a rude fort on the west side of Gloucester Harbor, called by its constructors, "Fort Conant." In 1625 or 1626 he had 200 under his charge, but the business proved unprofitable and he having heard of a place called Naumkeag, induced the company to close up at Cape Ann, and establish him at Naumkeag, which they did after a loss of 3,000 lbs. sterling. After a couple of years, he was superseded by John Endicott, in 1628, who came over from England, with a company of emigrants, representing a new company, who had purchased the interest of the Dorchester Company. In 1635-1636 he moved over to Beverly, to a 200-acre farm, which had been granted him, and built a house, which stood on the east side of Cabot, near Balch Street. Jonathan Conant (5th generation) was probably the last of the name who lived in it. He sold the northern part of the homestead farm to Dr. Ingalls Kittredge, who m. his dau., Sarah. Dr. Kittredge built a brick house, now standing. Roger Conant d. Nov. 19, 1679, in the 89th year of his age, place of burial unknown. Children were:

1. Sarah, d. in infancy.
2. Caleb, b. London, came with his parents to Massachusetts, returned to England and d. there in 1663.
3. Lot, m. Elizabeth Walton, and had sons, viz.: Nathaniel, John, Lot, William, Roger.

Roger's son Roger, b. Salem, 1626, first white child b. there.

Jonathan Conant, 5th generation from Roger (Jonathan, 4; Lot, 3; Lot, 2; Roger, 1), b. Beverly, Aug. 9, 1737. He lived in Beverly on the Roger Conant homestead till about 1783, when he removed to a farm on Cheny Hill. In 1791 he sold the Cheny Hill Farm and removed to Amherst (now Mont Vernon). On the breaking out of the Revolutionary War, he was chosen one of the Committee of "Correspondence and Safety." At the Lexington alarm he marched from Beverly to Boston under Capt. Peter Shaw, he was afterwards paymaster in Col. Francis' Regiment, and then in Col. Tupper's, serving four years or more. In 1787 he was one of the selectmen of Beverly, Mass., and soon after removed to Mont Vernon, where he d. He was the second justice of peace in Mont Vernon. He m. Jan. 30, 1758, Mercy Lovett. He d. in 1820. Children were:

1. *Jonathan, b. April 11, 1760, in Beverly.
2. *Lot, b. June 18, 1764, in Beverly.
3. Joseph, baptized Sept. 28, 1766, d. young.
4. *Israel, b. Nov. 15, 1767.
5. Sarah, baptized June 3, 1770, m. *Dr. Ingalls Kittredge.
6. Josiah, baptized July 7, 1776, supposed to have d. young.

Jonathan Conant, 6th generation (Jonathan, 5; Jonathan, 4; Lot, 3; Lot, 2; Roger, 1), b. Beverly, Mass., April 11, 1760, moved to Mont Vernon with his parents, where he d. Oct. 28, 1829. In 1803 his name appears in list of inhabitants of Amherst. In 1811 he settled in Antrim, N. H., where he remained un 1 1816, when he returned to Mont Vernon. He m.

WILLIAM CONANT.
Deacon from 1852 to 1875.

Polly Baker of Wenham, Mass., who d. April 26, 1834, age 69 years. Children:
1. *Israel Elliott, b. Oct. 6, 1789, in Mont Vernon.
2. Mehitable, m. (1) *Wm. Marvell, m. (2) 1843, *Ezekiel Upton.
3. Ruth, m. William Morgan of Beverly.
4. Nancy.
5. Mary, m. —— Marshall.
6. *William, b. Mont Vernon, Oct. 31, 1802.
7. Fanny, m. Feb. 24, 1828, Hiram Reed of Nashua.

Lot Conant, 2nd son of Jonathan Conant, Esq., and Mercy (Lovett) Conant, b. June 18, 1764, in Beverly, moved to Mont Vernon with his parents, where he d. 1833. He m. Mehitable Woodbury, who d. Dec. 6, 1844, age 77. She united with Mont Vernon Church, May 15, 1797. Children:
1. Jonathan, d. young.
2. Charlotte, baptized Aug. 16, 1801, m. Hezekiah Wallace of Beverly and had children.
3. Eliza, b. 1803, m. 1820, *Jesse Averill, Jr.

Israel Conant, 6th generation, 3rd son of Jonathan and Mercy (Lovett) Conant, b. Beverly, Nov. 15, 1767, went to Mont Vernon with his parents but returned and settled in Beverly, was a cooper, had wheelwright house and shop, which he built. It still stands on Federal Street. Joined Dane St. Church, 1820, d. 1845, m. about 1809, Elizabeth Chapman, dau. Capt. Isaac Chapman. In Aug., 1816, they lived in Mont Vernon. He m. (2) Mary Cross. He had one dau., Joanna, who probably was never married.

Israel Elliott Conant, son of Jonathan Conant, Esq., b. Oct. 6, 1789, in Mont Vernon. He moved to Antrim with his parents in 1811, and about the close of 1816 to New Haven, Vt. He d. Vergennes, Vt., 1857. He m. Eliza Holt of Antrim, Nov. 3, 1815, had five sons and two daughters. One of his daughters, Mary, m. 1820, Augustus Marshall of Dunstable.

Dea. William Conant, 7th generation, son of Jonathan and Polly (Baker) Conant, b. Mont Vernon, Oct. 31, 1802, removed to Somerville, Mass. He was deacon of the Mont Vernon church, forty-three years. He was a prominent citizen and worked earnestly for the town's development along the best lines, and was among those, who sought to give the community an exceptional position in regard of those who sought the best things. He m. Hannah Fornis of Beverly, Sept., 1828, b. Nov. 25, 1805. She d. Dec. 11, 1883. He d. at Somerville, Mass., Feb. 20, 1890. Children all b. in Mont Vernon.
1. *William Henry, b. June 5, 1829.
2. *Albert, b. Oct. 19, 1830.
3. *Charles Edwin, b. June 30, 1832.
4. *Walter Scott, b. June 8, 1834.
5. John, b. March 1, 1836, d. April 8, 1836.
6. *Harlan Page, b. March 3, 1837.
7. Martha Ellen, b. Nov. 30, 1842, d. Somerville, Mass., May 18, 1884.
8. Fanny Lovett, b. April 1, 1844, m. June 21, 1870, *Henry A. Kendall of Somerville, Mass., d. April 8, 1901.
9. Marcella Eliza, b. Dec. 3, 1845, m. *Dr. Charles M. Kittredge, d. Fishkill-on-the-Hudson, Aug. 4, 1892.

Deacon William Henry Conant, 8th generation from Roger Conant, son of Dea. William and Hannah (Fornis) Conant, b. Mont Vernon, June 5, 1829. He was deacon of the Congregational Church here since 1875, and was active in church matters. He was for many years a member of Conant Bros. Co. He d. May 3, 1903, he m. May 25, 1854, Sarah Emeline, dau. Thomas and Nancy (Stevens) Cloutman. She was b. Mont Vernon, May 6, 1834. Children b. Mont Vernon.

1. Ellen Frances, b. Dec. 18, 1857, m. Sept. 30, 1885, *Col. William H. Stinson of Mont Vernon, res. Goffstown.
2. Ada Emeline, b. Sept. 6, 1859, m. Jan. 6, 1884, *Francis C. Greenwood.
    3. Willie, baptized April. 1861, d. May 3, age 4 months.
    4. Cecil Franklin, b. Feb. 20, 1863, d. April 18, 1873.
    5. Mary Grace, b. March 24, 1865.
    6. Albert Fornis, b. May 6, 1869, m. Oct. 15, 1896, Beatrice E. Symonds of Salem, Mass., one daughter, resides in Boston.
    7. Freddie, b. Dec. 17, 1872, d. Aug. 16, 1873.
    8. Ruth Stevens, b. Nov. 26, 1876.

Deacon Albert Conant, 8th generation, son of Deacon William and Hannah (Fornis) Conant. b. Mont Vernon, Oct. 19, 1830, m. (1) Eliza Ann Beard, who d. Aug. 1, 1863, age 31 years, 7 months; m. (2) Susan Frances Bancroft, sister Dr. C. F. P. Bancroft. She was b. New Ipswich, Oct. 25, 1836, d. Charlestown, Mass., Jan. 30, 1885. Deacon Conant is a deacon in the Union Congregational Church, Boston, is a member of the firm of Conant Bros. Co., 73 Union Street, Boston. He has a summer residence in Mont Vernon. Children by first wife b. Mont Vernon.

1. Isabel Eliza, b. May 23, 1859, m. George Greenwood, son of Dexter Greenwood of Hollis. She d. East Orange, N. J., Sept. 2, 1890, age 31 years, 4 months.
2. Carrie Frances, b. Dec. 22, 1860, d. Dec. 27, 1860.
Children by second wife b. Charlestown, Mass.
3. Alice Bancroft, b. Oct. 19, 1868, m. April 20, 1899, Fred T. Wadleigh of Milford, resides in Milford and has two sons.
4. Annie Sanborne, b. Feb. 10, 1871, m. Nov. 20, 1901, William E. Horton of Boston, resides Boston.
5. Harry Winthrop, b. Feb. 5, 1875, is a law student.
6. John Bancroft, b. April 17, 1878, is an electrician.

Deacon Charles Edwin Conant, 8th generation, son of Deacon William Conant, b. Mont Vernon, June 30, 1832, m. March 28, 1860, Marion Crawford Wallace of Manchester. She was b. in Antrim, May 28, 1835. He resides in Boston. Children b. Winchester.

1. Charles Arthur, b. July 2, 1861, is a financial journalist.
2. Grace Wallace, b. Sept. 8, 1864, m. Rev. Frederick H. Page, pastor of the Trinity Congregational Church, Lawrence, Mass.

Deacon Walter Scott Conant, 8th generation, son of Deacon William Conant, b. Mont Vernon, June 8, 1834, d. June, 1900, New York City, buried in Mont Vernon. He was a Lieutenant in the War for the Union. For many years he was a manufacturer of wood, plush and leather boxes, and writing desks, in New York City, m. Mary Larkin Lewis of Boston. Children:

1. Mabel Frances, b. Charlestown, Mass., June 1, 1867.
2. Roger Lewis, b. April 1, 1873, at Jersey City, N. J., graduate of Columbia University, teacher in Porto Rico.

WILLIAM H. CONANT.
Deacon from 1875 to 1903.

Deacon Harlan Page Conant, 8th generation, son of Deacon William Conant, b. Mont Vernon, March 3, 1837. He is a member of Conant Bros. Co., Union Street, Boston, and resides in Somerville. He m. Feb. 16, 1864, Sarah P. Chase of Boston. Children:

1. Bertha Adams, b. Charlestown, Mass., Feb. 3, 1867.
2. William Chase, b. Oct. 4, 1868, Charlestown, Mass., m. Miss Harwood of Decatur, Ill.
3. Helen Pearson, b. Nov. 11, 1870 at Charlestown, Mass.
4. Sarah Florence, b. Somerville, Aug. 14, 1876.

Joseph Conant, 8th generation (Ezra, 7; John, 6; John, 5; John, 4; John, 3; Lot, 2; Roger, 1), b. May 16, 1816 at Beverly, Mass., by trade a cabinet maker. He removed from Beverly to Mont Vernon and bought a farm in the East District, where he now resides. He m. Sept. 19, 1844, Abigail. dau. of John and Mary (Stewart) Elliott, b. Mont Vernon, Feb. 9, 1826. Children:

1. Abigail J., b. Jan. 31, 1847, m. Stephen F. Hathaway of Beverly.
2. Mary, b. Dec. 23, 1848, resides with her parents, unm.
3. Alethea, b. May 20, 1850, m. John W. Bell of Beverly. She d. Sept. 27, 1900 at Beverly.
4. Joseph Frank, b. May 11, 1856, in business in Boston.
5. Charles E., b. Dec. 23, 1858, d. Woburn, Mass., Oct. 23, 1888, left a widow and children.
6. Josiephine, b. May 6, 1861, d. Sept. 4, 1861.
7. Willard E., b. March 21, 1866, d. New York City, March 22, 1893, was a teacher.

COX.

George Wilbert Cox, b. Upper Stewicke, Col. Co., Nova Scotia, July 9. 1856, m. Sept. 24, 1881, at Wolfeville, King's Co., N. S., Evangeline Davidson, b. Wolfeville, May 23, 1861. He graduated at Acadia College in 1880, taught school a few years, was then in business, took a post-graduate course at Harvard University, graduating in 1895. He was principal of McCollom Institute, Mont Vernon, N. H., 1895 to 1898, went to take charge of Bellows Falls Schools, Vt., in 1898, is now superintendent of schools, Ware, Mass. One child:

1. Laurie Wilbert, b. Londonderry, N. S., Aug. 18, 1883.

CROOKER.

James M., son Melzar and Abigail R. (Cox) Crooker, b. Amherst, Feb. 28, 1816, d. East part of Mont Vernon, April 3, 1888, m. Oct. 19, 1842, Sarah J. Smith, b. Augusta, Me., Jan. 15, 1817. Children b. Mont Vernon.

1. Mary E., b. Oct. 5, 1843, d. March 9, 1846.
2. Joseph H., b. May 23, 1845, d. Aug. 21, 1847.
3. James Henry, b. Aug. 3, 1847, m. Julia Hartshorn, Feb. 18, 1873, resides in Pennsylvania.
4. Olive J., b. Oct. 7, 1850, d. unm., April 26, 1870.
5. Sarah Ann, b. Oct. 24. 1853, m. (1) Oct. 7, 1871, C. A. Lowd, m. (2) David Rhodes, Aug. 17, 1879, lives in Amherst.
6. Clara M., b. Dec. 26, 1858, m. Jan. 17, 1882, Leander B. Barker, has one child.

CROSBY.

Joseph Fitch Crosby, son of Joseph and Sarah (Richardson) Crosby, b. Amherst, Sept. 16, 1819. He m. March 28, 1847, Helen M., dau. of James J. and Lucy W. (Burnham) Averill of Mont Vernon. She was b. March 15, 1827, d. Milford, Nov. 14, 1879. He moved to Mont Vernon in 1855, living on his father-in-law's farm 13 years, in the South District, then removed to Milford. He d. Milford, March 11, 1900. Children:
1. Grace Helen, b. Mont Vernon, June 13, 1858.
2. Catherine Belle. b. Mont Vernon, May 21, 1860, d. Oct., 1894.

CURTIS.

Jacob Curtis (or Curtice), b. Boxford, Mass., m. Mary Stiles of Boxford, Mass., May 26, 1752, settled first in Boxford, whence they moved about 1757 to Mont Vernon, served in the Revolution, was a taxpayer here, in 1804 moved to Antrim. He d. 1829, age 70. Children b. Mont Vernon.
1. Lemuel, a Revolutionary soldier, m. Mary Smith, Feb. 9, 1779, removed to Antrim in 1804, had six children.
2. Stephen, b. 1755, a Revolutionary soldier, m. Abigail, dau. of William Small of Amherst. She d. Jan. 10, 1782. He removed to Antrim in 1784, and d. there in 1832, had seven children.
3. Isaac Palmer, b. June 23, 1758, a soldier at "The Cedars," and at Bennington.
4. Ebenezer, b. June 9, 1760, a soldier in the Continental Army in 1781, m. Sarah Parker, Dec. 29, 1784.
5. Elizabeth, b. March 8, 1762, m. Isaac Carter, July 10. 1787.
6. Mary, b. April 15 ,1764.
7. John, b. Jan. 29, 1766.
8. Asaph, b. May 3, 1768, d. Jan. 4, 1769.
9. Asaph, b. Jan. 15, 1770.
10. Abel, b. July 8, 1772.
11. Sarah, b. Oct. 28, 1774.

Levi Curtis, son of Benjamin and Lydia Earle Curtis, b. Mont Vernon, 1792, m. Lydia Kinson (aunt of Geo. Kinson), of Mont Vernon. He moved to Antrim, Feb., 1825, d. there in 1861, leaving eight children of whom the seventh was Andrew J., b. Antrim, 1833, m. Lucy N. Barrett of Hadley, N. Y., May 4, 1856. Had eight children, the sixth of whom was Stillman E., b. Oct. 22, 1866, m. Lucy G. Murdough of Hillsboro', res. Mont Vernon. Children:
1. Homer E., b. Nov. 6, 1896.
2. Mabel M., b. Aug. 9, 1898.

CARR.

Alexander M. Carr, son of Dea. James and Ann (Patterson) Carr, was b. in Antrim, Dec. 15, 1791, m. Hannah McIlvaine, April 18, 1817, d. in Amherst, Jan. 28, 1869. She was b. Oct. 6, 1792, d. Bedford, July 11, 1879. They lived in various places in Antrim and Bedford, lived in Mont Vernon about five years, first on the "David Stiles" place in the East District, and then on the place now owned by Miss Lizzie R. Parker. He moved from here to Amherst, where he d. Jan. 28, 1869. Children:
1. Sabra G., b. 1818, m. Abram J. Twiss, lived in Mont Vernon and Manchester.

ALBERT CONANT.

2. Lorenzo C., b. Antrim, m. Caroline Hastings, d. Amherst, where he had lived 36 years, Feb. 22, 1903, age 82 years. One son, Edward N.

3. Elizabeth M., unm., lived in Bedford.

4. Mark M., m. (1) Emma Ferson of Goffstown, m. (2) Mary A. Clement of Hillsboro', d. Manchester, 1872.

5. Hannah J., m. Timothy Jones of Amherst.

6. Alexander M. Jr., d. unm., age 25 years.

DALAND.

Samuel Daland, m. Oct. 25, 1842, Sophia Goodridge, adopted dau. of Sardis and Charlotte Goodridge Johnson. She was b. in Bedford, Mass. He lived for many years on the farm now of George C. Hadley, moved to Milford, where he d. Sept. 17, 1887, age 76. She d. May 13, 1899, age 74.

DAVIS.

Benjamin F. Davis, son of Rev. Joseph and Alphia (Goldsmith) Davis, b. New London, N. H., July 4, 1826, m. Sept. 22, 1859, Caroline S., dau. of John and Hannah (French) Averill of Mont Vernon. She was b. in Mont Vernon, Nov. 15, 1832. They reside in Mont Vernon.

DEAN.

George Dean was son of Nathaniel and Abigail Ellis Dean, of Dedham, Mass., b. Oct. 3, 1766, m. Ruthy Morse, of Canton, Mass., March 7, 1800, and went to Francestown, N. H. to live. Mr. Dean was a farmer and miller by occupation and owned the saw-mill and grist-mill at Mill Village. In 1817 he moved to Hopkinton, and 1820 to Dunbarton; May, 1821, Mr. Dean moved to Mont Vernon, N. H., and bought the farm owned by the Rev. Stephen Chapin, directly south of the meeting house. Here he remained until his death, which occurred after a long and painful illness of over five years, Aug. 29, 1834; Ruthy Morse Dean d. Sept. 8, 1872, aged 91 years, 9 months. Caroline (their daughter), b. in Francestown, April 23, 1801, m. Capt. Pliny Whitney, of Milford, N. H., Oct. 23, 1823 and d. in Milford, May 8, 1886. George Ellis (their son), b. in Francestown, Oct. 18, 1808. George Ellis remained with his father on the farm in Mont Vernon, N. H., as long as he lived, and at the age of 24, was made Lieutenant of the 5th Regiment, N. H. Militia. June 11, 1837, m. in Mont Vernon, Augusta Kendall, of Leominster, Mass., dau. of Asa and Lydia (Adams) Kendall, and went to Concord, Mass., entering the business of stove dealer and plumber. Mr. Dean was made a deacon of the First Congregational Church and Superintendent of the Sunday School. In April, 1850, Mr. and Mrs. Dean returned to Mont Vernon, N. H., and June 10, 1855, Mrs. Dean died suddenly in Boston while attending a meeting of the American Board. June 30, 1857, Mr. Dean m. (2) Alma Holt Bruce, formerly of Milford, N. H., and bought the homestead of Asa Kendall, where he remained until he died. Mr. Dean was chosen Superintendent of the Sunday School, in which capacity he served for 35 consecutive years, also Deacon of the Church, which position he filled until his death. Deacon Dean was one of the 8 citizens of the town who formed the first board of trustees for the building of an academy, one of the building committee when McCollom Institute was built (formerly Appleton Academy), three years later and always remained an active trustee and promoter of the cause of education. He filled many town offices and always maintained the honor and respect of his fellow-men. Deacon Dean was one of the self-made men of his generation, and of the grand old Puritan stock. He d. Feb. 26, 1891. Alma Holt Dean d. Dec. 31, 1891. Helen Augusta (their dau.), was b. in June, 1858, and d. Nov., 1858. Harriet Alma (2nd dau.), b. Sept., 1860. Resides in Boston, Mass.

DEARBORN.

Dr. Samuel Gerrish Dearborn, b. Aug. 10, 1827, at Northfield, N. H., son of Edmund and Sarah Dearborn, educated at Sanbornton Academy, and New Hampshire Conference Seminary at Tilton. Graduated at medical department of Dartmouth College in Nov., 1849, located in practice at Mont Vernon, Feb., 1850, removed to Milford in June, 1853. While there he served one year, fall of 1861 to fall of 1862, in the Eighth New Hampshire Regt. of Volunteers in Mississippi and Louisiana, as surgeon. In summer of 1864 he served three months as surgeon in the 9th Corps Hospitals in front of Petersburg, Va. Later he was commissioned surgeon of the new 18th Regt., New Hampshire Volunteers, but the war ended before the regiment left the state. During Grant's first administration he was U. S. Pension Examining Agent for the Milford district. In 1868-1869 he was one of the two representatives for Milford in the state legislature. May, 1873, he removed to Nashua. He was one of the most eminent physicians in New Hampshire. He m. Dec. 5, 1853, Henrietta M., dau. of Dea. Joseph A. and Maria J. (Bruce) Starrett of Mont Vernon. She was b. in Mont Vernon, Sept. 29, 1834, d. in Nashua, June 29, 1893. He d. Nashua, May 8, 1903. Children :

1. Dr. Frank A., b. Milford, Sept. 21, 1857, a practising physician in Nashua, m. a Miss Clara K. Laton of Nashua, has one child.
2. Dr. Samuel S., b. Milford, Jan. 30, 1872, graduated Harvard University, 1894, graduated from its medical department in 1898, resides Nashua, m. Miss May Chandler, dau. of John D. Chandler, Esq., of Nashua.

DIKE.

Benjamin Dike, a Revolutionary soldier, was killed in battle at Bemis' Heights, Oct. 7, 1777. He m. Dorothy Stearns. She m. (2) William Hastings. Children, Benjamin and Dorothy Dike, were :

1. Betty, b. Aug. 18, 1772.
2. Samuel Stearns, b. July 5, 1774, m. —— Flanders.
3. Benjamin, b. Oct. 10, 1776.

Stephen Dike, probably a younger brother of Benjamin, was placed under the guardianship of Dr. Henry Codman, March 31, 1779, being then above fourteen years of age. He seems to have served in Col. Moses Kelley's regiment for the town of New Boston in 1779. He was a son of Benjamin Dike of Tewksbury.

DODGE.

Richard Dodge, one of two brothers (William and Richard), emigranted from Somersetshire, Eng., in 1638, and settled in the north part of Beverly, Mass., near the line of Wenham. He was b. in 1602, and d. in 1671, leaving a widow, Edith. He had five sons and two daughters.

Josiah Dodge, 5th generation (Jonathan, 4; Jonathan, 3; Edward, 2;

SAMUEL G. DEARBORN, M. D.

HENRY F. DODGE.

Richard, 1). b. Beverly, June 23, 1745. He lived on the old Dodge farm on Purgatory Hill. He lived awhile at Beverly, and went to sea till four years, after he was married. He m. May 14, 1771, Ellinor Edwards of Wenham, Mass., whose mother's maiden name was Abigail Allen. From Beverly he moved first to Wolfeboro', N. H., but in 1772, bought land in Mont Vernon. Children:

1. Abigail, b. Sept. 19, 1774, m. *Ezekiel Upton of Mont Vernon.
2. Molly, b. 1776, m. William Montgomery, went to Walden, Vt.
3. Eleanor, b. 1778, m. Thomas Needham, lived near Montpelier, Vt.
4. *Allen, b. Jan. 18, 1780.
5. Malachi, b. April 8, 1784, d. unm. on homestead, March 31, 1854.

Allen Dodge, 6th generation (Josiah, 5; Jonathan, 4; Jonathan, 3; Edward, 2; Richard, 1), son of Josiah and Abigail (Allen) Dodge, b. Mont Vernon, Jan. 18, 1780, d. Mont Vernon, Jan. 13, 1863, m. (1) April, 11, 1808, Abigail Langdell, dau. of *Joseph Langdell. She was b. Feb. 25, 1782, d. Oct. 17, 1812. He m. (2) Mary Upton of Mont Vernon. March 6, 1827, he m. (3) widow Rachel Emerson of Swansea, N. H., with nine children, one of whom was Robert Emerson, a prominent citizen of Nashua. She was b. April 20, 1780, d. July 27, 1868. He lived on Purgatory Hill on the homestead. No children by last marriage. Children by 1st wife:

1. *Henry Codman, b. Mont Vernon, March 7, 1811.
   Ch. by 2nd wife, b. Mont Vernon:
2. Allen, b. Aug. 7, 1820, m. Abby Hildreth, d. March 13, 1852.
3. Betsey Upton, b. March 12, 1822.
4. Mary Ann, b. April 3, 1824, m. Harvey Mason of Nashua, one son. She d. Nov. 2, 1858. One son, Charles A. Mason, b. May 3, 1853, yet living.

Henry Codman Dodge, 7 (Allen, 6; Josiah, 5; Jonathan, 4; Jonathan, 3; Edward, 2; Richard, 1), son of Allen and Abigail (Langdell) Dodge, b. Mont Vernon, March 7, 1811, taught school some when young, was a farmer in his native town, through a long life, was selectman for some years and representative in 1865. He d. Feb. 12, 1897. M. June 14, 1836. Sophia M., dau. of Robert and Rachel Emerson of Marlboro', N. H. She was b. Jan. 23, 1814, d. June 9, 1898. He lived on Purgatory Hill, moved to South District. Ch. all b. in Mont Vernon.

1. *Henry Francis, b. May 17, 1838.
2. Abby Sophia, b. July 1, 1840, m. March 20, 1866, William M. Hall of Bradford, Mass., who d. Dec. 9, 1871. She d. Dec. 13, 1875. One son, William H., b. Dec. 2, 1866, who is m. and lives in Bellows Falls, Vt.
3. Rachel Anna, b. June 27, 1842, resides with her brother, unm.
4. Emily Francilla, b. Aug. 15, 1845. She was an accomplished woman and a poetess of merit, m. Oct. 21, 1874, Thomas Simpson of Lawrence, Mass. He d. Jan. 25, 1885. She m. (2) James Simpson (her brother-in-law), of New York City, April 6, 1887. She d. July 22, 1887. He d. 1894. The Simpsons were of the firm of Simpson, Crawford and Simpson, large dry goods dealers in New York City. Two ch.:
   1. Oswald, L., b. Nov. 12, 1877, is m.
   2. Emily M., b. Oct. 31, 1879, is now Mrs. Hunt.

5. Ella Maria, b. Dec. 4, 1849, d. unm., March 5, 1871.

Henry Francis Dodge, 8th generation (Henry C., 7; Allen, 6;

Josiah, 5; Jonathan, 4; Jonathan, 3; Edward, 2; Richard, 1), son of Henry C. and Sophia (Emerson) Dodge, b. Mont Vernon, May 17, 1838, a farmer owning the homestead of his great grandfather, Joseph Langdell, in South District, received academic education, has held the office of selectman and representative, m. Jan., 1864, Laura Ruthy, dau. of William and Sarah (Smiley) Parker of New Boston, b. Dec. 20, 1844. Ch. b. in Mont Vernon.

1. Flora Lillian, b. May 29, 1865, d. June 11, 1865.

2. Fannie Laura, b. September 29, 1867, m. April 16, 1891, William D. Clark of Amherst, resides Amherst, and has two children.

3. Clara Ella, b. Sept. 24, 1873, m. April 12, 1899, Fred A. Holt of Milford, resides Milford and has one ch.

4. Allen Parker, b. Dec. 27, 1878, d. Jan. 12, 1879.

5. Abbie Sophia, b. Sept. 6, 1880.

DILLON.

Lawrence Dillon, b. Middlesex Village, Mass., in 1837, came here with his family from Waterbury, Conn., in 1881, lived on the farm now occupied by Stephen Carpenter, removed to Waterbury, Conn., in 1887, where he now resides. He is a mechanic, m. Katherine, dau. of Pierce Holt of Lyndeboro'. She was b. in 1847. Children:

1. Ulysses S., b. 1866, in Prospect, Conn., m. Nellie Humphrey of Waterbury, Conn., res. New Britain, Conn., is a tool-maker.

2. Hattie S., b. Waterbury, Conn., 1868, m. E. Willis Bradley, lives Waterbury, Conn. He is not living.

3. Walter, b. Waterbury, Conn., in 1872, is manager Boys' Club Work in Chelsea and Somerville, Mass.

4. George, b. Waterbury, Conn., Aug. 20, 1875, is a mechanic in New Britain, Conn.

5. Clara A., b. Jan. 1881, res. Waterbury, Conn.

DOUGLASS.

Daniel Douglass, m. Mehitable Johonnot of Goffstown. They lived in the valley in the East District. She d. Nov. 10, 1887, aged 80 years, 10 months. Ch. probably b. in Mont Vernon.

1. Sarah, m. a Hooper of New Boston, had ch.

2. Peter, lives in Henniker.

3. James, m. (1) Esther W. Smith, dau. James and Catherine (Caswell) Smith of Mont Vernon, m. (2) Emeline, dau. of John Stearns. He lives in New Boston.

George Oscar Douglass, son of Peter and Elizabeth (Bennett) Douglass, b. Mont Vernon, July 3, 1860, m. Rose Raymond of New Boston, Dec. 14, 1888. He resided East Dist., now res. Gorgeville. Ch. b. in Mont Vernon.

1. Ida, b. June 1, 1889.

2. Frances, b. June 1, 1890.

3. Ethel, b. May 20, 1891.

4. George, b. Feb. 19, 1893.

5. Arthur, b. April 22, 1895.

6. Daughter, b. April 14, 1897.

DUNBAR.

Stephen Dunbar, b. Peterboro', son of Rev. Elijah Dunbar of Peterboro', m. March 26, 1833, Jane, dau. of William and Hannah (Jones) Bruce of Mont Vernon. She was b. Mont Vernon, Jan. 1, 1816, d. Feb. 8, 1890. He was a member of the Fifth N. H. Regiment Volunteers. He d. Dec. 21, 1862, aged 54 years. He lived in Mont Vernon village a short time, was a resident of New Boston at time of death. They had several children, among them being Stephen H. Dunbar of Wilton, who m. for his second wife, Sarah E., dau. of Nathan and Sarah (Bruce) Richardson of Mont Vernon.

DUNLAP.

Thomas Dunlap, b. Antrim, Feb. 22, 1803, m. Mary B. Averill, dau. of Levi and Mary Averill of Mont Vernon. He d. Aug. 17, 1865. She d. June 18, 1874, age 70. They lived in Antrim. They had 13 children, of whom Jane, m. Asa B. Lyford of Lowell.

Thomas, b. Aug. 30, 1821, m. Lucinda Eaton, dau. James Eaton of Antrim. He d. 1848. She m. (2) *Albert C. French of Mont Vernon.

DURANT.

Benjamin Durant of Dracut, Mass., kept store in this village, failed about 1815, held the office of representative here, was selectman 6 years, representative 5 years, 1811, 1812, 1813, 1814, 1815. M. Jan. 15, 1804, Betsey, dau. Isaac and Hannah (Cole) Weston. She was b. Mont Vernon, 1779.

DUTTON.

David Dutton, b. Wilton, May 26, 1792, was a mechanic, engaged in clock-making, lived here many years, was an amiable and industrious man. He d. Medford, Mass., April 22, 1882, m. Delinda Saunders of Brookline. She d. March 29, 1862. She was b. Brookline, Jan. 31, 1793. Children b. in Mont Vernon.

1. Mary Ann, b. Oct. 5, 1814, m. Nov. 13, 1838, *Franklin Otis Kittredge of Mont Vernon. She d. July 31, 1902.

2. Harriet, b. May 12, 1826, m. Feb. 1845, *Ira Hill, d. Sept. 6, 1875.

3. *Andrew J., b. March 15, 1831.

Andrew J. Dutton, b. Mont Vernon, March 15, 1831, went to Boston, 1865, is a merchant in Boston. M. Oct., 1865, Mary Jane Atkins, b. Georgia, 1835. Children:

1. Charles K., b. 1861, d. 1881.
2. Belle Atkins, b. 1865, d. 1869.
3. Annie Atkins, b. Oct. 26, 1869, m. Alfred H. Colby.

ELLENWOOD.

A Mr. Ellenwood from Lyndeboro', a stone mason, built the house (burnt in 1896) near Geo. C. Hadley's, and lived there several years in the forties.

ELLIOT.

John Elliot, b. Newburyport, June 6, 1759, d. Mont Vernon, May 8, 1878, m. Feb. 14, 1814, Mary Stewart of Antrim who was b. Feb. 17,

1790, d. Feb. 11, 1879, at Mont Vernon. He came here about 1813, and settled on a farm, one mile east of Mont Vernon village. Children b. in Mont Vernon.

1. Thomas, b. Oct., 1814, d. Newport, N. H., March 3, 1890, left children.

2. John, b. July 5, 1816, d. Nov. 20, 1833.

3. James, b. Sept. 15, 1818, d. May 27, 1901, Westfield, Mass., left three children.

4. Mary Jane, b. July 27, 1820, resides on the homestead, unm.

5. Benjamin, b. Oct. 14, 1822, lives Cedar Rapids, Iowa, has one dau., who is m. and has three children.

6. Abigail, b. Feb. 9, 1826, m. Sept. 19, 1844, *Joseph Conant, lives in Mont Vernon.

7. Andrew, b. April 14, 1830, lived Salem, Mass., d. Goffstown, Jan. 24, 1898, had two children.

8. Samuel, b. Nov. 14, 1831, lived in Stockton, Cal., since 1853, has three children.

9. John, b. April 2, 1835, lived in Watertown, Mass., 25 years, resided in Mont Vernon since 1875, on the homestead, unm.

ESTEY.

Jesse Estey came from Dunstable, Mass., about 1810, kept the Ray Tavern in the village several years. He returned to Dunstable and d. there. He was a prominent citizen there. He had several sons, among them was Capt. Augustus, who was b. in Mont Vernon and d. in Galena, Ill., Oct. 30, 1882, age 72 years.

EMERSON.

Widow Rachel Emerson of Swansea, N. H., m. March 6, 1827, *Allen Dodge of Mont Vernon. Her children by first husband lived with her in Mont Vernon. She was b. April 20, 1780, d. July 27, 1868. Children b. Swansea:

1. Mary A., b. 1807, m. June 5, 1839, *Augustus B. French, d. Milford, May 16, 1880, four children.

2. Abbie F., d. Jan. 12, 1863, aged 55 years.

3. Lydia, b. Nov. 26, 1809, m. Nov. 9, 1842, George A. Nutt of Amherst. He d. July 6, 1845, for several years prior to her death she lived with her sister, Mrs. H. C. Dodge. She d. Jan. 18, 1897.

4. Rachel, b. Jan. 23, 1814, m. June 14, 1836.

5. *Henry C. Dodge, d. Mont Vernon, June 9, 1898.

6. *Joseph H., d. May 20, 1851, aged 35.

7. Fanny L., d. Oct. 27, 1836, aged 18 years.

8. Robert, b. June 1, 1824, learned the trade of a tailor in Amherst; was a merchant tailor in Nashua many years, d. there Feb. 13, 1903. He m. (1) Sept. 30, 1847, Frances H. Vaughan of Woodstock, Vt., who d. Dec. 29, 1859. He m. (2) Jan. 23, 1862, Hannah P. Bullard of Milford. No children.

Children of Joseph H. and T. Emerson.

1. Abby F., d. Aug. 15, 1850, aged 4 years.

2. George F., d. Aug. 21, 1850, aged 1 year, 5 months.

FAIRFIELD.

Henry M. Fairfield, son of Benj. and Eunice (McMillan) Fairfield,

b. New Boston, came here from New Boston in 1870, lived on the farm opposite East School house, moved to Nashua in 1885 where he died. He m. Sabrina, dau. Samuel and Eliza (Moore) Leach of New Boston, served in 16th N. H. Regiment in Civil War, from New Boston. Ch.:

1. Annie E., m. George W. Gross of Nashua, res. Nashua.
2. Sarah, m. Arthur M. Cotton of Nashua, res. Nashua.
3. Mary, m. Harry W. Spear of Nashua, res. Nashua, two children.
4. Benjamin, railroad engineer, is married, lives in Nashua.
5. Walter, res. in Lynn, is in the shoe business there, is married.

Miss Sarah Fairfield, dau. Benj. and Eunice (McMillan) Fairfield, d. in Mont Vernon, Jan. 5, 1894, age 67 years, 6 months. She was a sister of Henry M. Fairfield.

FARNUM.

Lt. Joseph Farnum settled on the farm now of Wallace D. Hooper, shortly after the incorporation of Amherst as a town. He was lieutenant in Capt. John Bradford's Co. at Bennington in Revolutionary War, and d. in Mont Vernon, May 10, 1824, aged 78. He m. (1) Mary Lyon by whom he had eleven children, m. (2) Mrs. Tabitha (Weston) Wilkins Baldwin, widow of Capt. Daniel Wilkins, Jr., and Jesse Baldwin, and daughter of Ebenezer and Mehitable (Sutherick) Weston. She was b. March 31, 1742, d. Mont Vernon, Jan. 1820. Her dau. Abigail Wilkins m. Timothy Dix of Boscawen, and was the mother of Gen. John A. Dix of New York. He m. (3) Edith Smith. She d. Nov. 12, 1862, age 88 years. Children by 1st wife b. in Mont Vernon.

1. Sally, b. June 22, 1766.
2. Abigail, b. Dec. 22, 1767, m. Peter Abbott, Oct. 25, 1788.
3. Mary, b. Jan. 19, 1770, m. Oliver, son of Dea. Oliver and Amy (Washer) Carlton, Sept. 24, 1789, had several children, moved to Acworth.
4. Phebe, b. May 12, 1772, m. *Lambert Bradford.
5. Joseph, b. March 4, 1774.
6. Susannah, b. March 27, 1776, m. Zachariah Bemis of Westminster, Mass., Jan. 10, 1797.
7. Thomas, b. Jan. 26, 1778.
8. Asa, b. Feb. 1, 1780, m. Arethusa Lovejoy, April 14, 1803.
9. Betty, b. March 24, 1784.
10. Lucy, b. May 3, 1786, m. a Benj. Fassett, July 10, 1811.
11. Martha, b. ——, m. *Silas Wilkins of Mont Vernon, Nov. 21, 1810.

Children by 2nd wife b. in Mont Vernon:

12. Gera, b. Feb. 26, 1795, m. Sophronia Bills, Oct. 17, 1817, d. Roxbury, Mass., April 14, 1864.
13. John, b. Aug. 15, 1796, m. Betsey Robbins of Nelson, N. H., d. Brighton, Mass., Sept. 30, 1845. Children: 1. John Robbins, b. May 12, 1823, at Nelson, N. H., d. Waltham, Mass. 2. Elizabeth Ann, b. June 14, 1825, at Mont Vernon.

Israel Farnum, m. (1) Phebe Sheldon, Feb. 15, 1787. She d. Dec. 2, 1824. He m. (2) May 17, 1825, Susanna, dau. Asa and Susanna (Town) Farnum. She was b. March 22, 1772. He d. 1842. Children b. Mont Vernon:

1. Phebe, b. March 31, 1788, m. July 10, 1811, Ebenezer Lamson of Mont Vernon.
2. *Israel, b. June 8, 1790.

3. Amos, b. May 17, 1792, d. Oct. 17, 1812.

Israel Farnum, son of Israel and Phebe (Sheldon) Farnum, b. Mont Vernon, June 8, 1790, m. Catherine Talbot. She was b. April 5, 1788, d. May 16, 1875. He d. Dec. 30, 1861. Ch. b. Mont Vernon:
    1. Amos, b. April 14, 1816, had a son, Geo. H. Farnum, b. Dec. 22, 1839, enlisted in the army from Milford in Civil War.
    2. Sarah J., b. Dec. 25, 1818, m. Oct. 27, 1842, Josiah Swinnington of Mont Vernon, d. Mont Vernon, Jan. 28, 1879. Five children.

FITZPATRICK.

William Fitzpatrick, b. Newport, R. I., Dec. 3, 1874, came to Mont Vernon in 1889, and worked for William Ryan twelve years, is now a medical student.

FLANDERS.

Elijah Clark Flanders, b. Dorchester, N. H., April 20, 1820, d. Sept. 11, 1901 at Mont Vernon, lived on a farm in the southeast part of the town, m. June 1, 1845, Lovicey H. Pollard of Canaan. She was b. Feb. 20, 1821. They moved to Mont Vernon, Nov., 1883. Children b. Canaan, N. H.:
    1. Julia A., b. March 2, 1846, unm.
    2. Augustus B., b. Nov. 9, 1850, d. July 28, 1863.
    3. Alice M., b. Oct. 9, 1853, m. Wallace G. Fogg of Canaan, one child, George.
    4. Middleton G., b. Feb. 20, 1856, is married and resides Mitchell, North Dakota, has children.

FLETCHER.

Dexter Fletcher, b. New Ipswich, April 19, 1799, d. Mont Vernon, April 13, 1883, m. (1) Miss Felt of New Ipswich, m. (2) Eliza —— of New Boston. No children. He lived several years on Edward G. Averill's place in West District.

George Howard Fletcher, b. East Washington, N. H., March 6, 1844, m. 1866, Luthera C. Barney of East Washington, moved to Mont Vernon in April, 1873, lived here about five years, where Chas. Henry Trow lives, left to take a position in Taunton Insane Asylum.

FLINT.

Simeon Flint, b. May 16, 1782, in Amherst, m. Sarah, dau. of Dea. Jacob and Sarah (Lamson) Kendall, Aug. 20, 1804. She was b. Jan. 17, 1784, m. (2) Aaron Wilkins, Jr., of Amherst, Sept. 16, 1824. She d. Sept. 14, 1861. Simeon Flint and wife settled in the easterly part of Mont Vernon. Children b. Mont Vernon:
    1. Simeon K., b. Feb. 5, 1805, d. Nov. 23, 1879. Moved to Wilton, was postmaster there.
    2. Nathan, b. Oct. 8, 1806.
    3. Grisey, b. Oct. 17, 1808, unm.
    4. Jacob, b. Dec. 8, 1810.
    5. Eliza, b. Feb. 18, 1813, d. Dec., 1814.
    6. Daniel K., b. May 15, 1815.

FOLLANSBEE.

John Follansbee, Sr., b. Londonderry, N. H., moved to Mont Vernon in 1856, lived many years where Henry F. Dodge lives, where he d. in Aug., 1877, aged 86 years. He m. Mary Eastman of Londonderry. She d. March 6, 1880, age 83.. Their ch. b. Londonderry:

1. Edwin, b. Londonderry, 1817, d. there, 1901.
2. *John, b. Aug. 6, 1819.
3. Frank served in the War for the Union and d. in a Southern prison. He m. Ruth Morse and had one dau., now Mrs. George G. Andrews of Hudson.
4. James.

John Follansbee, Jr., b. Londonderry, Aug. 6, 1819, m. Mary L. Nichols of Londonderry. She was b. Hudson, N. H., Aug. 17, 1824. She d. Mont Vernon, Feb. 13, 1875. He d. May 2, 1881, age 62. He lived where Henry F. Dodge does. He served as corporal in 8th N. H. Regiment in Civil War. Children:

1. Mary Ann, b. Nashua, April 8, 1847, m. May 7, 1868, Edward A. Lawrence of Londonderry, d. Jan. 31, 1902. Lived in Nashua and Wilton, two children.
2. Frances, b. Londonderry, Dec. 25, 1848, m. Jesse R. Wilkins, Oct. 14, 1871, three children, res. Milford.
3. Sarah Eliza, b. Londonderry, Sept. 18, 1852, m. Pierce Perham of Milford, one dau., Ada F., b. March 20, 1873, m. 1896, Frank W. Richardson of Milford. She d. March 15, 1878.
4. John Wesley, b. Sept. 20, 1858, m. Angeline Cheney of Lyndeborough, Sept. 6, 1887.

FORSAITH.

Charles Forsaith, b. Deering, m. Jan. 2, 1854, Almira L., dau. of Joseph and Sarah (Perkins) Trow. She was b. Mont Vernon, May 11, 1830, d. Mont Vernon, April 13, 1897. Carpenter. He resides with his dau. Mrs. Pinkham at Hyde Park, Mass. Ch.:

1. Caroline Frances, b. Oct. 30, 1854, m. Dec. 25, 1876, *William F. Pinkham of Nashua, resides Hyde Park, Mass., three children.

FOSTER.

Peter Foster, m. Lydia Farmer, Andover, Mass., 1787. He is said to have kept tavern in Mont Vernon. His wife d. in Lyndeboro' in 1840, and was interred in the southwest corner of cemetery, near the Baptist Church in Hillsboro', where he had been buried some years previous. Their ch. were:

1. Samuel, b. Oct. 22, 1787.
2. *Isaac, b. Aug. 5, 1790.
3. Betsey, m. a Mr. Abbott, b. Sept. 27, 1792.
4. Lydia, b. Nov. 16, 1794, m. a Mr. Haines, d. in Hooksett, March 9, 1893.
5. Abraham, b. July 3, 1797, went to New Orleans.
6. Hannah, b. May 27, 1799, m. a Mr. Berry.
7. Lucy, b. July 21, 1801, m. a Mr. Pike by whom she had one son. Peter F. Pike, m. (2) Oct. 23, 1836, Warren Williams of Mont Vernon. She d. Mont Vernon, May 2, 1892.
8. Sarah, b. June 12, 1804, m. (1) Francis Murdough of Hillsboro',

who d. Dec., 1841, m. (2) Mr. Abner Knowlton of Windsor, a widower. She had no children. She d. Mont Vernon, Sept. 10, 1890.

9. Permelia, b. Aug. 20, 1806, m. April 7, 1829, *Dr. Jesse K. Smith. She d. May 13, 1880.

Isaac Foster, son of Peter and Lydia (Farmer) Foster, b. Aug. 5, 1790, lived here a few years in the thirties, afterwards in Hillsboro', again in Mont Vernon, d. Wilton, April 10, 1872, kept tavern, was a shoemaker. He m. Feb. 1, 1821, Jane, dau. John and Jane Allds of Merrimack. She was b. May 31, 1801, d. 1874. Children:

1. Harriett J., b. Merrimack, April 16, 1822, m. Dec. 20, 1842, John F. Goss of Merrimack, six children, res. Milford.

2. *Newell Dean, b. Merrimack, July 21, 1833.
Twins.

3. Adaline, b. Mont Vernon, Nov. 2, 1825, d. Feb. 14, 1829.

4. Abraham, b. Mont Vernon, Nov. 2, 1825, d. Sept., 1826.

5. *Charles Abraham, b. Mont Vernon, March 6, 1828.

6. Isaac Newton, b. Hillsboro', Aug. 21, 1832, m. Lucy J., dau. of Leonard and Hannah (Foster) King. He had a tin-shop in Wilton with his two brothers. He d. Wilton, Jan. 16, 1885.

7. Samuel Kimball, b. Nashua, Feb. 9, 1838, m. Jan. 4, 1861, Hattie E., dau. Jeremiah Hood, lived Wilton where he d. Nov. 10, 1892, had four children.

Newell Dean Foster, son of Isaac and Jane (Allds) Foster, b. Merrimack, July 21, 1823, mechanic, m. Eliza M., dau. of Jesse, Jr. and Sarah (Leavitt) Averill, June 10, 1846. She was b. Mont Vernon, 1824, d. June 5, 1852. He m. (2) Harriet Orcutt of Cambridge. He m. (3) May 3, 1892, Mrs. Addie C. Leland of Bedford. He d. Wilton, May 7, 1893.

Children all b. in Mont Vernon.

Children by 1st wife:

1. Charlotte, b. ——, m. John S. Locke of Rye Valley, Oregon, lives Oregon, two children: one son and one daughter.

2. *George Barrett, b. 1849, d. ——.

3. *Charles Woodbury, b. Aug. 8, 1851.

N. D. Foster had two children by 2nd wife, Wm. and Florence.

Charles Abraham Foster, son of Isaac and Jane (Allds) Foster, b. Mont Vernon, March 6, 1828, m. (1) Clarinda J. Felch of Mason Village (now Greenville). She d. Milford, Feb. 11, 1870. He m. (2) June, 1870, Marietta Brigham of Nashua. He d. Concord, N. H., Jan. 12, 1882, age 53. Children by 1st wife b. Mont Vernon.

1. *Charles Alfred, b. March 23, 1854.

2. Etta, b. Aug. 20, 1857, m. March 18, 1876, Hiram Searles, lived in Milford, d. Goffstown, Nov. 24, 1902, three children.

3. Emma J., b. Jan. 1, 1860, m. June 8, 1876, *William Henry Marvell of Mont Vernon, had one child.

George Barrett Foster, son of Newell D. and Eliza M. (Averill) Foster, b. Mont Vernon, 1849, m. Mary Frances, dau. of Elbridge and Hannah E. (Philibrown) Foster, b. New Boston, May, 1851, d. Mont Vernon, Oct. 22, 1891. He d. Taunton, Mass., May 12, 1881, age 31 years, 9 months, one child.

1. Annie Parker, b. Mont Vernon, Nov. 17, 1880.

Charles Woodbury Foster, son of Newell D. and Eliza (Averill)

Foster, b. Mont Vernon, Aug. 8, 1851, m. Sept. 15, 1875, Jane Thompson. He removed to Concord, June, 1877. He d. Concord, N. H., Jan. 20, 1898. Children:

1. Evelyn Jane, b. Mont Vernon, June 28, 1876.
2. William Smith, b. Concord, Nov. 26, 1877.
3. Arthur John, b. Concord, Jan. 27, 1880.

Charles Alfred Foster, son of Charles Abraham and Clarinda J. (Felch) Foster, b. Mont Vernon, March 23, 1854, m. Oct. 21, 1886, Kate A. Garvin of Peterboro', has four children, lives in Hudson, N. H.

FOX.

John M. Fox, b. New Boston, March 5, 1836, son of Ephraim and Sarah (Parker) Fox, served in the War for the Union in the Second New Hampshire Regiment, moved here in 1857, thence to Milford and Amherst where he enlisted in 1861. He came back to Mont Vernon in 1864, and lived on a farm in the Southeast part of the town until 1887, when he purchased of the Wood Bros. the village store stock of goods. In 1899 he purchased a grocery store in Rochester, N. H., returned to Mt. Vernon, 1903. He was a town clerk here 23 years, and Representative in 1890. He m. Esther D. Fairfield, dau. of Benjamin Fairfield, Esq., of New Boston. She was b. New Boston, July 16, 1830, Children:

1. Frank, d. young.
2. Eunice Abbie, b. Amherst, Jan. 9, 1864, resides at home, unm.
3. William Henry, b. Mont Vernon, Nov. 25, 1868, m. Oct. 30, 1895, Jessie Alice, dau. of Arthur A. and Lucretia (Rideout) Trow, b. Mont Vernon, Jan. 24, 1875, ch., Esther Abbie, b. Jan. 18, 1902. He resides in Mont Vernon and is a mechanic.

FRENCH.

Abraham French, b. Lyndeboro', 1777, m. Naomi Wilkins, dau. of Benjamin and Naomi (Smith) Wilkins, of Lyndeboro', April 5, 1803. They lived in the West District many years. He d. April 26, 1863, age 86 years, 3 months. She d. Mont Vernon, Nov. 11, 1871, age 86 years, 3 months. Children:

1. Hannah, b. Mont Vernon, Jan. 9, 1804, m. Dec. 15, 1825, *John Averill, Jr. She d. July 10, 1855.
2. Albert Clinton, b. Mont Vernon, 1808, d. Milford, Sept. 1, 1878, age 70. He m. (1) Lucinda Eaton, dau. James Eaton of Antrim. She d. Feb. 11, 1848, age 32. He m. (2) Eliza Wilson of Weare, who d. Mont Vernon, July 29, 1892, age 81, children.

Frank B., b. Mont Vernon, Feb. 9, 1849, came to Milford, 1867, dealer in coal, wood, ice, m. May 4, 1870, Addie, dau. of John H. and Naomi (Wilkins) McConihe, b. Bedford, April 7, 1846, ch.:

1. Will F., b. Milford, May 15, 1873, in business with father, m. April 27, 1892, Nellie J., dau. Charles F. and Emeline W. (Smith) Holt of Antrim.

Augustus B. French, son Josiah and Rebecca (Blanchard) French, b. Milford, March 16, 1815, tanner, d. Milford, Aug. 9, 1884. He m. June 5, 1839, Mary A., dau. Robert and Rachel (Howard) Emerson. She was b. Marlboro', in 1807, d. Milford, May 16, 1860. Children:

1. Mary A., b. Milford, Sept. 7, 1840, m. June 23, 1859, Albert H. McIntire of Milford, d. March 4, 1881.

2. Hattie Lovica, b. Mont Vernon, Nov. 17, 1842, m. May 30, 1867, Geo. C. Farwell, res. Milford.

3. James W., b. Milford, Aug. 31, 1844, d. Jan. 25, 1846.

4. Helen L., b. Milford, Feb. 13, 1848, d. June 8, 1849.

FRINK.

Rev. Benson M. Frink, a native of Jackson, N. H., a graduate of Bangor Seminary, was settled here as Pastor of the Church two and one-fourth years from 1865 to 1867. He was subsequently settled in Portland, Me., Saco, Me., Beverly, Abington, and Shelburne Falls, Mass. He now lives at Brookfield, Mass. He had a wife and one child. For more extended account, see Ecclesiastical History in Manuscript of Town History.

FULLER.

Nathan Fuller, Jr., son of Nathan and Martha Fuller, b. Amherst, July 18, 1763, m. (1) Tamson Brown. She was b. Sept. 4, 1763, d. Sept. 1814. He m. (2) Feb. 28, 1815, Betsey, dau. of Nathan, Jr., and Esther (Butterfield) Jones. She was b. Mont Vernon, April 25, 1777, d. Feb. 8, 1829. He came to Mont Vernon about 1815, was a retired farmer, lived in the house in village now owned by Dr. C. H. Hallowell, d. Aug. 31, 1840. Children by 1st wife b. Amherst.

1. William B., b. May 15, 1786, d. Sept. 2, 1799.

2. Tamson, d. Nov., 1803, aged 8 years.

3. Tamson H., b. Aug. 27, 1804, m. *Matthew G. Rotch, d. Mt. Vernon, May 7, 1895.

Ch. by 2nd wife b. Mont Vernon.

4. Betsey, b. Feb. 9, 1816, m. Rufus Lounsbury, d. Rose Grove, Iowa, Jan. 26, 1871.

GERRISH.

Dr. Alfred A. Gerrish, 8th and youngest son of Joseph and Susan (Hancock) Gerrish, b. Franklin, N. H., July 4, 1829, fitted for college at Meriden, N. H., studied his profession with Dr. Nahum Wright of Gilmanton and Prof. E. R. Peaslee of Hanover, graduated at Bellevue Medical College, New York City, March, 1852, and immediately came to Mont Vernon as successor to Dr. Samuel G. Dearborn, and continued here in successful practice twelve years. In July, 1865, he removed to Lowell, Lake Co., Ind., where he has since resided. For many years he has held the position of surgeon for the Louisville, New Albany R. R. and its branches. He left an ample fortune. Dr. Gerrish was a bachelor. He d. Lowell, Ind., July 17, 1903.

GILBERT.

Adna A. Gilbert came from Francestown, was a carpenter by trade, lived several years with Justin Richardson in South District (where C. O. Ingalls now does), d. there, Dec. 3, 1883, age 43. His 2nd wife was Martha, dau. John H. and Martha J. (Gilmore) Lindsey. After his death she m. Joseph Whittemore, res. Providence, R. I. Children by 2nd wife:

DEA. JAY M. GLEASON.

1. Charles, druggist, Providence, R. I.
2. Frank.

GILES.

George B. Giles, b. Providence, R. I., lived in the South District, mechanic, m. Ann D. Chickering. He d. —— She d. Sept. 30, 1892, aged 78. Children:
1. John H., b. Mont Vernon, June 17, 1854, mechanic, res. Milford.
2. Olive, singer, m., res. Wilton.
Two other daughters.

GLEASON.

Jay Morton Gleason, son of Dr. E. V. and Almira H. Gleason, b. May 8, 1850, Dunham, Quebec, came to Mont Vernon in 1869, lives in village, is a farmer and ice-man, m. June 8, 1874, Mary C., dau. of Dea. Nathaniel and Elizabeth (Bruce) McIntire of Lyndeboro'. She was b. Lyndeboro', Feb. 20, 1851. Children b. in Mont Vernon.
1. Ernest Morton, b. June 5, 1875, m. Florence W. Gooding of Somerville, Dec. 29, 1902, Supt. of Schools in Unionville, Conn.
2. Marion Elizabeth, b. Oct. 22, 1887.

GOODRIDGE or GOODRICH.

Lieut. Allen Goodridge or Goodrich, owned and occupied the farm, late of Joseph H. Tarbell, in the South District. He served in the War for Independence, and d. Mont Vernon, Oct. 27, 1805, age 56. He m. Sarah, dau. of Capt. Josiah and Sarah (Fitch) Crosby. She was b. April, 1756, d. Mont Vernon of spotted fever, Jan. 27, 1812. Children b. Mont Vernon.
1. *Allen, b. 1782, d. Jan. 26, 1842, aged 60.
2. Sarah, b. —— m. —— Wallingford of Claremont, two children, Sarah and Elizabeth.
3. Fannie, m. Rev. Somerville, missionaries to the Indians of the West, had five children.
4. Joseph, m. (1) Abigail Emerson, of Amherst, N. H. She was b. Sept. 26, 1795, d. Boston, Jan. 24, 1835, m. (2) her sister Rebecca Parkman Emerson, b. Feb. 13, 1800. He d. Waltham, Mass., April 28, 1881. By his 1st wife he had two daughters, A. Frances and Elizabeth, Frances m. William S. Houghton of Boston, one dau., Elizabeth Houghton of Boston.
Twins presumably.
5. Crosby lived in Mont Vernon, d. unm., at an advanced age.
6. Sophia, not m. lived to advanced age.
7. Betsey, d. Feb. 27, 1803, aged 9 years.

Allen Goodrich, Jr., son of Lt. Allen and Sarah (Crosby) Goodrich, m. Mercy Emerson of Amherst, N. H., dau. Capt Nathaniel Emerson, March 20, 1814. She was b. Oct. 2, 1791. He lived on the homestead farm in the South District. He d. Jan. 26, 1842, age 60. She d. Dec. 16, 1841, aged 50. Children b. Mont Vernon.
1. Benjamin, b. 1815, m. April 4, 1839, Sophia, dau. Caleb and Rebecca (Converse) Boutell of Amherst. She was b. Dec. 26, 1812, d. Fairbanks, Iowa, Jan. 3, 1881. He d. Kier, Iowa, farmer. Children: 1.

Harriet, m. Owen Paine of Kier, Iowa. 2. William. 3. Ellen. 4. Sarah. 5. Asa.

2. Jarvis, b. Oct. 22. 1818, d. March 9, 1853, New York City, m. Mary J. Townsend of Waltham, Mass., May 30, 1849.

3. Sarah, b. Oct., 1822, m. Sewell K. Kidder of Pittston, Me. Children: Frank, Charles, Eugene. She d. Nov. 5, 1849, in Waltham.

4. Asa, b. Aug., 1824, d. unm., Feb. 11, 1852, in New York City.

5. John Franklin, b. Aug., 1826, grad. Harvard College, 1849, d. June, 1863, Vicksburg, Miss., m. —— Morrison of New York. Ch.: Frank Trueman, Edward Everett, and Fannie m. Richard Crowther of Waterloo, Iowa, one son. Keith Crowther.

6. Rebecca Frances, b. Aug., 1828, m. E. Wardwell Beal of Nelson, N. H. She d. March 24, 1865, in Waltham, Mass. Ch.: 1. Frank Wardwell; 2. Wm. Goodrich, m. Nettie L. Nichols of New Haven, N. Y., 2 ch.: Lois and Wm. G. Beal.

7. Mercy Ann Emerson, b. June 6, 1830, m. Augustus J. Beckwith, April 20, 1864, lives Waltham, Mass. Ch.: Mary F., b. Jan. 13, 1867, m. Charles D. Meserve of Hopkinton, Mass., lives Newton, Mass.

GOULD.

Stephen Gould, nephew Richard Gould of Topsfield, b. Topsfield, Mass., Feb. 6, 1754, d. 1825, at Hillsborough, m. Lydia Fuller of Middleton, Mass. She d. about 1810. They resided for some years on the farm, lately owned by James M. Crooker, in the east part of the town. They settled in Mont Vernon as early as 1785. About 1804 they removed to Hillsborough. Their ch. were:

1. Elijah, b. Boxford, Mass., May 13, 1780, m. (1) Miss Bradford, dau. of Samuel and Annie (Washer) Bradford of Hillsboro', had 3 ch., m. (2) Hannah Chapman, Sept. 18, 1823, had ch., d. in Antrim.

2. Stephen, b. Feb. 3, 1782, m. Polly Melendy of Amherst, d. Cambridge, Vt., Dec. 3, 1852, had 4 ch.

3. Lydia, b. April 7, 1784, m. Aaron Smith called "Hatter Smith," of Mont Vernon, had 2 sons.

4. Abner, b. Mont Vernon, Feb. 7, 1786, m. Almira Codman of Hillsborough, d. Hillsborough. He was taxed in Mont Vernon in 1813.

5. Timothy, b. Mont Vernon, May 2, 1789, m. Clarissa Bradford of Hillsboro', in 1815, was a blacksmith, had 4 ch., lived and d. in Hillsboro'. Children: 1. Leonora B., b. 1816, m. Walter McKean of Nashua, had 4 children; 2. Henry C., b. June, 1818, m. Miss Stratton of Bradford, had 3 children, lived and d. in Hillsboro', in 1900; 3. John M., b. June, 1821, d. 1895; 4. Frederick W., b. 1827, m. Eliza Smith, sister of Gov. John B. Smith, had one son. George. He was Deputy Sheriff many years. He d. 1901.

6. Thaddeus, b. Mont Vernon, Nov. 3, 1791, m. Mary Ann Hitchborn of Boston in 1812. He settled in Boston as jeweller, and d. in 1840.

7. Jonathan, b. Mont Vernon, June 21, 1799, m. Sabra Booth of Hillsboro', d. Hillsboro', Oct. 6, 1888, had 3 sons, the youngest of whom Edwin B. Gould is a lawyer in Nashua.

Mrs. Mary Gould, widow of Major Gould of Lyndeborough, d. 1842, in Mont Vernon, age 86. Her first husband was Rev. Joseph Appleton of North Brookfield, Mass. She was the mother of Hon. William Appleton of Boston. Sarah H. (Appleton) Burnham, wife John Burnham. Mary A. (Appleton) Stevens, wife Asa Stevens, and Abigail E. (Appleton) Starrett, wife of David Starrett.

GREEN.

George W. Green, son of Amos and Ruth (Hastings) Green of Amherst, b. Amherst, Aug. 21, 1807, m. (1) Oct. 6, 1838, Mary Upton of Mont Vernon, dau. of Ezekiel, Jr., and Abigail (Dodge) Upton. She d. April 29, 1841, age 36. M. (2) Hannah P., dau. of John Stearns. She was b. Mont Vernon, Sept. 28, 1817, d. Mont Vernon, July 11, 1900. He was a farmer and lived in the West District many years. He d. in Mont Vernon, 1881. Children by 1st wife b. Mont Vernon.
   1.   Addison, m. had ch., d. in Danville, N. H.
   2.   Edward.
   Child by 2nd wife, b. Mont Vernon.
   3.   Nancy J., b. Feb. 8, 1843, m. 1867, m. *G. Clifford Averill, d. Dec. 4, 1900. 3 children.

Nathan Green, son of Amos and Keturah (Stewart) Green, b. Amherst, July 15, 1778, m. Hannah, dau. of Joseph and Martha (Dodge) Trow, March 10, 1812. She was b. Mont Vernon, d. Boston, Sept. 8, 1862, age 76. He d. Lowell, Jan. 15, 1857, age 78 years. He lived in Mont Vernon, Plattsburg, N. Y., and Lowell, Mass. Ch.:
   1.   Antis, m. Luther Eastman, d. Bloomington, Ill., July 12, 1873, age 61.
   Twins.
   2.   *Cornelius, b. Sept., 1816, b. Mont Vernon.
   3.   Cornelia, b. Sept., 1816, b. Mont Vernon. Cornelia m. —— Varney of Lowell, Mass., had three girls and one boy. One dau. Martha m. William Bancroft of Newton, Mass.
   4.   Susan, m. Lewis Graves of Lowell.
   5.   Levi, m. Libel Nutting of Westford, Mass., niece of Mrs. Amasa Brown. He d. Dec. 9, 1892, at Lowell. One son, Willie.

Cornelius P. Green, son of Nathan and Hannah (Trow) Green, b. Mont Vernon, Sept., 1816, d. Mont Vernon, Feb. 24, 1875, m. Achsah Haseltine of Springfield, N. H., b. April 4, 1816, one adopted dau., Vienna, b. Sept. 16, 1861, m. *William P. Jenkins of Mont Vernon, Oct. 11 1882. Cornelius P. Green was a farmer.

Daniel H. Green, son of Edmund and Eliza (Withey) Green, b. Milford, Oct. 3, 1836, m. 1865, Antionette, dau. William and Elizabeth (Cook) Walker of Brighton, Mass. She was the widow of his cousin. Lived in Mont Vernon from 1871 to 1896. He was in the 2nd N. H. Regiment, d. Mont Vernon, Aug. 20, 1896.

GREENWOOD.

Francis C. Greenwood son of Dexter and Mary (Holden) Greenwood, b. Hollis, Nov., 1853, was for a number of years agent for firms in Boston and New York, who were in the West India fruit business, and about 1883 formed a connection in that trade in New York. In 1892 he came to Mont Vernon, was in the summer-boarding business four years at Conant Hall, three years Bellevue Hotel and two years at Lincoln Hall. He d. July 15, 1900. He m. Jan. 6, 1884, Ada E., dau. Dea. William H. and S. Emeline (Cloutman) Conant. She was b. Sept. 6 1859, res. Mont Vernon. Child b. Mont Vernon.
   1.   Miriam Conant, b. Jan. 29, 1895.

GURDY.

William P. Gurdy, b. Bristol, N. H., Feb. 12, 1836, m. Dec. 24, 1859, Adeline Caswell of Lowell, Mass., b. July 3, 1840. She d. Mont Vernon, April 28, 1900. He lived on the Peter Jones farm, in the southeast part of the town many years. Ch.:

1. William C., m. Miss Burnham of Amherst, is a U. S. Postal Clerk, on the route between New York and Boston, has one son, Charles W.

GUTTERSON.

Charles H. Gutterson, son John and Martha (Sawtelle) Gutterson, b. Milford, Oct. 29, 1837, m. (1) March 21, 1865, Mary, dau. William and Sarah D. (Russell) Sheldon, b. Wilton, March 31, 1837, d. Milford, May 17, 1876, m. (2) March 31, 1877, Mary E., widow James Langdell, and dau. Luke and Elizabeth (Langdell) Wilkins, b. Mont Vernon, Oct. 10, 1846. He has lived in Mont Vernon several years, mainly in the South District, farmer, ch.:

1. Charles W., b. Aug. 25, 1868, d. March 18, 1869.
2. Elmer Moody, b. Jan. 4, 1879, res. with his parents.

HADLEY.

Dr. Dewitt Clinton Hadley, son of Abijah and Mary (Whittemore) Hadley, b. Hancock, June 12, 1823, graduated Woodstock Medical College, 1850, d. Hancock, Feb. 11, 1859, m. Nov., 1851, Mary A. Haggett of Lyndeboro'. Ch. b. Hancock.

1. *George C., b. Sept. 3, 1852.
2. Andrew P., b. 1855, m. 1878, Clara Upton of Tyngsboro, Mass., lives in Tyngsboro and has two children.

George C. Hadley, son of Dr. Dewitt C. and Mary A. (Haggett) Hadley, b. Hancock, Sept. 3, 1852, fitted for college at Francestown and New Ipswich Academies, m (1) Sept. 23, 1880, Mary F., dau. of William P. and Frances C. (Bartlett) Burnham of Milford. She d. Dec. 15, 1881, age 25 years. He m. (2) Lizzie A. Goss of Kingston, N. H., dau. of Henry S. and Martha Goss. He moved to Mont Vernon in 1882, is a farmer. Ch. b. in Mont Vernon.

1. Bertha M., b. April 18, 1884.
2. Alice M., b. April 21, 1886.
3. Dewitt C., b. Nov. 15, 1888, d. Dec. 3, 1888.
4. Lura A., b. Oct. 15, 1889.

Gilbert Hadley, b. Goffstown, N. H., June 6, 1819, m. Nov. 11, 1851, Mary E. Wilson of Weare, lived on farm in East District. He d. Mont Vernon, June 12, 1891. She d. Mont Vernon, April 15, 1896. Ch. b. New Boston.

1. William Fred, b. Feb. 10, 1854, lived on his father's farm in East District, moved to Gloucester, Mass., in 1897, was selectman three years in Mont Vernon, m. Oct. 2, 1882, Emma Babson of Gloucester, Mass. He d. Gloucester, Feb. 10, 1903. Ch b. Mont Vernon. Ethel M., b. Feb. 5, 1883, res. Gloucester; Edward B., b. Oct. 16, 1888, res. Gloucester.
2. Frank Henry, b. Jan. 22, 1859, d. Goffstown, June 2, 1861.

HARTSHORN.

John Hartshorn, b. Lyndeboro,' lived on the farm owned by Maurice Herlehy in the South District several years in the thirties and forties. He m. (1) Susanah Curtis of Lyndeboro', by whom he had three ch. She d. Mont Vernon. He m. (2) Mehitable Carkin of Lyndeboro', no ch. She d. Feb. 19, 1881, aged 81 years. Ch.:

1. Susan E. R., b. Hancock, Vt., Dec. 9, 1818, m. Rodney K. Hutchinson, Nov. 12, 1840, 5 children, d. Milford, Aug. 17, 1853.

2. Sirepta J., b. Lyndeboro', June 21, 1826, m. after her sister's death, Rodney K. Hutchinson of Milford, Oct. 6, 1855, had 2 ch. She d. Nov. 2, 1901 in Milford.

3. John, emigrated to Ohio, carpenter, was a captain in the Civil War.

HARWOOD.

John Harwood, b. 1777, d. Mont Vernon, Nov. 13, 1845, age 68, lived in the "old red house" west of the village, now owned by Estate of William Stevens, m. April 4, 1799, Mary, dau. of Jeremiah and Lois (Hoyt) Carleton of Lyndeboro'. She was b. Aug. 3, 1779, d. April 18, 1834, at Mont Vernon. Ch. b. Mont Vernon.

1. Hannah, b. Feb. 6, 1800, m. Nov. 28, 1837, *Joseph Trow, d. July 21, 1862.

2. John, b. 1801, d. Littleton, Col., July, 1889, age 88 years, had two ch. b. Nashua, viz.: 1. Dr. John S. Harwood, a surgeon in the army d. in practice at Lowell, Mass. 2. Angeline, m. Henry Little.

3. Joseph, b. 1802 or 1803, m. Nancy Perham of Lyndeboro', April 7, 1837. He d. May 25, 1864, age 61. She afterwards m. Edward Fowle of Woburn, Mass., and d. there July 21, 1890, aged 73. She was b. April 7, 1817. One dau., Mary Jane Harwood, b. Mont Vernon, d. Feb. 24, 1862, age 23.

4. *Kilburn.

5. Mary, b. April 13, 1807, m. Sept. 13, 1827, *Luther Coggin. She d. Nov. 4, 1856.

6. Lois Hoyt, b. 1811, m. *Clinton Roby of Mont Vernon, d. June 11, 1857, age 46.

Kilburn Harwood, son of John and Mary (Carleton) Harwood, b. Mont Vernon, m. Sally Buss of Wilton. They lived in Fitchburg, Mass., had three sons and one daughter, viz.:

1. Junius of Fitchburg.

2. Theresa, m. a lawyer.

3. George.

4. Kilburn, m. Sally Reeme, lives Decatur, Ill., has three dau., viz.: 1. Josephine, m. William C., son of Harlan P. and Sarah (Chase) Conant of Somerville, Nov. 9, 1893, lives Somerville, Mass.; 2. Kate C.; 3. Mary Theresa.

HAZEN.

John Hazen, son of Horace and Betsey (Stevens) Hazen, b. Goffstown, Sept. 10, 1853, bought the Odell farm in the West District in 1885 where he has since lived, m. Dec. 22, 1880, Ida Abbie, dau. Calvin and Armindy J. (Tucker) Martin. She was b. Grafton, N. H., April 10, 1860. Ch.

1. Ida Belle, b. Goffstown, Feb. 9, 1884.
2. Lizzie Annie, b. Mont Vernon, Oct. 8, 1888.
3. Arthur Martin, b. Mont Vernon, May 8, 1894.

HERBERT.

Rev. Charles D. Herbert, youngest son of Hon. George Herbert of Ellsworth, Me., was b. at that place, Sept. 18, 1818, graduated at Bowdoin College in 1841, and three years later at Bangor Theological Seminary. He was immediately ordained and went as a home missionary to the West. After several years in this service he returned to New England. He commenced preaching in Mont Vernon, July 5, 1850, as successor to Rev. Bezaleel Smith, and was installed pastor of the church on the 6th of Nov., following. He closed his pastorate here in April, 1856, and shortly afterward was settled over the Congregational Church at West Newbury, Mass., remaining there until 1862.

He had qualified himself for the practice of medicine, and for some years practised as a physician at Rutland, Mass., preaching at the same time. In 1878 he was recalled to West Newbury, and was again pastor there eight years. In 1887 he became pastor of the Presbyterian Church in Hebron, N. Y., which he resigned on account of ill health. He d. Oct. 13, 1893, and was buried at Mt. Auburn, Mass., Oct. 17. In 1853 he m. Miss Sarah Flanders, dau. of Dr. Flanders of Durham, N. H. Two sons.
1. George Herbert, Esq., of St. Paul, Minn.
2. Rev. Charles E. Herbert, Esq., of Galway, N. Y.

HERLEHY.

David J. Herlehy, b. County Cork, Ireland, March 2, 1829, came to America in 1851, lived in Milford several years, bought the Milton McCollom farm in the East District, and has resided there since Nov., 1865. He m. (1) Ellen Ahearn of Milford. She was b. in County Limerick, Ireland, July, 1834, d. Mont Vernon in 1868. He m. (2) Margaret Murphy of Milford. She d. Nashua, Dec. 15, 1895, age 52. Ch. by 1st wife b. in Milford.
1. Mary A., lives in Mont Vernon, unm.
2. Patrick H., m. lives in Nashua, has 4 children.
3. Eliza Frances, d. April 16, 1883, age 22.
4. Benjamin John, lives in Cambridgeport, Mass., has 3 ch.
Children by 2nd wife b. in Mont Vernon.
5. David, d. young.
6. *Maurice, b. Jan. 24, 1873.
7. James, b. March, 1875, lives Mont Vernon.
8. Josephine, d. young.

Maurice Herlehy, son of David J. and Margaret (Murphy) Herlehy. b. Mont Vernon, Jan. 24, 1873, is a laborer and farmer, residing in South District, m. Sept. 21, 1898, Minnie A. Regan of Malden, Mass. Ch. b. Mont Vernon.
1. Abbie Catherine, b. Nov. 12, 1899.
2. Robert Everett, b. Feb. 8, 1901.
3. Walter Cecil, b. Nov. 9, 1902.

HERRICK.

Josiah Herrick, son of Josiah and Joanna (Dodge) Herrick, b.

Wenham, Mass., Nov. 10, 1733, d. in Mont Vernon in April, 1799. He m. Mary Low of Ipswich, who d. in Oct., 1806, aged 71. They settled in Mont Vernon in the East District about 1781. Children:

1. Mary, d. April 6, 1836, aged 80, unm.
2. Joanna, d. in Milford, unm.
3. Josiah, m. (1) Esther Tarbell, m. (2) Fanny Howard, March 16, 1841. He settled in Antrim and d. there April 8, 1853, leaving no children. He was a soldier in the war for Independence.
4. Lydia, b. April, 1765, m. John Cochran, Jr., of Amherst, Jan. 10, 1803, d. Sept. 23, 1836, 2 children.
5. William, b. Jan. 19, 1767, m. Elizabeth Kilman, settled in Essex, Mass., and d. there.
6. Betsey, b. May 7, 1769, m. Sept. 5, 1795, *Joseph Coggin, Jr., d. Mont Vernon, April 6, 1846, 6 children.
7. Daniel Low, b. Dec. 4, 1771, m. Hannah, dau. of Isaac and Hannah (Cole) Weston, resided in Merrimack, and d. there.
8. *Jonathan, b. Jan. 22, 1774.
9. *Joseph, b. Nov. 3, 1775.
10. Sarah, b. Feb. 28, 1778, m. Ebenezer Weston of Amherst, 3 ch., d. June 22, 1857.
11. Hannah, b. in 1780, d. young.

Joseph Herrick, son of Joseph and Mary (Low) Herrick, b. Wenham, Nov. 3, 1775, m. Mary Cox of Beverly, Mass., April 18, 1805. They settled in Beverly, rem. to Mont Vernon, lived in the East District, was a farmer, rem. to Antrim where he d. Jan. 18, 1833. Children were:

1. Joseph, b. in March, 1806, was m., lived in Antrim, had ch.
2. William Cox, b. in May, 1808, m. May 16, 1833, Sally Russell, lived in Nashua. Had one son, Fred, liquor dealer, Blackstone St., Boston, d. Brooklyn, N. Y.
3. Sarah Batchelder, b. Dec. 23, 1810.
4. Samuel D., b. Mont Vernon, Sept. 22, 1815, m. Dec. 12, 1841, Mary Elizabeth Abbott who was b. June 11, 1822. Lived in Beverly and Amherst, had 5 ch., d. Amherst, May 17, 1901.
5. Josiah, b. Sept. 27, 1818.
6. John, b. 1822, lived in Lyndeboro' and Peterboro', tanner, was m. twice and had ch.
7. Harriet, b. 1825, m. William H. Gilmore of Hillsboro', lived in Hillsboro', Lower Village.

Jonathan Herrick, son of Josiah and Mary (Low) Herrick, b. Wenham, Mass., Jan. 22, 1774, d. in Amherst, Aug. 28, 1858, m. Deborah Colburn of Dracut, Mass. She was b. Jan. 10, 1779, d. Oct. 18, 1860. They resided in Merrimack, Mont Vernon and Amherst. He was one of the selectmen of Mont Vernon several years. Their ch. were:

1. Mary C., b. Nov. 5, 1805, d. in Amherst, Dec. 12, 1871, unm.
2. Nancy, b. Nov. 19, 1810, m. April 7, 1831, Levi J. Secomb, had 2 ch.
3. Fanny C., b. March 27, 1816, m. Dec. 11, 1850, Daniel F. Secomb of Amherst. She d. Sept. 7, 1859.
4. Jonathan, b. June 26, 1822, d. in Francestown, Sept. 7, 1852, unm.

HEYWOOD.

Nathaniel Heywood was prominent in the organization of the northwest parish of Amherst (now Mont Vernon). He d. 1790. His will dated June 29, 1787, was presented for probate April 26, 1790. In it he names his wife, Annie and ch.

1. Sarah, m. William Manning.
2. Mary, m. Timothy Manning.
3. Nathaniel.
4. Abigail.
5. Huldah, m. William Burnam.
6. *Joshua, graduated at Dartmouth College in 1795, ordained and installed minister of Dunstable, Mass., June 5, 1799, d. there Nov. 11, 1814, age 51, m. Lydia French of Boston, Jan. 27, 1800.
7. *William.

Rev. Joshua Heywood was a large man, dark complexioned, dignified and courteous in his demeanor, and respected by all who knew him. Dr. Loring said of him at Dunstable, Sept. 17, 1873, "Of minister here or elsewhere can higher praise be uttered, than of Joshua Heywood, who, recognizing the burdens, which pressed upon his people, declined to avail himself of any statute for his pecuniary advantage, refused to make the stipulation between him and his people, a matter of speculation and appealed to their sense of honor to stand by the contract he had made with them, though it be to his own loss.

William Heywood, son of Nathaniel and Annie Heywood, lived in the South District. He m. Ely Parker. Ch.
1. Amy, b. April 15, 1791, m. Jan. 31, 1812, *Abial Wilkins. She d. Aug. 23, 1872.
2. Lucy, b. July 9, 1795, m. March 6, 1827, John Town of Milford, d. Milford, Feb. 13, 1879, had 5 ch.

HILDRETH.

Edward Hildreth, son of Mrs. Eliza Wheeler, b. Amherst, June 19, 1841, m. (1) Jane, dau. of Nahum and Keziah (Peabody) Bullard of Amherst, Aug. 30, 1864, m. (2) Jan. 1, 1894, Mrs. Isaphine (Jackson) Milliken, b. Bluehill, Me. Since 1868 (1902) he has lived in Mont Vernon. By 1st wife.
1. Albert, b. Mont Vernon, Jan., 1874, lives Sharon, N. H.

HILL.

Timothy Hill m. Judith Sherwin. He lived on the farm lately occupied by W. F. Hadley in the East District. Ch. b. in Mont Vernon probably. The sons were:
1. Ralph.
2. Samuel.
3. *James.
4. Calvin.
5. Mary, m. William Dodge, Nov. 27, 1806.
6. Sarah, dau., m. Alva Wilkins of Mont Vernon.

James Hill, son of Timothy and Judith (Sherwin) Hill, b. Mont Vernon, m. Huldah Peabody of New Boston. He lived on his father's farm in the East District and d. there Jan. 8, 1852, age 61 years, 6 months. She d. Nov. 2, 1854, age 56 years. Ch. b. Mont Vernon.
1. James, b. Jan., 1820, resides Malden, Mass., m. Mrs. Jones of Malden.

2. *Ira, b. Dec. 18, 1821.

3. Samuel Harris, m. a Miss Cram of Lyndeboro', lived and d. in Amherst, was an iron foundry man, had several ch.

4. Deborah J., m. Amos Putnam of Milford, had 5 ch.

5. William, b. 1827, was a merchant and prominent citizen in Tilton, N. H., d. 1891.

6. Mary, b. Sept. 7, 1826, m. *Charles Marvell, Oct. 16, 1851, d. April 29, 1880.

7. Granville, m. Harriet Whittemore, lived in Amherst, had 7 ch.

8. *Timothy B., b. June 22, 1832.

9. Joseph was a merchant associated in business with his brother William, in Tilton, N. H., had 3 ch.

10. Eliza, m. Mr. Mygatt of Nashua, had two sons, one of them, Harry, is a doctor in Franklin, N. H.

11. Hiram, d. Wakefield, Mass., had 4 ch.

12. Levi, unm.

13. Abby, d. unm.

Ira Hill, son of James and Huldah (Peabody) Hill, b. Mont Vernon, Dec. 18, 1821, m. Feb., 1845, Harriet, dau. of David and Delinda (Saunders) Dutton, b. Mont Vernon, May 12, 1826, d. Sept. 6, 1875. He m. (2) July, 1879, Arvilla J. Wilson, b. Weare, N. H., Dec. 3, 1825. He d. March 12, 1899. Ch. b. Mont Vernon.

1. Josephine Estelle, b. Dec. 18, 1847, d. Nov. 9, 1852.

2. Clarence Latimer, b. Aug. 10, 1856, m. Annie F. Raymond of Dunstable, Mass., Sept. 3, 1882, lives in Reed's Ferry, Merrimack, N. H. Cooper. Ch. 1. Flora Estelle, b. Jan. 17, 1888; 2. Lillian Pearl, b. Feb. 6, 1887.

3. Cleon Mortimer, b. Feb., 1863, m. Eva Robinson of Dover, N. H. Ch. b. Mont Vernon. 1. Hazel Maude, b. Feb. 23, 1887, d. Nov. 25, 1896; 2. Chrystabel Florence, b. Aug. 25, 1890.

4. George Edward, b. Sept. 19, 1865, m. Ida Shirley, dau. of Daniel C. and Julia A. (Chickering) Shirley of Amherst. She was b. March 19, 1871. They live in Amherst.

Timothy Barrett Hill, son of James and Huldah (Peabody) Hill, b. Mont Vernon, June 22, 1832, m. Aug. 26, 1862, Janette, dau. of Joel and Lucinda (Averill) Duncklee of Milford. He has resided Amherst, Gardner, Mass., Milford, d. in Amherst, May 27, 1903. Ch. b. Amherst.

1. Minnie B., b. March 14, 1864, m. Frank Boutelle of Milford.

2. Annie L., b. Aug. 20, 1866, m. John G. Boutelle of Pepperell, Mass., one son.

3. Katie, b. July 17, 1870, d. unm., July 29, 1891.

Benjamin Franklin Hill, b. Brookfield, Mass., May, 1822, m. Hannah, dau. of Daniel and Cynthia (Wilkins) Smith. He d. Nov. 5, 1860, age 66. She d. Dec. 1, 1866, age 68. Ch. b. Mont Vernon.

1. Rufus Franklin, d. Lowell, Mass., March 23, 1883, age 58. He m. Sarah Lawrence of Peterboro', 3 ch., viz.: Charles, Susan, Frank.

2. Daniel S., d. Peterboro', Jan. 7, 1867, age 42, left 2 dau., m. (1) Ellen O'Donald of Peterboro', 2 ch., Freeman and Caroline, m. (2) Caroline Stiles of Peterboro'.

3. Maria F., b. Oct. 16, 1829, m. Jan., 1865, Benjamin F. Livingstone, d. Sept. 13, 1880, left 3 dau.

4. Nancy E., b. Sept. 6, 1832, m. Dec., 1847, *Peter F. Pike of Mont Vernon.

William Orledge Hill, b. Meadville, Pa., March 22, 1846, m. Dec., 1879, at Milford, Etta May, dau. of Clinton and Elizabeth (Bennett) May. She was b. Jan. 25, 1863. He purchased the Hartshorn house in the East District, living there several years, leaving here in 1894 for Manchester, supposed to live in Haverhill. He is not living. Ch. b. in Mont Vernon.

1. Harry Orledge, b. Aug. 30, 1880.
2. Arthur Cordell, b. Sept. 19, 1882.
3. Fanny Cordell, b. July 6, 1885.
4. Gilbert Townsend, b. May 1, 1891.

HOLT.

Ebenezer, son of Samuel and Hannah (Farnum) Holt, was b. in Andover, Mass., April 8, 1705, m. Mehitable Stevens, Dec. 4, 1729. About 1750 they removed to Mont Vernon, where she d. May, 1805, aged 97. Their ch. all b. in Andover, were:

1. *Ebenezer, b. Sept. 7, 1730.
2. Mehitable, b. Sept. 3, 1733, m. James Holt, Jan. 2, 1755, d. March 4, 1767.
Twins.
3. Mary, b. June 15, 1737, m. Darius Abbott, had 9 ch.
4. Priscilla, b. June 15, 1737.
Twins.
5. Rachel, b. July 7, 1741, d. July 14, 1747.
6. *Ezekiel, b. July 7, 1741.
7. Reuben Holt, b. June 27, 1744, d. Landgrove, Vt., March 2, 1836, m. Lydia Small, had 6 ch.
8. Hepsibah, b. June 13, 1747, m. William Hartshorn, no ch. She d. Amherst, Jan. 11, 1851, aged 103½ years.

Ebenezer Holt, Jr., son of Ebenezer and Mehitable (Stevens) Holt, b. Andover, Sept. 7, 1730, m Lydia, dau. of Moses and Sarah (Holt) Peabody. She was b. July 5, 1731. They settled on the farm now occupied by W. L. Robinson, in Mont Vernon, where he d. in April, 1805. Ch. b. Mont Vernon.

1. Rebecca, b. Sept. 7, 1752, m. Jonathan Lamson, March 14, 1782, one son.
2. Sarah, b. 1757, m. Moses Peabody, May 25, 1786. She d. Mont Vernon, May 25, 1845, had 2 ch.

Ezekiel Holt, son of Ebenezer and Mehitable (Stevens) Holt, b. Andover, July 7, 1741, m. Mary Stewart, dau. of Samuel Stewart, and sister of David Stewart, who was County Treasurer from 1803 until 1821. She was b. Sept. 2, 1749. Ezekiel Holt was a citizen of Mont Vernon in 1804. Ch.

1. Elizabeth, b. July 8, 1773.
2. Mary, b. Dec. 11, 1775.
3. Sarah, b. Sept. 10, 1780.
4. Ezekiel, b. Aug. 19, 1782.
5. David, b. Feb. 27, 1792.

Stephen D. Holt, b. Andover, Mass., July, 1822, m. Nov. 29, 1849, Joanna Augusta, dau. of Franklin and Mary (Spaulding) Hadley of Lyndeboro'. He d. Lyndeboro', April 25, 1876. Mrs. Hadley removed to Mont Vernon village with her three ch. in fall of 1877. Ch.:

1. Charles Dexter, b. Francestown, Jan. 25, 1851, d. Mont Vernon, Oct. 4, 1881.

2. Frances Augusta, b. Francestown, March 17, 1854, resides Mont Vernon, unm.

3. George Franklin, b. Lyndeboro', Aug. 6, 1856, carpenter, resides Mont Vernon.

HOOPER.

Wallace D. Hooper, son of Nathaniel and Lucy (Carson) Hooper, b. New Boston, Jan. 27, 1838. Mrs. Lucy D. (Carson) Hooper d. Dec. 27, 1888, age 78. He came to Mont Vernon and bought the Fox farm, Jan., 1894. He m. (1) Mary Applebee. He m. (2) Martha Ann, dau. of Alexander and Margaretta (Hopkins) Carson. She was b. Mont Vernon, Feb. 28, 1846, m. May 9, 1878. Ch. by first wife:

1. Nathanial Frank, b. Fort Warren, Boston, Nov. 20, 1868, farmer, res. Mont Vernon, m. 1898, Nettie, dau. of Alexander and Margaretta (Hopkins) Carson. She was b. Mont Vernon, has one dau., Lucy, b. 1898. Ch. Lucy, b. Mont Vernon, March 30, 1898.

Ch. by second wife:

2. Wallace D., b. April 17, 1879, d. July, 1879.

HOPKINS.

James Hopkins, m. (1) Mary Beard. m. (2) Mary Taylor of Hollis, ch. were b. in Mont Vernon.

Ch. by first wife:

1. A dau.

Ch. by second wife:

2. Sarah, m. David Marshall of New Boston, June 6, 1796.

3. *James, b. June 10, 1781.

4. Mary, b. March 15, 1783, d. unm., Feb., 1803.

James Hopkins, Jr., son of James and Mary (Taylor Hopkins, b. Mont Vernon, June 10, 1781, m. Aug. 9, 1804, Azubah Curtis of Lyndeboro'. She d. Sept. 26, 1855, age 74. He m. (2) Mrs. Nancy Gould of Nashua. She d. 1857. He d. Sept. 26, 1862. He lived on the farm now owned by his son-in-law, Alexander Carson, in the South District. Ch. b. in Mont Vernon.

1. David, b. Jan., 1805, m. (1) Mary Gould. She d. Aug. 12, 1870, age 52 years, m. (2) Ede E., dau. Amos and Sarah (Whiting) Phelps. He d. Wilton, Oct. 13, 1888.

2. Mary, b. Jan. 9, 1806, d. May 16, 1867, m. *Noah Hutchinson. Twins.

3. *Jacob, b. March 12, 1809.

4. John W., d. July 29, 1811.

5. James W., b. Feb., 1813, m. 1836, Mary Jane Patch. She was b. Antrim, 1818, d. Mont Vernon, 1863. He d. New Boston, Sept. 10, 1890. They had six ch.—five sons and one dau., Fanny, all b. in Mont Vernon.

6. Sarah, b. 1816, m. *John J. Carson. She d. Nov. 18, 1887, age 71.

7 Olive, b. Feb. 5, 1819, m. Thomas Carr Kidder, had two sons and four daughters, who grew up. She d. in Milford, June 16, 1894.
8. Margaretta, b. Dec. 14, 1822, m. Dec. 23, 1843, *Alexander Carson.
9. Harriet N., b. April 26, 1824, m. *Joseph H. Tarbell, Aug. 23, 1844, res. Mont Vernon.

Jacob Hopkins, son of James and Azubah (Curtis) Hopkins, b. Mont Vernon, March 12, 1809, d. Feb. 24, 1881, was a shoemaker, m. Mary Marhsall of New Boston, who d. Nov. 12, 1840, aged 38. Ch.
1. Sarah A., d. June 7, 1843, d. young.
2. John A., d. Oct. 26, 1854, age 17.

HUMPHREY.

Leander F. Humphrey, son of Franklin and Mary (Lane) Humphrey, b. Barnston, Canada, May 7, 1855, came to Mont Vernon from Manchester in1894, owns and operates the stage route from Milford to Mont Vernon. He m. Sept. 2, 1894, Cora E. Davis, dau. Freeman and Caroline (Ryan) Davis. She was b. Richford, Vt., Feb. 27, 1866. She came to Mont Vernon from Manchester, m. 1894. Ch.
1. Carl Lawrence, b. Jan. 19, 1902.

HUTCHINSON.

Elisha Hutchinson, a Revolutionary soldier, was b. at Middleton, Mass., Dec. 6, 1751, d. at Milford, Oct. 12, 1800, m. Sarah Buxton, Nov. 10, 1772. She was b. at Middleton in 1751, d. Feb., 1828. They settled in that part of Amherst now Milford in 1779. Ch.
1. Andrew, b. Feb. 1, 1775, m. Martha Rayment (or Raymond, sister of George Raymond, who was grandfather of Charles H. Raymond), d. Milford, Oct. 22, 1862.
2. *Jesse, b. Middleton, Feb. 3, 1778.
3. Sarah, m. *William Marvell.

Jesse Hutchinson, son of Elisha and Sarah (Buxton) Hutchinson, b. Feb. 3, 1778, at Middleton, m. Mary, dau. of Andrew Leavitt. She was b. Mont Vernon, July 25, 1785, was m. Aug. 7, 1800, d. Milford, Sept. 20, 1868. He was a farmer, and lived in the North part of Milford on the Hutchinson farm, bought the Col. Burnham place in Milford, and d. there Feb. 16, 1851. Ch. b. in Milford.
1. Jesse, b. Feb. 25, 1802, d. April 11, 1811.
2. David, b. Oct. 11, 1803.
3. *Noah, b. Jan. 26, 1805.
4. Polly or Mary, b. June 7, 1806.
5. Andrew B., b. Aug. 19, 1808.
6. Zephaniah K., b. Jan. 6, 1810.
Twins.
7. Caleb, b. Nov. 25, 1811.
8. Joshua, b. Nov. 25, 1811.
9. Jesse, Jr., b. Sept. 29, 1813.
10. Benjamin Pierce, b. Oct. 3, 1815.
11. Adoniram Judson Joseph, b. March 24, 1817.
12. Sarah Rhoda Jane, b. March 14, 1819.
13. John Wallace, b. Jan. 4, 1821.
14. Asa Burnham, b. March 14, 1823.

NOAH B. HUTCHINSON.

15.   Elizabeth, b. Nov. 14, 1824.

16.   Abigail (Jemina) (Abby), b. Aug. 29, 1829.

Four of these children, three sons and one daughter, Judson, John, Asa and Abby, were the famous Hutchinson singers of the "Tribe of Jesse."

John W. Hutchinson is the only member of the family surviving. He lives at Lynn Mass.

Noah B. Hutchinson, son of Jesse and Mary (Leavitt) Hutchinson, b. Milford, Jan. 26, 1805, moved on to the Odell farm in South Dist. in 1822, now occupied by his son, Appleton, and lived there many years. He d. March 10, 1873. He m. April 5, 1827, Mary, dau. James and Azubah (Curtis Hopkins), of Mont Vernon. She was b. Mont Vernon Jan. 9, 1806, d. May 16, 1867. Ch.

1.   Frances J., b. Milford, May 21, 1828, d. Oct. 25, 1833.

2.   *Andrew Buxton, b. Milford, July 9, 1830

3.   Matthew Bartlett. b. Milford, April 16, 1832, d. unm. March 11, 1895, lived in Mont Vernon.

4.   Aaron Bruce, b. Mont Vernon Aug. 4, 1834, m. Dec. 31, 1868, Ellen, dau. of William W. and Lucinda (Hutchinson) Burns, of Milford. She was b. Aug. 5, 1848, d. Feb. 6, 1898. He lived in Milford, was a mechanic, d. there July 23, 1899.

5.   Ann Jane, b. Mont Vernon May 15, 1836, m. October 16, 1864, Daniel Sargent of Milford.

6   *Lucius Bolles, b. Mont Vernon Jan. 6, 1839.

7.   David Judson, b. Mont Vernon July 21, 1842, m. Oct. 26, 1881, Mary J., dau. Luther B.* and Dorothy (Keyes) Phelps, of that city. Was a broker. Retired. Resides New York City winters and Mont Vernon summers.

8.   Mary Victoria, b. Mont Vernon June 22, 1845, d. South Orange, N. J., May 14, 1864.

9.   Chestina Augusta, b. Mont Vernon Oct. 5, 1847, m. Hazen F. Wooster of Canaan, N. H., resides there, has two sons.

10.   *Henry Appleton, b. Aug. 16, 1850.

Andrew Buxton Hutchinson, son Noah B. and Mary (Hopkins) Hutchinson, b. Milford, July 9, 1830, carpenter, resided South Orange, N. J., d. there June 24, 1890, m. Dec. 5 1857, Ellen T., dau. Rev. David and Jane (Kirkpatrick) Kline, of Glen Gardner, N. J. Ch.

1.   Frank Stuart, b. April 29, 1870, d. Aug. 21, 1871.

2.   Florence K., b. Oct. 20, 1875.

Lucius Bolles Hutchinson, son of Noah B. and Mary (Hopkins) Hutchinson, b. Mont Vernon, Jan. 6, 1839, left here for New York City in 1856, was stock broker there, is now retired, resident of Mont Vernon, m. Jan. 6, 1864, Alice M., dau. Boynton Rollins, of New York City. Ch.

1.   Alice, b. June 22, 1867, m. Mr. Wallace.

2.   Mary, b. Aug. 28, 1871, m. Edw. Wendelstadt.

Henry Appleton Hutchinson, son of Noah B. and Mary (Hopkins) Hutchinson, b. Mont Vernon, Aug. 16, 1850, farmer and lumber dealer, resides on the homestead in South Dist., m. Oct. 14, 1871, Lucy J., dau. Luke and Elizabeth (Langdell) Wilkins, of Mont Vernon. Ch. b. Mont Vernon:

1.   Roy Wilkins, b. Aug. 4, 1872, m. (1) 1893, Katherine V. Welch of

Mont Vernon, one ch., Jean, b. 1894; m.(2) Mable Folsom of Greenville, Me., resides South Framingham, Mass.

2. Maude Lola, b. Oct. 22, 1872, m. May 21, 1896, Charles F. Isola, res. Mont Vernon.

3. Amy Victoria, b. March 28, 1878.

4. Ethelle, b. May 21, 1880.

5. Abby, b. Oct. 9, 1887.

Rodney K. Hutchinson, son of Alfred and Lydia (Foster) Hutchinson. b. Milford, Aug. 7, 1812. Was a carpenter, lived with his father-in-law, John Hartshorn, on a farm, now owned by Maurice Herlihy, in the South Dist., lived in Milford the greater part of his life, d. Milford, Jan. 24, 1890. M. (1) Nov. 12, 1840, Susan E. R., dau. *John and Susannah (Curtis) Hartshorn. She was b. Hancock, Vt., Dec. 9, 1818, d. Milford, Aug. 17, 1853. M. (2) Oct. 6, 1855. Sarepta J., a sister of his first wife, b. Lyndeboro, June 21, 1826, d. Milford, Nov. 2, 1901. Ch. b. Milford. Ch. by first wife:

1. Alfred Alonzo, b. Jan. 7, 1842, carpenter, res. Milford, m. Jan. 6, 1867. Hattie J. Fairfield of Hancock, one ch.

2. Rodney Lorenzo, b. Feb. 14, 1844, d. Aug. 27, 1847.

3. Mary Olivia, b. Oct. 3, 1846, m. March 21, 1888, John C., son John C. and Mary Fifield, res. Candia.

4. Susan Luella, b. Oct. 6, 1849, d. July 27, 1856.

5. Viletta Jane, b. March 2, 1853, d. July 17, 1856.

Ch. by second wife:

6. Susan Viletta, b. Nov., 1857, m. April 28, 1880, George L., son of George and Melinda Y. (Bent) Parker, res. Nashua.

7. John Curtis, b. Dec. 22, 1856, mechanic, res. Milford.

8. Willie Ellsworth, b. Dec. 21, 1861, mechanic, res. Milford, m. Dec. 21, 1890, Florence E., dau. Frank J. and Esther (Fuller) Smith, of Milford.

9. Grace B., b. June 7, 1866, m. Feb. 14, 1893, Charles A., son Charles and Laura A. (Hall) Baker, res. Milford.

HOLLIS.

Benjamin Hollis, shoemaker, came to Mont Vernon, from Braintree, Mass., in 1844, bought the house of Benjamin Nutter, then standing on the site where T. H. Richardson since lived; lived here until 1848, when he sold to Newell D. Foster and removed to Weare, thence to District No. 8, in Amherst, where he d. March 1, 1864. His widow, Abigail Hollis, d. at Weare, April 10, 1885. Their only ch.

Benjamin E., b. Braintree, Mass., November 16, 1833, removed from Amherst to Weare, Nov., 1865, m. Oct., 1887, Mrs. Harriet F., widow Alvah Buxton, keeps tavern in Weare.

INGALLS.

Charles Osmyn Ingalls, b. Hanover, N. H., May 5, 1862. Moved to Mont Vernon in 1894, farmer, owns and occupies the Justin Richardson farm in South Dist., m. Nov. 3, 1898, Hattie May, dau. of Daniel and Mary E. (Twiss) Richardson. She was b. Oct. 26, 1876, in Mont Vernon. Ch.

1. Mary Elizabeth, b. Mont Vernon, April 28, 1899.

LUCIUS B. HUTCHINSON.

IRELAND.

William H. Ireland, b. Park St., Boston, Jan. 28, 1818, m. (1) Sarah A. Stone, b. Cambridge, Mass., Aug. 1, 1820, m. Dec. 5 1839. She d. Newton Centre, Mass., Sept. 21, 1889. He m. (2) Francy Laubner, Oct. 7, 1890. She was b. Aug. 5, 1867, at Falkenstein, Bavaria, Germany. He d. at Newton Centre, February 16, 1900. He came from Newton, Mass., in the early forties to Mont Vernon and lived on a farm in the southeast part of the town. He returned to Newton in 1866. Ch. by first wife:

1. William Ezra, b. Dec. 14, 1840. drowned in Mississippi River, La., July 26, 1864.
2. *James Edward, b. Aug. 16, 1846.
3. *Charles Henry, b. Mont Vernon, Aug. 10, 1850.
4. Albert Frost, b. Mont Vernon, Sept. 12, 1852, m. April 12, 1896, Anna J. Richardson of Winchester, Mass., b. July 27, 1866, two ch. He was a large building contractor of the firm of C. H. and A. F. Ireland. D. Feb. 16, 1903.
5. George W., b. June 3, 1854. d. June 2, 1858.
6. Frank Fremont, b. Mont Vernon, July 8, 1856, drowned at sea, near coast of Japan, Sept. 12, 1885. He was mate of a large merchant vessel.
7. Sarah Anna, b. Mont Vernon, June 3, 1859, m. June 18, 1883, Charles E. Kendall of Winchester, Mass., one son, Frank Dana, b. Aug. 3, 1887.
8. Irving Whitney, b. Mont Vernon, July 24, 1863, m. Dec. 8, 1886, Olive E. Knowles of Newton, has three ch., is a mill owner and resides in Newton Centre. Ch. by second wife b. Newton Centre.
9. Josephine, b. Aug. 10, 1891.
10. Francy, b. March 6, 1893.
11. Frank Fremont, b. June 25, 1895.
12. Wm. Henry, b. 1897.
13. Helen, b. Dec. 16, 1899.

James Edward Ireland, son of William H. and Sarah (Stone) Ireland, b. Mont Vernon, Aug. 16, 1846, m. Oct. 9, 1871. Louisa G. Morgan, b. Bournemouth, Eng. He was a gardener in Milton, taking charge of a gentleman's greenhouses and grounds. Ch.
1. William Edward, b. July 31, 1872.
2. George Albert, b. June 25, 1874.
3. Agnes Freeland, b. March 11, 1876, d. May 30, 1880.
4. Gertrude Harriet, b. Sept. 17, 1880.
5. Frank F., b. Sept. 18, 1886.

Charles Henry Ireland, son of William H. and Sarah (Stone) Ireland, b. Mont Vernon, Aug. 10, 1850, m. Sept. 23, 1879, Eliza J. Kendall of Winchester, Mass., b. Oct. 14, 1858. He is a large building contractor of the firm of C. H. & A. F. Ireland, Newton Centre, Mass. Ch. b. Newton:
1. Marion K., b. July 6, 1880.
2. Lawrence Stone, b. May 1, 1882.
3. Mary Wyman, b. Oct. 9, 1884.
4. Alice Helen, b. June 22, 1886.
5. Ruth Linda, b. Jan. 12, 1889.
6. Wallace Raymond, b. June 13, 1891.
7. Grace Pearl, b. April 12, 1893.

ISOLA.

Charles F. Isola, b. Aug. 9, 1874, came from Pepperell in 1894.   **M.**
May 21, 1876, Maude L., dau. of Henry A. and Lucy (Wilkins) Hutchinson.   She was b. Mont Vernon, Oct. 22, 1873.   He built a costly house
in the South Dist., where he resides.

JAQUITH.

Asa Jaquith, b. 1792, Dec., son of Isaac and Prudence Jaquith, d.
Nashua, May 19, 1871, m. Mary J. Noyes, dau. of Silas Noyes. She was
b. Nov. 1806, d. Jan. 12, 1862.   They resided for some years on the farm
now owned by Charles E. Kendall in the East District.   Ch. b. in Mont
Vernon :
    1.   Asa, b. Aug. 23, 1823, voted here in 1845 and 1846; was a mer-
chant in Nashua, where he d. unm.
    2.   Ebenezer, b. April 4, 1825, m. Ellen J., dau. of William and
Naomi S. (Wilkins) Underwood, of Amherst.   He d. Nashua, May 6,
1870.
    3.   Mary Ann, b. Oct. 26, 1826, m. April 6, 1854, Calvin B. Duscomb,
d. Wilton, July 17, 1856.
    4.   Almina, b. April 10, 1833, unm.
    5.   Emeline b. Sept. 4, 1834, d. Oct. 2, 1854.

Isaac Jacquith, father Asa Jacquith, d. Oct. 2, 1789, aged 47 years.
Prudence, his wife, d. May 8, 1832, aged 84 years.   Prudence their dau.,
and wife of John Bragg, d. May 8, 1827, aged 42 years.   ·

JENKINS.

Micah Jenkins, b. in Andover, Mass., m. Betsey Mooar of Milford
in 1810.   She was b. Jan. 25, 1790, d. in 1825.   They settled on the farm
now occupied by Leander Barker.   Ch. probably b. Mont Vernon :
    1.   Osmore, b. December 3, 1815, watchmaker, resided in Plymouth
and Boston, Mass
    2.   Deborah, b. April 13, 1819, m. Jotham Clark, resided in Granby,
Mass.
    3.   Luther, b. Aug. 27, 1822, m. (1) ———— Putnam of Reading;
m. (2) ———— Putnam of Reading, resided in Reading.

William Patten Jenkins, b. Milton, N. H., April 16, 1811, m. June
16, 1836, Martha S. Rogers of Milton, lived in Hancock some years,
Greenfield seven years and moved to Mont Vernon in 1871, where he d.
June 12, 1884, aged 73.   His wife d. at St. Louis, Mo., January 5, 1889,
aged 73.   Their ch. were :
    1.   Mary Emily, b. April 14, 1837, m. Oct. 28, 1865, Calvin E. Stock-
bridge of Pelham.   She d. March 10, 1872.
    2.   Harriette A., b. May 17, 1839, m. June 30, 1869, Charles S. Free-
born; resides St. Louis.
    3.   Ellen M., b. March 21, 1841, m. Oct. 4, 1865, Milan E. Davis of
Hancock, has five ch.
    4.   Henry S., b. July 16, 1843, supercargo on a steamboat, d. at New
Orleans, Aug. 16, 1874.
    5.   Charles Albert, b. July 21, 1845, m. Sarah L. Heath, January 1,
1867; lives in Milford, farmer.   Ch.

1. Nettie L., b. Hancock, Feb. 7, 1870, m. Nov. 28, 1889, Edgar A. Littlefield of Wells, Me., res. Springfield, Mass.

2. Hattie M., b. Bennington, Aug. 11, 1871, m. May 10, 1897, Frank Davis, res. Springfield, Mass.

6. Elizabeth H., b. Aug. 12, 1847, m. June 4, 73, John M. Holt, lives in Haverhill, Mass.

7. Addie F., b. July 10, 1853, m. Edward S. Foster of Leverett, Mass., Nov. 24, 1875. They lived here some years, returning to Leverett, Mass., in 1885 have four ch.

8. Annie P., b. May 15, 1855, d. St. Louis, unm., Sept. 19, 1889. She was buried at Mont Vernon.

9. William P., b. May 23, 1857, m. Oct. 11, 1882, Vienna, adopted dau. of Cornelius and Aihsah (Heeltine) Green, of Mont Vernon. She was b. Sept. 16, 1861. Ch. b. Mont Vernon:

1. Annie May, b. July 16, 1883.
2. Viola Ida, b. May 18, 1885.
3. Eva Maria, b. Feb. 18, 1888.

JENNISON.

Rev. Edwin Jennison, b. Walpole, N. H., 1805, graduated Dartmouth College 1827, was minister at Walpole from 1831 to 1835. He was minister in Mont Vernon from 1836 until 1841. After a voyage to Europe he settled in Ashburnham, Mass., and was from 1847 to 1849 at Hopkinton, N. H. His frequent ill-health compelled his retirement from pastoral service. He located as a farmer in Alstead, N. H., supplying for a time one of the churches in that town, and from 1852 to 1854 the church in the adjoining town of Langdon, N. H. He d. in Conway, Mass., Dec. 5, 1887, age 82. He m. Miss Mary B. Shannon of Saco, Me., had ch. She d. Nov. 22, 1885, age 75 years.

JOHNSON.

Sardis Johnson, b. Jaffrey, N. H., moved here from Jaffrey, N. H., and lived many years on the farm now owned by George C. Hadley, where he d. April 22, 1865, age 69. His wife, Charlotte (Goodrich) Johnson, d. Aug. 13, 1852, age 62. Their adopted dau., Sophia Goodrich, b. Bedford, Mass., m. Samuel Daland, lived on her father's farm moved to Milford where he d. Sept. 17, 1887, age 76. She d. Milford, May 13, 1899, aged 74.

Warren D. Johnson, b. Boston, March 28, 1843, d. Mont Vernon, Sept. 6, 1893. He was a member of the Fifth N. H. Regt. in Civil War. He came here from Danbury, N. H., in 1870. He was a laborer. He m. Jan. 1, 1870, Martha A. Brown, b. Wilmot, May 30, 1851. Ch. b. Mont Vernon.

1. George F., b. February 10, 1872, m. March 28, 1895, Carrie Avery of Francestown.

2. James William, b. Mont Vernon, Nov. 28, 1876, teamster, res. Mont Vernon.

George T. Johnson, son of Warren D. and Martha A. (Brown) Johnson, b. Springfield, N. H., Feb. 10, 1872, m. (1) Carrie Avery of Francestown, who d. Nov. 1, 1901, m. (2) 1902, Nellie Wyman of Francestown. He resides New Boston, is a laborer. Ch.

1. Carl Avery, b. Francestown, June 23, 1897.
2. Carrie Gladys, b. New Boston, Oct. 26, 1901.

JONES.

Nathan Jones and Elizabeth Coburn were m. in Dracut, Mass., in
October, 1743, moved to the farm southeast of Mont Vernon village(now
owned by Sanborn P. Worthen) in 1760, where he d. Sept. 2, 1799. She
was a dau. of Josiah and Sarah Coburn and was b. June 24, 1724. They
had ten ch., of whom eight reached adult age:
    1. Elizabeth, b. Feb. 10, 1744, m. Matthew Parker of Litchfield June
1763. They were the grandparents of the late Hon. James U. and Nathan
Parker of Manchester.
    2. Thomas, b. March 20, 1746.
    3. *Nathan, b. Feb. 25, 1748.
    4. Rachel, b. Sept. 25, 1750, m. Jan. 2, 1772, Samuel Durant of Not-
tingham, West, now Hudson; d. 1786.
    5. Peter, b. March 1, 1753, d. young.
    6. *Timothy, b. July 27, 1755.
    7. Phinehas, b. Feb. 16, 1758, d. 1799, m. Sarah Hildreth, June 15,
1784, had four ch. After his death she m. *James Smith.
    8. Mary, b. April 21, 1760, m. Levi Kimball of Landgrove, Vt.
    9. *Peter, b. June 16, 1762, in Mont Vernon.
    10. Dolly, b. March 21, 1765, in Mont Vernon, m. ———— Dodge of
New Boston.

Nathan Jones, Jr., son of Nathan and Elizabeth (Coburn) Jones, b.
Dracut, b. Feb. 25, 1748, d. in Mont Vernon, Nov. 6, 1813, m. Esther Butterfield. They settled on what was since known as the McCollom place, in
the north part of Mont Vernon (buildings not standing now). Ch. b.
Mont Vernon were:
    1. Betsey, b. April 25, 1777, m. Feb. 28, 1815, Nathan Fuller of Am-
herst, one dau. She d. Mont Vernon Feb. 8, 1829.
    2. Dorcas, b. March 22, 1779, m. John Farrington.
    3. Dolly, b. Oct. 17, 1781, m. John Trow.
    4. Serviah, b. Oct. 1, 1783, m. *William Lamson.
    5. *Nathan, b. July 10, 1787.
    6. Rhoda, b. May 21, 1790, m. James Pike, May 7, 1812.

Timothy Jones, son of Nathan and Elizabeth (Coburn) Jones, b.
July 27, 1755, d. in Amherst in spring of 1793, m. June 13, 1782, Elizabeth,
dau. of Daniel Kendrick, of Hollis settled on a farm in the westerly part
of Amherst near Mont Vernon line. After his decease his widow m.
Andrew Leavitt of Mont Vernon. She d. May, 1818.   Ch.
    1. John, m. and settled in New Boston, where he d.
    2. Bowen, d. at sea, never m.
    3. Betsey, m. *Edmund Batchelder of Mont Vernon, settled in
Landgrove, Vt., d. in Peru, Vt., July 9, 1869, age 83 years three months.
    4. Rachel, m. Eben Batchelder, June 30, 1811, d. Amherst, Jan. 9,
1863, age 76.
    5. Hannah insane many years, d. at Concord Insane Asylum Aug.
12, 1847, age 55.
    6. Timothy Jones, Jr., b. July 28, 1793, d. June 24, 1882, m. (1)
Sophia, dau. of Reuben Stearns, Dec. 18, 1821. She d. July 7, 1830,
age 26. He m. (2) Hannah, dau. Alexander Carr, lived in Amherst, four
ch. by first wife.

Peter Jones, son of Nathan and Elizabeth (Coburn) Jones, b. Mont Vernon, Sept. 9, 1762, d. Amherst, Oct. 11, 1842 m. Betsey Woodbury, dau. of Peter and Elizabeth (Dodge) Ray Woodbury, June 5, 1787. She was an aunt of Julge Levi Woodbury and was b. Feb. 9, 1770, d. April 3, 1843. They settled on the frm occupied by his father, but removed thence to Amherst in 1825. Ch. b. Mont Vernon:

1. Mahala, b. 1788, m. Feb., 1809, *Mark D. Perkins. She d. June 24, 1843.

2. *Levi, b. Jan. 9, 1790.

3. Hannah, b. Nov. 20, 1793, m. December 1, 1814, *Capt. William Bruce, d. July 18, 1870.

4. Peter W., b. June 19, 1795, d. June 4, 1797.

Nathan Jones, 3rd., son of Nathan, Jr., and Esther (Butterfield) Jones, b. Mont Vernon, July 10, 1787 d. 1820, m. Sarah Bancroft. After his death she removed to Belleville, Canada, West, and d. there 1876, age 87. Her remains were brought to Mont Vernon and buried near those of her husband. Ch. were:

1. Nathan, 4th, lived in Belleville, Can., d. Ontario, April 22, 1892, age 47.

2. Timothy.

3. Adams.

4. Sarah, m. John D. Nutter, resided Montreal.

Col. Levi Jones, son of Peter and Betsey (Woodbury) Jones, b. Mont Vernon, Jan. 9, 1790, d. Amherst, Oct. 11, 1858, m. Sophia, dau. of Thomas Gilmore, June 11, 1815. She was a great-granddaughter of Rev. Daniel Wilkins of Amherst, and a cousin of Gen. John Adams Dix of New York. She was b. Jan. 27, 1796, d. April 13, 1875. They settled on the Jones homestead in Mont Vernon, but removed to Amherst in 1825. First four ch. b. Mont Vernon.

1. Peter Woodbury, b. March 30, 1817, m. Cynthia Marland Nov. 14, 1841. She d. Sept. 20, 1870, age 50. No ch. He d. Amherst, Dec. 6, 1886, age 69.

2. Nancy R., b. February 2, 1819, d. Aug., 1826.

3. Mary L., b. June 13, 1821, m. Elbridge F. Perkins, Jan. 31, 1854, d. Wilton.

4. Abby D., b. April 29, 1823, m. James H. Parmalee of New York, Jan., 1848, d. Manchester, Jan. 24, 1881.

5. George W., b. Feb. 2, 1825, was one of the city officers in Lowell, Mass., d. unm. in Amherst, Sept. 7, 1851.

6. Thomas, b. Feb. 3, 1827, lived in Amherst, d. there unm. Feb. 15, 1900; farmer.

7. Nancy R., b. Jan. 18, 1829, d. Lowell, April 20, 1843.

8. Charles F., b. March 12, 1831, d. Oct. 10, 1840.

9. Harriet N., b. Jan. 15, 1833, m. Dr. William E. Rogers of Westboro, Mass., March 4, 1861. 2 ch.

10. Jane M. W., b. April 3, 1835, m. Oct. 14, 1856, David R. Brant of Brooklyn, N. Y.

11. Amelia Frances, b. May 3, 1837, d. Oct. 10, 1840.

12. Daniel G., b. Aug. 3, 1839, d. Aug., 1840.

George Jones, son of ———, b. New Boston, m. 1831, Sarah, dau. of Samuel and Deborah (Atwood) Battles. He d. 1857, age 55. After

his death his widow lived in Mont Vernon, d. Jan. 2, 1894, age 80 years.
Ch. b. New Boston:

1. *Solomon, b. March 15, 1836.
2. Servilla, murdered at 16 yrs. of age, 1857.
3. *Plumer.
4. Sarah J., d. in infancy.
5. Eliza J., d. in infancy.
6. Rebecca, b. 1849, m. *Woodbury Averill. She d. March 23, 1885.
7. Elnora, b. March 22, 1851, m. 1871, Alonzo Winn of Antrim, res. Mont Vernon.
8. George Frank, b. July 4, 1854, m. April 3, 1889, Marianna, dau. Rufus Harwood of Lowell. She d. Oct. 29, 1895 age 44 yrs.

Bradley Jones, b. New Boston, Aug. 20, 1815, lived on the farm in East Dist. after his m. He built the house. Farm was known as the "Bradley Jones place." He was a carpenter. He d. Oct. 12, 1885, age 70 yrs. M. Mary W., dau. Daniel and Deborah (Battles) Kendall, March 7, 1843. She was b. Mont Vernon, April 30, 1820, d. May 18, 1882. Ch. b. Mont Vernon.

1. Emma Jane, b. March 1, 1848, m. Feb. 4, 1879, George H. Boardman of Lowell, res. Lowell, one ch., Blanche G., b. July 11, 1881.
2. Albert P., b. Aug. 31, 1851, d. Aug. 10, 1880.

Plumer Jones, son of George and Sarah (Battles) Jones, b. New Boston, m. Nancy M., dau. of Trask W. and Hannah W. (Perkins) Averill. She was b. Mont Vernon, Mar. 21, 1838, d. Nov. 16, 1876, lived in house in East Dist., now burnt, on left-hand side, between James Brown's mill and Stiles place. His widow, after his death, m. his brother, Solomon Jones. Ch.

1. Edwin Augustus, b. March 2, 1862, lived in Francestown, now res. Goffstown.

Solomon Jones, son of George and Sarah (Battles) Jones, b. New Boston, March 15, 1836, lived in smaller house on the best farm in East District, moved to Lowell, where he now res., was a farmer, hunter and laborer. M. (1) his brother's, Plumer Jones, widow, Nancy M., dau. Trask W. and Hannah W. (Perkins) Averill. She was b. Mont Vernon, May 21, 1838, d. Nov. 16, 1876. He m. (2) July 7, 1877, Martha Cook, by whom he has ch. Ch. by first wife b. Mont Vernon:

1. Annie Elletta, b. Sept. 10, 1867, m. Oct. 18, 1885, Frank Smith, son of Daniel H. and Mary J. (Holt) Smith, of Mont Vernon, res. Mont Vernon, two ch.
2. Samuel Prescott, b. Jan. 3, 1870.
3. Frank Eugene, b. April 30, 1874, d. Sept. 17, 1878.

KEELER.

Rev. Seth H. Keeler, graduate Middlebury College, Middlebury, Vt., was pastor at Windsor, Vt., So. Berwick, Me., and for many years at Calais, Me. From 1867 to 1875 he was settled at Mont Vernon. Removed to Somerville, Mass., in 1875, where he d. Sept. 26, 1886, aged 86 years. He m. a dau. of Peter Felt, of New Ipswich, where he taught in the Academy, prior to his settlement as a minister. They had three ch., one son and two dau.

KENDALL.

Capt. Thaddeus Kendall, son of Nathan and Rebecca (Colburn) Kendall, b. Amherst, Aug. 2, 1772, m. (1) Catharine, dau. of Robert Fletcher, Esq., Sept. 25, 1800. She d. April 27, 1801, age 22. m (2) Abigail, dau. Dea. Samuel and Abigail (Farwell) Wilkins, of Amherst, Nov. 13, 1808. She was b. April 30, 1773, in Amherst, d. Moble, Ala., Sept. 27, 1853. He settled in Mont Vernon, where he was a merchant several years. While here he was interested in the militia and under his leadership and instruction the North West Parish (or Mont Vernon) Company became one of the best in the old Fifth Regt. Leaving Mont Vernon he settled in Vergennes, Vt. He d. in Burlington, Vt., in 1843. Their ch. were:

1. *George Wilkins, b. Mont Vernon, Aug. 22, 1809.
2. Thaddeus Richmond, b. Mont Vernon. He m. Amanda Hutchins of Alabama, had several ch., two of whom are now living. He was a lawyer in Moble, Ala., also engaged in mercantile business there. He removed to Concord, N. H., thence to Binghamton, N. Y., where he d. Sept. 19, 1882.
3. Catherine, b. Mont Vernon, m. William Rix in 1837. They had several ch., only two now living—two dau. (married) live near her in Royalton, Vt. She lived in Mobile, Ala., until the war of 1860 broke out, when she moved to Vermont. Mr. R. is dead.

George Wilkins Kendall, son of Capt. Thaddeus and Abigail (Wilkins) Kendall, b. Mont Vernon, Aug. 22, 1809, d. on his ranch, "Post Oak Springs," near Boerne Kendall Co., Texas, Oct. 21, 1867. He learned the printer's trade while still a boy, which was a means for making a livelihood. From the age of 14 he earned his own living, pushing out far from civilization, seeking adventure and fortune. In 1837 he founded the New Orleans Picayune, a small, bright newsy sheet, that to this day exists and that for years was a power in the South and in all of its existence only suspended for a short time during the war of 1860-1865. The paper only passed out of the hands of the family after his death, when his share was purchased by a partner, whose heirs still have possession. He served in the Mexican War with great credit. He was a member of Gen. Edmund Worth's staff. After the end of the Mexican War he traveled extensively in Europe. During his travels he married his wife, Adeline de Valcourt, a French lady, and for several years they lived in Paris, France. He came back to America in December, 1855. From that time until 1860 the winters were spent in New Orleans and the summers on a ranch in Texas, where he engaged in raising fine sheep, many of which were imported from France. During the War of 1860 he remained on the Texas ranch, taking but little part in the conflict, the scarcity of men making it difficult to handle his large flocks of sheep, causing the Indians to grow very bold and for years making it dangerous to go about alone or unarmed.

After the war he spent the winters again in New Orleans, the paper showing to a marked degree the interesting articles, editorials and letters from his most versatile pen. In 1866 he made a flying trip to his old home in New Hampshire, visited many of the old-home scenes, and also spent a couple of months in Europe.

During the years he spent on the ranch he busied himself writing a History of the Mexican War and completed it but a few weeks prior to his death, which occurred after a short illness on Oct. 21, 1867, (the manuscript of said history is still in the hands of his heirs).

George W. Kendall was a man of very strong character, a man that stood six feet, with regular features and a most affable manner. He had a keen sense of humor and had, perhaps, the widest range of friends of any man in his community or indeed wherever he might find himself. He was enthusiastically fond of Texas and never tired extolling its opportunities, climate, etc., and was buried in the little cemetery in the town or village of Boerne, in Kendall Co., (named after him) in Texas, the state of his adoption. The printers from his paper erected to his memory a marble monument upon which are inscribed the following words: "He was a poet, journalist, author, and farmer, eminent in all."

Ch. b. France:
1. Georgina, b. 1851, m. a lawyer, Eugene J. Fellowes (a native of New Orleans), son of Thomas and Irene (Panavar) Fellowes, Dec. 15, 1873, at Binghamton, N. Y. Lived in Chicago, Ill. Now resides Spokane, Wash. She is a highly educated woman, speaking several European languages. One son, Kendall Fellowes, b. Chicago, Oct. 14, 1879, served in Spanish-American War, is now engaged in insurance business in San Francisco, Cal.

2. George Williams, b. 1853, d. 1878, unm.
3. Caroline Louise, b. 1854, d. Texas, July 4, 1898, unm.
4. Henry Fletcher, b. 1855, m. 1886, Mary A. Jordan, dau. W. H. (retired colonel 21st. Inf., U. S. A.,) and Mary Adiar, his wife, two ch. He graduated from West Point in 1878. He was promoted a major and assigned to the 12th cavalry. He served in the Spanish-American War, and is now stationed at Ft. Clark, Texas.

Dea. Jacob Kendall, b. Litchfield, 1758, d. Mont Vernon, June 3, 1823, m. June 25, 1782, Sarah, dau. of Jonathan and Mehitable (Holt) Lamson, of Amherst. She was b. March 20, 1761, d. Aug. 10, 1847. They removed from Litchfield to Mont Vernon about 1783 and lived on the farm in the East District, now occupied by Walter Bohonan. Ch. were:
1. *Amos, b. 1792, lived and d. in New Boston, Jan. 12, 1859.
These ch. b. Mont Veronn:
2. Sarah, b. Jan. 17, 1784, m. (1) Aug. 20, 1804, Simeon Flint of Mont Vernon, m. (2) Sept. 16, 1824, Aaron Wilkins of Amherst, d. Sept. 14, 1861.
3. *Jacob, b. April 15, 1785, lived for a time on the farm now owned by Daniel Richardson, had two dau., removed to Nashua and d. there.
4. Elizabeth, b. Aug. 11, 1788.
5. *Jonathan, b. Aug. 11, 1791.
6. *Josiah, b. Jan. 21, 1797, m. Polly Lovett, of Amherst.

Amos Kendall, son of Dea. Jacob and Sarah (Lamson) Kendall, b. 1782, m. an Adams of Londonderry, lived in Mont Vernon and New Boston, where he d. Jan. 12, 1859. Ch.
1. Delilah.
2. Sarah.
3. David.

Jacob Kendall, son of Dea. Jacob and Sarah (Lamson) Kendall, b. Mont Vernon, April 15, 1785, m. Ursula Jacquith, lived some years on the old Dr. Kittredge farm, now occupied by Daniel Richardson, moved to Nashua, where they both d. She d. 1873, age 82. He d. 1855. Ch. were:
1. Louisa, lives Nashua, unm.
2. Mary Ann, m. a Tyler, lived in Wilton.

Jonathan Kendall, son of Dea. Jacob and Sarah (Lamson) Kendall, b. Mont Vernon, Aug. 11, 1791, m. Dec. 7, 1815 Phebe dau. of Nathan and Phebe (Smith) Flint, of Amherst. He lived on his father's farm in the East District. He d. Oct. 24, 1859. She d. May 11, 1881, at Concord. Ch. b. Mont Vernon.

    1. Eliza, m. Benjamin Dodge of New Boston.

    2. Harriet, m. William Coffin of Concord.

    3. Marian, m. Dr. William P. Gambell of Boston, d. at Simeon F. Kendall's.

    4. *Simeon Flint, b. May 29, 1829.

    5. Charles A., m. Mary Hutchinson of Concord, lived Concord, one dau., Anna May.

Josiah Kendall, son of Dea. Jacob and Sarah (Lamson) Kendall, b. Mont Vernon, Jan. 21, 1797, m. Polly Lovett of Amherst. After rearing a family in Mont Vernon he moved to Antrim, lived there some years, moved to Tamworth, where he and his wife d. Ch. b. Mont Vernon.

    1. Elizabeth, d. young.

    2. Stephen Chapin, moved to Antrim in 1849 and engaged in the manufacture of doors, m. Alfreda Jackson of Tamworth, lives in Fitchburg, Mass.

    3. Adoniram J., went to Antrim, m. 1857, Amanda Abbott, went to Nashua in 1857, then to Manchester, where he and his wife d., leaving a son, Frank E.

    4. John L., worked some years for Rev. D. J. G. Davis in Amherst, moved to Antrim, m. 1851, Christiana Lovejoy, enlisted in the army from Antrim, and was lost overboard on the Potomac. Wife and ch. are all dead.

Simeon Flint Kendall, son of Jonathan and Phebe (Flint) Kendall, b. Mont Vernon, May 29, 1829, m. Sept. 20 1849 Mary C. Clark of Derry, b. July 24, 1828. He lived on the homestead, lived in Pennsylvania several years served in the war for the Union, and was wounded, returned to the farm in Mont Vernon, moved to Milford, where he d. Oct. 17, 1895. Ch. b. Mont Vernon.

    1. Frank Elmon, b. Aug. 10, 1850, m. Sarah Armstrong of Amherst, lives in Milford, is of firm of Ordway & Kendall, proprietors Livery Stable.

    2. Charles Edney, b. Nov. 20, 1853, m. Alice K. Dodge of Antrim, four ch., lives Milford, is of firm Kendall & Wilkins grocers and grain merchants.

    3. Edgar Irving, b. April 15, 1858, m. Miss Susan H. Kimball of Milford, Sept. 23, 1896, resides Milford is a lawyer, has one ch.

Daniel Kendall brother of Dea. Jacob Kendall, b. Litchfield, Jan. 18, 1760, d. Mont Vernon, Aug. 17, 1830, m. Sarah dau. Joseph and Patience (Bradford) Lovejoy. She was b. May 6, 1762, d. Aug. 14, 1847. He settled in 1785 on the farm owned afterwards by his son, Daniel, grandson, D. Porter K., and lately owned by his great-grandson, W. H. Kendall, in East Dist. Ch. b. Mont Vernon.

    1. *Daniel, b. Oct. 26, 1789.

    2. Mary, b. June 3, 1792, d. Nov. 3, 1813.

    3. Sarah, b. July 26, 1794, m. *John Battles, d. March 6, 1858.

    4. Nathan, b. 1796, d. Aug., 1798.

    5. Alice, b. Aug. 1, 1800, m. *Reuben K. Batchelder, d. June 26, 1846.

6. Zaccheus Nathan, b. June 2, 1803, d. Johnson. Vt., March 29, 1888.
7. *Ira, b. Jan. 9, 1805, d. March 20, 1863.

Daniel Kendall, son of Daniel and Sarah (Lovejoy) Kendall, b. Mont Vernon, Oct. 26, 1789, lived on his father's farm, d. Aug. 31, 1870, m. Dec. 31 1818, Deborah, dau. Samuel and Deborah (Atwood) Battles, of Mont Vernon. She d. April 24, 1871. Ch. b. Mont Vernon.
1. Mary W., b. April 30, 1820, m. *Bradley Jones of Mont Vernon, March 7, 1843. Two ch. D. May 18, 1882.
Twins :—
2. *Daniel Porter, b. Jan. 3, 1823.
3. Deborah J., b. Jan. 3, 1823, m. Alvin Chase of Milford, Oct. 18, 1855. He d. Aug. 1863. She d. E. Jaffrey, March 25, 1891. One dau., Jennie, b. Milford, May 26, 1857, m. June 28, 1882, at Mont Vernon Wm. Jacquith; has four boys; lives E. Jaffrey, N. H.

Ira Kendall, son of Daniel and Sarah (Lovejoy) Kendall, b. Mont Vernon, Jan. 9, 1805, lived on the farm with his brother, Daniel, d. March 20, 1863, m. May 10, 1832, Cyrene, dau. of Capt. John and Betsey (Batchelder) Batchelder. She was b. Oct. 17, 1803, in Mont Vernon, d. Goffstown, Dec. 16, 1872. Ch. b. Mont Vernon.
1. Emmeline, b. January 26, 1834, lives Goffstown, unm.
2. Cyrene Elizabeth, b. Jan. 14, 1836, lives Goffstown, unm.
3. Ira Kendrick, b. Jan. 26, 1838, m. March 29, 1864, Rebecca Warren of Goffstown, N. H., is a wealthy and prominent furniture manufacturer of Goffstown; has represented the town. Ch. b. Goffstown.
1. Frank Warren, b. October 16, 1866.
2. Annie May, b. Jan. 14, 1869.
3. Lewis B., b. May 25, 1877.
4. Nathan Franklin, b. Dec. 22, 1840, enlisted Co. C, 16th N. H. Regt. Vol., d. Aug. 15, 1863.

Daniel Porter Kendall, b. Mont Vernon, Jan. 3, 1823, settled on his father's farm, was representative in 1876, 1877, d. Aug. 27, 1891, m. May 30, 1850, Susan, dau. Thomas and Nancy (Stevens) Cloutman. She was b. March 13, 1823, d. Jan. 8, 1897. Ch. b. Mont Vernon.
1. Andrew P., d. Sept. 23, 1854, age 3 yrs. 4 mos.
2. Esther Cloutman, b. December 13, 1856, m. Sept. 26, 1882, Alonzo M. Carleton, has several ch., lives Goffstown.
3. William Henry, b. June 10, 1859, m. June 19, 1901, Clara H. Blood of Wilton, is a lumber dealer and resides in Mont Vernon Village; is also deacon of the church.
4. Andrew P., b. June 11, 1861, d. Aug. 25, 1876.
5. M. Susie, b. Feb. 3, 1867, m. April 26, 1898, Arthur Temple, resides Mont Vernon.

Asa Kendall, b. Leominster, Mass., June 10, 1778, m. Oct. 15, 1807, Lydia Adams of Townsend, b. Oct. 15, 1784, and sister of Dr. Daniel and Dea. J. S. Adams of Mont Vernon. Asa Kendall learned the saddler's trade off Ephraim Eager in his native town, and in 1799 succeeded his master in the business, which he carried on successfully until 1814, when he sold out, removed to Mont Vernon, and built the store, which is now part of the "Mont Vernon House," where he traded twenty years. In 1850 he removed to East Concord and resided in the family of his

WILLIAM H. KENDALL.
Deacon from 1891 (still serving, 1905).

son, Henry A., where he d. Dec. 13, 1863. His wife d. March 9, 1873, aged 88. Both were interred in Mont Vernon. Ch. b. Leominster.

1. Augusta, b. June 26, 1808, m. May 31, 1837, George E. Dean, d. June 10, 1855.

2. Henry Adams, b. Aug. 6, 1810, d. at Concord, March 27, 1894; fitted for college at Kimball Union Academy, was ordained pastor of a Trinitarian Church at Dublin, N. H., June 2, 1840, m. May 27, 1844, Harriet G. Appleton of Dublin, N. H. Ch. b. Dublin.

1. *Henry Appleton, b. March 29, 1845.
2. Samuel Adams, b. Dec. 27, 1846.
3. Sarah Harriet, b. East Concord, May 17, 1851.

Mary Ann Kendall, dau. Franklin Kendall, a sea captain, brother Asa Kendall, was b. Dec. 22, 1828. She was reared in family of Asa Kendall from seven years until her m., Aug. 8, 1848, to Wm. B. Richardson of Mont Vernon. She d. Newtonville, Mass., April 11, 1900.

Henry Appleton Kendall, b. Dublin, March 29, 1845, fitted for college at Henniker Academy, graduated at Dartmouth College, 1866, m. June 21, 1870, Frances L., dau. of Dea. William and Hannah (Fornis) Conant. She was b. Mont Vernon, April 1, 1844, d. April 8, 1901. He lives in Somerville, Mass. Ch. b. Somerville.

1. Gertrude Greenwood, b. Oct. 27, 1871.
2. Franklin Conant, b. April 29, 1875.
3. Marian Colby, b. April 5, 1879.
4. Marcella Fornis, b. December 18, 1882.

Mrs. Persis Kendall, mother of Asa Kendall, d. Nov. 15, 1829, aged 75.

KIDDER.

Thomas Karr Kidder, son of Ephraim and Betsey (Boffee) Kidder, born Lyndeborough, June 9, 1817. Was a farmer. Resided here in the forties and fifties in Centre and South District. He moved to Milford, where he d. Dec. 21, 1894. He m. Sept., 1839, Olive, dau. James and Azubah (Curtis) Hopkins, b. Mont Vernon, Feb. 15, 1819, d. Milford, June 16, 1894. Ch.

1. Hattie Frances, b. Milford, Dec. 22, 1841, m. April 16, 1863, Charles E., son of Nathaniel and Susan (Duncklee) Stone, res. Milford.

2. Newell Porter, b. Lyndeborough, Sept. 18, 1843, is a cooper and res. in Long Lake, Minn.

3. Abbie Jane, b. Mont Vernon, Oct. 12, 1846, m. April, 1865, Charles G. Burns of Milford, d. Jan. 20, 1866.

4. Mary Ann, b. Milford, June 6, 1848, d. Milford, March 25, 1868.

5. Eliza Ella, b. Mont Vernon, June 7, 1851, m. April, 1871, Lorenzo Cutter, of Milford, and res. in Webster, Mass.

6. Charles, b. in Lyndeborough, Sept. 6, 1856, is a laborer, res. in Brookline.

William L. Kidder, b. Billerica, Mass, April 13, 1775. m. Nov. 18, 1798, Nabby Jenkins of Andover, settled in Mont Vernon. Ch.

1. William Lambert, b. July 4, 1800.
2. Nancy, m. 1834, Amos Batchelder, d. in Goffstown.
3. Mahala, m. (1) Partridge; m. (2) Ambrose Smith, 1833, d. in Goffstown.

4. Francis, m. Susan Richardson, Aug. 19, 1830, d. Aug. 19, 1830, in Mont Vernon.

5. Charles, m. ——— Gowing, lived in North Reading, Mass.

William Lambert Kidder, Jr., b. July 4, 1800, d. in Amherst, Sept. 29, 1860, m. Mary Jane, dau. Parker Richardson of Mont Vernon, April 19, 1806, d. Amherst, August 27, 1880. He lived in Mont Vernon several years. Ch.

1. Ann Mary, b. April 28, 1827, m. June 14, 1857, Joseph F. Johnson, who d. Ship Island, May 27, 1862, was in the 8th N. H. Regt..

2. Mary Jane, b. March 10, 1836, d. April 9, 1836.

3. William Henry, b. June 22, 1837, m. Abby Burse of Shapleigh, Me., Nov. 26, 1868, machinst; res. Great Falls.

4. Andrew Jackson, b. May 23, 1840, m. Katy Greenleaf; farmer, res. in Hudson.

5. Emma Caroline, b. August 31, 1842, m. (1) W. H. Smith, Aug. 24, 1860; m. (2) ——— Reilly; m. (3) Eli A. Sawtelle; res. Amherst.

6. Alfred, b. April 22, 1847, d. at Providence, R. I., unm. Aug. 17, 1875.

John Kidder, b. Hudson, N. H., came to Mont Vernon from Milford, m. Eliza Wilkins of Antrim. He removed to Nashua, thence to Sacramento, Cal., where he d.

KIMBALL.

Porter Kimball came from Mass., kept tavern in village several years, was representative in 1836, was postmaster 1823, moved to Lowell, m. (1) Mary, dau. Jonathan and Mary Davis of Westford, Mass. She d. Feb. 26, 1820, aged 37 years. He m. (2) Fanny, dau. Dr. Zephaniah and Elizabeth (Stickney) Kittredge. She d. Sept. 16, 1821, age 22 yrs. Ch. by first wife buried Mont Vernon.

1. Son, d. Sept. 22, 1812.

2. ———

3. Jonathan, d. Dec. 12, 1815, aged 9 days.

4. Porter, d. Feb. 16, 1817, aged 20 days.

5. Porter, d. April 16, 1818, aged 9 weeks, 3 days.

6. John, d. June 20, 1819, aged 4 months.

KINGSBURY.

Rev. Nathaniel Kingsbury was ordained pastor here Nov. 8, 1823, was dismissed April 6, 1836. He was b. in Coventry, Conn., was a graduate of Amherst College. He removed to Wisconsin, where he d. at Prairieville, July 12, 1843, aged 48. His ministry here was prosperous, there being two great revivals, one in 1828, the other in 1831. He m. a Miss Dow of Coventry, Conn., and had several ch. Ch. buried Mont Vernon.

1. Mary F., d. June 29, 1833, aged 4 years.

2. Dwight L., d. July 15, 1833, aged 8 months.

3. Joseph, d. April 15, 1834, aged 8 months.

KINSON.

George Kinson, son of Ebenezer Kinson, b. Mont Vernon, April 1, 1800, d. Amherst, Oct. 2, 1867, m. Dec. 5, 1825, Martha M. Walker, sister

George Walker, Sr., of Amherst. She was b. New Ipswich, Jan. 20, 1805. They settled in Amherst in 1830, where he carried on the blacksmithing business, and was widely known as a skillful workman. He left six ch. His sister, Mary Kinson, b. Mont Vernon, m. Feb. 20, 1812, Luther, son of Simeon and Catherine (Wyman) Blanchard of Milford, d. Milford, Feb. 19, 1853. Had nine ch.

KITTREDGE.

The first we learn of the Kittredges coming to this country was in 1660, when Capt. John Kittredge fled from England to America. Capt. K. was in charge of a ship, which plied from England to some foreign port, and being of a surgical turn of mind, studied the medical receipts carefully. The tradition is that he began experimenting by breaking animals' limbs, then setting them, seeing how fast he could get them to heal. One of his men broke an arm and the captain set it. Soon after this another man broke a leg and asked the captain to set it. The captain said he would "if he would take a room and place himself entirely in his care," which he did. He became very successful. It became known to the authorities and as the laws were very stringent at that time, allowing no one to practice without a medical diploma, it became necessary for him to leave England. He came to this country and settled in Billerica, Mass., Sept. 25, 1660. The name was formerly spelled Keteredge. He m. Nov. 25, 1664, Mary Littlefield. He d. Oct. 18, 1676. He had five ch., all sons.

Solomon Kittredge, fifth generation from Capt. John Kittredge (Capt. John, 1; John, 2; John, 3; John, 4; Solomon, 5) b. Billerica, Mass., June 9, 1736, m. Tabitha Ingalls of Andover, May 14, 1755. They settled in Mont Vernon about 1766. He d. Aug. 24, 1792. She d. May 8, 1794, age 59 years, 1 month, 14 days. He was a blacksmith and a prominent man in the parish. He was in the French and Indian War. Ch.

    1. *Solomon, b. 1755, Aug. 3.
    2. *Zephaniah, b. Aug. 24, 1757.
    3. Tabitha, b. July 28, 1758, m. Benjamin Sawyer, settled in Nelson, N. H.
    4. *Josiah, b. July 26, 1761.
    5. Phebe, b. June 5, 1763, m. Aaron Townsend.
    6. *Stephen, b. June 27, 1765.
    7. Lydia, b. Aug. 29, 1767, in Mont Vernon, m. Joshua Kittredge, Nov. 29, 1787.

These ch. b. Mont Vernon:
    8. *Ingalls, b. Dec. 10, 1769.
    9. Betsey, b. Sept. 16, 1771, m. ———— Wheeler of Nelson, d. Nov. 9, 1865, age 94. She was the mother of the late Gilman Wheeler of Milford.
    10. Peter, b. Sept. 25, 1773.
    11. Asa, settled in Weare in 1803, was a physician, had five dau.
    12. Sally, b. April 19, 1779, m. Abial Stickney of Tewksbury, Mass., d. Aug. 28, 1847.

Solomon Kittredge, son of Solomon and Tabitha (Ingalls) Kittredge, b. Tewksbury, Aug. 3, 1755, m. (1) Anna Kittredge, Feb., 1777, by whom he had eleven ch. M. (2) Betsey Holt, April 13, 1815. He came to Mont Vernon with his parents, was a Revolutionary soldier, d. Mont Vernon, Oct. 22, 1845, age 90. Ch. b. Mont Vernon.

1.   Solomon, b. Sept. 28, 1778.
2.   Anna, b. March 13, 1780.
3.   Lucy, b. Jan. 25, 1783.
4.   Thomas, b. March 25, 1785.
5.   *Josiah, b. Feb. 26, 1787.
6.   Jeremiah, b. Jan. 26, 1789.
7.   Harriet, b. July 13, 1791.
8.   Hezekiah, b. Jan. 25, 1793.
9.   *Zephaniah, b. April 15, 1795.
10. Lucy, b. Feb. 8, 1797, m. Mr. Farrar, April, 1818.
11   Betsey, b. July 15, 1799, m. John Carter, Aug., 1818.

Dr. Zephaniah Kittredge, son of Solomon and Tabitha (Ingalls) Kittredge, b. Billerica, Mass., Aug. 24, 1757, m. Elizabeth Stickney of Tewksbury, Mass. She d. Mont Vernon Aug. 6, 1851, aged 90. He was long and favorably known as a skillful surgeon and physician. During his professional career he lived on the farm now owned by Daniel Richardson. He d. Aug. 17, 1843. Ch. b. Mont Vernon.

1.   Betsey, b. May 18, 1782, d. Aug. 5, 1786.
2.   Abigail or Nabby, b. March 22, 1784, m. June 28, 1804, *Jesse Smith. She d. May 7, 1866.
3.   *Zephaniah, b. Sept. 15, 1785.
4.   Betsey, d. March 5, 1799, age 11 years.
5.   Nancy, b. 1790, m. March, 1808, Uriah Wilkins, son Aaron and Lydia (Smith) Wilkins, d. Howe, Vt., Jan. 10, 1832.
6.   Fanny, m. Porter Kimball of Mont Vernon. She d. Sept. 16, 1821, age 22 years.

Josiah Kittredge, son of Solomon and Tabitha(Ingalls) Kittredge, b. July 6, 1761, came here with his parents, lived on the old poor farm, now owned by Edward Hildreth, which he owned and occupied many years, m. Oct. 13, 1792, Mary Baker. She d. Sept. 16, 1828, age 66 years, 3 months, 17 days. He d. May 23, 1850. Ch. b. Mont Vernon.

1.   *Josiah, b. Oct. 15, 1793.
2.   *Timothy, b. May 15, 1795.
3.   Lovey, b. Jan. 28, 1797.
4.   Alvah, b. May 15, 1798, lived Boston Highlands, ch. George went to Bombay; another son, Rev. Abbott E. Kittredge, pastor Madison Ave. Church, New York City, had three dau.
5.   Solomon, b. March 13, 1801, a graduate of Dartmouth College, was a minister; settled in Indiana.
6.   Mary, b. Dec. 17, 1803, m. Sept. 27, 1827, Rev. Ephraim Clark of Peacham, Vt. They went as missionairies to the Sandwich Islands; had ch.
7.   *Charles B., b. July 4, 1806, clergyman at Groton and Westboro, Mass., graduated at Dartmouth College and Andover Theological Sem.; m. Miss Brigham, d. Nov. 25, 1884.

Dr. Stephen Kittredge, son Solomon and Tabitha (Ingalls) Kittredge, b. Tewksbury, Mass., June 27, 1765, m. Mehitable Russell, Nov. 27, 1787. On the day of marriage they went to Francestown to reside moved to Hancock, Oct., 1790, where he d. Otc. 6, 1806. His widow m. (2) Daniel Bickford in 1811, and removed to Sedgewick, Me. Dr. K. was a successful physician and highly respected in Hancock. He had 11 ch. His eldest dau. Gratia m. Dr. Peter Tuttle his successor in Hancock, Sept. 9, 1808.

Dr. Ingalls Kittredge, son Solomon and Tabitha (Ingalls) Kittredge, b. Mont Vernon, Dec. 10, 1769, studied medicine with his elder brother, Zephaniah, first settled in Townsend, Mass., moved to Beverly in 1804, m. (1) Sarah, only dau. Jonathan and Mercy (Lovett) Conant. She was baptized June 3, 1770, d. Beverly, Oct. 7, 1833. He m. (2) Lydia Smith. He d. at Beverly. He owned the farm and estate for several years which he sold to Capt. Timothy Kittredge in 1837, which is now owned by the heirs of Dr. C. M. Kittredge in South Dist. Their second son, Dr. Ingalls Kittredge, b. Townsend, Mass., June 30, 1798, prepared for college at Phillips Academy, Andover, graduated at Dartmouth College, 1820, and at Harvard Medical College 1823, settled in Beverly, m. Sept. 22, 1824, Augusta Smith, who d. Jan. 12, 1871. He d. at Beverly, Feb. 14, 1867. "He was a strong anti-slavery man always ready with his purse to aid the cause as well as to assist refugee slaves. George Latimer and Fred Douglas ex slaves, were aided by him and introduced to Beverly audiences. He holds an eminent place in Beverly's history." He had seven dau. The eldest m. Charles W. Gallonpe and had two dau. Another m. Edward Leech Giddings of the banking firm of Tower, Giddings & Co., Boston.

Dea. Josiah Kittredge, son of Solomon and Anna (Kittredge) Kittredge, b. Mont Vernon, Feb. 26, 1787. He operated his uncle, Dr. Ingalls Kittredge's, farm many years. m. (1) Dec. 24, 1812, Hannah Mace. She was b. June 15, 1793, d. May 9, 1828. M. (2) Nancy Cochoran of Amherst, Dec. 16, 1828. She was b. Aug. 16, 1798, d. Feb. 19, 1830, age 31 years 11 mos. He m. (3) Sept. 2, 1830, Relief, dau. Capt. John and Betsey (Batchelder) Batchelder. She was b. Mont Vernon, Dec. 16, 1796, d. July 19, 1868. He d. Aug. 7, 1836, aged 49. Ch. b. Mont Vernon.

By first wife:

1. Hannah, b. Sept. 28, 1815, d. young.

2. Mary Ann, b. Nov. 8, 1818, m. Frank Lewis of Haverhill, Mass., had several ch., lived in Haverhill Mass.

3. Franklin F., b. Sept. 28, 1820, m. Miss Richardson of Pelham, served in the Union Army in the War for the Union and d. in Iowa. One dau.

4. Ingalls, b. Dec. 24, 1822, d. young.

5. Elizabeth, b. Nov. 27, 1824, m. Oct. 1, 1844, Benjamin Perry of Stoneham, Mass., lives Stoneham, has three sons, the eldest of whom Walter S. Perry has been professor drawing, Pratt Institute, Brooklyn, N. Y., many years.

6. Charles, b. July 31, 1827, d. July 15, 1828.

Ch. by second wife:

7. *Charles Alfred, b. Aug. 24, 1829.

Ch. by third wife:

8. Nancy Maria, b. March 9, 1832, m. March 18, 1854, *Samuel N. Stevens.

9. Harriet E., b. Sept. 22, 1834, unm., resides Stoneham, with her sister, Mrs. Perry.

Zephaniah Kittredge, son Solomon and Anna (Kittredge) Kittredge, b. Mont Vernon, April 15, 1795, m. Nancy Manning. He lived on the farm in the North District, now occupied by his son, Henry J. Kittredge. He d. Sept. 20, 1876, age 81 years, 6 mos. She d. March 26, 1868, age 68 years, 9 mos. Ch. b. Mont Vernon.

1.   Nancy Jane, b. Aug. 15, 1821, m. Jan. 1, 1849, *Albert D. Manning.   She d. Dec. 18, 1897.

2.   Eliza, d. Aug. 31, 1845, age 24.

3.   Lucy Maria, d. Lowell, May 22, 1895, age 68, unm.   Burial at Mont Vernon.

4.   Pamelia J., m. Charles E. Jackson of Tamworth, N. H., lives in Antrim, has three ch.

5.   *Henry J., b. March 1, 1830.

6.   *George W., b. Aug. 16, 1836, d. Nov. 1, 1869, age 33 years, 2 months, 16 days, m. ———— Flint, dau. John G. Flint of Antrim; lived Antrim.

7.   Sarah Frances.   Lived in Lowell, d. there Feb. 27, 1903, age 60 years, 11 months.

Zephaniah Kittredge, son of Dr. Zephaniah and Elizabeth (Stickney) Kittredge, b. Mont Vernon, Sept. 15, 1785; m. Oct. 26, 1809, Mary, dau. of Noah and Mary (Butterfield) Wheeler of Hancock (aunt of Charles James Fox of Nashua).   She was b. Hancock, Feb. 1, 1788, d. Feb. 25, 1880.   He d. Aug. 3, 1873.   He was a prominent and valuable citizen, was selectman five years, moderator five years, and representative in 1843. Ch. b. Mont Vernon.

1.   Mary, b. Sept. 7, 1810, m. April 14, 1846, Amaziah Wood of Francestown, lived Francestown; d. there Oct. 27, 1879; left two ch.

2.   *Franklin Otis, b. Nov. 28, 1813.

3.   *Zephaniah, b. July 18, 1815.

4.   Charles K., b. April 11, 1817, d. Sept. 26, 1819.

5.   Sarah Fox, b. Sept. 4, 1820; educated Literary and Scientific Institution, Hancock; taught in Hancock, Mont Vernon, New Ipswich, Charlestown, Mass., and St. Louis; m. Eleazer Block of St. Louis, who d. in 1865, had one dau., who m. T. A. Meysenburg of St. Louis.

6.   Elizabeth, b. Oct. 10, 1823, d. unm., Jan. 16, 1864.

7.   Abbie, b. April 3, 1827, m. April 27, 1849, Eben C. Batchelder of Milford, had six children, of whom one is living; res. Milford.

Dr. Josiah Kittredge, son of Josiah and Mary (Baker) Kittredge, b. Mont Vernon, Oct. 15, 1793; practised in Pembroke, Concord and Nashua, N. H., and Boston, moved to Glastonberry, Conn., where he d. October 29, 1872.   M. (1) Mary Blanchard, dau. David and Susannah (Lovejoy) Stewart of Amherst.   She was b. there Feb. 20, 1803, d. Pembroke, N. H.   He m. (2) Sarah Whiting French of Bedford, N. H.   M. (3) Sarah Baylies Brigham of Grafton, Mass., May 7, 1844.   Ch. by first wife:

1.   Mary Clark, b. Dec. 8, 1827.

Ch. by second wife:

2.   Charles S., b. Jan. 6, 1833, in Pembroke, m. Maria Chase of Haverhill, Mass., Oct. 20, 1864; resides Santa Barbara, Cal., has four ch.

3.   Sarah French, b. Nov. 15, 1834.

4.   Josiah Edward, b. Oct. 12, 1836, is a clergyman at Geneseo, N. Y., also a doctor of divinity, m. June 12, 1871, Emma McNair of Groveland, Mass., has four ch.

Capt. Timothy Kittredge, son of Josiah and Mary (Baker) Kittredge, b. Mont Vernon, May 15, 1795, m. Frances Marsh of Sharon, Vt.   She d. Aug. 28, 1870, age 62.   He d. Feb. 10, 1870.   He lived on his father's farm, afterwards sold it to the town for a poor farm (now owned and

FRANKLIN OTIS KITTREDGE.

occupied by Edw. Hildreth) and bought his uncle's, Dr. Ingalls Kittredge, farm, now owned by the estate of his son, the late Dr. C. M. Kittredge. He was a laborious and thrifty farmer. Ch. b. Mont Vernon

1. Albert B., d. July 21, 1835, aged three years, nine mos.
2. Mary Emeline, b. July 25, 1834, m. William Stearns of Amherst, Mass., a son of Pres. William Stearns of Amherst College; had several ch., one of their sons, Alfred E. Stearns, is principal Phillips Academy, Andover, Mass. She resides Amherst, Mass.
3. Maria Francis, d. Feb. 20, 1840, aged three years, six months.
4. *Charles Marsh, b. April 30, 1838.
5. George Dimick, fitted for college at Mont Vernon, graduated at Amherst College 1865, resided afterwards at New York City and Fishkill-on-the-Hudson. d. Andover, Mass., March 6, 1877, age 36. Interred at Mont Vernon.
6. Frances Adelia, b. Feb. 15, 1844, m. May 6, 1867, *Dr. Cecil F. P. Bancroft, d. Andover, Mass., March 29, 1898.
7. Maria Theresa, b. Dec. 1, 1850, teacher, res unm. Fishkill-on-Hudson, N. Y.

Charles Alfred Kittredge, son Dea. Josiah and Nancy (Cochran) Kittredge, b. Mont Vernon, Aug. 24, 1829, d. Jan. 7, 1899; m. May 18, 1853, Maria E. Chase of Lowell. She was b. May 29, 1829. He spent the greater part of his life in Lowell, Concord, Nashua, in which places he was grocer and meat man. He represented Nashua in the Legislature. A worthy and excellent man. Ch.

1. Charles Warren, b. June 3 1854. d. infancy, aged 10 weeks.
2. Adelaide Maria, b. May 4, 1856 is a physician, unm.
3. Frank E., b. Concord, N. H., May 18, 1862, m. December 21, 1887, Lizzie M. Coombs of Nashua, is a physician in Nashua.
4. Frederic Lincoln, b. Jan. 18, 1865, m. Oct. 24, 1893, Marian Nevens of Rochester, N. Y.; lives in Rochester, N. Y.

Henry J. Kittredge, son of Zephaniah and Nancy (Manning) Kittredge, b. Mont Vernon, March 1, 1830. M. (1) Mary Jane Chapman She d. April, 1861. M (2) Jane Murray. April 21, 1862. She was b. Oct. 6, 1839, at Shimogue, N. B.

Ch. by second wife b. Mont Vernon.

1. Ida E., b. Jan. 19, 1864, bookkeeper in Nashua.
2. Harriet, b. July 5, 1871, m. April 27, 1892. *Harry G. Blood of Mont Vernon; res. Mont Vernon.

Franklin Otis Kittredge, son Zephaniah and Mary (Wheeler) Kittredge, b. Mont Vernon, Nov. 28, 1813, d. March 20, 1902. For extended description see chapter on "Prominent Men" in Manuscript History. He m. Nov. 13, 1838, Mary Ann, dau. of David and Delinda (Saunders) Durton. She was b. Oct. 5, 1814, in Mont Vernon, d. July 31, 1902. Ch. b. Mont Vernon.

1. Charles Franklin, b. Feb. 24, 1841, graduated Dartmouth College, 1861, studied law with City Solicitor John P. Healey, Boston; Representative from Mont Vernon, 1867; is now a lawyer with a lucrative practice in Boston; m. Sept. 24, 1872, Adelaide F. Lee, dau. of David and Mary (King) Lee, of Barre, Mass. Ch.

1. Mabel Lee, b. Jan. 8, 1874, m. Charles Dunn of Boston, has one ch.
2. Florence Parmenter, b. March 12, 1876.
3. Louise Pierce, b. April 1, 1878.

4.   Charles Lee, b. May 24, 1883, d. Jan. 26, 1896.
(2.)   Laureta E., b. June 23, 1843, m. Butler H. Phillips, res. Mont Vernon.

Zephaniah Kittredge, son of Zephaniah and Mary (Wheeler) Kittredge, b. Mont Vernon, July 18, 1815; d. Tyngsboro, Mass., July 3, 1889. M. (1) March 19, 1840, Caroline McIntire of Lyndeboro'. She d. Lowell, Mass., Aug. 4, 1878. He m. (2) Caroline F. Tapley of Lowell, Feb. 5, 1885. Ch. b. Mont Vernon.
1.   Ellen J., b. Jan. 24, 1841, m. April 10, 1865 (1), John F. Drury of Columbus, Ohio, by whom she had one son, William R. Drury. She m. (2) Nov. 27, 1884, Oranius W. Burnham. They reside in Waltham, Mass.
2.   Darwin E., b. Jan. 15, 1846, m. Oct. 29, 1878, Amelia F. Filley. Mr. K. is in the boot and shoe business at Rochetser, N. Y. Ch. b. New Hampshire. Joseph P., b. Aug. 2, 1879; Frances, b. Sept. 12, 1881; Mary, b. Jan. 2, 1884.
3.   Harvey G., b. May 28, 1849, m. (1) June 15, 1870, Abbie S. Maxfield of Chester, Vt. They had one son, Arthur M., who d. infancy. She d. Lowell, Mass., Nov. 17, 1872. He m. (2) Feb. 2, 1875, Julia A. Spalding of Chester, Vt.; had two sons, Harry J. and Phillip H., both d. in infancy. He is a dentist in Waltham, Mass.
4.   Adna B., b. Oct. 31, 1851, is unm., is in the boot and shoe business at El Paso, Texas.

Dr. Charles Marsh Kittredge, b. Mont Vernon, April 30, 1838, d. Mont Vernon, Aug. 19, 1896; fitted for college at Appleton Academy, graduated at Amherst College 1862, entered the army in Sept., 1862, resigned his commission as lieutenant in the 13th N. H. Regt. in Nov., 1863; studied medicine with Dr. Edward Aiken of Amherst and at Hartford Retreat for the Insane, graduated Harvard Medical College in 1866; located Fishkill-on-the-Hudson in 1870, m. Dec. 5, 1869, Marcella Eliza, dau. Dea. William and Hannah (Fornis) Conant. She was b. Mont Vernon, Dec. 3, 1845, d. Aug. 4, 1892, at Fishkill. Ch. b. Fishkill-on-the-Hudson.
1.   William C., b. Nov. 28, 1870; d. Feb. 11, 1887.
2.   Charles Albert, b. April 26, 1872, a physician.
3.   Edward Walter, b. Oct. 2, 1873, d. July 29, 1874.
4.   Aida, b. Dec. 5, 1876, m. a Abbe.
5.   Harry Marsh, b. May 25, 1878.
6.   George Dimick, b. March 2, 1886.

KENNEDY.

Michael Kennedy, servant and coachman, came here from Boston and lived with Mr. Henry Bishop on Joseph Conant farm, in the forties and fifties, several years. He returned to Boston, where he d. He was a man of property, which he left by will to the Catholic Church.

La FOREST.

Samuel Otis La Forest, of Spanish origin, lived here in the fifties. He was a mechanic. He built the foundation and main part of A. W. Bragg's house, and lived there. He moved to Boston, served in the 47th Mass. Regt. in Civil War. He m. Mary Harrington. She d. March 4, 1885, age 67. They had several ch.

CHARLES M. KITTREDGE, M.D.

LEACH.

Capt. Lebbeus Leach came from Bridgewater, Mass., was a retired shipmaster, lived several years in the Campbell house, moved away about 1875. He d. Newtonville, Mass., May 25, 1884, aged 85 years. He m. Mrs. Elizabeth Wheelwright, second wife (sister of James Bruce). Ch.

1. John B., m. a Miss Bellows of Pepperell, Mass., lived in Mont Vernon several years. One son, Albert, who attended McCollom Institute.

2. Mary, m a ———— Loring of California.

3. Lebbeus.

LAMSON.

Samuel Lamson, b. Reading, Mass., Jan. 8, 1701. In company with Samuel Walton he settled on the Bryant Melendly place, a mile south of Amherst Village. Lamson afterwards removed to Mont Vernon, where he lived 25 years. In 1765 he removed to Billerica, Mass., where he d. about 1770. He m. Abigail Bryant, July 3, 1722.

1. Abigail, b. Feb. 12, 1723, m. Joseph Ellenwood.

2. Samuel, b. Oct. 24, 1724, m. Rebecca Crosby, Nov. 6, 1770.

3. *Jonathan, b. Sept. 29, 1726.

4. Rebecca, b. March 25, 1733.

5. Sarah, b. 1739, said to have been the first child b. of English parents in Amherst, m. James Gage of Amherst, had 10 ch.

Jonathan Lamson, son of Samuel and Abigail (Bryant) Lamson, b. Reading, Mass., Sept. 29, 1726, d. Mont Vernon, Dec., 1815; m. Mehitable Holt. She d. Feb. 16, 1826, age 92. Ch. probably b. Mont Vernon.

1. Mehitable, b. March 25, 1755, d. unm. in Nashua, April 18, 1844.

2. *Jonathan, b. Aug. 10, 1756.

3. Ebenezer, b. Aug. 20, 1759, d. June. 1760.

4. Sarah, b. March 20, 1761, m. June 25, 1782. *Dea. Jacob Kendall; d. Aug. 10, 1847.

5. Phebe, b. Jan. 9, 1763, d. Feb., 1773.

6. Elizabeth, b. Nov. 17, 1767.

7. Ebenezer, b. July 10, 1769, d. Jan. 18, 1770.

8. *John, b. March 10, 1771.

9. Jesse, b. Oct. 17, 1773.

Jonathan Lamson, son Jonathan and Mehitable (Holt) Lamson, b. Mont Vernon, Aug. 10, 1756, m. March 14, 1782, Rebecca, dau. Ebenezer and Lydia (Peabody) Holt. She was b. Sept. 7, 1752. He served in the War for Independence. Ch.

Ebenezer H. b. Dec. 23, 1784, m. July 10, 1811, Phebe, dau. Israel and Susanna (Farnum) Farnum. She was b. March 31, 1788.

John Lamson, son of Jonathan and Mehitable (Holt) Lamson, b. Mont Vernon, March 10, 1771, d. Mont Vernon, Oct. 12, 1841, m. Catherine Harris. She was b. Jan. 27, 1771, d. Dec. 10, 1853. Ch. b Mont Vernon.

1. Catherine, b. April 30, 1798, d. unm. at Groton, Mass., Feb. 26, 1884.

2. Hannah, b. Jan. 19, 1800, d. unm. Feb. 11, 1873.

3. Mehitable, b. Aug. 25, 1802; d. unm. Nov., 1854.

4. Betsey, b. July 24, 1805, m. Isaac Searles, June 27, 1824, had several ch., lived in Mont Vernon, d. March 18, 1884, at Milford.

5. Sarah, b. July 23, 1807; m. (1) Otis Marshall of Chelmsford, Mass., Nov. 14, 1834; he d. Aug. 29, 1837. She m. (2) William Cutler of Billerica, Dec. 17, 1846.

6. Levi Woodbury, b. July 13, 1813, d. in Amherst in July, 1856; m. Elizabeth Fuller of Lynn, Mass., had six ch.

7. Lois, b. July 13, 1813, m. Joseph Marshall of Chelmsford, Mass., Oct. 10, 1836.

8. John, b. Oct. 6, 1815, d. Oct. 6, 1821.

William Lamson, (of Danish origin) emigrated to here in 1637 and settled in Hamilton, Mass. He had a son, William, who was the father of Jonathan Lamson of Hamilton, who was b. in 1720, d. Aug. 16, 1808. His wife, Anna (Whipple) Lamson, d. Aug. 29, 1791. William, the eldest of their ch., b. Hamilton, March, 1746, d. Mont Vernon, Nov., 1800; m. Mary Summers of Hamilton, Mass. She was b. July 31, 1746, d. Dec. 10, 1835. He settled on the farm now owned by his great-grandson, Frank O. Lamson, about the year 1770. Ch. b. Mont Vernon.

1. William, b. Jan. 26, 1771, d. Oct. 5, 1775.

2. Porter, b. April, 1773, d. Sept., 1775.

3. Hannah, b. June 11, 1775, m. William Cogswell, May, 1794, d. Nov. 14, 1812.

4. Mary, b. July 15, 1777, d. Dec. 4, 1803.

5. Nancy, b. April 2, 1782, m. April 26, 1813, Nathan Smith of Templeton, Mass.; d. Feb., 1855.

6. *William, b. Feb. 15, 1785.

7. *John Lummus, b. July 15, 1787.

Capt. William Lamson, son of William and Mary (Lummus) Lamson, b. Mont Vernon, Feb. 15, 1785; m. Nov., 1807, Serviah Jones, dau. of Nathan, Jr., and Esther (Butterfield) Jones. She was b. Oct. 1, 1783, d. Jan. 10, 1851. He d. June 9, 1857. He inherited his father's farm. Ch. b. Mont Vernon.

1. *William Osborn, b. Sept. 15, 1808.

2. Mary, b. Aug. 17, 1810, d. unm., March 15, 1893.

3. Serviah, b. Jan. 15, 1815, m. Feb. 23, 1837, *Hiram Perkins. She d. March 1, 1871.

4. Augusta, b. March 9, 1817, m. July 21, 1841, *Capt. Chester B. Southworth. She d. Manchester, Feb. 1, 1879.

5. Adeline, b. July 25, 1821, d. unm., April 4, 1859.

6. Nancy, b. Oct. 7, 1827, m. Nov. 10, 1857, * George W. Averill.

John L. Lamson, son of William and Mary (Lummus) Lamson, b. Mont Vernon, July 15, 1787, m. Sept. 10, 1809, Nancy Bradford, dau. Enos Bradford of Mont Vernon. He settled on the farm, southeast of Mont Vernon Village, now owned by estate of E. C. Flanders. He d. March 5, 1878. Ch.

1. *William, b. Mont Vernon, 1809, m. Sarah, dau. of David Starrett of New Boston. She was b. Aug. 12, 1811. He was engaged for many years in his earlier life in the glass manufacture at Pembroke N. H., whence he removed to Matamora, Ill., opposite Peoria. He was there many years, subsequently removed Garden Grove, Orange Co., near Los Angeles, S. California, where he d. July 30, 1894 age 85. Ch.

1. William Bradford, b. June 16, 1836, m. Aug. 24, 1865, Eveline Tunnell, brick mason, five ch., res.

CAPT. WILLIAM O. LAMSON

2. George Starrett, b. Suncook, N. H., June 18, 1839, m. Hattie Henderson of Fairbury Ill., Dec. 26, 1865; d. Feb. 21, 1879, at Hamilton, Mo., was cashier of Hamilton Savings Bank and Judge of Caldwell Co. Court, left one son and two dau.

3. Justin W., b. Suncook, May 24, 1841. Physician; m. Susan M. Ritchey, Jan. 17, 1871, two ch., son and dau.

4. Sarah Frances, b. May 1, 1843, m. Oct. 13, 1874, Samuel B. Everett, a farmer, had two sons.

Capt. William Osborn Lamson, son of Capt. William and Serviah (Jones) Lamson, b. Mont Vernon, Sept. 15, 1808; farmer, resided on homestead in North Dist., where he d. July 12, 1896. He m. Jan. 10, 1849, Mrs. Orinda F. (Odell) Upton, wid. Josiah Upton and dau. of Luther and Betsey (Green) Odell. She was b. Feb. 16, 1819, d. Nov. 24, 1874. Ch. b. Mont Vernon.

Twins :—

1. Harriet Frances, b. April 6, 1850; m. Aug. 31, 1870, Henry A. Kelso of New Boston; one son, Walter L., b. Feb. 17, 1872. She res. New Boston.

2. Mariett Augusta, b. April 6, 1850; res. Mont Vernon, unm.

Twins :—

3. Ella Theresa, b. Dec. 9, 1851, m. Oct. 22, 1875, H. E. Hardy of Manchester; d. childless, June 13, 1877.

4. Ellen Orinda, b. Dec. 9, 1851, m. Dec. 25, 1871, Lendell Dodge of New Boston; res. New Boston; two ch.

5. Ida Henrietta, b. Sept. 20, 1853, m. L. Woodbury Perham of Wilton, Dec. 31, 1874; has two ch.

6. Frank Osborn, b. Oct. 20, 1858.

Frank Osborn Lamson, son Capt. Wm. B. and Orinda F. (Odell) Lamson, b. Mont Vernon, Oct. 20, 1858; m. Jan. 9, 1890, Marcia E. dau. Dea. George G. and Mary E. (Horne) Batchelder, she was b. Mont Vernon, March 3, 1864. Farmer; res. on homestead. Ch. b. Mont Vernon.

1. Albert Batchelder, b. July 31, 1891.

2. Ella M., b. March 5, 1895.

3. William Osborn, b. July 29, 1900.

LANGDELL.

William Langdell was an Englishman, settled in Beverly, Mass., came to Mont Vernon with his son, Joseph. He m. Maria Wittredge of Beverly, Mass., had 5 sons, two of whom were lost at sea in one vessel. His wife d. 1816. He finally settled in New Boston with his son, Livermore, who had settled there in 1771, and d. there in 1799.

Joseph Langdell, son of William and Maria, settled Mont Vernon, 1773, was selectman, removed to Wenham, Mass., in 1809, and d. there in May, 1829, aged 94. Ch. of Joseph Langdell, b. Mont Vernon.

1. Lucy, b. June 27, 1774.

2. Molly, b. April 27, 1776; m. John Bradford in April, 1798. He was an elder brother of Rev. E. P. Bradford of New Boston; lived in Hillsboro and Peterboro, where he d.; had six ch.

3. Rebecca, b. April 13, 1778, m. Feb. 19, 1796, (1) Dr. Henry Codman, Jr.; m. (2) Thomas Hamlin. She d. May 5, 1855.

4. Betsey, b. Nov. 15, 1780, m. Nov. 28, 1799,; John Ray, son of Ebenezer Ray.

5. Abigail, b. Feb. 25, 1782, m. April 11, 1808, *Allen Dodge, d.
Oct. 17, 1812.
6. Esther, b. May 14, 1783, m. June 5, 1807, Ebenezer Odell, Jr.
7. *Ezra, b. March 5, 1785.
8. Anna, b. March 9, 1788, m. July 2, 1810, Charles Cambridge.
9. *Mark D., b. May 6, 1792.

Ezra Langdell son of Joseph Langdell, b. Mont Vernon, March 5,
1785; m. his cousin, Rebecca, dau. of Livermore Langdell of New Boston.
She was b. March 20, 1792, d. Jan. 6, 1855. He d. Dec. 22, 1855. Ch. b.
Mont Vernon.
1 Aurelia, b. Aug. 13, 1810, m. *Charles Underwood, Oct. 8, 1829.
2. Nancy B., b. Sept. 28, 1812; m. Daniel Ordway; lives Francestown;
three ch.
3. Lucy A., b. Aug. 6 1814, m. *Gilman Alcott, June 24, 1837. She
d. March 12, 1838.
4. Edward D., b. Aug. 2, 1816, lived in New Boston.
5. Betsey, b. October 4, 1818.
6. *Stephen Chapin, b. Sept. 9, 1820.
7. Abby D., b. March 6, 1823, second wife Gilman Alcott.
8. Mary F., b. April 6, 1829.
9. Charles F., b. April 18, 1832, lived in Ohio.
10. John, b. May 16, 1835, d. young.

Mark D. Langdell, son of Joseph Langdell, b. Mont Vernon, May 6,
1792, m. Lucy, dau. of Paul and Betsey (Woodbury) Whipple of New
Boston, June 9, 1817. Was an inn-keeper. He d. Lyndeboro, Dec. 16,
1859. She was b. April 12 ,1798, d. Dec. 29, 1880, at Wilton. Ch.
1. James, b. Mont Vernon, May 27, 1818; m. Oct. 27, 1840, Mary,
dau. of James and Lydia (Glover) Stearns of Amherst; had three sons;
d. Lowell, where he lived, May 2, 1860.
2. Elizabeth, b. Mont Vernon, March 13, 1820, m. (1) *Luke Wilkins,
June 22, 1843; m. (2) Levi Curtis; d. Milford, May 28, 1897.
3. Esther M., b. Mont Vernon April 8, 1822, m. Isaac Richardson of
Milford, had two ch., d. Milford, Aug. 12, 1882.
4. Lucy M., b. Mont Vernon, May 9, 1824, m. June 9, 1844, George
E. Washer of Milford; d. Milford, Jan. 14, 1871; no ch.
5. Joseph, b. Mont Vernon, Sept. 30, 1826; lived Wilton, where he
d. Aug. 9, 1893; left a family.
6. Adaline, b. Amherst, July 15, 1828, d. Jan. 17, 1853, unm.
7. Clarinda, b. Lowell, December 13, 1853, d. Amherst, Sept. 29, 1855.
8. Hannah W., b. Lowell, March 15, 1835; m. Oct. 25, 1855, O. W.
Butler of Lyndeboro.
9. John D., b. Lowell, Feb. 14, 1837, d. Wilton, Aug. 5, 1892.
10. William, b. Nashua Nov. 26, 1841, d. at Andersonville, Ga., Sept.
25, 1864.

Stephen Chapin Langdell, b. Mont Vernon, Sept. 9, 1820, d. Sept. 25,
1895; m. Lucy B., dau. of James J. and Lucy W. (Burnham) Averill,
1844. She was b. Mont Vernon, Oct. 4, 1816, d. Feb. 9, 1903. Ch. b.
Mont Vernon.
1. James A., b. Sept. 14, 1845, m. Mary E., dau. Luke and Elizabeth
Langdell Wilkins, Dec. 15, 1869. She was b. Mont Vernon, Oct. 10, 1846.
He was acidentally shot April 2, 1870.

2. Helen M., b. Nov. 8, 1846, m. March 25, 1874, *George Fred Turbell, one dau.

3. Eunice B., b. March 31, 1851, m. August 21, 1869, Franklin E. Myers, b. North Adams, Mass., June 16, 1846; residence, Stoneham, Mass. No ch.

4. Jennie A., b. Oct. 23, 1853, m. Feb. 15, 1873, William H. Pratt of Stoneham, Mass. He d. 1899; res. Stoneham; one dau.

LEAVITT.

Andrew Leavitt, b. in the vicinity of Exeter in 1752, d. in Amherst, Aug. 24, 1846, aged 94; m. (1) Sarah Hastings; m. (2) Elizabeth (Kendrick) Jones, dau. of Daniel Kendrick of Hollis and widow of Timothy Jones; she d. May, 1818, aged 55. He m. (3) Mrs. Abigail (Rust) Hildreth, widow Jonathan Hildreth. She d. Feb. 12, 1834, age 66. He learned the housewright's trade of Dea. Ephraim Barker, and came with him as a journeyman to Amherst before the commencement of the Revolution, and afterward carried on the business here until disabled by age. He went to Amherst about 1800. He was present at the battle of Bunker Hill and was at Cambridge when Washington took command of the army. He was probably the last survivor of the Mont Vernon soldiers at Bunker Hill. He lived in Mont Vernon many years, coming here about the time of the Revolution. He built the house commonly known as the "Dr. Smith House" in Mont Vernon Village. Nine oldest ch. b. Mont Vernon by first wife.

1. Andrew, m. twice, served on board a privateer in the War of 1812, was taken prisoner and confined in Dartmoor prison, England, d. in Marblehead, Mass. after his liberation, of disease contracted while in prison.

2. Sarah, m. *Jesse Averill. The tradition is that she was a wonderful singer, with a voice of rare sweetness and remarkable power, though none of her descendants seem to have inherited this captivating gift. Following is an extract graphically describing the impression she made, from a letter of Prof. Reuben D. Muzzey (who, in his youth, was an attendant at the Mont Vernon Church) of Dartmouth College, written at Boston in 1862 to Rev. Dr. J. G. Davis of Amherst:

"There was one charm, which was peculiar, connected with the worship on that hill—it was the singing. There was a good choir, but the fascination came from a single voice, that of Miss Leavitt, an elder sister of Miss Leavitt, who afterward became the mother of the Hutchinson family, renowned in song. The choir of Mont Vernon Church met for practice on Sabbath morning, before the hour of worship. Miss Leavitt always sang the alto. How many times as striplings ascended the hill did we stop to drink in those rich and heavenly tones (oh, I can hear them now) which filled the whole atmosphere and seemed to come from an elevation far above that of the open windows. My dear sir, pardon my enthusiasm, I have since heard Madame Malibran, Madame Stontag, Jenny Lind and an oratorio in St. Xavier chapel from the choir of Pope Pius IX, on the evening of his coronation, and I have not yet heard a voice so rich and inspiring as that of Miss Leavitt. Does such a voice come as often as once in a century?"

3. Mary, b. July 25, 1785, m. Aug. 7, 1800, Jesse Hutchinson of Milford, d. in Milford, Sept. 20, 1868. She was the mother of 16 ch., among whom were the three brothers, Judson, John, Asa and one sister, Alby, who comprised the famous "Tribe of Jesse," who were renowned in Europe and America for their gift of song.

4. John, b. April 16, 1787, d. Amherst, Aug. 13, 1862; m. Nov. 17, 1816, Nancy Averill of Milford. She was b. March 24, 1793, d. Nov. 22, 1854. They lived in Amherst and had four ch.

5. Betsey, d. unm.

6. Benjamin was a painter, lived in Amherst, d. June, 1848, aged 54, m. (1) Clarissa, dau. Eleazer and Elizabeth (Bullard) Rhoads of Amherst, m. (2) Mary Ames, had five ch.

7. William, m. Sarah Burnham, d. Nov. 28, 1872.

8. Nathaniel, d. in California.

9. Hannah, m. John Adams.

Ch. by second wife b. Amherst.

10. Roxanna, m. John Marvell of Milford.

11. Daniel Kendrick, removed to Carmell, Ohio, where he d.

12. Nancy, m. Hiram Parker of Lexington, Mass., lived in Lowell, Mass.

LEWIS.

Rev. Thomas J. Lewis, b. Swansea, Wales, July 2, 1857, commenced preaching in Wales as a religious exhorter, at the age of 16 came to America in 1883, was student at Marietta College, Ohio, 1883 and 1884; was at Bangor Theological Seminary from 1884 to 1887, in which last year he was licensed to preach. Traveled one year in Europe; was located in the ministry two years from 1888 to 1890 at South West Harbor, Me. From 1890 to 1893 he was at East Andover, N. H. Commenced preaching at Mont Vernon, Oct. 21, 1894, closed his work here Dec. 5, 1897. Is now (1902) preaching at East Andover, N. H. M. Anna J. Daniels, b. 1855. Ch.

1. John Daniels, b. Wales, 1879.

2. William Edward, b. Wales, Aug., 1882.

3. Gladys, b. East Andover, N. H., Dec., 1892.

LIVINGSTONE.

Samuel A. Livingstone, m. Dec. 7, 1815, Hannah, dau. Samuel and Lydia (Adams) Twiss. He was killed by falling from the tannery of Samuel Trull, Esq., in New Boston, Oct. 30, 1827, age 69. His wid. m. John Hills in 1836. He d. 1873. She was b. New Boston, July 17, 1793, d. Mont Vernon, Dec. 8, 1891. Ch. b. New Boston.

1. Samuel F., b. Feb. 5, 1825, came to Mont Vernon when a lad and lived with John Battles, whose farm in the East District he ultimately owned. He m. (1) Feb. 20, 1859, Sarah J., dau. Galen and Sarah C. (Ames) Hamblett of Milford. She was b. Dracut, Mass., Nov. 30, 1834, d. Nov. 16, 1877. He m. (2) Mrs. Olivia (Haradon) Livingstone of New Boston. She d. May 11, 1902, aged 72 years, 10 months. He d. May 13, 1899. One son by first wife, Llewellyn H., b. Mont Vernon, Sept. 2, 1864, lives in Antrim.

2. Benjamin, T. b. Jan. 6, 1827, served in the Union Army in the 27th Mass. Regt. from Winchester, Mass., d. Chelsea, Mass., March 3, 1902. He m. Jan., 1865, Maria F., dau. Benjamin F. and Hannah (Smith) Hill She was b. Mont Vernon, Oct. 16, 1829; d. Sept. 13, 1880, at Chelsea, Mass

3. Dau. Adeline L., m. Irving Battles of Woburn; 2, Helen M., m Leonard S. Bean 3. Isabel, m Freeman D. Blake.

Charles A. Livingstone, son Col. E. W. Livingstone of Nashua, b. Nashua, was a blacksmith in Mont Vernon from April, 1876, until Sept. 1883, when he removed to Lowell where he d. May 4, 1892, age 52 years. He was twice married. He had two daughters by his first wife and one son by his second wife. His second wife, Mrs. Clara L. Livinstone, d. Lowell, Mass., June 3, 1896, age 47 years. A daughter, Josephine E., d. Lowell, Nov. 17, 1885, aged 10 years.

LOVEJOY.

Joseph Lovejoy, a soldier of the Revolution, d. in Mont Vernon, Oct. 18, 1814, aged about 80 years. He m. Patience, dau. of *William and Mary (Lambert) Bradford, July 9, 1761, she d. Amherst, May 1, 1826, aged about 85 years. He settled in Mont Vernon about 1761. Ch. probably b. Mont Vernon.

1. Sarah, b. May 6, 1762, m. Feb. 14, 1786, *Daniel Kendall; d. Aug. 14, 1847.
2. Edith, b. April 7, 1764, d. young
3. Patience, b. April 1, 1766, m. Feb. 1, 1787, William Small of Amherst; had 12 ch.; d. Morristown, Vt., Oct. 18, 1851.
4. Susannah, b. June 11, 1769, m. Feb. 9, 1796, David Stewart of Amherst, had 7 ch.; d. Amherst, Aug. 24, 1846.
5. Polly, m. James Dascomb, May 20, 1794; d. Wilton, Nov. 16, 1851; 4 ch.
6. Betsey, b. 1772, m. Oct. 10, 1794, *Benjamin Parker. She d. Amherst, Sept. 25, 1839; 6 ch.
7. Arethusa, m. Asa Farnum, May 25, 1803.
8. Joseph, m. Mrs. Baker, d. Salem, Mass., Nov., 1821

LOVEREN.

Alvah Loveren, b. Deering, moved to Medford, Mass., came to Mont Vernon Village, where he d. He m. Matilda K., dau. Isaac and Pamelia (Stevens) Smith of Deering. She d. Mont Vernon, March 7, 1885, aged 66. Ch.

1. Alva Dexter, b. Deering, d. in infancy.
2. Edgar H., b. Wendell, N. H., lives in Roxbury, Mass.; one ch.
3. Arthur D., b. Medford, Mass., lives in Philadelphia; has two dau.
4. Altia, d. young.
5. Charles D., b. Medford; is not livnig.

LORD.

Rev. Charles E. Lord, son John P. Lord and nephew Nathan Lord, President Dartmouth College, was b. South Berwick, Me., was pastor of the church here from 1856 to 1861, afterwards in the ministry at Chester, Vt., was some years a professor in training schools for divinity. He retired about 20 years before his death and resided at Salisbury, Mass., where he d. Feb. 9, 1902, aged 85 years. He m. 1856, Miss Eunice Pike of Newburyport. No, ch.

MANNING.

Albert D. Manning, son Jesse and Eleanor (Morgan) Manning, b. Billerica, Mass Dec. 20, 1820; m. Jan. 1, 1849, Nancy J., dau. Zephaniah

and Nancy (Manning) Kittredge. She was b. Mont Vernon, Aug. 15, 1821, d. Dec. 18, 1897. He settled on a farm in the North District in 1854. Ch.
    1. Albert Haskell, b. Oct. 4, 1849, d. Sept. 23, 1866.
    2. Lucy A., b. Sept. 23, 1853, d. April 25, 1865.
    3. Walter C., b. Feb. 15, 1861, in Mont Vernon, m. Sept. 11, 1886, Olive Bailey of Lunenburg. Mass. He d. Lunenburg. April 12, 1896; one ch.
    Pearl Ethel, b. Sept. 28, 1887.

Henry Manning, b. New Boston, Dec. 15, 1840 was a member of the 4th N. H. Regt. in the War for the Union, came to Mont Vernon in 1880 from Amherst, lived on the turnpike, moved to Milford in 1887, where he d. June 3, 1903; m. Oct. 2, 1867, Emily A. Braman of North-bridge, Mass. She was b. Grafton, Mass., June 1, 1849. Ch.
    1. Eugene H., b. Northbridge, Mass., Dec. 12, 1867, m. Miss Nettie Pond, lives Milford.
    2. Ruel D., b. Northbridge, Aug. 31, 1869, m. Miss Nellie Therrien; three ch.; lives Milford.
    3. James O., b. Mont Vernon, Sept. 13, 1871.
    4. Sadie M., b. Amherst, June 19, 1874, d. Milford, March 11, 1892.
    5. Louise A., b. Amherst, Sept. 27, 1879; res. Milf rd.
    6. Joseph, b. Mont Vernon, May 22, 1882; res. Milford.

Elisha R. Manning came from north part of state, m. Julia A., dau. Mrs. Charlotte Brown. They lived with Mrs. Brown, where J. M. Glea-son now does. Mrs. M. d. Sept. 9, 1877, aged 56. A dau, Julia M., d. Feb. 24, 1853, aged 20 months.

MARDEN.

Nathan Marden, son of Lemuel and Hannah (Greenough) Marden, a bricklayer by trade, moved to Mont Vernon from New Boston. He built the house in village now occupied by Mrs. Ellen Starrett. He d. here May 16, 1833, age 56. He m. Oct. 11, 1806, Susanna, dau. Calvin and Esther (Wilkins) Stevens. She was b. in Hillsboro, March 4, 1789, d. Mont Vernon, Aug. 20 1843. Ch. were:
    1. *Benjamin Franklin, b. New Boston, Sept. 7, 1807.
    2. *Nathan Richmond.
    3. Susanna m. Edwin M. Holt of Lyndeboro, Dec., 1834. They lived in Mont Vernon and Amherst. Three ch., viz: (1) Frank, d. in army in 1861; (2) Addie M., d. July 30, 1873, age 27; (3) George E., b. Jan. 20, 1848, is of Nashua.
    4. *William S., b. Nov. 22, 1820.
    5. Sarah C., b. 1824, m. Nov., 1844, Peter W. Haseltine; one son, Arthur. She d. Nov. 3, 1883, in Boston, aged 59. Was buried in Mont Vernon.

Benjamin Franklin Marden, son of Nathan and Susannah (Stevens) Marden, b. New Boston, Sept. 7, 1807, moved to Mont Vernon when young, having lived in Wilton, was a shoemaker; d. Mont Vernon, March 25, 1891. He m. May 20, 1834, Betsey Buss. She was b. Wilton, Aug. 3, 1810, d. Mont Vernon, Feb. 1, 1891. Ch. b. Mont Vernon.
    1. Sarah Luthera, b. May 9, 1835, m. March 9, 1868, *George G. Averill of Mont Vernon, res. Mont Vernon.

HON. GEORGE A. MARDEN.

2. Benjamin F., b. May 12, 1836, d. in infancy.

3. Susan, b. June 23, 1837, d. Jan. 2, 1859.

4. *George Augustus, b. Aug. 9, 1839.

5. Franklin, b. March 31, 1841, m. May 16, 1883, Frances M. Biddle, dau. Barrack Biddle of Concord. She d. Oct. 15, 1885, age 43. Has resided in Concord and Manchester, was shoe dealer, now resides Mont Vernon.

6. Maria Theresa, b. March 6, 1844, m. May 18, 1869, Capt. Elbridge Gerry Martin of East Boston. He was an efficient pilot, had summer residence in Mont Vernon. A very worthy man. He d. April 5, 1902. Ch. b. East Boston, where she resides. 1. Frank L., b. March, 1875; 2. Bertha V., b. March 20, 1878.

7. Katherine H., b. Dec. 16, 1846, m. Nov. 27, 1873, Samuel Sewall of Lowell. She d. Aug. 27, 1886. Two ch., Harry B., b. Aug. 9, 1875; Gertrude M., b. Oct. 19, 1879.

8. Wendell Phillips, b. May 6, 1850, m. Oct. 23, 1878, Malvina D., dau. of George L. Nutter of Concord, two ch., Edward L. and Mary, is a cashier in the Mass. State Treasury, resides Newton Centre, Mass.

Nathan Richmond Marden, son of Nathan and Susanna (Stevens) Marden, m. 1839, Abby, dau. of Dea. Abel Fiske of Wilton. Lived in Francestown for more than fifty years; was a shoemaker. Ch.

1. Richmond Fiske of Marblehead.

2. Sarah Caroline, m. R. P. Ordway of Francestown.

3. Edwin S. of Lowell.

4. Jennie M., m. Woodbury P. Hopkins of Francestown.

5. William R. of New Hampshire Cavalry, d. in Annapolis, 1863, from disease contracted while prisoner.

6. Charles N., of Lynn, has two ch.

7. Abby S., m. Sewall L. Brown of Francestown.

8. Hattie E., d. at nine years of age.

9. Jessie F., m. Wilton E. Osborne of Peterboro, N. H.

William S. Marden, son of Nathan and Susanna (Stevens) Marden, b. Nov. 22, 1820, m. (1) Eunice Evans, 1844. She d. March, 1845. He m. (2) Harriet M. Trefry of Dedham in 1849. He lived Marblehead. Ch. by first wife.

1. William H., b. March, 1845, lives Marblehead.

Ch. by second wife.

2. Louis W., of Salem, Mass.

3. Arthur of Portland, Me.

George Augustus Marden, son of Benjamin F. and Betsey (Buss) Marden, b. Mont Vernon, Aug. 9, 1839. Is editor Lowell Courier-Citizen and United States Sub-Treasurer, resides Lowell. For extended account see chapter on "Prominent Men," m. Dec. 10, 1867, Mary Porter, dau. Dea. David and Harriet (Nourse) Fiske of Amherst. She was b. Amherst, Dec. 9, 1841. Ch. b. Lowell.

1. Philip Sanford, b. Jan. 12, 1874, m. June, 1902, Florence, dau. Col. Edward Shirley of Goffstown, graduated Dartmouth, lives in Lowell, journalist.

2. Robert Fiske, b. June 14, 1876, m. June 12, 1901, Ella L. Pote of East Boston, Mass., graduated Dartmouth College, is in the insurance business.

Samuel K. Marden of Newton, m. Aug. 14, 1836, Eliza Ann Young, dau. of Mrs. Young (sister of William S. Stinson), Sr.

MARVELL.

William Marvell or Marble, b. Lyndeboro, lived in South Dist. (where D. J. Hutchinson now does) m. (1) Sarah dau. Elisha and Sarah (Buxton) Hutchinson of Milford; m. (2) Mehitable, dau. Jonathan and Polly (Baker) Conant. After his decease she moved here and became the second wife of Ezekiel Upton in 1843. Ch. by first wife:
    1. William, m. a Miss Whittemore of New Boston, lived Milford; no ch.
    Ch. by second wife.
    2. Eliot C., b. Feb. 9, 1809, m. Mary Marvell of Farmington, Me., settled in Farmington, Me.; had five ch.
    3. Mary H., b. Feb. 3, 1811, m. James Proctor of Nashua, lived Lynn, Mass., four ch.
    4. *Elbridge, b. Feb. 23, 1813.
    5. Nancy, b. Aug. 23, 1815, m. (1) Frances Lynch of Milford; m (2) Beri Bennett of Brookline, no ch., d. Lowell, July 11, 1803.
    6. Caroline, b. Sept. 21, 1817, m. (1) Joseph Bright of Pelham; m. (2) Peter Clark of Milford, May 23, 1878, d. Milford, Sept. 3, 1882.
    7. Maria F.,b. June 21, 1820.
    8. *Charles, b. Feb. 6, 1822.
    9. John B., b. May 17, 1824, d. Sept. 15, 1861.
    10. Henry Franklin, b. Oct. 8, 1826, settled Farmington, Me.
    11. James, b. Sept. 20, 1828, m. Charlotte Butterfield of Ashburnham, Mass., no ch., res. Goffstown.

Elbridge Marvell son of William and Mehitable(Conant) Marvell, b. Feb. 23, 1813, carpenter, d. Mont Vernon, Aug. 23, 1893; m. Nov. 17, 1836, Mary, dau. of David and Mary (Averill) Smith, b. Mont Vernon, Nov. 22, 1808, d. Aug. 5, 1895. Ch. b. Mont Vernon.
    1. Edwin A., m. Fanny Leach. He d. Oct. 26, 1872, age 30, 2 ch. b. Mont Vernon, (1) Caroline, m. Allie Austin, has two ch.; (2) Walter Elbridge.
    2. Mary Caroline, d. Jan. 28, 1855, age 16 years, 6 mos.

Charles Marvell, son of William and Mehitable (Conant) Marvell, b. Feb, 6, 1822, m. Mary Ann, dau. of James and Huldah (Peabody) Hill, Oct. 16, 1851. She was b. Sept. 7, 1826, d. April 29, 1880. Ch. b. Mont Vernon.
    1. *William Henry, b. Oct. 11, 1853.
    2. Helen, b. Nov. 22, 1855, m. Charles Searles, March 12, 1878, lived in Milford and Nashua, d. Haverhill, Dec. 27, 1899.
    3. George H., b. Sept. 26, 1859, d. Jan. 5, 1861, age 1 year, 5 mos.

William Henry Marvell, son of Charles and Mary A. (Hill) Marvell, b. Oct. 11, 1853, Mont Vernon, m. June 8, 1876, Emma J., dau. Charles and Clarinda J., (Felch) Foster. She was b. Mont Vernon, Jan. 1, 1860.
    Josie Leona, b. June 11, 1877, m. Jan. 31, 1900, *Edward W. Trow, one son.

MAY.

Clinton S. May was a shoemaker and lived in the East District with his wife's people. He m. Elizabeth, dau. John H. and Polly (Johnnot) Bennett. She was b. March, 1839, d. Nov. 29, 1888. He d. May 18, 1877, age 47 years. Ch. b. Mont Vernon.

1. Etta, b. Jan. 25, 1863, m. 1879, *William O. Hill.
2. Grace.
3. Harvey.
4. Harrie A., d. June 2, 1877, aged 10 months.

McCOLLOM.

Alexander McCollom, with wife Janet, came from Londonderry, Ire., and settled in Londonderry, N. H., about 1730. Had seven ch., the first Alexander, m. Elizabeth McMurphy, had five ch., of whom the fifth was Alexander, who retained the homestead in New Boston, m. 1787, Mary, dau. of Robert Patterson. He held the office of selectman in 1809 and 1811, and was an energetic and industrious citizen. He purchased the Peter Jones farm in the North part of Mont Vernon in 1820, occupying it until his death, June 1, 1843, age 77. His widow, b. Nov. 12, 1772, d. Jan. 4, 1852, age 79. Ch. b. New Boston.

1. John, b. April 30, 1788, m. Betsey Chase, settled in Claremont, d. Nov. 21, 1822; two ch.
2. Robert, b. Nov. 24, 1789, d. unm. Batavia, N. Y., May 17, 1825.
3. Elizabeth, b. Aug. 30, 1791, m. John McLane of Francestown, had ch. viz. Neil, Alexander, John, Charles, Rodney, Mary Isabel, Nancy Jane, George W., Elizabeth, Clara, Sarah, Helen, Marion and Robert E.
4. Rodney, b. March 27, 1793, m. Naomi Wilson, had three ch.
5. *Alexander, b. Feb. 5, 1795.
6. Fanny, b. Nov. 5, 1796, d. unm. Clinton, Mass., April 6, 1882.
7. A child b. March 12, 1798, d. young.
8. Elbridge, b. July 19, 1801, m. Mary Jane, dau. Jonathan Harvey of Sutton, lived in Sutton, had three ch.
9. *Milton, b. March 21, 1803.
10. Mary, b. Jan. 5, 1805, d. Nov. 13, 1825.
11. Haskell, b. March 19, 1807, m. and lived in Lancaster, Mass.; four ch.
12. Clarissa, b. Oct. 27, 1809, m. Lemuel Marden of New Boston, no ch., d. June 12, 1876.
13. George W. b. Jan. 14, 1812, d. Aug., 1814.
14. George W., b. Sept. 20, 1814, m. Oct. 4, 1842, Mary Ann, dau. of Asa and Mary A. (Appleton) Stevens. He was in the banking business in Indiana and in real estate in New York City; in 1872 endowed Appleton Academy with $10,000, with the condition that the name be changed to McCollom Institute, which was done. He also endowed an Episcopal College with the same sum. He d. Sept. 4, 1878. His wife d. 1865.

Dr. Alexander McCollom, son of Alexander and Mary (Patterson) McCollom, b. New Boston, Feb. 5, 1795, fitted for college under Rev. E. P. Bradford, New Boston, and with Prof. B. Towler, Bangor, Me., studied medicine at Bangor and Belfast, Me., and with Dr. Manning at Merrimack, N. H. attended medical lectures at Bowdoin and Dartmouth, and was in practice successively at Windsor, Palmero and Pittston, Me., at which place he d. Nov. 10, 1884, having resided there for 23 years. He m. Oct. 19, 1830, a niece and adopted dau. of Dr. Abel Goodrich of Merrimack. Ch.

1.   Mary G., b. Sept. 21, 1831, m. Oct. 18, 1860, Dr. Edward Mead of Cincinnati, Ohio.
2.   Abel Goodrich, b. Sept. 12, 1837, m. Aug. 4, 1861, Annie J. Davidson of Wiscasset, Me. Had one son, Edward, who fitted for college at McCollom Institute, graduated at Harvard in 1892, is a teacher in New Jersey.

Milton McCollom, son of Alexander and Mary (Patterson) McCollom, b. New Boston, March 31, 1803, d. Mont Vernon, Aug. 31, 1852; was an inn-keeper and farmer; lived where D. J. Herlehy lives in East District. He m. Sophronia, dau. of Joseph and Betsey (Perkins) Trow, June 18, 1829. She was b. Mont Vernon, June 4, 1806, d. Feb. 12, 1883. Ch. b. Mont Vernon.
1.   Mary E., b. May 5, 1830, m. Dec. 20, 1860, *Daniel R. Baker. He d. July 25, 1879.
2.   *Charles R., b. June 1, 1833.
3.   *John Trow, b. July 28, 1835.
4.   Frances Evelyn, b. Dec. 26, 1845, m. June 17, 1868, *William S. A. Starrett of Mont Vernon, two ch.

Charles R. McCollom, son of Milton and Sophronia (Trow) McCollom, b. Mont Vernon, June 1, 1833, m. (1) Jan. 1, 1861, Sarah R. Richards of Goffstown, who d. Aug. 15, 1876, m. (2) Louise Rundlett of Bedford, March 13, 1878, is a carpenter, resides Goffstown. Ch. by second wife b. Goffstown.
1.   Sarah Louise, b. June 15, 1879.
2.   Marion Sophronia, b. March 22, 1882.
3.   Mary Etta, b. Jan. 17, 1888.

John Trow McCollom, son of Milton and Sophronia (Trow) McCollom, b. Mont Vernon, July 28, 1835, is a carpenter and teamster and has always resided in town. M. (1) July 14, 1866, Emily J., dau. Dea. Joseph A. and Maria J. (Bruce) Starrett. She was b. Mont Vernon, Dec. 14, 1846, d. April 4, 1867, m. (2) Mrs. Theresa M. (Smith) Christy, widow Dea. Sumner L. Christy of New Boston, and dau. of Isaac and Pamelia (Stevens) Smith. She was b. Deering, Oct. 25, 1835. Ch. by first wife b. Mont Vernon.
1.   Mary Belle, b. Feb. 18, 1867, painter, m. Feb. 18, 1902, Julius Wurdeman of Chicago.

McCRILLIS.

Albert B. McCrillis of Lyndeboro', m. Harriet E. Cummings. She was b. Hancock, July 30, 1824. After his death she moved to Mont Vernon, where she d. Jan. 10, 1891, 3 ch.
1.   Ella, b. East Rindge, Nov. 19, 1848, m. George E. Boutell, 1868, resides Mont Vernon.
2.   Edwin A., m. April 29, 1891, Sarah W., dau. John Erastus and Sarah J. (Whittemore) Bruce, was a merchant in Milford, d. Milford, Jan. 9, 1902.
3.   Harriet E., milliner, res. Nashua.

McGOWN.

Rev. Richard H. McGown, b. North Ellsworth, Me., May 13, 1850, educated principally at the Easton State Normal School. Became a preacher of the Maine Methodist Conference, and as such was stationed at Dover, Tremont and Pembroke. March 7, 1882, he was ordained as a Congregational minister at Harrington, Me., was acting pastor at Turner, Me., from Dec., 1883 to Nov., 1885, and at Mont Vernon from Dec., 1885 to Feb. 26, 1888. Was two years each at Cornish, Me., and Northwood, N. H. Was pastor of a Congregational church in Everett, Mass., where he d. He m. Abby F. Rowe of Ellsworth, Me., ch.

1. Ruth M., b. 1876.
2. Ralph S., b. 1877.
3. Anna E., b. June, 1879.
4. Roy, b. Dec. 4, 1880.

McQUESTION.

Hugh N. McQuestion, b. Merrimack, Feb. 14, 1805, lived on the farm where Martin L. Wheeler now lives in the East District, d. Feb. 13, 1889, age 84; removed to farm near East School. He m. Sarah F. Hartshorn of Merrimack, April 2, 1829. She d. Oct. 18, 1877, age 72 years, 11 months, 19 days. She was b. Oct. 29, 1804. Ch. b. Mont Vernon.

1. Henry N., b. Feb. 15, 1830, m. Hattie Hunt, enlisted in the Fifth N. H. Regt. in the Civil War, d. diseased, Newport News, Va., June 6, 1862, one son, Fred.
2. *Thomas H., b. May 8, 1832.
3. Nathan P., d. March 26, 1842, age 7 yrs., 5 mos.
4. Harriet J., d. March 13, 1846, age 10 yrs., 2 mos.
5. Sarah F., b. Feb. 23, 1844, m. May 8, 1873, Wm. W. Grafton, Friendship, Me., res. Milford, d. Milford, Nov. 12, 1886; one dau.
6. Mary A., b. Feb. 2, 1846, d. unm. Milford, Dec. 19, 1893.

Thomas H. McQuestion, b. Mont Vernon, May 8, 1832, son Hugh M. and Sarah F. (Hartshorn) McQuestion. Lived on his father's farm near East School in East District, d. there Aug. 26, 1896, m. July 4, 1861, Hannah P., dau. Stephen and Hannah Gage of Amherst. She was b. 1838, res. Goffstown. Ch. b. Mont Vernon.

1. George N., b. Dec. 2, 1862, m. Addie S. Grant of Goffstown, April 28, 1891, who d. April 30, 1897, m. (2) Nov. 28, 1900, Carrie A. Richards; carpenter, res. Goffstown; one ch., Ruth E., b. Nov. 16, 1892.
2. William P., b. Sept. 1, 1867, m. Nov. 6, 1885, Edith Richards of New Boston; two ch., Ethel and Geo. R., res. Merrimack.
3. Bertha S., b. Dec. 13, 1868, m. Jan., 1885, Truman Parker, res. Lowell, Mass.
4. Mary J., b. June 10, 1876, m. Dec. 31, 1896, James E. Venio; one ch., Arthur E., b. Mont Vernon, Nov. 23, 1897, res. South Weare, N. H.

MILLS.

Capt. John Mills, the first of the family of six generations to the present day, was b. in Scotland. He is first found in Amherst, N. H., where he was married and settled in the Northwest Parish (now Mont Vernon). He is mentioned twelve times in Secombe's History of Amherst, and several times subsequently in petitions to prevent the settlement of a minister at Amherst Plain, insomuch as the Northwest Parish was without a Christian Church. On page 209 John Mills is mentioned as giving one shilling, four pence toward defraying the expenses of a delegate to the first Provincial Congress at Exeter. John Mills served in Col. John Hart's Co. at Crown Point in 1758, and in Col. John Goffe's Co. at Crown Point in 1760 in the French and Indian War. He was sergeant in Col. Reed's Regt., Capt. Crosby's Co. at Bunker Hill, was Second Lieut. in Col. T. Bedell's Regt. Dec., 1775. Joined army in New York to march northward to Canada, surrendered by Maj. Butterfield to the British and Indians at "The Cedars," was stripped and ran the gauntlet; May 19, 1776, exchanged and went to Crown Point. John Mills was First Lieut. in Col. Stark's Regt., Col. John Bradford's Co., at Battle of Bennington, was first company to attack. He went to Rhode Island in 1778 under Col. Nichols and Col. Josiah Crosby.

In autumn of 1781, Capt. John Mills led a company to Charlestown, N. H., to protect our frontier. The fighting done, Capt. John went to Winham, Vt., a place with which he was well pleased, having passed through it in his army marches, and settled with his family there for the rest of his life, dying in 1812, living there less than eight years.

He came to Mont Vernon prior to the Revolution, and made a homestead on the farm afterwards known as the Cloutman place, now occupied by Hon. Charles J. Smith. He lived here until about 1804, as there is no record of his living elsewhere. He was an active and prominent citizen of the then Northwest Parish. He m. Keziah Lyon about 1765. She d. in Windham, Vt., in 1824. Ch. b. Mont Vernon.

1. Abigail, b. Aug. 1, 1766, m. ———— Witherspoon, removed to Maine, where she d.
2. *Ebenezer, b. April 23, 1770.
3. *John, b. April 24, 1772.
4. Keziah, b. June 11, 1774, m. Jonathan Sherwin, moved to Landgrove, Vt., and d. there.
5. Betsey, m. John Dudley, they removed to Windham, Vt. She afterward removed to Canada with her son and d. there.

Ebenezer Mills, son Capt. John and Keziah (Lyon) Mills, b. Mont Vernon, April 23, 1770, m. Hannah W., dau. Ezekiel and Hannah (Washer) Upton of Mont Vernon, left his family with his son, Ebenezer, Jr., 20 years of age, went to Bellows Falls, Vt., to work. While there he enlisted in the War of 1812 from Rockingham, Vt. He d. in the army at Burlington, Vt., in 1812. His wife d. in Milford, Sept. 20, 1856, aged 83 years. Ch. b. Mont Vernon.

1. *Ebenezer.
2. Abigail, m. Daniel Bullard of Hyde Park, Vt., had two boys and three girls, and d. Hyde Park.
3. Annie or Rosanna, m. John Bullard, lived in Mont Vernon, three ch., Abbie, Edward and John
4. *Ezekial, b. Feb. 23, 1800.
5. Hannah, m. Dennis Holden of Milford. She d. Dec. 6, 1870, age 68 years, 5 months; six ch.
6. Lavina, b. Dec. 3, 1805, d. April 6, 1880, m. *Asa Wetherbee of Mont Vernon, May 1, 1824. Ch.
7. Salome, b. April 27, 1807, m. Gary W. Ober of Hyde Park, Vt., d. Sept. 14, 1883. He d. Sept. 2, 1857. Ch.
   1. Hannah, m. James Hunt, has two ch. lives Montana.
   2. Emily, m. Geo. V. Tarleton, two ch., son Geo., res. Nashua.
   3. Harriet, d. at 18.
   4. Everett, m. Emma McCauley of New Boston, d. Suncook, one dau., Etta.

5. Jennie D., b. Aug. 6, 1840, m. Kneeland C. White, res. Mont Vernon.

6. Helen L., b. July 25, 1842, m. (1) John Whipple of New Boston; m. (2) William Stevens of Mont Vernon, res. Mont Vernon.

7. Alma J., m. Charles Spencer of Pittsford, Vt., d. Milford; one dau., Mabel A., lived Mont Vernon; 14 years teacher.

8. John, b. Feb. 2, 1810, m. (1) Sarah Putnam, dau. Aaron K. Putnam of Wilton, 1835, lived in Wilton, came to Milford and engaged in boot and shoe manufacture till 1863, when he engaged in coopering and farming. Was a zealous antislavery man and Unitarian. His wife d. 1855. By her he had one dau., Sarah, who m. Hon. Charles H. Burns of Wilton, and two sons. He m. (2) 1858, Alvina Davis of Temple, by whom he had three sons and one dau. He d. March, 1892.

9. Aaron, b. April, 1812, m. Almira Bullard of Brookline, lived in Milford, was a boot manufacturer, farmer and cooper. He d. Aug. 5, 1893. His wife d. July 24, 1892. Six ch., only one living now (1903), Mrs. Geo. V. Tarleton.

John Mills, son Capt. John and Keziah (Lyon) Mills, b. Mont Vernon, April 24, 1772, m. Ednah Wilkins. He went to Nova Scotia to work upon a church, received his pay and started for home, which he never reached, was presumably murdered for his money. The story handed down is that a body was found in the vicinity of Lowell, thought to be that of John Mills. Ch. were:

1. Polly, b. Jan. 16, 1793.
2. Hezekiah, b. Dec. 15, 1795.

Ebenezer Mills, Jr., son of Ebenezer and Hannah W. (Upton) Mills, b. Mont Vernon, Aug. 4, 1792, enlisted from Rockingham, Vt., War of 1812, m. (1) Lovia P. Holden of Brookline, N. H., lived in Grafton, Vt., where nine ch. were born. She d. June, 1829. He then lived in Herkimer, N. Y., coming to Milford in 1844, where he worked at his trade as a carpenter the rest of his days. He m. (2) Jan. 10, 1830, Fanny Park of Grafton, Vt., had three sons by this wife. She d. in Milford, Aug. 8, 1864, aged 66 years, 8 months. Ch. by first wife b. Grafton, Vt., all but oldest:

1. Alphonse T., b. Weston, Vt., July 9, 1816, d. June 5, 1818.

2. Ebenezer U., b. Grafton, Feb. 23, 1818, lived in Boston, Mass., from boyhood, m. Sarah Stevens in 1844, who d. 1883. He d. June 12, 1882; one ch.

3. Maria A., b. Feb. 15, 1819, m. Lucius W. Woodard of Stratton, Vt., d. Manhattan, Kan., Dec. 25, 1891; had four ch.

4. Hannah, b. Oct. 16, 1820, m. John McIntire of Waterboro, Me., about 1844. She lived in Wilton and Boston, where she d. April 10, 1849; four ch.

5. John Frank, b. June 22, 1822. Went to Boston, was hotel-keeper, was proprietor of the Parker House from 1872 to 1876. He d. April 9, 1876. Wife d. Feb., 1864; eight ch.

6. Zenophon E., b. Oct. 18, 1823. Went to Milford, N. H., m. Harriet Russell Melzer of Milford, employed in J. & A. Mills shoe factory, was a quarryman, served three years as private in Co. C, 8th N. H. Regt., N. H. Volunteers; four ch.

7. Marion F., b. June 25, 1825, d. June 9, 1829.

8. Corydon S., b. Nov. 10, 1826, followed the sea for nine years in a whaler, went to the California gold mines about 1850, m. and was

killed Jan. 22, 1858, by a Uba mountain sliding.

9.   Loisa, b. Jan. 2, 1829, d. March 5, 1832.

Ch. by second wife b. Grafton.

10.   John Avery, b. Dec. 14, 1830, m. Emma Wheeler. Had one son
Edgar, who d. young. Was mill owner in Nashua and Manchester, and
shoe dealer in Penacook, Medford, Mass., and Milford, where he d. June
20, 1899. One adopted dau., Harriet.

11.   George Edgar, b. Oct. 27, 1833, followed sea seven years, lives
Medford, Mass., m. Frances, dau. James and Mary J. (Patch) Hopkins
of Mont Vernon; four ch.

12.   Henry Martin, b. Dec. 28, 1837, Lieut. in Co. C, Second N. H.
Regt. Vol., in Civil War, m. Nellie Jewett of Nashua, lived in Nashua
and Lowell; one son.

Ezekiel Mills, son of Ebenezer, Jr., and Hannah W. (Upton) Mills,
b. Mont Vernon, Feb. 23, 1800, m. Betsey Holt of Lyndeboro, lived in
Windham, Vt., and in Milford, was Milford tax collector 12 years, clerk
in store and kept boarding house. His wife d. Jan. 3, 1869. He d. June
18, 1881, Milford. Had two dau., Sarah R., m. Charles Buxton.

MITCHELL.

Joshua Mitchell, m. April 30, 1818, Mehitable Codman, dau. Thomas
and Tabitha (Wilkins) Gilmore of Mont Vernon. They lived where A.
W. Bragg does. He was a mechanic and moved to Woodstock, Vt., where
they d. Ch. b. Mont Vernon.

1.   Sarah Mehitable, b. Jan. 24, 1819.

2.   Thomas Gilmore, b. Nov. 19, 1820, a graduate of Dartmouth College, was a Congregational clergyman in Maine.

NICHOLS.

Jacob Nichols, son of Ensign S. and Sarah (Dinsmore) Nichols, b.
Londonderry, June 23, 1822. Mr. Nichols came to Mont Vernon about
1859, lived on the Reilly place on the turnpike, then on the old poor farm.
From 1867 to 1871 he lived on the farm in the South Dist., now owned
by Daniel Richardson, then in the village where A. W. Bragg, now lives.
He is a farmer, was formerly a merchant. Married (1) Sept., 1847, Ara-
bella E. Y., dau. of Henry Demeritt, b. in Boston, Mass., Feb. 22, 1822,
and d. in Mont Vernon, March, 1870; m. (2) Sept. 24, 1872, Georgia
E. Hall, widow of James Hall and dau. of Griffin and Elizabeth (Stevens)
Wilson, b. in Nelson, Aug. 4, 1842, and d. in Milford, July 6, 1900. Ch.

1.   Fannie Arabella, b. in Manchester, Feb. 21, 1850, m. March 22,
1877, Ellis H. Williams of Easton, Mass., and res. in Hyde Park, Mass.

2.   Henry James, b. in Manchester, Jan. 7, 1854, is assistant cashier
in Souhegan National Bank and res. in Milford; m. June 13, 1883, Nellie
M. Newman, widow of Henry A. Newman and dau. of George A. and
Diana (Woods) Graves of Cambridgeport, Mass.

3.   Carrie Maud, b. in Milford, May 22, 1874, m. June 28, 1891, Clarence A., son of John A. and Ella (Richards) Lovejoy of Milford; res. in
Concord Junction, Mass.

NEWMAN.

Moses Newman lived on James Reilly place, northeast of where Chas.

H. Trow now lives, in North Dist. He d. March 22, 1846, aged 70. His first wife, Polly, d. Aug. 21, 1825, age 40. His second wife, Abigail R., d. May 12, 1860, aged 77 years, 3 months. She was originally Abigail Haseltine (sister John Haseltine) of Amherst. She m. (1) Lt. John Weston, Sept. 27, 1802. He was killed by the falling of a mill-stone in 1810. She had five ch. by Lt. Weston. She m. Moses Newman, Jan. 31, 1826.

NUTTER.

Benjamin Nutter, son of John and Hannah (Dennett) Nutter, b. Barnstead, N. H., came to Mont Vernon in the thirties, engaged in the business of manufacturing organs. He removed to Belleville, Canada. He m. Sarah, dau. Benjamin Nathan and Sarah (Bancroft) Jones. Ch b. Mont Vernon.

1. George, m., not living lived in Belleville Canada.
2. Charles, m., lives Toronto, Canada.
3. Annette, m. ———— Booth, lived in Belleville, Canada, not living.

John D. Nutter, son of John and Hannah (Dennett) Nutter, b. Barnstead, N. H., 1811. He learned the trade of a cabinet maker in Rochester, N. H., and after attaining his majority came to Mont Vernon, where his elder brother, Benjamin Nutter had settled and engaged in the business of manufacturing organs for nearly ten years. In 1844 he removed to Nashua and here pursued the same industry some four years, returning to Mont Vernon in 1848 and remaining until 1853, when he went to Attica, Ind., and engaged in a banking business. In 1855 he sold out his business and returned to New Hampshire and for one or two years was a merchant at Nashua, removing thence to Montreal, where he resided some 31 years, extensively engaged in the lumber business. In 1888 he removed to Malden, Mass., where he d. Jan. 19, 1890, age 78 years. Aug. 8, 1844, he m. Harriet A., dau. Asa and Mary A. (Appleton) Stevens of Mont Vernon. She was b. Mont Vernon, May 22, 1821; res. Montreal.

1. John Appleton, b. Nashua, July 18, 1846, m. Katherine Howard of Hardwick, Mass., has five ch., res. Montreal.
2. Asa, b. Mont Vernon, d. unm. at 33 yrs. of age.
3. Dr. William D., b. Montreal, m. Charlotte Bartlett of Malden, res. Malden, Mass., physician; one dau.

O'BRIEN.

John O'Brien, son of Patrick and Mary (Magner) O'Brien, born in Limerick, Ireland, in 1837. Was a farmer. Lived here about 15 years, on the Purgatory Road, in a house now burnt down. He removed to Milford in 1870, where he d., June 30, 1889. Married Catherine, dau. of James and Margaret (Fox) Ryan, b. in Country Cork, Ireland. Ch.

1. James F., b. Mont Vernon, Nov. 15, 1856, d. here Dec., 1865.
2. Thomas C., b. Mont Vernon, Aug., 1859, d. here Dec., 1861.
3. John P., b. Mont Vernon in 1860, d. here Jan., 1862.
4. Joseph T. b. Mont Vernon, July, 1862, res. Milford; is a farmer; m. Nov. 18, 1896, Mary A., dau. of Jeremiah and Anistatia (Splain) Calnan of Woburn, Mass.
5. George N., b. Mont Vernon, May 15, 1867, d. Milford, April 4, 1881.
6. Mary F., b. Milford, Jan. 10, 1872.

ODELL.

William Odell was a resident of Souhegan West as early as 1759. Lived on the farm owned by John Hazen, in West District, d. **March, 1812**, age 85. He m. Phebe Boutelle. She d. Jan. 24, 1817, age 85. **Ch.** were:

1. Phebe, b. 1750, m. David Duncklee. She d. Jan. 6, 1839.
2. *William, b. 1752.
3. Martha, b. Aug. 6, 1754, m. John Lovejoy about 1775.
4. Ebenezer, b. May 22, 1756, m. Sarah Johnson, May 29, 1782.
5. John, b. Dec. 4, 1761, m. Edith Nourse, d. Nov. 5, 1844; nine ch.

William Odell, Jr., son of William and Phebe (Boutelle) Odell of Amherst, b. 1752, d. Aug. 26, 1829, m. Susannah, dau. Capt Hezekiah and Hannah (Phelps) Lovejoy of Amherst. She was b. July 25, 1756, d. March 17, 1831. Lived on his father's farm. Ch.

1. Susannah, b. Nov. 9, 1774, d. unm. Sept. 28, 1813.
2. William, b. Feb. 23, 1777, d. Nov. 7, 1850; had three ch.
3. Hannah, b. Aug. 9, 1779, d. Feb. 11, 1781.
4. Hannah, b. May 23, 1783, d. Jan. 5, 1830.
5. *Luther, b. Sept. 9, 1785.
6. Betsey, b. Sept. 28, 1787, m. Jacob Hildreth, Jr., of Amherst, May 15, 1807, d. Aug. 27, 1850; five ch.
7. Polly, b. Oct. 13, 1789, m. Henry Howard in 1809, d. Nov. 6, 1875; had 12 ch.

Luther Odell, son William, Jr., and Susannah (Lovejoy) Odell, b. Amherst, Sept. 9, 1785, lived on the farm now owned by John Hazen in West District, d. there July 6, 1862. He m. March 16, 1806, Betsey, dau. Amos and Keturah (Stewart) Green. She was b. Amherst, Oct. 15, 1783, d. Mont Vernon, Dec. 18, 1868. Ch. b.

1. Charles, b. Amherst, June 5, 1806, m. Maria J. Roberts of Wakefield, N. H., June 24, 1834, d. Biddeford, Me.; had eight ch.
2. *William, b. Amherst, July 13, 1808.
3. Luther, b. Amherst, July 18, 1816.
4. Orinda Felton, b. Amherst, Feb. 19, 1819; m. (1) Josiah Upton, Jan. 2, 1842; m. (2) Jan. 10, 1849, Capt William Osborn Lamson. She d. Nov. 24, 1874.
5. Susan, b. Goffstown, July 16, 1821, m. Nov. 15, 1845, Francis Brown of Lowell; had two ch., a son and dau.
6. Harriet, b. May 21, 1827, at Mont Vernon, m. Dec. 23, 1848, George Jones of Durham, N. H.; three ch.

William Odell, b. Amherst, July 13, 1808, son of Luther and B. (Green) Odell, lived on his father's farm in Mont Vernon, moved to Petrosky, Mich., where he d. Jan. 10, 1884; m. Mary Ann Kingsbury of Dedham, Mass. She d. Mont Vernon, July 5, 1877, aged 59 yrs., 4 mos. Ch. b. Mont Vernon.

1. Mary, b. Jan. 13, 1838, d. Jan. 15, 1838.
2. William, b. Dec. 1, 1842, d. same day.
3. Luther, b. 1844, m. Mrs. Green of Vermont, lives Petrosky, Mich.

Luther Odell, son of Luther and Betsey (Green) Odell, b. Amherst, July 18, 1816. Lived in Mont Vernon, Lyndeboro, Bennington and Hancock, where he d. Feb. 13, 1887. He was a carpenter and built the body of the house in Mont Vernon Village, now occupied as a summer residence by John F. Colby, m. March 21, 1844, Susan, dau. Jotham and Ruth (Cloutman) Richardson.

1. Susan Annette, b. Mont Vernon, Jan. 12, 1845, d. Lyndeboro, Dec. 24, 1859.

2. William Haskell, b. Mont Vernon, April 22, 1848, m Josie S. Kimball of Bennington, Dec. 7, 1875, lives Bennington; ch.: (1) Fred Wilton, b. March 11, 1877; (2) Ethel May, b. Dec. 24, 1882.

3. Hattie Elizabeth, b. Mont Vernon, Oct. 11, 1848, d. Wilton, Aug. 15, 1864.

Ebenezer Odell, Sr., d. 1824, age 75.

Ebenezer Odell, Jr., m. Esther Langdell, June 5, 1807.

ORDWAY.

Daniel Ordway, b. Pelham, N. H., April 5, 1813, m. Nancy B., dau. Ezra and Rebecca (Langdell) Langdell. She was b. Mont Vernon, Sept. 28, 1812, d She res. Francestown. He came to Mont Vernon rch ss one-half of the farm now occupied by George F. Tarbell, and lived there until 1859, when he purchased a farm in the east part of Francestown, where he resided until his death, April 19, 1900. He was a pious man and much respected. Ch. b. Mont Vernon.

1. Nancy.
2. Frances Rebecca.
3. Henrietta.

PARKER.

Lieut. Robert Parker and wife, Penelope, both from Andover, Mass., settled in the extreme south part of the town, where Charles H. Raymond did live, before the Revolution. He d. Mont Vernon, April, 1805, age 73. Ch.

1. William, b. April 26, 1757, Revolutionary soldier
2. *Robert, b. Sept. 3, 1759
3. Rachel, b. Oct. 19, 1761.
4. Deborah, b. May 3, 1764.
5. *Benjamin, b. March 18, 1766
6. Penelope, b. July 23, 1768.

Robert Parker, son of Robert and Penelope Parker, b. Sept. 3, 1759, m. Sept. 11, 1785, Rebecca, dau. Dea. Oliver and Amy (Washer) Carleton of Mont Vernon. She was b. Jan. 21, 1764. They moved to Barre, Vt., from Mont Vernon in 1805 and d. there. He was a Revolutionary soldier. Ch. all probably b. Mont Vernon.

1. Robert, m. Fanny Batchelder, dau. Ebenezer and Elizabeth T. S. Batchelder, May 29, 1806. She was b. July 8, 1785, moved to Landgrove, Vt.

2. Stephen lived in Newport, N. H., was a highly respected and prominent citizen, was Representative from that town.

3. Oliver.

4. Carlton, settled in Andover, Mass., m. a Miss Abbott, left five ch. viz: Carlton, George H., Charles S., Mary and Martha

5. George.
6. John.
7. Enoch.

The daughters:
8. Mary (Mrs. Damon of Pembroke Mass.).
9. Lucy (Mrs. Hewitt of Barre, Vt.),
10. Hannah (Mrs. Davis of Barre. Vt.)
11. Emma, unm.
12. Sarah, lived Brewer, Me

Capt. Benjamin Parker, son Robert and Penelope Parker, b. **Mont** Vernon, March 18, 1766, d. Jan., 1826; m. Oct. 10, 1794, Betsey, **dau.** Joseph and Patience (Bradford) Lovejoy of Mont Vernon. She d. **Am**herst, Sept. 25, 1859, was b. in 1772. Ch.
1. Nancy, m. Moses B. Stewart of Amherst. May, 1825, d. Bluffville, Ill., Sept., 1855, aged 59 years, 4 months.
2. Joseph, d. Dec. 26, 1823, aged 19.
3. Arethusa, d. Sept., 1830, age 25.
4. Thomas J., d. March 21, 1837, age 30, m.
5. Lucretia, d. April, 1834, aged 18.
6. Samuel, went West.

Caesar Parker (of colored blood) was from Weare, lived in a small house in the South part of the town several years, m. Margaret Spear of Weare. She d. Feb. 24, 1854, age 85 yrs.; had several ch. He d. 1855, age 99 yrs.
Nathaniel, b. 1802, went to live with David McCauley of Antrim in 1809, became a respected citizen of the town, d. there unm.
Humphrey Moore, d. June 28, 1861, age 53 years and 9 months
Mark.
Ross.
There were two dau., one m. a Baptist clergyman of Newport, R. I.
James, d. Dec. 4, 1839, age 27.

Granville Parker came from Nelson, lived on the Joseph H. Tarbell farm and on farm now owned by Estate of E. C. Flanders, southeast of the village. He moved to Deering. He m. Elizabeth, dau. Elisha and Betsey (Temple) Swinnington of Mont Vernon. She d.
Ira A., m. Harriet, dau. John J. and Sarah (Hopkins) Carson. She d. June 26, 1881, age 28. He m. (2) Miss Case; lives Deering.

Elbridge Parker, b. New Boston, March 27, 1815, son of William and Martha (Fox) Parker, m. Nov. 1844, Hannah Elizabeth Fillebrown, b. Lexington, Mass., July 29, 1819, d. Mont Vernon, March 11, 1898. They lived three years in Mass., then bought the John Fairfield farm in New Boston and lived there until 1885, when they moved to Mont Vernon. He d. June 12, 1886.
1. Henry Herbert, b. March 12, 1846, d. unm. May, 1871.
2. Mary Frances, b. New Boston, May 27, 1851, m. Nov. 3, 1875, *George N. Foster of Mont Vernon, who d. May 12, 1881. She d. Mont Vernon, Oct. 22, 1892; one dau., Annie P. Foster, b. Nov. 17, 1880.
3. Charles A., b. Sept. 6, 1856, in New Boston; lives Arlington, Mass., unm.
4. Lizzie R., b. New Boston, Nov. 9, 1861, lives Mont Vernon, unm.

PEABODY.

Col. Stephen Peabody, son of William and Rebecca (Smith) Peabody,

b. Sept. 3, 1742, m. Hannah, dau. of Thomas and Hannah(Goffe) Chandler of Bedford, in 1763. She d. in Montpelier, Vt., Aug., 1826, age 79 years. He was Adjutant of Col. Reed's Regiment in the Battle of Bunker Hill, aid to Gen. Stark at Bennington and Lieutenant-Colonel commanding a battalion sent to Rhode Island in 1778. The cellar of his large mansion on Purgatory Hill, one mile and one-half west of Mont Vernon Village can still be seen. He d. Sept. 19, 1780. Inscription on his tombstone in Mont Vernon Cemetery:

"In memory of Col. Stephen Peabody who, after he had displayed his martial abilities in the service of his country d. at home, 1782, age 38. Ch. b. Mont Vernon.

1. Thomas, b. Feb. 15, 1764, m. (1) Sarah Perkins, March 10, 1785; m. (2) Mrs. Bird, a sister of Gen. James Miller. He settled in Vermont. Near the close of the war for Independence he was surgeon in a regiment commanded by Col. Evans.

2. Dr. John, b. May 17, 1766, m. Keziah Hubbard, located Salem, Mass., had three ch.

3. Hannah, b. July 2, 1768, m. *Enoch Carleton of Amherst; had four ch.

4. Rebecca, b. July 17, 1770. She was a physician and surgeon, m. Gen. Perley Davis of Montpelier, Vt., Nov. 4, 1794, d. in East Montpelier, Feb. 5, 1853.

5. Stephen, b. Aug. 23, 1772, m. Martha, dau. Joseph and Martha (Dodge) Trow of Mont Vernon, Dec. 6, 1795. She was b. March 13, 1772. He was a physician in Orange, Vt.

6. Asenath, b. July 25, 1774, d. March 15, 1777.

7. Sarah, b. Dec. 2, 1776, d. suddenly on the day appointed for her marriage.

8. Asenath, b. Dec. 14, 1779, m. Lewis Parker of Cambridge, Vt., d. March, 1846.

Samuel Peabody, son of Moses and Sarah (Holt) Peabody, b. Sept. 1, 1741, d. Mont Vernon, Aug. 6, 1814, m. Elizabeth, dau. Joseph Wilkins of Amherst. They settled in Andover, Mass., removed to Mont Vernon, 1785.

1. *Moses.

2. Samuel, m. Huldah Stiles, June 11, 1790, d. June, 1825.

3. John, m. ———— Holt.

4. Joseph, b. Oct. 3, 1770 d. Nov. 1, 1853, m. (1) Olive Berry, Sept. 4, 1800; m. (2) Anna Flint, Oct. 22, 1805. They settled in Middletown, Mass., where he was deacon in the church several years; had seven ch.

5. Sarah, m. ———— Damon, settled in Marshfield, Vt.

6. Aaron, m. Edith Wilkins, d. in Mont Vernon, 1854, age 82. She d. 1863, aged 82. No ch.

7. Jacob, m. Sally Wilkins. They settled in Milford. Had a son, Horace, b. Mont Vernon, Jan. 28, 1814, lived in Milford.

8. Joel, b. 1778, m. Elizabeth Wilkins, settled Middletown, Mass.; five ch.

Moses Peabody, son Samuel and Elizabeth (Wilkins) Peabody, d. in Mont Vernon, Nov. 4, 1842, m. May 25, 1786, Sarah, dau. Ebenezer and Lydia (Peabody) Holt. She was b. in 1757, d. Mont Vernon, May 25, 1845. Ch. b. Mont Vernon.

1. Moses, m. Mary Marvell. He d. in the army at Burlington, Vt., in May, 1813.

2. Lydia H., m. *Azel W. Burnham, 1818.
Ch. Moses and Sarah H. Peabody:
1. Keziah, m. Nahum Bullard, 1830.
2. Mary Ann, b. July 2. 1812, m. April 19, 1830, Joshua F. Skinner
of Amherst, lived Amherst, four ch., a dau. d. in infancy.

PERKINS.

John Perkins, the emigrant ancestor of the Mont Vernon Perkinses,
was born in Newent, Gloucester, England, in 1590, sailed from Bristol,
England, for Boston, Dec. 1. 1630. Rev. Roger Williams was a fellow
passenger. Perkins had with him his family, consisting then of wife and
five children. Landed in Boston. Lived there about two years, where
another ch., Lydia, was born. Removed to Ipswich in 1633, became an extensive land owner in Ipswich, appears to have been one of the leading
men. Deputy to the General Court in 1636, d. 1654, age 64. His ch.
named in his will were John, Thomas, Mrs. Eliabeth Sargent, Mrs. Mary
Bradbury, Mrs. Lydia Bennett, Jacob Perkins. His wife, Judith Perkins,
to execute will.

Joseph Perkins (fifth generation from the first John Perkins, 1;
Jacob, 2; John, 3; Thomas, 4; Joseph, 5;), son of Thomas and Elizabeth
(Fowler) Perkins, b. Sept. 15, 1735, m. Emma Dodge of Beverly, May 12,
1761. They resided in Beverly some years after their marriage. He was
a tailor by trade. Probably came to Mont Vernon in 1776, not 1773, as
Lydia, the youngest of his four daughters, was baptized in Beverly, Dec.
10, 1775. He d. Mont Vernon, Dec., 1823.
His third dau., Betsey, m. *Joseph Trow of Mont Vernon. She d.
Aug. 22, 1851, age 83. His son, Capt. Joseph Perkins, Jr., b. Beverly,
Mass., Feb. 6, 1761, d. Mont Vernon. Nov. 22, 1822, came to Mont Vernon
with his parents when a lad. July 3, 1779, at 18, he enlisted in the army
and served one year. While in the service he was on a privateer vessel,
which was taken by the British and the crew was taken to England and
confined in what was called the Mill Prison. While in prison he worked
at his trade of tailoring, in which way he contrived to get some money,
which made his lot more tolerable than that of many others. Tradition
says that when he secured a guinea he would cover it with cloth and sew
it on his coat for a button. M. Hannah, third dau. of James and Hannah
(Trask) Woodbury. She was b. Oct. 5, 1766, d. April 15, 1856. He d.
Nov. 22, 1822. Ch. b. Mont Vernon.
    1. Hannah, b. Aug. 10, 1783, m. Levi Ray, Jan. 19, 1804.
    2. *Mark Dodge, b. June 5, 1785
    3. John Trask, b. Dec. 7, 1787, d. Mont Vernon, Jan. 16, 1859, unm.
    4. Lucretia, b. March 6, 1790, m. Jesse Woodbury of Weare, d. 1873
    5. Joseph, b. March 13, 1794, d. Aug. 19, 1797.
    6. *Joseph, b. April 18, 1796.
    7. James Woodbury, b. March 6, 1797, d. March, 1802.
    8. *James Woodbury, b. April 17, 1798, m. Fanny Cochran of New
Boston, dau. John Cochran, Esq., d. New Chester, Wis., March 30, 1874.
    9. Sarah, b. April 20, 1800, m. March 22, 1825, *Joseph Trow, d.
July 31, 1837; six ch.
    10. *Hiram, b. May 16, 1802.
    11. Solomon, b. March 2, 1804, d. March 19, 1804.
    12. Catherine, b. Sept. 15, 1805, m. May 4, 1826, Elijah Putnam, Jr.,
of Amherst; two ch. She d. March 18, 1884.

13. *Elbridge Fisk, b. Sept. 9, 1811.

Mark Dodge Perkins, son of Capt. Joseph and Hannah (Woodbury) Perkins, b. Mont Vernon, June 5, 1785, lived for many years in the house now burnt, which stood below A. W. Bragg's. Was Deputy Sheriff many years; m. (1) Feb., 1809, Mahala, dau. Peter and Betsey (Woodbury) Jones. She was b. 1788, d. June 24, 1843. He m. (2) Cynthia Johnson in 1842. She d. Feb. 19, 1867, aged 69. He d. Mont Vernon, July 22, 1881. Ch. by first wife b. Mont Vernon.

1. Betsey J., m. her second cousin, *Charles R. Beard, in 1829. She d. Dec. 26, 1850, aged 40 yrs.

2. Abigail F., m. Aug. 10, 1836, Zephaniah Hutchinson of Milford; had two ch. She d. Milford, April 20, 1848, aged 37.

3. Maria, m. Bradbury.

4. Hannah, m. Luke Beard, brother of Chas. R. Beard; four ch. viz: Albert, Horace, Emily, Luke. They lived in Wilton.

5. Peter J., d. unm. Aug. 10, 1843, aged 23.

6. Harriet N., d. Aug. 30, 1828, age 5.

7. Mahala, d. Aug. 23, 1828, aged 1 yr., 4 mos.

8. Emily L., m. *J. H. A. Bruce. She d. June 19, 1860, aged 26 yrs., 9 mos.

Joseph Perkins, son of Capt. Joseph and Hannah (Woodbury) Perkins, b. Mont Vernon, April 18, 1796, owned and occupied the Perkins farm in the North District; m. (1) Sally, dau. of Daniel and Granddau. of Dea. Daniel Smith. She d. June 4, 1830, age 32. He m. (2) Susanna B. Locke of Woburn, Mass. She was b. November 15, 1803, d. Mont Vernon, May 10, 1867. He d. Oct. 21, 1877. Ch. all b. Mont Vernon. Ch. by first wife:

1. Hannah, b. April 24, 1816, m. *Trask W. Averill, April 9, 1835; eight ch. She d. May 2, 1849.

2. James Woodbury, b. May 9, 1818, m. (1) Frances S. Bryant, July 9, 1837. She d. Nov. 3, 1855, age 39. He m. (2) Mrs. Jane Loveren. She d. Jan., 1873. He was a tin pedlar, lived in Amherst and Lowell, d. Lowell, Nov. 6, 1887.

3. *Daniel Smith, b. Sept. 22, 1821, m. (1) Jan. 28, 1842, Emeline F. Crosby. She d. July 18, 1868, age 45.

By second wife:

4. Joseph Elbridge, b. July 24, 1835, farmer, lived on his father's farm, m. April 6, 1862, Eleanor, dau. Jesse and Eleanor (Morgan) Manning. She was b. in Billerica, Dec. 15, 1841, d. June 29, 1902. He d. March 15, 1897; no ch. She m. after his death J. Henry Smith.

5. ?John Trask, b. June 28, 1839.

Dr. James Woodbury Perkins, son of Capt. Joseph and Hannah (Woodbury) Perkins, b. Mont Vernon, April 17, 1798, was installed as minister in Warner, N. H., March 4, 1840, dismissed in 1846. Fred Myron, Colby, in his sketch of Warner in History of Merrimack Co., characterizes him as having been an earnest, laborious and efficient pastor. He commenced his labors in Nooksett, Feb., 1846, was at Alstead, commenced preaching in Hillsboro in 1852 and at Deering in 1854, and finally left on account of ill health; was also a physician; m. Fanny, dau. John Cochran, Esq., and Frances (Gove) Cochran of New Boston. He d. New Chester, Wis., March 30, 1874. A son, Charles, went West, established a paper and lived in New Chester, Wis., where his father died.

Hiram Perkins, son of Capt. Joseph and Hannah (Woodbury) Perkins, b. Mont Vernon, May 16, 1802, owned and occupied the Lt. James Woodbury farm in the village many years (now owned by Estate of Dr. C. M. Kittredge. He m. Feb. 23, 1837, Serviah, dau. Capt. William and Serviah (Jones) Lamson. She was b. Mont Vernon, Jan. 15, 1815, d. March 1, 1871. He d. Nov. 13, 1880. Ch. b. Mont Vernon.

    1. Ann Augusta, b. Jan. 15, 1838, m. Nov. 27, 1862, *Clark Campbell. She d. Aug. 16, 1900.

    2. Mary F. B., b. Sept. 23, 1839, m. Feb. 15, 1866, Charles A. Hutchinson, lived Hilton Head, S. C., and at Jacksonville, Fla., where they both d. March 25, 1872. Ch., Chas. Everett, b. Hilton Head, S. C., Nov. 27, 1866, m., lives in Cal; two ch.; George M., b. Nov. 10, 1869, m.; one ch.; lives in Cal.

    3. Harriet Ida, b. Aug. 21, 1842, m. George W. Miller, Jan. 13, 1868, d. at Providence, R. I., March 7, 1869; one ch., Ada P., b. Providence, R. I., Feb. 14, 1869.

    4. Hiram Osborn, b. July 16, 1844, d. July 11, 1862.

    5. Elbridge Weston, b. Oct. 2, 1846, d. Oct. 3, 1847.

Elbridge Fisk Perkins, son of Capt. Joseph Perkins, Jr., and Hannah (Woodbury) Perkins, b. Mont Vernon, Sept. 9, 1811, m. (1) Abby, dau. Abiel and Emma (Howard) Wilkins, Sept. 10, 1830. She d. Oct. 4, 1853. Lived in Amherst and Wilton. Was a merchant tailor. He d. July 19, 1894. He m. (2) Jan. 31, 1854, Mary L., dau. Col. Levi and Sophia (Gilmore) Jones of Amherst. She was b. Amherst, June 13, 1821. Ch. by second wife b. Wilton:

    1. Levi Woodbury, b. March 26, 1855, m. Oct. 14, 1880, Lenore C. Emerson of Wilton.

    2. Hattie Sophia, b. Nov. 26, 1860.

John Trask Perkins, son of Joseph and Susanna B. (Locke) Perkins, b. Mont Vernon, June 28, 1839, m. April 18, 1860, Laura A., dau. of Nathan and Abigail (Weston) Richardson of Mont Vernon. She d. Jan. 19, 1873, age 30 years, 11 months. He m. (2) Sept. 14, 1878, Margaret W. Currier of Newburyport, Mass., res. Westboro, Mass. He served in 13th N. H. Regt. in War of '61-'65. Ch. all by first wife b. Mont Vernon:

    1. John Ellsworth, b. June 10, 1862, m. Nov. 3, 1892, Catharine Laws at Breckenridge, Col.

    2. Nellie Grace, b. July 21, 1867, m. at Newburyport, Mass., Feb. 18, 1892, Albert F. Swaine.

    3. Laura Etta, b. June 26, 1869, m. at Newburyport, Mass., Nov. 14, 1894, Arthur F. Ingram.

Daniel Smith Perkins, son of Joseph and Sally (Smith) Perkins, b. Mont Vernon, Sept. 22, 1821, m. Jan. 28, 1842, Emeline F., dau. Otis and Salome (Whipple) Crosby. She d. July 18, 1868, age 45. He resides Campton, N. H. Their ch. buried in Mont Vernon were:

    Joseph, d. 1845, age 4 yrs.

    Charles W., d. age 3 yrs., 6 mos.

    Eva F., d. at 18 mos.

    James W., d. July 24, 1851, age 3 yrs., 3 mos.

    Harriet, d. July 27, 1851, age 17 mos.

    Daniel Otis, d. April 22, 1852, age 6 yrs., 3 mos.

    Harriet E.

    Willis C., d. City of Mexico.

Edward lives in Mexico. m. Mrs. Spencer of Boston; 10 ch.

PIKE.

Peter F. Pike, son (name not known) and Lucy (Foster) Pike, b. Dec. 25, 1824, painter. m. Dec. 30, 1847, Nancy E., dau. Benjmain F. and Hannah (Smith) Hill. She was b. Mont Vernon, Sept. 6, 1832. He served in the 13th N. H. Regt. in the War for the Union. He d. Sept. 29, 1898. She res. Mont Vernon. Ch. b. Mont Vernon:

1. Ella M., b. Aug. 20, 1848, m. (1) Edwin N. Gutterson of Amherst, June 6, 1867. m. (2) Richard Beach; d. Oct. 2, 1888.
2. Almus W., b. April 7, 1851, d. April 29, 1865.
3. Frank L., b. March 12, 1860, m. Nov. 27, 1884, Mary A. Haridon of New Boston. They reside in Milford.
4. Alice B., b. Aug. 10, 1866, d. Jan. 29, 1867.
5. George W., b. Oct. 30, 1868, m. Feb. 24, 1892, Lura B., dau. Edward and Martha (Hardy) Colburn of Hollis. She was b. in Hollis. April 6, 1868. They reside in Mont Vernon.

Ephraim Pike lived on Battle's place in East Dist., before the Battles came, was moderator in 1813 and 1815. m. Sept. 10, 1809, Nancy, dau. James and Mehitable (Woodbury) Ray. She was b. Mont Vernon, March 24, 1791.

PINKHAM.

William F. Pinkham, b. Nashua, March 7, 1854. Has resided in Brideport, Ct. Lived here from 1890 to 1896. Now resides in Hyde Park, Mass. He is a civil engineer and speculator. He m. Dec. 25, 1876, Caroline Frances, dau. Charles and Almira L. (Trow) Forsaith. She was b. Oct. 30, 1854. Ch.

1. Ralph Howard, b. Jan. 16, 1880.
2. Charles Forsaith, b. July 14, 1881.
3. Henry Palmer, b. Mont Vernon, Jan. 16, 1894.

PREBLE.

Preble, b. Ossipee, N. H., d. Lawrence, 1850, age 51, m. Sally D. Barker of Marblehead. They lived here on the place now occupied by Charles J. Smith a few years in the forties. She now resides with her son Henry, in Lynn. Ch.

Henry, b. Mont Vernon, 1844, shoe cutter, resides Lynn.

PRENTISS.

John Prentiss came from Salem, Mass., to Mont Vernon about 1816. He was a most excellent penman. He was a merchant here. Removed to Amherst in 1825, where he was cashier of the Farmers' Bank through the whole of its existence. He was town clerk there and postmaster some years during the time. His wife, Mrs. Azubah Prentis, played the organ in the meeting house at Amherst several years. He d. in Claremont. March 2, 1868, aged 82 years, with his son, John J. Prentiss. Ch. were:

1. Howard.
2. John J., m. Mary Ann, dau. Hon. Edmund Parker; lawyer, set-

tled in Henniker and Claremont; was speaker in the N. H. House of Representatives; m. 1855. Lived in Chicago, Ill., afterwards.

3. Henry, d. young.

PERHAM.

Joel Frank Perham, son of Joel H. and Alice G. (Lynch) Perham, b. Wilton, Sept. 25, 1862, m. June 2, 1890, Annie E., dau. of Daniel H. and Mary J. (Holt) Smith of Mont Vernon. She was b. Mont Vernon, June 30, 1869. No ch. He is a cattle dealer and farmer and lives in village.

RAMSEY.

Dr. John Ramsey came here from Greenfield, succeeded Dr. Rogers Smith, was taxed here in 1815, practised here a few years, m. Miss Davis, dau. Jonathan and Mary Davis of Westford, Mass. He returned to Greenfield. Ch. probably b. in Greenfield.

1. Margaret, m. (1) Dr. George W. Moore of Amherst. He d. Sept. 8, 1866. She m. (2) Dr. Leonard French of Manchester, June 25, 1867.

2. John, farmer in Greenfield.

3. William, res. Wisconsin.

RAY OR REA.

James Ray, Esq., was the only ch. of James and Elizabeth (Dodge) Ray of Beverly, where he was b., May 1, 1759. His father d. shortly after his birth, leaving his mother a widow 17 years of age. In 1760 she m. Peter Woodbury and in 1773 the family moved to Mont Vernon, where James grew to manhood with his half-brothers, Levi, Jesse, Peter and Mark Woodbury. Here young Ray m. Mehitable, dau. James Woodbury, May 3, 1780. He was a noted inn-keeper and an active man in Mont Vernon. Trask W. Averill said that James Ray lived on the Dr. Adams place most of the time he lived here, and carried on the potash business, as well as keeping a tavern. In 1817 he moved to Amherst and kept the hotel afterwards known as the Nutt tavern until Jan., 1827. He d. Amherst, Jan. 15, 1830, age 70. His wid. d. in Francestown, Feb. 4, 1858. Ch. b. Mont Vernon:

1. James, b. July 9, 1780, m. Elsie Dana, April 26, 1810, lived on the New Boston road, had ch., d. April 2, 1857.

2. John, b. Aug. 13, 1781, d. Nov. 25, 1781.

3. Mehitable, b. April 15, 1783, d. Dec. 15, 1832, m. John Moor of New Boston, Aug. 25, 1804. One of her ch., Sabrina, was mother of Clark Campbell, Esq., of Mont Vernon.

4. Levi, b. July 13, 1785, m. his cousin, Hannah Perkins of Mont Vernon, Jan. 9, 1804.

5. Sabrina, b. Oct. 14, 1786, d. Dec. 11, 1802.

6. Henry Hammond, b. Sept. 9, 1789, d. Feb. 20, 1829.

7. Nancy, b. March 24, 1791, m. Sept. 10, 1809, Ephraim Pike.

8. Frances W., b. Jan. 13, 1794, m. James W. Haseltine of Francestown in 1814, d. Manchester, Dec. 12, 1877; had four ch.

9. John T., b. Nov. 15, 1795, d. 1797.

10. Elizabeth D., b. May 8, 1798, m. Newell Dean in Dec., 1828, d. Boston, Mass., July 7, 1858.

11. Mary, b. May 31, 1800, d. Feb. 22, 1802.

12. Peter W., b. Dec. 5, 1802, lived in Salem, Mass.
13. Horace, b. Nov. 5, 1807.

RAYMOND.

John Raymond of Beverly, b. about 1616, m. Rachel Scruggs, who d. 1666. He m. (2) Mrs. Judith Woodbury, wid. William Woodbury, Jr. She d. 1702, aged 75. His ninth ch. and the first by his second wife was 2Nathaniel, b. March 15, 1670, d. Jan. 8, 1749, m. Rebecca, dau. Lot Conant, b. Jan. 31, 1671, d. Dec., 1760. They had 10 ch., of whom 3Nathaniel was the ninth, b. April 1, 1712, m. Martha Balch, Oct. 3, 1735. They had eight ch., of whom the sixth was Nathaniel, 4th generation, b. Beverly, May 8, 1749, m. Phebe Dodge, dau. of Geo. Dodge, Hamilton, Mass. He d. Mont Vernon, 1800. He removed to Mont Vernon in 1773. He was a sailor. His wife d. Nov. 15, 1825, age 70. He lived on Raymond farm in South Dist. Ch.

1. Martha, m. Dea. Andrew Hutchinson of Milford, had sons, Nathaniel, Elisha and Stillman.

2. Mary, m. Nov. 15, 1800, David Goodell and settled in Hillsboro. d. Antrim, 1864, aged 85; had two sons, George D. and Jesse R. Goodell. George D. was the father of Dr. John Goodell of Hillsboro and Jesse R. Goodell, the father of Ex.-Gov. D. H. Goodell, of Antrim.

3. Sally, b. Jan. 26, 1781, m. Samuel Hartshorn of Lyndeboro, had six ch., of whom the first was Dea. Samuel, b. Feb. 25, 1810, d. Mason, Nov., 1846, was deacon Baptist Church, Lyndeboro, and Hancock.

4. *George, b. 1783.

5. *John, b. July, 1785.

6. *Jesse, b. 1792.

George Raymond, son of Nathaniel and Phebe (Dodge) Raymond, b. Mont Vernon, 1783, m. Dec. 19, 1809, Mary, dau. John and Polly (Bradford) Wallace of Milford. She was b. May 13 1785, d. Sept. 8, 1862. He was selectman, was representative in 1842; lived on the homestead in the South Dist., d. Dec. 14, 1853. Ch. b. Mont Vernon.

1. Mary, b. Jan. 5, 1811, was teacher and principal of the Female Seminary in Hancock, m. Jan. 19, 1839, Rev. Dura D. Pratt of Nashua, d. Aug. 8, 1902, at Evanston, Ill.

2. Phebe B., b. Sept. 13, 1812, m. Eugene Hutchinson of Milford, d. Nov. 13, 1837; one dau.

3. George, b. Nov. 3, 1814, d. Aug. 9, 1818.

4. *Andrew W., b. Oct. 19, 1817.

5. Sally, b. Oct. 3, 1818, d. Oct. 14, 1819.

6. *George, b. Aug. 9, 1820.

7. Nancy, b. April 25, 1824, m. May 11, 1847, Dana W. Pratt of Penacook, N. H., d. Feb., 1871; one son, Charles D., who d. at Milford, N. H.

John Raymond, son of Nathaniel and Phebe (Dodge) Raymond, b. Mont Vernon, July 23, 1785, m. Sally, dau. John and Polly (Bradford) Wallace of Milford. He d. April 22, 1850. They settled on the farm now of George F. Tarbell. In 1839 he sold his farm and moved to Union Co., Ohio, where he afterwards gave the name to the town of Raymond, where he and his wife, Sally, d. Ch. b. Mont Vernon:

1. Nathaniel, b. Sept. 19, 1811, was taxed here five years until 1838. Went first to Raymond, Ohio, thence to Champaigne, Ill., d. May 19, 1890.

2. John Wallace, b. March 5, 1815, m. Feb., 1839, Lucinda Smart d. Raymond, Ohio, June 30, 1841, without ch.

3. *Robert Burns, b. May 2, 1824.

Jesse Raymond, son Nathaniel and Phebe (Dodge) Raymond, b. Mont Vernon, 1792, m. Betsey Dale of Wilton, N. H. He d. July 14, 1862. He lived on the farm in South Dist., now occupied by C. F. Isola. Ch. b. Mont Vernon:

1. John Goodell, b. Sept., 1816, m. Oct. 8, 1839, Roxanna, dau. Alfred and Lydia (Foster) Hutchinson; m. (2) March 20, 1856, Abigail, dau. John and Rosanna (Mills) Bullard; m. (3) March 20, 1877, Mrs. Nancy J. (Cilley) Hill. He was a blacksmith, lived and d. in Milford, Jan. 14, 1885. His ch. were Abbie, m. Albert Conant of South Lyndeboro, and David E. of Peterboro.
2. David Goodell, d. Milford, Sept. 7, 1843, aged 24 years.

Andrew Wallace Raymond, son of George and Mary (Wallace) Raymond, b. Mont Vernon, Oct. 19, 1817, m. March 7, 1843, Abbie Stevens of Goffstown. She d. Feb. 23, 1883, age 65. He lived on the homestead, d. July 5, 1895. Ch. b. Mont Vernon:

1. Mary Frances, b. Jan. 7, 1844, m. March 4, 1863, Dodge G. Hartshorn of Milford, d. Milford, Aug. 17, 1899; one dau., Mrs. D. O. Handley of Milford.
2. *Charles Henry, b. Feb. 21, 1846.
3. *George Andrew, b. July 1, 1849.
4. Abbie E., b. Oct. 13, 1851, m. ——— Walker.
5. John W., b. April 6, 1857, m. April 14, 1886, Henrietta Colston; has two ch., lives in Concord, Mass.
6. Dana Pratt, b. Dec. 23, 1859, d. March 8, 1870.

George Raymond, son of George and Mary (Wallace) Raymond, b. Mont Vernon, April 9, 1820, lived in Antrim, Concord, N. H.; lives Rockbottom, Mass., m. Eleanor Pollard of Antrim. Ch.

1. *Edwin Herbert, b. Aug. 18, 1849.
2. Elsie A., b. Nov. 8, 1853, m. Nov. 30, 1882, Thomas J. Niles of Concord, N. H.

Nathaniel Raymond, son of John and Sally Bradford Raymond, b. Mont Vernon, Sept. 19, 1811, was taxed here five years until 1838. Went first to Raymond, Ohio, thence to Champaigne, Ill., d. May 19, 1890. Ch. of Nathaniel and his wife, Melissa, were:

1. Josephine, b. May 8, 1842, m. Sept. 29, 1868, William S. Maxwell.
2. Sally, b. April 22, 1844, m. June 14, 1871, Jona B. Green.
3. John E., b. Aug. 4, 1845, merchant Girard, Kan.
4. Isaac S., b. Jan. 29, 1849, m. Oct. 27, 1875, Edith Eaton.

Robert Burns Raymond, b. Mont Vernon, May 2, 1824, son of John and Sally (Bradford) Raymond, resides Monmouth, Ill., m. Sarah Lockwood 1846. Ch.

1. George, b. Jan. 9, 1847, d. Oct. 17, 1867.
2. Chas. W., of Monmouth, b. July 21, 1849, m. Dec., 1870; had two dau. Wife d. June, 1875. He m. (2) Hattie Hovier, Sept., 1879; has son and dau.
3. Pratt, b. March 29, 1852, d. Aug. 15, 1869.
4. David B., b. July 4, 1855, m. Dec., 1882, Alice Lake, one son.

Charles Henry Raymond, son Andrew W. and Abbie (Stevens) Ray-

CHARLES H. RAYMOND.

CHARLES H. RAYMOND.

mond, b. Mont Vernon, Feb. 21, 1846, lives on homestead, farmer, has been repeatedly selectman of the town, representative in 1900, member of Constitutional Convention 1902; m. Oct. 8, 1868, Matilda B. Pillsbury of Springfield, N. H. She was b. Feb. 2, 1843. Ch. b. Mont Vernon:

    1. Dana Charles, b. Feb. 15, 1870.
    2. Wallace Andrew, b. Dec. 14, 1872.
    3. Orie Matilda, b. Jan. 7, 1876, m. Jan. 7, 1903, John L. Bailey of Wakefield, Mass., res. Wakefield.
    4. Milon Henry, b. March 3, 1877, res. Mont Vernon.

George A. Raymond, son of Andrew W. and Abbie (Stevens) Raymond, b. Mont Vernon, July 1, 1849, res. Milford, m. May 11, 1880, Josie A. Bailey of Milford, dau. Jos. P. and Lucy A. (Woodbury) Bailey, b. S. Weare, March 31, 1862. Ch. b. Milford.
    Clarence A., b. Feb. 27, 1881, station agent Woonsocket, R. I.
    Grace B., b. May 31, 1884.

Edwin H. Raymond, son of Geo. and Eleanor (Pollard) Raymond, b. Aug. 18, 1849, lives at Antrim, Stafford Co., Kansas, m. Sept. 10, 1876, Eva G. Wheeler of Iowa. Ch.
    1. Mabel, b. April 6, 1878, d. 1878.
    2. George L., b. Jan. 31, 1881.
    3. Wadsworth P., b. Oct. 27, 1882.
    4. Mary, b. Jan. 31, 1885.

REED.

Jesse Reed lived in the East Dist., d. Oct. 25, 1875, age 75 years, 9 mos. His wife, Clarissa E., d. Nov. 23, 1860, age 59. Ch.
George W. His wife, Abbie H. Reed, d. Oct. 5, 1866, age 23.

REILLY.

James Reilly, b. Burke, N. Y., m. Nancy S., dau. of Thomas M. and Sarah M. (Manning) Harvell of Amherst, Feb. 24, 1873. She was b. Amherst, Feb. 24, 1853. They lived several years in the North Dist. Moved to Milford in 1885, where they now reside; stone mason. Ch.
    1. Mary E., b. Aug. 22, 1873, m. Nov. 26, 1892, Gustaf Hobinson of Milford, res. Milford, m. Sept. 29, 1901, Amelia Murray of Newton. Mass., lives in Somerville; two ch.
    2. Thomas J., b. Aug. 1, 1875.
    3. Frederic, b. Aug. 12, 1881, m. Feb. 17, 1900, Margaret Pequignot of Milford; res. Milford; two ch.

RICHARDSON.

Parker Richardson, b. Andover, Mass., one of 10 ch., nine sons and one dau., m. May 12, 1789, Susannah, dau. of Nathan and Martha Fuller. She was b. April 4, 1770, d. March 22, 1843. They lived chiefly on the Joseph Conant farm in the East Dist. He was a cabinet maker. Ch. b. Mont Vernon:
    1. *Jotham, b. April 23, 1790.
    2. Tamesin H., b. 1792, d. Dec. 7, 1815, m. Benj. H. Gage, settled in Lowell. A dau. m. a Norman Burnham and was the mother of William G. Burnham.

3.   Nancy D., b. Aug. 11, 1799, m. Nathan K. Seaton, Dec. 25, 1817, who was for many years employed in the Boston Custom House. He d. at Greenupsburg, Ky., March 11, 1859; no ch.

4.   Mary Jane, b. Dec. 31, 1801, d. Jan., 1802.

5.   Mary Jane, b. April 19, 1806, m. April 25, 1866, *William L. Kidder, d. Aug. 27, 1880.

6.   Susan, b. Nov. 10, 1809, m. Aug. 19, 1830, Francis Kidder; had ch., Addison, Susan, Henrietta, and Maria.

7.   Nathan, twin, d. young.

8.   Charlotte, twin, d. young.

Jotham Richardson, son of Parker and Susannah (Fuller) Richardson, b. Mont Vernon, April 23, 1790, m. Dec. 1, 1814, Ruthey, dau. Capt. Thomas and Susannah (Haskell) Cloutman. She was b. Marblehead, Mass., Oct. 23, 1791.   He d. Aug. 8, 1854.   He lived the most of his life near Beech Hill.   Ch. b. Mont Vernon.

1.   *Nathan Fuller, b. Jan. 5, 1816.

2.   *Thomas Haskell, b. May 19, 1817.

3.   Mark A. b. Sept. 30, 1818, m. Lydia Martin, d. Mont Vernon, Jan. 26, 1886; one dau., Carrie E., m. Augustus Nichols.   He operated the poor farm in Arlington, Mass.

4.   *John C., b. Jan. 12, 1821, lives Cambridgeport, Mass., has two sons.

5.   *William B., b. Aug. 8, 1822.

6.   Susan, b. Nov. 3, 1823, m. March 21, 1844, *Luther Odell; three ch.

Nathan Fuller Richardson, son of Jotham and Ruthey (Cloutman) Richardson, b. Mont Vernon, Jan. 5, 1816, m. Abigail Tuttle, dau. of *Thomas and Lucy (Wilkins) Weston.   She was b. Mont Vernon, March 4, 1815, m. in 1840.   She d. Nov. 16, 1853.   He m. (2) Lodema Semantha Butler of Antrim.   He lived in the North Dist. on farm now occupied by Chas. M. Hill.   He d. March 5, 1884.   Ch. b. Mont Vernon.

By first wife:

1.   Laura A., m. *John T. Perkins, d. Jan. 19, 1873, age 30 yrs., 11 mos.

2.   Eveline Frances, d. unm. Wilton, Jan. 24, 1884, age 35 yrs., 4 mos.

3.   John Franklin.

By second wife:

4.   Susan Inez, m. Frank M. Elliot of Milford.

5.   Estella, m. Benj. Chadwick, Marblehead, Mass.

6.   Mary Anna Evans, m. Frederic Hopkins of Greenfield.

7.   Emma Grace, m. ―――― Dalrymple of Marlboro, N. H.

8.   Clarence, m. Lula Sumner of Wilton, res. Milford.

9.   Mark Ambrose, m. Myra Parker, lives in Francestown.

Mark A., d. Oct. 14, 1858, age 4 yrs.

Geo. H., d. Sept. 9, 1854, age 9 mos.

Thomas Haskell Richardson, b. Mont Vernon, May 19, 1817, d. Sept. 21, 1890, m. Sept. 26, 1843, Nancy B., dau. Capt. Wm. and Hannah (Jones) Bruce.   She was b. Oct. 1, 1825, d. June 6, 1892.   He kept one of the stores for many years.   Ch. b. Mont Vernon.

Ellen B., b. Dec. 1, 1843, m. *William Gage Barnham.   She d. July 22, 1887.

John C. Richardson, son of Jotham and Ruthey (Cloutman) Richardson, b. Mont Vernon, Jan. 12, 1821, real estate business in Cambridgeport, Mass., m. Esther Bodwell of Danvers in 1852. Ch.
1. John Wilbur, pastor Centennial Baptist Church, Brooklyn, N. Y.
2. Willis K., lives at home, unm.

William B. Richardson, son of Jotham and Ruthey (Cloutman) Richardson, b. Mont Vernon, Aug. 8, 1822, m. Aug. 8, 1848, Mary Ann Kendall dau. Franklin Kendall. She was b. Dec. 22, 1828; was depot master Newtonville, Mass., d. there Aug. 13, 1886. Was buried here. She d. Newtonville, Mass., April 11, 1900. Ch.,
1. Catherine Augusta, b. July 9, 1850, d. Jan. 19, 1853.
2. Alice Ware, b. Feb. 3, 1854, d. July 7, 1900, at Newtonville, Mass.
3. Edward Austin, b. April, 1856.
4. Lydia Adams, b. June 9, 1860.

William Richardson, b. Billerica, Mass., came here from Milford about 1820, lived on the farm (owned by C. O. Ingalls) near the big maple on the Milford road; d. March 16, 1863, 84 yrs., 7 mos.; m. Phebe Batchelder of Greenfield. She d. Feb. 20, 1866, age 82 yrs., 3 mos. Ch. b. Mont Vernon.
1. William H., d. May 5, 1845, age 23, unm.
2. Justin E., b. March 23, 1823, lived on homestead, d. unm. Jan. 12, 1890.

Daniel Richardson, b. New Portland, Me., Feb. 23, 1836, m. May 9, 1857, Mary E. dau. Dimon and Harrie (Parmenter) Twiss. She was b. Antrim, June 20, 1838. He came here from Lowell about 1868. Carpenter and farmer; res. in South Dist. Ch.
1. Albert D., b. Sept. 26, 1860, d. Nov. 20, 1872.
2. Willie F., b. Oct. 2, 1862, m. Feb. 4, 1892, Anna G. Wheeler of Hollis. She d. March 7, 1901 in Mont Vernon. Carpenter. No ch.
3. Cora Belle, b. April 30, 1865, d. April 30, 1866.
4. Augustine, b. Dec. 1, 1868, d. Dec. 21, 1868.
5. Hattie May, b. Oct. 26, 1876, m. Nov. 3, 1898, Charles O. Ingalls; one ch.

RILEY.

Patrick Riley, b. Ireland, County Caban, m. there. His wife was b. in County Caban, Ire. They came to Mont Vernon in 1856 and lived in the big yellow house on the turnpike, moved to Winchester in 1881, where he d. Feb. 14, 1897, age 66. He worked in the tannery here and tannery in Milford while living here. His wife d. July 22, 1898, age 57. Ch. b. Mont Vernon.
1. Daniel, b. 1857, teamster, m., res. Somerville, Mass.; has three ch.
2. John, b. 1859, lives in Boston.
3. Anna L., b. Oct. 1, 1861, unm., res. Winchester.
4. Thomas, b. July, 1863.
5. Bridget H., b. Feb., 1865, m. Sept., 1899, James H. Cronin, res. Winchester, Mass.
6. Mary F., b. June, 1867, grad. Salem Normal School, was Prin. Rumford School, Winchester, is now Prin. Chapin School Winchester.
7. James, b. July, 1873, m., lives in Malden.

ROBERTS

Benjamin F. Roberts, son of Samuel and Almira (Berry) Roberts, b. Peabody, Mass., July 5, 1859, came to Mont Vernon when young, farmer and laborer, m. Feb. 2, 1884, Sarah E., dau. Samuel K. and Almira (Young) Russell of Nashua. She was b. Nashua, March 22, 1861. Ch. b. Mont Vernon.

1. Clarence F., b. Sept. 2, 1884.
2. Henry E., b. Jan. 20, 1886.
3. Carrie B., b. July 18, 1887.
4. Emma A., b. Nov. 12, 1888.
5. Helen S., b. Dec. 25, 1890.

ROBINSON.

Jesse Robinson of Bedford, Mass., b. Bedford, Mass., June 4, 1797, m. April 7, 1827, Asenath Buttrick of Pelham. She was b. Pelham, April 12, 1803, d. Dec. 28, 1880. He lived on Beech Hill, then on the farm now occupied by William Ryan. He d. Nov. 14, 1876. Ch. b. Mont Vernon.

1. Marion R., b. March 18, 1829, m. Feb. 24, 1850, Rev. Charles Pike, resided Waterbury, Conn., d. Sept. 6, 1887.
2. *Jesse Orrin, b. May 9, 1830.
3. Edwin Wallace, b. Feb. 12, 1832, m. Oct. 6, 1858, Caroline E. Nye of Littleton, Mass., res. Littleton, Mass.; had three ch.; d. Dec. 9, 1892.
4. Mary Elizabeth, b. June 17, 1833, m. May 19, 1856, James M. Hutchinson of Wilton; res. Wilton; had five ch., d. Oct. 27, 1896.
5. Harriet Ann, b. March 4, 1836, m. Oct. 6, 1858, Henry Nye of Littleton, Mass., res. Worcester, Mass., has one ch.
6. Sarah Jane, b. Dec. 15, 1839, m. Jan. 30, 1859, Frank Holcombe of Southwick, Mass., res. in Milford; has two sons, Dr. Chas. H. Holcombe of Brookline and Newton Holcombe of Hollis.
7. Charles Henry, b. April 27, 1842, served in 13th N. H. Regt. in Civil War, d. unm. May 23, 1864.

Jesse O. Robinson, son of Jesse and Asenath (Buttrick) Robinson, b. Mont Vernon, May 9, 1830, m. (1) April 30, 1858, Helen E., dau. Levi J. and Nancy (Herrick) Secomb of Amherst. She was b. July 13, 1833, d. June 27, 1861. He m. (2) March 27, 1862, Laura Frye, b. Manchester, Vt., May 14, 1827. He settled on the farm now occupied by his son in the East part of Centre Dist., d. Nov. 20, 1887. His wid. res. on the farm with her son, Willie. Ch. b. Mont Vernon.

Ch. by first wife:

1. George Alfred, b. March 21, 1859, m. Feb. 6, 1883, Anna E. Proctor, dau. Jacob and Nancy S. Proctor of Marlboro, N. H. She was b. Marlboro, Feb. 9, 1856, resides Marlboro; 1 ch.
2. Helen Elizabeth, b. May 11, 1861, res. Amherst, unm.

Ch. by second wife:

3. Willie Lincoln, b. May 1, 1864, res. on homestead, unm.
4. Jennie B., b. Oct. 7, 1865, milliner.

ROBY.

John Roby, b. Merrimack, 1743, m. 1771, Esther Blodgett of Chelmsford, Mass., d. Mont Vernon, June 8, 1826. They settled in Mont Vernon soon after their marriage on farm in East Dist., now occupied by

George F. Jones. She d. Dec. 21, 1819, aged 71 years. Ch. b. Mont Vernon.

    1. Lydia, d. unm., North Chelmsford, Mass.

    2. *John, Jr., b. Sept. 7, 1776.

    3. Hannah, b. Sept. 7, 1779, m. Joseph Gilbert, Aug. 29, 1799, d. Francestown, Aug. 14, 1858.

    John Roby, Jr., son of John and Esther (Blodgett) Roby, b. Sept. 7, 1779; lived on homestead in East. Dist., d. June 1, 1856, m. Hannah Haseltine. She d. Oct. 30, 1860, aged 85. Ch. b. Mont Vernon:

    1. Levi, b. Jan. 28, 1801, m. Louisa Trow, d. Nashua, April 16, 1855; three ch.

    2. Reuben, b. Jan. 5, 1803, d. May 5, 1805.

    3. Hiram, b. July 27, 1804, m. April 17, 1830, Rebecca Cummings, d. Nashua, June 7, 1868; left one dau.

    4. *Clinton, b. May 6, 1808.

    5. Hannah, b. Nov. 30, 1809, m. Asa McMillen, d. New Boston, Dec. 21, 1861.

    6. Luther, b. July 24, 1813, d. Aug. 14, 1826.

    7. Ira Roby, b. Oct. 20, 1815, m. Hannah Wilkins of Merrimack, April 27, 1847. He d. Jan. 9, 1888, in Amherst. He lived on the farm now owned by C. E. Kendall in East Dist., was representative in 1862, moved to Amherst, where he d. Jan. 9, 1888. No ch. She d. March 12, 1889, age 68.

    Clinton Roby, son of John, Jr. and Hannah (Haseltine) Roby, b. Mont Vernon, May 6, 1808, d. Oct. 25, 1870. Lived on the homestead in East. Dist. He m. (1) Lois, dau. of John and Mary (Carleton) Haywood. She d. June 11, 1857, age 46. He m. (2) Sarah Jenkins of New Boston. She d. May 5, 1868, aged 47 years. Ch. by first wife b. Mont Vernon.

    1. John Clinton, b. Aug. 10, 1835, m. Orinthia, dau. Thomas and Lucy (Stevens) Battles, March 14, 1861. Went to Illinois 1862. Res. Decatur, Ill. One son, Ira, b. Jan., 1874.

    2. Kilburn Harwood, b. Sept. 2, 1837, went West in 1858; lawyer and banker; res. Decatur, Ill., m. Dec. 1, 1862, Anna Haworth of Wilmington, Ohio, b. Dec. 24, 1839. Ch.

    1. Frank Clinton, b. June, 1865, m. Ida Worden, 1893, has a dau. Helen.

    2. Mary Lois, b. July, 1867, m. Frederic A. Brown of Tacoma, Wash.

    3. Kilburn H., b. Oct. 10, 1872.

    4. Luther Edward, b. Feb. 10, 1874.

    5. Sarah Jane, b. Jan. 14, 1876.

    6. Anna Haworth, b. April 10, 1878.

ROTCH

    Matthew Griffin Rotch, son of Samuel and Susannah (Johnson) Rotch, b. Boston, Sept. 24, 1806, d. Mont Vernon, July 24, 1878; m. July 7, 1835, Tamesin Hale, dau. Nathan and Tamesin (Brown) Fuller. She was b. Amherst, Aug. 27, 1804, d. Mont Vernon, May 7, 1895. He was a mechanic and lived in the village, in the house now "Syringa Cottage," owned by Hon. G. A. Marden. Ch. b. Mont Vernon:

    1. Maria Adelaide, b. Jan. 25, 1837, d. unm. Jan. 21, 1877; was a woman of good intellectual endowment, literary taste and fine education.

    2. Albert Atwood, b. May 5, 1840, d. Amherst, Dec. 10, 1890, m.

1859, Helen Reade, dau. of Dea. Edward D. and Mercy P. (Perkins) Boylston. She was b. Amherst, 1843. After his death she m. William Warren. He res. in Amherst, was editor Farmers' Cabinet and was in real estate business. Ch.

William Boylston Rotch, b. Amherst, June 6, 1859, m. Oct. 17, 1882, Grace Marston, dau. Joseph W. and Susan C. (Hunt) Burnell of Weymouth, Mass. He is editor and proprietor of the Milford Cabinet; res. Milford; one son, Arthur B.

RUSSELL.

Joseph Russell, b. Euston Sq., London, Eng., Jan. 20, 1863, came to America in 1883; m. Ellen V. Connors, dau. of Jeremiah Connors of Manchester, N. H., Oct. 30, 1866; lived in Mont Vernon near Purgatory, from winter of 1891-1892 to Dec. 1894, now resides Manchester. Ch.
    1.   Jennie V., b. June 27. 1887.
    2.   Joseph, b. Oct. 5, 1889.
    3.   Sarah E., b. Mont Vernon, June 15, 1891.
    4.   Anna Frances, b. Mont Vernon, April 3, 1894.

Walter Wood Russell, son of Walter and Caroline C. (Leonard) Russell, b. Watertown, Mass., May 27, 1835, teamster and farmer; lived in Watertown until 15 years of age, in Vermont 18 years, in Stowe, Mass., 4 years, in Charlestown. Mass., almost 25 years; came to Mont Vernon in 1894; m. April 14, 1858, Mary M., dau. Joseph and Mary (Sloan) Beede. She was b. Wilmington, Mass., Nov. 12, 1837. Ch.
    1.   Alice Shepard, b. Royalton, Vt., May 14, 1861, m. Frederick Bennett, lives in Waltham.
    2.   Carrie L., b. Stowe, Mass., Dec. 11, 1869; stenographer in Boston.

Catherine T. (Bond) Russell, widow Walter Russell, d. Dec. 11, 1887, age 84. She had lived with her dau., Mrs. Charles F. Stinson, several years. She was the step-mother of Walter W. Russell. She was b. in Watertown, Mass., May 14, 1803.
Josiah Russell, Jr., b. Mason, Sept. 1, 1799, m. Ruby Wyman, Oct. 8, 1826. She was b. Woburn, Mass., March 13, 1803. They lived in Derry. Lived in Mont Vernon several years in the thirties in the house in South Dist., now owned by estate Dr. C. M. Kittredge. He was selectman in 1835 and 1836. He moved to Amherst, d. at Lowell. Ch.
    1.   Maria Louisa, b. Derry, Sept. 23, 1827.
    2.   Almira Josephine, b. Derry, Sept. 28, 1830.
    3.   Edwin, b. Mont Vernon, June 13, 1833.
    4.   Albert Gallatin, b. Mont Vernon, April 3, 1835.

RYAN.

William Ryan, son of James and Margaret (Fox) Ryan, b. Kilworth, Cork Co. Ire., 1834, came to America in 1856, settled in Mont Vernon, 1858; m. at Nashua, Oct. 28, 1856, Catherine Oates. She was b. in Boyle, Ire., d. Feb. 17, 1885, age 47. He m. (2) Mrs. Mary Burns of Manchester, April 29, 1886. She d. Jan. 26, 1888, age 40. He m. (3) Ellen Murray, June 26, 1898. She was b. Ballynock, Ire., May 27, 1840. Ch. by his first wife:
    1.   James, b. Lowell, Aug. 24, 1857, unm., res. Mont Vernon.

2. Edmund, b. Mont Vernon, July 18, 1859, res. Worcester, m. Bridget Magnir of Worcester; one ch.

3. John, b. Mont Vernon, Dec. 11, 1861, res. Boston.

4. Wm. Bruce, b. March 12, 1864, d. Milford, May 26, 1887.

5. Mary, b. June 1, 1866, m. Nov. 26, 1888, Thos. P. Garrity, d. Feb. 21, 1896; two ch.

6. Katherine, b. Aug. 12, 1875, m. Jan. 11, 1900, James Cassidy of Milford, res. Milford; two ch.

SANBORNE.

George E. Sanborne, b. Reading, Mass., April 2, 1827, fitted for college at Andover, East Hampton and Monson, grad. Amherst College 1853, Andover Theological Seminary 1856, settled in Georgia, Vt., as pastor from 1856 to 1861; supplied at Portsmouth, came to Mont Vernon Dec. 1861, installed pastor April 10, 1862, left in June in 1865 to accept a call at Northboro, Mass., left there to accept the superintendency of the Orphan Asylum, Hartford. In May, 1885, he was appointed steward of Insane Retreat, Hartford, held that position until May, 1895. He m. June 10, 1858, Anna E., dau. Dea. John Knowlton of Portsmouth, N. H.; no ch. He d. Hartford, Jan. 7, 1900.

SANDERSON.

Henry Sanderson, b. Beverly, Mass., Feb. 19, 1810, m. Mary Frances, dau. Amos and Mary W. (Hartshorn) Hubbard, March 18, 1841. She was b. Amherst, Oct. 26, 1816, d. Milford, Dec. 13, 1893. He settled in Mont Vernon on a farm in the East Dist. in the forties, moved to Milford in the eighties. He d. there Dec. 13, 1888. Ch.

1. Sarah Frances, b. May 26, 1843, m. Charles Lovejoy of Milford, July 1, 1865, d. Dec. 2, 1893; had three ch.

2. Eliza A. H., b. May 17, 1845, m. March 19, 1866. Albert F. Boutell, res. Milford.

3. Henry Hubbard, b. Jan. 31, 1850, m. Helen Brown, 1881, res. Milford.

4. Leander Calvin, b. Mont Vernon, March 19, 1852, carpenter, came to Milford as a young man, res. village, m. Sept. 8, 1888, Mary L., dau. of James and Betsey (McQuestion) Sanderson. She was b. Milford, Jan. 7, 1859. Ch.

Gladys B., b. Leominster, Mass., Aug. 17, 1889.

SARGENT.

Daniel Sargent, Jr., son Daniel and Charlotte (Winslow) Sargent, b. Goffstown, Aug. 14, 1823; lived here a few years in the later sixties; came to Milford in 1844 from New Boston, quarryman, d. April 27, 1874, m. (1) Aug. 31, 1846, Nancy E., dau. John and Betsey (Moore) Wellman, b. Lyndeboro, Feb. 24, 1823; m. (2) Oct. 16, 1864, Ann Jane, dau. Noah B. and Mary (Hopkins) Hutchinson; she was b. Mont Vernon, May 15, 1836; resides Milford. Ch. by first wife:

Frank D., b. Milford, Oct. 29, 1853, d. Nov. 8, 1862

Ch. by second wife:

Edwin D., b. Mont Vernon, Sept. 2, 1867, mechanic; m. Feb. 28, 1899, Bertha, dau. Sylvester S. and Nettie (Schlim) Osborn of Nashua.

Mytie Ardelle b. April 21, 1869, m. May 30, 1893, Frank G. Easter; res. Milford.

Eva Bell, b. March 6, 1871, d. Milford, Dec. 28, 1875.

Thomas Sargent, son of Enoch P. and Jane (Jameson) Sargent, b. Nov. 5, 1828, m. Nov. 12, 1853, Elizabeth B. Tenney of Goffstown. She was b. Goffstown, March 31, 1837. He lived in Amherst, came to Mont Vernon 1888; lived on the Edward Hildreth farm until 1893, when he moved to Bedford, where he now lives. Ch.

1   Sarah Jane, b. New York, Nov. 16, 1858, m. William Schwartz, Dec., 1879; res. Bedford.

2   George W., b. Goffstown, Nov. 19, 1861, d. Feb. 20, 1865.

3   Cora E., b. Manchester, July 5, 1866; m. Harry S. Bagley, Oct. 17, 1887; lives Manchester.

4   *James W., b. Goffstown, April 19, 1870.

5   John M., b. Goffstown, Jan. 19, 1874, m. Aug. 21, 1898, Hannah A. Chase of East Deering, N. H.; two ch.; res. Bedford.

Orcutt J. Sargent, son of Dea. Enoch P. and Jane (Jameson) Sargent, b. Goffstown, Sept. 6, 1845; farmer; lived on the Best farm in East Dist. several years; moved to Milford in 1891. He m. Sept. 25, 1871, Mary C., dau. Nathaniel and Charlotte C. (Buxton) Lawrence, b. Tyngsboro, Mass., July 20, 1845.   Ch.

1   Lola L., b. Templeton, Mass., July 17, 1873; m. March 5, 1892, Sidney A., son Chas. M. and Susan J. (Wilkins) Pond of Milford, d. Milford, Jan. 8, 1896.

2   Edith B., b. Mont Vernon, Aug. 28, 1878; res. Milford.

3   Flossie I., b. Mont Vernon, Sept. 6, 1882, d. Milford, Jan. 4, 1895.

James W. Sargent, son Thomas and Elizabeth (Tenney) Sargent, b. Goffstown, April 19, 1870, m. Sept. 14, 1892, Emma Anderson. She was b. Germany; res. Bedford; has six ch.

SECOMBE.

Daniel Secombe, b. April 6, 1784, d. Jan. 19, 1816; settled on a farm in the East Dist., m. (1) Betsey Duncan, July 23, 1805. She d. Oct. 12, 1826, age 42. He m. (2) Elizabeth Austin, b. Sept. 28, 1828. Ch. b. Mont Vernon:

1   Mahala Jones, b. July 31, 1806, m. George C. Coburn, d. April 23, 1838; two ch.

2   Nancy Duncan, b. Sept. 27, 1812, d. Concord, Jan. 30, 1857, unm.

3   Mary, b. March 11, 1844, m. Charles Austin; lived in Lowell.

4   Jane, b. Oct. 27, 1821, d. Concord, Nov. 22, 1846.

By second wife:

5   Daniel Andrew Jackson, b. Sept. 16, 1829, m. Oct. 11, 1861, Emily A. Glover of Franklin, Vt.   He lived on the farm occupied by his wife and son, George, in south part of the town.   He d. Aug. 16, 1880.   One ch., George, unm.

6   John, b. Aug. 21, 1833, d. Aug. 18, 1835.

7   Charles, b. Jan. 16, 1836; lives Lowell, Mass., unm.

8   Harriet Newell, b. Sept. 9, 1838, m. April 9, 1866, John H. Coggin of Amherst; d. Jan. 8, 1882; two ch.

9   John, b. Feb. 20, 1840, d. Sept., 1844.

SHEDD.

Nelson E. Shedd, b. Hollis, Sept. 22, 1829, son Ebenezer and Betsey

Shedd; came here from Nashua in 1846, where he was overseer in mill of Nashua Manufacturing Co. He m. at Nashua, Oct. 13, 1842, Fidelia, dau. Paul and Betsey (Woodbury) Whipple. She was b. in Barre, Vt., Aug. 17, 1823, d. Mont Vernon, April 21, 1899. They lived on what is known as the Shedd farm on the turnpike in the West Dist. He d. Vineland, N. J., March 25, 1885. She m. (2) Nathaniel Cutter of Jaffrey. Ch. 5. Mont Vernon:

1. Sarah F., b. Mont Vernon, Nov. 18, 1847; m. Jan. 22, 1866, Milo R. Burnham; four ch.

2. Helen M., b. June 9, 1849, d. Aug. 23, 1851.

3. Frank, b. June 9, 1849, d. Aug. 28, 1851.

4. Franklin W., b. July 3, 1852, m. Anna Gilgua, Nov. 28, 1872. He lived in South Dist. He d. May 17, 1876, leaving three ch.

5. Celia M., b. July 17, 1855, m. Aug. 2, 1881, George W. Putnam; res. Lowell; no ch.

6. Henry Nelson, b. April 10, 1857, m. Oct. 4, 1886, Irene Christine of Washington, D. C.; res. Philadelphia; two ch.

7. Clarence A., b. Nov. 26, 1860; res. New York City; in insurance business.

SHATTUCK.

Noah Shattuck, b. Brookline, N. H., 1800, d. Aug. 7, 1843; m. Clarissa Saunders of Brookline (sister of Delinda Saunders that m. David Dutton). He lived in the village in the house J. M. Fox now owns. She d. Sept. 8, 1843. Ch. all but Samuel b. Mont Vernon.

1. Ingalls K., b. June 24, 1821; lives in Hudson, unm.

2. Quincy, b. May 16, 1824, m. Mary Chase, d. Bristol, Vt.; left one son, F. W. Shattuck of Bristol, Vt.

3. Dan, b. Jan. 9, 1826, d. infancy.

4. Milo, b. Sept. 18, 1827, d. New Britain, Conn., m.

5. Permelia, b. Jan. 10, 1829; m. May 26, 1858, George W. Trow, son of Jesse and Nancy (Cochran) Trow; lives Hudson, N. H.

6. Alfred, b. Sept. 22, 1831, m. (1) Rosemma Holden of Milford, m. (2) Mary E. Baker of Hudson; three ch., d. Nashua, Jan. 3, 1902.

7. Marion, b. June 22, 1833, d. in San Francisco, Cal., unm.

8. Samuel, b. New Boston, d. Nashua, m.; one ch.

9. Wallace, b. Mont Vernon, Aug. 28, 1838, d. San Francisco, Cal.

10. Henry K., b. Mont Vernon, enlisted in 13th N. H. Regt. in Civil War, d. diseased, Nov. 30, 1862.

11. Edwin, b. Mont Vernon; lives Mont Vernon, unm.

SIMONDS

Benjamin Simonds, m. Mary, dau. of John and Mary (Bradford) Averill. Settled in Mont Vernon, rem. to Antrim in 1793 and d. there in 1826, age 65. Four eldest ch. b. Mont Vernon:

1. Lucy, b. Jan. 30, 1784, m. Enoch Sawyer in 1802, d. June 7, 1853.

2. Polly, b. May 24, 1787; m. Sept. 1, 1812, Robert Burns; d. Oct. 3, 1857.

3. John, b. May 3, 1790, m. Sally B. Preston, Feb. 3, 1814, settled in Antrim; d. 1858.

4. Sally, b. March 8, 1792, m. May 7, 1812, William D. Atwood; rem. to Hartland, Vt., d. in 1836.

5. Benjamin, b. Antrim, June 5, 1796; m. Betsey Parsons of Windsor, d. Antrim, Oct. 27, 1850.

6. Nancy, b. Feb. 24, 1798, m. Simeon Buck, Dec. 29, 1818; d. in Windsor.
7. Sabrina, b. Feb. 25, 1803, m. Simeon Buck; d. in Windsor.
8. Mark, b. May 24, 1807, d. Nov. 1, 1807.

SMITH.

Cooley Smith, son of Thomas and Elizabeth Smith, b. April 9, 1709, m. Sarah, dau. Thomas and Eunice Burnham of Ipswich, Mass. They settled in Middleton, Mass. Ch. b. Middleton, Mass.
1. Ezekiel, b. June 3, 1731, d. Nov. 19, 1737.
2. Paltiah, b. Aug. 2, 1733; d. unm. 1762.
3. Sarah, b. May 17, 1736, m. (1) Ozemiah Wilkins, m. (2) Daniel Wilkins of Sutton.
4. *Aaron, b. April 24, 1738.
5. Lucy, b. June 20, 1740, m. Aquila Wilkins of New London, N. H.
6. Eunice, b. June 26, 1742; m. Abner Wilkins; d. in Middleton, Mass.
7. Jemima, b. April 22, 1744, m. Enos Wilkins of Middleton, Mass.
8. *Jacob, b. March 16, 1746.
9. *David, b. Dec. 5, 1748.
10. James, b. Feb. 14, 1750.
11. Lydia, b. Nov. 9, 1755, m. Aaron Wilkins of Amherst; d. March 25, 1837; nine ch.
12. Naomi, b. April 25, 1757, m. Benj. Wilkins; settled in Lyndeboro; d. May 11, 1850.

Aaron Smith, son of Cooley and Sarah (Burnham) Smith, b. April 24, 1738; m. (1) Mary Thomas; m. (2) Mrs. Bixby; settled in Mont Vernon. A son, Aaron, known as "Hatter Smith," was a hatter, m. Lydia, dau. Stephen and Lydia (Fuller) Gould. She was b. April 7, 1784. After his death she went to Hillsboro. She fell over a stove and was burnt to death. He d. Feb. 5, 1840, aged 60, at Mont Vernon. They had two sons.

Jacob Smith, b. March 15, 1746, son of Cooley and Sarah (Burnham) Smith; lived on the place now owned by Rufus A. Averill on the turnpike; d. in Mont Vernon, July 12, 1842; m. Hannah Upton of Middleton, Mass. Ch. b. Mont Vernon:
1. *Daniel.
2. *David, b. Oct. 9, 1782.
3. Jeremiah, farmer in Mont Vernon, went to Barre, Vt., m. a —— French; had ch.
4. *Jacob.

David Smith, son of Cooley and Sarah (Burnham) Smith, b. Dec. 5, 1748; m. —— Sweetser; settled South Reading, now Wakefield, Mass.; four ch. David, Noah, Archibald, Adam.

James Smith, son of Cooley and Sarah (Burnham) Smith, b. Middleton, Mass., Feb. 14, 1750; d. Mont Vernon, Jan. 29, 1831; m. (1) Moriah Rolfe of Middleton, Mass., in 1775. Removed to Mont Vernon in 1778, where she d. in Dec. 1802; m. (2) April 14, 1804, Mrs. Sarah (Hildreth) Jones, wid. Phinehas Jones and dau. Ephraim and Elizabeth (Ellenwood) Hildreth. She was b. June 6, 1765, d. Mont Vernon, Nov. 24, 1842. He first settled on the farm on the turnpike now owned by R. G. Averill, where his sons, Jesse, James and Luther, were b. He then purchased the farm in the North Dist. now occupied by W. M. Gilson. Ch. by first wife:

1. *Rogers, b. Middleton, Mass., June 12, 1776.
2. Rebecca, b. 1778, Amherst; m. Maj. Robt. Christie, son Dea. Jesse and Mary (Gregg) Christie, of New Boston; d. N. B., Sept. 6, 1804; left four ch., James, Mary, Jesse, Rebecca. They moved to Springfield, Clark Co., Ohio, where the sons were prominent citizens.
3. *Jesse, b. Mont Vernon, April 5, 1781.
4. *James, b. Mont Vernon, Feb. 8, 1784.
5. *Luther, b. Mont Vernon, Dec. 27, 1786.
6. Mary, d. infancy.
Ch. by second wife:
7. *Leander, b. Mont Vernon, Aug. 22, 1808.

Daniel Smith, son of Jacob and Hannah (Upton) Smith. He d. June 22, 1857, age 85 yrs., 6 mos.; m. his cousin, Cynthia, dau. of Daniel and Sarah (Smith) Wilkins of Sutton. She d. Aug. 8, 1864, age 84 yrs., 6 mos.; lived on his father's farm. Ch. b. Mont Vernon:
Hannah, m. May, 1822, Benj. F. Hill; d. Dec. 1, 1866, age 68.
John, known as "Big John Smith," lived on his father's farm, place near turnpike now owned by R. G. Averill. He was a peddler; m. Rebecca R. Hale of Bradford. She d. Jan. 30, 1890, aged 82 years. He d. Oct. 2, 1866, aged 64 years, 9 months; one ch., Elizabeth, b. Sept., 1833, m. *William Upton of Mont Vernon. She d. Mont Vernon, Aug. 8, 1882.
David Smith, son of Jacob and Hannah (Upton) Smith, b. Mont Vernon, Oct. 9, 1782, m. May 16, 1805, Mary, dau. Daniel and Mary (Weston) Averill. She was b. Mont Vernon, Oct. 26, 1783, d. Aug. 25, 1864. He lived on the turnpike above the village near his brother Daniel's house. He d. May 1, 1862. Ch. b. Mont Vernon:

1. Kilburn, b. Nov. 19, 1805, m. Maria Wood of Littleton, d. Lowell, Oct. 13, 1881, where he lived; one dau.
2. Cynthia W., b. March 14, 1807, m. *John Smith; d. June 15, 1884.
3. Mary, b. Nov. 22, 1808; m. Nov. 17, 1836, *Elbridge Marvell; d. Aug. 5, 1895.
4. David Orrin, b. Aug. 8, 1811; m. Mary Stone of Antrim; had two ch.; was a blacksmith. He moved to Antrim in 1846, thence to Concord in 1852, where he d. Dec. 15, 1897.
5. Emma Carleton, b. Aug. 19, 1813, d. unm. Feb. 6, 1875, in Mont Vernon.
6. *William Harrison, b. Oct. 22, 1815.
7. Richmond, b. Sept. 15, 1817; d. unm. at Concord, July 6, 1892; was a successful speculator and lived in Concord.
8. Mehitabel, b. May 7, 1821, m. Henry Ware of East Andover, N. H., d. there Dec. 10, 1898.
9. Sabrina, b. June 28, 1823, d. 1825.
10. Stephen Chapin, b. May 11, 1825; res. Boston; tailor; m. Augusta Straw of Lowell, d. Aug. 19, 1898; seven ch.
11. Nancy Lovett, b. March 19, 1828, m. April 2, 1860, Henry L. Walkup; res. Worcester, Mass.; had two ch.
Jacob Smith, son of Jacob and Hannah (Upton) Smith, b. Mont Vernon; lived on the turnpike, m. Katherine White of Lyndeboro; laborer.
1. *James.
2. Lewis, m. (1) Cynthia Mitchell; m. (2) Harriet, dau. John and

Sarah J. (Hodgeman) Stearns; four ch. After his death she m. David
Bumford of New Boston. Lewis Smith d. Feb. 14, 1886, aged 71 yrs.
   3. Samuel, lived in Orange, Vt.
   4. George, went West.
   5. One dau. m. a Meder of Saxonville, Mass.
There were four other dau.

   Dr. Rogers Smith, son of James and Moriah (Rolfe) Smith, b. Middleton, Mass., June 12, 1776; studied medicine with Dr. Jones of Lyndeboro, commenced practice in Amherst; removed thence to Mont Vernon,
where he resided until appointed surgeon in army; afterward to Greenbush, N. Y., and Weston, Vt., where he d. March 25, 1845. He m. Jan.
15, 1802, Sarah, dau. of Samuel and Sukey (Washer) Dodge. She was
b. Sept. 18, 1779, d. Weston, Aug. 1840. He was a surgeon in the U. S.
army in the War of 1812, and was stationed at Greenbush, N. Y.; was
town clerk and moderator. Ch. were:
   1. Samuel, b. Amherst, July 7, 1802, d. Sept. 24, 1804.
   2. *Asa Dodge, b. Amherst, Sept. 21, 1804; fitted for college at Kimball Union Academy, Meriden, graduated Dartmouth College, 1830; taught
in Limerick Academy, Me., one year; graduated Andover Theological
Seminary, 1834; was settled over the Brainard Presbyterian Church, New
York City, afterwards pastor of the Fourteenth St. Presbyterian Church
until 1863. He d. Hanover, Aug. 1877. He was eminent and popular as
a preacher.
   In 1863 he was chosen President of Dartmouth College, as successor
to Nathan Lord, D. D. Assuming this important trust at the age of 59
he devoted himself for 14 years with unflagging industry and energy to
the interests of the college. The period of his presidency is memorable in
the college annals as one of the most successful in its history. By his
personal efforts individuals of large means became interested in the college and contributed liberally to its finances. His arduous and incessant
labors seriously impaired his health and early in 1877 he resigned. He
was a man of gracious and kindly manners and he impressed his person-
ality upon his students, and his memory is cherished by them with warmest
affection.
   Among eminent men who graduated during his presidency are Ex-
Gov. Frank S. Black of New York, Col. Melvin O. Adams, Hon. George
Fred Williams, Hon. Samuel McCall of Massachusetts, Chief Justice Robert M. Wallace of New Hampshire and many others. He d. Aug., 1877.
He m. Sarah, dau. of John Adams, Esq., of North Andover, Mass. She
d. Sept. 24, 1882, age 76. Ch. were:
   1. Dr. William T., b. March 30, 1839, graduated Yale College, is
Dean of the Medical Dept. of Dartmouth College; m. Miss Susan Kellogg; res. Hanover, and has two ch.
   2. Sarah, unm., resides Hanover.
   3. Albert D., a retired merchant of New York City.
   4. Henry B., a graduate of Dartmouth College, is business manager
of Scribner's Magazine.
   5. Harriet, m. a Mr. Bigelow.
   Ch. of Dr. Rogers and Sarah (Dodge) Smith continued:—
   3. Sarah, b. Mont Vernon, Aug. 21, 1806, m. (1) John Dale of Weston, Vt., by whom she had one son, Geo. L. Dale; m. (2) Elijah Munson
of Wallingford, Vt. She d. Aug., 1854.
   4. Rebecca, b. Mont Vernon, Nov. 12, 1808, m. Cephas Dale of
Weston, Vt.; lived Wallingford, Vt.; had one dau., Ellen.

5. Annah R., b. Greenbush, N. Y., m. Rev. Dennis Chapin, 1840, a Universalist minister of Cambridge, N. Y.

6. Horace E., b. 1817 in Weston, Vt.; studied law at Broad Albin, N. Y., practised law in Boston, where he was partner of Henry M. Stanton; was a member of the Mass. Legislature; from 1879 to 1892 was dean of the law school at Albany, N. Y.; was a member of the New York Constitutional Convention of 1876. He was the most eminent lawyer in Fulton Co., N. Y. He was married three times and had several ch. He resided at Johnstown, N. Y., where he d. Oct. 19, 1902.

Rev. James G. Smith, b. Dec. 22, 1805, went to Claremont when young to live with his uncle (McLaughlin) there, grew up with Methodism there. He was granted a local preacher's license, April 8, 1826, at a quarterly meeting at Salem, N. H. He preached at Nashua and Manchester, went to Portsmouth in 1838, was superannuated in 1847, since which time he resided at Plymouth, N. H., where he d. April 10, 1888. He preached constantly. "He was an excellent singer, gifted in prayer, a strong and vigorous thinker, and expressed his thoughts with considerable force and effectiveness." He m. 1828, Mary Lathrop of Royalton, Vt., b. March 4, 1801, d. Nov. 26, 1879. Three ch., Joseph, Mary, and Col. Francis A. Smith, a graduate Wesleyan University, officer Union Army in Civil War, is now a successful lawyer in Essex Co., New York.

Jesse Smith, son of James and Moriah (Rolfe) Smith, b. Mont Vernon, April 5, 1781, d. April 14, 1862; lived where Mrs. M. J. Blood now does, afterwards Bridge cottage, m. June 28, 1804, Abigail or Nabby, dau. Dr. Zephaniah and Elizabeth (Stickney) Kittredge of Mont Vernon. She was b. March 22, 1784, d. May 7, 1866. Carpenter. Ch. b. Mont Vernon.

1. Jesse Kittredge, b. Oct. 29, 1804; m. April 7, 1829, Pamelia, dau. Peter and Lydia (Farmer) Foster. She was b. Aug. 20, 1806, d. Mont Vernon, May 13, 1880. He d. Dec. 24, 1851; a skilful surgeon and physician in Mont Vernon. Ch.

2. Ambrose, b. Sept. 10, 1808, m. 1833, Mahala, dau. William L. and Nabby (Jenkins) Kidder, widow —— Partridge. Blacksmith, lived in Goffstown where he d. Oct. 29, 1882. 3 ch., Chas. E., Perry and Almira.

3. *Norman, b. Oct. 13, 1811.

4. Laurania, b. Nov. 24, 1814, music teacher, d. unm. Mont Vernon, Jan. 19, 1887.

5. James, b. Sept. 23, 1817, d. Sept. 27, 1818.

James Smith, son of James and Moriah (Rolfe) Smith, b. Mont Vernon, Feb. 8, 1784; d. Mont Vernon, Sept. 26, 1809, m. Jan. 1, 1805, Susannah White of Lyndeboro'. Ch. were b. Mont Vernon.

1. James G., b. Dec. 22, 1805.

2. Luther, b. Oct. 6, 1807, m. Mary, dau. John and Elizabeth (Moore) Eaton of Hillsboro' Bridge, N. H. He was a foundryman, lived the greater part of his life in Manchester, where he d. March, 1862. He had three ch., two dau., Emily and Ellen, d. young, one son, Edwin R.

3. Moriah Rolfe, b. Jan. 11, 1810, d. infancy.

Dr. Luther Smith, son of James and Moriah (Rolfe) Smith, b. Mont Vernon, Dec. 27, 1786; studied medicine with his brother, Dr. Rogers

Smith, began practising at Hillsboro' Bridge, 1809, continued there until his death, Aug. 5, 1824. He m. July 22, 1817, Mary, dau. Dea. John and Judith (Weston) Carleton. She was b. Mont Vernon, Jan. 19, 1790. After her husband's death or from 1837 until her death, March 20, 1872, she resided in Mont Vernon. Ch. b. Hillsboro' Bridge.

　　1. Mary Ellen, b. May 7, 1818, teacher, d. June 10, 1853, unm., in Chesterfield Co., Va., where she was teaching.
　　2. *Charles James, b. Sept. 3, 1820.

　　Capt. Leander Smith, son of James and Sarah (Hildreth) Smith, b. Mont Vernon, Aug. 22, 1808; was selectman and representative of Mont Vernon several years; moved to Antrim in 1860, where he d. Dec. 22, 1884. He m. Dec. 15, 1832, Sophronia, dau. Silas and Martha (Farnum) Wilkins. She was b. June 22, 1812, d. Antrim, Nov. 25, 1882. Ch. b. Mont Vernon:

　　1. George W., b. April 19, 1835, d. in the army Oct. 15, 1863, being a soldier of the 16th N. H. Vol.
　　2. Augusta, b. June 5, 1837, m. (1) Moses Carr of Newport, N. H., who d. in 1864; m. (2) William N. Conn of Antrim, July 26, 1877, where she now res.; one son by first m., George M. Carr, b. Nov. 6, 1864.
　　3. Elbridge Franklin, b. Dec. 14, 1839, d. in the army at New Orleans, Dec. 15, 1862, member of the 8th N. H. Regt., Vol.
　　4. James McCauley, b. Sept 19, 1842, d. Antrim, July 15, 1865, from disease contracted in the army, member 9th N. H. Regt.
　　5. Emeline Willis, twin, b. Jan. 19, 1844, m. Chas. F. Holt of Antrim, Nov. 26, 1863; seven ch., d. Oct., 1883.
　　6. Emily Wilkins, twin, b. Jan. 19, 1844, m. Francis White of Boston, Nov. 7, 1865, lives in Boston; has two sons.
　　7. Arthur Linwood, b. July 29, 1885, m. Clara A. Conn of Antrim, Nov. 22, 1882, resides Antrim.

　　William Harrison Smith, son of David and Mary S. (Averill) Smith, b. Mont Vernon, Oct. 22, 1815. He worked in the box shop and resided on the Wilkins place in the valley in East Dist., moved to Milford in 1873, where he d. July 27, 1889. He m. Jan. 1, 1841, Lydia J., dau. of Timothy and Sally (Marshall) Baldwin. She was b. Mont Vernon, June 30, 1816, d. Mont Vernon, April 26, 1868. Ch. b. Mont Vernon:

　　1. Emeline M., b. Sept. 18, 1841, d. Aug. 13, 1847.
　　2. Lenora A., b. Feb. 27, 1845; res. Wilton, unm.
　　3. A. Josephine, b. Jan. 27, 1847; res. Wilton, unm.
　　4. Marcella, b. March 13, 1856, m. Feb. 25, 1880, Dr. Geo. W. Hatch; res. Wilton, where she d. March 17, 1899; two ch., Fred and Lydia.

　　James Smith, son of Jacob and Katherine (White) Smith, b. Mont Vernon, m. Catherine, dau. Charles and Catherine (Newton) Caswell. She was b. Boston, Vt. He lived in Francestown, afterwards in Mont Vernon in house now torn down near Scroobe's in South Dist. He afterward lived in West Dist., where he d. 1878. After his death she m. Aug. 26, 1885, Augustus Johnson of Bennington. She d. Mont Vernon, Oct. 12, 1901, age 84 yrs., 2 mos., 3 dys. Ch.

　　1. Deborah, m. Henry H. Joslin, an enterprising farmer of Lyndeboro, has a large family of ch.; res. Lyndeboro.
　　2. Andrew, res. Bennington.
　　3. Alvin, m. his cousin, dau. of Samuel Smith of Orange, Vt.; two ch.; is a rural mail-carrier and resides in New Boston.

4. James W., has resided in South Keene and Walpole, N. H., is m., has five ch.; res. Gilmanton.

5. Esther W., b. Nov. 25, 1853, m. (1) James Douglas, m. (2) *James C. Towne; res. Peterboro.

Dr. Norman Smith, son of Jesse and Nabby (Kittredge) Smith, b. Mont Vernon, Oct. 13, 1811. He grad. Vermont Medical College, Woodstock, in 1843, and the same year established himself in the practice of medicine and surgery at Groton, Mass. He acquired a wide practice in the surgical branch of his profession extending over the northern part of Middlesex Co., Mass., and the southern part of Hillsboro Co., in N. H. In April, 1861, at the outbreak of the Civil War he went out as surgeon of the 6th Mass. Regt. and was with it in its famous march through Baltimore, and during its first campaign of three months. In 1874 he went to Europe and passed one year attending medical lectures and hospital practice on the continent. Returning in 1875 he resided in Nashua. He purchased a fine estate near Groton, Mass., where he closed his busy and useful life May 24, 1888. During his earlier years Dr. Smith was proficient in music, which he taught with great success. He was a member of the Mass. Medical Society and was a public-spirited citizen, prominent in whatever promoted the welfare of the community in which he lived. In early life he united with the church in Mont Vernon, and was one of the oldest members of the evangelical church in Groton. He m. (1) May 1, 1838, Harriet, dau. John and Lydia Sleeper of Francestown. She d. Sept. 2, 1839. He m. (2) Nov. 6, 1843, Adeline Sleeper, a sister of his first wife, who d. July 6, 1846. He m. (3) Sept. 22, 1847, Abby Maria, dau. Ephraim and Sarah (King) Brown of Wilton. She d. July 17, 1852. He m. (4) Sept. 12, 1853, Sarah, dau. Solomon and Dorcas (Hopkins) Frost, who d. Dec. 4, 1856. He m. (5) Sept. 11, 1860, Mrs. Mary J. (King) Lee, wid David Lee of Barre, Mass., dau. Daniel and Rebecca (Parmenter) King of Rutland, Mass. She d. 1901, in Boston. Ch. by first wife:

1. Henry J., b. Aug. 26, 1836, d. Aug. 1855, at the age of nearly 19; a remarkably amiable and pious youth.

Ch. by third wife

2. Frank, b. Aug. 2, 1851, d. July 27, 1860.

Ch. by fifth wife:

3. Norman K., Sept. 28, 1868; res. Boston

4. Frederic L., Feb. 26, 1871; res. Boston.

5. Laura K., Oct. 27, 1872; res. Boston.

Honorable Charles James Smith, son of Dr. Luther and Mary (Carleton) Smith, b. Hillsboro Bridge, N. H., Sept. 3, 1820, attended the public schools until 1835; attended the Hopkinton, N. H., Academy three years and Milford Academy a few months. In Jan., 1839, he entered the law office of Albert Baker, Esq., (brother of Mrs. Mary (Baker) Eddy, the founder of Christian Science) at Hillsborough, and continued with him until Mr. Baker's death in Oct., 1841, pursuing the study of law and general literature. He subsequently spent a few months in the office of George Barstow, Esq., then at Hillsborough, but he never entered upon the practice of law. From 1842 until 1853 he was for the larger part of the time occupied in school teaching in New Hampshire and Massachusetts, with the exception of three years, serving in 1846 as register of deeds for Hillsborough county and in 1850 and 1851 he was employed in the office of the U. S. military engineers at Boston. In April, 1853, he was appointed an inspector in the Boston custom house, holding the position until July, 1857

He has sustained remarkable reverses of fortune, losing heavily in the great fires of Chicago and Boston, in the latter of which he was financially overwhelmed by the loss of over $40,000 in insurance stocks, owning 252 shares in 13 of what was, prior to the fire, the strongest companies in New England. Since 1873 he has been engaged in fire insurance, having an office in Boston several years. An historical sketch of his native town, entitled, "Annals of Hillsborough," from his pen, was published in 1841. He contributed to the History of Hillsborough County, published in 1885, the historical sketch of Mont Vernon. He has had a voting residence in Mont Vernon since 1842 and has held the offices of selectman four years, town clerk six years, moderator 16 years, and for over 20 years had the supervision of his schools. He was a representative in 1860 and 1861, member of the Senate in 1863 and 1864, and of the Constitutional Convention in 1876 and 1889. From 1845 to 1871 he resided with his mother in the house now owned by the Dr. C. M. Kittredge Estate in South Dist. In 1871 he purchased the "Cloutman place" of Mrs. C. L. Wilkins, southeast of the village, where he now resides. June 6, 1878, he m. Mrs. Marguerite (Haymand) Burt of Plymouth, Mass. She was b. Feb. 15, 1847. Ch. b. Mont Vernon:

1. Mary Ellen Rolfe, b. May 13, 1879, is a teacher.
2. Edward Lorhair, b. Jan. 24, 1881, has a position with a publishing company in Lowell and Lawrence, Mass.
3. Lelia Eugenie, b. Oct. 15, 1882, stenographer in Boston.
4. Helen Adelaide, b. Oct. 1, 1884, d. Aug. 24, 1885.

Mr. Smith's stepson, Charles J. Smith, Jr., b. Feb. 4, 1871, has resided in Somerville since 1889; is a foreman in a large teaming establishment in Boston; m. Feb. 6, 1897, Ada K., dau. John K. and Mary (Sexton) Stinson of Somerville; one ch.

Dea. Daniel Smith, lived west of McCollom Hill in North Dist., m. (1); m. (2) Polly Carleton of Lyndeboro. He d. Sept. 1, 1829, age 80. His wife, Polly, d. June 13, 1847, age 59. Ch. by first wife b. Mont Vernon.
1. William, a tanner, settled in Greenfield. His widow, Clara, m. Charles Richardson of Amherst. She d. July 16, 1863.
Ch. by second wife b. Mont Vernon.
1. *John, b. Sept. 12, 1809.
2. Sarah, m. Asa Goodale of Antrim, a man of wealth; one dau., Olive Jane, m. Melvin Temple of Windsor; had two ch.
3. Mindwill, m. *Simeon Story, moved to Antrim, 1860; one ch.
4. Hiram, m. Eliza Bertram, went from Antrim to Minnesota in 1854.

John Smith, son of Dea. Daniel and Polly (Carleton) Smith, b. Mont Vernon, Sept. 12, 1809; m. Cynthia W., dau. of David and Mary (Averill) Smith. She was b. Mont Vernon, March 4, 1807, d. June 15, 1884. He lived in the village. He d. July 5, 1881. Ch. b. Mont Vernon:
1. John Henry, b. Aug. 5, 1835, served in 2nd and 13th N. H. Regts. in Civil War, m. (1) Aug. 13, 1862, Almira Fletcher of Antrim, who d. June 29, 1861; m. (2) Mrs. Sarah R. Sargent, wid. William Sargent of Amherst and dau. Dea. Enoch and Jane (Jameson) Sargent. She was b. Goffstown, March 5, 1833, d. May 14, 1896. He m. (3) Mrs. Eleanor M. Perkins, wid. Joseph E. Perkins and dau. Jesse and Eleanor (Morgan) Manning, Sept. 6, 1900. She was b. Billerica, Mass., Dec. 13, 1841, d. June 29, 1902. He m. (4) Nov. 22, 1902, Mrs. Bridget (Quinn) Gould.
2. *Daniel Harrison, b. March 15, 1838.
3. Emma Angeline, b. Oct. 11, 1840, d. unm. Sept. 12, 1881.

4. Charles Richmond, b. April 4, 1844, d. unm. June 29, 1901.
5. Nancy Maria, b. Oct. 26, 1848, m. Russell Farrington; res. near Livermore Falls, Me.; has two dau.

Daniel Harrison Smith, son of John and Cynthia (Smith) Smith, b. Mont Vernon, March 15, 1838. He is a farmer and resides at the upper end of village at "Pine Grove Farm." He m. June 1, 1858, Mary J., dau. Daniel and Olive (Proctor) Holt of Milford. She was b. Milford, Jan. 27, 1840. Ch. b. Mont Vernon:
1. Richmond, b. July 11, 1863, m. Nov. 2, 1887, Jessie B. Nye. He is a meat and provision dealer in Boston; res. in Dorchester, Mass., has one ch.
2. *Frank, b. Aug. 20, 1865.
3. L. Belle, b. Feb. 16, 1867, m. July 3, 1893, Peter W. Pattee of Goffstown; res. Goffstown; one ch., Wardner.
4. Annie E., b. June 30, 1869, m. June 2, 1890, *J. Frank Perham; res. Mont Vernon.
5. Grace H., b. June 16, 1872, m. Nov. 8, 1894, Louis H. Hall of Milford; res. Milford.
6. Harry A., b. Dec. 13, 1874, res. Mont Vernon with his parents.

Frank Smith, son of Daniel H. and Mary J. (Holt) Smith, b. Mont Vernon, Aug. 20, 1865. He resides in the village, is a carpenter; m. Oct. 18, 1885, Annie E., dau. Solomon and Nancy (Averill) Jones. She was b. Sept. 10, 1867, in Mont Vernon. Ch. b. Mont Vernon.
1. Cecil Frank, b. April 4, 1886.
2. Alice Belle, b. June 18, 1889.

Rev. Bezaleel Smith (for more information see chapter on "Ecclesiastical History"), grad. Dartmouth College in 1825, came to Mont Vernon from Rye, N. H., in Aug., 1841. He m. 1829, Eliza E. Morrison of New Hampton, N. H. She d. March 21, 1847, age 35. He closed his ministry here in 1850, removed from here to Roxbury, N. H., thence to New Alstead, N. H., thence to Hanover Centre, N. H., d. May 15, 1879, age 82, at Randolph, Vt. He m. (2) Miss Davis of Royalston, Vt. Ch.
1. John B., grad. Dartmouth College, 1854, d. Nashua, June 17, 1858, age 27 years.
2. Horace Morrison, merchant tailor in Boston, m. a dau. of Ira Gay of Nashua, lived in Malden, where he d. April 25, 1884, age 51.
3. Caroline Eliza, d. Nov. 23, 1850, age 16.
4. *Huntingdon Porter, b. Jan. 11, 1837.
5. Martha Haven, d. March 3, 1866, age 26 years, seven months.
6. George Henry, b. Mont Vernon, 1842, m. Sept. 9, 1866, Jane L. Fletcher of Antrim; laborer, lived in Lebanon, d. 1898, age 56.
7. Levi W., d. Aug. 12, 1846, age seven months.
8. Daniel A., d. May 28, 1844, age five months; seven ch.

Huntingdon Porter Smith, son of Rev. Bezaleel and Eliza E. (Morrison) Smith, b. Rye, N. H., Jan. 11, 1837, m. Anna D. Berry, dau. Dr. Chas. T. Berry of Pittsfield, N. H. He is a merchant of woolen cloth in Boston; res. Cambridge. He is an elocutionist of considerable ability. Ch.
1. Charles P., b. 1867.
2. Chadbourne, b. 1869, d. at 18 months.
3. Winifred B., b. 1871.
4. Bertha M., b. 1875, d. May, 1887.
5. Robert L., b. 1883.

SPAULDING.

Otis M. Spaulding, son of Stephen and Sarah (Blodgett) Spaulding, b. Tyngsboro, Mass., Aug. 23, 1841, was a stone mason in Milford, came to Mont Vernon in 1886; lives on his father-in-law's (Josiah Swinnington) farm in South Dist.; m. Jan. 18, 1869, Hannah E., dau. Josiah and Sarah (Farnum) Swinnington. She was b. Mont Vernon, Oct. 4, 1850. Ch. b. Milford:

1. Minnie B., b. Sept. 1, 1869, m. Nov. 25, 1891, Joseph G. Carleton of Mont Vernon, res. Mont Vernon; five ch.
2. Wilbert O., b. Jan. 14, 1874, laborer.
3. Frank C., b. July 27, 1876, m. Dec. 24, 1901, Mrs. Mary Storer of Rochester, N. H., res. Nashua; one son.
4. Ernest Holmes, b. May 30, 1882, res. at home.

SOUTHWORTH.

Capt. Chester B. Southworth was b. in West Fairlee, Vt. He lived there until 21 years of age. In 1836 he came to Mont Vernon and worked for some years at his trade of currier in the tannery of Dea. Joseph A. Starrett. While thus employed a permanent injury to his left arm compelled a change of occupation, and he was engaged as a travelling merchant for S. Thayer & Co. of New Ipswich, and later through the remainder of his life very successfully, on his own account. During his 25 years' residence in Mont Vernon, from 1836 to 1861, he owned and occupied the place just above the cemetery, now occupied by Kneeland C. White. In 1861 he removed to Manchester, where he d. May 26, 1893, age 78 years. He m. (1) Augusta, dau. Capt. William and Serviah (Jones) Lamson, July 21, 1842. She was b. Mont Vernon, March 9, 1817, d. Manchester, Feb. 1, 1879; no ch. He m. (2) Miss Southworth of Thetford, Vt., who d. shortly after. He m. (3) Mrs. Harriet Holbrook of Bedford, N. H., who still lives in Manchester.

SPOFFORD.

Abijah Spofford was a teacher and singer. He was a tax-payer in 1804.

STARRETT.

David Starrett, b. Francestown, N. H., April 21, 1774, grad. Dartmouth College 1798; was lawyer in Hillsboro. He m. Abigail Ellery Appleton, dau. Rev. Joseph Appleon of North Brookfield, Mass. She d. Mont Vernon, May 3, 1858, age 73. Mrs. Starret with three ch. came here in 1813. Ch. b. Hillsboro:

1. *Joseph A., b. Aug. 31, 1804.
2. Emily Caroline, b. Jan. 20, 1807, m. Rev. David Stowell of Townsend, Mass., Oct. 26, 1837; had one ch., Dr. David P. Stowell of Waterville, Me., d.
3. *Albert Gardiner, b. Oct. 21, 1810.

Dea. Joseph A. Starrett, son of David and Abigail E. (Appleton) Starrett, b. Hillsboro, Aug. 31, 1804, was deacon of the Congregational Church; came to Mont Vernon in May, 1813, learned the tanner's trade, operated the tannery. D. May 22, 1894, m. Dec. 10, 1833, Maria J., dau. Dea. John and Dolly (Durant) Bruce of Mont Vernon. She was b. Mont Vernon,

JOSEPH A. STARRETT.
Deacon from 1836 to 1858.

Aug. 21, 1814. She d. Oct. 20, 1869. He lived in the brick house in the village. Ch. b. Mont Vernon:

1. Henrietta M., b. Sept. 29, 1834, m. Dec. 5, 1853, *Dr. Samuel G. Dearborn. She d. Nashua, June 29, 1893; two ch.

2. Josephine, b. March 12, 1836, d. March 11, 1846.

3. *William Sullivan A., b. June 4, 1838.

4. Emily J., b. Dec. 14, 1846, m. *John T. McCollom, July 14, 1866, d. April 4, 1867; one ch.

Albert Gardiner Starrett, son of David and Abigail E. (Appleton) Starrett, b. Hillsboro, Oct. 21, 1810; worked in the shops here, lived in village, d. Mont Vernon, March 24, 1855, m. Sept. 17, 1845, Mary M., dau. of Daniel and Tabitha (Sawyer) Stevens. She was. b. May 17, 1826, Stoddard, N. H., d. Mont Vernon, Nov. 11, 1896. Ch. b. Mont Vernon:

1. Albert Appleton, b. Aug. 8, 1847, d. July 31, 1848.

2. George Gardiner, b. May 27, 1849, m. Dec. 28, 1882, Ellen Sinnicks, b. Five Leagues, Labrador, Oc. 27, 1851. He d. Sept. 24, 1887. His wid. res. Mont Vernon. Lived in his father's house in village; farmer. Ch. b. Mont Vernon:

1. Alice Gardner, b. Oct. 6, 1883.

2. William Appleton, b. Sept. 14, 1885.

William Sullivan A. Starrett, son of Dea. Joseph A. and Maria J. (Bruce) Starrett, b. Mont Vernon, June 4, 1838, m. June 17, 1868, Frances E., dau. Milton W. and Sophronia (Trow) McCollom of Mont Vernon. She was b. Mont Vernon, Dec. 26, 1845. He res. in the brick house in village, owned by his father. Ch. b. Mont Vernon:

1. Emily C. A., b. March 15, 1871; teacher in Milford.

2. Henrietta M., b. Sept. 1, 1872, m. June 6, 1903, Fred Auryansen of New York City; res. Brooklyn, New York.

William A. Starrett, cousin Dea. Joseph A. Starrett, came here from Francestown, worked in the tannery, m. Emily Frances, dau. Dea. John and Dolly (Durant) Bruce of Mont Vernon. She d. Aug. 19, 1853, aged 23. He d. Oct. 10, 1854, aged 30. Both buried in Mont Vernon.

STEARNS.

John Stearns m. Nancy Wetherbee of New Boston. He d. June 5, 1860, aged 69. They lived in the West Dist. Ch. b. Mont Vernon.

1. Hannah Pettengill, b. Sept. 28, 1817, George Green; one ch. d. July 11, 1900.

2. *John W., b. July 29, 1819, d.   He m. Sarah Jane Hodgeman.

3. *Daniel, b. 1823.

4. *Seth P., b. Oct. 14, 1826.

John W. Stearns, son of John and Nancy (Wetherbee) Stearns, b. July 29, 1819, lived in Mont Vernon in West Dist., m. Sarah Jane Hodgeman. Ch. were:

1. Reuben, d. unm.

2. Hannah, m. Daniel Boardman.

3. Emeline, m. James Douglas; had several ch., lived New Boston.

4. Harriet, m. (1) Lewis Smith, had ch.; m. (2) David Bumford.

5. Frank, d. young.

6. Sarah, m. Abbott of Milford.

7. Ida M., m. ——— Flagg of Mason.
8. John Frank, lives Lyndeboro.
9. Alfred, d. 1894.
10. Granville, lives Lyndeboro.

Daniel Stearns, son of John and Nancy (Wetherbee) Stearns, b. 1823, d. Feb. 18, 1899; lived in the West Dist., m. Nancy J. Mills. She was b. Chester, N. H., d. Aug. 23, 1897, age 82 yrs., 7 mos. Ch. b. Mont Vernon:
  1. Caroline, m. David Ritter, lives in Washington, D. C.; four ch.
  2. Daniel Augustus, m. Georgia Hartshorn of Merrimack, July 3, 1882, d. July 26, 1883, age 33.
  3. Charles.
  4. George, res. in West Dist.; m. (1) ——— Christie, dau. John Christie of New Boston; m. (2) Aug. 12, 1895, Josie, dau. Peter and Emeline (Stearns) Douglass of N. B.

Seth P. Stearns, son of John and Nancy (Wetherbee) Stearns, b. Oct. 14, 1826; m. Feb. 23, 1852, Mary E. Brown of Lyndeboro, b. April 23, 1832. She d. Oct. 18, 1895, age 63 yrs., 5 mos., 25 dys. He d. Jan. 26, 1902. Lived in the West Dist. Ch. b. Mont Vernon.
  1. Harvey Page, b. Aug. 16, 1855, lives in West Dist., unm.
  2. Almira, d. infancy.
  3. Andrew Jason, b. June 26, 1862, m. May 7, 1893, Cora E. Mason of Tamworth; lives in Tamworth.
  4. Elizabeth A., b. Feb. 2, 1872, unm.

STEVENS.

Calvin Stevens was a native of Rutland, Mass., where he was b. Jan. 27, 1753, but removed to Carlisle, Mass., in infancy, where he was bred. He removed to Hillsboro, N. H., in 1776. He fought in the Revolution and was in the Battle of Bunker Hill. His mind was naturally inquisitive, abounded in anecdote, and was much improved by reading. He was for many years a town officer and civil magistrate, and in these relations was distinguished for his correctness and integrity. He was a kind husband, a tender father and an humble and consistent Christian. He removed from Hillsboro to Mont Vernon in 1821, where he d. Feb. 22, 1833. He m. in 1773 Esther Wilkins of Carlisle, Mass., by whom he had 13 ch., 10 of whom survived him. She d. Aug. 24, 1828. He m. (2) his sister-in-law, Mrs. Hannah (Brown) Wilkins, wid. James Wilkins. She d. Carlisle, Feb. 8, 1852. Ch. all but eldest b. Hillsboro:
  1. Isaac, b. Oct. 2, 1774, drowned at sea, Oct. 15, 1802; left a widow and two sons.
  2. Polly, b. March 13, 1778, m. in Hillsboro to David Dodge, a noted and accomplished schoolmaster, a native of Amherst, subsequently located in Charlestown, Mass., and was town clerk there more than 25 yrs. He kept a select school at Hillsboro Center. He was a brother of the mothers of Gov. Jos. A. Gilmore of N. H. and Pres. Asa Dodge Smith of Dartmouth College (president from 1864 to 1877). He d. at Carlisle, Feb. 8, 1852. Mrs. Dodge d. July 10, 1846, leaving five dau. and one son.
  3. Luther, b. Sept. 2, 1779, was by trade a copper-plate printer, settled in Boston, m. but had no ch., d. at Mont Vernon. Aug. 13, 1858.
  4. Calvin, b. Feb. 5, 1781, d. unm. Nov. 20, 1803, at Boston, of yellow fever.
  5. William, b. Jan. 21, 1783, m. ——— Pulsifer, d. Aug. 12, 1813, in

New York City of wound received in War of 1812. He left two dau., viz: Adeline, m. John H. Osgood, a noted auctioneer of Boston, and Mary Ann, m. S. A. Ranlet of St. Louis, Mo.

6. Matilda, b. Dec. 14, 1785, m. George Killom of Hillsborough, moved to Buffalo, N. Y., and d. there Nov. 9, 1827, leaving five ch.

7. *Asa, b. Feb. 5, 1787.

8. Susanna, b. March 4, 1789, m. Oct. 11, 1806, *Nathan Marden, res. Mont Vernon and New Boston (res. New Boston first). She d. Mont Vernon, Aug. 20, 1843; eight ch. She was the grandmother of Hon. Geo. A. Marden.

9. Hannah, b. Feb. 1, 1791, m. May 22, 1814, *James Whittemore of Weymouth, Mass. She d. Mont Vernon, Oct. 31, 1866; six ch.

10. Zadock, b. March 9, 1793, settled in Texas, Oneida Co., N. Y. He d. there leaving ch.

11. Samuel, b. Feb. 15, 1796, settled first in Mont Vernon, removed to Clyde, N. Y., m., had no ch. While on a visit to New England he d. at Billerica, Mass., March 31, 1872, was buried at Mont Vernon.

12. Pamelia, b. Sept. 11, 1797, m. 1817, Isaac Smith; settled in Deering. He d. Jan. 27, 1855. She d. Oct. 8, 1861; 10 ch.

13. Nancy, b. Feb. 11, 1800; m. *Thomas Cloutman of Mont Vernon, d. Feb. 15, 1877; 11 ch.; six dau. grew to womanhood and were m.

Asa Stevens, son of Calvin and Esther (Wilkins) Stevens, m. Mary Ann, dau. Rev. Joseph Appleton of Brookfield, Mass. He was b. Hillsboro, Feb. 5, 1787, d. Mont Vernon, Jan. 9, 1863; farmer and shoemaker, lived on the place now occupied by his descendants. His wife d. Nov. 17, 1867, aged 76. Ch. were b. Mont Vernon:

1. David, b. June 8, 1812, d. Oct. 28, 1826.

2. Calvin, b. May 28, 1814, m. Catherine E. Boynton of East Cambridge, Mass., d. in New York City in March, 1877. He was a millionaire; three ch., one son, C. Amory Stevens, and two dau., Catherine and Mrs. Grace Richardson. The dau. in 1896 gave $5000 towards the buildings of the new church here, in memory of their father.

3. *William, b. July 28, 1816.

4. Mary Ann C., b. July 22, 1818, m. Oct. 4, 1842, George W. McCollom and d. in New York City in 1865, leaving no ch. Her husband, as a memorial to her, donated $10,000 to the Institute at Mont Vernon.

5. Harriet A., b. May 22, 1821, m. John D. Nutter, Aug. 8, 1844; has three sons and resides in Montreal, Canada.

6. Sarah Frances, b. Aug. 9, 1823, m. Ignatius Tyler, res. Montreal; no ch. He d. Aug. 25, 1889.

7. Asa, b. Jan. 23, 1825, m. (1) Harriet O. Howard, by whom he had one son and three dau. m. (2) Mrs. S. J. Tremere; was a merchant in New York City, d. April 10, 1888.

William Stevens, son of Asa and Mary A. (Appleton) Stevens, b. Mont Vernon, July 28, 1816. He was was a provision merchant in New York City many years. In June, 1865, he retired and returned to Mont Vernon, where he d. Jan. 5, 1887. For extended sketch of his life see chapter on "Prominent Men." He m. (1) Louisa W. Dye of Newark, N. J. He m. (2) Jan. 4, 1876, Helen L. (Ober) Whipple, wid. John Whipple of New Boston, and dau. Gary W. and Salome (Mills) Ober. She was b. July 25, 1842. Ch. by first wife:

1. Mary Ann.

2. Ella L.

3. Katherine.
4. Frances E.

Daniel Stevens, son of Daniel and Phebe (Durant) Stevens, b. **Stod-**
dard, N. H., March 26, 1785. His parents were from Billerica, **Mass.**,
where most of their ch. were b. He m. Tabitha, dau. Benjmain **and**
Tabitha (Kittredge) Sawyer, b. Nelson, N. H., July 16, 1792, **d. Mont**
Vernon, Jan. 26, 1883. He moved from Stoddard to Mont Vernon in
1839 and d. Sept. 24, 1844. Ch. b. Stoddard:
1. James, b. 1810, d. Sept. 17, 1838, unm., at Daysville, Ill.
2. Elizabeth, b. March 22, 1814, m. Griffin Wilson of Peterboro **who**
d. Nashua, Jan. 26, 1861. She m. (2) Ebenezer Fiske of Lyndeboro. **She**
d. Milford, Dec. 30, 1893, age 79 yrs., 9 mos. By her first husband she **had**
two ch., Mrs. Jacob Nichols and Albro M. Wilson.
3. Elmira, d. at the age of three years.
4. Joshua D., d. Daysville, Ill., unm., Oct. 4, 1838.
5. Levi, m. Caroline Warren of Dublin, N. H., Nov. 9, 1848. She d.
Charlestown, Mass., Dec. 2, 1872. He m. (2) Jan. 6, 1874, Mary E. Moore.
He d. Boston, July 9, 1890.
6. Sarah B., b. ——, m. June 9, 1846, Samuel G. Parker of Lowell.
She d. Lowell, Jan. 10, 1865; three dau., Alice C., Evie M. and Lena S.
7. Lydia, m. June 18, 1848, George W. Wilkins of New Boston, d.
May 16, 1857; one son.
8. *Hon. George W., b. Oct. 23, 1824, d. Lowell, June 6, 1884, m. **Sept.,**
1850, Elizabeth Kimball of Littleton, Mass. She d. Oct. 26, 1891, at St.
Paul, age 59; three ch., the eldest, George H., was b. Mont Vernon, **July,**
1851, lawyer in Lowell.
9. Mary M., b. May 17, 1826, m. Sept. 17, 1845, *Albert G. Starrett
of Mont Vernon. She d. Nov. 11, 1896; two ch.
10. *Samuel N., b. March 13, 1828.
11. Adeline, m. Thomas C. Ryder of Dunbarton, March 23, 1847, d.
Feb. 19, 1852; one ch., George H. Ryder.
12. Caroline A., m. March 16, 1865, Dr. John P. Brown of Raymond,
N. H., now Supt. of Insane Asylum, Taunton, Mass.; one dau., Gertrude, **m**

Samuel N. Stevens, son of Daniel and Tabitha (Sawyer) Stevens, **b.**
Stoddard, March 13, 1828, provision dealer; moved to Milford 1867, **rem.**
to Mont Vernon 1895, m. March 19, 1854, Nancy M., dau. Dea. Josiah and
Relief (Batchelder) Kittredge, b. Mont Vernon, March 9, 1832. Ch. b.
Mont Vernon:
1. Josephine M., b. May 30, 1855, m. Sept. 27, 1883, William F., **son**
of Francis J. and Betsey A. (Robinson) French of Milford and res. there.
2. Charles Newell, b. July 10, 1857, is a hotel steward, res. in Philadelphia, Pa., m. Jan. 11, 1892, Jennie J. Shattuck of Brooklyn, N. Y.
3. Hattie Adella, b. May 6, 1860.

SAWYER.

Hon. Aaron Flint Sawyer was b. April 24, 1780, at Westminster, **Mass.**
grad. Dartmouth College, 1804, commenced practice of law in Mont Vernon in 1807, removed to Nashua about 1828, d. there Jan. 4, 1847. Represented Mont Vernon in 1827, and Nashua in 1847; m. Aug. 30, 1811, Hannah, granddaughter Rev. Samuel Locke, D. D., president of Harvard College from 1770 to 1773. Ch. b. Mont Vernon.
1. Samuel Locke, m. Mary Cathaway; had two sons and one dau.,

lived Independence, Mo., where he d. March 30, 1890, age 77 yrs., 4 mos. He was a leading member of the bar of Missouri, a circuit judge and member Congress one term.

    2. Charlotte, b. July 1, 1816, m. Aaron P. Hughes, Esq., of Nashua, Nov. 17, 1845; ch., James A. D., b. Sept. 6, 1846, grad. Dartmouth 1869, m. Emma Mininger; for many years was an Episcopal clergyman in Mo., now a farmer there.

    2. Aaron, b. Feb. 20, 1849, grad. Dartmouth 1871, res. Nashua, unm.
    3. *Aaron W., b. Oct. 11, 1818.
    4. Flint H., b. Nov. 2, 1821, m. Martha J. Colburn; no ch.
    5. Catherine, b. April 25, 1825, m. John Taft of Worcester, two ch. lived in Worcester.

    Hon. Aaron Worcester Sawyer, son of Hon. Aaron F. and Hannah (Locke) Sawyer, was b. in Mont Vernon, Oct. 11, 1818, and d. in Nashua, Aug. 23, 1882. The first few years of his life was passed in Mont Vernon, from which place his father removed about 1828 to Nashua. He was educated at the public schools of Nashua and the academies of Hancock, Derry and Nashua. Afterwards he taught school several years, also studied law. He was admitted to the bar in 1844, and in 1846 began the practice of law in Nashua. From that time until 1872 his professional career was continuous, uninterrupted and successful. He served as Representative from Nashua and Senator in the State Legislature, and from 1867 until July, 1876, he held the office of register in bankruptcy. On the 22d of July, 1876, he received from Governor Cheney his commission as associate justice of the Supreme Court, but failing health obliged him to resign his office within two years. Judge Sawyer was not only an eminent lawyer and jurist, but also a devoted laborer in the vineyard of Christ. He was a licensed minister of the Congregational faith, active and useful in all Christian work. He m. (1) Mary Frances Ingalls of New York City, m. (2) Fanny, dau. of Francis and Almira (Stetson) Winch, of Nashua, Sept. 12, 1855. Their ch. were: Fanny Ingalls (deceased), Fanny Locke, m. Dr. Bowers a dentist in Nashua; Aaron Frank (deceased), and William Merriam, b. Sept. 9, 1873, fitted for college, Exeter, N. H., graduated Williams College, 1893, Boston Law School, 1898, admitted to bar at Concord, m. June 23, 1898, Marion Stimpson.

STILES.

    David Stiles, b. Feb. 4, 1811, d. Jan. 24, 1881, m. Margery M. Goodridge, May 13, 1841, of Lyndeboro. She was b. April 23, 1810, d. Dec. 31, 1884. He came to Mont Vernon about 1840, occupied the farm now occupied by Wm. Ryan, afterwards in East Dist., moved to Lyndeboro, was killed by railroad, Jan. 24, 1881. Ch. b. Mont Vernon:

    1. Benjamin G., b. Jan. 9, 1845, d. Jan. 28, 1845.
    2. Maria, b. Jan. 2, 1847, d. Jan. 2, 1847.
    3. *David A., b. June 24, 1849.
    4. Maria E., b. May 11, 1851, d. April 5, 1868.
    5. Lucie S., b. March 28, 1854; teacher; res. Minneapolis, Minn.

    David A. Stiles, son of David and Margery M. (Goodridge) Stiles, b. Mont Vernon, June 24, 1849, d. Wilton, April 11, 1899, m. Nov. 27, 1873, Eugelia J. Brooks of Greenfield, N. H. She was b. Dublin, N. H., Sept. 30, 1854, res. Wilton. Mr. Stiles was a schoolmaster, taught Antrim, Greenfield and Mont Vernon; moved from here to Wilton. Ch.

1. Lillian F., b. Francestown, May 15, 1877.
2. Edith M., b. Francestown, Jan. 23, 1879.
3. Annabel M., b. Antrim, June 13, 1883.
4. Lucie G., b. Mont Vernon, Nov. 21, 1886.
All the ch. live in Wilton.

Cyrus Stiles, b. Middleton, Mass., May 13, 1753, d. in Amherst, Aug. 24, 1831, m. Oct. 29, 1789, Hannah Berry. She was b. in Middleton, March 14, 1771, d. Amherst, Sept. 28, 1852. They lived in the East Dist. but afterwards rem. to Amherst. He was a voter here in 1804. Ch.
1. Cyrus, b. Middleton, Mass., Feb. 25, 1790, d. Amherst, 1794.
2. Hannah, b. Middleton, Mass., April 1, 1792, m. Nov. 29, 1813, Joseph Prince of Amherst, rem. to Warren, Pa., d. Jan. 13, 1837.
3. Hiram, d. young.
4. Mary, m. Peter McNeil of New Boston, Sept. 23, 1818, d. New Boston, 1882.
5. Abby, d. Mont Vernon, aged 14.
6. Cynthia, d. Mont Vernon, aged 14.
7. Elizabeth B., d. March 13, 1874, aged 74, unm.
8. Lydia, b. May 10, 1804, m. April, 1838, George H. Shaw of Amherst. She d. July 20, 1884, aged 80 years.
9. Josiah, d. Lynn. Mass., Aug. 3,; 1868, age 59 yrs.

STINSON.

William Stark Stinson, b. July 9, 1792, came to Mont Vernon from Dunbarton; lived in village; jeweller; d. Feb. 23, 1845, age 56 yrs., 7 mos., 14 dys. He m. (1) Sept. 12, 1816, Lois, dau. Rev. John and Lois (Wilkins) Bruce of Mont Vernon. She was b. 1793, d. Oct. 5, 1823. He m. (2) Anna Gray, who d. July 26, 1829, age 29. He m. (3) Sarah Twiss of Dunbarton. She was b. May 4, 1798, Dunbatron, d. Dunbarton, July 12, 1884. Ch. all b. Mont Vernon.
Ch. by first wife:
1. Mary L., b. June, 1817, d. July, 1818.
2. *William A., b. Feb. 22, 1819.
3. Bruce, was a shoemaker in Stoneham.
4. Washington, minister, lived in Illinois.
Ch. by third wife:
5. Sarah A., b. Dec. 21, 1835, m. David Story of Dunbarton, d. Dunbarton, March 4, 1887; three ch.
6. Mary A., b. March 18, 1838, d. July 14, 1875, unm.
7. *Charles F., b. Oct. 24, 1840.

William A. Stinson, son of William S. and Lois (Bruce) Stinson, b. Mont Vernon, Feb. 22, 1819; lived in his father' house in village; worked in Conant's box shop, d. Sept. 10, 1876; m. Sept. 24, 1846, Nancy A., dau. Thomas and Nancy (Stevens) Cloutman. She was b. Mont Vernon, Oct. 26, 1824, d. Mont Vernon, Oct. 18, 1898. Ch. b. Mont Vernon:
1. *Thomas Henry, b. Nov. 18, 1848.
2. Emmie F., b. April 1, 1855, m. Dec. 5, 1883, Guilford U. Carlton of Goffstown; res. Minneapolis, Minn.
3. Annie F., b. April 22, 1860, d. June 30, 1872.

Major Charles Frederick Stinson, son of William S. and Sarah (Twiss) Stinson, b. Mont Vernon, Oct. 24, 1840, d. Mont Vernon, March

MAJOR CHARLES F. STINSON.
Deacon from 1891 to 1893.

10, 1893; m. Nov. 28, 1867, Ella Louise Russell, dau. Walter Russell of Watertown, Mass. She was b. Aug. 27, 1846, d. March 3, 1900. He was in the 13th N. H. Regt. in Civil War, afterwards Major of a colored company. He was a partner with his nephew, T. H. Stinson, in Boston, in manufacture of boxes, etc.; came to Mont Vernon 1882. Ch. b. Charlestown, Mass.

    1. *William Stark, b. Jan. 22, 1870.
    2. Charles Frederick, b. May 24, 1876; has a position in a chemical factory in Boston.
    3. Lucy Russell, b. Aug. 17, 1877; res. Waltham, Mass.

    Thomas Henry Stinson, son of William A. and Nancy A. (Cloutman) Stinson, b. Mont Vernon, Nov. 18, 1848; m. Sept. 24, 1874, Nellie M. Woods of Hollis, N. H. He d. Jan. 3, 1895, Winchester. He was in the real estate business for a few years; in business in the manufacture of boxes with G. F. Stinson, afterwards was town clerk of Winchester. Ch.
    1. William H., b. July 7, 1875.
    2. Annie E., b. Nov. 10, 1876.
    3. Mabel W., b. Feb. 19, 1878.
    4. Charles Pressy, b. July 19, 1880, d. July 6, 1900.
    5. Richard L., b. July 22, 1881.
    6. Helen E., b. May 19, 1887.

William Stark Stinson, son of Major Charles F. and Ella L. (Russell) Stinson, b. Charlestown, Mass., Jan. 22, 1870; m. June 13, 1893, Myra W., dau. Henry and Myra (Woodman) Clement of Winterport, Me. She was b. Winterport, Me., Feb. 28, 1872. Res. Mont Vernon. Ch. b. Mont Vernon:
    1. Clement Russell, b. Dec. 2, 1894.
    2. Mildred Louise, b. May 30, 1896.
    3. Katherine Shepard, b. Feb. 8, 1898.

    Col. William H. Stinson, son of William C. and Sarah E. (Poor) Stinson, b. Dunbarton, July 2, 1851, m. Sept. 30, 1885, Ellen F., dau. Dea. William H. and S. Emeline (Cloutman) Conant of Mont Vernon. She was b. Mont Vernon, Dec. 18, 1857. Was Master of State Grange; was a member of Gov. Chas. H. Bell's staff; was a statistican several years; moved from Mont Vernon to Dunbarton in 1895, now resides at Goffstown. Ch.
    1. Daniel Chase, b. Mont Vernon, June 9, 1886.
    2. William Conant, b. Mont Vernon, Dec. 9, 1888.
    3. Grace Isabel, b. Mont Vernon, April 9, 1891.
    4. Cecil Ray, b. Dunbarton, May 28, 1893.
    5. Dorothy May, b. Dunbarton, Dec. 16, 1896.

STORY.

    Simon Story lived in the North Dist., near the New Boston line, m Mindwill Smith, dau. Dea. Daniel and Polly (Carleton) Smith. They moved to Antrim in 1860.
    William, b. Mont Vernon, Feb. 13, 1846, m. Nellie Brooks, now of Antrim; one ch., William.
    Albert T., d. Nov. 2, 1850, aged 1 year.

SWINNINGTON.

Elisha Swinnington, m. (1) Betsey Temple. She d. July 25, 1840, age

45. He m. (2) Sarah Hood, dau. Joseph and Eleanor (Woodbury) Hood of Milford, b. Milford, Jan. 25, 1807, d. June 28, 1883, age 76. He d. May 6, 1870, age 80. He lived on the farm in the South Dist. afterwards owned by his son, Josiah, now by his granddaughter, Mrs. O. M. Spalding. He d. May 6, 1870, age 80. Ch. b. Mont Vernon.
    Ch. by first wife:
    1. *Josiah, b. Dec. 4, 1819.
    2. Hannah, d. of consumption.
    3. Elizabeth, m. *Granville Parker; d.

Josiah Swinnington, son of Elisha and Betsey (Temple) Swinnington, b. Mont Vernon, Dec. 4, 1819, d. April 21, 1902; lived on and owned his father's farm in South Dist., m. Oct. 27, 1842, Sarah J., dau. Israel and Catherine (Talbot) Farnum. She was b. Mont Vernon, Dec. 25, 1818; d. Mont Vernon, Jan. 28, 1879. Ch. b. Mont Vernon.
    1. Martin L., b. Feb. 10, 1844, d. Feb. 25, 1845.
    2. Abby T., b. Dec. 23, 1848, m. Nov. 20, 1879, *Franklin Trow, d. June 1, 1886; one son.
    3. Hannah E., b. Oct. 4, 1850, m. Jan. 18, 1869, *Otis M. Spalding; res. Mont Vernon; four ch.
    4. Albert E., b. May 30, 1855, m. June 29, 1881, Kate, dau. Eli Clark and Betsey A. (Curtis) Curtis of Lyndeboro; res. Lyndeboro; one dau., Clara B.
    5. Ida B., b. May 25, 1860, m. Nov. 23, 1875, *John A. Bullard of Mont Vernon; three ch.; res. Lyndeboro.

Abigail Swinnington (sister Elisha) m. Dec. 11, 1825, Jesse Averill of Mont Vernon.
Mary Swinnington (sister Elisha) m. Jan. 22, 1824, John Phelps, Jr., of Wilmot.
Job Swinnington (brother Elisha) m. 1818, Betsey Clark.

TARBELL.

Joseph H. Tarbell, son of William and Lydia (Spaulding) Tarbell, b. Exeter, N. H., Aug. 25, 1822, d. Dec. 25, 1898; m. Aug. 23, 1844, Harriet N., dau. James and Azubah (Curtis) Hopkins Hopkins. She was b. Mont Vernon, April 26, 1824. At the age of four he entered the family of an uncle, Col. Benj. Hutchinson of Milford, where he lived until 18 years of age. He located here upon marriage, lived on a farm in South Dist. Ch. b. Mont Vernon:
    1. George Fred, b. Oct. 19, 1848, m. March 25, 1874, Helen M., dau. Stephen C. and Lucy (Averill) Langdell. She was b. Nov. 8, 1846, in Mont Vernon; farmer; res. South Dist. Ch.
    1. Alice Grace, b. Mont Vernon, June 22, 1882.
    2. Emma, b. Aug. 29, 1855, m. Charles L. Perham of Lyndeboro, Feb. 14, 1878; res. Lyndeboro; one dau., Bertha, b. Oct. 20, 1884.

TEMPLE.

Arthur Prince Temple, son of George T. and Hattie A. (Prince) Temple, b. Milford, May 12, 1875. He has resided in Mont Vernon since 1895 and is a junior partner of the firm of Blood & Temple, village grocers. He is a lineal descendant on his mother's side of Lieut. Joseph Prince, one of the proprietors of that part of Souhegan West, which is now

Mont Vernon. He m. April 27, 1898. M. Susie, dau. of D. Porter and Susan (Cloutman) Kendall. She was b. Mont Vernon, Feb. 3, 1867. Ch. Blanche E., b. Aug. 12, 1900, d. Sept. 29, 1900.

THORPE.

Rev. John Thorpe, b. May 4, 1845, Newton Heath, Manchester, Eng., son of Joel and Sarah (Brown) Thorpe, both silk weavers. John was the sixth of 11 ch. seven girls and four boys; m. 1869, Emily A. Bennett; came to Mont Vernon as minister in 1888; remained until Sept., 1894; is now preaching at Centre Harbor, N. H.; no ch.

TODD.

George W. Todd, b. Rindge, N. H., Nov. 9, 1828. He obtained his earlier education there. He grad. at the Law School, Poughkeepsie, N. Y. Was admitted to the bar in 1856. Was engaged in the practice of his profession eight years principally in Glover, Vt. In this place he was also Principal of the Orleans Institute for seven years. During this time and previously he had acquired a good knowledge of medicine, so that when he decided upon teaching for his life work as being best adapted to his taste and inclination he brought to that profession a general knowledge that was invaluable to him as an instructor. To teaching he devoted his talents, his large experience, his life. He taught 6000 students in the grammar, high schools and academies of Vermont, New Hampshire and Massachusetts. He was a Supt. of Schools 16 years. In 1872 he came to McCollom Institute and continued here six years. He began with less than 30 students and by his energy and constant exertion increased the number to 100 several terms. His enthusiasm for the success of the school was almost boundless. He infused new life into every department. Interest in the classics and higher English branches was revived and the standard of the institution improved. The dull were encouraged, and for those who needed he always had a helping hand and a kind word. In May, 1878, he resigned, but having been elected a State Senator for two years he did not change his residence until the Spring of 1880, when he removed to Rindge, teaching there until 1884, when he accepted the principalship of Eaton's Commercial College, Norwidgewock, Me., where he d. of typhoid pneumonia, April 15, 1884. Mr. Todd represented Rindge in the N. H. Legislature two years. In Aug., 1857, he m. Miss Mary J. Blodgett of Jaffrey, N. H. She d. Sept., 1864. In 1869 he m. Miss Sarah J., dau. of Dea. Henry Chapin of Holyoke, Mass., and a successful teacher in her native city. She resides in Holyoke. Ch. by first wife:

1. Frank T., b. 1863, d. Sept. 30, 1864, aged 15 months.

Ch. by second wife:

2. Geo. Frank Chapin. b. Rindge, N. H., July 9, 1880; res. Holyoke, Mass.

TOWLE.

Charles A. Towle, b. Epsom, N. H., grad. Dartmouth College 1864, Principal McCollom Institute from 1864 to 1866; studied at Andover Theological Seminary two years and one year at Chicago, grad. Chicago Theological Seminary, 1869; pastor in Sandwich, Ill., four years and in Chicago nine years, and in Monticello, Iowa, was Supt. Congregational Sunday School and Publishing Society for Iowa, with residence at Ginnell in that State. He d. Feb. 22, 1899.

TOWNE.

James D. Towne, son of Samuel Towne, b. Mont Vernon, April 23, 1810; lived in the South Dist., in the house near Trow's Pond; was selectman, farmer and miller; d. Dec. 10, 1856, age 46 yrs., 7 mos., 17 dys. He m. Jane E., dau. Jesse and Nancy (Cochran) Trow of Mont Vernon, July 11, 1839. She was b. Mont Vernon, Dec. 2, 1818, d. April 5, 1856. Ch. b. Mont Vernon:

1. James D., b. Jan. 4, 1840, enlisted as private in 1861 in the Second Regt., U. S. Vol. Sharpshooters, d. Washington, D. C., Dec. 20, 1861.
2. George E., b. March 22, 1842.
3. Nancy Jane, b. Feb. 12, 1844, d. Mont Vernon, March 26, 1883.
4. Pamelia Annett, b. March 13, 1851, d. March 14 1855.
5. Willie E., d. Aug., 1856, age five mos.

George E. Towne, son of James D. and Jane E. (Trow) Towne, b. Mont Vernon, March 22, 1842; lived in South Dist., in Mont Vernon; moved to Amherst, 1887; lives on a farm which he owns (formerly of Amos Green) on Christian Hill, Amherst, m. Nov. 28, 1882, Sarah E. Cullen of Glenham, N. Y. She was b. Feb. 23, 1851. Ch.

1. Laura Ella, b. Mont Vernon, April 27, 1884.
2. Alice Emma, b. Amherst, Sept. 8, 1887.
3. Guy Everett, b. Amherst, Nov. 19, 1889.
4. Maud Ethelyn, b. Amherst, Dec. 12, 1891.

James C. Towne, b. Greenfield, N. H., Aug. 2, 1822; m. (1) Mary Jane Swinnington, 1849. She was a native of Mont Vernon and a dau. of Job Swinnington. She d. 1852. He m. (2) Margaret Walker of Antrim, who d. 1868. He m. (3) Jan. 9, 1873, Mrs. Esther W. (Smith) Douglass, dau. James and Catherine (Caswell) Smith. She was b. Mont Vernon, Nov. 25, 1873. He came here from Hancock, lived on the Reilly place on the turnpike several years; was a butcher; moved to Peterboro in 1891. Ch. by first wife:

1. Lizzie B., twin, b. 1852, res. Peterboro.
2. George A., twin, b. 1852, res. Greenfield.

Ch. by third wife:

3. James Otis, b. Hancock, July 22, 1873; m., res. Dunbarton.
4. William W., b. Hancock, Nov. 6, 1874.
5. Charles A., b. Hancock, Nov. 4, 1876.
6. Laura Josephine, b. Hancock, Nov. 26, 1878.
7. Bessie M., b. Mont Vernon, May 7, 1881.
8. Ida Belle, b. Mont Vernon, Nov. 9, 1882.
9. Frederic H., b. Mont Vernon, Nov. 26, 1886.
10. Daisy, b. Mont Vernon, Dec. 3, 1889.
11. Winnie, b. Mont Vernon.
12. Ernest, twin, b. Peterboro.
13. Elmer, twin, b. Peterboro.

TRAVIS.

Alonzo Travis, son of William and Lydia (Sargent) Travis, b. Hillsborough, Oct., 1816, m. Maria, dau. of James and Abigail (Pollard) Baldwin of Hillsboro, April 3, 1846. She was b. Hillsboro, Jan. 24, 1821, d. Mont Vernon, Sept. 20, 1891; was moderator 14 years, town clerk 10 years, selectman four years, Representative in 1853, 1854 and 1855, also justice of peace. He d. Aug. 22, 1891. Ch.

CAPT. JOHN TREVITT.

1. Addie M., b. Mont Vernon, Oct. 16, 1846, m. John G. Dodge of Goffstown, d. Jan. 14, 1883, at Goffstown, aged 36; no ch.

Jennie W. Beal, an adopted dau. of Mr. and Mrs. Travis, m. Elmer E. Smith of Manchester, in 1892.

TREVITT.

Richard Trevitt came from England and was killed by the Indians at Fort William Henry. He left a little son, Henry Trevitt, b. at Marblehead in 1755, who at ten years of age came to Mont Vernon with his stepfather, Amos Steel, and here grew to manhood, engaged in active service in the War of the Revolution and fought under Stark at Bennington. He moved to Ohio and died in Licking Co., Aug. 27, 1850, aged 96. His ch. were nine, seven sons and two dau. His wife, Jane, b. 1761, d. Oct. 28, 1816.

Capt. James Thompson Trevitt, eldest son of Henry and Jane (Steel) Trevitt, led a company at Portsmouth in 1814 (War of 1812). He lived on the farm now occupied by his dau.-in-law, Mrs. John Trevitt. He d. Aug. 2, 1858, aged 72. He m. June 29, 1815, Sally, dau. of Jonathan and Margaret Gillis of Greenfield, N. H. She was b. Greenfield, Jan. 10, 1788, d. Mont Vernon, Dec. 10, 1867. Ch. b. Mont Vernon:

1. Margaret, d. July 18, 1817, aged one day.
2. Sarah Jane, b. Sept. 22, 1818, m. Dec. 17, 1874, *Dr. Sylvanus Bunton of Mont Vernon. She d. Mont Vernon, Dec. 26, 1899.
3. Henry Flint, b. April 23, 1820, d. Dec. 31, 1820.
4. *John, b. Oct. 9, 1821.
5. *Henry, b. Aug. 10, 1823.
6. James T., b. Sept. 23, 1825, d. Oct. 14, 1825.

Capt. John Trevitt, son of Capt. James T. and Sally (Gillis) Trevitt, b. Mont Vernon, Oct. 9, 1821. In Sept., 1837, he went to Perry Co., Ohio, to study medicine with his uncle, Dr. Wm. Trevitt. From there he was appointed a cadet to West Point Military Academy, which he entered in 1840, graduating in 1844. He entered the army as Lieut. of Infantry. He served successfully on garrison duty at Plattsburg, N. Y., in the Mexican War, and on frontier service. From 1850 to 1853 he was in charge of the recruiting service in the Third Infantry in Boston. In Dec., 1860, he resigned and returned to Mont Vernon, where he lived on his father's farm. He was a farmer and fruit grower. In 1874 and 1875 he was Representative, and was selectman five years, was also Trustee of McCollom Institute. He m. Feb. 24, 1862, Ellen W. Stayner, dau. of Henry M. Stayner of Lyndeboro. She res. Newtonville, Mass., and Mont Vernon. Ch. b. Mont Vernon.

1. Lucia Ellen, b. June 17, 1863, m. June 11, 1891, George W. Auryansen of Newtonville, Mass.; res. Newtonville, Mass.
2. Mary Victoria, b. Dec. 23, 1864; res. Mont Vernon and Newtonville, Mass.

Dr. Henry Trevitt, son of Capt. James T. and Sally (Gillis) Trevitt, b. Mont Vernon, N. H., Aug. 10, 1823, completed his medical studies at Columbus, Ohio, returned to New Hampshire in 1861, settled in East Wilton and practised there until his death, July 3, 1898. Jan. 27, 1874, he m Eleanor Winslow Benedict, dau. John and Margaret (Winslow) Benedict of Boston. She was b. May 11, 1850. Ch. b. Wilton.

1. Carita, b. Sept. 25, 1875.
2. Lotta T., b. Jan. 3, 1879, d. Aug., 1903.
3. Harry B., b. May 3, 1881.
4. Annie L., b. May 21, 1883.

Eli Trevitt, son of Henry and Jane Trevitt, m. (1) Sally Stinson of Johnson, Vt., Feb. 4, 1825. She was b. Dunbarton, N. H., March 4, 1800, d. Alexandria, Ohio, Jan. 14, 1846. He m. (2) Sept. 7, 1847, Mary Richards, b. Jan. 18, 1813. He removed from Johnson, Vt. to Mont Vernon in 1829. In 1842 they went to Alexandria, Ohio, where he d. Ch.
1. David, b. Dec. 13, 1825, m. Usena Ames. He d. Ohio, May 2, 1880; 2 ch., Frank and Lina.
2. Victor, b. May 2, 1827. In 1846 he entered the printing office of Col. Medary in Columbus, Ohio. In 1846 he went to the Mexican War. In 1851 he emigrated overland to Oregon, and resumed his trade in Oregon City. In 1882 he m. the widow of Judge Miller in Idaho. He d. in San Francisco, Cal., Jan. 22, 1883, whence he had gone for the benefit of his health.
Dr. William Trevitt, youngest son of Henry and Jane Trevitt, b. Mont Vernon, Feb. 7, 1809, lived in Columbus, Ohio. (For extended account of him see Chapter on "Prominent Men," in History Manuscript), m. Lucinda Butler in Columbus, Ohio, had 6 ch., only two of whom are living, Butler and Carlos. He d. Feb. 8, 1881.

TROW.

Joseph Trow, b. Beverly, m. Martha Dodge, May 21, 1767. He was a minute man of the Revolution. He settled on the farm now occupied by his grandson, Arthur A. Trow, in the South District. He was a shoemaker, and probably came here in the early eighties. His older children were born at Beverly, the youngest ones at Mont Vernon. He d. May 8, 1833, aged 93. His wife d. Nov. 30, 1843, aged 97. Ch.
1. *Joseph, b. Feb. 13, 1768.
2. George, b. Feb. 21, 1770, grew up.
3. Martha, b. March 31, 1772, m. Dec. 6, 1795, Dr. Stephen Peabody, son of Col. Stephen Peabody, settled in Orange, Vt.
4. Molly, b. March 5, 1774.
5. John, b. March 10, 1776.
6. Josiah, b. March 20, 1778, of Barre, Vt.
7. Joanna, b. Feb. 28, 1780, m. March 11, 1802, Nathaniel Phillips of Vermont.
8. John, b. Oct. 24, 1782.
9. Allen, b. Sept. 13, 1784, m. Sarah, dau. Phineas and Sarah (Hildreth) Jones of Amherst.
10. Hannah, b. July 21, 1786, m. March 10, 1812, *Nathan Green of Mont Vernon. He d. Lowell, Jan. 15, 1857. She d. Boston, Sept. 8, 1862. Five ch.
11. *Jesse, b. Mont Vernon, July 20, 1788.
12. Levi, b. Mont Vernon, Nov. 18, 1790, m. May 7, 1812, Betsey Averill. Settled in Goshen.
13. Anstis, b. Mont Vernon, Feb. 17, 1795, m. a Mr. Frost of Cambridge.

Joseph Trow, son of Joseph and Martha (Dodge) Trow, b. Feb. 13, 1768, came with his parents to Mont Vernon, m. Betsey, dau. Joseph and

Emma (Dodge) Perkins, m. Feb. 10, 1791. She d. Aug. 22, 1851, age 83. He d. Aug. 1, 1859. He lived on the farm now occupied by his great grandson, Charles H. Trow, in the North District. Ch. b. Mont Vernon.
1. Emma, b. Aug. 18, 1791, m. March 2, 1815, *Charles W. Wilkins. She d. Lowell, Jan. 26, 1868.
2. *Joseph, b. Jan. 28, 1794.
3. Martha D., b. Feb. 7, 1796, m. July 3, 1825, *Stowell Bancroft. She d. Dec. 15, 1876.
4. Betsey, b. Jan. 28, 1798, d. unm., May 16, 1879.
5. Sabrina, b. Oct. 15, 1800, m. Joseph Underwood, June 30, 1844, of Mont Vernon. She d. Lancaster, Mass., May 22, 1890, no ch.
6. Sophronia, b. June 4, 1806, m. June 18, 1829, Milton McCollom of Mont Vernon. She d. Feb. 12, 1885, 4 ch.
7. Perkins, d. Aug. 30, 1842, aged 5 years, 4 months.

Jesse Trow, son of Joseph and Martha (Dodge) Trow, b. Mont Vernon, July 20, 1788, m. Nov. 16, 1815, Nancy, dau. of John and Nancy (Washer) Cochran. She d. Sept. 25, 1878, age 86. He lived on the homestead in the South District. d. May 20, 1866. Ch. b. Mont Vernon.
1. Nancy, b. May 29, 1816, d. July 22, 1838.
2. Jane E., b. Dec. 2, 1818, m. James D. Towne, July 11, 1839, d. April 5, 1856.
3. *Franklin, b. Oct. 27, 1821.
4. George W., b. Aug. 12, 1823, m. Permelia, dau. Noah and Clarissa (Saunders) Shattuck of Mont Vernon, lived in Hudson in 1858, farmer, d. there Feb. 28, 1903, had 2 sons.
5. Martha Ann, b. March 10, 1825, m. June 14, 1848, Horace S. Boutell of Hillsboro' Bridge, d. Amherst, Aug. 18, 1893. Ch.: 5 sons.
6. James C., d. Dec. 15, 1829, aged 2 years, 4 months.
7. *Arthur Allen, b. Aug. 9, 1829.
8. Mary A., b. Aug. 10, 1831, d. Nov. 10, 1836.
9. *Daniel Webster, b. March 15, 1835.

Joseph Trow, son of Joseph and Elizabeth or Betsey (Perkins) Trow, b. Mont Vernon, Jan. 17, 1794, d. Sept. 22, 1875, lived on the farm now occupied by Stillman Curtis in North District. He m. (1) Sarah, dau. of Joseph and Hannah (Woodbury) Perkins, March 22, 1825. She was b. Mont Vernon, April 20, 1800, d. July 31, 1837. He m. (2) Nov. 28, 1837, Hannah, dau. Joseph and Mary (Carleton) Harwood. She d. July 21, 1862, age 62 years, 5 months. He m. (3) Mrs. Abigail (Carson) Andrews, of New Boston. She d. Feb. 14, 1885, age 80. Ch. all by first wife b. Mont Vernon.
1. *Joseph Perkins, b. Sept. 26, 1826.
2. Irene Augusta, b. Aug. 10, 1828, d. Sept. 5, 1847.
3. Almira Lucretia, b. May 11, 1830, m. Jan. 2, 1854, *Charles Forsaith, one dau. She d. April 13, 1897.
4. Abigail Frances, b. Jan. 1, 1832, d. Aug. 9, 1837.
5. *Henry Hiram, b. Feb. 12, 1834.
6. *Elbridge Fisk, b. Oct. 24, 1835.

Franklin Trow, son of Jesse and Nancy (Cochran) Trow, b. Mont Vernon, Oct. 27, 1821, was a stone mason, hunter and farmer. After marriage, lived in the house near Trow's pond, m. Nov. 20, 1879, Abby, dau. Josiah and Sarah (Farnum) Swimington. She was b. Mont Vernon, Dec. 23, 1848. He d. Nov. 22, 1882. She d. June 1, 1886. Ch. b. Mont Vernon.

1. Elmer, b. Nov. 5, 1880, lives Nashua, m. Florence McDonald of Nashua.

Arthur Allen Trow, son of Jesse and Nancy (Cochran) Trow, b. Mont Vernon, Aug. 9, 1829, m. Jan. 23, 1872, Lucretia H. Rideout, dau. Gardiner and Lucretia (Wilson) Rideout. She was b. March 5, 1849, d. March 23, 1901. Lives on his father's farm in South Dist. Ch. b. Mont Vernon:

1. Charles Arthur, b. Aug. 29, 1872; civil engineer, lives in Utah; m. Aug. 10, 1902, Jennie E. Gracier of San Francisco.
2. *Louis Allen, b. Nov. 19, 1873.
3. Jessie Alice, b. Jan. 24, 1875, m. Oct. 30, 1895, *William H. Fox, one ch.
4. Edward Wilson, b. Aug. 17, 1877, m. Jan. 31, 1900, Josie L., dau. William H. and Emma J. (Foster) Marvel. She was b. Mont Vernon, June 11, 1877; resides with his father; one ch., Arthur William, b. July 9, 1902.

Daniel Webster Trow, b. Mont Vernon, March 15, 1835, m. June 12, 1859, Mary Emily, dau. Samuel L. and Mary Ann (Ober) Shepard of Amherst. She was b. April 5, 1840, d. Feb. 24, 1902, at Amherst. He lived for many years on a farm which he owned in Amherst, where he d. April 24, 1899. Ch. b. Amherst.

1. *Jesse S., b. April 23, 1862, m. April 23, 1891, Helen P., dau. Benj. B. and Minday S. (Peaslee) Whiting of Amherst. She was b. May 10, 1864.
2. Kate E., b. Dec. 30, 1864, res. Milford.
3. Emma, b. June 2, 1868, m. Arthur G. Burns of Lowell; res. Lowell, one ch.

Joseph Perkins Trow, son of Joseph and Sarah (Perkins) Trow, b. Mont Vernon, Sept. 26, 1826, m. Jan. 8, 1856, Lenora F., dau. William and Naomi (Wilkins) Underwood. She was b. New Boston, June 10, 1836. They settled in Amherst in 1857 and occupy the farm formerly occupied by Capt. Elijah Putnam on Christian Hill. Ch.

1. Clarence L., b. Nov. 13, 1860, m., resides Milford.
2. Geo. A., b. Dec. 18, 1862, res. Milford.

Henry Hiram Trow son of Joseph and Sarah (Perkins) Trow, b. Mont Vernon, Feb. 12, 1834, m. Oct. 8, 1856, Harriet C., dau. Jesse and Eliza (Glidden) Clement. She was b. Lowell, Dec. 8, 1830, d. March 31, 1897. Lived and owned a farm in the North Dist. for many years, where he d. April 2, 1903. Ch. b. Mont Vernon:

1. *Charles Henry, b. June 22, 1858.
2. Emma F., b. Aug. 20, 1860, m. Sept. 23, 1893, Harlan P. Odell of Amherst, d. Milford, March 19, 1902.
3. Milton J., b. Sept. 9, 1868, d. Nov. 13, 1890.

Elbridge Fisk Trow, son of Joseph and Sarah (Perkins) Trow, b. Mont Vernon, Oct. 24, 1835, m. Jan. 1, 1863, Hannah M., dau. Dimon, and she was b. Oct. 17, 1840, d. New Boston, March 28, 1892. He lived for many years on the Cleaves farm in South Dist., now owned by Jesse S. Trow, moved to New Boston and was proprietor of the tavern there, d. March 19, 1892. Ch.

1. Frank Dimond, b. April 22, 1866.

2. Albert Fisk, b. May 4, 1874, m. Miss Clark of New Boston; res. New Boston.

Louis Allen Trow, son of Arthur A. and Lucretia H. (Rideout) Trow, b. Mont Vernon, Nov. 19, 1873, m. Oct. 15, 1895, Millie A. Goodrich of Lyndeboro. She was b. Lyndeboro, Sept. 9, 1876. They live on the farm of heirs of Dr. C. M. Kittredge in South Dist. Ch. b. Mont Vernon.
1. Harold Arthur, b. Jan. 10, 1897.
2. Sewall Atwood, b. Feb. 2, 1898.
3. Amy Irene, b. June 26, 1899.
4. Jesse Everett, b. Dec. 27, 1901.

Charles Henry Trow, son of Henry H. and Harriet C. (Clement) Trow, b. Mont Vernon, June 22, 1858, m. Dec. 19, 1882, Carrie E., dau. Geo. W. and Nancy E. (Lamson) Averill. She was b. Mont Vernon, Aug. 24, 1861. He lives on and owns the Joseph Trow, Sr., farm in North Dist. Ch.
1. Herbert Averill, b. Amherst, Nov. 17, 1885.

Jesse S. Trow, son of Daniel W. and Mary E. (Shepard) Trow, b. April 23, 1862, in Amherst; bought farm of E. F. Trow in 1890, on Cleaves farm, lives in the South Dist.; farmer, m. April 23, 1891, Helen P., dau. Benj. B. and Minday S. Peaslee Whiting of Amherst. She was b. May 10, 1864. Ch. b. Mont Vernon.
1. Norman Daniel, b. May 10, 1895.
2. Lila Whiting, b. April 7, 1899.

TUPPER.

Tyler Tupper, b. Dec. 13, 1812, son Royal Tupper, Esq., of Lyndeboro, came here from Claremont, lived in the South Dist., where he d. Aug. 17, 1853. He m. (1) April, 1834, Anna H., dau. Hon. Jedidiah K. and Anna (Henchman) Smith of Amherst; three ch.; m. (2) Almira, dau. Abiel and Amy (Heywood) Wilkins of Mont Vernon, b. Jan. 17, 1825. She d. Dec. 13, 1852, age 27; two ch.
1. Abby S., d. April 6, 1869, age 32 years, 6 months.
2. Henry B., d. April 25, 1856, age 6 years, 7 months.

TUTEN.

Robert P. Tuten was b. in Boston, Mass., Feb. 6, 1806, d. Cambridge, Mass., Sept. 7, 1851, age 46; m. Nancy S., dau. Isaac and Pamelia (Stevens) Smith. She was b. Deering, April 14, 1820, d. Bellefonte, Pa., March 14, 1883. After her husband's death she purchased the Dr. Adams place and came to Mont Vernon in 1852, lived here until her death, March 14, 1883, age 62; ch. all b. in Cambridge, brought up in Mont Vernon. Ch.
1. Edward T., b. Sept. 18, 1841, m. Feb. 10, 1870, Maria P. (Fifield) Gray wid. Edw. L. Gray, E. Cambridge, Mass.; one ch., Earle C., b. Shelburn Falls, Mass., Dec. 4, 1870. Mr. Tuten has lived in Bellefonte, Pa., many years, where he is now editor and proprietor of the "Bellefonte Republican."
2. Maria N., b. Sept. 20, 1843, m. May 31, 1865, *Alonzo S. Bruce; three ch., res. Mont Vernon.
3. Susan R., b. July 14, 1845, res. Ayer, Mass.
4. Robert P., b. April 11, 1847, m. Miss Amy Mason of Galesburg.

Ill., left Mont Vernon in 1861, has resided at Iron Mt., Mich., now resides Burlington, Mo., one ch.; is a printer.

    5. Sarah, b. Oct. 23, 1848, treasurer Ayer Savings Bank, Ayer, Mass.

    6. Esther P., b. Oct. 11, 1850, matron of Children's Home, Dover, N. H.

TUTTLE.

Charles Bell Tuttle, son of Dr. Peter and Gratia (Kittredge) Tuttle, b. Hancock, May 9, 1818, m. (1) June 8, 1843, Lydia Ann, dau. Joshua and Elizabeth (Lincoln) Cleaves. She was b. Mont Vernon, April 8, 1823, d. July 26, 1866. He m. (2) Cornelia E., dau. Hon. Leonard and Mary G. (Dickey) Chase of Milford, Sept. 4, 1867. She was b. Milford, May 19, 1839. He lived for a few years in Mont Vernon with his father-in-law, Joshua Cleaves. Ch. by first wife:

    1. Charles W., b. Oct. 27, 1847, d. Aug. 19, 1866.

    2. Catherine A., b. June 19, 1849, m. June 18, 1847, Frank W. Chase of Milford.

    3. Charlotte E., b. July 25, 1851, d. June 14, 1852.

    4. Caroline L., b. Aug. 3, 1854, d. Sept. 6, 1854.

    5. Edward S., b. July 8, 1849, d. Sept. 12, 1860.

    6. Anna L., b. March 19, 1862, d. Oct. 6, 1862.

    7. Isabella L., b. Feb. 12, 1865, d. July 22, 1866.

Ch. by second wife b. Milford:

    8. Morton C., b. June 2, 1875, res. Boston.

    9. Leonard W., b. Aug. 30, 1877, res. Boston.

    10. Donald D., b. May 29, 1879, res. Milford.

TWISS.

Dimon Twiss, son of Dimon C. and Sarah (Ireson) Twiss, b. Antrim, Aug. 4, 1803, m. (1) Harriet, dau. George Parmenter of Antrim, Oct. 30, 1831. She d. 1844. He m. (2) June 10, 1845, Mehitable Hills. She d. June 4, 1874. He was a blacksmith and carried on business in Antrim several years, thence he rem. in 1868 to Mont Vernon where he d. Nov. 10, 1888, age 85 years. Ch. b. Antrim.

    1. Harriet M., b. Jan. 29, 1836, m. Dr. W. H. Hinds of Milford, Aug. 23, 1861. She d. Milford, Feb. 7, 1870, leaving two sons.

    2. Mary E., b. June 20, 1828, m. May 9, 1857, Daniel Richardson, res. Mont Vernon; two ch.

    3. Hannah M., b. Oct. 18, 1840, m. Jan. 1, 1863, El'Dridge F. Trow, d. New Boston, March 28, 1892; left two sons.

Abraham G. Twiss (half-brother to Dimon), son Dimon C. and Mary (Jones) Twiss, b. Antrim, May 19, 1818; m. Sabra G., dau. Alexander M. and Hannah (McIlwaine) Carr. She was b. 1818. He lived on the "David Stiles" place in East Dist. with his father-in-law several years, moved to Manchester, where he d. April 8, 1876; one ch., dau., m. Henry M. Parker of Amherst; res. Amherst.

THOMPSON.

Alpha Thompson had a blacksmith's shop on a brook in the North Dist., when a young man, moved to Woburn, Mass., and after it was an incorporated city became its first mayor. He lived to be an old man.

UPTON.

Ezekiel Upton, Sr., d. 1835, age 90, lived in house afterwards of John O'Brien, burned in 1871, on Purgatory Road, m. Hannah, dau. John and Hannah (Wilkins) Washer. Ch. b. Mont Vernon.

Mary, m. *Allen Dodge of Mont Vernon.

*Ezekiel, Jr.

Other ch.

Hannah, m. *Ebenezer Mills, Sr., and had nine ch. She d. Milford, Sept. 20, 1856, aged 83 years.

Ezekiel Upton, Jr., son of Ezekiel, Sr., and Hannah (Washer) Upton, d. Feb. 2, 1863, age 87; lived on Beech Hill; m. Abigail, dau. Josiah and Ellinor (Edwards) Dodge. She was b. Sept. 19, 1774, d. June 26, 1837. He was selectman 15 years and representative five years. He m. (2) 1843, Mehitable, dau. Jonathan and Polly (Baker) Conant, and wid. of Wm. Marvel. She d. 1873, age 80. Ch. b. Mont Vernon.

1. Mary, m. Geo. W. Green, Oct. 6, 1838. She d. April 29, 1841, age 36.

2. *Josiah.

3. *David.

4. Alvan, d. unm. May 18, 1883, aged 75 yrs., 5 mos.

5. Abigail, m. Hiram Nichols of Lowell, Nov. 20, 1832.

Ezekiel E., d. Sept. 24, 1818, age three yrs., six mos. Hannah, d. Jan. 29, 1827, age 17. Daniel, d. Dec. 6, 1834, age 27.

Josiah Upton, son of Ezekiel and Abigail (Dodge) Upton, d. Dec. 27, 1845, age 27; lived on his father-in-law's farm, Wm. Odell, Jr., in West Dist., m. Jan. 2, 1842, Orinda F., dau. Wm., Jr. and Susannah (Lovejoy) Odell. She was b. Mont Vernon, Feb. 19, 1819. After his death she m. Jan. 10, 1849, Capt. Wm. Lamson. She d. Nov. 24, 1874. Ch.

1. Alvan, b. Feb. 17, 1845, d. Sept., 1845.

2. William Henry, b. New Boston, Sept. 22, 1842, enlisted in 16th N. H. Regt., d. in Carrolton, La., Feb. 18, 1863.

David Upton, son of Ezekiel and Abigail (Dodge) Upton, m. Rebecca Avery of Lyndeboro. She was b. Nov. 14, 1809, d. June 29, 1896, age 89. Ch.

David E., b. Oct. 3, 1830, res. New Boston, m. Emily L., dau. John J. and Sarah (Hopkins) Carson of Mont Vernon. She was b. Milford, Jan. 16, 1843, resides on farm in the southwest part of New Boston. Ch.

1. Chas. H., b. Aug. 11, 1865.

2. Alvan E., b. Oct. 27, 1868, d. Aug. 4, 1898.

3. John E., b. Jan. 30, 1877.

4. Emily Josephine, b. Oct. 27, 1883.

Enos Upton.

James Upton, son of Enos Upton, b. St. Stephens, N. B., Oct. 11, 1792, lived on the farm on Purgatory Road, afterwards occupied by his son James Upton, m. March 14, 1822, Jane Bixbie of Litchfield. She was b. Feb. 7, 1799, d. Feb. 19, 1868. He d. July 12, 1831. Ch.

1. Mary Elizabeth, b. St. Stephens, N. B., June 24, 1823, d. unm., June 9, 1881.

2. Jane, b. May 7, 1825, m. Amos Melvin; three ch.; lives Concord, Mass.

3. Sarah Ann, b. July 27, 1826, m. (1) Albert Decatur, m. (2) *Hiram Batchelder. She d. Goffstown, June 22, 1897.

4. James, b. Feb. 16, 1829, representative 1872, 1873, selectman eight years, now res. Amherst.

5. William, b. Aug. 9, 1830, d. July 10, 1877, m. Elizabeth, dau. John and Rebecca (Hale) Smith. She d. Aug. 8, 1882, age 49. Ch. b. Mont Vernon.

Willis, d. July 23, 1879, aged about 18.

John, b. 1868, res. Providence, R. I.

UNDERWOOD.

Joseph Underwood came to this town, was a stone mason, lived where Mrs. Mary J. Blood now does in the village where he d. Feb. 13, 1871, age 68. He m. June 30, 1844, Sabrina, dau. of Joseph and Betsey (Perkins) Trow, b. Mont Vernon, Oct. 15, 1800, d. Lancaster, Mass., May 22, 1890; no ch.

Charles Underwood, son of Thomas and Mehitable (Gage) Underwood, b. Amherst, lived in the South Dist., where J. H. Tarbell since lived; rem. to Lowell, where he d.; m. Aurelia, dau. Ezra and Rebecca (Langdell) Langdell, Oct. 8, 1829. She was b. Mont Vernon, Aug. 13, 1810. Ch. b. Mont Vernon.

1. Charles Henry, b. Feb. 9, 1833, m. Nov. 9, 1859, Elvira L. Hewey, b. Jan. 4, 1837; lived in Lowell; four ch.

WALLACE.

Andrew Wallace, second son Dea. John and Polly (Bradford) Wallace of Milford, b. Milford, March 28, 1783, d. Amherst, Sept. 23, 1856; m. Hepsibah Cummings, Dec., 1820. She was b. 1794, d. Sept. 17, 1874. After fitting for the practice of law he settled in Mont Vernon in 1814, which town he represented 1816; rem. to Hancock 1817, where he remained until April, 1824, when he received the appointment of Clerk of the Courts in Hillsborough County and rem. to Amherst, where he spent the remainder of his life. He resumed the practice of law Nov. 1, 1839. He was moderator and representative of Mont Vernon in 1816, school committee 1815 and 1816. Was school commissioner in Hancock in 1818 and 1822, representative of there in 1822, 1823 and 1824. He was greatly respected as a man and citizen. Ch.

1. Horace W., b. Hancock, March 25, 1822, d. Oct. 9, 1826.
2. Charles A., b. Amherst, Aug. 5, 1825, d. March 8, 1832.
3. Mary C., b. Amherst, May 30, 1828, d. Aug. 14, 1833.
4. Henry H., b. Amherst, Jan. 10, 1831, d. Aug. 18, 1833.
5. Mary C., b. Amherst, July 4, 1834, d. Jan. 4, 1846.
6. Charles Henry, b. Amherst, Sept. 14, 1835, grad. Dartmouth College, 1857; studied law; d. June 21, 1861.

Milton W. Wallace, son of George O. and Olive (Wilkins) Wallace, b. Bedford, N. H., 1829, lived Reed's Ferry from 1851 to 1855; went to California 1855; returned to Reed's Ferry 1863; moved to Nashua 1868, and to Mont Vernon March, 1882, on a farm on Beech Hill; m. May, 1851, Margaret P., dau. Robert and Ruth A. (Clark) Mears. She was b. Reed's Ferry, N. H., 1829. He d. March 5, 1902. Ch.

1. Effie V., b. Reed's Ferry, N. H., Aug. 24, 1902, m. George P. Nutter of Nashua, Nov., 1878.

2.   Carrie L., b. Reed's Ferry, July 23, 1854, m. July 4, 1876, David W. Duncklee of Nashua, d. Nashua, Feb. 25, 1882.

3.   Sherman E., b. Reed's Ferry, June 2, 1864, m. Feb. 15, 1890, Julia A. Cody, res. Providence, R. I.

4.   *Miles E., b. Manchester, Feb. 24, 1867.

5.   Mytelle M., b. Nashua, May 27, 1869; res. Mont Vernon.

6.   Minnie O., b. Nashua, July 19, 1871, m. Ira R. Brown of Lyndeboro, Nov. 25, 1896; res. Lyndeboro.

Miles E. Wallace, son of Milton W. and Margaret P. (Mears) Wallace, b. Manchester, N. H., Feb. 24, 1867. He is a carpenter; came to Mont Vernon from Milford in 1897; m. April 17, 1886, Ida B., dau. Leonard G. and Nancy D. (Larkin) Brown. She was b. Lyndeboro, July 25, 1865. Ch.

Maud Ethel, b. Lyndeboro, April 21, 1890.

WESTON.

Ebenezer Weston, b. Reading, Jan. 28, 1702, m. Mehitable, dau. Isaac Sutherick, Nov. 29, 1726. She was b. Oct., 1706. They settled in Souhegan West, now Amherst, in 1752. Ch.

1.   Mehitable, b. Nov. 27, 1727, m. Sept. 30, 1751, Timothy Nichols of Amherst; three ch.

2.   Elizabeth, b. Oct. 6, 1729, m. ———— Larrabee.

3.   Ebenezer, b. Feb. 10, 1731, m. (1) Eliza Hildreth, by whom he had three ch.; m. (2) Sarah Herrick; had three ch.; d. June 12, 1846; lived in Amherst; was on Committee of Safety in Revolutionary War.

4.   Ann, b. March 31, 1734, d. Sept. 3, 1751, unm.

5.   Daniel, b. Oct. 11, 1735.

6.   Hepsibah, b. June 11, 1738, d. unm. advanced age.

7.   Sarah, b. Sept. 7, 1740, d. Sept. 22, 1751.

8.   Judith, b. June 3, 1742, d. Aug. 31, 1751.

9.   *Thomas, b. June 26, 1744.

10.   *Isaac, b. May 11, 1746.

11.   Tabitha, b. March 31, 1748, m. (1) Daniel Wilkins, Jr., m. (2) Jesse Baldwin, m. (3) Lt. Joseph Farnum, d. at Mont Vernon, Jan., 1820. Her dau., Abigail (Wilkins) Dix, was the mother of of Gen. John A. Dix, War Governor of New York.

12.   Sutherick, b. Nov. 19, 1751, m. Mary Lancy; Revolutionary soldier; seven ch., d. Antrim, May 11, 1831.

Daniel Weston, son of Ebenezer and Mehitable (Sutherick) Weston, b. Reading, Mass., Oct. 11, 1735; came to Amherst with his parents about 1752; m. April 20, 1762, Mary, dau. David and Sarah (Phelps) Hartshorn, who came from Reading as early as 1747. He was a soldier in the French and Indian War; d. 1768. His wid. m. Thomas Carleton, by whom she had four ch. Ch. b. Mont Vernon.

1.   Judith, b. March 30, 1763, m. Dea. John Carleton, d. Mont Vernon, Nov. 25, 1824; 12 ch.

2.   Daniel, b. July 8, 1764, grad. Harvard College 1795, was a clergyman nearly 40 years at Gray, Me., where he d. May 28, 1837, aged 72.

3.   Mary, b. Feb. 20, 1766, m. Daniel Averill of Mont Vernon.

4.   David, b. Oct. 13, 1767, d. in infancy.

Thomas Weston, son of Ebenezer and Mehitable (Sutherick) Weston,

b. Reading, June 26, 1744, m. 1769, Ruth Tuttle, d. Dec. 27, 1822; settled on the farm in Mont Vernon occupied more than 100 years by his descendants, now owned by Cleon M. Hall. Was on Com. of Safety in Revolutionary War. Ch. b. Mont Vernon.

    1. Ruth, b. Nov. 17, 1769, d. unm.
    2. *Thomas, Jr., b. Jan. 20, 1773.
    3. Sarah, b. 1776, d. March 17, 1777.
    4. Sarah, b. July 21, 1779, m. John Worthley.

Isaac Weston, son of Ebenezer and Mehitable (Sutherick) Weston, b. Reading, May 11, 1746, m. Hannah Cole. She d. June 1, 1834, age 80; lived in the East Dist.; was on Com. of Safety in Revolutionary War. Ch. Mont Vernon.

    1. *John, b. July 17, 1775.
    2. Hannah, b. 1777, m. Daniel L. Herrick, Sept. 27, 1802.
    3. Betsey, b. 1779, m. Benjamin Durant of Mont Vernon, Jan. 15, 1804.
    4. Susannah, b. 1781.
    5. Isaac, Jr., b. Nov. 27, 1781, m. Aug. 20, 1812, Mehitable Batchelder; lived in Amherst; three ch.; d. Jan. 23, 1869.
    6. Luther, b. 1785, d. infancy.
    7. Luther, b. 1787, d. about 1808.

Thomas Weston, Jr., son of Thomas and Ruth (Tuttle) Weston, b. Mont Vernon, Jan. 20, 1773; settled on the homestead in North Dist., Mont Vernon; d. Nov. 22, 1840, m. 1775, Lucy Wilkins, dau. Abijah and Lucy (Averill) Wilkins. She was b. March 27, 1777, d. Feb. 18, 1851. Ch. b. Mont Vernon.

    1. Ira, b. Feb. 18, 1796, m. Miriam Chellis in 1825; physician in Windham and Bradford, N. H., d. Oct. 12, 1868.
    2. Lucy, b. Sept. 7, 1799, d. Oct. 26, 1851.
    3. John, b. Dec. 13, 1801, d. unm. May 15, 1857.
    4. Thomas, b. Oct. 27, 1803, killed by lightning, May 30, 1840.
    5. Jason, b. May 17, 1805, m. Eliza Wilkins in 1832; lived in Manchester.
    6. Langdell, b. March 24, 1808, d. March 16, 1844.
    7. Sarah, b. Sept. 12, 1810, m. Elbridge G. Fairfield in 1836.
    8. Abigail Tarbell, b. Oct. 13, 1813, d. March 27, 1814.
    9. Abigail Tuttle, b. March 4, 1815, m. *Nathan F. Richardson of Mont Vernon in 1840, d. Nov. 16, 1853.

Lt. John Weston, son of Isaac and Hannah (Cole) Weston, b. July 17, 1775, was killed by the falling of a mill-stone in his mill, which was on the site of J. A. Brown's mill in the East Dist., in 1840; m. Sept. 27, 1802, Abigail Haseltine, sister John Haseltine of Amherst. She m. (2) Jan. 31, 1826, Moses Newman of Mont Vernon. She d. May 12, 1860, age 77 yrs., 8 mos. Ch. b. Mont Vernon.

    1. *James, b. Dec. 5, 1803.
    2. Hannah, b. Oct. 25, 1805, d. unm. March 14, 1859.
    3. Thirza, b. Sept. 5, 1807, d. unm. March 23, 1840.
    4. Abigail, b. June 25, 1809, d. Aug. 31, 1873; m. —— Arlin; had ch., lived in Lowell.
    5. Mary, b. June 24, 1811, d. July 22, 1877, at Chelsea; m. *Reuben K. Batchelder.

James Weston, son of John and Abigail (Haseltine) Weston, b. Mont Vernon, Dec. 5, 1803; lived in North Dist. a few years; moved to California, where he d. Sept. 11, 1852; m. (1) Diantha Chapin; m. (2) Mary Haraden. Ch. by first wife:

1. John, d. infancy.
2. Diantha Maria, b. Sept. 2, 1830, d. April 1, 1889.
3. James Franklin, b. Aug. 16, 1832, d. June 23, 1892; lived in Boston and Lowell, was a belt manufacturer.
4. Mary Jane, b. Jan. 6, 1835; was Female Supt. of State Hospital for Insane at Jacksonville, Ill., and for many years Matron of the Old Ladies' Home, Lowell, where she d. unm., March 26, 1900.

Ch. by second wife:

Abigail R., b. Aug. 2, 1848; res. Lowell, unm.

WETHERBEE.

Asa Wetherbee, son of Joseph Wetherbee, b. July 18, 1802, Wilton; farmer; came here from Lyndeboro and lived about 17 years here; moved to Milford about 1849, d. Milford, April 13, 1885; m. May 1, 1824, Lavina, dau. Ebenezer and Hannah (Upton) Mills. She was b. Mont Vernon, Dec. 3, 1805, d. Milford, April 6, 1889. Ch.

1. John F., b. Milford, March 13, 1825; hotel-keeper; res. Leed, Me., m. Lucinda J. Caldwell of Hudson.
2. William W., b. Wilton, March 11, 1827, m. Elizabeth Parker, dau. Robt. Parker of Milford; res. Milford; four ch.
3. David G., b. Lyndeboro, Jan. 21, 1829, d. Milford, Sept. 22, 1852; shoemaker; m. Mary J. Gerald of Milford.
4. James Addison, b. Mont Vernon, April 7, 1832, m. Nov. 27, 1856, Harriet E., dau. Joseph and Indiana (Barnes) Duncklee, b. Milford, Aug. 1, 1838; one son, Dr. Fred M. Wetherbee of Milford; J. A. d. Milford, Sept. 27, 1895; was a merchant.
5. Henry M., b. Mont Vernon, May 31, 1836, d. July 14, 1837.
6. Henry P., b. Mont Vernon, July 10, 1838; laborer, res. Milford, unm.
7. Emma A., b. Mont Vernon, Dec. 6, 1843, m. June 18, 1865, Marcellies M. Marvell of Milford, d. Feb. 6, 1880.
8. Mary C., b. Mont Vernon, April 15, 1845, m. Jan. 28, 1866, John R. Perkins of Weare; res. Milford.

Jesse Wetherbee, son of Joseph Wetherbee, m. Permelia Osborn Gleeson. She d. March 16, 1884, age 82, at Merrimack; lived in the house afterwards known as Conant Hall, moved to Nashua, then to Merrimack; was partner of Asa Stevens at Nashua in the manufacture of shoes; one son.

Joseph Wetherbee, son of Joseph Wetherbee and brother of Asa and Jesse Wetherbee, m. Clarissa Heywood, dau. Wm. Heywood; lived in Mont Vernon several years; came here from Lyndeboro. Ch. were:

1. Joseph, b. Mont Vernon, m. (1) Nancy Tuttle of Wilton, m. (2) Mrs. Nancy (Gould) Flint Barnes of Wilton, dau. Benjamin and Nancy Gould. He d. June, 1870, in Wilton; had five ch.
2. Abbie, d. unm. in Boston.

WHITE.

Kneeland C. White, son of Aaron and Louisa (Crane) White, b. Deering, N. H., Dec. 30, 1835; lived New Boston, Brandon, Vt., 25 years; came

to Mont Vernon in 1888, worked before coming to Mont Vernon seal-
ing scales in scale shop; m. June 28, 1859, Jennie D. Ober of New Boston, dau. Gary and Salome (Mills) Ober. She was b. Johnson, Vt., Aug.
6, 1840; no ch.

William White came here from Weare, lived about 42 years in East
Dist., moved to Wilton about 1858. He m. Mary, dau. Isaac and Eunice
(Flagg) Colby of Amherst, Oct. 6, 1835. She was b. June 27, 1810. Ch.
   1. Stillman C., b. July 8, 1839; lives Wilton.
   2. Henry, lives Wilton.
   Eliza J., b. Mont Vernon, Jan. 8, 1849, m. Jan. 26, 1870, Horatio C.
Shaw, son Christopher C. and Rebecca P. (Hutchinson) Shaw of Milford;
res. Milford; one ch.

WILKINS.

Bray Wilkins a large land owner in Middleton, Mass., was the ancestor of all of that name who have lived in Amherst or in any of the
towns severed from that town.

Joshua Wilkins, fourth generation from Bray Wilkins, b. Middleton,
Mass., Aug. 26, 1718. He and his wife, Ruth, were residents of Amherst
(now the East Dist., Mont Vernon), March, 1776. Ch.
   1. Aspath, b. March 17, 1738.
   2. Eli, b. Sept. 24, 1741, d. young.
   3. Sylvester, b. Jan. 11, 1744, d. young.
   4. Joshua, b. Oct. 12, 1746.
   5. Elizabeth, b. Nov. 16, 1748, d. young.
   6. *Abijah, b. Oct. 7, 1751.
   7. *Eli, b. April 6, 1753.
   8. Sylvester, b. Nov. 24, 1757, a Revolutionary soldier, d. Easton, Pa.
   9. Ruth, b. March 24, 1761.
   10. Elizabeth, b. June 15, 1764.

Abijah Wilkins, son of Joshua and Ruth Wilkins, b. Middleton, Mass.,
Oct. 7, 1751; lived in the North Dist. on the farm now owned by S. E.
Curtis; d. Mont Vernon, July, 1833, age 81; m. (1) Lucy Averill, May 7,
1772. She was b. Dec. 18, 1752. He m. (2) Sarah Farmer, Sept. 30, 1788.
She d. Feb. 8, 1818, age 59. Ch. by first wife:
   1. *Abijah, b. Sept. 18, 1771.
   Probably b. Mont Vernon:
   2. Lucy, b. March 27, 1777.
   3. Jason, b. Dec. 7, 1780.
   4. Asaph.
   Ch. by second wife probably b. Mont Vernon:
   5. *Charles W., b. Oct. 30, 1791.
   6. George, b. Dec. 12, 1793, d. unm. Holliston, Mass., May 4, 1826;
studied medicine, was licensed by the N. H. Medical Society in 1820, practised two years at Littleton, Mass., and from thence went to Holliston.
By his premature removal the community lost a faithful physician and a
citizen of uprightness and integrity.
   7. Esther, b. Nov. 28, 1797, d. May 19, 1820, a very pious and amiable
young lady.
   8. Ruth K., b. Dec. 17, 1801, d. unm. Nashua, Aug. 18, 1871.

Eli Wilkins, son of Joshua and Ruth Wilkins, b. April 6, 1753, m.
—— —— Leach; settled in Amherst (now East Dist., Mont Vernon), school

teacher, selectman from 1781 to 1788 inclusive; was for many years Justice of the Peace; was made Justice in 1787. Ch. b. Mont Vernon:

1. Eli.
2. *Ira.
3. *John L.
4. Joshua.
5. Tryphosa, m. Gerry Knights of Francestown.
6. *Alvah.
7. Nathaniel.

Abijah Wilkins, son of Abijah and Lucy (Averill) Wilkins, b. Sept. 18, 1771, d. 1856; settled in Boston before 1800 and there he was for many years an industrious carpenter and masterbuilder, a Christian very much respected. He left one son and two dau.

Charles Warren Wilkins, son of Abijah and Sarah (Farmer) Wilkins, b. Mont Vernon, Oct. 30, 1791; settled in Lowell, d. there June 16, 1871; m. March 2, 1815, Emma D. Trow, dau. Joseph and Sarah (Perkins) Trow. She was b. Aug. 18, 1791, d. Lowell, Jan. 26, 1868. Ch. b. Lowell, probably.

1. Chas. P., b. 1815, m. (1) Abigail Brown; m. (2) Grace Puffer; removed from Lowell to Auburn, N. Y., d. there April, 1889, leaving seven ch.
2. Sarah A., b. 1818, m. Elijah Perry, d. 1845.
3. Esther, b. 1822, d. unm. Lowell, June 6, 1841.
4. Martha, b. July 15, 1825, m. June 16, 1849, Theophilus D. Berry of Lowell, who d. Nov. 29, 1885.
5. Elizabeth, b. 1827, d. unm. Sept. 1, 1848.
6. Geo. Henry, b. 1829, d. 1842.
7. Joseph A., m. Mrs. Anna Hunt; has seven ch. lives Whitefield, N. H.

Ira Wilkins, son Eli Wilkins, m. Anna P., dau. Nathan and Sarah (Kendrick) Kendall of Amherst. She was b. July 17, 1787, m. July 11, 1815. He d. Burlington, Ohio, July 16, 1849. He lived for a time where C. O. Ingalls now does; four dau.

John L. Wilkins, son Eli Wilkins. He lived in East Dist., (on place now burnt, formerly occupied by Bradley Jones). He moved to New Boston and d. at the poorhouse there; m. Susan Weston.

Ira Wilkins (his son) lived in East Dist., m. Feb. 18, 1835, Nancy, dau. Isaac and Eunice (Flagg) Colby of Amherst. She was b. Oct. 29, 1813, d. April, 1858. He d. Wilton, June 20, 1888, age 78 yrs., 3 mos.; one dau. Mrs. Dunbar; one son, Ira Gardner was a captain in Civil War, lived in Fitchburg, Mass.

Alvah Wilkins, son Eli Wilkins, lived in East Dist., m. (1) Sarah, dau. James Hill. She d. Oct. 19, 1857, age 64. He m. (2) Mrs. Sarah S. Gould, Sept. 25, 1860. He d. Oct. 5, 1862, age 65. Ch. by first wife, a dau. m. Peter Douglass; had one ch.

Jonathan Wilkins, son of Rev. Daniel and Sarah (Fuller) Wilkins; a Revolutionary soldier, served on board the armed ship Hague, was wounded in battle with British vessel. He d. Mont Vernon, April 18, 1824, aged 75. Susannah, his first wife, d. Dec. 23, 1778, age 30. Ch. were.

1. Polly, m. Bradford.
2. David G., lived Addison, Vt.
3. Jonathan, lived Goffstown.
4. Samuel, lived New Albany, Ind.
5. Robert, lived Jaffrey, N. H.
6. James, b. Dec. 15, 1784, was apprenticed to James McKean of Amherst, whence he took the name of McKean. He rem. to Maine with Mr. McKean, where his education was neglected. When he returned to Amherst at the age of 19 he was unable to read or write. Determined to have an education he applied himself vigorously to study, fitted for college, grad. at Dartmouth College in 1812, read law with Hon. Daniel Abbott of Dunstable and practised many years in Bedford and Manchester. He served as Representative, Senator and Councillor, and d. Manchester unm. Jan. 18, 1855.

Abiel Wilkins, b. Jan. 6, 1778. Was the son of Wm. Wilkins of English descent, whose mother lived in Salem, Mass. She was accused when a girl of being a witch, went home from church and when they followed her, her father fought them with pitch fire brands and thus saved his child. Very little is known of Wm. Wilkins. Abiel removed from Salem, or that vicinity, after the Revolutionary War, settled on the farm in the South Dist., now owned by Jesse R. Wilkins. Abiel had five sons who reached manhood. Ch.
1. *William.
2. James, moved to Antrim in 1799, m. Lydia Whipple (probably sister to his brother William's wife). He d. June 13, 1804. James, his eldest child, d. Weston, Vt., had nine ch. His youngest son, Dea. Joel Wilkins of Antrim, m. (1) his cousin, Betsey Wilkins; m. (2) H. B. Crombie. He d. Nov., 1865; had 11 ch.
3. Enoch, m. Sally Case, lived in Antrim. He d. June 13, 1851, age 75. She d. 1852.
4. *Abiel, b. Jan. 6, 1778.
5. Jesse, d. of spotted fever, 1812, age 30 years.
6. Phebe, m. John Heywood, March 27, 1825.

William Wilkins, son of Abiel, moved from Mont Vernon to Antrim in 1798, m. (1) Sarah Whipple of Hamilton, Mass.; m. (2) Elizabeth Hopkins of Antrim. He d. May 15, 1837, age 63. He had five ch. by first wife and two ch. by second wife. His second ch., Betsey, b. 1801, became first wife of her cousin, Dea. Joel Wilkins. His seven ch., Maria Eliza, m. John Kidder of Mont Vernon, Sept. 15, 1837, is still living.

Abiel Wilkins, son Abiel Wilkins, b. Jan. 6, 1778, lived on homestead where he d. July 31, 1859; m. Amy or Emma Heywood, dau. Wm. Heywood, Jan. 31, 1812. She was b. April 15, 1794, d. Aug. 23, 1872. He d. July 31, 1859. Farmer. Ch. b. Mont Vernon.
1. Abigail, b. May 10, 1812, m. March, 1832, *Elbridge F. Perkins, b. July 29, 1811. She d. Oct. 4, 1853.
2. Jesse, b. Sept. 24, 1813, d. Sept. 10, 1818.
3. Eliza, b. Nov. 24, 1815, m. Sept., 1837, George E. Robbins of Wilton.
4. *Luke, b. April, 1818.
5. Emma J., b. Aug. 4, 1820, d. July 17, 1854, m. April 10, 1844, William P. Duncklee of Milford, who was b. Aug. 28, 1817.
6. Almira Wilkins, b. Jan. 17, 1825, d. Dec. 13, 1852, m. *Tyler Tupper of Mont Vernon.

Luke Wilkins, son of Abiel and Amy (Heywood) Wilkins, b. Mont Vernon, April, 1818, d. May 8, 1857; lived on Wilkins farm in South Dist., m. June 22, 1843, Elizabeth, dau. of Mark D. and Lucy (Whipple) Langdell. She was b. March 13, 1820. She m. (2) Levi Curtis, Nov. 28, 1867, d. Milford, May 28, 1897. Ch. b. Mont Vernon.

1. *Jesse R., b. Dec. 13, 1844.
2. Mary E., b. Oct. 10, 1846, m. (1) Dec. 15, 1869, James A. Langdell, who d. April 2, 1870; m. (2) Chas. H. Gutterson, March 31, 1877; one son; res. Mont Vernon.
3. Lucy J., b. Nov. 29, 1848, m. Oct. 14, 1871, Henry Appleton Hutchinson of Mont Vernon, res. Mont Vernon; five ch.
4. Emma E., b. July 22, 1855, m. Nov. 30, 1876, Marcus C. Gutterson of Milford, d. Milford, Dec. 10, 1884; one ch., Alburen.
5. Luke A., d. June 27, 1862, aged 10 yrs., 9 mos.

Jesse R. Wilkins, son Luke Elizabeth (Langdell) Wilkins, b. Mont Vernon, Dec. 13, 1844, m. Oct. 14, 1871, A. Frances, dau. John and Mary (Nichols) Follansbee. She was b. Londonderry, Dec. 25, 1848. He lived in South Dist. until 1891, when he moved to the north part of Milford; farmer. Ch. b. Mont Vernon.

1. Willie A., b. Oct. 28, 1872, meat cutter, m. June 30, 1896, Cora Belle, dau. George and Abbie (Flanders) Stone of Greenville, res. Milford.
2. Frances M., b. May 10, 1874, m. March 5, 1896, Louis A., son Thos. B. and Adaline A. (Crosby) Hall of Milford; res. Milford; two ch.
3. Clarence E., b. Aug. 17, 1888.

Benjamin Wilkins, m. Naomi, dau. Cooley and Sarah (Burnham) Smith. She was b. April 25, 1757, d. May 11, 1850; settled in Lyndeboro; several ch., a dau., Naomi, m. Abraham French, d. Nov. 11, 1874, aged 86 yrs., 3 mos.

His son, Benjamin Wilkins, settled in Hillsboro, m. Nov. 27, 1806, Lydia, dau. Ebenezer and Elizabeth T. S. Batchelder. She was b. Nov. 21, 1786, m. Nov. 27, 1806; several ch.

Silas, son of Benjamin and Naomi (Smith) Wilkins, lived in West Dist., m. Martha, dau. Lt. Joseph and Mary (Lyon) Farnum of Mont Vernon, Nov. 21, 1810. He d. Oct. 29, 1851, age 64. His wife d. April 14, 1840, age 51. Ch. b. Mont Vernon.

1. Sophronia, b. June 22, 1842, m. Dec. 15, 1832, Capt. Leander Smith, d. Antrim, Nov. 25, 1882.
2. Naomi S., b. Feb. 9, 1844, m. (1) Jan. 10, 1833, Wm. Underwood of Amherst, had three ch. He d. Nov. 28, 1844. She m. (2) John H. McConihie of Amherst; two ch. She d. July 25, 1900.
3. Hannah, b. May 11, 1846, m. *Trask W. Averill, Oct. 14, 1849; one ch. She d. Feb. 28, 1900.
4. Silas, b. July 3, 1849, m. Helen M. Tappan, lived in Bradford and Newport.
5. James, b. June 8, 1823; stable-keeper, Nashua.
6. Emily M., b. Sept. 15, 1826, m. May, 1847, Walter M. Gilson; res. Nashua and Mont Vernon.

Charles Lucien Wilkins, son of Frederick and ——— (Marston) Wilkins, b. Montgomery, Vt., lived in a house which stood between the Bellevue and Dr. Hallowell's, and where C. J. Smith now does; was a house painter; moved to Milford in 1871, thence to Amherst, Mont Vernon and New Boston, where he d. by drowning Aug. 13, 1888, age 65. He m. Mary Mills of Chester, N. H. He served in 8th N. H. Regt. in Civil War. Ch.

    Charlena M., m. May 1, 1878, Waler Wilkins of Omaha, Neb., resides Omaha, Neb.

WINCHESTER.

    Lemuel Winchester, son of Isaac and Deborah Winchester, b. Tewksbury, Mass., May 13, 1740, m. Lydia Flint of Reading in 1760, served in French and Indian War; moved to Mont Vernon between 1768 and 1775; settled on farm in East Dist., served in the Revolution from Amherst, now Mont Vernon, was a corporal, promoted to sergeant; moved to Danvers, where he d. Feb., 1841, aged 101 years. Ch.

    1. Silas, m. Dolly Wilson, lived and d. in Danvers, Mass.

    2. Lemuel, b. 1768, lived and d. in Andover, Mass.

    3. Isaac, twin, b. Mont Vernon, April 19, 1770, m. Polly Balch; ch. lived in Providence, R. I.

    4. Deborah, twin, b. Mont Vernon, April 19, 1770, m. Elias Cheney of Antrim, moved to Vermont. Among her ch. were two sons, Franklin Cheney, who was the father of Rev. William P. Cheney, Rector Church Good Shepherd, Oakdale, Mass., and Jesse Cheney, father of Benj. P. Cheney, who was a famous expressman in Boston and became a millionaire.

    5. Lydia, b. 1771, b. Geo. Sumner, descendants live in Hill, N. H.

    6. Betsey, b. 1779, m. Samuel Sargent of Hill.

WINN.

    Alonzo Winn, son of Benjamin and Clarissa (Foote) Winn, b. Antrim, Dec. 22, 1849, m. 1871. Elnora, dau. George and Sarah (Battles) Jones. She was b. March 22, 1851, in New Boston. He resided in the East Dist. several years; rem. to Wilton; now lives Mont Vernon; is a farmer; no ch.

WOODBURY.

    John Woodbury came to Cape Ann, Gloucester in 1624, moved to Beverly in 1626, was an energetic, faithful and worthy man, d. 1641, probably not above 60 years of age. We regard him as standing next to Conant in intelligence and usefulness in the colony. His son, Humphrey, b. 1608, during his residence in Somersetshire, Eng., came over in 1628, was head of a family in 1638. His descendants were Peter, 1; Josiah, 2; Josiah, 3; Peter, 4; Peter, 5. They were all thrifty and substantial citizens. John Woodbury at death owned a house in Salem, where he had first settled, though he probably then resided at the farm near the pond being East of and adjoining Roger Conant's. The five planters were Conant, Woodbury, Palfrey, Balch and Trask.

    William Woodbury was b. England, 1589, John, his brother, was for some 10 years his servant. John settled at Cape Ann 1624, and was one of the old planters, who settled Salem 1626. He was second of the five old planters to whom 1000 acres was granted in that part of Salem afterwards incorporated as Beverly, where he and his brother, William, who came to Massachusetts in 1634, planted and their descendants multiplied.

John Woodbury's 200 acres is still owned by one of his descendants, Levi Woodbury.

Peter Woodbury, son of Peter and Hannah (Perkins) Woodbury, b. Beverly, Mass., March 28, 1738, d. in Antrim, Oct. 11, 1817; m. Mrs. Elizabeth (Dodge) Rea or Ray in 1760, wid. of James Ray. She d. Antrim, April 19, 1812, age 69 years. They settled in Amherst, now Mont Vernon. He rem. to Antrim in 1799 or 1800. From C. L. Woodbury in New England Historical and Genealogical Register Jan., 1894: "As Peter Woodbury signed a petition in 1770 relative to town affairs in Amherst, he was already living there. He was an ardent rebel. His name is fifth of those who in April, 1776, pledged to resist with arms and fortune the encroachments of the British Parliament on American Liberty. He was of the Legislature who formed the first constitution of New Hampshire, and was frequently on the Committee on Public Safety. Two of his sons, Levi and Jesse, served in the army and were afloat under the flag. Peter, the third son, enlisted at 13, but his father stopped him."

His cousins, Josiah and James, were at Lake George, and tradition says that he was out one campaign in the French War. He passed some years as a sea-faring man and in 1760 m. a widow of 17 years, with one son, a woman of shrewdness and energy, who d. in Antrim, April 9, 1812, age 69 years. He served as Representative to the General Court and joined in the convention which made the first constitution of New Hampshire. He lived on the place afterwards known as the Dr. Adams place in the village. He probably moved to Antrim about 1800. Ch.

1. Levi, b. Beverly, Jan. 20, 1761, captured on the privateer Essex and carried a prisoner of war to England, where he d. at Plymouth.
2. *Jesse, b. Oct. 2, 1763, d. Texas, about 1835.
3. *Peter, b. Jan. 9, 1767.
4. Betsey, b. Mont Vernon, Feb. 9, 1770, m. June 5, 1787, Peter Jones of Amherst, d. April 3, 1843; four ch.
5. Hannah, b. Mont Vernon, Feb. 14, 1772, d. young.
6. *Mark, b. Mont Vernon, Jan. 1, 1775.

Peter Woodbury, son of Peter and Elizabeth (Dodge) Woodbury, b. Jan. 9, 1767; lived and d. in Francestown, Sept. 12, 1834; m. April 23, 1787, Mary, dau. James and Hannah (Trask) Woodbury. She was b. Mont Vernon, Aug. 15, 1769, d. Francestown, Dec. 31, 1839. Ch. b. Francestown.

1. Mary, b. Oct. 28, 1787, m. (1) Dr. Adonijah Howe of Jaffrey; m. (2) Dr. Luke Howe of Jaffrey; d. Jan. 18, 1875.
2. Levi, b. Dec. 2, 1789, Governor of New Hampshire, Secretary of Treasury under Jackson and Van Buren, Secretary of Navy, first term of Jackson; Associate Justice Supreme Court, U. S.; d. Sept. 4, 1851; m. a Miss Clapp of Portland, Me.; three dau. and one son, Chas. Levi Woodbury of Boston.
3. Peter P., b. Aug. 8, 1791, physician in Bedford; d. Dec. 5, 1860. He was an ancestor of Gordon Woodbury of Manchester.
4. Antress B., b. May 29, 1793, m. Nehemiah Eastman of Farmington, d. Sept. 10, 1847; had ch.
5. Martha, b. Aug. 14, 1796, m. Thomas Grimes of Windsor, Vt., d. Dec. 25, 1854; had ch.
6. Hannah T., b. March 17, 1799, m. Isaac O. Barnes of Boston, Mass., d. Feb. 28, 1855; no ch.
7. James Trask, b. May 9, 1803, lawyer and clergyman, d. Acton, Mass., Jan. 16, 1861.

8. Harriet, b. May 1, 1805, m. Perley Dodge of Amherst; three ch.
9. Jesse, b. May 17, 1807, m. Hannah Duncklee; had ch.; lived in Francestown.
10. Adeline, b. April 22, 1809, m. Edwin F. Bunnell of Boston. They went to California.
11. George Washington, b. June 2, 1811; physician in Yazoo Co., Miss., d. Feb., 1876.

Mark Woodbury, son of Peter and Elizabeth (Dodge) Woodbury, b. Mont Vernon, Jan. 4, 1775, d. in Antrim, March 17, 1828; a successful merchant in Antrim; m. Alice Boyd of Antrim. Ch. b. Antrim.
1. Luke, b. Dec. 25, 1800, d. Aug. 27, 1854; was Judge of Probate for Hillsboro Co., and at time of his death was Democratic candidate for Governor of New Hampshire.
2. Sabrina, b. Feb. 4, 1804, m. George W. Hill of Montpelier, Vt., d. May 8, 1862.
3. Mary, b. Dec. 8, 1805, m. Joshua C. Dodge of Francestown, d. May 3, 1836.
4. Betsey, b. May 8, 1808, d. in infancy.
5. Betsey, b. May 8, 1809, m. Benj. B. Muzzey of Boston, d. March 20, 1849.
6. Mark B., b. May 9, 1841, d. Oct. 24, 1874; merchant in Antrim.
7. Fanny, b. Nov. 14, 1843, d. Oct. 15, 1855.
10. Nancy, b. Oct. 28, 1847, m. (1) A. N. Moore; m. (2) George C. Trumball, d. Boston, Oct. 21, 1855.
11. Levi, b. Aug. 18, 1820, d. Antrim, Aug. 10, 1865.
12. John B., b. Aug. 13, 1823; lived in Antrim.

Lt. James Woodbury. (Line of descent: 1. John Woodbury, who d. 1641; 2. Peter, youngest ch. of Edward, born d. 1700, m. Abigail Batchelder; 3. Peter, b. Dec. 12, 1656, m. wid. Mary Dodge, b. about 1673. She d. Nov. 20, 1703; left three sons and four dau.; 4. Peter, b. June 20, 1705, m. Hannah Batchelder.) Their son, Jones, b. Beverly, June 4, 1738, d. Francestown, March 3, 1828, m. Nov. 5, 1761, Hannah, dau. Josiah and Abigail Trask. She was b. Beverly, Sept. 28, 1741, d. Francestown, Oct. 5, 1819.
When he was about 20 years old, March 31, 1758, he enlisted in Col. Bagley's Regt. Mass. Rangers, and marched to Lake George, where he participated in all the hard fighting and scouting of that campaign. Lord Howe was with this regiment fighting at the front, when he was killed. James again enlisted in Col. Bagley's regiment, which went to Louisburg, and part of it to Quebec, where it was at the battle of Abraham Heights with Wolfe. James was wounded in this battle, where he was a subaltern officer. After a few years of sea-faring he had a share of the proprietors lands in what is now Mont Vernon, where he moved apparently in 1767, as he ceased being taxed in Beverly in 1767. In March, 1776, he was one of the signers of the declaration of resistence, was active on town committees during the Revolution to levy the quota, to provide for the families of soldiers in the field, and on the Committee of Public Safety. He freely advanced his money for the service. He was taxed in Mont Vernon until 1810, when he removed to Francestown and lived in the family of his son-in-law, Peter Woodbury, where he d. March 3, 1823. He owned and lived on the place below the town house, now owned by Estate of Dr. C. M. Kittredge. He gave the land on which the church and town-house now stands, for church purposes; also the cemetery. Ch.

1. Mehitable, b. Aug. 15, 1762, m. *James Ray of Mont Vernon, May 5, 1780, d. Francestown, Feb. 14, 1858.

2. Abigail, b. March 13, 1765, m. Eben Fisk of Wilmot, was a grand-mother of Gov. E. A. Straw of New Hampshire.

3. Hannah, b. Beverly, Oct. 5, 1766, m. *Capt. Joseph Perkins of Mont Vernon, d. Mont Vernon, April 15, 1856.

4. Mary, b. Mont Vernon, Aug. 15, 1769, m. April 23, 1787, Peter Woodbury, d. Francestown, Dec. 31, 1839.

5. Sarah, b. Mont Vernon, May 5, 1771, m. (1) Josiah Beard, Dec. 3, 1793; m. (2) Isaac Andrews of Hillsboro, d. Francestown, March 25, 1863; had ch.

6. Anna, b. Mont Vernon, Aug. 4, 1774, m. John Averill, Jr., of Mont Vernon, d. May 9, 1858.

7. Betsey, b. Mont Vernon, Aug. 11, 1777, m. Oct. 10, 1795, Paul Whipple of New Boston. They are grandparents of J. Reed Whipple, proprietor of Young's Hotel, Touraine and Parker House, Boston; 10 ch.

8. Lucy, b. Mont Vernon, Oct. 4, 1779, d. June 25, 1782.

9. Lucy, b. Mont Vernon, Aug. 15, 1783, m. Sept. 7, 1806, John S. Tyler, d. New York, May 12, 1843.

Jesse Woodbury, son of Peter and Mrs. Elizabeth (Dodge) Ray, b. Oct. 2, 1762, in Beverly, Mass., moved with his parents to Amherst (now Mont Vernon) about 1773, served in the Revolutionary War in 1780, m. Abigail Boutell of Lyndeboro in 1784, moved to South Weare about 1785. He was in trade in South Weare from 1789 till his death, Oct. 6, 1802. His wife d. March 24, 1862. They had seven ch.

WOODWELL.

Rev. William H. Woodwell, son of Hon. David T. Woodwell and Mary (Haskell) Woodwell, b. Newburyport, Mass., Sept. 9, 1844, fitted for college at Newburyport High School, afterwards learned the printer's trade in the office of the Boston Transcript, entered Bowdoin College in 1865, grad. in 1869, pursued a full theological course at Andover Seminary, grad. in 1872, was ordained pastor Congregational Church, Wells, Me., June 12, 1873, dismissed in the Autumn of 1875. In Nov. 1875 he came to Mont Vernon and was engaged to supply the pulpit for one year with reference to a permanent settlement. His ministry here continued nearly four and one-half years, he delivering his farewell discourse March 28, 1880. From Jan., 1881, to July, 1883, he was employed in teaching at the Sandwich Islands. From 1883 to July, 1887, he was in the ministry at Orient, Long Island. Since March, 1889, he has been pastor of the Congregational Church, Sandwich, Mass. (He was there at last accounts.) When not a resident minister to a parish he has resided in his native city, supplying various churches temporarily as opportunity offered. He m. Miss Martha Haskell of Newburyport, Mass., April 18, 1873. Ch.

1. Julian Ernest, b. Jan. 7, 1874.
2. Eva Cecilia, b. Mont Vernon, March 2, 1878.
3. Willie Herbert, b. Sandwich Island, May 3, 1881.
4. Auber Roscoe, b. May 23, 1883.
5. Carolus Sylvester, b. Feb. 9, 1889.

WOODS.

Walter Woods, son of Moses and Alice (Lynch) Woods, b. New Boston, Sept. 27, 1819, m. Lucy Patterson of Amherst, Feb. 9, 1845. She was b. Jan. 6, 1823; ch. all b. in New Boston. They moved to Mont Vernon in 1884.

1. Francena E., b. July, 1846, m. Jan. 22, 1873, Chas. H. Clark of Francestown, res. Francestown; one ch., Dell F., b. Feb. 8, 1882.

2. Charles W., b. Sept. 1, 1848, d. Sept. 5, 1869.

3. Edward C., b. Oct. 2, 1851, lived Mont Vernon, d. unm. June 4, 1903.

4. John A., b. Sept. 3, 1857, m. Dec. 20, 1882, Abby M. Richardson of Lebanon; commercial traveler; res. Manchester; one ch., Bertha L., b. Mont Vernon, May 20, 1884.

5. Frederic H., b. May 2, 1860, d. July 18, 1861.

6. Willard Patterson, b. Oct. 5, 1862; commercial traveler.

7. Mary Emma, b. Sept. 15, 1865; stenographer in Nashua.

WYMAN.

Charles Wyman, b. Greenville, N. H., came to Mont Vernon in 1871 and purchased the farm now owned by Estate of Dr. C. M. Kittredge; rem. to Amherst in 1894, where he now resides, m. (1) Eliza Felch of Sutton. She d. Wilton, March 17, 1902. M. (2) Mrs. Priscilla (Page) Bacon.

Ch. by first wife:

1. Emma, m. Willis H. Abbott of Wilton.

2. Katherine, d. young.

3. Frank, went to Mexico.

4. Fred, lives Boston.

Ch. by second wife:

Edith, b. Mont Vernon.

Henry O. Wyman, brother Charles Wyman, b. Greenville, N. H., 1822. Was a merchant tailor in Lowell, Manchester and other places; lived in Mont Vernon 12 years, d. there Aug. 24, 1894, was a widower when here, m. a dau. of City Marshall Shedd of Lowell; had ch.

WINTERS.

Thomas Winters, son of Thomas and Esther (Jeans) Winters, b. Liverpool, Nova Scotia, Dec. 15, 1847, m. May 5, 1871, Mary A., dau. Charles A. and Esther S. (Cloutman) Gray of Mont Vernon. She was b. Mont Vernon, Sept. 8, 1849. He lived in Worcester on the place in village now occupied by Kneeland C. White, moved to Milford, 1887; is a contractor and builder. Ch.

1. Charles B., b. Worcester, Mass., Aug. 14, 1872, lives Syracuse, N. Y.

2. Mabel A., b. Worcester, July 7, 1874, m. April 18, 1900, Dr. Quincy H. Merrill, res. Leominster, Mass.

3. Fred G., b. Worcester, Dec. 10, 1876; res. Syracuse, N. Y.

4. Cora G., b. Mont Vernon, Feb. 1, 1879.

5. Alice E., b. Mont Vernon, April 29, 1894

WARD.

Richard Ward, son of Ephraim and Mary (Haven) Stone Ward, b. Newton, Mass., Sept. 9, 1739, m. Peggy Chandler of Bedford, Sept. 16,

J. FRANK WELLINGTON.

1764, and settled in Mont Vernon. Here they continued until Feb., 1794, when they removed to Chester, Vt., where he d. Dec. 27, 1795. She d. in March, 1812. He seems to have taken quite an active part in the formation of the Northwest Parish (now Mont Vernon) in 1780, and was one of the first members of the church here. Ch.

1.   William, b. 1765, was a physician, d. in Maine.
2.   Margaret, b. 1767, d. in Andover, Vt., in 1841, unm.
3.   Sally, b. July 26, 1769, m. Caleb Barton of Chester, Vt., in 1798, d. July 26, 1799, had one child.
4.   Sarah, b. 1772, d. in 1792.
5.   Richard, b. in 1774, m. Hannah Smith in 1798, d. June 6, 1832, had four ch.
6.   Zachariah Chandler, b. in 1781, m. Elizabeth Willard in 1802, d in Bolton, Warren Co., New York, Aug. 14, 1842, had eight ch.
7.   John, b. in 1782, m. Sally Lord, resided in Hague, N. Y.
8.   Sally, m. (1) Jonas Putnam of Windham, Vt., both became Mormons. After his decease she m. again and settled in New York.
9.   Thomas, b. in 1788, m. Rebecca Gerald, resided in Northfield, Vt., had no ch.

WRIGHT.

James Wright came here from Pepperell, Mass., lived a few years in the house near Purgatory Brook in West District, where he d. Feb. 10, 1873, age 56. He m. Elizabeth Fox of Vermont, who lived there until 1890. She m. (2) George Towne, son of James and Mary J. (Swinnington) Towne; m. (3) Nathaniel Morrison of Peterboro. She m. (4) 1890, Franklin Grace of Tamworth, N. H., where she now resides.

WILLIAMS.

Warren Williams, b. Greenfield, lived here most of his life; lived in South District and village; farmer; d. Mont Vernon, July 25, 1883, age 77 years; m. Oct. 23, 1836, Lucy, dau. Peter and Lydia (Farmer) Foster, of Mont Vernon. She was b. July 21, 1801, d. Mont Vernon, May 2 ,1892. Ch.

1.   Lucy A., d. Aug. 9, 1856, aged 17 years.
2.   Sarah M., d. Feb. 12, 1849, aged 5 years, 9 months.

Hannah Williams, a sister of Warren Williams, m. Morris Bane, March 28, 1839. They moved to Milford.

ROLLINS.

John Rollins lived in East District, where John D. Brown afterwards lived. He m. Mary, dau. of Daniel and Ruhama (Cutter) Smith of Milford. She was b. Milford, Aug. 22, 1789, d. Mont Vernon, April 8, 1824 He d. in 1860, aged 80 years.

SEARLES.

Isaac Searles, m. June 27, 1824, Betsey, dau. John and Catherine (Harris) Lamson. She was b. Mont Vernon, July 24, 1805, d. March 18, 1884, at Milford. He was a laborer, lived in the house which stood north of the Bellevue, which is now the Golf Club House. Ch

1.   ²Charles.
2.   George was killed by a kick from a horse in 1872, m., had one dau., who m. Lucien Durant of Litchfield, N. H., res. Litchfield, N. H.
3.   Levi, ―― d. March 18, 1876.
4.   Hiram, m. Etta, dau. of Charles A. and Clarinda J. (Felch) Foster. She was b. Mont Vernon, Aug. 20, 1857, d. Goffstown, Nov. 24, 1902, 3 ch. d.
5.   Samuel, went to New Jersey.

Charles Searles, son of Isaac and Betsey (Lamson) Searles, m. (1) ―――― Stevens, m. (2) ―――― ――――, lived in Dunstable, Mass. One son, Charles, m. Helen, dau. Charles and Mary A. (Hill) Marvell, March 12, 1878. She was b. Mont Vernon, Nov. 22, 1855, d. Haverhill, Mass., Dec. 27, 1899, had several ch.

STEEL.

Joseph Steel, a wheelwright, settled in that part of Souhegan West, now Mont Vernon, before the incorporation of Amherst (1760). He died Feb. 23, 1788, in his 82nd year. He is buried in Mont Vernon. His will was presented for probate March 24 of that year. In it he names his wife, Sally, and children.

He was one of the petitioners, from what is now Mont Vernon, who, in 1753, petitioned for the incorporation of what was afterwards the town of Amherst.

INDEX

TO GENEALOGY.

INDEX.

A.

B.

C.

H.

INDEX.

I.

J.

K.

M.

R.

S.

INDEX TO PORTRAITS

The following portraits were added after the index was made out.

INDEX TO PORTRAITS

Lightning Source UK Ltd.
Milton Keynes UK
UKHW040807040520
362748UK00001B/142